OXFORD MEDIEVAL TEXTS

General Editors

C. N. L. BROOKE D. E. GREENWAY

M. WINTERBOTTOM

ORDERICI VITALIS HISTORIA ÆCCLESIASTICA

THE ECCLESIASTICAL HISTORY OF ORDERIC VITALIS

VOLUME IV

BOOKS VII AND VIII

EDITED AND TRANSLATED
BY
MARJORIE CHIBNALL

CLARENDON PRESS · OXFORD

Oxford University Press, Walton Street, Oxford OX2 6DP
London Glasgow New York Toronto
Delhi Bombay Calcutta Madras Karachi
Kuala Lumpur Singapore Hong Kong Tokyo
Nairobi Dar es Salaam Cape Town
Melbourne Auckland
and associates in
Beirut Berlin Ibadan Mexico City Nicosia

Published in the United States by
Oxford University Press, New York

First published 1973
Reprinted 1983

Printed in the United States of America by
Edwards Brothers, Inc., Ann Arbor, Michigan

PREFACE

WITH the appearance of the present volume this edition of the *Ecclesiastical History* approaches the half-way mark. It is an appropriate moment to review the plan of the whole edition, and indicate any modifications that have been introduced at the request of other scholars since the publication of Volume II in 1969.

The practice of dividing the work into numbered chapters, with a table of contents, begun in Volume III, will be continued throughout the edition. But I am convinced that it is not desirable to attempt to introduce dates in the margins. The work is not chronicle, but history; it moves very freely in time, and marginal dates would have to be so softened by question-marks and wide dating limits as to be of very little use if they were not to be positively misleading. Even Le Prévost's cautious running headings have caused errors to creep into textbooks through hasty reading. The dates, as far as they can be established, are given with relevant evidence in the footnotes or Introduction. Dates of English abbots and priors given without further reference have been supplied by Professor Brooke from the list of heads of religious houses on which he has been engaged (David Knowles, C. N. L. Brooke and Vera London, *The Heads of Religious Houses, England and Wales 940–1216* (Cambridge, 1972)).

The index in each volume is designed to enable the reader to identify persons and places, and to find his way through a narrative that is far from systematic. I recognize the need for a much fuller *index uerborum*, but have decided that this would be more satisfactory and more useful if it were compiled as a single index for the whole work, or at least for Books III to XIII. I hope to provide this at a later date.

My debt to other scholars constantly increases. In particular, it is a pleasure to thank Professor C. N. L. Brooke for the many corrections and suggestions which I owe to his exact and far-ranging scholarship, and for the generosity with which he gives his time and help. Dr. Rosalind Brooke and Dr. Beryl Smalley have provided me with a number of references. To Dr. Diana Greenway

I am grateful for permission to cite her forthcoming edition of the Mowbray charters, and to Dr. A. J. Holden, who is preparing a new edition of the *Roman de Rou*, for discussing his conclusions with me. Mr. T. A. M. Bishop very kindly helped me with the identification of hands in the Paris manuscripts.

The travel necessary for this volume was made possible by a grant from the Leverhulme Trust; and my work was facilitated by those in charge of the manuscripts in the Bibliothèque nationale, the Vatican Library, the Bibliothèque municipale at Rouen, the Bibliothèque municipale at Alençon, and the Stadtbibliothek at Bern. Lastly, I am particularly grateful to Clare Hall, Cambridge, for the research fellowship that has enabled me to work in the lively and learned society of the college.

M. C.

Clare Hall, Cambridge
February, 1972

CONTENTS

ABBREVIATED REFERENCES

MANUSCRIPTS

Caen MS.	Vatican, MS. Reginensis lat. 703^{B}.
lat. 4861	Bibliothèque nationale, MS. latin 4861.
Vespasian A xix	British Museum, MS. Cotton Vespasian A xix.

PRINTED BOOKS

AA.SS.	*Acta Sanctorum*, ed. J. Bollandus and others (Antwerp, Brussels, 1643 etc.).
Alexiad	Anna Comnena, *Alexiad*, ed. B. Leib (Paris, 1937–45).
Anal. boll.	*Analecta bollandiana*.
Bede, *HE*	Bede, *Ecclesiastical History of the English People*, ed. B. Colgrave and R. A. B. Mynors (Oxford, 1969).
BHL	*Bibliotheca Hagiographica Latina*, ed. Socii Bollandiani, vols. 1, 2, and suppl. (Brussels, 1898–1911).
Bouquet	*Recueil des historiens des Gaules et de la France*, ed. M. Bouquet *et alii* (Paris, 1869–1904).
BSAN	*Bulletin de la Société des Antiquaires de Normandie*.
CDF	*Calendar of Documents preserved in France*, vol. i, ed. J. H. Round (London, 1899).
Chalandon, *Alexis I Comnène*	F. Chalandon, *Essai sur le règne d'Alexis I Comnène* (Paris, 1900).
Chalandon, *Domination normande*	F. Chalandon, *Histoire de la domination normande en Italie et en Sicile*, 2 vols. (Paris, 1907).
Cod. dip. bar.	*Codice diplomatico barese* (Bari, 1897–1935; Trani, 1936 ff.).
Cottineau	L. H. Cottineau, *Répertoire topo-bibliographique des abbayes et prieurés*, 2 vols. (Macon, 1936–7).
David, *Robert Curthose*	C. W. David, *Robert Curthose, Duke of Normandy* (Cambridge, Mass., 1920).
DB	*Domesday Book*, 4 vols. (Record Commission, 1783–1816).
Depoin, *Cartulaire de Pontoise*	J. Depoin, *Cartulaire de l'abbaye de Saint-Martin de Pontoise* (Pontoise, 1895).

DHGE	*Dictionnaire d'histoire et de géographie ecclésiastiques*, ed. A. Baudrillart, A. de Meyer, E. van Cauwenbergh *et alii* (Paris, 1909 ff.).
Douglas, *Domesday Monachorum*	D. C. Douglas, *The Domesday Monachorum of Christ Church Canterbury* (London, 1944).
Douglas, *WC*	David C. Douglas, *William the Conqueror* (London, 1964).
Ducange	Ducange, *Glossarium mediae et infimae latinitatis*, 10 vols. (rev. edn., Niort and London, 1884–7).
Dugdale, *Mon. Ang.*	William Dugdale, *Monasticum anglicanum*, ed. J. Caley, H. Ellis, and B. Bandinel (London, 1817–30).
EHR	*English Historical Review.*
E. M. Jamison, 'Some notes . . .'	Evelyn M. Jamison, 'Some notes on the *Anonymi Gesta Francorum*, with special reference to the Norman contingents from South Italy and Sicily in the First Crusade', in *Studies in French Language and Medieval Literature presented to Professor M. K. Pope* (*Manchester*, 1939).
EYC	*Early Yorkshire Charters*, i–iii, ed. W. Farrer (Edinburgh), and iv–xii, ed. C. T. Clay (Yorkshire Archaeological Society, 1914–65).
Fauroux	*Recueil des actes des ducs de Normandie (911–1066)*, ed. Marie Fauroux (Mém. Soc. Ant. Norm. xxxvi, Caen, 1961).
Fliche, *Philippe I*	A. Fliche, *Le règne de Philippe Ier, roi de France* (Paris, 1912).
Fliche et Martin, viii	A. Fliche, *La réforme grégorienne et la reconquête chrétienne* (Fliche et Martin, *Histoire de l'Église*, vol. viii) (Paris, 1950).
Foreville	Guillaume de Poitiers: *Histoire de Guillaume le Conquérant*, ed. Raymonde Foreville (Paris, 1952).
Freeman, *William Rufus*	E. A. Freeman, *The Reign of William Rufus*, 2 vols. (Oxford, 1882).
FW	Florence of Worcester, *Chronicon ex chronicis*, ed. B. Thorpe (Eng. Hist. Soc., London, 1848–9).
GC	*Gallia Christiana* (rev. edn., Paris, 1715–1965).
GEC	*The Complete Peerage of England, Scotland, Ireland*, by G. E. C., rev. edn., 13 vols. in 14 (1910–59).

GM	Geoffrey of Malaterra, *De rebus gestis Rogerii Calabriae et Siciliae comitis*, ed. E. Pontieri (Rerum Italicarum Scriptores, v, pt. 1) (Bologna, 1928).
GR	William of Malmesbury, *De Gestis Regum Anglorum*, ed. W. Stubbs, 2 vols. (RS, 1887–9).
Halphen, *Anjou*	L. Halphen, *Le comté d'Anjou au XIe siècle* (Paris, 1906).
Haskins, *Norman Institutions*	C. H. Haskins, *Norman Institutions* (Cambridge, Mass., 1925).
John of Bari	John of Bari, *De translatione S. Nicolai episcopi* in L. Surius, *De probatis sanctorum historiis*, iii (Cologne, 1579).
Knowles, *MO*	David Knowles, *The Monastic Order in England* (2nd edn., Cambridge, 1963).
Lair	Dudo of Saint-Quentin, *De moribus et actis primorum Normanniae ducum*, ed. J. Lair (Mém. Soc. Ant. Norm. xxiii, Caen, 1865).
Latouche, *Maine*	R. Latouche, *Histoire du comté du Maine pendant le Xe et le XIe siècle* (Paris, 1910).
Lemarignier, *Le gouvernement royal*	J.-F. Lemarignier, *Le gouvernement royal aux premiers temps capétiens (987–1108)* (Paris, 1965).
Lemarignier, *L'hommage en marche*	J.-F. Lemarignier, *Recherches sur l'hommage en marche et les frontières féodales* (Lille, 1945).
Le Prévost	*Orderici Vitalis ecclesiasticae historiae libri tredecim*, ed. A. Le Prévost (Société de l'Histoire de France), 5 vols. (Paris, 1838–55).
Le Prévost, *Eure*	A. Le Prévost, *Mémoires et notes pour servir à l'histoire du département de l'Eure*, ed. L. Delisle et L. Passy, 3 vols. (Évreux, 1862–9).
Loyd	L. C. Loyd, *The Origins of some Anglo-Norman Families* (Harleian Society, ciii, 1951).
Luchaire, *Louis VI*	A. Luchaire, *Louis VI le Gros* (Paris, 1890).
Mansi	*Sacrorum conciliorum nova et amplissima collectio*, ed. J. D. Mansi (Florence, Venice, and Paris, 1759 ff.).
Marx	Guillaume de Jumièges, *Gesta Normannorum Ducum*, ed. J. Marx (Société de l'Histoire de Normandie, 1914).
Mathieu	Guillaume de Pouille, *La geste de Robert Guiscard*, ed. M. Mathieu (Istituto siciliano di studi bizantini e neoellenici; Testi e monumenti. Testi, iv) (Palermo, 1961).

Mém. Soc. Ant. Norm.	Mémoires de la Société des Antiquaires de Normandie.
MGH SS	*Monumenta germaniae historica, Scriptores.*
MGH SS Rer. Meroving.	*Monumenta germaniae historica, Scriptores rerum Merovingicarum.*
Migne, *PL*	*Patrologiae cursus completus, series latina*, ed. J. P. Migne.
Musset, *Abbayes caennaises*	L. Musset, *Les actes de Guillaume le Conquérant et de la reine Mathilde pour les abbayes caennaises* (Mém. Soc. Ant. Norm. xxxvii, Caen, 1967).
Nitti di Vito, *La ripresa*	F. Nitti di Vito, *La ripresa gregoriana di Bari, 1087–1105* (Trani, 1942).
Porée	A. A. Porée, *Histoire de l'abbaye du Bec*, 2 vols. (Évreux, 1901).
PUF	J. Ramackers, *Papsturkunden in Frankreich*, N.F. ii, *Normandie* (Göttingen, 1937).
Regesta	*Regesta regum Anglo-Normannorum*, vol. i, ed. H. W. C. Davis (Oxford, 1913); vol. ii, ed. C. Johnson and H. A. Cronne (Oxford, 1956); vols. iii and iv, ed. H. A. Cronne and R. H. C. Davis (Oxford, 1968–70).
Ritchie, *Normans in Scotland*	R. L. G. Ritchie, *The Normans in Scotland* (Edinburgh, 1954).
Roman de Rou	Wace, *Roman de Rou*, ed. H. Andresen (Heilbronn, 1877–9).
RS	Rolls Series.
RSB	*Regula sancti Benedicti.*
R. Tor.	*Chronique de Robert de Torigni*, ed. L. Delisle, 2 vols. (Société de l'Histoire de Normandie) (Rouen, 1872–3).
Sanders	I. J. Sanders, *English Baronies* (Oxford, 1960).
Southern, *Medieval Humanism*	R. W. Southern, *Medieval Humanism and Other Studies* (Oxford, 1970).
Southern, *St. Anselm*	R. W. Southern, *Saint Anselm and his Biographer* (Cambridge, 1963).
TRHS	*Transactions of the Royal Historical Society.*
TSAS	*Transactions of the Shropshire Archaeological Society.*
VCH	*Victoria History of the Counties of England.*

INTRODUCTION

Books VII and VIII are among the most famous in the *Ecclesiastical History*, and contain some of its finest passages. In them Orderic embarked without restraint on a plan to write a general history of the Normans, which was to fill altogether seven more books of his life's work. He looked back reflectively to the achievements of William the Conqueror in Normandy and Robert Guiscard in Apulia, giving his own interpretation of their value. Both in this recapitulation and in the narrative he began to unfold of events after 1087 he carried on in a much wider context the traditions of William of Poitiers and William of Jumièges. His work laid the foundations of the epic of the Normans, not only in Normandy and England, but from Scotland to Apulia, through the Balkans to Constantinople and the Holy Land, which, in some ways, was to influence all subsequent historians of them, from Wace and Benoît of Sainte-Maure in the twelfth century to C. H. Haskins and D. C. Douglas eight hundred years later.

(i) *Text*

Books VII and VIII have not survived in the exact form in which Orderic wrote them. The autograph manuscript of this section probably became separated from the other three volumes in the fifteenth century and is now lost. About the third quarter of the twelfth century a transcript of most of it was made for the abbey of St. Stephen's, Caen; this copy was later acquired by Queen Christina of Sweden, and is now in the Vatican Library.[1] It forms the basis of the present edition, as of the earlier editions of Duchesne and Le Prévost.

The scribe appears to have omitted the beginning of Book VII;

[1] Vatican MS. Reginensis lat. 703^{B}, described by Delisle in 'Notice sur vingt manuscrits du Vatican' in *BEC* xxxvii (1876), 491–4. The first part of the MS. contains the annals of Caen. Ff. 57–100^{v} containing the work of Orderic have been reproduced in facsimile in a presentation volume for L. Delisle, *Orderici Vitalis historiae ecclesiasticae libri VII et VIII e codice Vaticano reg. 703*^{A} (Paris, 1902). The MS. has recently been rebound in two volumes; the second, containing Orderic's work, has been renumbered 703^{B}.

there is no introduction, and the extract begins abruptly in the year 1083 with an account of Henry IV's attack on Rome. That the scribe also omitted some passages in Book VIII is clear from a marginal note in a late fourteenth- or early fifteenth-century hand in the final volume of the *Ecclesiastical History*: 'In secunda parte Vitalis, ad unum tiretum inuenietis quomodo Serlo, predecessor Rogerii abbatis, non potuit habere benedictionem ab episcopo Lexouiensi.'[1] This episode is not mentioned in the Caen MS. The note is evidence that at the date it was written the original complete text was still at Saint-Évroul.

A fourteenth-century copy of part of Book VII, including a fragment of the account of Odo of Bayeux's arrest and trial, and the long narrative of William I's death, was made directly from the Caen MS. and is in the British Museum.[2] It was carefully written and lavishly decorated with gold leaf; William's name was written in gold wherever it occurred. According to Camden, who printed it in 1603 as an anonymous fragment, it was brought from France with other booty in the reign of Henry V.[3] It is now bound up with a number of separate works belonging to the abbey of Ely. Although not an independent source, it occasionally corrects slips made by the Caen scribe.

The treatise on the origins of the new monastic orders, inserted towards the end of Book VIII, also exists in an early thirteenth-century manuscript, which at one time belonged to the abbey of Saint-Taurin-d'Évreux.[4] Some passages are omitted in this version, and a number of textual variations suggest that it was not derived from the Caen MS. It may have been copied directly from Orderic's manuscript at Saint-Évroul; but there is a possibility that this treatise, which was also utilized by Robert of Torigny, circulated separately.[5]

[1] Bibl. nat. MS. lat. 10913, p. 157 (Le Prévost, iv. 63). See also below, p. 170 for evidence of the omission of Lanfranc's epitaph.

[2] Brit. Mus. MS. Cotton Vespasian A xix, ff. 104–121v. The heading runs: 'Que sequntur de uita et gestis gloriosi Guillermi ducis Normannorum ac uictoriosissimi regis Anglorum extracta fuerunt de quodam libro antiquo monasterii sancti Stephani de Cadamo cuius monasterii fundator quondam extitit.'

[3] William Camden, *Anglica, Normannica, Hibernica, Cambrica a veteribus scripta* (Frankfort, 1603), pp. 29–35 and dedicatory epistle. Camden failed to notice that some folios were missing, and ran the two passages together without comment.

[4] Bibl. nat. MS. lat. 4861, ff. 125v–128v.

[5] See *Millénaire monastique du Mont Saint-Michel*, ii. 137

The volume containing Books VII and VIII had presumably disappeared from the library of Saint-Évroul by the beginning of the sixteenth century, when the first proposals for publishing the work were made. Out of six transcripts[1] made between this time and 1619, when Duchesne's edition[2] appeared, not one contained anything that can be assigned with certainty to any part of these two books. The four transcripts latest in date prefaced Book VII with a fragment, subsequently published by Duchesne and Le Prévost as chapters 1–3 of Book VII. Both palaeographical and internal evidence, however, are against this ever having formed part of Orderic's *Ecclesiastical History*.

The transcript made by Dom William Vallin for Abbot Felix de Brie (1503–46) some time before 1536 does not include this fragment. Vallin omitted the whole of Books VII and VIII, though his re-division and renumbering of the books made his 'edition' appear complete.[3] A copy of Books IX–XIII made by an anonymous scribe in the late fifteenth or early sixteenth century, and now MS. Bongars 555 in the Stadtbibliothek of Bern, also omits the fragment, though with a significant difference. The scribe copied it separately at the end of the manuscript (ff. 276–283ᵛ), without a heading and without any suggestion that it might have formed part of the *Ecclesiastical History*. The presumption is, therefore, that by this date five or six folios containing the material had already become bound into the same volume as Books IX to XIII.

Not many years later, possibly in 1536,[4] a transcript of the whole of Books I–VI and IX–XIII (Bibl. nat. MS. lat. 5122) introduced the fragment as part of Book VII or VIII.[5] It thus secured a position in the work which it has retained up to the present time. Three other sixteenth-century manuscripts appear to have been

[1] For a description of these MSS. see L. Delisle, 'Notice sur Orderic Vital', in Le Prévost, v, pp. xcviii–civ; H. Wolter, *Ordericus Vitalis* (Wiesbaden, 1955), pp. 9–10.

[2] *Historiae Normannorum scriptores antiqui*, ed. A. Duchesne (Paris, 1619), pp. 319–925.

[3] The three volumes, beautifully written in a humanistic hand, are now Bibl. nat. MS. lat. 12713 (Books I–II, numbered I–III); Berlin, Phillipps 1836 (Rose 140) (Books III–VI, numbered IV–VII); and Bibl. nat. MS. Dupuys 875 (Books IX–XIII, numbered VIII–XIII).

[4] Bibl. nat. MS. lat. 5122, f. 302ᵛ.

[5] Ibid. f. 303, 'Liber [VII] (crossed out), VIII. Anno ab incarnatione domini DC. LXXXVIII' etc.

copied from MS. lat. 5122,[1] and all include the fragment as part of the missing books. Duchesne, who produced his edition in 1619, used the Caen MS. and MS. lat. 5122 for Books VII and VIII, and treated the fragment as the first three chapters of Book VII. In this he was followed by Le Prévost. Yet the whole long tradition seems to stem from an over-hasty assumption made by the scribe of MS. lat. 5122.

The volume containing the fragment, together with Orderic's last five books, has since been rebound, and a few folios have been lost.[2] The end of Book XIII, including the Epilogue, has gone, and of the preliminary fragment only four folios, in a separate quire, remain. Palaeographically they are not uniform with the holograph of the *Historia Æcclesiastica*. The hand is not Orderic's; and although it is not unlike a hand that appears constantly in association with his and even wrote the first few folios of Book III[3] the writing is coarser and more irregular. The scribe copied carelessly and the corrections are rough. The pages are the same size as those of the other volumes (24 cm × 15½ cm), but the margin is more cramped and thirty-nine lines are ruled on each page. The normal number of lines in the volumes of the *Ecclesiastical History* was thirty-three to a page, increasing in places to thirty-four and occasionally to thirty-five or thirty-six. Orderic sometimes squeezed in extra lines of writing when he had left too short a space for a later entry, but he never ruled as many as thirty-nine. There is no early pagination of any kind in the fragment. In the remainder of the volume two medieval paginations occur: contemporary (red) Roman numerals on the verso of ff. i–xxi, xxv, and xxx; and fifteenth-century Roman numerals (black) in the lower right-hand corner of the recto of each folio throughout the book. In brief, the fragment, though visibly a product of the same scriptorium, does not appear to have formed part of the same work as the remainder of the volume, and was presumably bound in after the date of the second pagination.

The evidence of the contents supports this conclusion. There are three elements:

1. A literal copy of the *Historia Francorum Senonensis*: this

[1] Bibl. nat. MSS. lat. 5123, lat. 5124 (2 vols.); Rouen, Bibl. municipale, MSS. 1175 and 1176 (a single copy in two volumes). Both the Rouen MS. and MS. lat. 5124 abbreviate the text.

[2] Bibl. nat. MS. lat. 10913.

[3] I hope to discuss this more fully later, in the General Introduction.

corresponds almost verbatim with other versions of the chronicle. The only significant variation is that Duke William Longsword is substituted for William archbishop of Sens in the mission to bring back Charles the Simple's son, Louis, from England. This extract occupied slightly more than four folios of the book, and it is inconceivable that Orderic would have padded out his history by copying at such length from another chronicle. He might copy documents, such as charters or the canons of councils; when he used the works of other historians he invariably rephrased them in his own rhythmic prose and retained only short sentences or phrases unchanged. Moreover he did use much of the material copied here, reshaping it, in Book I.[1]

2. Some notes on the history of Normandy under William the Bastard, and on his children. These are the only part of chapters i–iii that, in my opinion, could ever conceivably have formed part of the *Historia Æcclesiastica*, but they contain material to be found in other books, and may be no more than first drafts, later rejected. Since the folio on which they were originally written is now lost there is no palaeographical evidence either way.

3. An incomplete genealogy of the kings of England from mythical beginnings. The whole genealogy up to Edward the Confessor was copied, possibly from the lost part of this MS., in an early thirteenth-century MS. of Saint-Évroul, which was seen at Alençon and described by Delisle,[2] but has since disappeared. Like chapter i, it is source material, not finished history.

These fragments have all the marks of materials assembled in the course of writing the *Historia Æcclesiastica*; there is no proof that they were ever part of Book VII. Consequently I have not included them in this edition, but have printed them separately in Appendix I. It is impossible to be sure what Orderic wrote in the lost part of Book VII; but whenever he outlined his intentions he was fairly consistent. When he began Book V he intended to include in that book the history of Normandy and of Saint-Évroul up to the death of William the Conqueror.[3] When he changed his plan and expanded the internal history of the monastery to let it run on right through Book VI he assigned general Norman history to a second 'volume'. In the epilogue to Book VI, which was actually written when the whole work was completed or

[1] Cf. Le Prévost, i. 166–75, 179.

[2] Le Prévost, v, pp. li–liv.

[3] See above, iii. 6.

nearing completion, he stated that the second 'volume' contained seven books (VII–XIII) 'in which I have described at length the death of King William and the deeds of his three sons, and have added an account of the Crusade to Jerusalem and various events of our own times'.[1] The general plan of this volume, in its final form, was chronological; the surviving part of Book VII begins about 1083, approximately where Orderic had dropped his account of general Norman affairs in Book V, and the book ends with the death of the Conqueror. It is arguable that little except the prologue has been lost; even though this would leave Book VII exceptionally short (about thirty folios) the other books are not uniform in length and vary from about forty to ninety folios.

One possible explanation is that Book VII represents the truncated remains of at least two changes of plan. The material that it now contains was certainly at one time envisaged as the second half of Book V. After deciding to separate the history of Saint-Évroul from more general Norman history Orderic may have intended to begin his 'second volume' with a chronological survey of earlier history. This, however, was finally incorporated in Book I. Possibly Book VII was finally prefaced with a brief synopsis of Norman history, of which chapter 2 represents one fragment.[2] Duchesne thought so, but I share the doubts of Le Prévost who, while recognizing the existence of a gap, considered it impossible to pronounce on its length, or its content, or the place it occupied in the original plan of the author.[3] It may even be tendentious to speak of an original plan, for Orderic's 'plan' seems to have evolved and changed as the history proceeded. The loss of the preface to Book VII and of any preface to the 'second volume' as a whole is greatly to be regretted. Only because a few folios of miscellaneous historical material have accidentally been bound into a volume of the *Ecclesiastical History* has it become customary to assume that Book VII in its final form began with some kind of a summary of earlier history.

[1] See above, iii. 360.

[2] It was written after the death of Henry I (cf. Delisle, in Le Prévost, v, p. xlvii) and is therefore almost certainly later than the main part of Book VII, but it could belong to the period when Orderic finally remodelled his work.

[3] Le Prévost, iii. 161 n. 3.

(ii) *Date and sources*

There is no internal evidence of the date when Book VII was written. The passage cited as evidence by Delisle, which was written after the death of Henry I, may never have formed part of this book. In suggesting that the epilogue was written after Henry's death, H. Wolter seems to me to overstrain the meaning of the words;[1] but in any case the brief epilogue could have been added later. Planned as the continuation of Book V, Book VII was probably written after that book, and possibly after the early part of Book VI, which can be dated about 1130.[2] But certain sections could have been written separately, and one can never be sure that the order in which the component parts appear in Orderic's final work represents the order in which he wrote them. With this proviso it is a reasonable assumption that the main part of Book VII was written before Book VIII. The latter at least contains some hints of date: Henry I was certainly still alive when Orderic wrote in one of the early chapters that John, son of Odo of Bayeux, was serving in Henry's court.[3] A few pages later he stated that Henry had been king for about thirty-three years, which implies that it was then about 1133.[4] There is strong internal evidence that the treatise on the new monastic orders, almost at the end of Book VIII, was written in 1135 or possibly 1136.[5] The final note on the family of Grandmesnil may have been added some time later on a blank page: if Robert of Grandmesnil died a full thirty-eight years after his father it was added in or after 1136.[6] But Orderic's numerical calculations are liable to error, and he appears sometimes to have counted a fraction of a year as a whole year. Book VIII may have been completed during the lifetime of Henry I. A reasonable hypothesis is that Book VII was written between 1130 or 1131 and 1133, and Book VIII between 1133 and 1135, possibly with additions a year or two later.

The date of composition has a particular interest, because of the very strong views on the descent of the kingdom and duchy expressed in these two books. The evidence suggests that they were written under the shadow of the last years of Henry I's reign, amid the uncertainties of the impending succession. The statement attributed to William I, that he could not take back Normandy

[1] H. Wolter, *Ordericus Vitalis*, p. 70.
[2] See above, iii, p. xiv.
[3] See below, p. 116.
[4] See below, p. 120.
[5] See below, p. 324.
[6] See below, p. 338.

from Robert because Robert was his eldest son and had received the homage of almost all the Norman lords, may have been coloured by knowledge of the fealty sworn to Henry's daughter Matilda at the Christmas court of 1126–7 rather than by any evidence of what had happened in 1087. Indeed there is a possibility, suggested by the near-contemporary account of a monk of Caen, that William's first intention at that moment was to disinherit Robert altogether.[1] The arguments attributed to the Norman barons in 1088 on the disadvantages of divided allegiance for those holding lands in Normandy and England under two different lords,[2] though couched in biblical terms, are evidence of a dilemma that was as acute when Orderic wrote as in 1088 and became an immediate practical issue when Henry died. The passage has much in common with Orderic's account in Book XIII of events at Neubourg immediately after Henry's death.[3] There he relates that the barons were about to give their allegiance to Stephen's brother Theobald, when they heard that Stephen had been accepted in England, and resolved 'to serve under one lord on account of the honors they held in both lands'. But if Book VIII was indeed written in Henry's lifetime it cannot have been influenced by anything said or done at Neubourg. If so, the imaginary speeches attributed to the rebels of 1088 may have expressed views widely held by the Norman barons towards the end of Henry's reign: views that are very likely to have induced them to act at Neubourg as Orderic said they did. How far they represent views held in 1088 is harder to assess.

Orderic wrote with hindsight: the imaginary speeches and the interspersed moral reflections give the interpretations of a man writing between forty and fifty years after the events discussed. In describing events, however, he attempted to record them truly; he could succeed only in so far as his sources were reliable. Of written sources, for this part of the work, he had few. For his recapitulation of the events of William the Conqueror's reign he drew partly on William of Poitiers and William of Jumièges, cited as a rule from memory. He had seen Eadmer's *Vita Anselmi*, and probably took the account of Anselm's election from it. His chapter on Robert of Rhuddlan made use of charters of

[1] Cf. J. H. Le Patourel, 'The Norman succession, 1066–1135', in *EHR* lxxxvi (1971), 232.

[2] See below, pp. 120–4.

[3] Le Prévost, v. 54–7; cf. J. Le Patourel in *EHR* lxxxvi (1971), 247.

Saint-Évroul; and for the lives of contemporary abbots he gleaned something from mortuary rolls, epitaphs, and obituaries. He used hagiographical material for particular sections of the work. His account of the translation of St. Nicholas of Myra to Bari is essentially an abbreviation of the narrative of John, archdeacon of Bari.[1] For his treatise on early monasticism he used the *Vita S. Pauli eremitae* of Jerome, the *Vita Columbani* of Jonas, and the forged *Vita* of St. Maur attributed to Faustus.

But for most events in Normandy, England, and southern Italy in the years 1083–95 he relied very little on written sources. Although he had seen the chronicle attributed to Florence of Worcester,[2] which incorporated parts of the Anglo-Saxon Chronicle, he appears not to have relied on it for this part of his work. The monastic annals of this period are thin: those of Saint-Évroul revive only in 1095 when Orderic himself began to write them.[3] Neither William Rufus nor Robert Curthose patronized historical writing as their father had done, and up to that time Norman history had derived its inspiration from the dukes. Odo of Bayeux was a patron of letters, but of poetry and philosophy[4] rather than of history. The immediate impetus to historical writing came shortly afterwards with the Crusade, which deflected interest from Normandy itself. Consequently the history of the last two decades of the eleventh century was written up for the first time in the next generation, by William of Malmesbury, Orderic Vitalis, Henry of Huntingdon, and Robert of Torigny.

One other possible, lost, source has been suggested by the earlier editors of Wace's *Roman de Rou*. In some places Orderic's narrative is remarkably close to that of Wace. This is particularly so in the account of William the Conqueror's death and burial and the recapitulation of Norman history put into his mouth by Orderic. Le Prévost and Deeping suggested a common source for the two; Andreson postponed judgement.[5] Haskins showed a similar caution, merely noting: 'Whether Wace and Ordericus are

[1] See below, Appendix II.

[2] See above, ii. 186.

[3] Bibl. nat. MS. lat. 10062, f. 194^{r-v}. Entries in Orderic's hand are from 1095 to 1140; a few entries for this period are in later hands.

[4] Cf. for example A. B. Scott, *Hildeberti Cenomannensis episcopi carmina minora* (Leipzig, 1969), pp. xxxii, 45.

[5] *Roman de Rou*, ii, pp. 748–9. Dr. A. J. Holden, however, who is preparing a new edition of the *Roman de Rou* informs me that he too has come to the conclusion that Wace used Orderic in certain passages.

entirely independent is a matter which needs investigation.'[1] The evidence that for some information they are not independent of each other is indeed compelling. In one passage, describing King Henry I's visit to Fécamp at the beginning of his reign both appear to have used William of Jumièges, but both differ from him in placing the visit positively at Easter and in stating that Henry enfeoffed Duke Robert with the Vexin.[2] They agree on a wide range of subjects; on the wrongs done by William in taking England by conquest,[3] on the moral character of the Normans, said to need a strong hand if they are to show their best qualities,[4] on the arguments used by William the Conqueror when he arrested Odo of Bayeux,[5] all of which are characteristic of Orderic's opinions. They also agree on exact figures: both say, wrongly, in contradiction to the evidence they themselves produce, that William the Conqueror lived for sixty-four years;[6] both fix the amount bequeathed to Prince Henry by his father at five thousand livres,[7] the sum paid to Ascelin son of Arthur for the Conqueror's place of burial at sixty shillings,[8] and the sum paid by Helias for the county of Maine at ten thousand shillings.[9] Even if we allow that both Wace and Orderic used *chansons de geste* this is not the kind of material likely to be found in them. The evidence all points in one direction: Wace used a number of written sources, and among them must surely have been Book VII at least of the *Ecclesiastical History*, and possibly Book VIII. As a canon of Bayeux who had been educated at Caen he would have had easy access to the books of St. Stephen's, Caen: and amongst these, between 1160 and 1183 when he was writing the *Roman de Rou*, was undoubtedly the copy of these two books that is now MS. Vatican Reginensis lat. 703^{B}.

If this is accepted we need seek a lost written source no further: for the events in Normandy and England described in these two books Orderic probably relied almost exclusively on oral sources, and on his own memory.

1 Haskins, *Norman Institutions*, p. 272 n. 37.
2 See below, pp. 74–6; *Roman de Rou*, ii, ll. 2551–66, 2587–94.
3 See below, p. 94; *Roman de Rou*, ii, ll. 9167–74.
4 See below, p. 82; *Roman de Rou*, ii, ll. 9143–58.
5 See below, pp. 40–2; *Roman de Rou*, ii, ll. 9232–40.
6 See below, p. 80; *Roman de Rou*, ii, ll. 9259–60.
7 See below, p. 94; *Roman de Rou*, ii, ll. 9181–2.
8 See below, p. 106; *Roman de Rou*, ii, ll. 9359–62.
9 See below, p. 198; *Roman de Rou*, ii, l. 9776.

Orderic came to Normandy as a boy of ten in 1085; two years later he may have heard the dramatic account of the events at William the Conqueror's funeral from his abbot, Mainer, who was among those present. Episodes in the fighting near his abbey during the years that followed, such as the murder of Gilbert of Laigle as he rode away from his visit to Moulins-la-Marche, and the capture of the castle of Saint-Céneri during the absence of its lord, when the attackers found the tables laid and the food cooking in the kitchen as the few defenders fled, may have been told to him at the time and stored in his memory. Other happenings may have been described later by his fellow monks or the lords, visitors to the abbey, who had taken part in them. He was always dependent on the accuracy of his reporters, and with time various kinds of distortion might creep in.

First, his recollection of exact dates may have been uncertain, and his presentation adds to the confusion. Events are introduced by such vague terms as 'about the same time', 'soon afterwards', 'in those days'. Because Orderic gave an illusion of chronological sequence by beginning some new sections with a precise date historians using his work have sometimes attributed wrong dates to him. In fact his method was to move from one theme to another in some way associated with it, treating each one in depth and often over a considerable number of years before he left it. Even when he attempted to give an exact year memory might fail him. Thanks to details in obituaries, or to the weather that aided or hindered particular military operations, he was more likely to be right about the day or the time of year than the year itself. His counting was not always reliable: he was quite capable of saying that William the Conqueror was eight years old when he succeeded to the duchy in 1035 and sixty-four when he died in 1087. Sometimes, but not always, he appears to have counted both terminal dates in a time sequence, so that thirty-three years from 1100 may be either 1132 or 1133. It is possible too that at times he used figures in a general way, without precision: three years appears frequently to describe the duration of a long war or siege or time of exile, even when the true duration cannot have been more than one or two years; expressions such as 'fifteen years' or 'thirty years' were perhaps used in the sense of 'half-a-generation' or 'a generation', to indicate a rough span of time rather than an exact number of years.

Secondly, events might be distorted, possibly unintentionally, by his informants. A man fighting in a battle sees only a small corner of the field: a participant in a campaign depends on others for movements of other sections of the army. Precise and accurate detail of some episodes may be combined with vague or garbled accounts of others. Further, it may reasonably be asked how Orderic's informants collected their stories, and how they may have remodelled them before passing them on.

Secular Norman society, in the late eleventh and early twelfth centuries, was a seeding ground of vernacular epic and romance.[1] The earliest *chansons de geste* were taking shape: the written romances were still to come, but the themes were being developed. History, sometimes Latin, sometimes vernacular, had a place in the courts of great lords like Count Roger of Sicily,[2] or of men of modest standing, such as Ralph fitz Gilbert for whose wife, Constance, Gaimar wrote the *Estoire des Engleis* shortly before 1140.[3] Legends of warrior saints might be related to young lords by an earl's chaplain.[4] The Welsh, near neighbours of Earl Hugh of Chester and Robert of Rhuddlan, took their bards into battle with them, and perhaps depended on them for the stories of the engagements to be handed down to future generations.[5] If William of Malmesbury is to be believed, the Normans had their *jongleur* at the battle of Hastings.[6] Orderic gives an account of knights seated in a hall around Isabel of Tosny, telling stories 'as men do' of their dreams;[7] they might equally well have been telling stories of their battles.

Readers of Orderic cannot fail to be struck by the number of allusions to current legends of Troy and Thebes, of Roland and Charlemagne; and by the number of episodes that, though told as history, have the ring of epic or romance. Mabel of Bellême

[1] For the literary background see: John H. Fisher, *The Medieval Literature of Western Europe* (London, 1965), pp. 130–40; R. Bezzola, *Les origines et la formation de la littérature courtoise en occident* (Paris, 1960); J. Bédier, *Les légendes épiques* (Paris, 1908–13); E. Faral, *Les jongleurs en France au moyen âge* (Paris, 1910); Italo Siciliano, *Les origines des chansons de geste* (Paris, 1951); Foreville, pp. xliii–xlix; R. Louis, 'Les ducs de Normandie dans les chansons de geste' in *Byzantion*, xxviii (1958), 391–419; M. de Bouärd, 'A propos des sources du *Roman de Rou*' in *Recueil des travaux offerts à M. Clovis Brunel* (Paris, 1955), i. 178–82; D. C. Douglas, 'The "Song of Roland" and the Norman Conquest of England', in *French Studies*, xiv (1960), 99–116.

[2] GM, p. 4.

[3] Geffrei Gaimar, *L'Estoire des Engleis*, ed. A. Bell (Oxford, 1960).

[4] See above, iii. 216.

[5] See below, p. xxxviii.

[6] *GR* ii. 302.

[7] See below, p. 218.

murdered after her bath; Bertrade of Montfort entertaining her former and present husbands at the same banquet and serving them herself; Garnier of Montmorillon giving a sick beggar the pair of costly gloves he had received from his lady; Robert Guiscard haranguing his followers in the language of heroic song, are only a few. There can be few if any of Orderic's informants who never listened to *jongleurs*,[1] and legends of warrior saints and historical *gesta* of contemporary heroes were materials suitable even for the strictest moralists. It is possible that some episodes in the *chansons de geste* were derived from contemporary events: Henri Grégoire has produced an impressive body of evidence to suggest that the Baligant episode in the *chanson de Roland* could have been based on the Illyrian campaign of Robert Guiscard in 1081–5.[2] Even if contemporary experience was only exceptionally formalized and elaborated to such an extent, the stories of campaigns were passed from man to man in the milieu that produced the *chansons*. They must have become dramatized in the minds of the knights who took part in them, so that by the time they reached Orderic they were already contaminated by literary conventions. While his interpretations were moral and ecclesiastical, devoid of the cruelty and brutality of epic, he probably accepted the narratives much as he received them, respecting the tellers as eyewitnesses. But history and poetry could not be kept apart, in a society where both provided the main entertainment of knights in the hall. This does not mean that Orderic is wholly unreliable: often his dramatic stories can be confirmed. But he reflects the knowledge and ideas of his informants, and sometimes his work is more important as evidence of what they believed than as a literal record of fact.

(iii) *The contents of Books VII and VIII*

A full consideration of the contents of these books would involve rewriting the whole history of the period, for which they are a primary source of first importance. But certain topics need fuller treatment than is possible in footnotes, and since Orderic's handling

[1] Ansold of Maule was probably the most puritanical; see above, iii. 182.

[2] H. Grégoire, 'La chanson de Roland de l'an 1085', in *Bull. de l'académie royale de Belgique; Classe des lettres et sciences morales et politiques*, 5ᵉ sér. xxv (1939), 211–73; H. Grégoire and R. de Keyser, 'La chanson de Roland et Byzance', in *Byzantion*, xiv (1939), 265–301; with some corrections by M. de Bouärd in *BSAN* xlviii (1942), 608.

of them is an introduction to his methods and the materials available to him they are discussed here rather than in an Appendix.

1. *Robert Guiscard's campaign against Alexius Comnenus*

Orderic's account of south Italian history, as in earlier books, is full of errors in chronology and interpretation, yet valuable for the information he gives about the lives of individual Normans whose families were connected with Saint-Évroul. Although it has sometimes been suggested that he had seen the *De rebus gestis* of Geoffrey of Malaterra[1] there are no verbal echoes, and the contradictions in the works of the two men are hard to explain unless Orderic knew of Geoffrey's work only at second hand. He wrote from the angle of a Norman in Normandy. His view of Robert Guiscard's expedition against Durazzo as a heroic achievement and a pre-Crusade is out of tune with the works of writers nearer to the scene, who were aware of its extreme unpopularity with Italians, Greeks, and Normans alike in southern Italy.[2]

One remarkable parallel suggests the nature of some of his oral sources. The speech attributed by Anna Comnena to Robert Guiscard before his final assault on Durazzo in 1081[3] has three elements in common with the speech that Orderic puts into Guiscard's mouth on his death-bed in 1085.[4] In both Guiscard points out that he has undertaken the campaign in the interests of the deposed Emperor Michael and to avenge the slight to his daughter, betrothed to Michael's son. He reminds the Normans of how they have left their homes and ventured out with courage, and how they prosper when God gives them the victory. Lastly, he urges them to elect a single leader and obey him implicitly. This final proposal, which seems out of place in Anna's narrative, since in 1081 Guiscard was in good health and the unquestioned leader of his men, is turned by her into an invitation for a renewed show of confidence under the pretext of an offer to accept the will of his followers. It is the kind of gesture that might be expected from a leader in a *chanson de geste*. And in this, perhaps, may be explained the resemblances between works written independently some fifty years after the events in places as far apart as Constantinople and Normandy. After the collapse of the campaign Norman lords scattered to take service in both places, carrying with them not

[1] Cf. Mathieu, p. 74.
[2] Cf. Mathieu, p. 15.
[3] *Alexiad*, IV. v. 5.
[4] See below, pp. 36–8.

only their memories of events, but also the formalizing and embroidering of these events in *chansons*. Anna used a speech from one of these to illustrate the duplicity of Guiscard. Orderic wove it into a literary set piece: a death-bed speech recalling the achievements and ambitions of his rule and recognizing the hand of God in everything. This is a device that Orderic was to use again and develop further in imagining the last hours of William the Conqueror.

2. *Odo of Bayeux*

The trial and imprisonment of Odo of Bayeux in 1082 are among the most obscure events in William I's reign. The earliest sources give no indication of the nature of the charges against him: the Anglo-Saxon Chronicle merely says under 1082, 'In this year the king seized Bishop Odo',[1] and under 1087, in the account of William I's character, that in spite of Odo's power and influence the king put him in prison. Gregory VII wrote two letters of protest in 1083: one to the king, in moderate language,[2] and a second, much more strongly worded, to Archbishop Hugh of Lyons,[3] but both complain only of the disrespect for Odo's sacerdotal dignity and say nothing of the alleged offence. Leaving aside for the moment the Durham tractate, *De iniusta vexatione Willelmi episcopi*, whose date has been questioned,[4] and which was likewise concerned only with the justification for laying hands on Bishop Odo and not with the actual charge, more detailed stories come only some forty or fifty years later, in William of Malmesbury's *Gesta Regum*, Orderic's *Ecclesiastical History*, and the Hyde chronicle.[5] By this time these historians must have depended on reports that had lost their freshness and become contaminated by rumours of doubtful reliability. But at least they appear not

[1] Copied by Florence of Worcester (FW ii. 16) and much later by the Winchester and Waverley annalists (*Ann. Mon.* (RS), ii. 33, 194).

[2] *Das Register Gregors VII*, ed. E. Caspar (Berlin, 1920–3), ii. 630–1.

[3] P. Jaffé, *Monumenta Gregoriana* (Berlin, 1865), pp. 570–1.

[4] Symeon of Durham, *Opera*, ed. Arnold (RS 1882–5), i. 170–95. An account of the trial of William of Saint-Calais, bishop of Durham, on a charge of treason in 1088, it has normally been accepted as a near contemporary document. H. S. Offler in *EHR* lxvi (1951), 321–41 argued a case for a date in the second quarter of the twelfth century, but Southern, *St. Anselm*, p. 148 n. 1 reasserted the probable contemporaneity of the tract.

[5] *GR* ii. 360–1; below, pp. 40–2; *Liber monasterii de Hyda*, ed. E. Edwards (RS 1886), p. 296 (cf. *EYC* viii. 4).

to have depended on each other, and so their combined testimonies, together with record sources and the evidence for Odo's extortions, add up to something very near positive evidence.

All three historians allege that Odo was spending lavishly in Rome in a bid for the papacy, and that he had secured the support of many Norman magnates, amongst whom Orderic alone names Hugh earl of Chester. The Hyde chronicler[1] and Orderic refer to an oath; William of Malmesbury and Orderic suggest that the attempt to take so many of the king's knights overseas for his own schemes constituted an offence. They both allege that a distinction was made between the bishop and the earl, though Orderic attributes it to the king and Malmesbury to Lanfranc.[2] Orderic alone specifies that Odo was arrested in the Isle of Wight. He and the Hyde chronicler both refer to the trial: the Hyde chronicler with a brief statement that Odo was summoned to a council and found guilty, Orderic with a dramatic reconstruction embellished with imaginary speeches. The Durham tractate also contains a passing reference to the trial, saying that the king had seized Odo as a count and his brother, not as a bishop.[3] The variations in the details of these accounts indicate that the Hyde chronicler and Orderic cannot have taken their information from William of Malmesbury, whose *Gesta Regum* was the earliest of the three works, and that the most likely source lies in reports, possibly at second or third hand, of the arrest and trial. Any of the three, particularly Orderic, may have allowed a knowledge of Odo's later treason in 1088 to colour the account of his fall in 1082. But it is likely that the charges common to all three sources were in fact made at the trial; they may have been the pretext for Odo's imprisonment, even if the real cause went deeper. That anything as positive as treason was proved seems unlikely from the history

[1] 'Denique ubi plures Norman-Anglorum (*sic*) principes occulta persuasione et sacramento sibi associavit, ignorante rege, Anglia discedere decrevit, sed manifestata ejus versutia, ab eodem rege in consilium vocatur, devincitur, carceri mancipatur' (*Liber monasterii de Hyda*, p. 296).

[2] *GR* ii. 360–1: 'Cum olim Willelmus senior apud Lanfrancum quereretur se a fratre deseri, "Tu" inquit, "prende eum et vinci." "Et quid" respondit ille, "quia clericus est?" Tunc archiepiscopus, lepida hilaritate . . . "Non" dixit "episcopum Bajocarum capies, sed comitem Cantiae custodies."'

[3] The author attributes the following remark to Lanfranc during the trial of the bishop of Durham in 1088, 'Nos non de episcopio sed de tuo te feudo iudicamus, et hoc modo iudicavimus Baiocensem episcopum ante patrem huius regis de feudo suo, nec rex vocabat eum episcopum in placito illo sed fratrem et comitem' (Symeon of Durham, *Opera*, i. 184).

of his estates. There was certainly disorder and some transfer of allegiance on the Norman lands; the treatment of Odo's fee in Domesday Book and other assessment lists of the time is too inconsistent for any firm conclusions to be drawn about the English lands, except that royal action apparently stopped short of confiscation.[1] But there must surely have been a suspicion that the gathering of a large number of knights bound by an oath on the Channel coast might have been used for causes less remote than an Italian expedition. William had enemies in France, Maine, Brittany, and Normandy; his eldest son, Robert, had been in arms against him in 1079 and was so far from satisfied that he quarrelled again with his father a few months after the arrest of Odo.[2] William may have found the imprisonment of his over-mighty and over-ambitious half-brother a necessary precaution for his own safety. There is no contemporary warrant for the suggestion that Odo aimed at the Crown; the story first appears *c.* 1108 in Guibert of Nogent and later in Wace,[3] who possibly embroidered Orderic's vague suggestions of treachery.

Of Odo's exactions and oppressions there is ample evidence: the great trial on Penenden Heath was only one of a series of land-pleas in which he became involved, and a hundred years later the Evesham chronicler remembered with bitterness his invasions of church lands and considered his imprisonment a just judgement of God.[4] There may have been talk of injustice and maladministration at the trial. Yet this was not a justification for imprisonment. William seems to have taken a firm line in his later years on the duties of his knights to be available for service: if Orderic is to be believed he confiscated the estates of Baudry son of Nicholas for going to fight in Spain without permission, and only restored them on his

[1] Cf. H. Navel, 'Recherches sur les institutions féodales en Normandie', in *BSAN* li (1948–51), 17; R. S. Hoyt, 'A pre-Domesday Kentish assessment list', in *A Medieval Miscellany for D. M. Stenton*, ed. P. M. Barnes and C. F. Slade (Pipe Roll Society, 1962), p. 195; Douglas, *Domesday Monachorum*, p. 25; *VCH Kent*, iii. 220–42.

[2] There is no suggestion of any collusion between Robert and Odo before 1088, when they came together as allies in the very different conditions of a new reign; but Robert's last quarrel with his father and his departure from Normandy towards the end of 1083 may have been due in part to a fear of sharing the same fate as Odo. It has never been fully explained. See David, *Robert Curthose*, pp. 36–8, and above, iii. 112.

[3] Cf. *Recueil des Historiens des Croisades* (Paris (1841–1906)), *Historiens Occidentaux*, iv. 232–3; *Roman de Rou*, ii, ll. 9199–9248.

[4] *Chronicon abbatiae de Evesham*, ed. W. D. Macray (RS 1863), pp. 96–7.

death-bed.[1] Disinheritance as a penalty for failure in service was traditional; imprisonment was not. When William's prisons were opened after his death the men released were hostages, convicted traitors, and Odo of Bayeux. It is hard not to believe that Odo was under very grave suspicion of treason.

In questioning the early date of the Durham tractate, H. S. Offler has thrown doubt on whether Lanfranc in fact made the distinction between the functions of bishop and earl in 1082, suggesting that if the story of Lanfranc's remarks at the trial of William of Saint-Calais did not come from the author's immediate genuine knowledge 'it is not easy to know whence he had it, if not from the *Gesta Regum* of William of Malmesbury'. But Orderic and the Hyde chronicler certainly did not depend on Malmesbury, and their accounts tip the balance in favour of the distinction having been made, if not in 1082, at least shortly afterwards. Moreover Gregory VII voiced his objections in no uncertain terms in 1083; Lanfranc was too good a canonist not to have given considerable thought to the legality of the arrest of a bishop[2] before the bishop of Durham came under suspicion of treason in 1088. If he did not make the distinction in 1082, almost certainly he made it retrospectively in 1088. At least some of the stories of the trials current in the next generation were likely to have been based on reliable contemporary accounts of what took place.

3. *The Vexin and the frontier with France*

From the closing years of the reign of William I until the loss of Normandy in 1204 the frontier on the river Epte, which divided the Vexin into two parts, was one of the chief centres of conflict between France and Normandy.[3] The position of the French Vexin was in some ways anomalous: during the early eleventh century it was the only substantial part of the province of Rouen not in Normandy and the count of the Vexin, who was the immediate neighbour of the duke of Normandy until 1077, held, not directly of the king of France, but as his subtenant under the abbot of Saint-Denis.[4] Up to that date relations between the dukes of Normandy and the counts of the Vexin were usually friendly.

[1] See below, p. 100.

[2] Cf. Z. N. Brooke, *The English Church and the Papacy* (Cambridge, 1931), pp. 129–30.

[3] See Lemarignier, *L'hommage en marche*, pp. 39 ff.

[4] J. Flach, *Les origines de l'ancienne France* (Paris, 1886–1917), iii. 525–7, 529.

Under Ralph IV (1053–74), count of Amiens and Valois as well as of the Vexin, who took as his third wife Anne of Russia, the widow of King Henry I of France, the power of the counts constituted a challenge to the Capetian kings.[1] But the whole situation changed in 1077, when Ralph's successor Simon (later St. Simon of Crépy), who was without heirs, entered a monastery, and King Philip retained the Vexin in his own hand, holding it as a fief of the abbot of Saint-Denis. From that date Chaumont and Mantes, and to a lesser extent Pontoise, became of major importance in the defence and fortification of the region.[2] The attack of William the Conqueror on Mantes in 1087 must be seen in the context of this reshuffle of power on a vital frontier.

Orderic's account of the origins of this war, though probably unreliable on particular points, shows an appreciation of the underlying political realities in the region. He must have had sources of local information: Saint-Évroul had acquired priories at Parnes and Neufmarché during the 1060s,[3] and the monks of these cells were in touch with the frontier lords, including the vassals of the châtelain of Chaumont. From 1085 Orderic himself was in Normandy, growing up in contact with these men. He knew, therefore, something of the actual fighting and of the popularly held justification of the war. There is no reason to doubt that William I laid claim to the Vexin, at least to the extent of producing a legal claim for the satisfaction of his own vassals. Whether such a claim rested on any solid basis of fact is much more doubtful.[4]

Orderic alleges that, when Henry I of France took refuge in Normandy at Easter, 1033, and received Norman help to put down a rebellion among his vassals, he rewarded Duke Robert by granting him the whole Vexin, with the full consent of Drogo, count of the Vexin. Henry's flight to Normandy is a well-attested fact: it is recorded by William of Jumièges[5] and proved by Henry's

[1] See P. Feuchère, 'La principauté d'Amiens-Valois au xie siècle', in *Le Moyen Âge*, lx (1954), 1–37.

[2] Lemarignier, *L'hommage en marche*, p. 43.

[3] See above, iii, pp. xviii–xix.

[4] Historians have differed on the interpretation of the scanty evidence: J. Dhondt, 'Les relations entre la France et la Normandie sous Henri Ier' (*Normannia*, xv (1939), 466–7), considers Orderic's account trustworthy; Lemarignier, *L'hommage en marche*, p. 42, gives arguments for rejecting it.

[5] Marx, pp. 104–5. The value of William of Jumiège's account of Duke Robert's reign and of the other sources is discussed in Haskins, *Norman Institutions*, pp. 265–76.

subscription to three surviving charters.[1] William of Jumièges adds that the duke asked his uncle Mauger, count of Corbeil, to give assistance to Henry. Orderic says nothing of this, but describes an attack on Orleans. Wace, who probably made use of Orderic for the story of Henry's flight, gives an independent account of the subsequent suppression of the rebellion, saying that Robert had Henry escorted back to France by way of Gisors, and making no mention of Orleans.[2] Possibly the two men relied on different oral traditions for the later events; Orderic's source of information was certainly reliable, for Robert duke of Normandy subscribed a charter given at Orleans in King Henry's court in 1032.[3]

That Henry owed a debt of gratitude to Duke Robert can be proved; that he enfeoffed him with the Vexin cannot. Similarly, Count Drogo of the Vexin was undoubtedly a friend of the duke of Normandy, but there is no evidence that he was his vassal in any sense, and that he held the Vexin from him as a fief is far from certain. Drogo married Edward the Confessor's sister Goda (or Godgifu), who was a Norman protégée;[4] he appeared in Rouen in 1024,[5] and Duke Robert confirmed one of his charters in 1030,[6] but as this was concerned with rights of the abbey of Jumièges in Normandy the confirmation does not necessarily imply vassalage, and the charter was given at Mantes, not in Normandy. Finally Drogo accompanied Robert on his pilgrimage and died with him at Nicaea. If he ever became Robert's vassal for the Vexin it is strange that there is no mention of the fact in William of Jumièges. When one considers that at the time William was writing, before 1077, there was no incentive to invent a story of enfeoffment his silence becomes all the more significant. Not until 1077 did William the Conqueror need to look for a plausible pretext to prevent the strengthening of the frontier which, particularly after the siege of Gerberoy in 1079, was a threat to Normandy. Like Robert Guiscard about to attack Durazzo, he probably made

[1] Fauroux, nos. 55, 63, 69; no. 69 runs: 'Signum Henrici regis qui tunc temporibus profugus habebatur in hac terra.'

[2] *Roman de Rou*, ii, ll. 2575–85.

[3] Cf. Fauroux, no. 91; dated 1032 by O. Guillou, *Le comte d'Anjou et son entourage au xie siècle* (Paris, 1972), ii. 49–50.

[4] Cf. *Encomium Emmae Reginae*, ed. A. Campbell (Camden third ser. lxxii 1949), pp, xlix–l.

[5] F. Lot, *Études critiques sur l'abbaye de Saint-Wandrille* (Paris, 1913), pp. 37–8.

[6] Fauroux, no. 63.

a claim to legality and spread the story among his supporters; it may have been wholly unsound, but it passed into tradition and Orderic most likely reported it in good faith.

Other accounts of the causes of William's attack on Mantes in 1087 are more superficial. William of Malmesbury's suggestion that it was the Conqueror's reply to a derisive joke of Philip I's proves nothing but Malmesbury's inability to resist a good story.[1] Robert of Torigny suggested that William was exasperated at the help given by Philip to the rebellious Robert Curthose.[2] This may have added fuel to the fire: but Orderic goes deeper. He was aware of the far more fundamental causes of hostility on the Vexin frontier; and the disorder that arose from the situation where local French châtelains could raid across the Epte into Normandy may well have been the real cause of William's retaliatory raid on Mantes, backed by a presumptuous claim to the whole Vexin. In spite of errors in the details of his story, Orderic shows here a deeper awareness of political reality than other historians of his day.

The same cannot be said of his handling of the civil conflicts that arose in the early years of Robert Curthose's rule, which appeared to him in a different context. To him they were evidence of Robert's incompetence to govern and, to a lesser extent, of the iniquities of Odo of Bayeux and Robert of Bellême. In region after region, particularly along the frontiers, he shows how civil strife broke out, dwelling on personal feuds, private rivalries, and the inability of Robert to maintain the firm rule of his father or to follow any steady course of action. He wrote a tacit defence of Henry I's seizure of Normandy and imprisonment of his brother in 1106, and failed to explain the underlying motives either of the king of France or of most of the lords engaged in mutual war.

As far as the events on the north-east frontier can be reconstructed, it seems that Robert Curthose turned to his overlord, Philip I, for support against his vassals in that region, while they received support from William Rufus. Whether William or Robert took the initiative is not clear. Charter evidence shows that Robert was at Vernon on his way into France for a campaign on 24 April 1089.[3] In the course of the summer Robert besieged the

[1] *GR* ii. 336. Wace repeats the same story (*Roman de Rou*, ii, ll. 9087–9112).

[2] Marx, p. 265.

[3] *Regesta*, i, no. 308.

principal castle of the count of Eu[1] and, with the help of King Philip, Gerard of Gournay's castle at La Ferté. In return for Philip's help Robert gave him the manor of Gisors, which was in fact a property of the archbishop of Rouen, and which Archbishop William Bonne-Âme was not prepared to surrender without a struggle.[2] William Rufus, always more of a political realist than his elder brother, appreciated the danger of allowing the king of France to gain a footing on this important frontier of Normandy. His first efforts in 1089–90 were directed to securing the support of the lords in this region, and this remained a vital part of his strategy. When some of them became involved in Robert of Mowbray's rebellion in 1095 his most severe vengeance fell on the count of Eu.[3] The climax of his fortification of that frontier was reached in 1097 when, with the help of Robert of Bellême, he built a strong castle at Gisors.[4] Up to the time that Robert Curthose's departure on Crusade in 1096 gave him a free hand in Normandy he was steadily increasing his grip on other parts of the frontier, by securing the allegiance of Ralph of Tosny, and making an alliance with his brother Henry after the latter was established in Domfront. If the king of France failed to gain anything from the internal struggles in Normandy the credit must go to William Rufus.

Orderic, while consistently denouncing the incompetence of Robert, describes these events as isolated episodes, and seems to have had no appreciation of the political role of the king of France. Occasionally, in passing, he mentions the presence of French troops in a particular engagement. It seems likely that for an appreciation of political motive he was dependent on clear-sighted informants, or on political propaganda. And, since of William's sons only the youngest, Henry, had any skill as a political propagandist, Orderic was thrown back either on his own judgements which were inherently moral, or on Henry's justification of his appropriation of Normandy in 1106.

4. *The date of the death of Robert of Rhuddlan*

Robert of Rhuddlan's death has generally been assigned without question to the year 1088, on the evidence of Orderic, and other

[1] *Regesta*, i, no. 310.

[2] *GC* xi. *Instrumenta*, col. 18. There is no convincing evidence for the suggestion in Fliche, *Philippe I*, p. 293 n. 3, that the date should be 1090 or 1091.

[3] See below, p. 284.

[4] Le Prévost, iv. 21.

events in Welsh history have been dated on the assumption that Robert's conquests in Wales, which were said by Orderic to have lasted fifteen years, began in 1073. Yet Orderic never stated that Robert of Rhuddlan was killed in 1088; indeed he was positive only on the day, 3 July, and never mentioned the year at all. The date has been deduced partly from a hasty reading of his account, and partly from his inclusion of Robert in the list of those who died 'about the same time as William the Conqueror', which could mean a few years later.[1]

Orderic tells how Robert of Rhuddlan returned after the siege of Rochester in 1088 and found that his lands had been ravaged by King Gruffydd ap Cynan;[2] since his death is also attributed to Gruffydd historians have deduced that Robert at once set out on a punitive expedition in which he lost his life. This deduction is unwarranted. Orderic held together the separate elements in his *History* by association of ideas and persons: his mention of Robert led him to a full account of Robert's whole life, from the time that he served as a squire in the court of Edward the Confessor and was knighted by him, through service under his cousin and overlord, Hugh of Chester, and his independent Welsh campaigns up to the time when he fell under a shower of Welsh darts by the Great Orme. Here, as in his account of Scottish affairs, he moves ahead from the episode in his roughly chronological narrative to finish the story some years later.

The difficulty of reconciling the date 1088 with the narrative in the *History of Gruffydd ap Cynan*, written probably in the lifetime of his son Owain Gwynedd (1137–71),[3] was clearly noted by J. E. Lloyd.[4] The writer of this history, working probably not long after Orderic but without knowledge of his work, makes many statements that are consistent with both Orderic's narrative and the evidence of Domesday. Though the writer gives no dates and tends to be vague in his chronology the sequence of events described by him does not normally conflict with these sources.[5] But he states

[1] See below, p. 112. Robert's name possibly crept in by association with his cousin, Hugh of Grandmesnil.

[2] Below, pp. 134–6.

[3] *The History of Gruffydd ap Cynan*, ed. and trans. Arthur Jones (Manchester, 1910), pp. 18–23.

[4] In *Transactions of the Honourable Society of Cymmrodorion*, 1899–1900, p. 155 n. 2.

[5] In 1086 Gruffydd's lands were certainly in the hands of the Normans, after his capture. The Domesday survey (*DB* i. 269a; J. Tait, *The Domesday Survey*

in one place that the captivity of King Gruffydd, who fell into the hands of Hugh of Chester shortly after securing the crown of Gwynedd in 1081, lasted twelve years; a little later, if the existing manuscripts are correct, he describes the period as sixteen years.[1] Sixteen could be a mistake for twelve, particularly if the figures in the lost original manuscript were given in Roman numerals; but if Gruffydd was active in 1088 even twelve must be wrong. Historians have assumed either that both figures are rhetorical exaggerations, or that the Gruffydd who raided Robert of Rhuddlan's lands and caused his death was not Gruffydd ap Cynan.[2]

Yet we may accept twelve years as the true length of Gruffydd's captivity without discarding anything in Orderic's account except the statement that Gruffydd was responsible for the attacks on Robert's Welsh lands during his absence at the siege of Rochester, and on this point Orderic may easily have been wrong. On the other hand, since Orderic's informant was Robert's brother Arnold, who went to Chester some years later to arrange for the transfer of his remains to Saint-Évroul, it is unlikely that he was mistaken in saying that Robert's body was first buried in the monastery of St. Werburgh, which Hugh earl of Chester had established shortly before under the abbot Richard, a monk of Bec. And St. Anselm did not visit Chester to take, at Hugh's request, the first steps for turning the church of secular canons into a monastery colonized by monks of Bec until the early autumn of 1092.[3] This would make 3 July 1093 the earliest possible date for Robert's death, and indeed it is the most probable. There is no mention of Robert of Rhuddlan among the lords who gave lands to St. Werburgh's from late 1093 onwards, and Hugh himself gave lands in Rhos that had been held *in capite* by Robert at the time of Domesday. By 1094, therefore, Robert was almost certainly dead.[4]

of Cheshire (Chetham Society, N.S. lxxv, 1916), pp. 38–9, 45), shows that the castle, borough, vill, berewicks, and appurtenances were divided between Hugh of Chester and Robert of Rhuddlan; and that Robert held *in capite* Rhos and Rhuvoniog in farm from the king for £40.

[1] *The History of Gruffydd ap Cynan*, ed. A. Jones, p. 133.

[2] Ibid., pp. 63–9, where the date of Robert's death is unaccountably given as 1089; A. H. Williams, *An Introduction to the History of Wales* (Cardiff, 1941), ii. 5 n. 1; J. E. Lloyd, *A History of Wales from the Earliest Times*, 3rd edn., ii. 390 n. 109.

[3] *The Life of St. Anselm by Eadmer*, ed. R. W. Southern (Edinburgh, 1962), p. 63 n. 2; J. Tait, *The Chartulary of St. Werburgh, Chester* (Chetham Society, 1920), pp. xxiii–xxv.

[4] The 'foundation' charter was written later, and the gifts of lands cannot be

Gaimar's statement that William Rufus gave Hugh of Chester North Wales has sometimes been taken to refer to a formal investiture after Robert's death. Standing alone the evidence of Gaimar would hardly be acceptable; but the context is interesting, since he certainly had some contact with the royal court during the reign of Henry I.[1] He places Hugh's investiture at festivities at Westminster in the new great hall,[2] and says that while the king was holding his court the news of the murder of King Malcolm of Scotland was received.[3] The great hall at Westminster was not completed until 1099,[4] and the poet may have compressed two courts into one; but Malcolm was murdered in November, 1093,[5] just at the time when, if Robert of Rhuddlan had lost his life in the previous July, the king might have been investing a successor with authority in Rhos and Rhuvoniog.

If Robert was killed in 1093 his assailant could have been Gruffydd, at liberty after twelve years in Chester prison, and his death might have been one of the first episodes in Welsh attacks on the Normans in Gwynedd that reached their climax in the year 1094.[6] Indeed there is a striking parallel in the Welsh *History of Gruffydd*[7] at about this time. After plundering the castle of Aberlleriog, Gruffydd 'returned to another place in Anglesey where he had three ships. The men of the castle and the men of Mor pursued him throughout the day, fighting behind him valiantly. And as before they went back with the plunder and with the French and Saxons bound by them, and prisoners; and they killed several of their pursuers in the long battle. On Gruffydd's side there fell Gellon, the chief harpist and musician in the fleet.' The editor's comment is that in this unsatisfactory account of the opening of the Welsh reaction of 1094–8 the writer seems to confuse this expedition with 'the earlier one against Robert of Rhuddlan at Deganwy'.[8] In fact, if we substitute the estuary of the Conway for 'another place in Anglesey', this could be the same episode. The absence of comment on the death of the redoubtable

dated precisely; see *The Chartulary of St. Werburgh, Chester*, pp. 13–37, but there is no suggestion that Robert had ever made any gift.

[1] Geffrei Gaimar, *L'Estoire des Engleis*, ed. A. Bell (Oxford, 1960), pp. x–xi.

[2] Ibid., ll. 5972–3, 6037.

[3] Ibid., ll. 6105–7.

[4] Ibid., p. 274.

[5] Anglo-Saxon Chronicle (1093).

[6] Anglo-Saxon Chronicle (1094), FW ii. 35.

[7] *History of Gruffydd ap Cynan*, ed. A. Jones, p. 139.

[8] Ibid., p. 174 n. 9.

Robert of Rhuddlan may seem surprising, but it is possible that the Welsh were ignorant of the identity of the man they had killed. If he had rushed out in haste without his armour and with only one attendant he would hardly have been taken for a great marcher lord, and the ferocity of the attack must have made the body quite unrecognizable even before the head was hacked off. The Welsh record noted only the name of the harpist they themselves had lost; and the harpist's death perhaps deprived them of a full account of the episode.

But even if this was a different episode the case for 1093 rather than 1088 as the date of Robert's death is not seriously weakened. There is nothing in the known history of Wales at this period inconsistent with the revised date. The appointment of Hervey as bishop of Bangor about 1092[1] points only to Norman influence in the region, not specifically to control by Hugh of Chester. Other dates, such as the attack on Rhuddlan castle in 1075,[2] seem to have been derived by historians from the supposition that Robert's campaigns in Wales began fifteen years before 1088, and so about 1073. But Orderic's 'per xv annos intolerabiliter Britones protriuit' is vague enough, and may even date from the building of the castle at Deganwy. Robert's activities in the marches began with his service under Hugh, possibly as sheriff in Chester, included a phase of conquest jointly under Hugh, leading to the shared lordship of Rhuddlan, and ended with his independent warfare against the Welsh from his bases at Rhuddlan and Deganwy. The last two phases no doubt overlapped. It is impossible to tell from which point in Robert's activities Orderic began his calculation, if it was a calculation, and it is just as likely to have been a rough estimate. No other events should be dated by it.

5. *Herlequin's* (*Hellequin's*) *hunt*

The story of the priest of Bonneval's encounter with the *familia Herlechini* is one of the fullest and most theological expositions of a piece of popular folklore of great antiquity and widespread occurrence. Stories of nocturnal hosts of the dead, sometimes armies, sometimes hunts, that swept across the country with fear-

[1] Hugh the Chantor, *History of the Church of York*, ed. C. Johnson (Edinburgh, 1961), p. 7.

[2] J. E. Lloyd, *History of Wales*, ii. 382 ff.

ful shrieks, occur in various forms in most parts of western Europe. They have given rise to an extensive literature: a good, scholarly introduction to the folklore basis is L. Sainéau's article 'La Mesnie Hellequin',[1] and some of the more literary aspects of the legend have been critically examined by F. Lot in 'La Mesnie Hellequin et le comte Ernequin de Boulogne'.[2] Among twelfth-century references are the account in the Peterborough chronicle of the gigantic, black hunters seen and heard at night in the woods round Peterborough after the appointment of Abbot Henry of Poitou,[3] Walter Map's account of King Herla and mention of 'phalanges noctiuage quas Herlethingi dicebant' which ceased to appear after the first year of Henry II,[4] and Peter of Blois's comparison of worldly clerks to 'milites Herlewini'.[5]

Orderic treated the vision of the priest of Bonneval as historical fact. It satisfied the first criterion of historical veracity for a historian of his day: it was an eyewitness account given by a trustworthy man. William of Malmesbury accepted the story of the witch of Berkeley on similar grounds.[6] Whatever underlay the priest's experience, and it is at least possible that his first fears[7] were justified and that he was so severely manhandled by troops of ruffians riding to the siege of Courcy that the subsequent vision was the product of delirium, he undoubtedly believed in the reality of the phenomena he had seen. He was an educated man, whose brother had put out large sums of money to provide for his schooling in France, and he must have known the teaching on penance, the efficacy of the Mass, and the pains of purgatory, which provided the interpretation of these phenomena. When Orderic wrote down the story some thirty years after the priest died his own long reflections on the subject-matter may have added some precision to the interpretations, just as the rolling periods of his rhythmic prose spelled out more clearly the terror and sombre magnificence of the vision. In the form he has passed it on to us it is as much a moral and social tract or sermon, coloured by the penitential teaching of the early twelfth century, as a piece of

[1] *Revue des traditions populaires*, xx (1905), 177–86.

[2] *Romania*, xxii (1903), 422–41.

[3] Anglo-Saxon Chronicle (1127).

[4] *De Nugis Curialium*, ed. M. R. James (Oxford, 1914), pp. 13 ff., 186.

[5] Migne, *PL* ccvii. 44.

[6] *GR* i. 253–4.

[7] See below, p. 238.

folklore. It is also one of the most unforgettable passages in the *Ecclesiastical History*.

6. *The treatise on the new monastic orders*

Orderic lived through the years when the older monasticism came under attack from newer houses, where the Benedictine Rule was interpreted more literally, without regard to historical change or climatic differences. These attacks came both from the 'orders' of Cîteaux, Savigny, and Tiron as they gained strength, and from groups of monks in individual monasteries, like those of Coulombs, who were the subject of a wise and understanding letter from Ivo of Chartres.[1] The great debate on the interpretation of the Rule reached its climax in the third and fourth decades of the twelfth century, with a spate of letters and treatises in addition to those of the two chief protagonists, Peter the Venerable of Cluny and St. Bernard of Clairvaux.[2] It is unlikely that Orderic ever saw the famous *Letter 28* of Peter the Venerable, which seems to have been a treatise intended for publication rather than a private letter,[3] but he certainly heard Peter the Venerable expound his views in the chapter of March, 1132, attended by representatives of all Cluniac houses and houses with Cluniac customs.[4] This was the chapter where Peter proposed a number of reforms for the whole order, but agreed to mitigate some of the more severe restrictions under pressure from the traditionalists. Orderic, in his comments on this meeting of two hundred priors and seven hundred and twelve monks which he attended in person, shows himself one of the traditionalists. Nevertheless he was an admirer of St. Bernard, and must have received a first-hand account of his character from his abbot, Warin, who had visited him and consulted him on the affairs of Saint-Évroul in 1131.[5]

[1] Migne, *PL* clxii. 198–22 (Ep. 192).

[2] The chronology of the documents in this controversy has been carefully established by André Wilmart, 'Une riposte de l'ancien monachisme au manifeste de saint Bernard' in *Revue bénédictine*, xlvi (1934), 296–344, J. Leclercq, 'Nouvelle réponse de l'ancien monachisme aux critiques des Cisterciens', in *Revue bénédictine*, lxvii (1957), 77–94, and Giles Constable, *The Letters of Peter the Venerable* (Cambridge, Mass., 1967), ii, Appendix E (pp. 270–4).

[3] Printed, G. Constable, *The Letters of Peter the Venerable*, i. 52–101; commentary, ii. 115–20.

[4] Le Prévost, v. 29–31.

[5] See above, iii. 338–40.

He knew therefore the best in both the old and the new ideals, and he attempted to express it in his account of Robert of Molesme's efforts to secure a literal observance of the Rule, which led to the founding of Cîteaux.[1] But his exposition shows that he had little direct knowledge of the events of 1098–9. He knew that there was a bull commanding Robert to return to Molesme, and he either knew or guessed that some kind of canonical restriction was put on future movements of monks between Molesme and the new monastery. But comparison of Urban II's real bull, or even the letter of the legate Hugh,[2] with the pseudo-bull of Urban II invented by Orderic shows that he interpreted the events in terms of 1135 rather than 1099. If the reference to the horrible dangers of schism might have been equally appropriate at either date, the use of the term 'Cistercian', which had not been coined in 1099, was an anachronism. Orderic's narrative cannot be taken as evidence of the obscure and controversial early history of Cîteaux; it is much more likely to reflect the arguments that he had heard in his own cloister and in other monasteries. On the other hand, Tiron and Savigny were nearer to Saint-Évroul, and their history was less clouded by controversy. Orderic's brief accounts of the lives of Bernard of Tiron and Vitalis of Savigny are earlier than the official *Vitae* of these great abbots, and have the value of independent and contemporary testimony.

He made no reference to other treatises and pamphlets, and may not have seen any. The one document he cited explicitly was a satirical poem by Pain Bolotin,[3] a canon of Chartres, written only a few years earlier, which attacked the hypocrites to be found among the genuine reformers in the new movement. He himself wrote as a historian, explaining and interpreting the growth of monasticism from its origins in the deserts of Egypt, not as a satirist or pamphleteer. Some historians have charged him, unjustly, with attacking St. Bernard or the Cistercians. In fact his strictures,

[1] For a guide to some of the extensive literature on the subject see David Knowles, 'Cistercians and Cluniacs', in *The Historian and Character* (Cambridge, 1963), pp. 50–75; id., *Great Historical Enterprises* (Edinburgh, 1963), pp. 198–222; J. Winandy, 'Les origines de Cîteaux et les travaux de M. Lefèvre', in *Revue bénédictine*, lxvii (1957), 49–76; F. Masai, 'Les études cisterciennes de J. A. Lefèvre', in *Scriptorium*, xi (1) (1957), 119–23.

[2] See below, pp. 322–4; *Analecta Sacri Ordinis Cisterciensis*, vi (1950), 9–10.

[3] J. Leclercq, 'Le poème de Payen Bolotin contre les faux ermites', in *Revue bénédictine*, lxviii (1958), 52–86.

like those of Pain Bolotin, were not directed against any particular individual or order. He gave high praise to the joys of Cistercian life at its best, in abbeys whose very names proclaimed the spiritual delights to be found in them, while criticizing individual pharisees or hypocrites, who brought the whole of monasticism into ill repute by their unholy lives. Tares were mixed with the good corn, and this is no worse than he said in his account of life in his own monastery. His treatise is a balanced summing up of the views of a traditional Benedictine historian on the purpose of the institution in which his whole life was spent: it is a defence, and not a polemic.[1]

(iv) *Note on the editing*

When Duchesne was preparing his edition the Caen MS. was still in France, and he transcribed and edited it. Le Prévost and Delisle did not have the same advantage. They used the edition of Duchesne and a transcript made by La Porte du Theil, which was in the Bibliothèque Nationale (Collection Moreau, no. 1275). Duchesne either misread words or deliberately provided editorial emendations which changed the sense in a number of places. La Porte du Theil's transcript is sometimes closer to the original than Duchesne's edition, but it contains a number of misreadings. Delisle did not see a facsimile of the MS. until long after the appearance of the edition with which he was concerned.

I have kept my edition as close as possible to the Caen MS. (MS. Vatican Reginensis lat. 703^{B}), and this involves in places substantial differences from earlier editions. This MS. is a fairly careful copy and was corrected; but the scribe had lapses, and his conventions were slightly different from Orderic's. He was careless in his use of the cedilla, and sometimes inserted abbreviations or suspensions out of place. While on the whole he preserved the periods of Orderic in his punctuation, he sometimes broke up the work into shorter sentences and seems occasionally to have used his medial stops indiscriminately. Where the punctuation corresponds neither to the sense nor to the rhythm I have slightly

[1] J. Lefèvre, 'Le vrai récit primitif des origines de Cîteaux est-il l'*Exordium Parvum*?', in *Le Moyen Âge*, lxi (1955), 329–61, argued that the treatises of Orderic and William of Malmesbury were Benedictine propaganda, which provoked a Cistercian response in the *Exordium Parvum*; but he modified this in *Analecta Bollandiana*, lxxiv (1956), 72–3, where he treated Orderic as accepting the Cistercian position.

emended it. There are some obvious mistakes in words, particularly noticeable where Orderic was quoting from another work, or in the fragments for which an alternative early copy exists, and these have been corrected. I have also made some minor adjustments, for instance by changing final *e* to *æ* where Orderic's own usage was consistently different from that of the scribe. Where substantial emendations have been made the readings of the Caen MS. are given in the textual notes.

HISTORIA ÆCCLESIASTICA

CONTENTS OF BOOKS VII AND VIII

BOOK VII

BOOK VIII

BOOK VII

4

ANNO ab incarnatione domini millesimo octogesimo quarto,
iii. 162 indictione vii.' Henricus teutonicus rex multitudinem Saxonum, Alemannorum, Lotharigensium, aliarumque gentium coaceruauit, Italiam uiolenter ingressus penetrauit, Romam obsedit et expugnauit. Porro Romanis pro cupiditate munerum quæ illis spoponderat sese dedentibus urbem cepit, Gregorium septimum de sede apostolica expulit.' et Witbertum Rauennatium metropolitam ei nefarie subrogauit.[1] Tunc Gregorius Beneuentum secessit.' et maxima dissensio in orbe orta magnum filiis æcclesiæ detrimentum generauit, et ad multorum perniciem diu permansit. Gregorius enim papa qui Hildebrannus in baptismate dictus fuerat a puero monachus fuit[2] omnique uita sua sapientiæ et religioni admodum studuit.' assiduumque certamen contra peccatum exercuit. Per singulos gradus æcclesiasticorum ordinum usque ad summi pontificatus apicem ascendit.' in quo sedecim annis[3] legem Dei uigilanter obseruare studuit. Zelo quippe ueritatis et iusticiæ inflammatus omne scelus arguebat.' nullique contra rectitudinem pro timore seu fauore parcebat. Inde persecutionem et exilium ab indomitis et iugo domini contrariis pertulit.' nec tamen ab eis qualibet arte uinci usque ad mortem potuit.

iii. 163 Henricum ergo Teutonicorum regem quia diuinæ legis preuaricator erat incorrigibilis sepe admonuit.' corripuit, ad postremum excommunicauit.[4] Nam princeps prefatus uxorem suam Eustachii Boloniensium egregii comitis filiam reliquit, et sordidis

[1] Henry gained possession of the whole of Rome except the castle of Sant' Angelo on 21 March 1084; and the anti-pope, Wibert of Ravenna, who had been elected on 25 June, 1080, was enthroned on Palm Sunday (24 March), 1084. See A. Fliche, *La réforme grégorienne et la reconquête chrétienne* (Fliche et Martin, *Histoire de l'Église*, viii), pp. 154–7; G. Meyer von Knonau, *Jahrbücher des deutschen Reiches unter Heinrich IV und Heinrich V* (Leipzig, 1890–1909), iii. 276–7, 521 ff.

[2] He had been a monk only for a very short time in 1047–8, probably at Cologne. See above, ii. 298–9 and note; H. E. J. Cowdrey, *The Cluniacs and the Gregorian Reform* (Oxford, 1970), pp. 148–9.

BOOK VII

4

IN the year of our Lord 1084, the seventh indiction, the German king, Henry, summoned a great host of Saxons, Swabians, Lotharingians, and other peoples and, invading Italy by force, overran the country and besieged and stormed Rome. The Romans, greedy for the gifts he promised, surrendered to him and he took the city, drove Gregory VII from the papal throne and impiously set up Wibert, archbishop of Ravenna, in his place.[1] Gregory then withdrew to Benevento; and a general schism began all over the world, causing great harm to Christians and lasting so long that it brought many to damnation. Pope Gregory, who had been baptized with the name of Hildebrand, had been an oblate monk;[2] he was an active promoter of learning and monasticism all his life and unremittingly waged war on sin. He rose through the lower ecclesiastical orders to the highest peak of the papacy, and there for sixteen years[3] he devoted all his endeavours towards upholding the law of God. Fired with a passion for truth and justice he attacked every kind of wickedness, sparing no offenders through fear or favour. Consequently he endured persecution and exile at the hands of insubordinates who rejected the Lord's yoke; but up to the time of his death they were never able to overthrow him, try as they would.

Because Henry, king of the Germans, was an incorrigible rebel against the divine law, he repeatedly admonished and corrected, and finally excommunicated him.[4] This monarch deserted his wife, a daughter of the renowned Count Eustace of Boulogne, and gave

[3] Gregory VII was elected pope on 22 April 1073, and died on 25 May 1085, just over twelve years later. In an earlier book Orderic wrongly gave the length of his pontificate as seventeen years (above, ii. 298).

[4] Gregory pronounced sentence of excommunication and deposition on Henry in the Lenten synod of 1080 for his open and protracted disobedience to papal authority (E. Caspar, *Das Register Gregors VII* (Berlin, 1920–3), pp. 483–7). The remainder of the paragraph is completely untrue. Henry IV's wife was Bertha of Savoy; he never married a sister of Godfrey of Bouillon. Orderic made the same mistake in Book IV (above, ii. 207 n. 4). Many defamatory stories circulated among Henry's enemies after his excommunication.

adulterii uoluptatibus ut porcus luto gaudens inhesit.' Deique legibus et bonorum exhortationibus omnino infestus obstitit. Godefridus autem Lotharingiæ dux turpi repudio sororis suæ mestus bellum contra Henricum commouit.' et multis in unum milibus congregatis cum eo conflixit, ipsumque cum dedecore uictum de campo fugauit, et sic iniuriam sororis suæ uindicauit.

Sepe idem rex proceres suos quorum uxores seu filias uel predia concupiscebat, ad curiam suam fraudulenter accersiebat.' et occulte premissis satellitibus suis in uia securos perimebat. His aliisque multis nequitiis fœdus rex se interficiebat.' et innumeros complices pariter perditionis ad perniciem secum trahebat. Gregorius papa tantorum scelerum querelas ut audiuit.' prefatum uirum ut uitam suam emendaret plerumque obsecrauit, sed illo nequiter medicum et doctorem subsannante nichil profecit. Sepe multorum presulum sinodum adunauit.' et de Christiano imperio quod iam turpiter et nefarie polluebat qualiter corrigeretur
iii. 164 tractauit. Denique Henricum sepius admonitum et in facinoribus pertinaciter resistentem iudicio sinodi excommunicauit, et sub anathemate obduratum potestate regni damnabiliter usurpata exspoliauit, et Conradum comitem auctoritate apostolica per plurimorum manus presulum in regem consecrauit.[1] Priuatus itaque Henricus per unum annum in domo propria conticuit, et comitatu quem hereditario iure a parentibus susceperat potitus delituit.' sed auxilia multa sumptibus de thesauro quem copiosum olim congesserat dapsiliter datis procurauit. Deinde multis milibus complicum aggregatis commune decretum contempsit.' publicus hostis rebellauit, contra Conradum regem pugnauit, ipsumque deiectum iugulauit, et exercitum eius uaria clade quassauit.

Henricus itaque hac uictoria elatus imperium quod amiserat inuasit, rebelles cohercuit.' magnisque sibi uiribus adauctis Romam obsedit, totumque conatum contra Gregorium papam exercuit. Menti eius ut reor penitus exciderat quod Absalon ingentes turmas contra Dauid patrem suum congesserat, consilio Achitophel Gilonitis arma leuauerat.' ipsoque patre cum suis discedente

[1] Orderic presumably wrote without reliable sources and confused different events. He certainly had in mind Rudolph of Swabia, elected in 1080 and killed in battle the following year. The revolt of Henry's son Conrad against his father

himself up to the sordid pleasures of adultery, like a pig wallowing in the mire, obstinately and persistently defying both the laws of God and the exhortations of good men. However Godfrey, duke of Lotharingia, affronted by the shameful repudiation of his sister, took action against Henry; mustering a great army he engaged him in battle and drove him in dishonourable flight from the field, thereby avenging the injury to his sister.

King Henry often treacherously summoned to his court those of his nobles whose wives or daughters or estates he coveted, and had them ambushed and murdered by his minions as they journeyed on their way, imagining themselves safe. By these and many other crimes the faithless king destroyed himself, dragging countless accomplices to destruction and damnation along with him. When Pope Gregory heard complaints of such terrible crimes, he urgently besought this man to amend his life; but Henry, impiously scorning his physician and teacher, profited nothing. Gregory frequently summoned many bishops to synods, and discussed with them how the Christian Empire, which was so shamefully and evilly corrupted, might be reformed. Finally, after repeatedly cautioning Henry, who obstinately persisted in his crimes, he excommunicated him according to the sentence of a synod; and since he remained obdurate under anathema, deposed him from the throne which he had culpably usurped, and had Count Conrad anointed as king by several prelates with papal authority.[1] For a year after his deposition Henry remained quietly at home, skulking in the county which he had inherited from his ancestors; but he secured powerful allies by lavishly distributing subsidies from the wealth that he had already amassed. Then, when he had assembled a great host of supporters, this public enemy defied the general sentence, rebelled, fought against King Conrad, defeated and slew him, and scattered his army in utter defeat.

Then Henry, flushed with victory, usurped the imperial power he had forfeited, coerced the rebels and, reinforcing his army with strong troops, besieged Rome, flinging his whole might against Pope Gregory. It had, I think, totally escaped his memory how Absalom gathered great forces against his father David, waged war by the advice of Achitophel the Gileonite, attacked Jerusalem while his father withdrew his forces, and finally destroyed many

did not take place until 1093 and he was crowned king of Italy at Milan in the time of Urban II (Fliche et Martin, viii. 245).

iii. 165 Ierusalem inuaserat, ac ad ultimum multa bellatorum milia pessundederat, sed nefaria uoluntate in multis completa miserabiliter perierat.[1] Sic iste contra patrem suum arma sustulit.' meritoque postea diram a prole sua persecutionem pertulit. Inquirentibus uero cur tam horrenda contra caput æcclesiæ presumpserat, hanc tantæ discordiæ causam inter se et papam esse cum cachinno asserebat.' quod medicus ægrotum nimis acriter curare inpatientem nisus fuerat.

Obsidionem ergo ualidam rex effrenis Romæ applicuit,[2] Romanos uiribus et minis terruit, muneribus et promissis leniuit, et his modis ciues aliciens urbem optinuit. Deficientibus itaque Romanis Gregorius papa Apuliam expetiit.' ibique a Normannis honorifice susceptus quattuor annis[3] habitauit, et mandata uitæ filiis æcclesiæ propinans finem laborum peregit. Tunc Henricus augustus Witbertum Rauennatium metropolitanum quem Clementem nuncupauerunt in ouile Domini contra fas intrusit.' et hac de causa grauis in mundo et diutina dissensio multos duplici morte multauit. Mediolanenses et Maguntini et multi alii qui Witberto fauebant.' Gregorianos omnes anathematizabant[a] armis quoque crudeliter impugnabant. E contra Gregorius cum suis errantes Witbertinos ad unitatem æcclesiæ reuocabat.' et redire contempnentes secundum ius æcclesiasticum excommunicabat.

iii. 166 Odo Sutriæ comes inuasoris Witberti nepos erat,[4] omnesque tam peregrinos quam indigenas quos poterat.' ad nefariam partem deflectere ui precibusque elaborabat, et resistentes indebitamque subiectionem heretico denegantes torquebat, aut morte ferali puniebat. In tanta obscuritate catholica gemebat æcclesia, orans Deum qui uera lux est et iusticia.' ut prostratis et ablatis discordiæ auctoribus, pacem et ueritatem conferret in terra bonæ uoluntatis hominibus.

5

In diebus illis eloquens Grecia graui bellorum turbine quatiebatur.' et ingentibus damnis afflicta timore et luctu affatim

[a] anathemazabant, *Caen MS*.

[1] Cf. 2 Samuel, chs. 17, 18.

[2] The siege of Rome began in May 1081. Henry had to retire during the summer heat in 1081 and 1082, and the city finally fell in March 1084.

[3] Gregory left Rome in 1084 and died at Salerno on 25 May 1085, only one year later.

[4] After Wibert of Ravenna (the anti-pope Clement III) made his nephew, Otto, count of Sutri the county of Sutri seems to have been an important centre

thousand warriors; but nevertheless, after he had wrought his evil will on many, himself died a wretched death.[1] Similarly Henry took up arms against his father and afterwards endured harsh persecution at the hands of his own son. When anyone asked why he had ventured to make such a shocking attack on the head of the Church, he replied, roaring with laughter, that the reason for this breach between him and the Pope was that the doctor had attempted a cure that was too harsh for an unruly patient.

The turbulent king invested Rome closely,[2] terrorized the Romans by his power and threats, tempted them with gifts and promises, and, after winning over the citizens by such means, captured the town. As the Romans had defected, Pope Gregory sought refuge in Apulia, where he was received with honour by the Normans and lived for four years.[3] There, providing salutary laws for the sons of the Church, he brought his labours to a close. Meanwhile the Emperor Henry unlawfully thrust Wibert, archbishop of Ravenna, who was given the name of Clement, into the Lord's sheepfold, and by so doing caused a terrible schism, widespread and enduring, which destroyed many in body and soul. The people of Milan and Mainz, together with many other supporters of Wibert, anathematized all the Gregorians and attacked them savagely. On the other hand Gregory and his supporters demanded the return of the erring partisans of Wibert to the unity of the Church; and when they refused to comply excommunicated them in accordance with canon law.

Otto, count of Sutri, who was a nephew of the intruder Wibert,[4] strove by force and persuasion to win all men, both natives and foreigners, to the erring side; he either tortured or punished with a cruel death those who resisted and refused to give unlawful obedience to a heretic. So the universal Church suffered in great darkness, praying God, who is true light and justice, to destroy and remove the fomentors of discord and grant peace and truth on earth to men of good will.

5

At this time Greece, the home of oratory, was shaken by the fierce storms of war, suffered great injuries, and was filled with

of his power. See G. Meyer von Knonau, *Jahrbücher des deutschen Reiches*, iv. 269, v. 81.

replebatur. Butinacius enim Grecus nimiæ cupiditatis et proteruiæ spiritu inflatus imperium inuasit, Michahelem Constantinopolitanum imperatorem de regno expulit, et filium eius qui in regno ei succedere deberet oculis priuauit, et in carcere compedibus constrinxit,[1] filias duas Roberti Wiscardi quarum unam idem iuuenis desponderat.'[2] custodiæ mancipauit. Perturbatus uero Michahel in Italiam confugit.' auxiliumque Normannorum sibi sobolique suæ humiliter efflagitauit. Magnanimus autem Wiscardus dux augustæ maiestatis exulem honorifice suscepit, obse-
iii. 167 quiis et fauoribus leniuit, et multiplex ei adiutorium alacriter spopondit. Nec mora sicut pollicitus est.' eum ulcisci uehementer molitus est. Verum multa laboriosa nolente Deo frustra commentatus est.' sed ei ad effectum rei quam summopere flagitabat perducere permissum non est.

Alexius princeps militiæ iussu Michahelis in Paflagoniam ierat.' secumque contra Turcos Niceam Bithiniæ urbem obsidere captantes exercitum Greciæ duxerat.[3] Qui dum audisset expulsionem ingenui imperatoris, et temerariam tirannidem perfidi presumptoris.' exercitum alloquitur, et quid agendum sit percunctatur. Erat enim prudens et probus, audax et largus, et amabilis omnibus. Omnes igitur ei fauent.' eiusque iussui se promptos exhibent. Ille mox hortatur ut unanimes Bizantium obsideant.' et imperiale ius uecordi tiranno uiriliter auferant. Obsidione itaque Constantinopolis aliquot diebus uallata est.' sed per Raimundum Flandrensem qui precipuus custos et ianitor urbis erat consulto ciuium patefacta est.[4] Alexius augustale palacium intrauit, Butinatium de regali throno precipitauit, prolixam ei barbam de-

[1] For the political troubles which led to the forced abdication of Michael VII and his replacement by Nicephorus Botaneiates, who claimed descent from Phocas, see G. Ostrogorsky, *History of the Byzantine State* (Oxford, 1956), pp. 307–8. Michael retired to the Studite monastery; he did not go to Italy. His young son Constantine was not blinded; on the contrary Nicephorus married his mother, the Empress Maria, and he was kept at court and later betrothed to Anna Comnena (B. Leib, 'Nicephore III Botaniatès (1078–1081) et Marie d'Alanie', in *Actes du VI*[e] *congrès international d'études byzantines*, i (1950), 129–40). Geoffrey of Malaterra has a similar story, with varying details (GM iii. 13, pp. 64–5). These stories were put out by the pseudo-Michael (below, p. 16 n. 4) and by Robert Guiscard himself, to justify his attack on Durazzo.

fear and mourning. For the Greek Botaneiates, spurred on by his unquenchable greed and presumption, seized the imperial power, drove Michael, the emperor of Constantinople from the throne, and blinded and flung into close imprisonment the son who should have succeeded him in the Empire.[1] He also kept in close custody the two daughters of Robert Guiscard, one of whom was betrothed to the young man.[2] Michael in his distress fled to Italy and humbly begged the Normans to help him and his son. The illustrious duke, Guiscard, received the imperial exile honourably, comforted him with offers of allegiance and goodwill, and readily promised every kind of assistance. Without delay he set about fulfilling his vows of revenge. But since it was not God's will all his laborious preparations were undertaken in vain, and he was not permitted to bring the enterprise he was pursuing so ardently to fruition.

Alexius, the commander of the army, had gone by Michael's command into Paphlagonia, leading a Greek force against the Turks, who were endeavouring to besiege Nicaea, a town of Bithynia.[3] When he heard of the expulsion of the young emperor and the rash acts of the faithless pretender, he harangued the army and demanded to know what ought to be done. He was a wise and upright man, brave and generous and universally beloved; accordingly all applauded him and professed their eagerness to obey his commands. He then urged that they should unite to lay siege to Byzantium and by their power deprive the crazy tyrant of the imperial rule. So Constantinople was closely besieged for a number of days; but on the advice of the citizens the gates were opened by Raymond the Fleming, a captain of the guard and gatekeeper of the city.[4] Alexius entered the imperial city, thrust Botaneiates from the royal throne, cut off his flowing beard, and kept him

[2] A daughter of Robert Guiscard was betrothed to Michael VII's young son, Constantine Porphyrogenitus, in 1074 (Mathieu, p. 306); he must have been betrothed at birth since, according to Anna Comnena, he was in his seventh year in 1081 (*Alexiad*, III. i. 1 (p. 104)). For the marriage see also P. Charanis, 'Byzantium, the West and the origin of the first crusade', *Byzantion*, xix (1949), 17–36.

[3] Orderic apparently confuses the events of the revolutions of 1078, when Nicephorus rose to power, and 1081, when Alexius Comnenus, who had at first been his principal supporter, replaced him.

[4] According to Anna Comnena the Charisios gate was opened for Alexius by Gilpracht, commander of the Nemitzi, or German, guard (*Alexiad*, I. ix. 3–4 (pp. 92–4)).

truncauit.' et carcerali custodiæ illesum commendauit. Ipse cunctis
gaudentibus imperiale sceptrum et diadema sumpsit.' regnumque
iii. 168 xxx annis in aduersis et prosperis strenue nobiliterque rexit.[1]
Erat enim multum sapiens et misericors pauperibus, bellator fortis
et magnanimus.' affabilis militibus munerumque dator largissimus,
diuinæque legis cultor deuotissimus. Ipse mox ut regnare cepit.'
filium Michahelis quem cecatum retuli de uinculis sustulit, et
abbati cœnobii sancti Ciri tutandum tradidit. Ille uero utpote
mundo inutilis monachus ibidem factus est.' omnique uita sua cum
seruis Dei commoratus est.[2] Filias quoque Wiscardi prefatus heros
ac si ipse genuisset eas amauit, blanditer et pie tractauit.' et fere
xx annis sub tutela sua in deliciis educauit. Officium illarum erat
mane dum imperator de suo stratu surrexisset manusque suas
ablueret.' mappulam et pectinem eburneum afferre, et barbam
imperatoris pectere. Nobiles puellæ facili gratoque seruicio a
liberali principe deputatæ sunt.' quæ post longum tempus Rogerio
comiti Siciliæ augusto fauenti ut amico redditæ sunt.[3] Cotidie
mundi rota uersatur titubantis. Vera probate feri mortales dicta
iii. 169 tonantis, 'Eadem mensura qua mensi fueritis.' remetietur uobis.'[4]
Ecce sicut Michahel pepulit Diogenem uitricum suum de regali
solio, sic ipse de eodem culmine precipitatus est a Butinatio.' qui
nichilominus simili repulsa deiectus est ab Alexio.[5]

Alexius cum patriarcha regiæ urbis ac sapientibus et senatoribus regni Grecorum consilium habuit, et rebus gestis tam priscis quam modernis profunde perscrutatis communi decreto definiuit.' ne sanctum imperium redderetur Michaheli[6] qui ad hostes publicos confugerat, et malefidis se et omnia sua Normannis commiserat.' quibus moris est imperium sociis non reddere, sed aufferre et quos ab aliis debent liberare.' atque ad optinendum debitos fasces adiuuare.' crudeli ritu demptis honoribus sibi penitus

[1] Alexius was emperor from 1081 to 1118: a total of thirty-seven years.

[2] All this is untrue; cf. above, p. 13 n. 2.

[3] No other historian suggests that more than one of Guiscard's daughters went to Constantinople; and Orderic is the sole source for the romantic and improbable account of their duties there.

[4] Luke vi. 38.

unharmed in close confinement in prison. He himself assumed the imperial sceptre and diadem amid general rejoicing, and reigned with firmness and dignity in prosperity and adversity for thirty years.[1] He was a man of great wisdom, merciful to the poor, a brave and illustrious warrior who was genial to his soldiers, open-handed in giving, and a most diligent servant of the divine law. As soon as he had begun to reign he released from his fetters the son of Michael, who, as I have related, had been blinded, and gave him into the safe keeping of the abbot of the monastery of St. Cyrus. Since he was now useless in the world, he became a monk and remained there all his life with the servants of God.[2] As for Guiscard's daughters, Alexius loved, cherished, and honoured them as if he had been their father. For about twenty years he brought them up in luxury under his protection. Their duty each morning was, when the Emperor had risen from his couch and was washing his hands, to fetch a towel and an ivory comb and comb his beard. This light and easy service was assigned to the noble girls by a generous prince; much later they were sent back to Roger count of Sicily, who was amicably disposed towards the Emperor.[3] Daily the wheel of the reeling world revolves; cruel mortals, learn the truth of the Thunderer's words, 'With the same measure that ye mete it shall be measured to you again.'[4] For, just as Michael drove his stepfather Diogenes from the Empire, so he himself was flung down from the same eminence by Botaneiates, who likewise in his turn was dethroned by Alexius.[5]

Alexius took counsel with the patriarch of the imperial city and the wise men and counsellors of the Greek realm; after a thorough examination of precedents both old and new he decreed, with general consent, that the holy Empire should not be restored to Michael,[6] who had fled to enemies of the state and had entrusted himself and all that he had to the treacherous Normans. For the Normans are accustomed never to restore power to their allies; instead they take it from them and, by a refinement of cruelty, deprive of their dignity and force into utter subjection those whom they ought to liberate and help to recover their rightful authority.

[5] William of Apulia, Amatus of Monte Cassino, and other contemporary historians drew similar morals from the revolutions of this time (cf. Mathieu, pp. 296–7).

[6] Michael was by this time a monk-archbishop of Ephesus; there was no question of his restoration.

subiugare. Anglos igitur qui perempto Heraldo rege cum proceribus regni Albionem reliquerant, et a facie Willelmi regis per
pontum[1] in Traciam nauigauerant.' Alexius in amiciciam sibi
asciuit, eisque principale palacium regiosque thesauros palam
commendauit.' quin etiam eos capitis sui rerumque suarum
iii. 170 custodes posuit.[2] A quattuor mundi climatibus innumeræ bellatorum cohortes contra eum conuenerunt, ipsumque uita regnoque
priuare multum conatæ sunt.' sed frustra uehementer laborauerunt.
Nam ipse multas inimicorum insidias protegente Deo euasit.'
et in senectute sua Iohannem filium suum consortem imperii
fecit.[3] Sic cunctis sapienter intuentibus perspicue lucet, quod
quem Deus defensat ac refouet.' nemo deicere uel adnichilare
preualet.

Procellis itaque tot motionum ut diximus in Illirico seuientibus,
et Michahele Italos ad auxilium sui sollicitante lacrimis et questibus.'[4] Robertus Wiscardus ex omni ducatu Apuliæ et Calabriæ
fortem exercitum Normannorum et Langobardorum contraxit, et
ualida classe parata portum Otrente intrauit. Deinde prosperis
uentis spirantibus per mare Dyracio applicuit.' et oppidanis
uiriliter obstantibus in fine Iunii mensis urbem obsedit.[5] In
exercitu quippe suo non plus quam x milia bellatorum habebat,[6]
nec in numero sed in fortitudine uirorum aduersarios terrebat.' et
iii. 171 bellicosam a priscis temporibus Adrasti et Agamemnonis[7] Greciam
inuadebat. Robertus Gifardus et Guillelmus de Grentemaisnilo[8]
aliique probissimi tirones qui nuper de Neustria uenerant.' huic
expeditioni aderant. Marcus Buamundus Wiscardi filius ex Normannica matre patrem iuuabat, partem exercitus absente patre

[1] Since Orderic did not use capitals for proper names it is uncertain whether he meant 'sea' or 'Black Sea' here. Elsewhere he speaks of crossing the Black Sea as 'trans pontum maris' (Le Prévost, i. 386). Whatever his intention, a route across Russia and the Black Sea is a likely one for the English to have taken (cf. A. A. Vasiliev, in *Annales de l'Institut Kondakov*, ix (1937), 39–70 and Jonathan Shepard, 'The English and Byzantium . . .', forthcoming in *Traditio*, xxix (1973)).

[2] Cf. above, ii. 202–3.

[3] John Comnenus was designated successor to his father at his birth in 1092; he received power only when Alexius was on his death-bed (G. Ostrogorsky, *History of the Byzantine State*, p. 334).

[4] An impostor passing himself off as Michael VII was in Italy in July 1080, and deceived Gregory VII, who asked the bishops of Apulia and Calabria to give him aid (E. Caspar, *Das Register Gregors VII* (Berlin, 1920–3), ii. 6). Most of the Italian chroniclers recognized the imposture (Mathieu, pp. 314–15). Anna Comnena gave two versions of the story: either a monk called Rector had carried off the deception, or Guiscard himself had produced him to justify the war (*Alexiad*, I. xii. 5 ff.). Malaterra records that many in the palace who had seen the real Michael knew this man was a fraud; but Robert himself concealed his suspicions (GM iii. 13, pp. 64–5).

So Alexius received into his trust the English who had left England after the slaughter of King Harold and the lords of the kingdom, and in their flight from King William had sailed across the sea[1] to Thrace. He openly entrusted his principal palace and the royal treasures to their care,[2] even making them guards of his own person and all his possessions. Countless attacking armies marched against him from the four corners of the earth, attempting to slay him and seize his kingdom, but they struggled in vain. For by God's care he escaped again and again from the snares of his enemies, and when he had grown old he associated his son John with himself as ruler of the Empire.[3] In this way it is clearly demonstrated to all thinking men that none can overthrow or destroy a man defended and cherished by God.

While the storms of the revolutions I have described were raging in Illyria, and Michael was imploring help from the inhabitants of Italy with tears and complaints,[4] Robert Guiscard raised a powerful army of Normans and Lombards from all parts of the duchy of Apulia and Calabria and, after equipping a strong fleet, entered the harbour of Otranto. From there he crossed the sea with a favourable wind and landed at Durazzo. Here the garrison put up a stout resistance and at the end of June he laid siege to the city.[5] His army was not more than ten thousand strong;[6] it was, therefore, not by numbers but by the courage of his men that he struck terror into the hearts of his adversaries and launched an invasion of Greece, which had been renowned as a warlike country from the earliest days of Adrastus and Agamemnon.[7] Robert Giffard, William of Grandmesnil,[8] and other courageous young knights who had recently come from Normandy took part in this expedition. Mark Bohemond, Guiscard's son by his Norman wife, helped his father, commanded part of the army with

[5] Cf. GM iii. 24, pp. 71–2; William of Apulia (Mathieu, pp. 214–16) for other accounts of the expedition. The siege of Durazzo began on 17 June 1081 (Chalandon, *Alexis I Comnène*, p. 74 n. 1).

[6] Estimates of numbers vary; Anna Comnena exaggerates (30,000) (*Alexiad*, I. xvi. 1); Orderic, whose figure is the smallest, possibly underestimates. The core of the army probably consisted of about 1,300 knights (GM iii. 24, p. 71), and the total was unlikely to have been more than 15,000 (Chalandon, *Alexis I Comnène*, p. 65).

[7] These heroes were well known through the stories of Thebes and Troy, which were among the cultural commonplaces of Norman feudal society (cf. above, iii. 100 n. 2).

[8] Cf. below, p. 32. For an account of William's later career see E. M. Jamison, 'Some notes. . .', pp. 199–200. Cf. also GM iv. 22, pp. 100–1.

prouido regimine ducebat.' et in omnibus prudenter agens futuræ uirtutis specimen prestabat.[1] Rogerius autem frater eius cognomento Bursa iussu patris in Apulia remanserat.' et ducatum sibi ex hæreditate matris debitum custodiebat.

Alexius imperator Diracianorum planctu excitus ingentem exercitum aggregauit.' et obsidentes urbem suam terrestri naualique prælio conterere sategit. Interea dum augustales ueredarii undique mitterentur, et cohortes bellatorum de insulis maris et de ad-
iii. 172 iacentibus prouinciis contraherentur, quadam die Marcus Buamundus cum quinquaginta militibus pabulatum perrexit,[2] et quingentis militibus qui obsessis adminiculari exercitum expediti[a] præibant forte obuiauit. Mox ut sese mutuo uiderunt acre certamen inierunt. Porro Danai Normannorum impetum non ferentes terga uerterunt.' multasque manubias amiserunt. Tunc æream crucem perdiderunt.' quam Constantinus imperator pugnaturus contra Maxentium uisa cruce in cœlo fecerat.[3] Redeuntes itaque de conflictu Normanni gaudium ingens et uictoriæ spem sociis retulerunt, Pelasgi autem grauissimum dolorem et diffidentiam pro amissa cruce Domini habuerunt.' quam maximo auri talento redimere multum laborauerunt. Verum Wiscardus talem mercatum agere indignum duxit.' quia æs in cruce pro uirtute Christi preciosius omni auro estimauit. Hanc itaque crucem secum in multis periculis portauit.' quam post mortem eius cenobium sanctæ Trinitatis Venusiæ reuerenter usque hodie custodit, et cum aliis sanctorum pignoribus excolit.

Mense Octobri Alexius imperator Diracio appropriauit.' et legiones suas ex multis nationibus accitas ad bellum ordinauit. Deinde commisso prælio magna sanguinis effusio facta est.' et ingens detrimentum utrique parti seuo Marte furente collatum
iii. 173 est. Denique fidelem paucitatem et instantiam occidentalium peregrinorum dominus de cœlo respexit, eisque uictoriam concessit.' copiasque orientales quæ in uirtute sua confidebant terruit, et cum dedecore fugauit. Deinde Robertus dux tam nobili triumpho

[a] expeditus, *Caen MS.*

[1] The best account of the campaign is given by William of Apulia (Matthieu, pp. 214 ff.); modern accounts by Chalandon (*Alexis I Comnène*, pp. 72–94) and Karl Schwartz (*Die Feldzüge Robert Guiscard's gegen das byzantinische Reich* (Fulda, 1854)) need to be corrected by it.

[2] Orderic may refer here to the first successful engagement of Bohemond's forces at Butrinto, otherwise described only by William of Apulia, who put the number of Greeks at 2,000 (Mathieu, pp. 36, 223, 320; H. Grégoire, 'La chanson de Roland de l'an 1085', in *Bulletin de l'académie royale de Belgique, Classe des lettres et sciences morales et politiques*, 5e sér. xxv (1939), 271).

[3] This story of the making of the famous banner, the Labarum, by Constantine the Great derives from Eusebius. The standard captured by Robert

great skill during his father's absence, and gave a foretaste of the qualities he was to show later by the wisdom of all his actions.[1] His brother Roger, nicknamed Borsa, had remained in Apulia at his father's command and was responsible for the duchy, destined to be his by inheritance from his mother.

The Emperor Alexius, in response to an appeal from the citizens of Durazzo, assembled a great army and prepared to harry the forces besieging his city with an attack on both sea and land. One day, while the imperial messengers were hurrying in all directions, summoning troops of fighting-men from the islands of the sea and the adjacent provinces, Mark Bohemond set out with fifty knights on a foraging expedition;[2] by chance he encountered five hundred lightly armed soldiers, who were the advance guard of the army sent to relieve the besieged. As soon as they sighted each other the forces engaged in bitter conflict. But the Greeks, unable to stand up to the Norman onslaught, turned tail abandoning much booty. On this occasion they lost the bronze cross which the Emperor Constantine had had made when he set out to fight Maxentius, after seeing a cross in the sky.[3] Consequently when the Normans returned from the fray they spread jubilation and high hopes of victory among their comrades, whereas the Greeks were filled with sorrow and misgivings because they had lost their Lord's cross, and strove desperately to redeem it by offering a great sum of gold. But Guiscard would not deign to consider such a bargain, holding the bronze in the cross more precious through Christ's merits than all the gold in the world. He carried this cross with him in many perils; and since his death the monastery of Holy Trinity at Venosa has preserved it with other relics of the saints.

In the month of October the Emperor Alexius approached Durazzo and drew up his legions, composed of men of many nations, in battle-order. When fighting began blood flowed freely and both sides suffered heavy losses in the fierce engagement. At length the Lord in Heaven, having regard for the faithfulness, perseverance, and small numbers of the western pilgrims, granted the victory to them, and terrified the eastern forces, who had trusted in their own strength, putting them to shameful flight. Duke Robert, elated by such a glorious victory, then left Durazzo

Guiscard was certainly not the original Labarum (Cabrol–Leclercq, *Dictionnaire d'archéologie chrétienne et de liturgie* (Paris, 1907–53), viii. 940–54).

exhilaratus Diracium reliquit, longiusque cum exercitu suo progressus in Bulgaria hiemauit. Regionem enim circa Diracium obsidione trium mensium[1] deuastauerat.' et nichil ibi unde homines uel equi subsistere possent dimiserat.

Tunc legati Romanæ æcclesiæ ad Robertum ducem cum litteris apostolicis[2] uenerunt.' eumque suppliciter salutantes dixerunt, 'Gregorius papa, O strenuissime dux ut pater filium te humiliter et obnixe obsecrat.' ut apostolicæ sedi festinanter inuincibilis tua probitas subueniat, nec ullam huic subuentioni pro amore Dei excusationem præponat. Henricus enim Alemannorum rex Romam obsidet.' et papam cum clero sibi adhærente in arce Crescentis inclusum cohercet. Ibi nimirum papa circumseptus cum turma fidelis populi timet defectione Quiritum qui nimis cupidi sunt et uersipelles deludi.' et manibus inimicorum irreuerenter tradi. Ad te igitur ab illo missi sumus.' celeremque opem tuam ad tantam necessitatem requirimus. Fortitudo tua super omnes inimicos tuos diuinitus sullimata est.' nec ei mortalis manus resistere potest, quamdiu Deo militaueris.' et uicario sancti Petri principis apostolorum obedieris.'

iii. 174 His auditis magnanimus heros ualde anxiatus est. Nam uenerando papæ a proteruis leonibus profligato sicut Petro in carcere Herodis succurrere desiderat.' et exercitum suum quem numero paucissimum inter multos hostes et callidos atque atroces computat in terra aliena sine duce uelut agnos inter lupos relinquere uehementer hesitat. Tandem erectis luminibus mentis ad Deum a quo omne bonum procedit.' conuocatis agminibus suis cum Buamundo filio suo ait, 'Semper obsecundare Deo qui per communem catholicæ æcclesiæ pastorem alloquitur nos oportet. Auxiliante Deo iussioni papæ obediam.' et quam citius potero ad uos redire satagam. Interea uos prudenter in hac prouincia requiescite.' et inter hostes undique circumspecti estote. Si quis presumpserit bello uos impetere.' in uirtute Dei uiriliter resistite. Vos tamen cauete ne bellare incipiatis nec occasionem præliandi hostibus detis.' neque indigenas quousque regressus fuero contra uos lacessatis. Iniunctam michi a domino seruitutem inibo.' et si uita comes fuerit celeriter redibo. Per animam Tancredi patris mei

[1] The battle was fought on 18 October (Chalandon, *Alexis I Comnène*, p. 79); the siege had then lasted for four months.

[2] Gregory VII wrote to Robert Guiscard to ask for aid in the late autumn of 1081, during the early stages of the siege of Rome, before he was forced to retire to the castle of Sant' Angelo in 1083 (E. Caspar, *Das Register Gregors VII* (Berlin, 1920–3), ii. 597–8). The tone is very different from that in the version invented by Orderic; it is a stern reminder of earlier promises. Cf. GM iii. 23, p. 77; Suger, *Vie de Louis le Gros*, ed. A. Molinier, pp. 21–2. In fact Guiscard's

and, advancing further with his army, wintered in Bulgaria. He had already devastated the whole region round Durazzo during the three months' siege,[1] leaving no provisions there for the support of either men or horses.

At this time legates of the Roman Church visited Duke Robert, bringing papal letters.[2] Greeting him as petitioners, they said, 'Valiant duke, Pope Gregory humbly and earnestly begs you, as a father his son, to come at once to the aid of the apostolic see with your invincible strength, letting no excuse whatsoever delay your succour, for the love of God. Henry, king of the Germans is besieging Rome, and is closely investing the Pope with the clergy who remain loyal to him in the castle of Sant' Angelo. The Pope, shut up there with a throng of faithful people, fears that he may be betrayed by the defection of the Romans, a notoriously avaricious and fickle people, and sacrilegiously handed over to his enemies. Therefore he has sent us to you to beg for immediate help in such great need. By divine aid your strength has been made to triumph over all your enemies and no human force can resist it, as long as you continue to fight for God and obey the vicar of St. Peter, the chief of the apostles.'

When he heard these words the illustrious lord was deeply disturbed. He wished to rescue the venerable Pope, who lay at the mercy of raging lions like Peter in Herod's prison; yet he had grave misgivings about leaving his army leaderless in a foreign country, knowing his men to be few in number among a great many cunning and cruel enemies, like lambs among wolves. However he turned his thoughts to God, from whom all good proceeds, and sending for his troops and his son Bohemond, he said: 'We are bound at all times to obey God, who speaks to us through the universal shepherd of the catholic Church. With God's help I will obey the Pope's summons and do my best to return to you at the earliest opportunity. Whilst I am away, since you are surrounded by enemies, lie low in this province and act with the utmost restraint. If anyone attempts to attack you, resist courageously trusting in God's strength. But take care not to strike the first blow or give the enemy any pretext for battle or provoke the people in any way until I return. I will undertake the task laid on me by my Lord, and if my life is spared I shall soon return. I swear by the soul of

return was necessitated by revolts in south Italy, encouraged by Alexius (Mathieu, pp. 230–2, 324–5, 353; E. M. Jamison, 'Some notes . . .', pp. 198–9).

iuro, et hoc iureiurando uobis firmiter assero.' quod donec reuersus ad uos fuero, non utar balneo.' barba mea non radetur neque cesaries michi tonsorabitur.'

Post hæc uerba bellicosus miles cum paucis commilitonibus mare mox ingressus est.' Deoque ducente in Apuliam profectus est, et inde assumptis armatorum cœtibus Romam aggressus est.[1]
iii. 175 Porro Henricus imperator ut ueraci rumore comperit quod Robertus dux Constantinopolitanum imperatorem superauerit, ac ad subuentionem papæ quasi fulgur cum nimio impetu ex improuiso aduenerit.' uariis euentibus sollerter consideratis ualde timuit, iamque facta cum quibusdam Romanorum proceribus pace partem urbis recepit.' ac postmodum occiduas regni sui partes repetiit. Maluit quippe sanus et liber honeste discedere.' quam furibundum agonithetam expectare, et repentini certaminis inuolui turbine.

6

Dum tam graues tumultus et tot bellorum tempestates in mundo seuirent.' et regna terrarum ut puppem inter pelagi fluctus agitarent.' uenerabilis Robertus abbas sanctæ Eufemiæ postquam de bello Diraceno in Calabriam rediit, ueneno ut fertur in esca sumpto, ii° kal' Decembris egrotare cœpit.[2] Nam quidam genere Sarracenus arte pistoria Brixensi[3] cenobio seruiebat. Hic sororem
iii. 176 Willelmi prioris filii Ingranni[4] in matrimonio habebat.' et pro quadam latenti causa satisque parua occultum contra abbatem odium gestabat. Vnde instinctu diaboli ferculum eius ueneno corrupit.' imitatus Ismahelem[5] patrem suum qui ferali ludo simplicem Isaac grauare studuit. Deinde uir Dei monachis lugentibus xiii diebus eger iacuit.' dataque confessione sanctaque sumpta communione ii° idus Decembris obiit. In æcclesia sanctæ Dei genitricis Mariæ quam ipse a fundamento construxit sepultus est.' et per singulos annos anniuersarius dies reuerenter celebrari ob memoriam eius constitutus est.[6] Hoc libenter agitur a monachis

[1] Orderic's account is greatly distorted. Robert Guiscard returned to Apulia in 1082; he first put down the Apulian rebels and turned to Rome only in 1084. Henry IV retired on 21 May, and Guiscard entered the city on 28 May. Cf. William of Apulia (Mathieu, pp. 234–6, 325–6); Geoffrey of Malaterra (GM iii. 33, 37, pp. 77, 79–80), William of Malmesbury (*GR* ii. 321).

[2] For Robert of Grandmesnil, abbot of Saint-Évroul and later of St. Eufemia, see above, ii. 100; L.-R. Ménager, 'Les fondations monastiques de Robert Guiscard', in *Quellen und Forschungen*, xxxix (1959), 4–19.

[3] See above, ii. 100 n. 3.

[4] William son of Ingran was later abbot of Mileto (above, ii. 102).

[5] The name *Ishmaelites* was at first confined to certain tribes living east of

my father Tancred, and so swearing firmly declare to you, that until I return to you I will not take a bath, nor allow my beard to be shaved or my hair to be cut.'

After making this speech the brave warrior hastened to embark with a small bodyguard and, with God as his guide, reached Apulia, where he raised an army and marched on Rome.[1] The Emperor Henry, hearing the true report of how Duke Robert had overcome the Emperor of Constantinople and was coming to the rescue of the Pope with the force of a thunderbolt that strikes from the blue, carefully weighed up the situation and felt grave apprehension. Having already made a treaty with some of the Roman nobles, he received part of the city and then retired to the western provinces of his kingdom. He had decided that it was better to retreat in good order of his own free will than to wait for the avenging champion, and face the doubtful issue of a pitched battle.

6

While these terrible dissensions and the tempests of countless wars were raging all over the world and the kingdoms of the earth were tossed up and down like ships on a stormy sea, the venerable Robert, abbot of St. Eufemia, after returning to Calabria from the battle of Durazzo, ate food alleged to have been poisoned and fell sick on 30 November.[2] It happened that a man of Saracen blood served as a baker in the Brescian[3] monastery; he had married a sister of Prior William the son of Ingran[4] and for some unknown but trivial reason nourished a grudge against the abbot. So at the instigation of the devil he put poison in his food, imitating his father Ishmael,[5] who in an ominous game tried to harm the unsuspecting Isaac. In consequence the man of God lay sick for thirteen days while the monks wept; after making confession and receiving Holy Communion he died on 12 December. He was buried in the church of the blessed Mary, mother of God, which he had built from its foundations and an anniversary, to be celebrated every year, has been established in his honour.[6] This is

Egypt, who claimed descent from Ishmael, but in the twelfth century it was loosely applied to all Saracens. The reference is probably to Genesis xx. 8–10, though Ishmael did not in fact cause any harm to Isaac.

[6] His obit was celebrated at Saint-Évroul on 11 December (Bouquet, xxiii. 490).

quos ipse in domo Dei ut pater filios educare molitus est.' pauperibus quoque uberem elemosinam ipso die pro defuncto pastore largiri mos est.

7

Appropinquante Wiscardo turgentes Romani conuenerunt, et quod ab aduenis piscatoribus caput orbis impugnaretur indignum duxerunt. Multis igitur hortatibus animati cum armis obuiam processerunt.' sed statim a Normannis in re militari nimis obduratis facto impetu repulsi sunt. Deinde uictores ciuibus mixti fugientibus urbem intrauerunt.' iussuque feruidi ducis ignem tectis iniecerunt. Sic Wiscardus ferro et flammis sibi aditum Romæ patefecit.' nec ullus ciuium postea contra eum mutire ausus fuit. Deinde perueníenti ad turrim Crescentis papa cum clero obuiam exiit, pro labore et subuentu gratias egit, pro obedientia a reatibus absoluit.' et æternam ei a Deo benedictionem peroptauit.

iii. 177 Post alternam heroum collocutionem, post depromptam a papa querelarum relationem.' iratus dux subintulit huiuscemodi comminationem, 'Romani ciues pessimi sunt et infidi.' Deoque et sanctis eius pro innumerabilibus beneficiis sibi collatis sunt et erunt semper ingrati. Roma quæ mundi caput et peccatorum medicina olim dicta est.' nunc habitatio draconum et totius nequitiæ fouea facta est. Hanc ergo speluncam latronum ferro seu flamma destruam.' sordidos nefariosque habitatores eius perimam. Persecutionem in Christum quam Iudei ceperunt.' Romani pertinaciter perficere conati sunt. Nonne sicut Iudei Christum crucifixerunt, sic Romani membra Christi Petrum et Paulum martirizauerunt? Quid dicam de Lino et Cleto, Clemente et Alexandro, Sixto et Thelesphoro, Calixto et Vrbano, Cornelio et Fabiano? Omnes hi pontificali cura mederi languentibus studuerunt.' et a propriis ciuibus quos saluare nitebantur iniuriose perempti sunt. Denique quid referam de Sebastiano, quem sagittatum in cloaca suspenderunt gumfo?[1] Quid de Laurentio quem crati ferreæ imposuerunt, et prunis suppositis ut piscem assauerunt? Quid de

[1] Cf. *Acta sancti Sebastiani* (*AA.SS.*, January, ii. 278), 'in cloaca . . . invenies corpus meum pendens in gompho.'

gladly observed by the monks whom he laboured to bring up in the house of God, and to whom he was like a father; in addition it is customary to distribute generous alms to the poor the same day on behalf of the dead abbot.

7

At Guiscard's approach the angry Romans assembled, indignant that the chief city of the world should be attacked by men they reckoned foreign fishermen. Incited by many harangues they took arms and advanced to meet him, but were thrown back at the first onslaught by the experienced Norman veterans. The victors pressed on to enter the city on the heels of the citizens as they fled and at the command of the angry duke they set fire to the houses. So Guiscard forced an entry into Rome with fire and sword, and not one of the citizens ever dared to raise a voice against him afterwards. When he reached the castle of Sant' Angelo the Pope came out to meet him with the clergy, thanked him for his help and all his labours, absolved him from his sins because of his obedience, and prayed fervently that God might bless him eternally.

After these great men had spoken together, and the Pope had given an account of his injuries, the angry duke voiced this threat: 'The Roman citizens are evil and treacherous to the core; they are and always will be ungrateful to God and his saints for the many benefits conferred on them. Rome, which used to be called the capital of the world and the balm of sinners, has now become a den of serpents and a pit of all evil. Therefore I will destroy this robbers' den with fire and sword and will slaughter its ignoble and wicked inhabitants. The Romans have attempted to bring to completion the persecution of Christ which the Jews began. Did not the Romans martyr Peter and Paul, the members of Christ, in the same way that the Jews crucified Christ himself? What shall I say of Linus and Cletus, Clement and Alexander, Sixtus and Telesphorus, Calixtus and Urban, Cornelius and Fabian? All these endeavoured to heal the sick by their pastoral care and were vilely slaughtered by those very citizens they strove to save. Then what can I say of Sebastian, pierced with arrows and hung in chains[1] in a sewer? What of Laurence, whom they placed on a gridiron and roasted like a fish over burning coals? What of

Ypolito quem alligatum equis indomitis discerpserunt? Quid de
iii. 178 Hermete, Tiburcio, Xenone, Valentino aliisque sanctis quorum numerus humanæ noticiæ est incomprehensibilis? Fama[a] refert et astipulatur[b] assertione multorum, quod tota Roma perfusa est precioso cruore martirum: et in latrinis Romanorum innumera latent corpora sanctorum. Eadem crudelitas quæ tunc grassabatur in paganis, nunc debachatur in falsis christianis: qui cupiditate illecti fauent prophanis, et contra catholicam æcclesiam auxiliantur hereticis insanis. Nulla igitur eis pietas impendenda est. Vltore gladio impios puniam, cruentam ciuitatem igne succendam: et transalpinis gentibus replendam opitulante Deo meliorem restituam.'

Tunc papa ad pedes ducis corruit: lacrimisque profusis ait, 'Absit hoc a me: ut Roma destruatur pro me. Non enim ad destructionem urbis: sed ad saluationem electus sum plebis. Malo dominum nostrum Iesum Christum morte sequi: quam peccatoribus punitis iniurias meas nequiter ulcisci. Creatori quippe nostro contrarii sunt: qui statuta eius despiciunt, et ordinem æcclesiæ truculenter impediunt, dominicumque gregem ut lupi rapaces dispergunt. Ipsius nimirum est iniuria et ultio: seruitus quoque et retributio. Nouit pios clientes: et abhorret aduersarios furentes. Eius igitur omnipotentiæ nos et nostra commendamus, et corde beniuolo exoramus: ut legi sacræ aduersantia censorio ense recidat, et nos ad beneplacitam uoluntatem suam infatigabiliter dirigat.'

iii. 179 Sic iratum ducem papa leniuit, acceptoque consilio de turre Crescentis cum clero sequaci exiuit: et comitante duce cum ualida manu ductus Albam adiuit.[1] Hanc itaque urbem Ascanius Iulus Æneæ filius condidit: et Constantinus Augustus sancto Siluestro papæ dedit.[2]

Dux autem apostolica benedictione accepta iter ad mare accelerauit: et trans pontum cœtus suos festinanter ut eis iurauerat expetiit. Interea callidus imperator Grecorum ut Robertum adiisse Italiam cognouit: ratus quod Normannos absente duce destitutos debilitare posset insurrexit, multas cohortes adunauit, et inuitos ad bellum Normannos coegit. Commisso autem prælio

[a] famam, *Caen MS.* [b] astipulatus, *Caen MS.*

[1] Robert Guiscard escorted Gregory from the castle of Sant' Angelo to the Lateran Palace, and from there by way of Monte Cassino and Benevento to Salerno, which he reached towards the end of June (G. Meyer von Knonau, *Jahrbücher des deutschen Reiches*, iii (Leipzig, 1890–1909), 554–60). No other source mentions Albano.

Hippolitus, whom they bound to wild horses and tore to pieces? What of Hermes, Tiburtius, Zeno, Valentine, and the other saints, too many to be accounted for in human knowledge? The story runs and is supported by the evidence of many men, that Rome is soaked in the precious blood of the martyrs and that countless bodies of saints are hidden in the sewers of Rome. The cruelty that was once nourished in pagans now shows itself in false Christians, who, succumbing to their greed, support godless men and give their aid to mad heretics to attack the catholic Church. No mercy therefore is due to them. I will punish the impious with an avenging sword; I will burn the bloody city to ashes and, repeopling it with men from the north, I will with God's help make it a better place.'

Then the Pope fell at the duke's feet, bathed in tears, and said, 'Never let Rome be destroyed for my sake. I have been chosen for the salvation of the people, not for the destruction the city. I would rather follow our Lord Jesus Christ in death than avenge my wrongs cruelly after the sinners have been punished. The enemies of the Creator are those who despise his laws, aggressively interfere with the order of the Church, and scatter the Lord's flock like ravening wolves. For injury and vengeance, service and reward alike are in his hand. He recognizes his dutiful servants and spurns his raging enemies. Therefore we commit ourselves to his almighty power and beseech him, with goodwill in our hearts, to cut out opposition to the divine law with the sword of judgement and guide our steps unfailingly in accordance with his holy will.'

So the Pope appeased the angry duke, and after taking counsel left the castle of Sant' Angelo, followed by the clergy. Accompanied by the duke and a strong bodyguard, he was escorted to Albano.[1] This city was founded by Ascanius Iulus, son of Aeneas, and given by the Emperor Constantine to Pope Silvester.[2]

After receiving the papal blessing the duke made all speed to the coast and hurried overseas to the help of his forces. Before this, however, the cunning Greek emperor had learnt that Robert had gone to Italy and, believing that he could weaken the Normans while they were left leaderless, he took the field, gathered a great army, and forced battle on the unwilling Normans. In the early

[2] The legend of the founding of Alba Longa by Ascanius Iulus, son of Aeneas, is derived from Virgil (*Aeneid*, viii. 43–9).

Normanni debiles in primis reperti sunt, et multis ex causis in inicio certaminis territi et pene uicti sunt. Nam ut paucitatem sui et absentiam fortunati ducis et multitudinem hostium perpenderunt.' pene fugam ante pugnam inierunt. Sed cum Buamundus in conflictu cum turmis sui uacillans trepidaret, et anxius Deum ex corde inuocaret.' diuinæ pietatis auxilium affuit, et uox huiuscemodi desuper intonuit, 'Buamunde quid agis? Præliare fortiter. Nam ille qui patrem tuum iuuit, te similiter adiuuabit.' si in illo confisus fueris, eique fideliter militaueris.' Hac uoce Normanni
iii. 180 recreati et confortati sunt.' et in antea progressi Pelasgos acriter impulerunt, quorum impetu Achiui repente repulsi sunt.' et terga uertentes spolia multa indigentibus peregrinis dimiserunt.[1]

Regressus de Tuscia Wiscardus suos hac uictoria sat hilares inuenit.' ipse quoque tam nobili tripudio exultans Deo gratias egit. Buamundum uero qui uulneratus fuerat in certamine.' ut curaretur misit ad medicos Psalerniæ, quorum fama per orbem admodum diuulgatur excellentia medicinalis peritiæ.[2]

Porro Diraceni dum Normannos perpendunt in Bulgariam longe progressos, pluresque prouincias de imperio Bizanteo militari manu adeptos, seseque ab auxilio Tracum seu Macedonum omniumque affinium suorum penitus remotos, diffidentes mutuo sepe tractant.' qualiter sibi nimis in arto positi consulant. Tandem procaciores quid agant uicissim diffiniunt, legatos ad ducem clam mittunt, pacem poscunt.' et quod asilum urbis satellitibus eius tradant ueraciter promittunt. At ille quod postulant concedit, et ccc milites ad recipiendam urbem mittit. Noctu itaque uenientibus Normannis ciuitas aperta est.' quibus receptis pax inter utrosque et securitas firmata est.[3]

iii. 181 Sichelguada uxor Roberti Wiscardi, filia erat Guaimalchi ducis Psalernitani, sororque Gisulfi.' qui ducatu priuatus fuerat per auidam inuasionem sororii sui. Hæc Buamundum priuignum suum odio habebat, metuens ne per eum quia fortior erat, et sensu multaque probitate pollebat.' Rogerius filius suus amitteret ducatum Apuliæ et Calabriæ, qui sibi competebat hereditario

[1] For the course of the campaigns of 1082–4 see William of Apulia (Mathieu, pp. 236–40, 328–34). Bohemond successfully penetrated as far as Larissa, but a victory by the emperor Alexius finally forced his army back on Valona and Castoria. See also R. Manselli, 'Normanni d'Italia alla prima crociata' in *Japigia*, xi (1940), 50–3.

[2] William of Apulia, after speaking of an epidemic that ravaged the Norman army, relates that Bohemond was ill and returned to Italy for medical treatment (Mathieu, pp. 228–30).

[3] Durazzo had in fact capitulated on 21 February 1082, and the citadel remained in Norman hands until Guiscard's death (Chalandon, *Alexis I Comnène*, p. 83; Mathieu, pp. 228–30, 330).

stages of the engagement the Normans proved weak; for a time they had every cause to fear and were almost vanquished. When they considered their small numbers, the great host of the enemy, and the absence of their duke, the friend of fortune, they almost fled before the fight. But, when Bohemond and his troops were wavering uncertainly in the thick of battle, Bohemond called inwardly on God in his distress, and help came by divine grace; a voice from Heaven was heard, saying, 'Bohemond, what are you about? Fight on bravely. He who helped your father will likewise help you, if you put your trust in him and fight faithfully in his service.' The Normans were revived and encouraged by this voice; pressing forward they fell upon the Greeks and drove them back with their sudden onslaught, so that they turned and fled, abandoning much booty to the needy foreigners.[1]

On his return from Italy Guiscard found his men elated by this victory; he too, rejoicing at so glorious a triumph, gave thanks to God. He sent Bohemond, who had been wounded in the battle, to be treated by the doctors of Salerno, who were famed all over the world for their surpassing skill in medicine.[2]

Then the citizens of Durazzo, realizing that the Normans had penetrated deeply into Bulgaria and wrested several provinces from the Byzantine Empire by force of arms, whereas they themselves were cut off from all hope of help from Thracians or Macedonians and all their neighbours, began to lose heart and debated repeatedly among themselves how they might extricate themselves from an impossible situation. Finally the boldest spirits determined for their part what should be done, secretly sent ambassadors to the duke, sued for peace, and promised faithfully to hand over the defence of the city to his men. He granted their requests and sent three hundred knights to receive the city. The gates were opened to the Normans, who came by night, and when they had been received peace was made and trust was established between the parties.[3]

Robert Guiscard's wife Sichelgaita was a daughter of Gaimar, duke of Salerno, and sister of Gisulf, who had been deprived of the duchy by the attack of his covetous brother-in-law. This woman conceived a hatred for her stepson Bohemond, fearing that, because he was stronger than her son Roger and excelled in judgement and valour, he might cause Roger to lose the duchy of Apulia and Calabria, which was his due by hereditary right. Therefore she

iure. Vnde ipsa letiferam potionem confecit.' et Psalernitanis archiatris misit, inter quos enutrita fuerat et a quibus ueneficiorum eruditionem perceperat.[1] Protinus ipsi uoluntatem dominæ et alumnæ suæ cognouerunt.' et Buamundo quem curare debuerant uirus mortis contulerunt. Quo percepto ad mortem egrotauit.' patrique suo per nuntium languorem suum protinus intimauit. Callidus uero dux dolos uxoris suæ subito animaduertit.' ipsamque ante se tristis accersiens sic interrogauit, 'Viuitne Buamundus dominus meus?' Quæ respondit, 'Nescio domine.' At ille, 'Afferte' inquit 'michi textum sancti euangelii et gladium.' Quibus allatis gladium accepit, et super sacra sic iurauit, 'Audis Sichelguada. Per hoc sanctum euangelium iuro, quod si Buamundus filius meus hoc morbo quo detinetur mortuus fuerit, hoc ense interficiam te.' Porro illa tali allegatione nimis territa salubre antidotum preparauit.' et medicis suis per quos mortem parauerat Psalerniam confestim transmisit, nunciumque ut sibi periclitanti adminicularetur blanditiis et precibus obnixis sollicitauit. Archiatri detectam
iii. 182 fraudem et angustiam herilem audientes, et in futurum ne terribiles minæ ducis complerentur precauentes.' toto nisu iuueni quem leserant, in omni exercitio phisicæ artis mederi certabant. Opitulante Deo qui per eundem Turcos et agarenos Christianæ fidei hostes comprimere decreuerat eger conualuit.' sed tamen omni uita sua pro ueneno quo infectus fuerat pallidus permansit.

Interea uersipellis et ingeniosa mulier multa secum reuoluebat, nimioque metu indesinenter stimulata considerabat.' quod si legatus suus ad transfretandum mare tardaret, et egrotus ante aduentum eius emigraret.' illa iuratam sibi mortem ense mariti non euaderet. Igitur aliam e contra tergiuersationem truculentam et omnino execrabilem excogitauit. Veneno uirum suum proh dolor infecit.[2] Protinus ut ille egrotare cœpit, et ipsa de ineuitabili casu eius non dubitauit, conuocatis parasitis suis cum reliquis Langobardis noctu surrexit, ac ad mare progressa naues optimas cum omnibus suis intrauit.' et omnes reliquas naues ne Normanni eam prosequerentur incendit. Dum uero litus Apuliæ attigit.' quidam

[1] For the rumours of attempted poisoning cf. below, n. 2.

[2] Robert Guiscard died in the north of Cephalonia, probably at Cape Atheras. Accounts of his death, probably from fever, differ greatly (cf. Mathieu, pp. 334–5, 336). William of Malmesbury also alleged that he was poisoned by Sichelgaita (*GR* ii. 321); the rumours were probably spread in France by Bohemond himself. They reflect the active hostility of Normans and Lombards in south Italy, but are unlikely to be true. According to William of Apulia (Mathieu, p. 254) Sichelgaita sailed after her husband's death, taking his body with her to Apulia in the fastest ship. William also says (ibid., p. 256) that the larger boats had been burnt, but offers no explanation.

brewed a deadly potion and sent it to the physicians of Salerno, amongst whom she had been brought up and from whom she had acquired great skill in the preparation of poisons.[1] On receiving it they understood the will of their mistress and pupil, and administered the deadly poison to Bohemond, whom they should have attempted to cure. After taking it he sickened to the point of death and hastily sent a messenger to tell his father of his illness. The shrewd duke immediately recognized his wife's evil-doing and, sending for her with a heavy heart, asked her, 'Does my lord Bohemond live or not?' To which she answered, 'I do not know, my lord.' 'Bring me', he said, 'the text of the Gospels and a sword.' When they had been brought, he took the sword and swore on the holy books in these words, 'Listen, Sichelgaita: by this holy Gospel I swear that if my son Bohemond dies of the sickness that afflicts him I will slay you with this sword.' At this, terrified by the fearful vow, she prepared a sound antidote and dispatched it hastily to the doctors at Salerno, who had been her instruments in the intended murder, earnestly pressing the messenger with promises and entreaties to rescue her from her perilous position. When the physicians heard that the treachery was discovered and their mistress in distress, they took measures to prevent the execution of the duke's terrible threats and exerted all their arts of healing to cure the young man they had harmed. With the help of God, who intended him to be the scourge of the Turks and Saracens, the enemies of the Christian faith, the sick man recovered; but he remained pale all his life as a result of the poison that had been administered to him.

Meanwhile the shifty, cunning woman turned over many schemes in her mind; haunted day and night by terror she knew that if the messenger she had sent were delayed in crossing the sea so that the sick man died before his arrival she would not escape death by her husband's sword, as he had vowed. Consequently she devised another plot, which was cruel and utterly depraved. Terrible to relate, she administered poison to her husband.[2] The moment his sickness began, when she was sure that he could not escape death, she sent for her dependants and the other Lombards and set out at dead of night to the coast, where she embarked in the best ships with all her partisans. To prevent the Normans from following her she burned the remaining ships. As soon as she reached Apulia, a certain knight from among her dependants

miles de satellicio eius clam egressus Psalerniam noctu uenit, et
Buamundum festinanter aggressus ait, 'Surge cito et fuge.' et
salua te.' Cumque ille causam inquireret.' nuncius respondit, 'Pater
tuus mortuus est.' et nouerca tua in Apulia est. Huc autem festinat
uenire.' ut occidat te.' Nec mora Buamundus tam graui rumore
turbatus asinum ascendit, clam urbem exiuit.' ad Iordanum princi-
iii. 183 pem Capuæ consobrinum suum[1] confugit, a quo amicabiliter receptus fraudes et minas nouercæ suæ sic euasit. Illa uero ut
Psalerniam peruenit, et egresso quem querebat delusam se
comperit, uehementer contristata est.' et Rogerius filius eius cognomento crumena amplum citra mare ducatum ex successione
maiorum adeptus est.[2]

Vndique nimiis anxietatibus aggrauati sunt in peregrina regione
Normanni, dum maximum ac strenuissimum ducem suum uident
muliebri dolo periclitari.' et robur exercitus sui defectione Langobardorum qui cum domina sua clam discesserant imminui, et se
non posse in Italiam quia naues eorum combustæ erant sine graui
mora et difficultate proficisci. Magnanimus itaque dux Robertum
comitem Lorotelli, et Goisfredum de Conuersana nepotes suos,
Hugonem monoculum de Claro monte, et Guillelmum de Grente-
masnilo, Odonem quoque bonum marchisum sororium suum,
aliosque cognatos proceresque suos ad se conuocauit.'[3] et quid
acturi essent interrogauit. Cumque omnes inter se mussitarent, nec
certum quid proferrent.' ait 'Vltio diuina pro peccatis nostris nos
iii. 184 percutit.' et a nimiis cupiditatibus nostris nos reprimit. Iuste
nos ut dominus seruos suos uerberat.' et prospicue quod mundi
gloria non sit appetenda nobis insinuat. Gratias illi pro omnibus
quæ nobis impertiri dignatus est agamus.' et ut nostri semper
misereatur toto corde appetamus. Ecce nos de pauperibus in-
fimisque parentibus processimus.' et sterile rus Constantini
uacuosque necessariis rebus penates reliquimus, et profecti
Romam cum magno timore uix pertransiuimus. Deinde donante
Deo magnas et multas urbes optinuimus.' sed hoc non nostris
uiribus nec meritis sed diuinæ ordinationi imputare debemus.

[1] Jordan, prince of Capua, was the son of Robert Guiscard's sister (Mathieu, p. 199; Chalandon, *Domination normande*, i. 112).

[2] For the succession of Roger Borsa and his rivalry with his half-brother Bohemond see Mathieu, p. 13; Chalandon, *Domination normande*, i. 286–95; R. Manselli in *Japigia*, xi (1940), 55–9.

[3] Since Orderic knew the kinsmen of some of the magnates named he is probably correct in saying that they were near Guiscard in his last moments. Robert of Loritello was the son of Guiscard's brother Geoffrey, and Geoffrey of Conversano of his sister. William of Grandmesnil, son of Hugh of Grandmesnil, a founder of Saint-Évroul, married Guiscard's daughter Mabel (cf. below, p. 338). Odobonus Marchisus 'probably belonged to one of the sub-

stole away and came to Salerno under cover of darkness. Hastily seeking out Bohemond, he said, 'Rise at once, take flight and save yourself.' When Bohemond asked the reason, the messenger replied, 'Your father is dead and your stepmother is in Apulia: she is coming as fast as she can to kill you.' Without delay Bohemond, alarmed by this disturbing report, secretly left the city mounted on an ass and fled to his cousin Jordan, prince of Capua,[1] who welcomed him warmly. In this way he escaped from the toils and threats of his stepmother. She for her part, on reaching Salerno and learning that her intended prey had escaped her, was deeply mortified. Her son Roger, called Borsa, took possession of the extensive duchy in Italy by hereditary succession.[2]

The Normans were now beset with every kind of anxiety, for they found themselves in a foreign land with their great and invincible leader brought low by a woman's treachery and the strength of his army undermined by the desertion of the Lombards, who had crept away with their mistress. Since their ships had been burnt they themselves could not return to Italy without many difficulties and delays. So the valiant duke called to his bedside Robert count of Loritello and Geoffrey of Conversano, his nephews; Hugh 'Le Borgne' of Chiaromonte and William of Grandmesnil, Odobonus the Marquis his brother-in-law, and other kinsmen and nobles,[3] to ask them what they would do. As they only muttered to each other, uncertain what they should propose, he spoke these words: 'Divine vengeance now strikes us down for our sins and restrains us from our presumptuous ambitions. It rightly chastises us, as a master his servants, and providently teaches us not to pursue worldly fame. Let us give thanks to God for all that he has deigned to make known to us and beseech him from our hearts always to show us mercy. Consider: we were born of poor and humble parents and left the barren country of the Cotentin and homes which could not support us to travel to Rome with great toil and danger. Afterwards by God's will we won many great cities, but we ought to attribute this not to our own strength or deserts but to God's ordinance. Finally we conquered

alpine marchional families who settled in southern Italy and Sicily with the Normans' and was the father of Tancred; he married Robert Guiscard's sister Emma. Orderic always writes his name as if it had been Odo 'the good Marquis', and he may have been so nick-named; he occurs in witness lists as 'Odobonus Marchisus'. For the careers of William and Odobonus see E. M. Jamison, 'Some notes . . .', pp. 196–7.

Denique de imperio Constantinopolitano pro reatibus indigenarum inuasimus quantum potest in quindecim peragrari diebus. Optime nostis quod in sui presidium inuitatus sum a Michahele imperatore, quem ciues sui de solio regni nequiter expulere, quia filiam meam filio eius tradidi legitime.[1] Constantinopolim quam possidet imbellis populus deliciisque seruiens et lasciuiæ·ʼ decreueram si Deo placuisset catholicis pugnatoribus subiugare, qui sanctam Dei ciuitatem Ierusalem Turcis auferrent·ʼ æthnicisque bello repulsis Christianum imperium dilatarent.[2] Propter hoc desiderium tam magnum laborem et tam periculosum agonem iniui·ʼ sed hoc aliter ordinauit irreprehensibilis uoluntas omnipotentis Dei. Dauid templum Deo Ierusolimis construere uoluit, sed hoc a Salomone filio eius peragi cum ingenti tripudio Deus disposuit.[3] Sic labor meus ut autumo futuris temporibus consummabitur, et fructus laboris quandoque manifestabitur, et incitamentum tantæ probitatis utiliter posteris nostris propinabitur. Nunc igitur
iii. 185 O uiri fortes sapiens consilium accipite·ʼ pristinamque uirtutem uestram quam in arduis et angustis rebus multotiens expertus sum perdere nolite. Vnus homo sum ac ut reliqui mortalis·ʼ uos autem multi estis, multisque carismatibus largiente Deo uigetis. Famosa uero gesta quæ longe lateque diuulgata sunt uos fecistis·ʼ nec unquam maiora a tam paucis et infimis hominibus leguntur in aliquibus historiis, quam iuuante Deo facta sunt a uobis. Fortiorem itaque et sapientiorem de uobis eligite·ʼ[4] ipsumque uobis ducem constituite, ne perdatis fecundam tellurem quesitam magno labore sed paruo tempore. Buamundus filius meus si uita et sospitate uiget·ʼ quantocius uobis succurrere sataget.'

Hæc et his similia duce prosequente·ʼ Petrus francigena[5] aliique contubernales ducis dicta subtiliter intuentes dixerunt, 'In hoc negotio quod nobis imperas ingens discrimen est et maxima difficultas. Innumeri sunt hostes et nos pauci sumus, nimiumque nobis aduersatur imperator potens et callidus·ʼ quem te cohibente grauiter in multis sepe offendimus. Fortitudini eius latæque potentiæ nequiuimus resistere. Multis enim dominatur regnis et

[1] Cf. the speech attributed to Robert Guiscard at Durazzo by Anna Comnena (*Alexiad*, IV. v. 5).

[2] For Orderic's view of Guiscard as a 'crusader before the Crusades' see Mathieu, pp. 6–7; M. Mathieu, 'Normands et Byzantins', in *Archivio storico pugliese*, xii (1959), 39–40.

[3] Cf. 2 Samuel vii. 2–16.

[4] Cf. above, Introduction, pp. xxvi–xxvii.

[5] Possibly Orderic had in mind Peter of Alifa, one of Guiscard's captains, who subsequently took service with Alexius and founded the family of Petralifas in Byzantium. For his career see Marquis de la Force, 'Les conseillers latins d'Alexis Comnène', in *Byzantion*, xi (1936), 158–60. His origins are uncertain; Marquis de la Force suggests that he may have been a brother or son of Robert,

from the empire of Constantinople, because of the crimes of its people, as much territory as can be traversed in fifteen days. You know well that I was asked by the Emperor Michael to come to his aid, because his subjects had unjustly driven him into exile and my daughter was betrothed to his son.[1] I had resolved to subject Constantinople, which is held by an effeminate race given up to luxury and wantonness, if God so willed, to warriors of the catholic faith so that they might capture God's holy city, Jerusalem, from the Turks, conquer the infidels and extend the bounds of the Christian empire.[2] To achieve this end I undertook this great labour and perilous enterprise: but the mysterious will of almighty God has determined otherwise. David wished to build a temple of God in Jerusalem, but God willed that this should be accomplished by his son Solomon with great triumph.[3] So my work, I declare, will be completed at some future time; the fruits of our labour will appear one day and this great valour of ours will inspire our descendants. So now, my brave followers, take prudent counsel and do not lose your former courage that has helped me in so many difficulties and dangers. I am only one man and mortal like the rest of us; you are many and enjoy many blessings from the hand of God. You have performed famous deeds which are renowned far and wide; in all the histories that men read never were greater things achieved by such a small band of obscure men as, by God's help, have been performed by you. Choose the bravest and wisest among you and make him your leader;[4] avoid in this way losing the fertile land conquered by great efforts in a short space of time. If my son Bohemond is alive and safe, he will do his best to help you.'

As the duke put forward these and similar proposals, Peter the Frank[5] and other companions of the duke carefully weighed his words and said, 'The course which you impose on us is very hazardous and difficult. Our enemies are numberless and we are few; a powerful and experienced emperor is our relentless foe, for in spite of your restraints we have given serious offence to him on many occasions. We cannot resist the great might and far-flung power of one who rules over many kingdoms and nations. Our

lord of Chiazza and Alifa, a Norman lord. The term 'Franci' was freely applied to the Normans of south Italy (cf. A. Gallo, *Aversa Normanna* (Naples, 1938), pp. 7–8). His later career would make him a suitable mouthpiece for the party opposed to continuing the fight.

nationibus. Vtinam ad domos nostras unde discessimus.' cum pace et salute regredi ualeamus.'

His auditis dux ualde ingemuit.' Deumque cum fletu inuocare
filiumque suum sic lugere cœpit, 'Heu me miserum tot infortuniis
circumdatum. Olim multis nocui et iniuste multa peregi. Nunc
simul mala inuenerunt me.' quæ promerui longo tempore. Summe
Deus nunc parce michi, pie Deus miserere michi peccatori, fortis
Deus succurre populo tuo, quem huc adduxi. Fili mi Buamunde,
iii. 186 uirtute et sensu Thebano par Epaminundæ, ubi reperiam te?
Nobilis atheleta Buamunde, militia[a] Thessalo Achilli seu franci-
genæ Rollando[1] equiparande, uiuisne an detineris pernicie? Quid
tibi contigit, quid probitas tua deuenit? O si sospes qualem te dum
Tusciam adirem dimisi presto adesses.' opulentam Bulgariæ
regionem armis nostris optentam possideres. Scio nanque quod
tanta si uiuis strenuitate polles, ut si morti meæ diuino nutu
interesses.' ius quod bello adquisiui iuuante Deo nullatenus
amitteres. Eia commilitones optimi caute uobis consulite, et quod
a laribus uestris ualde remoti estis perpendite. Recolite quam
magna Normanni fecere, et quod parentes nostri Francis et
Britonibus et Cenomannensibus multotiens restitere, et fortiter
uicere. Ad mentem reducite quam magna me duce gessistis in
Italia et Sicilia, Psalerniam et Barum, Brundisium et Tarentum,
Bisinnanum[2] et Regium.' Siracusam et Palernum, Cosentiam et
Castrum Iohannis aliasque multas urbes et oppida optinuistis.
iii. 187 Gisulfum quoque Salernitanum ducem,[3] et Wazsonem Neapolita-
num comitem,[4] aliosque principes fortissimos me duce per Dei
iuuamen superastis. Nunc igitur ne uilescatis amisso pristinæ
magnanimitatis conamine.' eleccione communi unum ex uobis ut

[a] militiam, *Caen MS.*

---

[1] Versions of the *chanson de Roland* were popular among the Normans from the late eleventh century; H. Grégoire has made a strong case for the composition of the Baligant episode about 1085; many of the names can be identified as places near to Durazzo, and the contingents of Baligant's army have names suggesting races and peoples serving in the Greek army of Alexius (H. Grégoire and R. de Keyser, 'La chanson de Roland et Byzance', *Byzantion*, xiv (1939), 265–301). In this context Orderic's comparison of Bohemond to Roland has a special interest.

[2] Le Prévost's reading (*Bismanno*) prevented him from identifying the place correctly as Bisignano, in the Val di Crati. Guiscard's capture of Bisignano assumed legendary proportions (cf. Mathieu, p. 3 n. 1; GM i. 17, pp. 17–18).

[3] Gisulf II of Salerno, Guiscard's brother-in-law, was forced to surrender to Guiscard after the siege of Salerno in 1076–7 (Mathieu, pp. 186–8).

only wish is to be allowed to return in peace and safety to the homes we have left.'

Hearing this the duke was sad at heart and, weeping, began to call on God and mourn his son in these words, 'How wretched I am, in the midst of so many misfortunes. There was a time when I injured many and acted unjustly in numerous ways. Now all my evil deeds have come home to me together, according to my deserts. Most high God, spare me now; gracious God, have mercy on me, a sinner; mighty God, help your people whom you have led to this place. O my son Bohemond, equal to the Theban Epaminondas in courage and judgement, where shall I find you again? O Bohemond, noble champion, comparable in the art of war to Achilles the Greek or Roland the Frank,[1] are you alive or treacherously slain? What has happened to you, what has become of your prowess? If you were well and strong, as you were when I left you to go to Italy, you would soon be here to take possession of the rich province of Bulgaria, conquered by our arms. So great is your valour that, if life remains in you and God willed that you should witness my death, I know you would never surrender the right that I have won in war by God's help. Come then, my chosen comrades-in-arms, take good counsel with each other and consider that you are very far from your own homes. Remember what prodigies the Normans have performed; remember that our parents often took arms against Frenchmen and Bretons and men of Maine and valiantly conquered them. Call to mind what great deeds you have done under my leadership in Italy and Sicily, when you conquered Salerno and Bari, Brindisi and Tarento, Bisignano[2] and Reggio, Syracuse and Palermo, Cosenza and Castro-Giovanni and many other towns and fortresses. Under my command and by God's help you also overcame Gisulf, duke of Salerno,[3] the Neapolitan count Wazo[4] and other powerful princes. So do not forget now the challenge of your former greatness and become underlings; appoint a leader from among yourselves by

[4] This allusion is obscure. In his interpolations in William of Jumièges Orderic referred to the murderer of Drogo of Hauteville in 1051 as 'Wazso Neapolitanus comes' (Marx, pp. 189–90); but the only other writer to use this name is Benoît of Sainte-Maure, who probably copied from Orderic. Geoffrey of Malaterra calls the assassin Risus (GM i. 13, p. 14), and the murder was avenged by Drogo's brother Humphrey, not by Robert Guiscard (Amatus of Montecassino, *Storia de' Normanni*, ed. V. de Bartholomaeis (Rome, 1935), pp. 136 n. 2, 137 n. 1).

dixi ducem constituite, uberesque prouincias quas iam nacti estis insigniter uobis retinete.'

Nullus eorum qui rebus istis interfuere.' ausus fuit ducatum huiusmodi suscipere sed omnes de fugæ presidio maluerunt cogitare. Deinde anno ab incarnatione domini millesimo octogesimo quinto, Robertus Wiscardus Apuliæ dux insignis, nostrisque temporibus pene incomparabilis.' facta confessione a peccatis mundatus, et salutaris Eucharistiæ perceptione munitus.' non militari robore prostratus, sed liuore femineo corruptus.' quo primus Adam est de paradisi sede proiectus, non armis sed ueneno lesus.' adueniente mortis hora mundo est sublatus. Quo defuncto Normanni corpus eius sallierunt.' et cum pace reditum in patriam suam ab imperatore petierunt. Imperator autem licet
iii. 188 lætaretur quia liberatus a terribili hoste fuerit.' defunctum tamen
ducem qui nunquam de bello fugerat ex pietate multum planxit. Licentiam his qui redire in Italiam uellent cum cadauere principis sui et omnibus rebus suis benigniter concessit.' aliis uero qui secum remanere sibique seruire uellent larga stipendia pepigit. Bizantio ex tunc itaque fideliter famulati sunt.' qui antea fortiter impugnauerunt.[1] Remeantes autem in Apuliam corpus ducis Venusiæ detulerunt.' ibique in cœnobio Sanctæ Trinitatis cum luctu magno sepelierunt. Venerabilis Berengarius abbas filius Ernaldi filii Helgonis eidem monasterio præerat.' quem Teodericus archimandrita pius apud Vticum educauerat, et inde Robertus abbas secum in Calabriam adduxerat. Deinde ab Alexandro papa Venusiensi monasterio abbas consecratus est.' atque post aliquot annos pro merito uitæ et sapientiæ doctrina ad pontificatum præfatæ urbis a papa Vrbano promotus est.[2]

8

Dum furerent in orbe tempestates quæ superius memoratæ sunt.' quidam sortilegi Romanorum quis in papatu succederet Hilde-
iii. 189 branno indagarunt, et quod post transitum Gregorii Odo Romanis
papa foret compererunt. Hoc audiens Odo presul Baiocensis qui cum fratre suo Guillelmo rege Normannis dominabatur et Anglis, paruipendens potestates et diuitias regni occidentalis, nisi iure

[1] For the Normans who entered the imperial service after Robert's death see Marquis de la Force, in *Byzantion*, xi (1936), 153–65; Mathieu, pp. 256, 335–6. According to Anna Comnena many Normans had passed into the service of Alexius at Castoria in 1083 (*Alexiad*, VI. i. 4).

[2] For Berengar's career see above, ii. 20, 50, 96, 100–2. He came to Calabria with Robert of Grandmesnil.

common consent, as I have advised, and honourably retain for yourselves the rich provinces which you have already won.'

Not one of those who witnessed these events dared to undertake such a leadership; on the contrary all preferred to turn their minds to making good their escape. So in the year of our Lord 1085 Robert Guiscard, the illustrious duke of Apulia, almost without equal in our own times, made his confession, received absolution from his sins, and was fortified by taking the saving Eucharist. He was not struck down by military might, but was destroyed by the envy of woman, by which the first Adam was driven from Paradise; he departed from the world when the hour of death came, the victim not of arms, but of poison.

When he was dead the Normans preserved his body in salt and petitioned the Emperor for a safe-conduct to return home. Although the Emperor was greatly relieved at being delivered from his terrible foe, yet out of respect he could not refrain from mourning the dead duke who had never fled from battle. He graciously gave leave to depart to those who wished to return to Italy with the body of their prince and all their belongings, and offered generous wages to others who were willing to remain with him and enter his service. From that time those who had once valiantly attacked the Byzantine Empire now gave it faithful service.[1] But the others, returning to Apulia, carried the body of their leader to Venosa and buried it there in the abbey of Holy Trinity with great lamentations. The monastery was governed by the venerable abbot Berengar, the son of Arnold son of Heugon, who had been educated at Saint-Évroul by the holy father Thierry and brought to Calabria by Abbot Robert as one of his companions. Later he was blessed as abbot of Venosa by Pope Alexander; some years later he was promoted by Pope Urban to be bishop of the same city because of his good life and sound doctrine.[2]

8

While the storms I have described disturbed the world, certain soothsayers at Rome, in an attempt to discover who would succeed Hildebrand in the papacy, ascertained that Odo was to be pope in Rome after Gregory's death. When the news reached Odo, bishop of Bayeux, who with his brother King William ruled the Normans and English, he counted all the power and wealth of the

papatus dominaretur Latiis et omnibus terrigenis; Romam misit, palacium sibi emit, senatores Quiritum magnis muneribus datis sibi amicicia copulauit, palaciumque suum multis sumptibus et superfluis apparatibus exornauit.[1] Hugonem Cestrensium comitem magnamque cohortem precipuorum militum asciuit, ut secum in Italiam proficiscerentur obsecrauit; et ingentia precibus promissa prodigus addidit. Illi uero quia Normanni leues et extera uidere cupidi sunt; protinus presumptori episcopo cui principatus Albionis et Neustriæ non sufficiebat assenserunt. Ingentes quoque fundos quos in occiduis climatibus possidebant deserere decreuerunt, ac ut prefato presuli trans Padum comitarentur per fidem spoponderunt.

Apparatum huiuscemodi prudens rex Guillelmus edidicit, sed non approbauit, regnoque suo multisque aliis ualde nociturum estimauit. Vnde festinanter in Angliam transfretauit, ac Odoni episcopo cum grandi pompa nauigare in Normanniam cupienti ex insperato in insula Vecta obuiauit. Ibi nimirum congregatis in
iii. 190 aula regali[2] primoribus regni rex ita locutus est.

'Egregii proceres uerba mea diligenter audite, et salubre consilium michi queso tribuite. Antequam transfretassem in Normanniam, regimen Angliæ fratri meo Baiocensi episcopo commendaueram. In Normannia multi contra me surrexerunt; et ut ita dicam intimi et forinseci me inuaserunt. Robertus filius meus et tirones quos enutriui et quibus arma dedi contra me rebellauerunt; eisque mei malefidi clientes et finitimi hostes gratanter adheserunt. Verum Deo cuius seruus sum me protegente nil profecerunt; nec de meo aliquid nisi ferrum in uulneribus suis optinuerunt. Conglobatos in me Andegauenses paratus ad bellum terrore compressi; parique modo rebellantes Cenomannos armis et uiribus

[1] There are similar stories of intrigues in Rome in William of Malmesbury (*GR* ii. 334) and the Hyde Chronicle (*Liber Monasterii de Hyda*, ed. E. Edwards (RS 1866), p. 296). The exact causes of Odo's fall are obscure; see above, Introduction, pp. xxvii–xxx.

[2] In dramatizing the trial of Odo Orderic went beyond the known facts, and the implication that Odo was seized in the Isle of Wight and tried on the spot need not be taken too literally. Indeed the proceedings were speeded up progressively in legend as time advanced; Wace (*Roman de Rou*, ii, ll. 9241–4, 'Ici fu pris e retenu . . . Prez fu la nef, boen fu li venz, E li evesques fu mis enz') imagined the bishop bundled straight on board ship and taken to Rouen. The Hyde chronicler (p. 296) has a slightly different version, without placenames: 'manifestata eius versutia, ab eodem rege in consilium vocatur, devinci-

western kingdom for nothing, wishing only to have authority as pope over the Latins and all the peoples of the earth. Sending to Rome, he bought himself a palace, secured the alliance of the leading Roman families by scattering lavish gifts and embellished his palace at great expense with superfluous furnishings.[1] He sent for Hugh, earl of Chester, and a great force of distinguished knights, invited them to set out with him for Italy and recklessly backed up his request with lavish promises. Because the Normans are restless and always eager to see foreign lands they readily agreed to support the presumptuous bishop, who was not to be satisfied with dominion over England and Normandy. So they resolved to abandon the great estates that they possessed in the western parts and took an oath to accompany the bishop to lands beyond the Po.

King William, wise monarch that he was, learned of these preparations but did not approve of them; he judged that they would cause great damage to his kingdom and many others. Crossing immediately to England, he came without warning on Bishop Odo in the Isle of Wight, where he was making preparations to sail to Normandy in great state. There the king assembled the magnates of the kingdom in the royal palace[2] and spoke these words:

'Great lords, I invite you to listen carefully to my words and give me good counsel. Before crossing to Normandy I entrusted the government of England to my brother, the bishop of Bayeux. In Normandy many rebelled against me and both natives and foreigners, so to say, attacked me. Robert my son and the young men whom I had trained as squires and invested with arms rebelled against me; both my faithless dependants and the enemies on my frontiers readily supported them. In fact, since God whom I serve protected me, they accomplished nothing and got nothing from me save weapons in their wounds. I prepared for war and struck terror into the hearts of the Angevins, who were massed against me; in like manner I crushed the rebellious men of Maine

tur, carceri mancipatur.' There was considerable flexibility in the *curia regis*, and the court that tried Odo may have assembled anywhere; but the word 'consilium' is a shred of evidence in favour of one of William I's great courts at Winchester, Westminster, or Gloucester. If Odo was imprisoned just after Christmas 1082 or even Easter 1083 then Orderic is not far wrong in giving the length of his incarceration as four years.

compescui. His nimirum occupationibus ultra mare irretitus fui.' ibique diu moratus publicis utilitatibus laboriose deseruiui. Interea frater meus Angliam uehementer oppressit, et æcclesias fundis et redditibus exspoliauit, ornamentis ab antecessoribus editis nudauit, militesque meos qui contra Danos et Hibernenses et alios hostes michi nimis infestos Angliam tutare debuerant seduxit, et trans Alpes in extera regna me contempto pertrahere
iii. 191 disponit. Nimius dolor cor meum angit.' precipue pro æcclesiis Dei quas afflixit. Christiani reges qui ante me regnauerunt, æcclesiam Dei amauerunt.' honoribus et exeniis multi generis locupletauerunt, unde nunc ut credimus in amena sede felici retributione gaudentes requiescunt. Adelbertus et Eduinus, ac sanctus Osualdus, Athulfus ac Alfredus, Eduardus senior et Edgarus, cognatusque meus et carissimus dominus Eduardus dederunt opes æcclesiæ sanctæ quæ est sponsa Dei, et frater meus cui tocius regni tutelam commendaui.' uiolenter opes diripuit, crudeliter pauperes oppressit.' friuola spe milites modo surripuit, totumque regnum iniustis exactionibus concutiens exagitauit. Quid inde agendum sit caute considerate, et michi queso insinuate.' Cumque omnes tantum uirum timerent, et sententiam in illum proferre dubitarent.' magnanimus rex ait, 'Noxia temeritas semper comprimenda est.' nec uni ad detrimentum rei publicæ pro aliquo fauore parcendum est. Hunc ergo uirum qui terram turbat comprehendite.' et ne in deterius preualeat sollerter custodite.' Cumque nullus in episcopum auderet inicere manum.' rex ipse primus apprehendit eum. Illo autem reclamante 'Clericus sum et minister Dei.' non licet tibi pontificem damnare sine iudicio papæ', prouidus rex ait, 'Ego non clericum nec antistitem damno, sed comitem meum quem meo uice mea proposui regno.' rationem commissæ uillicacionis audire uolens comprehendo.'[1]

Sic regia potestas prefatum præsulem cepit, in Normanniam
iii. 192 deduci fecit, et in arce Rotomagensi incarcerauit, ibique intrusum iiii annis scilicet usque ad finem uitæ suæ diligenter custodiuit. Capite uero inquietudinis deiecto, militum motio conquieuit.' probique regis prouidentia regnum suum intus et extra fortiter muniuit.

[1] Cf. Luke xvi. 2 ff.; and see above, Introduction, pp. xxviii–xxx. For the suggestion that William treated Odo as a lay lord see A. Morey and C. N. L. Brooke, *Gilbert Foliot and his Letters* (Cambridge, 1965), p. 177 n. 2.

by force of arms. Such enterprises delayed me overseas and I remained there for a long time, labouring for the public good. All this time my brother was oppressing England cruelly, robbing churches of their estates and revenues, stripping them of the ornaments given by his predecessors and misleading my knights, whose duty was to guard England against Danes and Irishmen and other enemies who hate me, and planning to lead them to foreign kingdoms beyond the Alps regardless of my interests. My heart is full of bitter grief, in particular for the churches of God which he has oppressed. The Christian kings who ruled before me loved the Church of God and enriched it with estates and gifts of many kinds; now therefore, as we firmly believe, they rest and enjoy their precious reward in a blessed place. Æthelbert and Edwin, St. Oswald, Ethelwulf and Alfred, Edward the Elder and Edgar and Edward, my kinsman and dear lord, all gave wealth to the holy Church which is the bride of God; my brother, to whom I entrusted the regency of the whole realm, violently seized the riches, cruelly oppressed the poor, just now suborned the knights with empty hope and tormented the whole kingdom, shaking it to its foundations with unjust exactions. Give serious thought to what should be done and tell me, I beg you, what you decide.' As all feared the great man and hesitated to pronounce sentence on him, the illustrious king said, 'Harmful ambition should always be checked and it is never right to spare one man against the public interest through any partiality. Arrest this man, who stirs up trouble in the land, and guard him closely for fear of even worse deeds.' As no one dared to lay a hand on the bishop the king himself seized hold of him first of all. When he protested, 'I am a clerk and a priest of God; you have no right to condemn a bishop without papal judgement', the prudent king replied, 'I condemn neither a clerk nor a bishop, but arrest my earl, whom I have made viceroy in my kingdom, desiring to hear an account of the stewardship entrusted to him.'[1]

So the king in his royal might arrested the bishop, and had him taken to Normandy and imprisoned in the tower of Rouen, where he kept him under close guard for four years, until the end of his own life. Once the instigator of the disturbance had been overthrown, the tumult among the knights died down; and the upright king, by his foresight, buttressed his kingdom against attack from within or without.

Ecce in hoc homine palam completum uidemus, quod in libro mittologiarum[1] dicit Fulgentius, 'Qui plus querit quam licet: minus erit quam est.' Præsulatus Baiocensis et comitatus Cantiæ ingentibus gazis abundans, et per totam Angliam atque Normanniam regia potestas cum fratre communis[2] uni clerico non sufficiebat, qui uniuerso mundo preferri satagebat: quem ad hoc non cogebat diuina assumptio, nec canonica electio, sed insatiabilis cupiditatis immoderata presumpcio. Ergo quod habebat perdidit, et inclusus diu gemuit, exemplumque posteris ne similibus inhient dereliquit.

9

His temporibus indictione septima, Mathildis regina Anglorum
egrotauit, diutina infirmitate anxia reatus suos cognouit, et
obnixe defleuit, omnibusque rite peractis quæ mos Christianus
iii. 193 exigit, salutari sacramento munita, iii° non' Nouembris[3] obiit.
Deinde corpus eius ad cœnobium sanctæ Trinitatis quod ipsa
sanctimonialibus apud Cadomum construxerat delatum est: et ab
episcopis ac abbatibus multis inter chorum et altare uenerabiliter
tumulatum est. Exequias eius celebrarunt monachi et clerici cum
pauperum agmine: quibus ipsa uiuens frequenter profuit in
Christi nomine. Memoriale eius super ipsam ex auro et gemmis
mirifice constructum est: et epitaphium huiusmodi litteris aureis
comiter exaratum est.

Egregie pulchri tegit hæc structura sepulchri,
Moribus insignem germen regale Mathildem.
Dux Flandrita pater huic extitit, Hadala[a] mater,
Francorum gentis Roberti filia regis,
Et soror Henrici regali sede potiti.
Regi magnifico Guillelmo[b] iuncta marito,
Præsentem sedem, præsentem fecit et ædem,
Tam multis terris quam multis rebus honestis,
A se ditatam, se procurante dicatam.

[a] Adala, *original* [b] Willelmo, *original*

[1] The *Mitologiae* of Fulgentius (ed. R. Heim, *Fabii Planciadis Fulgentii Opera*, Leipzig, 1898), a brief and inaccurate account of various episodes in classical mythology, with fanciful allegorical interpretations, enjoyed great popularity in the ninth century and for some time afterwards (see M. L. W. Laistner, 'Fulgentius in the Carolingian age', in *The Intellectual Heritage of the Early Middle Ages*, ed. C. G. Starr (Ithaca, 1957), pp. 202–15). This trite quotation does not occur in the work; and Orderic probably accepted the attribution at second hand.

[2] For Odo's authority in England see above, ii. 264–6.

In this man you may see fulfilled the saying of Fulgentius in his book on mythology,[1] 'He who seeks more than his deserts will sink below his present station.' The bishopric of Bayeux and the earldom of Kent, with its abundant resources, and a share with his brother in the royal power over all England and Normandy,[2] were not enough for one churchman who aspired to be set over all the earth, though he was drawn towards this end neither by divine choice nor by canonical election, but only by the unrestrained presumption of his insatiable ambition. Consequently he lost what he had and for years pined in captivity, leaving an example to future generations to deter them from such undertakings.

9

About this time, in the seventh indiction, Matilda, queen of England, fell sick; growing apprehensive because her illness persisted, she confessed her sins with bitter tears and, after fully accomplishing all that Christian custom requires and being fortified by the saving sacrament, she died on 3 November.[3] Her body was carried at once to the abbey of the Holy Trinity, which she had founded at Caen for nuns, and was reverently buried by many bishops and abbots between the choir and the altar. Monks and clergy celebrated her obsequies, attended by a great throng of poor people, for in her lifetime she had often been their benefactress in the name of Christ. A monument was erected over her, wonderfully worked with gold and precious stones, and this epitaph was lovingly engraved in letters of gold.

The lofty structure of this splendid tomb
Hides great Matilda, sprung from royal stem;
Child of a Flemish duke; her mother was
Adela, daughter of a king of France,
Sister of Henry, Robert's royal son.
Married to William, most illustrious king,
She gave this site and raised this noble house,
With many lands and many goods endowed,
Given by her, or by her toil procured;

[3] In fact Matilda died on 2 November 1083 (Musset, *Abbayes caennaises*, p. 15); the date is correctly given in the epitaph. Orderic made the same mistake in his interpolations in William of Jumièges (Marx p. 183), possibly because Matilda's obit was celebrated at Saint-Évroul on 3 November (Bouquet, xxiii, 490).

Hæc consolatrix inopum pietatis amatrix,
Gazis dispersis pauper sibi, diues egenis.
Sic infinitæ petiit consortia uitæ,
In prima mensis post primam luce Novembris.[1]

iii. 194 Cadomense cœnobium sanctæ et indiuiduæ Trinitati dicatum Mathildis abbatissa per annos xlvii strenue rexit, atque Ceciliam regis filiam aliasque plures in Dei famulatu sollerter educauit, et regulariter instruxit.[2] Qua defuncta nobilis Cecilia successit, et pluribus annis tempore fratris sui Henrici regis officium matris gessit. Deinde filia Guillelmi consulis filii Stephani Blesensis regimen eiusdem æcclesiæ suscepit: sed immatura morte preuenta paruo tempore tenuit.[3]

10

Post obitum gloriosæ Mathildis reginæ Guillelmus rex pene quatuor annis quibus superuixit: multis procellis tribulationum contra eum insurgentibus uehementer laborauit. Nam quidam Cenomannensium qui quasi naturali semper inquietudine agitantur, et mobilitate sua pacem turbant ipsique turbantur: contra regem Guillelmum arma sumpserunt, sibique multisque aliis dispendia magna procurauerunt.[4] Hubertus enim uicecomes[5] gener Guillelmi Niuernensium comitis quibusdam paruis occasionibus regem
iii. 195 prius offendit, sed postmodum in maius crescentibus castra sua Bellummontem et Fredernaicum reliquit: et cum uxore sua omnibusque suis ad castrum quod Sancta Susanna uocatur, ut publicus hostis secessit. Illud nempe municipium ad quod confugit, super Arua fluuium situm est in ardua rupe: in confinio Cenomannensium et Andegauensium. Illuc militarem manum sibi accersiit: et Normannis qui Cenomannensem pagum tutari conabantur dampna dampnorumque formidinem non segniter intulit. Erat enim nobilitate clarus, sensu et probitate precipuus: ingenti uirtute et audacia feruidus, et pro his insigniis longe

[1] Matilda's tombstone with the epitaph carved round it can still be seen in the choir of Holy Trinity Church at Caen, before the high altar. Apart from a few minor variations of spelling the epitaph is exactly as Orderic copied it. See the reproduction in *Histoire de la Normandie*, ed. M. de Bouard (Toulouse, 1970), plate 13.

[2] Matilda died, according to the tradition of the abbey, on 6 July 1113. On the varying figures given for the length of her term of office see Musset, *Abbayes caennaises*, pp. 13–14, and above, iii. 10 n. 1. Cecilia died on 13 July 1127 (ibid.).

[3] Isabel or Elizabeth was abbess for only a year. For her father, William, the eldest son of Stephen count of Blois, see above, iii. 116.

Comforter of the needy, duty's friend;
Her wealth enriched the poor, left her in need.
At daybreak on November's second day
She won her share of everlasting joy.[1]

The Abbess Matilda vigorously ruled the nunnery at Caen dedicated to the holy and undivided Trinity for forty-seven years; she carefully brought up the king's daughter Cecilia and many others in the service of God, instructing them in life under a rule.[2] After her death the nobly-born Cecilia succeeded her and was reverend mother to the convent for a number of years during the reign of her brother, King Henry. Next a daughter of Count William, the son of Stephen of Blois, undertook the government of the church; but she was cut off by premature death after holding office for only a short time.[3]

10

After the death of his illustrious queen, Matilda, King William, who survived her for almost four years, was continually forced to struggle against the storms of troubles that rose up against him. Some of the men of Maine, who are always so rebellious that they are virtually turbulent by nature and by their unruliness disturb the peace and trouble each other, took up arms against King William, with consequences disastrous to themselves and many others.[4] For Hubert the vicomte,[5] son-in-law of William count of Nevers, who had first given offence to the king for a number of petty reasons, afterwards for more serious causes abandoned his castles of Beaumont-le-Vicomte and Fresnay-sur-Sarthe and, becoming a public enemy, withdrew with his wife and all his adherents to the castle of Sainte-Suzanne. This fortress in which he took refuge is built on a steep crag above the river Erve, on the frontiers of Maine and Anjou. There he gathered an armed force round him and all too often injured or threatened to injure the Normans who were busy protecting the county of Maine. He was a man of very high birth, remarkable for his judgement and integrity, conspicuous for his valour and daring, and renowned far

[4] For the insurrection in Maine in late 1083 or early 1084 see Latouche, *Maine*, p. 39; Halphen, *Anjou*, p. 186.

[5] Hubert of Sainte-Suzanne, vicomte of Le Mans. See above, ii. 118; Latouche, *Maine*, p. 39.

lateque famosus. Custodes autem Cenomannicæ urbis et circum-
iii. 196 iacentium oppidorum infestationibus Huberti frequenter laces-
siti sunt.' regique Guillelmo querelas infortunii sui retulerunt, et ab
eo auxilium poposcerunt. Rex igitur exercitum Normannorum
actutum asciuit, partemque Cenomannorum qui sibi cohærebant
accersiit, et hostilem patriam cum ualida manu adiuit. Sed castrum
Sanctæ Susannæ quod inaccessibile erat pro rupibus et densitate
uinearum quibus circumdabatur obsidere nequiuit.' nec hostem qui
intus erat ad libitum coartare ualuit, quia fortiter sibi procurabat, et
amplos aditus habebat. Rex itaque quoddam municipium in
ualle Beugici construxit, ibique magnam militum copiam ad
arcendum hostem constituit.' ipse uero pro magnis regni negociis
in Neustriam rediit. Regis familia cui Alannus Rufus Britonum
comes[1] preerat, diuitiis equis et bellicis sumptibus prestabat.' sed
castrensis cuneus eis uirtute et multitudine equiparari satagebat.
Nam de Aquitania et Burgundia aliisque prouinciis Galliæ probati
milites ad Hubertum conuolabant.' eique totis nisibus auxiliari
suamque probitatem ostentare feruenter optabant. Vnde factum
iii. 197 est ut ex detrimentis Beugicorum Susannense castrum ditaretur.'
et cotidie ad resistendum magis magisque confortaretur. Multotiens opulenti Normannorum et Anglorum proceres capiebantur,
quorum redemptionibus uicecomes et Robertus Burgundio[2] cuius
neptem in coniugio habebat aliique adiutores sui honorifice dita-
bantur. Sic tribus annis Hubertus Normannis restitit.'[3] et inimicorum opibus locuples inuictus permansit.

In hac guerra Robertus de Veteri Ponte[4] et Robertus de Vxeio
aliique egregii Normannorum milites multumque lugendi occisi
sunt. Nam xiiii° kal' Decembris dum Normannica cohors impetum
in hostes faceret.' quidam puer inberbis qui secus uiam inter
uebres absconditus erat sagittam emisit, et Richerium de Aquila
Engenulfi filium[5] letaliter sub oculo percussit. Furentes autem
socii cucurrerunt.' et puerum statim comprehenderunt, atque
iii. 198 pro uindicta nobilissimi baronis occidere uoluerunt. Sed moriens

[1] Alan the Red, lord of Richmond, one of William the Conqueror's leading Breton followers. See *EYC* iv. 84–100, for his English possessions.

[2] Robert the Burgundian, lord of Craon and Sablé, was the brother of William of Nevers, whose daughter, Ermengarde, married Hubert on 6 December 1067 (Bertrand de Broussillon, *La maison de Craon* (Paris, 1893), i. 23).

[3] The length of the siege impressed contemporaries, but Orderic's figures cannot be taken literally. Elsewhere (below, p. 52) he speaks of a conflict of four years, which must be an overstatement. Peace was made between Hubert and William between 23 May 1085 and 20 April 1086 (Halphen, *Anjou*, p. 186 n. 4; Latouche, *Maine*, p. 39 n. 8); hostilities at most lasted a little over two years.

[4] Probably the same man as Robert of Vieux-Pont who was sent to the aid of John of La Flèche against Fulk of Anjou (above, ii. 308).

and wide for these qualities. The custodians of the city of Le Mans and the neighbouring strongholds, suffering from the injuries repeatedly inflicted on them by Hubert, carried complaints of their wrongs to King William and begged for his help. The king quickly raised an army of Normans, summoned those among the men of Maine who were loyal to him and advanced on the enemy country with a strong force. But he could not blockade the castle of Sainte-Suzanne, which was made inaccessible by the crags and a thick growth of creepers surrounding it, neither could he bring effective pressure on his enemy in the castle, since Hubert was strong enough to procure supplies and controlled many entrances and exits. The king therefore built a castle in the valley of Beugy, posted a strong force of men-at-arms there to contain the enemy and himself returned to Normandy to deal with the urgent business of his realm. The king's garrison, under the command of a Breton count, Alan the Red,[1] was well provided with supplies, horses, and war equipment; but the troops in the castle equalled them in courage and numbers. Experienced knights had flocked to Hubert from Aquitaine and Burgundy and other French provinces and were striving with all their might to help him and show their worth. As a result the castle of Sainte-Suzanne was stocked with booty taken from the defenders of Beugy and each day became better equipped for defence. Wealthy Norman and English lords were frequently captured and Hubert the vicomte and Robert the Burgundian, whose niece he had married,[2] and their other supporters made an honourable fortune out of the ransoms of these men. In this way Hubert kept the Normans at bay for three years,[3] growing rich at the expense of his enemies and remaining unvanquished.

In the course of this war Robert of Vieux-Pont[4] and Robert of Ussy and many other famous and much-lamented knights were slain. On 18 November, when a Norman force made an onslaught on the enemy, a certain beardless boy, hidden among thorn bushes beside the path, shot an arrow which struck Richer, son of Engenulf of Laigle,[5] just below the eye, wounding him fatally. His furious companions were on the spot at once and laying hands on the boy proposed to kill him to avenge the noble lord. But Richer, who

[5] Richer was the second son of Engenulf of Laigle, who fell at Hastings (above, ii. 176). His family were benefactors of Saint-Évroul.

Richerius ei subuenit. Nam dum uellent eum iugulare.' uulneratus quanto potuit conatu exclamauit, 'Sinite illum pro amore Dei. Peccatis meis exigentibus sic debeo mori.' Mox dimisso percussore lugendus heros peccata sua sodalibus suis confessus est.' et sic antequam presbiter adduci potuisset mortuus est. Deinde corpus eius delatum est ad quoddam monachorum monasterium, quod Engenulfus pater eius in sua possessione construxerat in honore sancti Sulpicii presulis Bituricensium.'[1] ibique cum ingenti luctu parentum et affinium tumulatum est a Gisleberto uenerabili episcopo Ebroicensium.

Merito uir iste a notis plangebatur.' quia multis bonis in uita sua decorabatur. Erat enim corpore fortis, pulcher et agilis, in lege Dei fidelis, religiosis hominibus supplex et humilis, in negociis uero seculi cautus et facundus, et in omni conuersatione sua tranquillus et dapsilis. Hic habuit coniugem Iudith, Ricardi Abrincatensis cognomento Goz filiam sororem scilicet Hugonis Cestrensium comitis.' ex qua genuit Gislebertum Aquilensem et Engenulfum et Matildem, et alios plures filios et filias. Gislebertus autem solus aliis decidentibus paternæ probitatis et honoris heres successit, ac Iulianam strenuissimi comitis Mauritaniæ Goisfredi filiam
iii. 199 coniugem duxit.' quæ Richerium et Engenulfum ac Goisfredum et Gislebertum peperit, quorum duo medii cum Guillelmo adelino Henrici regis filio aliisque multis nobilibus vii° kal' Decembris naufragio perierunt.[2] Mathildis autem potenti uiro Roberto de Molbraio comiti Nordanhumbrorum nupsit, qui eodem anno contra Guillelmum Rufum regem Anglorum rebellauit, sed paulo post captus fere xxxiiii annis in carcere prefati regis et Henrici fratris eius sine prole consenuit.[3] Nunc ad rem unde parumper disgressus sum remeabo.

Mense Ianuario Guillelmus de Warenna et Baldricus de Chitreio[4] Nicholai filius atque Gislebertus de Aquila cupiens mortem Richerii fratris sui uindicare, cum ualida manu Normannorum impetum facere super oppidanos conati sunt.' sed nichil preter ferrum in uulneribus suis lucrati sunt. Tunc Guillelmus Ebroicensium comes
iii. 200 captus est.' et Mathiellus de Guitot filius Godefridi parui[5] letaliter uulneratus est. Deinde a lugentibus armigeris et commilitonibus ad hospitium suum reportatus est.' et mox accersito sacerdote

[1] Saint-Sulpice-sur-Risle, where there was a small priory (Cottineau, ii. 2897).

[2] In 1120.

[3] See below, pp. 278–84.

[4] See above, iii. 114 n. i, 250, and below, p. 100. He was a benefactor of Saint-Évroul's priory at Auffay, and his sister married Otmund of Chaumont, a benefactor of the abbey's priory at Parnes (above, ii. 154).

lay dying, saved him; when they were on the point of cutting the boy's throat the wounded man summoned all his strength and cried out, 'Spare him for the love of God. I deserve to die for my sins.' The assailant was released and the lamented lord at once confessed his sins to his companions and died in this way before a priest could be summoned. His body was taken to a monastery that his father Engenulf had founded on his estates in honour of St. Sulpice, bishop of Bourges,[1] and there, greatly mourned by his kinsmen and neighbours, he was buried by Gilbert, the venerable bishop of Évreux.

This man deserved to be lamented by his friends for he was distinguished by virtues during his lifetime. He was physically strong and athletic, obedient to God's law, submissive and humble to men of religion, provident and eloquent in worldly affairs, calm and generous in all his conduct. He married Judith, the daughter of Richard Goz of Avranches and sister of Hugh earl of Chester, and by her he had Gilbert of Laigle, Engenulf, Matilda, and several other sons and daughters. But Gilbert, since the others died, inherited his father's estates and dignity as sole heir. He married Juliana, daughter of Geoffrey, the valiant count of Mortagne, and she bore him Richer, Engenulf, Geoffrey, and Gilbert; of these boys the middle two perished in a shipwreck with King Henry's son, Prince William, and many other nobles on 25 November.[2] As for Matilda, she married the mighty Robert of Mowbray, earl of Northumbria, who rebelled against William Rufus, king of England, in the very same year; he was captured almost immediately and spent about thirty-four years in the prisons of King William and Henry his brother, growing old without offspring.[3] Now I will return to the matter from which I have digressed somewhat.

In January William of Warenne and Baudry of Guitry,[4] the son of Nicholas, and Gilbert of Laigle, seeking to avenge the death of their brother Richer, attempted an onslaught against the garrison with a strong force of Normans; but they gained nothing except iron in their wounds. On that occasion William, count of Évreux, was taken prisoner, and Matthew of Vitot, son of Godfrey the Small,[5] was mortally wounded. He was carried back to his quarters by his grief-stricken attendants and comrades-in-arms; there,

[5] For the family of Matthew of Vitot see above, ii. 120.

reatus suos confessus est, et sacro uiatico communitus obitumque suum prestolari preparatus est.

Normanni qui munitionem in ualle Beugici custodiebant: grauibus damnis afflicti et fortissimorum casibus tironum imminuti deteriora sibi adhuc formidabant, et quia Hubertum nec probitate nec felicitate superare ualebant: mutato consilio studioque ad regis amiciciam eum reuocare temptabant. Ille nichilominus licet in hac guerra diuitiis et potestate admodum esset corroboratus: serenæ tamen pacis securitatem preoptans prudenter annuit sequestrorum conatibus. Nec mora legati ad regem in Angliam missi sunt. Rex autem ut Herueum Britonem quem magistrum militum[1] constituerat et Richerium aliosque pugiles acerrimos interiisse audiuit suumque aduersarium felici fortuna prouehi cotidieque contra se confortari comperit: nimia procacitate in deteriorationem precipitari res suorum precauit. Prudenter igitur omnes preteritos reatus Huberto indulsit. Ille autem accepta securitate ad regem transfretauit, et facta inter eos amicicia omne
iii. 201 paternum ius honorifice recepit. Normanni et Cenomannenses gaudebant: qui quadriennio[2] conflictu multipliciter uexati fuerant. Deinde quamdiu rex Guillelmus uixit, prefatus heros ei fidus extitit: honoremque suum libertate plaudens gratanter tenuit, filiisque suis Radulfo et Huberto moriens dimisit.

II

His temporibus miliciam Anglici regni rex Guillelmus conscribi fecit,[3] et sexaginta milia militum inuenit: quos omnes dum necesse esset paratos esse precepit. Nam Chunutus iunior rex
iii. 202 Dacorum ingentem classem tunc parabat, et in Angliam quam parentes sui Suenus et Chunutus olim sibi subiugarant uenire et ius suum repetere disponebat.[4] Erat enim ante Deum pietate deuotus, et inter homines potentia magnus, multarumque probitatum laude dignus. Hic nimirum minis et apparatibus suis Normannos qui Angliam incolebant terruerat: sed uariis euentibus

[1] Orderic uses the term *magister militum* so imprecisely (cf. G. H. White in *TRHS* 4th ser. xxx (1948), 150) that it is not possible to be sure what the exact office of Hervey was, or how his duties were related to those of Alan the Red, described as commander of the *familia regis* (above, p. 48).

[2] See above, p. 48 n. 3.

[3] This reference to the surveys made in England in 1085–6 is in line with the comments of Florence of Worcester ('quot feudatos milites', FW ii. 18), and the account of the Anglo-Saxon Chronicle (1085) of William quartering his French and Breton troops on his English vassals. Domesday Book itself was not directly concerned with military service (cf. V. H. Galbraith, *The Making of Domesday Book*, Oxford, 1961, p. 50); but records preserved by individual

when a priest had been summoned, he confessed his sins and prepared to meet his death fortified by the last sacrament.

The Normans guarding the castle in the valley of Beugy, who had suffered great losses and declined in numbers through the misfortunes of their bravest knights, began to fear even worse disasters. Since they were unable to overcome Hubert either by daring or by luck they changed their plan and attempted to win him back to the king's friendship. He, in spite of the considerable gains in wealth and power he had made during this war, considered the security of peace far more desirable, and prudently consented to the proposals of the mediators. Messengers were sent to the king in England without delay. When the king learnt that Hervey the Breton, whom he had appointed captain of the knights,[1] and Richer and other valiant warriors had been killed, and that his adversary was carried along by good fortune and daily grew stronger to resist him, he took care not to risk worsening his position still further through obstinacy, and shrewdly pardoned Hubert for all his offences. Hubert received a safe-conduct and crossed the Channel to the king; when peace had been restored between them he received all his father's inheritance with honour. The Normans and men of Maine were jubilant, for they had suffered a great deal during the four years' conflict.[2] From that time, as long as King William lived, Hubert remained loyal to him; he freely enjoyed the full possession of his honor and transmitted it to his sons, Ralph and Hubert, on his death-bed.

II

At this time King William had a record made of the military strength of England,[3] and found that there were sixty thousand knights, all of whom he commanded to be ready for service if need arose. For Cnut the younger, king of Denmark was then preparing a great fleet, and making arrangements to invade England, conquered in earlier days by his ancestors Swein and Cnut, and claim his right.[4] He was a devout man in the sight of God, very powerful among men and commendable for his many virtues. He caused great alarm among the Normans living in England by his threatening

estates at the time of the Inquest certainly were (cf. Douglas, *Domesday Monachorum*, pp. 26–7). Orderic gives the same exaggerated figure in Book IV (above, ii. 266).

[4] Cf. FW ii. 18; Anglo-Saxon Chronicle (1085).

impeditus uiuente notho rege ad effectum non attigerat.[1] Regnante
iii. 203 autem Guillelmo iuniore dum multæ naues paratæ in littore starent, idoneoque uento iam flante in Angliam nautæ per naues armatum exercitum collocarent.' rex Chunutus uelle Dei exploraturus æcclesiam intrauit, ante altare humiliter procubuit.' Deumque ut iter suum secundum beneplacitam uoluntatem suam dirigeret cum lacrimis orauit. Deinde frater eius templum ingressus est. Qui dum regem solum ante aram prostratum perspexit cogitare cœpit.' quam magnus labor et quam graue periculum tot milibus per unum hominem immineret, et si idem aufferretur cita uehemensque mutatio fieret. Nec mora gladium abstraxit, et orantis regis caput abscidit.' statimque in exilium aufugit. Porro tam tristi nuncio mox exercitus dispersus est.' et ad proprium unusquisque negocium reuersus est. Denique seniores populi Calomanoth fratrem regis parricida exulante regem constituerunt. Corpus uero Chunuti regis honorifice in basilica sepelierunt.' ad cuius tumulum multa miracula diuinitus facta sunt. Ibi grande cenobium monachorum constructum est, et monasticus ordo sicut in Anglia apud Eoueshamium seruatur regulariter constitutus est.[2]
iii. 204 Inde nimirum primi monachi Danos adierunt.' et cenobiale ius barbaris mirantibus diligenter ostenderunt.

Merito prefatus rex a monachis aliisque religiosæ uitæ uiris honoratur. Primus enim ipse ritus gentis suæ quæ neophita nimiumque
iii. 205 effrenis erat correxit, et metropolitanas sedes ac episcopales secundum scita canonum constituit.' monachosque qui prius inuisi et incogniti Danis erant accersiit, et opportunæ habitationis locum in regno suo liberaliter eis delegauit.[3]

12

Anno ab incarnatione Domini M°LXXX° VII° indictione decima.' nono die Maii corpus sancti Nicholai archiepiscopi et confessoris de Mirrea in Barum translatum est. Quam translationem qualiter et a quibus facta sit.' Iohannes archidiaconus Barensis æcclesiæ

[1] In fact Cnut's invasion was planned in 1085 but was delayed, and the fleet was dispersed; he was murdered in the summer of 1086 by a band of rebels. See F. M. Stenton, *The First Century of English Feudalism* (Oxford, 1932), pp. 149–50; *Aelnothi monachi historia . . . sancti Canuti regis Daniae* in Langebek, *Scriptores rerum Danicarum* (Copenhagen, 1772–1878), iii. 371–3.

[2] Relics of St. Alban were removed from Ely by King Cnut, probably in 1070, and placed in the church at Odense, where he was later murdered (see Richard Vaughan, *Matthew Paris* (Cambridge, 1958), pp. 202–3). A priory was formally founded there in 1095–6 and colonized with twelve monks from Evesham (Knowles, *MO*, p. 164).

[3] This attributes too much to Cnut: his father, King Swein Estridson, was

preparations, but circumstances prevented him from achieving anything while William the Bastard lived.[1] During the reign of William Rufus however, when a great fleet was waiting off-shore, and the sailors, taking advantage of a favourable wind for England, were embarking an armed force in the ships, King Cnut entered a church to seek out the will of God, humbly prostrated himself before the altar, and prayed with tears that he might be guided according to God's gracious will. His brother came into the church; when he saw the king alone, prostrate before the altar, he began to think to himself that great toil and terrible danger threatened many thousands because of one man, and that if that man were removed their fortunes would be wholly transformed at a stroke. Without delay he drew his sword, cut off the king's head as he prayed, and immediately fled into exile. On learning this sad news the army soon dispersed and each one returned to his own affairs. Then the leaders of the people chose the king's brother Calomanoth as king, since the fratricidal murderer was in exile. Cnut's body was honourably buried in the church, and by God's will many miracles were performed at his tomb. A great abbey of monks was built, the monastic order was established there, and the same customs were observed as at Evesham in England.[2] It was from Evesham that the first monks had come to Denmark, and they resolutely showed the monastic way of life to the wonder of the uncivilized people.

King Cnut is deservedly honoured by monks and other men of religious life. He was the first to correct the religious customs of his people, who were newly converted and lacked discipline; he established archbishoprics and bishoprics according to canon law and sent for monks, who had previously been unknown in Denmark, generously providing them with a suitable site for a monastery in his kingdom.[3]

12

In the year of our Lord 1087, the tenth indiction, on 9 May, the body of St. Nicholas, archbishop and confessor, was translated from Myra to Bari. John, archdeacon of the church of Bari, has vividly described how and by whom the translation was carried

the great organizer of the Danish church, though Cnut himself was an active promoter of canon law (A. J. Otto in *New Catholic Encyclopaedia*, iv. 767).

luculenter describit.[1] Ex eius dictis libet parumper excerpere, et mentionem tam gloriosæ rei huic opusculo inserere.' ad noticiam studiosorum qui nondum dicta Iohannis uidere, si forte contingat ut istud dignentur inspicere.

Tempore Alexii imperatoris Turci aliique paganorum populi rabiem suam exercere uolentes fines suos exierunt.' Deoque permittente Liciam aliasque regiones Christianorum depopulati sunt. Æcclesias propter peccata Christianæ plebis destruxerunt, cruces et imagines Christi atque sanctuaria multis modis uiolauerunt.' et multas urbes cum ciuibus suis incendio tradiderunt. Sic per
iii. 206 multos annos debachati sunt.' et innumeras strages Christianorum peregerunt.

Mirrea itaque metropolis Liciæ Turcorum dominio subacta est.' propriisque ciuibus peccatis ut reor exigentibus euacuata est. [2]Barenses autem qui tribus cum nauibus Antiochiam negocii causa proficisci disposuerunt.' ut Mirreum lætantes ad territorium accesserunt, peregrinum quemdam[3] ad basilicam beati Nicholai quæ in castro est[4] exploraturum premiserunt. Qui rediens multos Turcorum renunciauit adesse.' et ad exequias principis castri qui defunctus ibidem iacebat conuenisse. Quo audito Barenses carbasa expanderunt, ilico uersus Antiochiam proras ratium direxerunt.' paucibusque diebus secundo cursu ad eam[a] adierunt. Ibi nauem Veneticorum inuenerunt.' et de pluribus ut mos est mutuo
iii. 207 percunctari cœperunt. Erant enim de Barensibus quidam Veneticis noti et amici qui ceperunt de corpore sancto alternatim confabulari. Venetici autem quod dudum conceperant animis non dubitarunt edere uerbis. Palos quoque ferreos et malleos se habere preparatos confessi sunt et quod[b] temptare deberent consilium habitum illic[c] pandere non distulerunt. Quod cum audissent Barini, ad hoc incipiendum et perficiendum maiori desiderio sunt accensi.' non tam sui pro gloria et honore tociusque patriæ magnitudine quam pro tam excellentissimi confessoris amore.[5] Negocium

[a] Mirream, *Caen MS.*; ad eam, *John of Bari* [b] quia, *Caen MS.*; quod, *John of Bari* [c] illis, *John of Bari*

[1] For the sources of the history of the translation of St. Nicholas to Bari in 1087 and the historical background see below, Appendix II.

[2] From this point Orderic abbreviates the account of John of Bari (printed by L. Surius, *De probatis sanctorum historiis*, iii (Cologne, 1579), 172–81).

[3] The ships carried a certain number of pilgrims to the Holy Land as passengers.

out.[1] I have been able to take extracts, albeit somewhat hastily, from his account, and to include a record of this glorious event in my modest work, for the information of scholars who are not familiar with John's writings, if they should ever chance to cast their eyes over mine.

In the time of the emperor Alexius the Turks and other pagan races, wishing to vent their fury, burst across their frontiers and, by God's sufferance, depopulated Lycia and other Christian countries. They destroyed churches because of the sins of the Christian people, desecrated crosses and images of Christ and sanctuaries in various ways, and committed many towns with their inhabitants to the flames. In this way they ravaged for many years, slaughtering countless numbers of Christians.

So it happened that Myra, the chief city of Lycia, was subjected to Turkish rule and emptied of its own citizens as a punishment, it seems to me, for their sins. [2]Certain citizens of Bari, who had decided to set out on a trading expedition to Antioch with three ships, reached the territory of Myra with rejoicing, and sent one of the pilgrims[3] in advance to the church of St. Nicholas which is in the city,[4] to spy out the land. Returning, he announced that a great many Turks were near at hand, and had assembled for the funeral rites of the governor of the city, who was lying there dead. On hearing this the men of Bari hoisted sail and turned the prows of their vessels without delay towards Antioch, which they reached a few days later with a favourable wind. There they found a ship manned by Venetians and, as men do, they began to ask each other questions. Among the men of Bari were some who were acquaintances and friends of the Venetians, and they began to talk together about the holy relics. The Venetians moreover did not hesitate to speak openly about the plan they had just made. They admitted that they had iron crowbars and hammers ready for use, and disclosed then and there the undertaking on which they were already resolved. When the men of Bari heard it they burned with desire to carry it out from start to finish, not so much for their own renown and honour and the fame of their country as for love of the most worthy saint.[5] So, completing the business

[4] John of Bari's words were 'in castro quo sancti erat basilica' (p. 174), possibly meaning that the church was within the territory of a city; later (p. 176) he said that the church was about a mile from the 'castrum'.

[5] Here Orderic's interpretation differs from John's, see below, Appendix II.

igitur ob quod Antiochiam ierant expleuerunt.' et inde quantocius ducente Deo remeauerunt. Cum uero prospere[a] Mirreum ad littus appropinquarent.' iamque a priore deficientes ardore ultra transire uellent.' imperante Deo contrarius uentus a boreali parte surrexit, nautasque Barinos austro quiescente ibi remorari coegit. Voluntatem itaque Dei intelligentes.' arma continuo comprehenderunt, paucosque qui rates interim custodirent acie facta relinquunt.' et reliqui muniti ac prouidi uelut hostibus obuiarent, festinant ad æcclesiam ire, quæ longe quasi spacio trium miliariorum erat a littore.

Denique claustrum æcclesiæ introeunt, arma deponunt.' edemque sanctam humiliter subeunt, sanctumque presulem flagitare
iii. 208 satagunt. Finitis uero singulorum precibus cœperunt edituos percunctari.' ubi iaceret corpus sancti Nicholai. Qui mox locum ostendunt.' et de liquore sancto extrahentes illis tribuunt.[1] Tunc Lupus Barensis presbiter de oleo sancto in uitrea ampulla suscipit.' ipsamque in alto ut ibi tutius seruaretur ponit.' quæ casu dum loquerentur pauimentum super marmoreum cecidit sed illesa non sine admiratione omnium permansit. Porro Barenses cum tribus monachis qui ad custodiendas reliquias relicti erant, quasi attemptantes colloqui cœperunt. 'Volumus hinc sanctum corpus tollere.' nostramque ad patriam transportare. Hac enim pro causa Romano missi a pontifice uenimus tribus aduecti nauibus. Si consentire nobis hoc[b] uolueritis.' dabimus uobis de unaquaque puppi centum aureos solidos.'

Audientes autem hæc monachi, statim stupefacti et pauidi dixerunt, 'Qualiter hoc audemus incipere, cum nullus mortalis hactenus hoc ualuerit impune temptare? Quis temerarius tanti commercii esse poterit emptor uel uenditor? Quæ tam preciosa res et admirabilis tanto thesauro comparabitur? Si domini terrarum non temerarie sed precibus et supplicationibus istud non inchoare temptauerunt, qualiter uos ualebitis operari?[2] Sinite ergo amplius
iii. 209 tantum nefas persequi, quia diuinæ placitum non est maiestati. Tamen probate, ecce locus.' Hoc dicentes non posse fieri putabant, quod illi uolebant. Nam fere ducentarum olimpiadum curricula

[a] prospero austro, *John of Bari* [b] in hoc, *John of Bari*

[1] The 'miraculous fluid' was traditionally offered to pilgrims by the custodians of the shrine.

[2] The story of the saint's unwillingness to leave Myra was an important element in the legend: amongst others the Emperor Basil is said to have attempted unsuccessfully to secure a portion of the relics. See B. Leib, *Rome, Kiev et Byzance à la fin du XIe siècle* (Paris, 1924), pp. 54–5; *Anal. boll.* iv (1885), 171.

which had brought them to Antioch, they re-embarked as quickly as possible with God as their guide. When however they were approaching the shores of Myra with a favourable wind and, as their first ardour had cooled, were anxious to press on, a contrary wind sprang up from the north at God's behest, and forced the mariners of Bari, as the south wind dropped, to remain there. Recognizing the hand of God they immediately seized their weapons and, leaving a few men to keep a look-out and guard the ships while they were away, the remainder formed a line and, armed and equipped as if to face an enemy, hastened to the church, which was some three miles distant from the shore.

When they reached the precinct of the church they laid down their arms, and humbly entering the hallowed building they addressed their entreaties to the holy bishop. When all had finished their prayers they turned to ask the sacristans where the body of St. Nicholas lay. These men showed them the place at once, and drawing off some of the holy liquid offered it to them.[1] Then Lupus, a priest of Bari, poured some of the holy oil into a glass bottle and placed it in a high place so that it might be safer; by chance while they were talking it fell on to the marble floor but remained unbroken to everyone's amazement. Next the men of Bari began to talk with the three monks who had been left to guard the relics, and pretended to make a proposition, 'We would like to take the holy body away from here and carry it to our own country. In fact we have been sent by the Roman pontiff for this purpose, sailing in three ships. If you are ready to give your consent to this we will pay you a hundred shillings in gold from each ship.'

Hearing these words the monks, amazed and trembling, immediately replied, 'How could we dare to undertake something which no living man has undertaken with impunity up to this day? What madman could be buyer or seller in such a trade? What is so precious and wonderful that it can be compared to such a treasure? If the lords of the earth have never attempted such an undertaking even with prayers and supplications, let alone brazenly, how can you expect to carry it out?[2] Desist, therefore, from pursuing this act of sacrilege, for it is displeasing to God. But try and you will see: here is the place.' When they said this they believed that the mariners wished to attempt something that was impossible. For almost eight hundred years had passed since the death of Nicholas,

transierant, ex quo Nicholaus qui in Nicena sinodo sub beato Siluestro papa et Constantino principe facta fuisse legitur de mundo migrauit.'[1] nullusque de reliquiis eius uel occulte furari uel manifeste uiribus rapere, uel a domino precibus ualuit hactenus impetrare. Barenses uero pauebant, quia in extraneo loco pauci inter multos erant.' et sol ad occasum uergebat, reditusque ad naues formidabilis erat. Sed tamen diuinitus confortati primo monachos comprehendunt tentosque sollerter custodiunt. Speculatores quoque cautius exponunt qui undique uenientes prospiciant.' et ipsi hinc et inde cum armis diuisi per tramites stant. Audacter itaque probissimi iuuenes xl et iiii[2] foris ad obsistendum parati stant, et duo presbiteri Lupus et Grimoaldus cum paucis aliis in æcclesia quæ agenda sunt procurant, et preces quæ lætaniæ uocantur inchoant. Sed nimio timore correpti quod inchoarant.' clarius exprimere non poterant.

iii. 210 Interea Mathæus[3] unus ex nautis[4] ferreum uiriliter malleum arripuit, marmoreum pauimentum percussit et fregit, sub quo cementum reperit, quo diminuto et eiecto.' urnæ dorsum marmoreæ statim apparuit. Hinc ergo exorta læticia magis magisque infodere, ueteremque iuncturam calce[a] colligatam quadam cum asciola rumpere ac dissipare, fragmentaque non tardabant eicere. Quibus eiectis foris pilaque detecta.' et a predicto iuuene malleo percussa, unoque in latere fracta, flagrantissimus[b] odor exiit.' qui mira eos qui aderant delectatione suauitatis impleuit. Porro prefatus iuuenis manum immisit.' nimiumque liquorem adesse primo sensit, quo urna eadem quæ non erat parua plena quasi usque ad medium uidebatur esse. Deinde dexteram immersit, preciosissimumque thesaurum quem summo desiderio querebat inuenit.' celeriterque impauidus extrahere cœpit. Denique pro capite querendo totus in multitudinem liquoris intrauit, et pedibus ac manibus ut necesse erat caput hinc inde requirens inuenit, ac demum de salutifero latice uestibus et toto corpore madefactus exiuit. Hoc itaque post obitum sancti Nicholai fere post dccc annos xii° kal' Maias actum est.

[a] cale, *Caen MS.*; calcis, *John of Bari* [b] fragrantissimus, *John of Bari*

[1] St. Nicholas is known to have been bishop of Myra in the first half of the fourth century, but otherwise there is no trustworthy evidence among the many legends that surround his life. See G. Anrich, *Hagios Nikolaos* (Leipzig, 1913–17), especially ii. 299–303.

[2] The total number of 'translators' can be calculated from a list of those later receiving pensions for their share in the enterprise: it contains 62 names (Nitti di Vito, *La ripresa*, pp. 276–7; *Cod. dip. bar.* v. 279–81). Orderic took the

who is said to have taken part in the Council of Nicaea under the blessed pope Silvester and the emperor Constantine,[1] and in all that time no one had been able to steal covertly, or snatch openly, or secure from the Lord by prayers any part of the relics. Fear struck the men of Bari, for they were few among many in a foreign land, and the sun was setting and the road back to their ships was beset with perils. However they received strength from God, and laying hands on the monks they kept them under close restraint. They placed look-outs at key points, where they could see anyone approaching from any side, and taking up their arms stationed themselves along the paths. So while forty-four seasoned young men[2] waited boldly outside, ready to put up a fight, two priests called Lupus and Grimoald with a few others undertook what was necessary in the church, and began to recite the prayers known as litanies. But they were so shaken by fear that they could find no way of expressing clearly what they had begun to recite.

Meanwhile one of the mariners[4] called Matthew[3] boldly took up an iron hammer, and striking the marble paving broke it, revealing cement underneath; when this had been chipped away the side of a marble urn came into sight. Then with mounting joy they dug deeper and deeper and hurriedly broke up the old casing mixed with lime with a hatchet, throwing out the fragments. When these had been cleared away a marble case was found; as young Matthew struck it with a hammer and broke one side a wonderful fragrance spread from it, which filled the bystanders with marvellous joy at its sweetness. The young man thrust in his hand and at once perceived a great quantity of liquid, apparently half filling the urn, which was a large one. Thereupon he plunged his right hand into it, found the precious treasure that he sought with such zeal and quickly and fearlessly began to pull it out. Finally, to seek the head, he stepped right down into the liquid and, feeling about with feet and hands as need arose, found the head; not till then did he emerge with his clothes and his whole body drenched with the holy fluid. All this happened on 20 April, nearly eight hundred years after the death of St. Nicholas.

number of forty-four young men directly from John of Bari; in addition there were the priests and the men who had been left to guard the ships.

[3] Matheus is named among the translators (*Cod. dip. bar.* v. 280).

[4] In the early sources the terms 'nautae' and 'marinarii' are used interchangeably, to describe all participants in the enterprise, whether merchants, men of substance, priests, or sailors.

Deinde quia loculus deerat, et res inopinata tam cito euenerat.'
iii. 211 sanctas reliquias tunica[1] Lupi presbiteri prout poterant inoluerunt, ipsumque Lupum ferentem sacrum onus secuti sunt. Laudantes itaque Deum pro sanctissima preda quam non de hostibus sed dominico de gazophilacio sumpserant.' ad littora maturabant. Frusta quoque de marmorea urna quam ruperant quidam asportauerunt, ex quibus a multis pontificibus per Italiam multa altaria tabulæque itinerariæ consecratæ sunt. Ad portum autem ut uenere.' orta est contentio in cuius naue mitteretur onus desiderabile. Optabant enim secum omnes tantum sodalem et patronum habere. Omnibus tandem pacifice placuit ut Mathei nauis illud ueheret.' si tamen ipse prius iureiurando de bona societate fidem illis faceret.[2] Quod ita factum est.

Ratem itaque leti ascendunt, reliquias alio panno nouo et candido inuoluunt.' et in uasculo ligneo quo nautæ sibi temetum seruare solebant recondunt. De dolore uero Mirræensium pro damno sibi facto dum notum illis factum est.' multa referre necesse non est. Nam ut huiusmodi famam incolæ Mirrei castri quod non longius
iii. 212 miliario uno ab æcclesia in monticulo quodam situm est audiunt, undique uelociter concurrunt.' irati nimium ac tristissimi ad littora tendunt, raptoque de pastore dominoque lugentes crines et barbas euellunt, et conclamantes lugubre carmen depromunt.

[3]Tempore quid miseris heu nobis accidit isto?
Quod patriæ nostræ dedecus aspicimus?
Munera nanque Dei multos seruata per annos.'
Tam facili rapto perdidimus subito.
Hactenus hoc fuerat Liciæ ditata superno
Thesauro tellus ac decorata nimis.
Laudibus eximiis totum celebrata per orbem,
Et munita patris magnanimi meritis.
Infelix Mirrea tuis spoliata manebis
Cultibus et donis.' mestaque semper eris.
O Nicholae pater toto uenerabilis orbe
Cur patriam nostram deseris immo tuam?
Hic genitus fueras sanctisque parentibus altus,

[1] John of Bari adds, 'quae alias paludamentum vocatur'; his account implies that it was Grimoald's.

[2] John of Bari is more explicit, 'ea tamen conditione ut prius iusiurandum darent se sine caeteris nihil de sancto corpore acturos vel constituturos'. But Orderic's use of 'societas' is opportune, for later the mariners formed a 'societas' or gild, initially of a religious and beneficial nature, and it probably had its origin in a sworn association made in the course of the enterprise. For a discussion of the nature of the gild see G. Antonucci, 'Per la storia giuridica della Basilica di S. Nicola de Bari', in *Japigia*, v (1934), 244–58; F. Babudri, 'Sinossi critica dei traslatori nicolaiani di Bari', in *Archivio storico pugliese*, iii (1950), 3–94.

Since their success was so unexpected and so sudden and they had no coffin, they wrapped the holy relics as best they might in the tunic[1] belonging to Lupus the priest and followed Lupus as he led the way carrying the sacred burden. And in this way, praising God for the most holy prize they had taken, not from enemies but from the Lord's treasure-house, they hastened to the shore. Some men also carried away fragments of the marble urn which they had broken, from which many altars and portable altars were consecrated by many bishops all over Italy. When they reached the harbour they began to dispute about whose boat was to carry the precious burden, for everyone wished to have a companion and patron of such worth with him. In the end all agreed peaceably that Matthew's ship should carry it, provided that he first swore a solemn oath to act only in close association with them;[2] and this is what they did.

They boarded the ship in good spirits, wrapped the relics in another new white cloth, and hid them in a wooden barrel in which the sailors normally kept their wine. There is no need to dwell on the distress of the Myreans when they learnt of the harm done to them. When the inhabitants of the town of Myra, which is situated on a hill not more than a mile from the church, heard the report they rushed together from all quarters and hurried in great grief and anger to the shore; lamenting their lost bishop and lord, tearing their hair and their beards, and calling aloud in their grief they chanted this song:

[3]Alas, what blow has struck us, helpless wretches,
Now, as we see our holy father's shame?
The gifts of God, preserved through many ages,
Are in an instant, by swift rapine, gone.
Our land, Lycia, with this heavenly treasure
Was once enriched and splendidly adorned,
Honoured through all the world with signal praises,
And by its father's merits fortified.
Unhappy Myra! spoiled of all your riches,
Devotions, gifts, henceforward dwell with woe.
Nicholas, world-renowned, most holy father,
Why do you leave our country, which is yours?
Here you were born, brought up by holy parents,

[3] This long lament is taken verbatim from John of Bari.

Hic puer et iuuenis uirque senexque pius,
Hic pater et dominus, pastor custosque benignus,
Hactenus hac patria uiuus et exanimis.
Quælibet hanc miseram quotiens aduersa premebant.’
Auxilium petiit mox pater alme tuum.
Rebus in aduersis aderas spes una salutis.’
Munimen tribuens supplicibus populis.
Quorum tu precibus presens uenerande fauebas
Votaque suscipiens quæque rogata dabas,
Vndique currebant cunctis e partibus orbis.’
Ad sacrum tumulum sepe salutiferum.
Nouerit heu uacuum simul hac quod turba fidelis
Omnis cessabit cultus et omnis honor.
Munera quippe Dei deerunt et gratia prima,
Historiæ solum nomen erit ueteris.
Pastor oues proprias cui nos committis alendas?
Te linquente gregem.’ mox lupus adueniet.
Virtus, solamen, nostrum decus omne leuamen
Tu spes una salus, causaque læticiæ.
Ve nobis miseris, hæc omnia perdimus, at nos
Hinc subit et luctus, perpetuusque dolor.
Heu cui tale nefas fuit hæc permissa potestas
iii. 213 Efficere.’ et tantum sic uiolare locum?
Et male tractauit cuius temeraria dextra?
Fecit et hoc furtum quis modo sacrilegus?
Sed fortunati qui predam fertis opimam,
Nos infelices occupat omne malum.

Mirreis itaque nimium lugentibus, luctumque suum ulcisci non ualentibus.’ læti Barenses celeriter rudentes exoluunt, et remigantes nocte illa insulam quæ Cacabum dicitur adeunt.’ et inde Maiestras ad insulas profecti sunt. Hinc uero discedentes nimia cum fatigatione remorum ad loca ubi Macri dicitur applicuerunt.’ ibique triduo propter boream sibi contrarium permanserunt.[1] Vnde nimium turbati sunt.’ et dubitare utrumne corpus sancti Nicholai secum haberent an ipse ab eis ultra ferri uellet ceperunt. Tunc Eustasius[2] unus ex illis per uisionem de dubietate correptus est.’ et nimis dum in uisu irudinum[3] morsibus lingua eius cruentaretur territus est.

[1] A more detailed account of the route is given by Nicephorus (cf. Nitti di Vito, *La ripresa*, p. 258 n. 2). After leaving Makry they went by way of Monemvasia and Methoni.

[2] Stasius Scannoria (*Cod. dip. bar.* v. 281).

[3] The Caen MS. reads 'irudinum' (leeches); John of Bari has 'hyrundines' (swallows) and the omission of the 'n' may be a copyist's slip. However in this

Lived as boy, youth and man to pious age;
Here lord and father, bishop, loving guardian
Were you, in life and death, of this your land.
Whenever perils threatened in our weakness
Swift help was sought, kind father, from your hand;
In all distress, our only hope of safety,
You came and brought your suppliant people aid.
You, worthy father, heard the prayers they offered,
Received their vows, bestowing what they sought;
From every earthly region men came flocking
In search of healing to your holy tomb.
Alas, the tomb is bare, the faithful scattered,
All reverence and homage now will cease;
God's gifts and grace will disappear for ever,
Only the ancient legend's name be left.
Who now will cherish us, your sheep, O shepherd?
As you desert the flock the wolf is near;
You were our might, aid, honour, consolation,
Our only hope and refuge, strength and joy.
Woe to us wretches! all is lost; we suffer,
Bowed down in grief and everlasting woe;
Alas, to whom was fatal power given
To do this deed, profane this holy place?
Whose hand in rash presumption wrought this evil?
What sacrilegious man has robbed this grave?
Fortunate you who carry off this treasure;
Nothing remains to us but tears and grief.

As the Myreans lamented, unable to avenge their wrongs, the men of Bari, rejoicing, quickly cast off their moorings and, rowing hard, reached the island called Kakava that night. From there they proceeded to the island of Megista. Continuing further, but exhausting the rowers in the effort, they touched shore at the place called Makry and were detained there for three days by a contrary north wind.[1] Their anxiety mounted because of the delay, and they began to wonder whether they really had the body of St. Nicholas with them, or alternatively whether he wished them to take him further. Then one of their number named Eustace[2] was reproved for his doubt in a dream, and at the same time was terrified by seeing in the vision his tongue streaming with blood from the bites of leeches.[3]

cryptic account of Eustace's vision leeches would seem just as appropriate as swallows.

Deinde communi decreto minutas reliquiarum particulas quas
furtim sibi quidam eorum subtraxerant protulerunt.' et cum
iii. 214 iureiurando quod nil de reliquiis sibi peculiariter retinerent
asseruerunt, Romoaldus[1] duos de dentibus et de minutis articulis
quos occultos habuerat manifestauit. Sic omnes alii particulas
quas sibi clam sequestrarant attulerunt, et cæteris artubus resti-
tuerunt. Denique prospero uento flante latumque carinis equor
sulcantibus.' Disigio[2] uni nautarum in somnis sanctus Nicholaus
apparuit, confortauit.' et quod xx° die ex quo corpus eius abstulerunt Barinum portum intraturi essent predixit. Ille uisum sociis
narrauit.' et ipsis inde magna confidentia inhæsit.

Auicula quædam ex improuiso nautis in naui uolitans apparuit, eosque frequenti aduentu suo lætificauit. Sepe etiam odorem suauissimum nautæ sentiebant, aliisque delectabilibus indiciis roborati gaudebant et læti ad sua littora appropinquabant.

Ducente Deo ad portum sancti Georgii qui quasi quinque
iii. 215 miliariis a Barinis mœnibus abest aduenerunt.' et inde ad clerum
Barensem et populum nuncios premiserunt. Tota ergo ciuitas
inopinato gaudio confestim repleta est.' et mox uterque sexus et
omnis etas ad littora egressa est. Porro nautæ capsellam cum reliquiis commendarun treligioso Heliæ abbati cenobii sancti Benedicti.'[3] quod supra portum situm est. Ille uero sacra pignora
reuerenter suscepit, in prefatam æcclesiam cum fratribus nono die
mensis Maii deposuit, et tribus diebus diligenter custodiuit.

Tunc Vrso Barinorum archiepiscopus uir religiosus Deo dignus
Italicisque dominis notissimus et familiaris amicus aberat. Nam
iii. 216 apud Tranum nauis preparata stabat quam idem presul post diem
alterum disposuerat ingredi, causaque orationis Ierusalem proficisci. Sed legatus cum litteris a ciuibus ad illum aduenit.' nunciumque tanti gaudii protinus intimauit. Ille igitur dimisso quod
incepit itinere.' gaudens Barum non distulit properare. Corpus
itaque sancti Nicholai a Barensibus susceptum est.' et solennitas
translationis eius vii° idus Maii constituta est. Tunc ad curiam

[1] Romoaldus Bulpannha (*Cod. dip. bar.* v. 280).
[2] Disigius de Alberto (*Cod. dip. bar.* v. 280).

So by general agreement every man surrendered the small fragments of the relics which some of them had surreptitiously appropriated; all solemnly swore that they would keep back no part of the relics for themselves. Romoald[1] produced two teeth and various small fragments that he had hidden away; and all the others likewise offered the small bones that they were hiding and reunited them with the other limbs. When this had been done a favourable wind sprang up, and as the keels ploughed through the calm surface of the sea St. Nicholas appeared in a dream to Disigius,[2] one of the sailors, comforted him, and foretold that they would sail into the harbour of Bari on the twentieth day after they had taken his body. He told the dream to his companions, and they were greatly heartened by it.

A certain small bird unexpectedly appeared to the mariners, flying about in the ship, and cheered them by its frequent visits. Often too the mariners smelled a most fragrant perfume and were reassured by other delightful portents, so that they drew near to their own shores filled with gladness and rejoicing.

With God's guidance they reached the port of St. George, which is about five miles from the walls of Bari, from where they sent messengers ahead to the clergy and people of Bari. The whole city was at once filled with unexpected joy, and immediately men and women of all ages flocked to the shore. Then the mariners entrusted the receptacle with the relics to Elias, the pious abbot of the monastery of St. Benedict[3] which stands above the harbour. He received the blessed relics reverently, with the help of his monks, placed them in his church on 9 May, and guarded them carefully for three days.

At that time Ursus, archbishop of Bari, a man of sound religion, acceptable to God, and known and loved as a friend by the lords of Italy, was absent from the city. Indeed a ship was standing ready at Trani, which the prelate was preparing to board the very next day in order to go on a pilgrimage to Jerusalem. But when a messenger arrived with letters from the citizens, announcing the glad tidings, he abandoned the journey he had begun and hastened back, rejoicing, to Bari. In this way the body of St. Nicholas was received by the inhabitants of Bari, and the feast of his translation was established on 9 May. Afterwards it was carried

[3] For Abbot Elias and his relations with Archbishop Ursus of Bari, see below, Appendix II; Nitti di Vito, *La ripresa*, pp. 53–104.

iii. 217 catepani[1] portatum est.' ibique in æcclesia beati Stephani prothomartiris[2] quæ ante tres annos fabricata fuerat ab archiepiscopo nautis petentibus et cunctis ciuibus reuerenter positum est.

Deinde propriam basilicam sancto Nicholao cœperunt, sanctumque corpus et oblationes fidelium et opus basilicæ uenerando Heliæ abbati commiserunt, ipsumque prepositum consensu archiepiscopi et fauore omnium super omnibus quæ agenda erant constituerunt. Protinus diuersæ multitudines de uniuersis tocius Hesperiæ prouinciis concurrunt.' innumera quoque signa et miracula cotidie diuinitus fiunt. Nam in primo die dum sanctum corpus in æcclesia sancti Benedicti ut dictum est depositum fuit.' amplius quam xxx infirmantes utriusque sexus et omnis etatis a multimodis infirmitatibus liberantur perfectaque sanitate recepta cum gratiarum actione læti et incolumes ad propria remeant. Aliis quoque diebus sequentis temporis quot demoniaci uel surdi, quot claudi seu muti siue cæci, quot denique alii multigenis egritudinibus oppressi, penitusque alleuiati sunt et sanati, notis particulatim signare nequimus et numerare. Infinitus enim est ut equipollenti significatione preostendimus.' et nobis incognitus numerus.[3]

iii. 218 Præfatus Iohannes Barensis diaconus[a] ex cuius libro breuiter hæc excerpsi, duodecim preclara miracula scripto signauit.' sed nec ipse nec alius omnes sanitates et alia subsidia posteris notificare potuit, quæ Deus omnipotens pro meritis sanctissimi pontificis Nicholai seruis suis fideliter petentibus usque hodie clementer exhibuit. Denique permittente Deo plures æcclesiæ de sanctis reliquiis prefati presulis optinuerunt, et non solum Itali et Pelasgi sed et aliæ gentes sanctis pignoribus habitis Deo grates concinunt.

Christoforus[4] enim quidam miles qui translationi nobilis Nicholai interfuit.' unam costam in manica sua sibi retinuit. Nec multo post infirmatus ad Venusiense[5] cenobium confugit, monachatum a Berengario archimandrita requisiuit et impetrauit.' secumque

[a] *Presumably a slip for* 'archidiaconus'

---

[1] The exact movement of the relics has been a source of much controversy, complicated by a series of later forgeries designed to buttress the pretended authority of the cathedral over the church of St. Nicholas. These forgeries imply that Archbishop Ursus made a grant of the *curia catepani*, which in fact was not his to give as it was under ducal authority; none of the earliest authorities hints at any such cession, and neither does Orderic in his abbreviation (cf. Nitti di Vito, *La ripresa*, pp. 271–3, 285–8; *Anal. boll.* iv. 187).

[2] This misrepresents John of Bari's statement, 'de medio curiae abstulit, et in ecclesia beati protomartyris Stephani . . . deposuit.' The Kievan legend says that the relics were placed in the church of St. John the Baptist (*Japigia*, viii (1937), 395–6).

to the catapan's residence[1] and there, at the request of the mariners and all the citizens, it was reverently placed in the church of St. Stephen, the first martyr,[2] which had been built by the archbishop three years previously.

They then set about building a church for St. Nicholas himself, entrusting the holy body and oblations of the faithful, as well as the building works, to the venerable Abbot Elias, whom, with general approval and the archbishop's consent, they placed in charge of everything that had to be done. Immediately great crowds flocked from every country in the western world, and countless wonders and miracles were performed daily by God's help. The very first day that the holy body was placed in St. Benedict's church, as I have described, more than thirty men and women of all ages, afflicted with different diseases, were healed and completely restored to health, so that they returned home well and joyful, giving thanks to God. But I cannot enumerate and describe in detail in these brief notes how many, in the days that followed, who were possessed with demons, or deaf, or lame, or dumb, or blind, or oppressed by other infirmities of all kinds, were completely restored and healed. For the number, as I have already clearly shown, is very great, and unknown to me.[3]

John, the archdeacon of Bari, from whose treatise I have, as I said before, taken these brief extracts, gave details of twelve remarkable miracles, but neither he nor anyone else could record all the cures and other aids which almighty God in his mercy has granted to his servants when they ask in faith, by the merits of the most holy bishop Nicholas. Later God allowed many churches to secure some of the holy relics of the saintly bishop; and in addition to the Italians and Greeks many other peoples sing praises to God for their share in the sacred treasure.

A certain knight called Christopher,[4] who was present at the translation of St. Nicholas, kept a rib for himself hidden in his sleeve. Falling sick shortly afterwards, he took refuge in the monastery of Venosa,[5] and at his request was clothed in the monastic habit by Abbot Berengar. At the same time he presented

[3] The abbreviation of John of Bari ends here.

[4] No Christopher occurs in any list of mariners who took part in the translation (*Cod. dip. bar.* v. 279–81; Nitti di Vito, *La ripresa*, pp. 276–7).

[5] For the foundation of the abbey of Holy Trinity, Venosa, and its abbot Berengar see above, ii. 100–2. Orderic's information about the relics there came from monks of Saint-Évroul who visited the abbey.

costam sancti Nicholai sanctæ Trinitati presentauit, et de morbo conualuit.

13

Eodem tempore Stephanus cantor cœnobii quod Fulco senior comes apud Andegauiam urbem in honore sancti Nicholai construxerat[1] Apuliam abiit, et per licentiam domni Natalis abbatis sui monachile scema ex industria dimisit. Deinde ut clericus Bari habitauit.' magnamque familiaritatem ac postmodum potestatem inter edituos basilicæ sancti pontificis optinuit. Tandem conspecta facultate brachium sancti Nicholai quod apte argento tectum erat, et extra mausoleum ad signandum populum serua-
iii. 219 batur[2] furtim arripuit.' et in Gallias aufugere patriamque suam cenobiumque suum tanto thesauro ditare sategit. Verum quia mox ut tale latrocinium sibi factum Barenses compererunt, longe lateque ueredarios suos ad confines suos et amicos atque patronos miserunt, omnesque tramites quibus itur in Franciam sollicite tutari ne fur huiuscemodi elongaretur conati sunt.' Stephanus Venusiam diuertit, ibique timidus latere uolens hiemauit.' et serenum uer expectans egrotare cœpit. Deinde deficiente sibi censu necessario.' coactus est pro uictu distrahere argentum de sancto brachio. Interea per totam Italiam et Siciliam fama uolitauit.' quod a Gallis surreptum esset brachium beati Nicholai. Denique dum de tali furto crebra locutio populos moueret, et a quibusdam Venusiensibus famulisque monachorum argentea
iii. 220 tectura uisa et cognita esset, et in conuentu monastico rumor huiusmodi perstreperet.' Erembertus impiger cœnobita cum famulis monasterii ad exmonachum languentem accurrit, subitoque frendens impetu brachium sancti Nicholai ac si eidem commendasset atrociter exposcit. At ille deprehensum se uidet, et in tanto turbine nescius quo se uerteret.' pallidus et tremens perurgenti monacho preciosum pignus exhibet. Quod ille cum ingenti gaudio recipit et mox ad cenobium sanctæ Trinitatis monachis et cunctis ciuibus Deum laudantibus deuehit.' ibique sanctus Nicholaus usque hodie pignora sua fideliter poscentibus in multis

[1] The abbey of St. Nicholas, Angers, was founded by Fulk Nerra in 1020. Noël was abbot from 1080 to 1096 (Halphen, *Anjou*, pp. 86–7, 312, 325).

[2] The Kievan legend records that after the building of the basilica a hand of

the rib of St. Nicholas to the abbey of Holy Trinity, and recovered from his sickness.

13

At this time Stephen, cantor of the monastery which Count Fulk Nerra had founded at Angers in honour of St. Nicholas,[1] had come to Apulia, and with the consent of his abbot Noël had deliberately abandoned the monastic life. He lived afterwards as a clerk at Bari, and became very influential amongst the clergy of the church of St. Nicholas, whose confidence he won. Finally, seizing his opportunity, he secretly stole an arm of St. Nicholas, which was handsomely covered with silver and kept outside the shrine for blessing the people,[2] and attempted to escape to France to enrich his country and his own monastery with this rare treasure. However, as soon as the citizens of Bari discovered that this shocking theft had been perpetrated, they sent out their messengers in all directions to their neighbours and friends and patrons, and took steps to have all the roads leading to France carefully watched so that the guilty man could not escape. Stephen therefore turned aside to Venosa, and as he hid there in fear, waiting for the spring, he fell ill. As he had not enough money with him, he was obliged to sell the silver from the holy relic. Meanwhile the news spread through Italy and Sicily that an arm of St. Nicholas had been stolen by the French. The story of the theft, frequently repeated, became known to all, and finally the silver case was seen and recognized by some men of Venosa and servants of the monks. When the report of this was heard in the monastery, a bold monk, named Erembert, with some of the monastic servants, burst in upon the ex-monk as he lay sick, and with dire threats demanded the arm of St. Nicholas as confidently as if he had himself entrusted it to his keeping. The man realized that he had been found out; pale and trembling, not knowing where to turn in such a predicament, he revealed the precious relic to the importunate monk. Erembert received it with great joy, and at once took it to the abbey of Holy Trinity amidst the acclamations of the monks and all the citizens. There St. Nicholas miraculously helps those believers who visit his holy relics in

St. Nicholas was exposed for the veneration of the people (*Japigia*, viii (1937), 396).

necessitatibus mirifice succurrit. Prefatus autem Erembertus erat natione Normannus, ante conuersionem miles strenuus, postmodum uero monachus in ordine feruidus.

Hisdem temporibus quidam miles de Normannia Guillelmus cognomento Pantulfus[1] in Apuliam abiit, et quia sanctum Nicholaum ualde diligebat de reliquiis eius multum quesiuit.' Deoque iuuante procurationem eius a reliquiarum translatoribus unum dentem et duo frusta de marmoreo tumulo optinuit. Erat enim in armis strenuus, ingenio preditus.' inter collimitaneos sensu diuitiisque[a] maximus, Angliæ Italiæque dominis notissimus. Dentem itaque tanti baronis nactus in Normanniam rediit.' et ad proprium predium quod Noron dicitur plures personas ut congrue reliquias susciperent denunciato die accersiit. Anno itaque dominicæ in-
iii. 221 carnationis MºXCºIIº indictione xvª dens almi confessoris Nicholai cum aliis sanctorum reliquiis a Guillelmo Pantulfo de Apulia delatus est.' et in basilica Noronensi in honore sancti Petri prisco tempore condita honorifice susceptus. Ad hanc utique susceptionem Rogerius Vticensis abbas et Radulfus tunc temporis Sagiensis abbas sed postmodum Cantuariensis archiepiscopus accersiti sunt.' et cum ingenti studio monachorum ac tripudio laicorum sanctas reliquias mense Iunio susceperunt, et in argentea pixide a supradicto milite liberaliter parata diligenter coaptauerunt. Frequenter a multis febricitantibus et ab aliis egrotantibus sepedicta pignora requisita sunt.' meritisque almi presulis Nicholai pie postulantes optatam sanitatem adepti sunt.

Non multo post prefatus heros nouæ basilicæ fundamenta iactauit.' datisque uiginti marcis argenti magnam operis partem edidit, sed pluribus infortuniis insurgentibus opus impeditum est ac ad effectum primo fundatore cadente perductum non est. Ipse quidem xviº kal' Maii[2] et Leelina uxor eius xiº kal' Octobris defuncti sunt.' et ibidem in claustro monachorum sepulti requiescunt, sed Philipus ac Rodbertus ac Iuo et Arnulfus filii eorum studia parentum in æcclesiasticis rebus perfecte assequi nondum intenderunt.[3] Hæc itaque de translatione corporis sancti Nicholai
iii. 222 ueraciter operi nostro inseruimus, ipsumque mirabilium opificem

[a] *Omit* que, *Caen MS.*

[1] For William Pantulf and his foundation of a priory at Noron see above, iii. 156–8, 162–4.

[2] The year of William's death is uncertain: he was still alive in 1112, but probably died soon afterwards (cf. R. W. Eyton, *Antiquities of Shropshire* (London and Shifnal, 1854–60), ix. 161).

[3] See above, iii. 164.

their many needs. Erembert, of whom I have spoken, was a Norman by birth; he had been a brave knight before his conversion, and devoted himself fervently to the monastic life afterwards.

At about this time a certain Norman knight, William Pantulf,[1] travelled to Apulia and, since he had a great reverence for St. Nicholas, sought resolutely for some part of his relics. Since God favoured his quest he obtained a tooth and two fragments of the marble tomb from the men who had translated the relics. He was a man of great courage in battle, keen-witted, outstanding among his fellow countrymen for his discretion and riches, and respected by the lords of England and Italy. Having obtained the tooth of the great patron he returned to Normandy to his own patrimony at Noron and summoned many people to receive the treasure honourably on the appointed day.

So in the year of our Lord 1092, the fifteenth indiction, a tooth of the beloved confessor, Nicholas, was brought from Apulia with other relics of the saints by William Pantulf, and honourably received in the church of Noron, which he had founded previously in honour of St. Peter. On this occasion Roger, abbot of Saint-Évroul, and Ralph, then abbot of Séez but afterwards archbishop of Canterbury, were invited to attend and, while the monks showed their great devotion and the laymen their joy, they received the holy relics in the month of June, and carefully placed them in a silver casket generously provided by the knight William. The relics were often visited by many who suffered from fevers and other infirmities, and by the merits of the beloved Bishop Nicholas those who asked in faith recovered their health according to their desires.

Not long afterwards this knight laid the foundations of a new church, giving twenty marks in silver, and completed a great part of the work; but it was interrupted by various misfortunes that assailed him, and has still not been brought to completion after the death of its first founder. He himself died on 16 April[2] and his wife Lesceline on 21 September, and both lie buried there in the monks' cloister; but Philip and Robert and Ivo and Arnulf their sons have not yet shown any signs of following in the footsteps of their parents in love for the church.[3]

I have now included a true account of the translation of St. Nicholas in my work and, in complete faith, I beseech him who has worked so many miracles that, being mindful of those who

fideliter deposcimus: ut suorum memorum memor nostri misereatur, et pro nobis Deum indesinenter deprecetur. Nunc ad inceptam unde aliquantulum digressi sumus redeamus materiam.

14

Antiquo rancore inter Normannos et Francos renouato bellorum incendium exortum est:[1] unde grauissimum pondus detrimentorum clericis et laicis male infixum[a] est. Hugo namque cognomento Stauelus et Radulfus Malus Vicinus[2] aliique oppidani Madantensis castri contra regem Guillelmum insurrexerunt, et magna manu latrunculorum aggregata: plures discursus in Normanniam fecerunt. Aucturam fluuium dirimentem a Francia Neustriam noctu cum satellicio suo pertransibant: et in Ebroicensem diocesim ad nocendum crudeliter parati protinus irruebant. Terram maxime Guillelmi de Britolio circa Paceium: et Rogerii de Ibreio deuastabant: ductisque armentorum gregibus et captis
iii. 223 hominibus Normannos subsannantes immoderate turgebant. Vnde bellicosus rex Guillelmus uehementer iratus totam Wilcassinam prouinciam calumniari cepit: Pontisariam et Caluimontem atque Madantum reddi sibi a Philippo rege Francorum requisiuit. Et nisi ius suum sibi reddatur: terribilibus minis in hostes euehitur. Ratio calumniæ huiusmodi est.

Rex Henricus Roberti Francorum regis filius, dum post mortem patris iure primogeniti deberet redimiri regni fascibus: sed a regina Constantia matre sua nouercali odio insequeretur,[3] eique ipsa in regno Gallorum preponere Robertum fratrem suum ducem Burgundionum conaretur: consultu Amalrici senioris de Monteforti filii Guillelmi Hanoensis Fiscannum cum xii satellitibus uenit,[4] et Robertum Normannorum ducem ut sibi materna fraude miserabiliter exulanti[b] subueniret humiliter expetiit. Quem prefatus dux utpote naturalem dominum suum liberaliter suscepit: et secum donec pascalis festiuitas expleretur[5] gratanter detinuit.

[a] interfectum, *Caen MS.* [b] exultanti, *Caen MS.*

[1] For the hostilities on the Vexin frontier see above, Introduction, pp. xxx–xxxii.

[2] Both these men were moderately wealthy and powerful châtelains; see Lemarignier, *Le gouvernement royal*, p. 135. Ralph Mauvoisin's daughter married Ansold of Maule (cf. above, iii. 180).

[3] Cf. William of Jumièges (Marx, pp. 104–5), 'a matre Constantia novercali odio est affectus.'

[4] Cf. ibid. 'cum duodecim clientulis apud Fiscannum Normannorum ducum adiit.' The reference to Amaury of Montfort does not occur in William of Jumièges.

commemorate him, he may look on us with pity and perpetually intercede with God on our behalf. Now I will return to my subject, from which I have digressed somewhat.

14

An ancient dispute between the Normans and French was revived,[1] and the fires of war were once more ignited, bringing a heavy burden of woe to oppress clergy and laity alike. Hugh Estevel and Ralph Mauvoisin[2] and other knights of the garrison of Mantes began an attack on King William and, collecting a great force of brigands, made several raids into Normandy. They led their rabble by night across the river Eure, which divides France from Normandy, and then overran the diocese of Évreux, prepared for savage destruction. They ravaged the lands of William of Breteuil and Roger of Ivry around Pacy most severely, driving away herds of cattle and taking prisoners; as they grew bold in their arrogance they taunted the Normans. This provoked the warlike King William to anger, and he laid claim to the whole Vexin, demanding from King Philip that Pontoise and Chaumont and Mantes should be returned to him, and uttering terrible threats against his enemies unless his rights were restored to him. The grounds for his claim were as follows.

When King Henry, son of Robert, king of France, ought by right of primogeniture after his father's death to have been invested with the symbols of government of the kingdom, he was thwarted by the hatred of his stepmother, Queen Constance,[3] who tried instead to thrust his brother Robert duke of Burgundy on to the throne of France. On the advice of the elder Amaury of Montfort, son of William of Hainault, Henry came with twelve attendants to Fécamp,[4] and humbly begged Robert duke of Normandy to help him, since his mother's injustice had driven him wretchedly into exile. Duke Robert received him munificently as his natural lord, and was happy to entertain him until the end of the Easter festivities.[5] Then he summoned his Norman forces

[5] The year was 1033 (cf. above, Introduction, pp. xxxi–xxxii); William of Jumièges does not mention Easter, but as Robert frequently spent Easter at Fécamp this is likely to be true. Wace adds, on what authority is not known, that he arrived the day before Palm Sunday and stayed a week (*Roman de Rou*, ii, ll. 2554, 2567), and Dhondt dates his stay, with greater precision than the facts warrant, as 13–20 April (*Normannia*, xv (1939), 466). In 1033 Good Friday fell on 20 April.

Deinde Normannorum agmina undique aggregauit, acerrimam expeditionem in Galliam fecit, et Aurelianensem urbem Normannico impetu ignem immitens incendit. Damnis itaque incomparabilibus ceruicositatem Francorum confregit.' quibus cohercitis
iii. 224 repulsum clitonem regno suo restituit. Henricus autem in regno confirmatus Roberto duci gratias egit.' eique pro beneficio suo totum Vilcassinum a fluuio Isara usque ad Eptum donauit. Hoc nimirum Drogo eiusdem prouinciæ comes libentissime concessit, hominioque facto dum uixit[a] prefato duci fideliter seruiuit.[1] Ambo consules stemmate uirtutum pollebant, et sese uicissim admodum diligebant, mutuaque honoratione et prouectu tripudiabant.

Præfatus Drogo erat ut dicunt de prosapia Caroli magni regis Francorum,[2] eique sepedictus dux in coniugium dederat consobrinam suam Godiouam sororem Eduardi regis Anglorum, ex qua orti sunt Radulfus et Gaulterius comites ac uenerandus Fulco presul Ambianensium.[3] Hæc nimirum puella cum fratre suo in Neustria exulabat.' dum Chunutus Danorum rex Angliam uirtute bellica inuaserat, et genuinos heredes Alfredum et Eduardum effugauerat.' ac Edmundum et Eduinum clitonem Edrici dolis peremerat.[4]

Post aliquot annos defuncto Roberto duce apud Niceam Bithiniæ urbem, rebellauerunt proceres Normanniæ contra Guillelmum infantem.' qui dum pater eius cum Drogone comite iter iniit Ierusolimitanum octo solummodo erat annorum.' et a patre com-
iii. 225 missus tutelæ Alanni consanguinei sui comitis Britonum.[5] Roberto itaque et Drogone defunctis in peregrinatione, et Alanno dum Montem Gomerici obsideret[6] per fraudem Normannorum letaliter corrupto uenenosa potione, et eorum heredibus nefarie priuatis necessaria tuitione, Henricus rex consilio Francorum qui semper Normannis aduersantur Vilcassinum pagum auide repetiit, iurique suo postmodum semper mancipauit. Guillelmus autem tunc pro puerili debilitate ius uendicare suum non potuit, postea uero maioribus sibi curis in Cenomannenses uel Anglos crescentibus

[a] auixit, *Caen MS.*

---

[1] There is no confirmation of these statements; see above, pp. xxxii–xxxiii.

[2] Drogo's family were indirect descendants of Charlemagne (see P. Feuchère, 'La principauté d'Amiens-Valois au xie siècle', in *Le Moyen Âge*, lx (1954), 8).

[3] For Drogo's marriage and children see *Encomium Emmae Reginae*, ed. A. Campbell, Camden 3rd ser. lxxii (1949), p. xlix; J. H. Round, *Studies in Peerage and Family History* (London, 1901), pp. 147–9; Frank Barlow, *Edward the Confessor* (London, 1970), pp. 40, 50, 76, 93–4.

[4] Cf. Anglo-Saxon Chronicle *s.a.* 1013 for the flight of Edward and Alfred to Normandy. The invasion began under Swein, who was not succeeded by

from all quarters, made a fierce attack on France and, capturing Orleans at the head of his Normans, burned it to the ground. By such terrible deeds he broke the obstinacy of the French and forced them to restore the young prince in his kingdom. When Henry had been confirmed in his rule he showed his gratitude to Duke Robert, and gave him the whole Vexin from the river Isère to the Epte as a reward for his service. Drogo, count of the Vexin, readily assented to this grant, did homage to the duke, and served him faithfully as long as he lived.[1] Both counts were distinguished by courage and nobility; they held each other in great affection and throve in mutual respect.

Count Drogo was reputed to be descended from Charlemagne, king of the Franks;[2] and Duke Robert gave his cousin Goda, sister of Edward king of England, to him in marriage. Their children were the counts Ralph and Walter and the venerable Fulk bishop of Amiens.[3] The girl Goda had gone into exile in Normandy with her brother when Cnut, king of Denmark, conquered England by force of arms, drove out the true heirs Alfred and Edward, and defeated Edmund and Prince Edwy through the treachery of Eadric.[4]

Some years later Duke Robert died in the city of Nicaea in Bithynia and the Norman lords rebelled against young William, who was only eight years old when his father set out for Jerusalem with Count Drogo, leaving him in the guardianship of his kinsman Alan, count of Brittany.[5] When Robert and Drogo had died on their pilgrimage, and Alan had been poisoned by Norman treachery at the siege of Montgomery[6] so that their heirs were foully deprived of the protection they needed, King Henry, on the advice of the French counsellors, who always oppose the Normans, greedily took back the Vexin, which thereafter he always held as his by right. At that time William, who was only a weak boy, could not defend his rights; afterwards, as his greater interests in Maine

Cnut until 1014. Eadric's treachery, as the Anglo-Saxon Chronicle tells, took place in 1015 and 1016.

[5] The guardianship of Alan count of Brittany is not mentioned in William of Jumièges. Wace probably took the fact from Orderic, but adds further details about Alan (*Roman de Rou*, ii, ll. 2979–2994). Cf. Haskins, *Norman Institutions*, pp. 269, 270, 272.

[6] Although Montgomery was described simply as 'uicus' in a charter of 1028–35 it may have been fortified by the early years of William I's reign. See J. Yver, 'Les châteaux forts en Normandie', in *BSAN* liii (1955–6), 53.

conticuit, et contra Henricum dominum suum seu Philippum filium eius pro Vilcassino pago arma leuare distulit.

Igitur anno xxi° ex quo super Anglos regnauit.' requisitionem et calumniam de Vilcassino comitatu Philippo regi Francorum fecit.[1] Ille autem sediciosorum friuolis sophismatibus usus est.' et Anglige̜næ regis petitiones omnino spernens frustratus est. Guillelmus ergo ultima mensis Iulii septimana[2] cum exercitu suo Madantum ex improuiso uenit, et cum castrensibus mixtim intrauit. Milites enim et uulgus exierant ut uiderent conculcationem segetum suarum et extirpationem uinearum.' quas Ascelinus Goellus pridie
iii. 226 quam rex aduenisset cum Normannorum uiribus deuastauerat.[3] Irruens itaque exercitus regis cum opidanis portas pertransiuit, et per rabiem armigerorum immisso igne castrum cum æcclesiis et edibus combussit, ac sicut fertur hominum multitudo uiolentia ignis deperiit.

Tunc ibi ex nimio estu et labore pinguissimus rex Guillelmus infirmatus est.'[4] et sex ebdomadibus languens grauiter anxiatus est. Inde quidam qui paci aduersabantur gaudebant.' et liberam permissionem furandi seu res alienas rapiendi expectabant. Porro alii qui securitate pacis exultabant.' pacifici patroni mortem multum formidabant. Ille uero qui semper in omni uita sua sapientum consilio usus fuerat, Deumque ut fidelis seruus timuerat.' sanctæque matris æcclesiæ indefessus defensor extiterat, usque ad mortem laudabili memoria uiguit, et sicut uita sic etiam finis uenerabilis extitit. In egritudine sua usque ad horam mortis integrum sensum et uiuacem loquelam habuit, scelerumque penitens peccata sua sacerdotibus Dei reuelauit,[5] ac secundum morem Christianitatis Deum sibi placare humiliter studuit. Circa illum presules et abbates et religiosi uiri commorabantur.' et
iii. 227 morituro principi salubre consilium perennis uitæ largiebantur. Et quia strepitus Rotomagi quæ populosa ciuitas est intolerabilis erat

[1] See above, Introduction, pp. xxxii–xxxiii.

[2] There seems no reason to doubt the accuracy of Orderic's consistent statements that William attacked Mantes in the last week of July 1087, and that he was ill for six weeks before his death on 9 September. This is compatible with the vague statement in the Anglo-Saxon Chronicle (1087), copied by Florence of Worcester (FW ii. 20), that William went to France 'before the feast of the Assumption' (15 August).

[3] Ascelin Goel, a vassal of William of Breteuil, may have retaliated privately for the raids of Hugh Estevel and Ralph Mauvoisin; but his raid may have been undertaken as part of William's more general war.

[4] Orderic, like the Anglo-Saxon Chronicle (1087) and the *De obitu Willelmi*

and England demanded his attention, he held his peace and put off making an armed attack on his lord Henry or Henry's son Philip to recover the Vexin.

At last in the twenty-first year of his reign in England he laid claim to the Vexin and demanded its return from Philip king of France.[1] Philip however put forward the frivolous sophistries suggested by traitors, utterly rejecting and disregarding the petitions of the English king. In the last week of July,[2] therefore, William unexpectedly came to Mantes with his army and effected an entrance in company with some of the garrison. It happened that the soldiers and townsfolk had gone out to assess the damage done by Ascelin Goel and his Norman forces the day before the king's arrival, when they had trampled down the corn and torn up the vines.[3] So the king's army burst in through the gates as the garrison re-entered; and the troops, getting out of control, set fire to the castle and burnt it together with churches and houses; it is said that a great number of men perished in the consuming flames.

It was there that the king, who was very corpulent, fell ill from exhaustion and heat;[4] and for six weeks he lay sick in a very serious condition. Some enemies of the peace took heart at this, foreseeing an opportunity of pillaging and plundering to their heart's content. But others who preferred the safety of peace dreaded the death of the peace-loving ruler. He indeed, who all his life long had relied on the counsel of wise men, feared God as a faithful servant should, and stood firm as the tireless defender of holy Mother Church, kept his renown untarnished to the end; his death was as noble as his life. Ill as he was he kept all his faculties and his power of lively speech up to the hour of his death; repenting of his misdeeds he confessed his sins to the priests of God[5] and humbly endeavoured to cleanse himself in God's sight by the Christian rites. Bishops, abbots, and monks stood at his bedside, and gave saving counsel of eternal life to the dying prince. Because the noise of Rouen, which is a very crowded city, was intolerable for a sick

written by a monk of Caen (Marx, p. 145; D. C. Douglas and G. W. Greenaway, *English Historical Documents 1042–1189* (London, 1953), pp. 279–80), speaks of William's fatal illness without reference to any injury received at Mantes. William of Malmesbury (*GR* ii. 336–7) says that he was injured internally by being thrown against the pommel of his saddle.

[5] Cf. Eadmer, *Historia Novorum*, ed. M. Rule (RS 1884), pp. 24–5, 'mortuus est, non tamen, ut dicitur, inconfessus.'

egrotanti, extra urbem ipse rex precepit se efferri.' ad æcclesiam sancti Geruasii in colle sitam occidentali, quam Ricardus dux auus eius dederat cenobio Fiscannensi.[1] Ibi Gislebertus Luxouiensis episcopus[2] et Guntardus Gemmeticensis abbas cum quibusdam aliis archiatris sedulo excubabant.' et de spirituali cum corporali salute regis sollicite tractabant.

[3]Denique rex morbo nimium ingrauescente dum sibi mortem uidet ineuitabiliter imminere.' pro futuris quæ non uidebat, sed intimo corde reuoluendo pertimescebat.' crebro cum suspiriis
iii. 228 ingemiscebat. Filios itaque suos Guillelmum Rufum et Henricum qui aderant et quosdam amicorum conuocauit.' et de regni ordinatione sapienter ac multum prouide tractare cepit. Robertus enim filius eius qui maior natu erat, multotiens olim contra patrem suum litigauerat, et tunc nouiter pro quibusdam ineptiis similiter stomachatus ad regem Francorum discesserat.[4] Verum sapiens heros in futurum sibi multisque commoda facere non distulit.' omnesque thesauros suos æcclesiis et pauperibus Deique ministris distribui precepit. Quantum uero singulis dari uoluit callide taxauit.' et coram se describi a notariis imperauit. Clero quoque Madantensi supplex ingentia dona misit.' ut inde restaurarentur æcclesiæ quas combusserat. De fide et iusticia seruanda, de lege Dei et pace tenenda.' de priuilegiis æcclesiarum et statutis patrum obseruandis omnes qui presentes erant admonuit, et allocutionem perenni memoria dignam admixtis interdum lacrimis eloquenter sic edidit.

15

'Multis' inquit 'O amici grauibusque peccatis onustus contremisco.' et mox ad tremendum Dei examen rapturus quid faciam ignoro. In armis enim ab infantia nutritus sum.' et multi sanguinis effusione admodum pollutus sum. Nullatenus enumerare possum mala quæ feci per sexaginta quatuor annos[5] quibus in hac erumnosa

[1] See Fauroux, no. 34.

[2] For Gilbert Maminot, bishop of Lisieux, see above, iii. 18–22.

[3] Orderic's account of the death and burial of William the Conqueror is corroborated at some points by the *De obitu Willelmi*, a nearly contemporary account (see above, p. 78 n. 4), by Eadmer's *Historia Novorum* (RS, pp. 24–5), and by William of Malmesbury (*GR* ii. 337–8). In the imaginary speech Orderic presents his interpretation of the reign; his assignment of motives is subjective, but he is trustworthy for some of the events of 1087 (cf. above, Introduction, pp. xix–xx). For some criticism of Orderic's interpretations see J. H. Le Patourel, 'The Norman succession, 996–1135', in *EHR* lxxxvi (1971), 231–4.

man, the king himself commanded that he should be carried out of the city to the church of St. Gervase, standing on a hill to the west, which his grandfather Duke Richard had given to the abbey of Fécamp.[1] There Gilbert bishop of Lisieux,[2] Gontard abbot of Jumièges, and several other physicians watched ceaselessly over him, and attended to both the spiritual and the corporal needs of the king.

[3]Finally, as the king's sickness grew worse and he realized that death would soon overtake him, he grew fearful of the things to come, which were hidden from his sight but continually present in his mind, and gave way to repeated sighs and groans. He called to his bedside his sons William Rufus and Henry, who were near at hand, and certain friends, and began to speak wisely and fully about the affairs of his kingdom. But his son Robert, who was the eldest, had often quarrelled with his father and again quite recently taking offence for some trivial cause, had gone off to the king of France.[4] Like the wise man that he was the king did not defer doing good to many others and himself as well, but commanded all his wealth to be distributed to the poor and the ministers of God. He prudently fixed the exact sums that he wished to be given to each, and ordered them to be written down in his presence by notaries. He sent great gifts as a penitent to the clergy of Mantes, so that they might restore the churches he had burnt. He adjured all present to keep faith and do justice, follow the law of God and keep the peace, and respect the privileges of churches and the laws of their fathers. Then, weeping, he uttered this eloquent last speech, which deserves to be remembered for all time.

15

'O my friends,' he said, 'I am weighed down with the burden of my sins and tremble, for I must soon face the terrible judgement of God and do not know what I shall do. I was brought up in arms from childhood, and am deeply stained with all the blood I have shed. The ills that I have done in the sixty-four years[5] I have

[4] See above, iii. 112.

[5] If William was eight when his father died he would have been sixty in 1087. The *De obitu Willelmi* states that he was in his fifty-ninth year. See Douglas, *WC*, p. 380. Wace (*Roman de Rou*, ii. 9259–60), repeats Orderic's mistake.

uita uixi.' pro quibus absque mora rationem reddere nunc cogor equissimo iudici. Dum pater meus sponte proficiscens in exilium,
iii. 229 commisit michi Normanniæ ducatum.' tenellus eram puer utpote octo annorum, ex quo tempore usque nunc semper subii pondus armorum ipsumque iam ducatum fere quinquaginta sex annis[1] gessi in discrimine bellorum. Mei quibus preeram michi sepe insidiati sunt.' et damna grauesque iniurias michi nequiter intulerunt. Turchetillum nutricium meum[2] et Osbernum Herfasti filium Normanniæ dapiferum.' comitemque Gislebertum patrem patriæ cum multis aliis rei publicæ necessariis fraudulenter interfecerunt.[3] His itaque rebus gentis meæ fidem expertus sum. Noctibus multotiens cognatorum timore meorum a Gaulterio auunculo meo[4] de camera principali furtim exportatus sum.' ac ad domicilia latebrasque pauperum ne a perfidis qui ad mortem me querebant inuenirer translatus sum.

iii. 230 'Normanni si bono rigidoque dominatu reguntur strenuissimi sunt, et in arduis rebus inuicti omnes excellunt, et cunctis hostibus fortiores superare contendunt. Alioquin sese uicissim dilaniant atque consumunt.' rebelliones enim cupiunt, seditiones appetunt, et ad omne nefas prompti sunt. Rectitudinis igitur forti censura coherceantur.' et freno disciplinæ per tramitem iusticiæ gradi compellantur. Si uero ad libitum suum sine iugo ut indomitus onager ire permittuntur.' ipsi et princeps eorum penuria et confusione probrosa operientur. Pluribus hoc experimentis iamdudum edidici. Proximi consanguineique mei qui debuissent contra omnes mortales me omnimodis tutari.' frequenti conspiratione facta in me insurrexerunt, et pene omnem patris mei hereditatem michi abstulerunt.

'Guido Rainaldi Burgundionum ducis ex Adeliza amita mea filius, malum michi pro bono reddidit. Nam ego eum de alia regione aduentantem benigniter susceperam, ac ut unicum fratrem honoraueram, atque Vernonum et Brionnam partemque Normanniæ non modicam donaueram. Ille uero uerbis et actibus michi derogauit, me nothum degeneremque et principatu indi-
iii. 231 gnum detestatus indicauit.' et hostiliter diffamauit. Quid plura

[1] Orderic repeats his mistake in calculation; the correct figure is 52.

[2] Thurkill of Neufmarché, father of Geoffrey of Neufmarché (see above, ii. 130, iii. 254).

[3] For the murders of Osbern the Steward and Gilbert of Brionne see William of Jumièges (Marx, p. 116) and Orderic's interpolations (ibid., p. 156).

passed in this troubled life cannot be numbered; and for them I must soon render account before the most just Judge. When my father decided to go on a pilgrimage and committed the duchy of Normandy to me I was still a young boy, only eight years old; from that day to this I have always borne the burden of arms, and by now I have ruled the duchy for almost fifty-six[1] years in strife and war. My own subjects have often risen in revolt against me, and have perfidiously harmed and wronged me. They treacherously slew Thurkill my tutor,[2] Osbern son of Herfast, steward of Normandy, and Count Gilbert, father of his country, with many other loyal servants of the duchy.[3] By such acts as these I learnt what the fealty of my people meant. Many times, for fear of my kinsmen, I was smuggled secretly at night by my uncle Walter[4] out of the chamber in the castle, and taken to the cottages and hiding-places of the poor, to save me from discovery by traitors who sought my death.

'If the Normans are disciplined under a just and firm rule they are men of great valour, who press invincibly to the fore in arduous undertakings and, proving their strength, fight resolutely to overcome all enemies. But without such rule they tear each other to pieces and destroy themselves, for they hanker after rebellion, cherish sedition, and are ready for any treachery. So they need to be restrained by the severe penalties of law, and forced by the curb of discipline to keep to the path of justice. If they are allowed to go wherever they choose, as an untamed ass does, both they and their ruler must expect grave disorder and poverty. I have learnt this by now through repeated experience. My closest friends and my kinsmen, who ought to have defended me with all their might against all men, frequently conspired and rebelled against me, and robbed me of almost all the inheritance I had received from my father.

'Guy, son of Reginald duke of Burgundy and my aunt Adeliza, rendered me evil for good. For I received him favourably when he came to me from another province, honoured him like my only brother, and gave him Vernon and Brionne and a considerable part of Normandy. Yet he spoke and acted without respect and slandered me disloyally, calling me a bastard and declaring me base and unfit for rule. What more shall I tell? Breaking his oath

[4] Walter was one of Herleve's brothers and occurs occasionally as a witness to charters (Fauroux, nos. 102, 134).

referam? Fidem suam michi mentitus in me rebellauit,[1] proceresque meos Rannulfum Baiocensem ac Haimonem Dentatum et Nigellum de Constantino aliosque multos michi subtraxit.' secumque periuros esse nefario monitu coegit. Immemor itaque hominii et fidelitatis quam michi iurauerat.' totam Normanniam auferre sategit. Sic igitur adhuc imberbis in illum coactus sum arma leuare.' et in planicie apud Valesdunas contra consobrinum
hominemque meum dimicare. Tunc auxiliante Deo qui iustus
iii. 232 iudex est inter Cadomum et Argentas[a] hostes uici.'[2] quibus nutu
Dei subrutis patrium ius libere possedi. Deinde munitionem Brionnæ obsedi, Guidonem uulneratum et de bello fuga elapsum inclusi.' nec inde discessi donec hostem publicum de Neustria expulerim, et cuncta eius munimenta optinuerim.

'Non multo post alia michi grauissima aduersitas oborta est. Patrui namque mei Malgerius Rotomagensis archiepiscopus, et Guillelmus frater eius cui Archas et comitatum Talogii gratis dederam me uelut nothum contempserunt.'[3] et Henricum regem ac Engelrannum comitem Pontiui[4] contra me accersierunt. Mox
ego ut in Constantino[5] huiusmodi rumores audiui.' multis dis-
iii. 233 suadentibus iter iniui. Aliquantos milites qui feruentiores ad ictus
dandos erant Archas premisi.' et ipse cum exercitu non grandi subsecutus arduam munitionem[6] obsedi. Sed antequam rura quæ inter duo flumina sunt Sedam et Guarennam attigissem.' precursores mei preoccupauerunt Engelrannum comitem[7] in castrum intrare festinantem, ipsumque fortiter pugnantem quia miles erat asperrimus occiderunt, et agmina eius fugauerunt. Obsidione graui castrenses cohercui.' et periurum comitem exulare coegi, nec in omni uita sua redire ad id quod omiserat permisi. Proteruum quoque presulem qui nec Deo deuotus nec michi fidus erat de pontificali sede per decretum papæ deposui.' et Maurilium

[a] Baiocas, *Caen MS., corrected in a fourteenth-century hand to* Argentas; Argentas *MS. Vespasian A xix*

[1] Cf. William of Poitiers (Foreville, pp. 14–16), who names Ralph of Briquessart, vicomte of Bayeux, Nigel, vicomte of the Cotentin, and Hamo-aux-Dents, lord of Torigny, as Guy's associates in his revolt.

[2] For accounts of the battle of Val-ès-Dunes (1047) see Douglas, *WC*, pp. 49–51.

[3] Cf. Le Prévost, i. 184 for a similar statement. Orderic is the earliest source to say that Mauger was an abettor of William of Arques (cf. *Roman de Rou*, ii,

of fealty he rebelled against me,[1] corrupted my barons Ralph of Bayeux and Hamo-aux-Dents and Nigel of the Cotentin and many others, and by his infamous arguments persuaded them to share in his treason. Heedless of his homage and the fealty sworn to me he tried to seize all Normandy. I therefore, though still a beardless boy, was forced to raise arms against him and join battle in the plain of Val-ès-Dunes against my cousin and vassal. Then by the help of God, that most just Judge, I defeated my enemies between Caen and Argences[2] and, dispossessing them by the will of God, I regained full control of my inheritance. Afterwards I besieged the castle of Brionne, closely investing Guy, who had fled there wounded from the field of battle, so that he could not escape, until I had driven him from Normandy as a public enemy and gained possession of all his castles.

'Only a few years later another serious rebellion broke out against me. My uncle Mauger, archbishop of Rouen, and his brother William, to whom I had freely given Arques and the county of Talou, denounced me as a bastard[3] and secured the support of King Henry and Enguerrand count of Ponthieu[4] against me. As soon as the news of this reached me in the Cotentin[5] I set out against them, though many sought to dissuade me. I sent ahead a few of my more experienced and warlike knights to Arques and, following myself with a relatively small army, laid siege to the well-fortified castle.[6] But before I reached the open country between the rivers Scie and Garenne my advance-guard encountered Count Enguerrand[7] as he hastened to enter the castle, and, though he fought bravely as a valiant knight should, slew him and put his troops to flight. By a close investment I forced the garrison to surrender and compelled the perjured count to go into exile, refusing to allow him to return to his lost fiefs as long as he lived. As for the treacherous bishop, who had been neither faithful to God nor loyal to me, I deposed him by papal decree from the

ll. 3417–18), but William of Poitiers hints at unspecified crimes (Foreville, pp. 130–1). For William of Arques see D. C. Douglas, 'The earliest Norman counts', in *EHR* lxi (1946), 146.

[4] William of Arques had married a sister of Enguerrand II, count of Ponthieu.

[5] Cf. William of Poitiers (Foreville, p. 54), 'Quae postquam duci comperta sunt Guillelmo, e Constantino pago . . . properabat.'

[6] The castle of Arques was built shortly after William received the county of Le Talou *c.* 1038 (Foreville, p. 54 n. 1; J. Yver in *BSAN*, liii (1955–6), 50).

[7] Enguerrand was killed on 26 October, either 1052 or, more probably, 1053 (Douglas, *WC*, pp. 388–9).

uenerabilem cenobitam quem michi Deus de Florentia ciuitate Italiæ transmiserat in loco eius subrogaui.[1]

'Henricus regali potentia fretus, et militari audacia feruidus, hostiumque meorum derogationibus admodum stimulatus.' sepe
iii. 234 nisus est me uelut inermem conculcare, multisque modis proterere, et indebita michi iura imponere. Sepius cum ingenti armatorum manu terram meam ingressus est.' sed nunquam de preda spoliisque meis hominumque captura meorum gauisus est. Cum grandi pompa minisque terribilibus plerumque fines meos intrauit.' sed nunquam letus nec sine dedecore ad sua repedauit. Plures secum probitate ualentes huc adduxit.' quos quia meo meorumque gladio proh dolor perierant non reduxit.

'Quondam nimis contra me inflammatus, ingentem exercitum Galliæ in duas partes diuisit rex Henricus.' ut nostros opprimeret fundos geminis irruptionibus. Ipse unam phalangem in Ebroicensem diocesim ut usque ad Sequanam omnia deuastaret introduxit, aliamque Odoni fratri suo ac Rainaldo de Claromonte[2] et duobus consulibus Radulfo de Monte Disderii[3] atque Widoni de
iii. 236 Pontiuo commendauit.' ut per uada Eptæ Neustriam cito introirent, Braium et Talogium atque Calcegium totumque Rotomagensem pagum inuaderent, ferro et flamma necne rapinis usque ad mare penitus deuastarent. Hæc itaque comperiens ego e contra non segnis processi contra regis mappalia per litus Sequanæ cum meis me semper opposui.' et ubicumque conaretur cespitem meum depopulari, armis et bello calumniam paraui. Robertum uero Aucensium comitem et Rogerium de Mortuo mari[4] aliosque milites probatissimos misi contra Odonem eiusque legiones. Qui dum penes castrum quod Mortuum mare dicitur[5] occurrissent Francis utriusque partis agminibus paratis, terribile prelium commissum est, et ex utraque parte multum sanguinis effusum est. Vtrobique enim bellatores erant strenui.' et usque ad mortem cedere nescii. Hinc seuiunt Galli pro cupidine adquirendi.' illinc
iii. 237 feriunt Normanni spe feruentes euadendi, et se suosque lares defendendi. Tandem iuuante Deo uicere Normanni.' et fugere

[1] See above, iii. 86–90.

[2] For the family of Reginald of Clermont see P. Feuchère, 'La principauté d'Amiens-Valois au xie siècle', in *Le Moyen Âge*, lx (1954), p. 26 n. 89.

[3] Orderic is the only historian to describe Ralph of Crépy, count of Amiens, Valois, and the Vexin, as 'of Montdidier' (ibid., pp. 6, 12).

archbishopric and appointed in his place the worthy monk Maurilius, whom God had sent to me from the city of Florence in Italy.[1]

'Henry, trusting in his royal power and boldness in war and much encouraged by the slights of my enemies, often tried to attack me without provocation, harass me in many ways, and impose unjust customs on me. Often he invaded my land with a huge army, but never succeeded in carrying off booty or plunder or capturing my men. On several occasions he crossed my frontiers in great force, uttering terrible threats; but he never returned to his lands with any profit or without shame. Many of the valiant men he brought with him failed to return because, I grieve to tell, they perished by my sword and the swords of my men.

'On one occasion when he was particularly aggressive towards me he divided a great French army into two parts and planned to overwhelm my lands by invading at two different points. He himself led one division into the diocese of Évreux, intending to ravage the country as far as the Seine, and he entrusted the other to his brother Odo and Reginald of Clermont[2] and the two counts Ralph of Montdidier[3] and Guy of Ponthieu, who were to cross the Epte into Normandy and overrun Bray and Le Talou and the Pays de Caux and the whole province of Rouen, laying it waste with fire and sword and rapine as far as the sea. Getting wind of this plot I lost no time in advancing against him, stationed myself with my men opposite to the king's encampments along the banks of the Seine, and prepared to meet him in battle wherever he might attempt to devastate my country. I sent Robert count of Eu and Roger of Mortemer[4] and other tried knights against Odo and his forces. When they fell in with the French near to the castle of Mortemer[5] both armies drew up their battle lines and a terrible conflict took place; many were slain on both sides, for each army contained valiant warriors, who would fight to the death without a thought of yielding. The French on one side fought avidly to conquer; the Normans on the other, determined to avert the threat, passionately defended their lives and their own homes. Finally by God's aid the Normans won the victory, and

[4] For Roger of Mortemer see GEC ix. 266; *EYC* viii. 3 n. 1.

[5] The details given by Orderic suggest the existence of a castle at Mortemer in 1054 (cf. J. Yver in *BSAN* liii (1955–6), 56).

Franci. Hoc itaque bellum transequanam in hieme ante quadragesimam fecere, octauo anno post Valesdunense.[1]

'Tunc Wido Pontiui comes captus est.' et Odo cum Rainaldo aliisque qui uelocitate pedum[2] uiguerunt fugatus est. Radulfus quoque comes pariter caperetur.' nisi Rogerius princeps miliciæ meæ[3] illi suffragaretur. Hominium enim iamdudum illi fecerat. In tali ergo necessitate pulchrum illi et competens seruitium impendit, dum in castro suo illum triduo protexit, et postea saluum ad sua perduxit. Pro hac offensa Rogerium de Normannia eieci, sed paulo post reconciliatus illi ceterum honorem reddidi. Castrum tamen Mortui maris in quo inimicum meum saluauit illi iure ut reor abstuli.' sed Guillelmo de Guarenna consanguineo eius[4] tironi legitimo dedi. Widonem uero comitem Baiocis quamdiu placuit in carcere habui, et post duos annos hominium ab eo tali tenore
iii. 238 recepi.' ut exinde michi semper fidelis existeret, et militare seruitium ubi iussissem cum centum militibus[5] michi singulis annis exiberet. Deinde muneribus illum magnis donaui.' et honoratum cum pace dimisi.

'Peracto certamine mox ut certos rumores comperi, per Radulfum de Toenia quæ trans Sequanam contigerant regi Francorum mandaui.[6] Quibus auditis ille protinus noctu surrexit.' et cum exercitu suo uelociter aufugit, nec unquam postea securus in terra
iii. 239 mea pernoctauit. Sic a puericia mea innumeris pressuris undique impeditus sum.' sed per gratiam Dei de omnibus honorifice ereptus sum. Inuidiosus igitur omnibus uicinis meis factus sum.' sed auxiliante Deo in quo semper spem meam posui a nullo superatus sum. Hoc sepe senserunt Britones, et Andegauenses, hoc astipulantur Franci atque Flandrenses, hoc grauiter experti sunt Angli et Cenomannenses.

'Goisfredus Martellus comes Andegauorum, et Conanus princeps Britonum, atque Robertus Fresio satrapa Morinorum michi

[1] In February 1054 (Halphen, *Anjou*, p. 77).

[2] This must not be taken to mean that they were unhorsed; William of Poitiers, whom Orderic echoes here, wrote 'equorum velocitate' (Foreville, p. 72).

[3] Cf. the use of the term 'princeps militiae' in William of Poitiers (Foreville, p. 74).

[4] The exact relationship between Roger of Mortemer and William of Warenne has not been established (*EYC* viii. 3 n. 1; GEC ix, Appendix A).

[5] Orderic's figure cannot be checked and may be wrong; but as the Bayeux Inquest of 1133 proves the prevalence of a five- and ten-knight unit it may contain some truth. See Haskins, *Norman Institutions*, p. 18.

the French fled. This battle was fought on the other side of the Seine in winter before Lent, in the eighth year after Val-ès-Dunes.[1]

'On that occasion Guy count of Ponthieu was taken prisoner, and Odo, Reginald, and others escaped only because they ran away fast enough.[2] Count Ralph would have been taken prisoner also, if Roger, the commander of my army,[3] had not spared him. He did so because he had done homage to him. So, in his lord's hour of need, he performed a just and seemly service by protecting him in his own castle (of Mortemer) for three days and then escorting him back to his lands. I banished Roger from Normandy for this offence, but became reconciled with him soon afterwards and restored the rest of his honor to him. I withheld from him, however, the castle of Mortemer in which he had preserved my enemy, acting—I believe—rightly; and gave it to his kinsman William of Warenne,[4] a loyal knight. As for Count Guy, I kept him in prison at Bayeux at my good pleasure, and two years later received homage from him on these terms: that in the future he would always be faithful to me and would perform military service for me each year wherever I commanded with a hundred knights.[5] Then, loading him with gifts, I sent him away honourably, in peace.

'As soon as I received a trustworthy account of the victory, I informed the king of France by the mouth of Ralph of Tosny of what had taken place across the Seine.[6] The night after he had heard the news he struck camp, beat a hasty retreat with his army, and never again presumed to pitch camp on my domain. You see how from my boyhood I have always been threatened by many dangers, but by the grace of God I have escaped with honour from them all. As a result I became an object of hatred and enmity to all my neighbours, but none could ever defeat me, for God, in whom I always placed my trust, was my strength. This the Bretons and men of Anjou experienced on many occasions, to this French and Flemings are witnesses, this the English and men of Maine learnt to their cost.

'Geoffrey Martel, count of Anjou, Conan duke of Brittany, and Robert the Frisian, count of Flanders, hatched many plots against

[6] In his interpolations in William of Jumièges Orderic gives a dramatic account of the announcement of the defeat by Ralph of Tosny (Marx, pp. 179–80). William of Poitiers describes the announcement of the news without naming the messenger (Foreville, pp. 72–4).

multis machinationibus insidiati sunt.' sed custodiente Deo licet multum optassent, et plures insidias perstruxissent, nunquam uoti compotes effecti sunt. Diadema regale quod nullus antecessorum meorum gessit adeptus sum, quod diuina solummodo gratia non ius contulit hereditarium. Quantos ultra mare labores et periculosos conflictus pertulerim contra Exonios.' Cestrenses et
iii. 240 Nordanhimbros, contra Scotos et Gualos.' Nordwigenas et Dacos,[1] et contra cæteros aduersarios qui conabantur me regno Angliæ spoliare.' difficile est enarrare, in quibus omnibus prouenit michi sors uictoriæ. Sed quamuis super huiuscemodi triumphis humana gaudeat auiditas, me tamen intrinsecus pungit et mordet formidinis anxietas.' dum perpendo quod in omnibus his grassata est seua temeritas. Vnde uos O sacerdotes et ministri Christi suppliciter obsecro ut orationibus uestris me commendetis omnipotenti Deo.' ut peccata quibus admodum premor ipse remittat, et per suam infatigabilem clementiam inter suos me saluum faciat. Thesauros quoque meos iubeo dari æcclesiis et pauperibus.' ut quæ congesta sunt ex facinoribus dispergantur in sanctis sanctorum usibus. Debetis enim recolere quam dulciter uos amaui.' et quam fortiter contra omnes emulos defensaui.

'Æcclesiam Dei matrem scilicet nostram nunquam uiolaui.' sed ubique ut ratio exegit desideranter honoraui. Æcclesiasticas dignitates nunquam uenundedi.' simoniam detestatus semper refutaui. In electione personarum uitæ meritum et sapientiæ doctrinam inuestigaui.' et quantum in me fuit omnium dignissimo æcclesiæ regimen commendaui. Hoc nimirum probari ueraciter potest in Lanfranco Cantuariensium archipresule, hoc in Anselmo Beccensium abbate, hoc in Gerberto Fontanellense et Durando Troarnense, et in aliis multis regni mei doctoribus, quorum celebris laus personat in ultimis ut credo terræ finibus. Tales socios ad
iii. 241 colloquium elegi, in horum contubernio ueritatem et sapientiam inueni.' ideoque semper gaudens optabam eorum consiliis perfrui.

'Nouem abbatiæ monachorum et una sanctimonialium[2] quæ a patribus meis in Normannia fundatæ sunt.' me adiuuante cum auxilio Dei creuerunt, et gloriose multarum augmentis rerum quas

[1] See above, ii. 210–14, 216–36.

[2] Lists of monastic foundations were made by Orderic elsewhere (above, ii. 8 ff.) and by Robert of Torigny in his interpolations in William of Jumièges (Marx, pp. 252–4; cf. Foreville, p. 122 n. 1). The numbers do not quite tally: Orderic probably had in mind Jumièges, Fécamp, Mont Saint-Michel, Saint-Ouen (Rouen), Saint-Wandrille, Bernay, Cérisy, and possibly Bec-Hellouin and

me; but though they hoped for great gain and laid cunning traps they never secured what they desired, for God was my help. I won a royal crown, though no ancestor of mine had worn one; it came to me by divine grace, not hereditary right. It is difficult to describe all the toils and perilous conflicts that I endured across the Channel against the men of Exeter and Chester and Northumbria, against the Scots and Welsh, Norwegians and Danes,[1] and against all the adversaries who strove to wrest my English kingdom from me; in all of them the fortunes of victory came to me. Although ambitious men rejoice in such triumphs, fear and dread now clutch me and gnaw at my heart when I consider what cruel brutality was unleashed in these conflicts. Therefore, priests and ministers of Christ, I humbly beg you to commend me to almighty God in your prayers, asking him to forgive the sins by which I am so sorely burdened and, by his unfailing mercy, to bring me to salvation among his own. I command that my treasures be distributed among churches and the poor, so that what I amassed through evil deeds may be assigned to the holy uses of good men. For you should remember how warmly I have loved you, and how resolutely I have defended you against all your enemies.

'I have never harmed the Church of God, which is our mother, but have always been glad to honour her as our duty requires. I never sold ecclesiastical offices, and always hated and forbade simony. In making elections I inquired carefully into the good conduct and sound doctrine of the candidates, and as far as I was able entrusted the government of the church to the most worthy of them. The truth of this shines forth in the persons of Lanfranc, archbishop of Canterbury, Anselm, abbot of Bec, Gerbert of Saint-Wandrille and Durand of Troarn, and in many other religious teachers of my realm, whose praise resounds, I believe, to the furthest corners of the earth. These are the men I chose as my constant companions; I learnt truth and wisdom in their society, and so was always happy to follow their good counsels.

'With God's help I further enriched the nine abbeys of monks and one of nuns[2] which my ancestors founded in Normandy, so that they grew yet greater in renown through the abundant gifts

La Trinité-du-Mont (Rouen), which were founded with ducal consent by vassals. Possibly Saint-Taurin (Évreux) should be included, but it is not specified in the other lists and none of William's known charters made any grants to it. The nunnery was Montivilliers.

dedi magnificatæ sunt. Deinde ducatus mei tempore decem et septem monachorum atque sanctimonialium sex cenobia constructa sunt.'[1] ubi magnum seruitium et plures elemosinæ pro summi regis amore cotidie fiunt. Huiusmodi castris munita est Normannia.' et in his discunt terrigenæ preliari contra demones et carnis uitia. Horum quippe aut ego inspirante Deo fui conditor.' aut fundatorum feruidus adiutor, et beniuolus incentor. Omnes quoque res quas in terris uel aliis redditibus proceres mei Deo et sanctis eius dederunt pro salute spirituali.' in Neustria et Anglia benigniter concessi, et cartas largitionum contra omnes emulos et infestatores principali auctoritate gratis confirmaui.

iii. 242 'Hæc studia sectatus sum a primeuo tempore.' hæc heredibus meis relinquo tenenda omni tempore. In his filii mei me iugiter sequimini.' ut hic et in æuum coram Deo et hominibus honoremini. Hoc precipue uos uiscera mea commoneo, ut bonorum et sapientum indesinenter inhereatis sodalicio, et eorum in omnibus si diu gloriosi uultis persistere obediatis imperio. Piorum sophistarum doctrina est bonum a malo discernere, iusticiam omnimodis tenere, nequitiamque omni molimine cauere, infirmis et pauperibus ac iustis parcere et subuenire, superbos et iniquos comprimere ac debellare,[2] et ab infestatione simplicium refrenare, æcclesiam sanctam deuote frequentare, diuinitatis cultum super omnes diuitias amare, et diuinæ legi nocte dieque[3] id est in aduersis et prosperis infatigabiliter obtemperare.

'Ducatum Normanniæ antequam in epitimio[4] Senlac contra Heraldum certassem Roberto filio meo concessi.' cui quia primogenitus est et hominium pene omnium huius patriæ baronum iam recepit concessus honor nequit abstrahi.[5] Sed indubitanter scio quod uere misera erit regio.' quæ subiecta fuerit eius dominio. Superbus enim est et insipiens nebulo.' trucique diu plectendus infortunio. Neminem Anglici regni heredem constituo.' sed

[1] It is not quite certain which houses were included in Orderic's list (cf. above, p. 90 n. 2). The most probable list is St. Stephen's (Caen), Montebourg, Grestain, Saint-Pierre-de-Préaux, Saint-Pierre-sur-Dives, Lire, Saint-Sauveur-le-Vicomte, Saint-Évroul, Séez, Conches, Troarn, Lessay, Le Tréport, Cormeilles, Saint-Sever, Saint-Victor-en-Caux, and Fontenay. The nunneries were Holy Trinity (Caen), Saint-Léger-de-Préaux, Almenèches, Saint-Sauveur-d'Évreux, Saint-Amand (Rouen), and Notre-Dame-du-Pré (Lisieux). Le Prévost (iii. 241 n. 2) suggests Saint-Georges-de-Boscherville and Bonne-Nouvelle (Rouen); but these were priories.

[2] Cf. Virgil, *Aeneid*, vi. 854 (H. Walther, *Carmina Medii Aevi posterioris latina* (Göttingen, 1959–69), no. 20670).

I gave them. Further, while I was duke, seventeen abbeys of monks and six of nuns were built,[1] where every day full offices are performed and abundant alms are given for love of the most high King. These are the fortresses by which Normandy is guarded: in these men learn to fight against devils and the sins of the flesh. Of all of these I was either the founder under God's guidance, or the ready friend and eager sponsor of the founder. Further I willingly conceded all the lands and revenues which my barons gave to God and his saints for their spiritual salvation, in both England and Normandy. By my royal authority I freely confirmed the charters preserving these gifts against all who might covet or attack them.

'These have been my concerns from the beginning of my life; these I bequeath to my heirs to be cherished for ever. In these things, my sons, follow in my footsteps, so that you may deserve honour before God and men now and for ever. I specially urge you who are my own flesh and blood, to keep to the society of good and wise men and obey their precepts in all things if you wish to prosper long and honourably. The teaching of holy philosophers is to know good from evil, preserve justice in all things, shun evil with determination, be merciful and helpful to the sick and poor and law-abiding, overthrow and punish the proud and wicked,[2] refrain from harming the humble, be a devout worshipper in the Church, cherish the service of God above all riches, and obey the divine law by night and day,[3] that is, in adversity and prosperity.

'I invested my son Robert with the duchy of Normandy before I fought against Harold on the heath[4] of Senlac; because he is my first-born son and has received the homage of almost all the barons of the country the honor then granted cannot be taken from him.[5] Yet I know for certain that any province subjected to his rule will be most wretched. He is a proud and foolish fellow, doomed to suffer prolonged and grim misfortune. I name no man as my heir

[3] Psalm i. 2; cf. above, iii. 3.

[4] Orderic is, as far as I can discover, the only writer to use the very rare word 'epitimium' in the sense of 'field' or 'heath'. It occurs in Isidore's *Etymologies* with the meaning, 'flower of thyme' (cf. Ducange, iii. 281).

[5] This is the clearest statement in the *Ecclesiastical History* of Robert's rights as Orderic saw them; his interpretation is typical of the date at which he wrote. Cf. M. Chibnall in 'Compte rendu de la Semaine de Droit Normand, Alençon 1969', in *Revue historique de droit français et étranger*, xlviii (1970), 347. See J. H. Le Patourel in *EHR* lxxxvi (1971), 231–4 for the suggestion that William's division of his lands represented an unwilling compromise.

iii. 243 æterno conditori cuius sum et in cuius manu sunt omnia illud commendo. Non enim tantum decus hereditario iure possedi.' sed diro conflictu et multa effusione humani cruoris periuro regi Heraldo abstuli, et interfectis uel effugatis fauctoribus eius dominatui meo subegi. Naturales regni filios plus æquo exosos habui, nobiles et uulgares crudeliter uexaui, iniuste multos exhereditaui, innumeros maxime in pago Eborachensi fame seu ferro mortificaui. Deiri enim et transhumbranæ gentes exercitum Sueni Danorum regis contra me susceperunt.' et Robertum de Cuminis cum mille militibus intra Dunelmum aliosque proceres meos et tirones probatissimos in diuersis locis peremerunt.[1] Vnde immoderato furore commotus in boreales Anglos ut uesanus leo properaui.' domos eorum iussi segetesque et omnem apparatum atque supellectilem confestim incendi, et copiosos armentorum pecudumque greges passim mactari. Multitudinem itaque utriusque sexus tam diræ famis mucrone multaui.' et sic multa milia pulcherrimæ gentis senum iuuenumque proh dolor funestus trucidaui.[2] Fasces igitur huius regni quod cum tot peccatis optinui.' nulli audeo tradere nisi Deo soli, ne post funus meum adhuc deteriora fiant occasione mei. Guillelmum filium meum qui michi a primis annis semper inhesit, et michi pro posse suo per omnia libenter obediuit.' opto in spiritu Dei diu ualere, et in regni solio si diuina uoluntas est feliciter fulgere.'

16

iii. 244 Hæc et his similia dum rex Guillelmus multa dixisset, et stupor adsistentes callideque futura dimetientes inuasisset.' Henricus iunior filius ut nil sibi de regalibus gazis dari audiuit, merens cum lacrimis ad regem dixit, 'Et michi pater quid tribuis?' Cui rex ait, 'Quinque milia libras argenti[3] de thesauro meo tibi do.' Ad hæc Henricus dixit, 'Quid faciam de thesauro, si locum habitationis non habuero?' Cui pater respondit, 'Equanimis esto fili et confortare in domino. Pacifice patere.' ut maiores fratres tui precedant

[1] See above, ii. 220–2. Orderic there gives the number of knights in Durham as five hundred.

[2] See above, ii. 230–2. Orderic regarded the harrying of the north as the blackest of William's crimes.

[3] William of Malmesbury (*GR* ii. 468) says that Henry received 3,000 marks. Wace (*Roman de Rou*, ii, ll. 9182–3) gives the same sum as Orderic.

to the kingdom of England; instead I entrust it to the eternal Creator to whom I belong and in whose hand are all things. For I did not come to possess such a dignity by hereditary right, but wrested the kingdom from the perjured king Harold with bitter strife and terrible bloodshed, and subjected it to my rule after killing or driving into exile all his partisans. I treated the native inhabitants of the kingdom with unreasonable severity, cruelly oppressed high and low, unjustly disinherited many, and caused the death of thousands by starvation and war, especially in Yorkshire. This was because the men of Deira and Northumbria welcomed the army of Swein king of Denmark when he attacked me and slew Robert of Commine and many men-at-arms in Durham, together with my other magnates and experienced knights.[1] In mad fury I descended on the English of the north like a raging lion, and ordered that their homes and crops with all their equipment and furnishings should be burnt at once and their great flocks and herds of sheep and cattle slaughtered everywhere. So I chastised a great multitude of men and women with the lash of starvation and, alas! was the cruel murderer of many thousands, both young and old, of this fair people.[2] I dare not transmit the government of this kingdom, won with so many sins, to any man, but entrust it to God alone, for fear that after my death my evil deeds should become the cause of even worse things. I hope that my son William, who has always been loyal to me from his earliest years and has gladly obeyed me in every way he could, may long prosper in the Lord, enjoy good fortune, and bring lustre to the kingdom if such is the divine will.'

16

When King William had spoken these words and others to the same purpose, and the assembled company stood dazed with grief at the realization of what lay in store for them, Henry, his younger son, who had heard that no share of the royal wealth was to come to him, said sorrowfully and with tears to the king, 'And what, father, do you give me?' The king answered him, 'I give you five thousand pounds in silver[3] from my treasure.' To which Henry said, 'What shall I do with treasure, if I have no place to make my home?' and his father replied, 'Be satisfied, my son, and take comfort in the Lord. Patiently allow your elder brothers to take

te. Robertus habebit Normanniam.' et Guillelmus Angliam. Tu autem tempore tuo totum honorem quem ego nactus sum habebis, et fratribus tuis diuitiis et potestate prestabis.' His ita dictis, metuens rex ne in regno tam diffuso repentina oriretur turbatio.' epistolam de constituendo rege fecit Lanfranco archiepiscopo, suoque sigillo signatam tradidit Guillelmo Rufo filio suo.' iubens ut in Angliam transfretaret continuo.[1] Deinde osculatus eum benedixit, et trans pontum ad suscipiendum diadema properanter direxit. Qui mox ad portum qui Witsant dicitur peruenit.' ibique iam patrem obiisse audiuit. Henricus autem festinauit denominatam sibi pecuniam recipere, diligenter ne quid sibi deesset ponderare, necessariosque sodales in quibus confideret aduocare, munitumque gazofilacium sibi procurare.

Interea medici et regales ministri qui languidum principem custodiebant, proceresque qui ad eum uisitandi gratia ueniebant.'
iii. 245 ceperunt pro uinctis quos in carcere tenebat eum affari, ac ut misereretur eis et relaxaret suppliciter deprecari. Quibus ipse ait, 'Morcarum nobilem Anglorum comitem iam diu uinctum tenui et iniuste, sed pro timore ne per eum si liber fuisset turbaretur regnum Angliæ.[2] Rogerium uero de Britolio quia ualde contumaciter contra me furuit, et Radulfum de Guader sororium suum et multos alios in me prouocauit in uinculis artaui, et quod in uita mea non egrederetur iuraui.[3] Sic multos uinculis inieci ex merito propriæ peruersitatis.' aliosque plures pro metu futuræ seditionis. Hoc enim censura rectitudinis exigit, et diuina lex per Moisen rectoribus orbis precipit.' ut comprimant nocentes ne perimant innocentes.[4] Nunc autem in articulo mortis positus sicut opto saluari, et per misericordiam Dei a reatibus meis absolui.' sic omnes mox iubeo carceres aperiri, omnesque uinctos preter fratrem meum Baiocensem episcopum relaxari.' liberosque pro amore Dei ut ipse michi misereatur dimitti. Nexi tamen tali tenore de carcere procedant ut antea iureiurando securitatem rei

[1] William's accession and coronation were in fact carried out with the minimum of formality and the support of Lanfranc. See A. Morey and C. N. L. Brooke, *Gilbert Foliot and his Letters* (Cambridge, 1965), p. 110 and n. 2. Of the earliest chroniclers Eadmer alone (*Historia Novorum* (RS), p. 25) suggests that Lanfranc showed some reluctance.

[2] See above, ii. 256–8.

precedence over you. Robert will have Normandy, and William, England. But you in your own time will have all the dominions that I have acquired and be greater than your brothers in wealth and power.' Having said this the king, fearing that rebellion might suddenly break out in a realm as far-flung as his, had a letter to secure the recognition of the new king addressed to Archbishop Lanfranc and sealed with his seal. Giving it to his son William Rufus, he ordered him to cross to England without delay.[1] Then he gave him his blessing with a kiss, and sent him post-haste overseas to receive the crown. He had barely reached the port of Wissant when he heard that his father had died. Henry for his part made haste to secure the money assigned to him, having it carefully weighed to make sure that nothing was withheld, secured the aid of the trustworthy companions he needed, and provided himself with a strong treasure-house.

Meanwhile the doctors and royal officials who were watching over the dying prince, and the magnates who had come to pay their respects to him, began to plead the cause of the prisoners whom he kept in captivity, and to beg him to pardon and release them. In reply he said, 'I have already kept the noble Earl Morcar a prisoner for many years, not for any just cause but for fear that if he were free he would stir up rebellion in England.[2] As for Roger of Breteuil, I flung him into prison and swore that he should never leave it as long as I lived, because he treacherously rebelled against me and carried with him his brother-in-law, Ralph of Gael, and many others.[3] In this way I have condemned many to captivity deservedly for their own disloyalty, and many others for fear of future treachery. Right custom requires, and the divine law given through Moses commands, earthly rulers to restrain evildoers so that they cannot injure the innocent.[4] But now that I am at the point of death, as I myself hope to be saved and by the mercy of God pardoned for my sins, I command all prisons to be opened immediately, and all prisoners released except my brother the bishop of Bayeux. I set them free for the love of God, so that God may have mercy on me. But before they leave prison they shall first enter into an obligation by taking an oath to the officials

[3] See above, ii. 318, where the translation should read 'as long as I live', not 'as long as he lives'.

[4] The reference here seems to be general; it could apply to several parts of Leviticus (e.g. chs. 24, 26).

publicæ ministris faciant.' quod pacem in Anglia et Normannia omnibus modis teneant et pacis aduersariis pro posse suo uiriliter resistant.'

Cumque Robertus Moritolii comes audisset regali sententia
iii. 246 fratrem suum perpetuo uinciri.' multum contristatus est. Herluinus quippe de Contauilla Herleuam Roberti ducis concubinam in coniugium acceperat.' ex qua duos filios Odonem et Robertum genuerat. Guillelmus autem dux et postea rex uitricum suum magnis et multis honoribus in Normannia et Anglia ditauerat, et filios eius Radulfum quem de alia coniuge[1] procreauerat, fratresque suos uterinos Odonem et Robertum maximis possessionibus sullimauerat. Nam postquam Guillelmum cognomento Werlengum Moritolii comitem filium Malgerii comitis pro minimis occasionibus de Neustria propulerat.' Roberto Herluini filio fratri suo comitatum Moritolii dederat.[2] Defuncto quoque Hugone Baiocensi episcopo Radulfi consulis[3] filio.' predictum presulatum concesserat Odoni fratri suo, quem postmodum in Anglia preposuit Cantiæ regno. Denique hunc pro nimietate sua ut superius pleniter relatum est,[4] rex Guillelmus in insula Vecta cepit, quattuor annis in carcere tenuit.' nec etiam in morte pro insolentia sua
iii. 247 relaxare uoluit. Vnde prefatus Moritolii comes admodum merebat.' et pro fratre suo per se et per amicos suos suppliciter interpellabat, precibusque languentem fatigabat.

Cumque multi obnixe pro Baiocensi presule rogarent.' tantorum suplicatione fatigatus rex ait, 'Miror quod prudenter non indagatis.' quis uel qualis est uir pro quo supplicatis. Nonne pro tali uiro petitis, qui iamdiu contemptor extitit religionis, et argutus incentor letiferæ seditionis? Nonne hunc iam cohercui quattuor annis episcopum, qui dum debuerat esse iustissimus rector Anglorum, factus est pessimus oppressor populorum, et monachilium destructor cenobiorum? Seditiosum liberando male facitis.' et uobismet ipsis ingens detrimentum queritis. Euidenter patet quod Odo frater meus leuis est et ambitiosus, carnis inherens desideriis et immensis crudelitatibus, et nunquam mutabitur a lenociniis et noxiis uanitatibus. Hoc perspicue in pluribus expertus sum.'

[1] Ralph was one of the two sons of Fredesendis, who was probably Herluin's second wife. He may be the Ralph of Conteville described in the Exon. Domesday as holding land in Somerset and Devon; he certainly occurs in charters of Grestain and Marmoutier (see Douglas, *Domesday Monachorum*, pp. 33–4).

[2] See above, ii. 312. For the origins of the county of Mortain and the forfeiture of William Werlenc see L. Musset, 'Compte rendu de la Semaine de

of the realm to preserve the peace in England and Normandy in every way, and to resist enemies of the peace stalwartly with all their might.'

When Robert count of Mortain heard that his brother was to suffer perpetual imprisonment by the royal decree, he was sad at heart. Herluin of Conteville had taken Duke Robert's concubine Herleve to wife, and had had two sons, Odo and Robert, by her. Duke William, afterwards king, had enriched his stepfather with many great honors in Normandy and England, and had lavished extensive estates on his sons. These were Ralph, his son by another wife,[1] and Odo and Robert, William's own half-brothers. After he had banished William Werlenc, count of Mortain and son of Count Mauger, from Normandy on some trivial pretexts, he gave the county of Mortain to his brother Robert, Herluin's son.[2] And after the death of Hugh bishop of Bayeux, son of Count Ralph,[3] he bestowed the bishopric of Bayeux on his brother Odo, whom he later made earl of Kent in England. But afterwards because of his excessive ambition, as I have already fully described,[4] King William took him into custody in the Isle of Wight, kept him in prison for four years, and even at the point of death refused to release him because of his presumption. Therefore the count of Mortain was deeply grieved, begged for mercy for his brother both in person and through his friends, and wearied the dying man with his entreaties.

When many persons had pressed the case of the bishop of Bayeux the king, exhausted by the importunities of so many, said, 'I am amazed that you do not appreciate what kind of man this is for whom you plead. Are you not interceding for a man who has long been an enemy of the church and a cunning instigator of treacherous rebellion? Have I not kept under restraint for four years this bishop who, when he should have been a most just viceroy in England, became the worst oppressor of the people and destroyer of monasteries? You are ill advised to free this traitor, and you are asking for serious trouble for yourselves. It is all too clear that my brother Odo is frivolous and ambitious, devoted both to delights of the flesh and to deeds of great cruelty, and he will never give up his vices and frivolities. I have discovered

Droit normand', in *Revue d'histoire de droit français et étranger*, xxix (1951), 150; J. Boussard, 'Le comté de Mortain', in *Le Moyen Âge*, lviii (1952), 258–68

[3] Ralph of Ivry, count of Bayeux. [4] See above, pp. 40–2.

ideoque constrinxi non antistitem sed tirannum.[1] Absque dubio si euaserit, totam regionem turbabit./ et multis milibus perniciem subministrabit. Hæc non ex odio ut hostis profero./ sed ut pater patriæ plebi christianæ prouideo. Si enim caste et modeste se haberet, sicut sacerdotem et Dei ministrum ubique condecet./ cordi meo maior quam referre possim læticia inesset.'

Spondentibus autem cunctis emendationem pontificis./ rex iterum ait, 'Velim nolim uestra fiet petitio./ quia me defuncto uehemens subito rerum fiet mutatio. Inuitus concedo ut frater meus de carcere liberetur./ sed scitote quod multis per eum mors
iii. 248 seu graue impedimentum incutietur. Baldrico autem Nicholai filio quia seruitium meum insipienter reliquit, et sine mea licentia in Hispaniam abiit./[2] totam terram suam pro castigatione abstuli, sed nunc illi reddo pro amore Dei. Illo melior in armis tiro reor non inuenitur, sed prodigus et leuis est ac per diuersa uagatur.' Sic Guillelmus rex licet nimio ilium dolore grauiter angeretur./ sana tamen mente ac uiuaci loquela efficaciter fruebatur, et in omnibus de negociis regni poscentibus promptum et utile consilium impertiebatur.

Denique quinto idus Septembris feria quinta, iam Phebo per orbem spargente clara radiorum spicula./ excitus rex sonum maioris signi audiuit in metropolitana basilica. Percunctante eo quid sonaret./ responderunt ministri, 'Domine, hora prima iam pulsatur in æcclesia sanctæ Mariæ.' Tunc rex cum summa deuotione oculos ad cœlum erexit, et sursum manibus extensis dixit, 'Dominæ meæ sanctæ Dei genitrici Mariæ me commendo./ ut ipsa suis sanctis precibus me reconciliet carissimo filio suo domino nostro Ihesu Christo.' Et his dictis protinus exspirauit.[3] Archiatri autem et ceteri coessentes qui regem sine gemitu et clamore quiescentem tota nocte seruauerunt, et nunc ex insperato sic eum mox migrasse
iii. 249 uiderunt./ uehementer attoniti et uelut amentes effecti sunt. Porro ditiores ex his ilico ascensis equis recesserunt./ ac ad sua tutanda properauerunt. Inferiores uero clientuli ut magistros

[1] Here Orderic goes even further in justifying the seizure of Odo than the 'non clericum nec antistitem . . . sed comitem meum' of his earlier account.

[2] He was in the king's service during the war in Maine in 1085 (above, p. 50 n. 4). He may have gone to Spain to take part in the fighting against the Almo-

this for certain on many occasions; I imprisoned not a bishop but a tyrant.[1] If he goes free, without doubt he will disturb the whole kingdom and bring thousands to destruction. I declare this not through hatred as an enemy, but as the father of my country providing for the welfare of my Christian subjects. If he could conduct himself chastely and modestly, as befits any priest or minister of God, my heart would be filled with a greater joy than I am able to express.'

But as all gave security for the future good conduct of the bishop, the king went on, 'Whether I will or no you will get your wish, for once I am dead there will be sudden and violent changes. Unwillingly I grant that my brother may be released from prison, but I warn you that he will be the cause of death and grievous harm to many. Also for the love of God I restore to Baudry son of Nicholas all his land, which I confiscated as a punishment, because he foolishly abandoned my service and went to Spain without my consent.[2] I do not think any knight can be found who fights better than he, but he is extravagant and capricious and given to wandering abroad.' So though King William suffered great internal agony he kept a clear mind and all his powers of speech, and gave sound and practical advice to all who consulted him about the affairs of the kingdom.

At last on Thursday, 9 September, the king awoke as the sun was beginning to shed its clear rays over the earth and heard the sound of the great bell in the cathedral church. When he asked what hour it was sounding, the attendants replied, 'My lord, the hour of prime is being rung in the church of St. Mary.' Then the king raised his eyes to heaven with deep devotion, and looking up with outstretched hands said, 'I commend myself to my Lady, the blessed Mary, mother of God, that by her holy prayers she may reconcile me to her most dear Son, our Lord Jesus Christ.' As soon as he had spoken these words he died.[3] The physicians and others present, who had watched the king as he slept all night without a sigh or groan, and now realized that he had died without warning, were utterly dumbfounded and almost out of their minds. But the wealthier among them quickly mounted horse and rode off as fast as they could to protect their properties. The lesser

ravides early in 1087, in which many foreigners, including some Normans, were involved.

[3] For Wace's use of this passage in Orderic see above, Introduction, pp. xxi–xxii.

suos sic manicasse perspexerunt.' arma uasa uestes et linteamina omnemque regiam suppellectilem[a] rapuerunt, et relicto regis cadauere pene nudo in area domus aufugerunt. Cernite precor omnes.' qualis est mundana fides. Vnusquisque quod potuit, de apparatu regio ut miluus rapuit.' et confestim cum preda sua aufugit. Impietas itaque iusticiario labente impudenter prodiit.' et rapacitatem circa ipsum ultorem rapinæ primitus exercuit.

Fama de morte regis pernicibus alis uolauit.' et longe lateque gaudium seu merorem audientium cordibus infudit. Nam mors Guillelmi regis ipso eodem die quo Rotomagi defunctus est in urbe Roma et in Calabria quibusdam exheredatis nunciata est.' ut ab ipsis postmodum ueraciter nobis in Normannia relatum est. Malignus quippe spiritus oppido tripudiauit.' dum clientes suos qui rapere et clepere uehementer inhiabant per occasum iudicis absolutos uidit.

O secularis pompa quam despicabilis es.' quia nimis uana et labilis es. Recte pluuialibus bullis equanda diceris, quæ in momento ualde turgida erigeris, subitoque in nichilum redigeris. Ecce potentissimus heros cui nuper plus quam centum milia militum[1] auide seruiebant, et quem multæ gentes cum tremore metuebant, nunc a suis turpiter in domo non sua spoliatus est.' et a prima usque ad terciam supra nudam humum derelictus est. Ciues enim audito Rotomagenses lapsu principis ualde territi sunt.' et pene
iii. 250 omnes uelut ebrii desipuerunt, et palam ac si multitudinem hostium imminere urbi uidissent turbati sunt. Vnusquisque de loco ubi erat recessit.' et quid ageret a coniuge uel obuio sodali uel amico consilium quesiuit. Res suas quisque aut transmutauit, aut transmutare decreuit.' pauidusque ne inuenirentur abscondit.

Religiosi tandem uiri clerici et monachi collectis uiribus et intimis sensibus processionem ordinauerunt, honeste induti cum crucibus et thuribulis ad sanctum Geruasium processerunt.' et animam regis secundum morem sanctæ Christianitatis Deo commendauerunt. Tunc Guillelmus archiepiscopus iussit ut corpus eius Cadomum deferretur.' ibique in basilica sancti Stephani prothomartiris quam ipse condiderat tumularetur. Verum fratres eius et cognati iam ab eo recesserunt, et omnes ministri eius eum ut barbarum nequiter deseruerunt. Vnde nec unus de regiis

[a] suppectilem, *Caen MS.*; suppellectilem, *MS. Vespasian A xix*

---

[1] A rhetorical exaggeration.

attendants, seeing that their superiors had absconded, seized the arms, vessels, clothing, linen, and all the royal furnishings, and hurried away leaving the king's body almost naked on the floor of the house. Behold, I beg you all, of what earthly loyalty is made. Each one of them, like a bird of prey, seized what he could of the royal trappings and made off at once with the booty. So when the just ruler fell lawlessness broke loose, and first showed itself in the plunder of him who had been the avenger of plunder.

News of the king's death flew swiftly far and wide, bringing joy or sorrow to the recipients. King William's death was revealed to certain exiles in the city of Rome and in Calabria on the very day he died at Rouen, and later we heard this for a fact from their own lips in Normandy. Then the evil spirit rejoiced greatly, seeing that his followers whose whole aim is to plunder and steal were left free by the death of the just judge.

O worldly pomp, how despicable you are, how utterly vain and fleeting! It is right to compare you to watery bubbles, one moment all swollen up, then suddenly reduced to nothing. See how that most mighty lord, who once commanded the eager service of more than a hundred thousand[1] men-at-arms, who was feared and dreaded by many peoples, is now shamefully despoiled by his own followers in another's house, and abandoned on the bare ground from the hour of prime to that of terce. When the citizens of Rouen heard of the loss of their duke terror seized them; almost all acted like drunken men and appeared as confused as though they had seen an enemy horde threatening the city. Everyone rushed hither and thither to ask his wife or some passing acquaintance or friend what he ought to do. Each individual either moved or planned to move his goods, hiding them to keep them safe from discovery.

At length the religious, both canons and monks, mustering their courage and coming to their senses, formed a procession and, clad in vestments with crosses and censers, moved to St. Gervase, where they commended the king's soul to God according to Christian rites. Then Archbishop William decreed that the body should be taken to Caen and buried there in the church of St. Stephen the first martyr, which the king himself had founded. By then his brothers and kinsfolk had left him, and all his servants had shamefully abandoned him as if he had been a barbarian. So not one of the royal dependants could be found to prepare his

satellitibus est inuentus.' qui curaret de exequiis corporis ipsius. Tunc Herluinus quidam pagensis eques naturali bonitate compunctus est.' et curam exequiarum pro amore Dei et honore gentis suæ uiriliter amplexatus est. Pollinctores itaque et uispilliones ac uehiculum mercede de propriis sumptibus conduxit.' cadauer regis ad portum Sequanæ deuexit, impositumque naui usque Cadomum per aquam et aridam perduxit.

Tunc domnus Gislebertus abbas cum conuentu monachorum ueneranter obuiam feretro processit, quibus flens et orans multi-
iii. 251 tudo clericorum et laicorum adhesit.' sed mox sinistra fortuna omnibus pariter maximum terrorem propinauit. Nam enorme incendium de quadam domo protinus erupit, et immensos flammarum globos eructauit.' magnamque partem Cadomensis burgi damnose inuasit. Omnes igitur ad ignem comprimendum clerici cum laicis cucurrerunt.' soli uero monachi ceptum officium compleuerunt, et soma regis ad cenobialem basilicam psallentes perduxerunt.

Denique ad sepeliendum maximum ducem et patrem patriæ.' congregati sunt omnes episcopi et abbates Normanniæ, ex quibus ad notitiam posteriorum libet quosdam nominare.' et presenti breuiter in pagina denotare. Guillelmus Rotomagensis archiepiscopus, Odo Baiocensis episcopus, Gislebertus Ebroicensis, Gislebertus Maminotus Lexouiensis, Michahel Abrincatensis, Goisfredus Constantiniensis et Girardus Sagiensis. Abbates quoque hi sunt, Anselmus Beccensis, Guillelmus de Ros Fiscannensis, Gerbertus Fontinellensis, Guntardus Gemmeticensis, Mainerius Vticensis, Fulco Diuensis, Durandus Troarnensis, Robertus Sagiensis, Osbernus Bernaicensis, Rogerius de Monte Sancti Michahelis in periculo maris, Rotomagenses archimandritæ Nicholaus de sancto Audoeno, et Gaulterius de Monte Sanctæ Trinitatis, et alii plures quos nominatim proferre perlongum est. Omnes hi ad exequias famosi baronis conuenerunt.' ipsumque in presbiterio inter chorum et altare sepelierunt.

Expleta missa cum iam sarcofagum in terra locatum esset, sed
iii. 252 corpus adhuc in feretro iaceret.' magnus Gislebertus Ebroicensis episcopus in pulpitum ascendit, et prolixam locutionem de magnificentia defuncti principis eloquenter protelauit, quod ipse fines Normannici iuris strenue dilatauerit, gentemque suam plus quam omnes antecessores sui sullimauerit, iusticiam et pacem sub omni ditione sua tenuerit, fures et predones uirga rectitudinis utiliter castigauerit.' et clericos ac monachos et inermem populum

body for burial. At last a certain country knight called Herluin was moved by natural goodness, and actively took charge of the funeral preparations for the love of God and honour of his race. He brought persons to lay out the corpse and bearers and a conveyance, paid for them out of his own resources, transported the king's body to the port on the Seine and, placing it on a boat, took it by water and land to Caen.

Then Dom Gilbert the abbot came out reverently in procession with all his monks to meet the bier, and with them came a great multitude of clergy and laity, weeping and praying. But soon a terrible disaster caused general panic. A raging fire suddenly broke out in one of the houses, sending up great balls of flame, and spread destruction through the greater part of the town of Caen. All, therefore, clergy and laity alike, rushed to put out the fire; the monks alone completed the half-finished office and, chanting psalms, escorted the king's body to the abbey church.

There at last all the bishops and abbots of Normandy were assembled for the funeral of the great leader and father of his country. For the information of later generations I will name some of them in a brief list here: William archbishop of Rouen; Odo bishop of Bayeux; Gilbert of Évreux, Gilbert Maminot of Lisieux, Michael of Avranches, Geoffrey of Coutances, and Gerard of Séez. The abbots were Anselm of Bec; William of Rots of Fécamp; Gerbert of Saint-Wandrille; Gontard of Jumièges; Mainer of Saint-Évroul; Fulk of Dives; Durand of Troarn; Robert of Séez; Osbern of Bernay; Roger of Mont Saint-Michel in peril of the sea; the abbots of Rouen, Nicholas of Saint-Ouen and Walter of La Trinité-du-Mont; and many others whom it would be tedious to enumerate. All these assembled for the obsequies of the famous lord, and buried him in the sanctuary between the choir and the altar.

When the Mass had been completed and the coffin had been lowered into the earth, but the body still lay on the bier, Gilbert, the famous bishop of Évreux, mounted into the pulpit and preached a long and eloquent sermon on the great eminence of the dead duke, telling how he had valiantly extended the frontiers where Norman law prevailed; how, more than all his ancestors, he had brought greatness to his people; how he had maintained justice and kept the peace in all his dominions, had effectively chastened thieves and robbers with the rod of law, and bravely protected clerks and monks and the defenceless populace with his strong

uirtutis ense fortiter munierit. Finita uero locutione plebem rogauit, et pro pietate multis flentibus ac uerba eius attestantibus adiecit, 'Quia nullus homo mortalis potest in hac uita sine peccato uiuere, in caritate Dei uos omnes precamur pro defuncto principe: ut propter illum apud omnipotentem Deum studeatis intercedere, eique si quid in uobis deliquit benigniter dimittere.'

Tunc Ascelinus Arturi filius de turba surrexit, et uoce magna querimoniam huiuscemodi cunctis audientibus edidit, 'Hæc terra ubi consistitis area domus patris mei fuit: quam uir iste pro quo rogatis dum adhuc esset comes Normanniæ patri meo uiolenter abstulit, omnique denegata rectitudine istam edem potenter fundauit.[1] Hanc igitur terram calumnior et palam reclamo: et ne corpus raptoris operiatur cespite meo, nec in hereditate mea sepeliatur ex parte Dei prohibeo.'

Hoc ut episcopi et proceres alii audierunt, et uicinos eius qui eundem uera dixisse contestabantur intellexerunt, hominem ac-
iii. 253 cersierunt, omnique remota uiolentia precibus blandis lenierunt:
et pacem cum eo fecerunt. Nam pro loculo solius sepulturæ lx solidos ei protinus adhibuerunt. Pro reliqua uero tellure quam calumniabatur equipollens mutuum eidem promiserunt:[2] et post non multum temporis pro salute specialis eri quem diligebant
iii. 254 pactum compleuerunt. Porro dum corpus in sarcofagum mittere-
tur, et uiolenter quia uas per imprudentiam cementariorum breue et strictum erat complicaretur: pinguissimus uenter crepuit, et intolerabilis fœtor circum astantes personas et reliquum uulgus impleuit, fumus thuris aliorumque aromatum de thuribulis copiose ascendebat: sed teterrimum pudorem excludere non preualebat. Sacerdotes itaque festinabant exequias perficere: et actutum sua cum pauore mappalia repetere.

Ecce subtiliter inuestigaui, et ueraciter enucleaui quæ in lapsu ducis pie ostendit dispositio Dei. Non fictilem tragediam uenundo, non loquaci comedia cachinnantibus parasitis faueo: sed studiosis lectoribus uarios euentus ueraciter intimo. Inter prospera[a] patuerunt aduersa, ut terrerentur terrigenarum corda. Rex quondam potens et bellicosus, multisque populis per plures prouincias

[a] prosperas, *Caen MS.*

[1] The truth of Orderic's account is well attested. There is documentary evidence for the existence of houses on the site where the abbey was built, for the acquisition of land from Arthur, and for the renunciation by Ascelin's son Ralph of his right to the land 'intra ecclesiam et circa'. See Musset, *Abbayes caennaises*, pp. 45–6.

[2] Wace (*Roman de Rou*, ii, l. 9359) also states that he was given sixty shillings for the place of burial; possibly he took the figure from Orderic. William of Malmesbury's figure, £100 (*GR* ii. 337), is obviously an exaggeration.

sword. When he had ended his oration he made a request to the people, saying to the multitude who wept out of respect and listened attentively, 'Since no mortal man can live all his life without sin, I beg you all for the love of God to intercede with almighty God for the dead duke, and if he has ever done you any wrong to forgive him freely.'

Then Ascelin son of Arthur came forward from the crowd, and made this complaint in a loud voice, in the hearing of all, 'This ground where you stand was the site of my father's house, which this man for whom you intercede, when he was still only duke of Normandy, violently took away from my father; refusing him all redress he founded this church in the fullness of his power.[1] Therefore I lay claim to this land, and openly demand it, forbidding in God's name that the body of this robber be covered by earth that is mine or buried in my inheritance.'

When the bishops and other magnates heard these words and learnt from the testimony of neighbours that he had spoken the truth they had the man brought to them, and far from treating him roughly appeased him with gentle words and made peace with him. For the place of burial alone they offered him sixty shillings on the spot, and for the rest of the land that he claimed they promised a sum of equivalent value.[2] Shortly afterwards they fulfilled their bargain out of concern for the salvation of the great lord whom they loved. Next, when the corpse was placed in the sarcophagus, and was forcibly doubled up because the masons had carelessly made the coffin too short and narrow, the swollen bowels burst, and an intolerable stench assailed the nostrils of the bystanders and the whole crowd. A thick smoke arose from the frankincense and other spices in the censers, but it was not strong enough to conceal the foul ignominy. So the priests made haste to conclude the funeral rites, and immediately returned, trembling, to their own houses.

See now, I have carefully investigated and truthfully described what God's ordinance providently revealed in the duke's last days. I neither compose a fictitious tragedy for the sake of gain, nor entertain cackling parasites with a wordy comedy, but truly record events of different kinds for studious readers. Adversity showed itself in the midst of prosperity, so that the hearts of mortal men might be chastened. A king, once powerful and warlike, feared by many peoples in various lands, lay naked on the

metuendus in area iacuit nudus, et a suis quos genuerat uel aluerat destitutus. Ære alieno in funebrio cultu indiguit.' ope gregarii pro
iii. 255 sandapila et uispillionibus conducendis eguit, qui tot hactenus et superfluis operibus nimis abundauit. Secus incendium a formidolosis uectus est ad basilicam.' liberoque solo qui tot urbibus et oppidis et uicis principatus est caruit ad sepulturam. Aruina uentris eius tot delectamentis enutrita cum dedecore patuit.' et prudentes ac infrunitos qualis sit gloria carnis edocuit. Inspecta siquidem corruptione cenosi cadaueris quisque monetur.' ut meliora quam delectamenta sunt carnis quæ terra est et in puluerem reuertetur, labore salutaris continentiæ mercari feruenter conetur.

Diuitis et pauperis par est conditio, et similiter ambos inuadit mors et putredo. Nolite ergo confidere in principibus falsis O filii hominum.' sed in Deo uiuo et uero qui creator est omnium.[1] Veteris et noui testamenti seriem reuoluite, et exempla inde multiplicia uobis capessite.' quid cauere quidue debeatis appetere. Nolite sperare in iniquitate, et rapinas nolite concupiscere. Diuitiæ si affluant.' nolite cor apponere.[2] Omnis enim caro ut fœnum.' et omnis gloria eius ut flos fœni. Exaruit fœnum et flos eius decidit.' uerbum autem Domini manet in æternum.[3]

Hic septimo[4] libro Vticensis historiæ placet cum fine regis terminum dare.' et in octauo de filiis eius et multimoda perturbatione quæ diu Neustriam uehementer et Angliam afflixit aliquid uolo posteris enodare.

[1] Psalm cxlvi (cxlv), 3–6.
[2] Psalm lxii. 10 (lxi. 11).
[3] Cf. Isaiah xl. 6.
[4] The transcript gives no indication whether this was the original or the revised numbering of books.

ground, abandoned by those who owed their birth and position to him. He who until that time had enjoyed the possession of unlimited wealth now needed borrowed money for his funeral rites, and was dependent on the resources of a common man to procure a bier and bearers. He was carried to the church through a conflagration by terrified attendants, and he who had ruled over so many towns and castles and villages lacked a plot of free earth for his own burial. His bowels, nourished with so many delicacies, shamefully burst, revealing to wise and foolish alike how vain is the glory of the flesh. All who beheld the corruption of that foul corpse learnt to strive earnestly through the salutary discipline of abstinence to earn better rewards than the delights of the flesh, which is earth, and will return to dust.

Rich and poor are of the same nature; both alike fall victims to death and decay. Therefore put not your trust in false princes, O sons of men, but in the true and living God who is the creator of all things.[1] Meditate on the books of the Old and New Testaments, and from them heap up examples to teach you what to shun and what to pursue. Trust not in oppression and become not vain in robbery. If riches increase, set not your heart upon them.[2] For all flesh is grass, and all the goodliness thereof is as the flower of grass. The grass withers and the flower thereof falls, but the word of the Lord shall stand for ever.[3]

Here, with the king's death, it is fitting to conclude the seventh book[4] of the history of Saint-Évroul. In the eighth I propose to unfold for posterity an account of his sons and of the various disorders which shook Normandy and England terribly for many years.

BOOK VIII

I

iii. 256 ANNO ab incarnatione Domini millesimo octogesimo septimo, indictione decima, Guillelmus nothus rex Anglorum quinto idus Septembris Rotomagi defunctus est.' et corpus eius in æcclesia sancti Stephani prothomartiris Cadomi sepultum est. Robertus autem filius eius Normannorum dux et Cenomannorum princeps nomine tenus multis annis factus est.' sed torpori et ignauiæ subactus nunquam ut decuit in uirtute et iusticia principatus est. Guillelmus Rufus epistolam patris sui Lanfranco archiepiscopo detulit.' qua perlecta idem presul cum eodem iuuene Lundoniam properauit, ipsumque ad festiuitatem sancti Michahelis archangeli in ueteri basilica sancti Petri apostoli quæ Westmonasterium dicitur regem consecrauit.[1] Hic xii annis et decem mensibus regnauit.' patremque suum in quibusdam secundum seculum imitari studuit. Nam militari probitate et seculari dapsilitate uiguit, et superbiæ libidinique aliisque uiciis nimium subiacuit, sed erga Deum et æcclesiæ frequentationem cultumque frigidus extitit.

Hic auri et argenti gemmarumque copiam Othoni aurifabro[2]
iii. 257 erogauit.' et super patris sui mausoleum fieri mirificum memoriale precepit. Ille uero regiis iussis parens insigne opus condidit.' quod ex auro et argento et gemmis usque hodie competenter splendescit.[3] Egregii uersificatores de tali uiro unde tam copiosum tema uersificandi repererunt.' multa concinna et preclara poemata protulerunt, sed solius Thome archiepiscopi Eboracensis uersus huiusmodi pro dignitate metropolitana ex auro inserti sunt.

Qui rexit rigidos Normannos, atque Britannos
Audacter uicit[a] fortiter optinuit,
Et Cenomannenses uirtute cohercuit enses,
Imperiique sui legibus applicuit,
Rex magnus parua iacet hac Guillelmus in urna[b]
Sufficit et magno parua domus domino.

[a] Armis deuicit, *De obitu Willelmi* [b] parua hac tumulatur in urna, *De obitu Willelmi*

---

[1] See above, p. 96 n. 1.

[2] Otto the goldsmith held the manor of Gestingthorpe (Essex) and other

BOOK VIII

I

In the year of our Lord 1087, the tenth indiction, William the Bastard, king of the English, died at Rouen on 9 September and his body was buried at Caen in the church of St. Stephen the first martyr. Robert his son became duke of Normandy and count of Maine in name for many years, but he was so idle and frivolous that he never governed justly and effectively as he ought to have done. William Rufus took his father's letter to Archbishop Lanfranc; after reading it the archbishop hurried to London with the young man and anointed him king on the feast of St. Michael the archangel in the old church of St. Peter the Apostle called Westminster.[1] William reigned for twelve years and ten months and endeavoured to imitate his father in some matters of a secular nature. He was a man of military valour and worldly magnificence, though far too prone to pride, lust, and other vices; but he remained indifferent to God and attendance at church and divine worship.

He provided a generous supply of gold and silver and precious stones for Otto the goldsmith,[2] instructing him to erect a tomb over his father as a splendid memorial. Otto obeyed the king's orders, and completed a noble tomb, which to this day shines with gold and silver and precious stones in handsome style.[3] Distinguished poets proffered many rhymes and notable poems about this great man, who provided such a rich theme for poetry; but these verses of Thomas archbishop of York, chosen because of his metropolitan dignity, were the only ones to be inscribed there in gold.

He governed the proud Normans; his firm hand
Constrained the Bretons conquered by his sword;
The men of Maine were beaten to submission,
Kept in obedience to his rule and right;
William, great king, lies in this little urn,
So small a house serves for a mighty lord.

properties in Domesday Book (*DB* ii. 97–8). He and his descendants were hereditary masters of the mint (*VCH Essex*, i. 350–1).

[3] The author of the *De obitu Willelmi* (Marx, p. 148) describes it in the words 'arca argentea deaurata super tumulum ejus'.

Per[a] septem gradibus se uoluerat atque duobus
Virginis in gremiis Phebus et hic obiit.[1]

Eodem anno multi Normannorum nobiles regi suo morte comi-
tati sunt. Nam dum rex adhuc egrotaret, cognatus eiusdem Gul-
iii. 258 bertus Alfagiensis filius Ricardi de Hugleuilla[2] uir bonus et simplex
xix kal' Septembris defunctus est.' et in æcclesia sanctæ Mariæ ubi
sex monachos ex Vticensi cenobio constituerat[3] sepultus est. Ibi
etiam post quatuor annos religiosa mulier Beatrix uxor eius ii^{o}
nonas Ianuarii tumulata est.[4] Moriente duce suo Normanni multas
lacrimas fuderunt.' et si non pro illo saltem pro amicis et cognatis
suis qui tunc mortui sunt. Simon de Monteforti gener Ricardi
iii. 259 comitis Ebroicensium,[5] et Guillelmus Paganellus,[6] Hugo quoque
iii. 260 iuuenis strenuissimus Hugonis de Grentemaisnil filius,[7] et cognatus eius Robertus de Rodelento[8] atque Guillelmus de Abrincis
iii. 261 filius Witmundi[9] aliique illustres uiri obierunt. Beati qui bene
mortui sunt.' qui erumnas desolatæ regionis ac defensore carentis
non uiderunt.

Tunc in Normannia subito facta est nimia rerum mutatio.'
gelidusque timor inermi inhesit populo, et potentibus importune
flagrans ambitio. Robertus de Bellisma festinabat ad curiam regis
colloqui cum illo de rebus necessariis. Perueniens ad introitum
Brionnæ, audiuit regem mortuum esse. Qui mox cornipede re-
girato Alentionem uenit.' et improuisos regis satellites statim de
iii. 262 pretorio eiecit. Hoc quoque fecit Bellismæ et in omnibus aliis
castellis suis.' et non solum suis sed et in uicinorum suorum quos

[a] *Sic in Caen MS.*; *possibly an error for* Ter

[1] In the *De obitu Willelmi* (Marx, p. 148) the seventh line is completely different: 'Addiderat septem ter quinis Scorpius, unam / Virginis . . .' There are obscurities in both versions. The belt of the Zodiac was divided into twelve signs of 30 degrees, each degree corresponding very nearly to a day. The sun was thought to enter the sign of Virgo on 23 or 24 August, and 9 September fell on the sixteenth or seventeenth day. The version copied in the Caen MS. is plainly garbled; by substituting 'ter' for 'per' it can be made to construe, but the calculation (twenty-three days) is wrong. Marx (p. 148 n. 1) made the ingenious suggestion that the first part of the line in the *De obitu* might refer to William's birth, giving a date in mid November; and that in the second part the repetition of certain words must be understood, 'unam [addiderat ter quinis] Virginis in gremiis Phebus', which would mean that William died on the sixteenth day of Virgo's sign. I cannot improve on this.

[2] For Gilbert of Auffay and his family see above, iii. 250–60. The date of his death is there given as 15 August.

[3] See above, iii. 246 ff. for the founding of the priory of Auffay.

The sun had travelled twenty-three degrees
In the Virgin's sign when last he saw the light.[1]

Many Norman lords died in the year of the king's death. Whilst the king was lying sick his kinsman, Gilbert of Auffay the son of Richard of Heugleville,[2] who was a good, single-hearted man, died on 14 August. He was buried in the church of St. Mary, where he had established six monks from Saint-Évroul.[3] Four years later his pious wife Beatrice was also buried there on 4 January.[4] The Normans shed copious tears when their duke died, if not for him then at least for their friends and kinsmen who died about the same time. Simon of Montfort, the son-in-law of Richard count of Évreux,[5] and William Paynel;[6] also young Hugh, the valiant son of Hugh of Grandmesnil,[7] and his kinsman Robert of Rhuddlan,[8] and William of Avranches son of Wimund[9] and many other famous men died. Blessed are they who made a good end and did not see the sorrows of the unhappy land which was deprived of its defender.

At that time a great revolution suddenly took place in Normandy; cold fear gripped the helpless people while unbridled ambition consumed the mighty. Robert of Bellême was hastening to the king's court to speak with him on important matters when, coming to the gates of Brionne, he heard that the king was dead. Instantly wheeling round his horse he galloped to Alençon, caught the king's men off their guard, and drove them out of the stronghold. He did the same at Bellême and in all his other castles; and not only in his own but in those of his neighbours also, for he would not

[4] Cf. above, iii. 256. Orderic there said that she died three years after her husband; probably therefore the date was 4 January 1091, in the fourth year of her widowhood.

[5] Simon of Montfort married as his third wife Agnes, daughter of Richard count of Évreux (above, iii. 128; GEC vii. 710–11).

[6] William Paynel was probably lord of Moutiers-Hubert. His son Ralph held extensive English lands in 1086. His grandson William married a daughter of William son of Wimund (*EYC* vi. 1–6, 97–8; Loyd, p. 77).

[7] Hugh died young and was buried at Saint-Évroul (see below, p. 338).

[8] Robert of Rhuddlan was the son of Humphrey of Tilleul and Adelina of Grandmesnil; see above, Introduction, pp. xxxiv–xxxviii, and below, pp. 136–42.

[9] William of Avranches was a son of Wimund, lord of La Haye-Pesnel. He married a daughter of Baldwin of Meules, sheriff of Devon (*DB* iv. 272). His son was Robert of Avranches and his granddaughter, Matilda, acquired a share in the honor of Le Sap (*EYC* vi. 97–8; GEC xi. 108–9; Sanders, p. 69). The family is not to be confused with that of William of Avranches, lord of Folkestone, or that of Hugh of Avranches, earl of Chester.

sibi pares dedignabatur habere municipiis.' quæ aut intromissis clientibus suis sibi subiugauit, aut penitus ne sibi aliquando resistere possent destruxit. Guillelmus etiam comes Ebroicensis de dangione regios expulit excubitores, et Guillelmus de Britolio ac Radulfus de Conchis aliique omnes in sua ditione redegerunt munitiones, ut unusquisque libere posset contra uicinum suum et collimitaneum exercere inimicicias damnabiles.[1] Sic proceres Neustriæ de munitionibus suis omnes regis custodes expulerunt.' patriamque diuitiis opulentam propriis uiribus uicissim exspoliauerunt. Opes itaque quas Anglis aliisque gentibus uiolenter rapuerunt.' merito latrociniis et rapinis perdiderunt.

Omnes ducem Robertum mollem esse desidemque cognoscebant, et iccirco facinorosi eum despiciebant, et pro libitu suo dolosas factiones agitabant. Erat quippe idem dux audax et ualidus, militiæque laude dignus.' eloquio facundus, sed in regimine sui suorumque inconsideratus. In erogando prodigus, in promittendo diffusus, ad mentiendum leuis et incautus. Misericors supplicibus, ac ad iusticiam super iniquos faciendam mollis et mansuetus, in definitione mutabilis, in conuersatione omnibus nimis blandus et tractabilis.' ideoque peruersis et insipientibus despicabilis. Corpore autem breuis et grossus.' ideoque 'breuis ocrea' est a patre cognominatus.[2] Ipse cunctis placere studebat, cunctisque quod petebant aut dabat aut promittebat uel concedebat. Prodigus dominium
iii. 263 patrum suorum cotidie imminuebat insipienter tribuens unicuique quod petebat, et ipse pauperescebat, unde alios contra se roborabat. Guillelmo de Britolio dedit Ibericum ubi arx quam Albereda proauia eius[3] fecit fortissima est.' et Rogerio de Bellomonte qui solebat Ibericum iussu Guillelmi regis custodire concessit Brionnam quod oppidum munitissimum et in corde terræ situm est.[4]

Odo Baiocensis episcopus postquam de carcere liber egressus est.' totum in Normannia pristinum honorem adeptus est, et consiliarius ducis uidelicet nepotis sui factus est. Erat enim eloquens et magnanimus, dapsilis et secundum seculum ualde strenuus. Religiosos homines diligenter honorabat.' clerum suum

[1] Orderic's account shows the speed with which the greater Norman barons reacted against William the Conqueror's attempt to keep the principal castles of the duchy in his own control, under royal officers. See J. Yver, 'Les châteaux forts en Normandie', in *BSAN* liii (1955–6), 62–5.

[2] Cf. above, ii. 356.

[3] Aubrée, wife of Ralph of Ivry, Richard I's half-brother.

[4] It is very likely that Roger of Beaumont then received the castle of Brionne as a fief; this represented a complete break with the policy of the Conqueror. Cf. J. Yver in *BSAN* liii (1955–6), 67.

suffer any man to be his equal. Either he effected an entry for his own men and gained control over the castles, or he razed them to the ground so that they could offer no resistance to him. In like manner William count of Évreux drove the king's watchmen out of the keep, and William of Breteuil and Ralph of Conches and others gained control of all the castles in their domains, so that each man could practise abominable acts of hostility against the neighbour whose lands adjoined his.[1] So the magnates of Normandy expelled the king's garrisons from their castles and, plundering each other's lands with their own men-at-arms, they stripped the rich country of its wealth. They justly lost by robbery and violence all the riches which they had taken as plunder from the English and other peoples.

All men knew that Duke Robert was weak and indolent; therefore trouble-makers despised him and stirred up loathsome factions when and where they chose. For although the duke was bold and daring, praiseworthy for his knightly prowess and eloquent in speech, he exercised no discipline over either himself or his men. He was prodigal in distributing his bounty and lavish in his promises, but so thoughtless and inconstant that they were utterly unreliable. Being merciful to suppliants he was too weak and pliable to pass judgement on wrongdoers; unable to pursue any plan consistently he was far too affable and obliging in all his relationships, and so he earned the contempt of corrupt and foolish men. Since he was short in stature and stout he was nicknamed 'Curthose' by his father.[2] Through his wish to please all men he either gave or promised or granted whatever anyone asked. He diminished his inheritance daily by his foolish prodigality, giving away to everyone whatever was sought; and as he impoverished himself he strengthened the hands of others against him. To William of Breteuil he gave Ivry, where the almost impregnable fortress built by his great-grandmother Aubrée[3] stands; and to Roger of Beaumont who had been appointed castellan of Ivry by King William he granted Brionne, a well-fortified castle in the heart of the duchy.[4]

After Odo bishop of Bayeux was released from prison he recovered the whole of his former honor in Normandy, and became a close counsellor of his nephew, the duke. He was a man of eloquence and statesmanship, bountiful and most active in worldly business. He held men of religion in great respect, readily

acriter ense et uerbo defendebat, æcclesiamque preciosis ornamentis copiose per omnia decorabat. Hoc attestantur edificia quæ construxit.' et insignia ex auro et argento uasa et indumenta quibus basilicam uel clerum ornauit. In adolescentia pro germanitate ducis datus est ei Baiocensis presulatus.' in quo plus quam quinquaginta annis pollens diuersa est operatus.[1] In quibusdam spiritus ei laudabiliter dominabatur, in nonnullis uero spiritui caro
iii. 264 miserabiliter principabatur. Carnali ergo ardore stimulatus genuit filium nomine Iohannem.' quem nunc in curia Henrici regis uidemus eloquentia magnaque probitate pollentem.[2]

Sed quamuis in quibusdam prefatum Odonem secularis detinuisset leuitas.' multum tamen exterius ipse res emendauit æcclesiasticas. Æcclesiam sanctæ Dei genitricis Mariæ a fundamentis cepit.' eleganter consummauit, multisque gazis et ornatibus affatim ditauit. Ad æcclesiam sancti Vigoris episcopi Baiocensis quæ sita est extra murum urbis monachos posuit,[3] eisque religiosum et sapientem Robertum de Tumbalenia patrem preposuit. Qui inter reliqua peritiæ suæ monumenta.' breuem et luculentam sensuque profundam super Cantica Canticorum expositionem dimisit in æcclesia.[4] Verum postquam prefatus pontifex ut predictum est clausus fuit in carcere.' predictus abbas relictis omnibus perrexit peregre.' ueniensque Romam a Gregorio septimo papa detentus honorifice, usque ad mortem Romanæ fideliter seruiuit æcclesiæ. Fundatore itaque episcopo uinculis mancipato et abbate
iii. 265 in Latias partes abeunte nouicius grex monachorum dispersus est.' et quesitis prout quisque potuit sedibus ad idem cenobium nunquam reuersus est.

[1] Odo became bishop of Bayeux between October 1049 and 23 April 1050 (V. Bourrienne, *Antiquus cartularius ecclesie Baiocensis* (Soc. Hist. Norm., Rouen, 1902–3), i. 6–8); the date of his birth is uncertain. In his interpolations in William of Jumièges (Marx, p. 157) Orderic stated that his mother Herleve married Herluin of Conteville after the death of Duke Robert on pilgrimage to the Holy Land in 1035; if so Odo was probably born in 1036. Douglas (*WC*, pp. 381–2, and *Domesday Monachorum*, p. 33) has questioned the date on the ground that if he had become a bishop at the age of fourteen his promotion would have aroused comment; but in 1050 this would not necessarily have been thought scandalous. William of Malmesbury (*GR* ii. 333–4) said that Herleve's marriage took place before Duke Robert's death; if this is true Odo might have been slightly older. He held the see for not more than forty-eight years.

[2] John of Bayeux, chaplain, attested many charters of Henry I between 1104 and 1131, including one which settled a tithe dispute between the bishop of Évreux and the monks of Saint-Évroul in 1131, very shortly before Orderic wrote this passage (*CDF*, no. 287). Both Haskins (*Norman Institutions*, pp. 294,

defended his clergy by words and arms, and enriched his church in every way with gifts of precious ornaments. There is evidence of this in the buildings that he raised and the furnishings—gold and silver vessels and precious vestments—which he lavished on cathedral and clergy. As a young man he was given the bishopric of Bayeux because he was the king's brother; and he did both good and evil during the fifty years and more that he ruled over the see.[1] Sometimes the spirit triumphed in him to good ends, but on other occasions the flesh overcame the spirit with evil consequences. Yielding to the weakness of the flesh he had a son named John, who may now be found in the court of King Henry and is renowned there for his ready speech and great integrity.[2]

But although in some things Bishop Odo was a slave to worldly trivialities, externally he brought about many improvements in the church's welfare. He began to build the church of St. Mary the mother of God and completed it in a handsome style, enriching it with great wealth and treasures. He placed monks in the church of St. Vigor, bishop of Bayeux, which is outside the walls of the town,[3] and appointed as their superior Robert of Tombelaine, a learned and pious man. Among other evidences of his skill Robert left for the church a short, lucid, and profound commentary on the Song of Songs.[4] But after Bishop Odo was imprisoned, as described above, Abbot Robert gave up everything and went into exile to Rome, where he was given an honourable welcome by Pope Gregory VII and remained to serve the Roman church to the end of his life. Since the founding bishop lay in fetters and the abbot had gone away to Italy, the newly-established community was dispersed. The monks scattered as best they might to other monasteries, never to return to that house.

296) and Round (*CDF*, nos. 287, 792, 793, 795) identify him in the Index as Odo's son, and I am in agreement with them; the editors of the *Regesta* unaccountably call him 'probably the son of Richard, bishop of Bayeux 1107–33' (*Regesta*, ii, p. x). Orderic later says (Le Prévost, iv. 482) that Odo's son John brought the news of William Clito's death to Henry I.

[3] For the refoundation of Saint-Vigor see J. Yver in *BSAN* lvii (1963–4), 216 n. 6; Abbé Faucon, *Essai historique sur le prieuré de Saint-Vigor-le-Grand* (Caen, 1861), pp. 66–76. Robert Curthose's charter of confirmation is printed by V. Bourrienne, *Antiquus cartularius ecclesie Baiocensis* (Rouen, 1902–3), i, no. vi.

[4] For the life of Robert of Tombelaine and his *Commentary*, often wrongly attributed to Gregory the Great, see Paul Quivy and Joseph Thiron, 'Robert de Tombelaine et son commentaire sur le Cantique des Cantiques', in *Millénaire monastique du Mont Saint-Michel*, ii (Paris, 1967), 347–56; also Migne, *PL* cl. 1363. See also below, pp. 304–6.

Denique presul Odo Grentoni Diuionensium abbati dedit predictum monasterium.' ibique usque hodie cella floret Diuionensium.[1] Sic euidenter patet.' quod antistes Odo monasticum ordinem ualde dilexisset. Dociles quoque clericos Leodicum mittebat, et ad
iii. 266 alias urbes ubi philosophorum studia potissimum florere nouerat.' eisque copiosos sumptus ut indesinenter et diutius philosophico fonti possent insistere largiter administrabat. De discipulis quos ita nutrierat fuerunt Thomas archiepiscopus Eborachensis,[2] atque Samson frater eius episcopus Wigornensis.'[3] Guillelmusque de Ros abbas Fiscannensis,[4] et Turstinus Glestoniensis,[5] multique alii qui nostris temporibus in æcclesia Dei floruerunt, et subiectis ouibus pabulo doctrinæ radiisque uirtutum sollerter profuerunt. Sic Odo pontifex licet secularibus curis admodum esset irretitus, multa tamen laudabilia permiscebat illicitis actibus.' et quæ facinorose aggregarat largitus est æcclesiis et pauperibus. Tandem nutu Dei compunctus dominicæ incarnationis anno millesimo xc°vi° indictione quarta omnia reliquit.' et iter Ierusolimitanum cum Roberto duce nepote suo ut in sequentibus uolente Deo plenius dicemus[6] arripuit, et presente Gisleberto Ebroicensium episcopo in urbe Panormitana obiit. Corpus uero eius in basilica Sanctæ Mariæ sepultum est.' super quod insigne opus a Rogerio comite Siciliæ factum est.[7]

Robertus Normanniæ dux opes quas habebat militibus ubertim
iii. 267 distribuit.' et tironum multitudinem pro spe et cupidine munerum sibi conexuit.[8] Deficiente erario Henricum fratrem suum ut de thesauro suo sibi daret requisiuit.' quod ille omnino facere noluit. Dux autem mandauit ei.' quod si uellet de terra sua uenderet illi. Henricus ut audiuit quod concupiuit.' mandato fratris libenter

[1] Bishop Odo's charter was confirmed by Robert Curthose on 24 May 1096 (Haskins, *Norman Institutions*, pp. 66–7, 75). At that date Gerento, abbot of Saint-Bénigne, Dijon, was papal legate in Normandy (Hugh of Flavigny, *Chronicon*, in *MGH SS* viii. 475; David, *Robert Curthose*, p. 91).

[2] Thomas was treasurer of Bayeux and from 1070 to 1100 archbishop of York. See Hugh the Chantor, *History of the Church of York*, ed. Charles Johnson (Edinburgh, 1961), p. 1.

[3] See above, ii. 300–2; V. H. Galbraith, 'Notes on the career of Samson, bishop of Worcester (1096–1112)', in *EHR* lxxxii (1967), 86–101; C. N. L. Brooke, 'Gregorian Reform in action', *Cambridge Historical Journal*, xii (1956), 12 n. 39.

[4] See above, ii. 292–4; Le Prévost, iv. 269–71.

[5] Thurstan's rule at Glastonbury was disastrous; see above, ii. 270 and n. 1.

[6] See Le Prévost, iv. 16–18.

[7] The cathedral of Palermo was rebuilt in the last quarter of the twelfth century; some of the bones of noble Normans buried there were removed to the Capella della Maddalena, but the tombs disappeared in the rebuilding (A. Zanca, *La cattedrale di Palermo* (Palermo, 1952), pp. 7–14). Odo had intended the

Finally Bishop Odo gave the monastic house to Gerento, abbot of Dijon,[1] and to this day a cell of Dijon flourishes there. This clearly demonstrates Bishop Odo's great affection for the monastic order. He also sent promising clerks to Liège and other cities where he knew that philosophic studies flourished, and supported them generously there so that they might drink long and deeply from the springs of knowledge. Among the pupils whom he educated in this way were Thomas, archbishop of York,[2] and Samson his brother, bishop of Worcester,[3] William of Rots, abbot of Fécamp,[4] Thurstan abbot of Glastonbury,[5] and many others who have occupied high positions in the Church of God in this present age, and have diligently led their flocks, feeding them on sound doctrine and lighting their paths with virtues. So Bishop Odo, although to some extent entangled in worldly preoccupations, nevertheless performed many praiseworthy actions among less creditable ones; and though he accumulated wealth by dubious methods he bestowed it generously on churches and the poor. Finally at God's prompting, in the year of our Lord 1096, the fourth indiction, he abandoned everything and set out for Jerusalem with Duke Robert his nephew, as I hope, God willing, to describe more fully in a later book,[6] and died in the town of Palermo with Gilbert bishop of Évreux at his death-bed. His body was buried in the church of St. Mary, and Roger count of Sicily had a splendid tomb erected for him there.[7]

Robert duke of Normandy lavishly distributed the wealth he possessed among his men-at-arms, and gathered round himself a crowd of young knights greedy for gain, who were attracted by his promises.[8] When his treasure was exhausted he asked his brother Henry to give him some of his wealth, which Henry flatly refused to do. The duke then offered to sell him a portion of his land if he would like to buy it. This was precisely what Henry desired, and as soon as he heard his brother's offer he accepted it.

priory of Saint-Vigor at Bayeux as his place of burial (Abbé Faucon, *Essai historique sur le prieuré de Saint-Vigor-le-Grand*, pp. 75–6).

[8] This suggests two elements in Robert's dependants: the paid mercenary soldiers, the kind of men that William of Malmesbury (*GR* ii. 468) calls 'stipendiarii', and the young men of noble birth and knightly training, many of them younger sons, who had no prospect of an adequate landed inheritance (cf. Eadmer, *Vita Anselmi*, ed. R. W. Southern (Edinburgh, 1962), pp. 94–6). Orderic normally uses the word *tiro* (when in the military and not the allegorical sense of monks) of men who were either training for knighthood or had been dubbed knights. His use of *miles* is much more varied and ambiguous.

adquieuit. Pactio itaque inter fratres firma facta est.[1] Henricus duci tria milia librarum argenti erogauit, et ab eo totum Constantinum pagum quæ tercia Normanniæ pars est recepit. Sic Henricus Abrincas et Constantiam Montemque Sancti Michahelis in periculo maris, totumque feudum Hugonis Cestrensis consulis quod in Neustria possidebat[2] primitus optinuit. Constantiensem itaque prouinciam bene gubernauit.'[3] suamque iuuentutem laudabiliter exercuit. Hic in infantia studiis litterarum a parentibus traditus est.' et tam naturali quam doctrinali scientia nobiliter imbutus est.[4] Hunc Lanfrancus Dorobernensis archiepiscopus dum iuuenile robur attingere uidit, ad arma pro defensione regni sustulit, eumque lorica induit, et galeam capiti eius imposuit.' eique ut regis filio et in regni stemmate nato[6] militiæ cingulum in nomine domini cinxit.[5] Hic xii annis quibus super Anglos Guillelmus Rufus regnauit.' laboriosam per uarios mobilis fortunæ
iii. 268 rotatus uitam transegit, et tristibus seu lætis exercitatus multa edidicit. Denique defuncto fratre suo regni culmen conscendit.' quod iam fere xxxiii annis tenuit.[7] Mores eius et actus suis in locis donante Deo si uita comes fuerit enodabo. Nunc uero ad narrationis ordinem redire decerno.' et quæ nostris temporibus acta sunt posteris intimabo.

2

In primo anno principatus duorum fratrum optimates utriusque regni conueniunt.' et de duobus regnis nunc diuisis quæ manus una pridem tenuerat tractare satagunt.[8] 'Labor' inquiunt 'nobis

[1] Charter attestations provide supporting evidence for the friendly relations of the brothers in the year following their father's death (David, *Robert Curthose*, pp. 48–9).

[2] The origin and composition of the holding of Hugh of Avranches are discussed by L. Musset, in *La Normandie bénédictine au temps de Guillaume le Conquérant* (ed. J. Daoust, Lille, 1967), pp. 358–68. Robert of Torigny, in his interpolations in William of Jumièges, mentions one report that the Cotentin was not given to Henry, but pledged in return for a loan (Marx, p. 269).

[3] The complaints of the nuns of Holy Trinity, Caen, about Henry I's depredations on their property show that his administration was not altogether blameless (Haskins, *Norman Institutions*, pp. 63–4; David, *Robert Curthose*, pp. 79–80).

[4] Both Orderic and William of Malmesbury (*GR* ii. 467) describe Henry's learning in fulsome terms; scholars have since whittled down his claims to learning (see C. W. David, 'The claim of Henry I to be called learned', in *Anniversary Essays in Medieval History by Students of C. H. Haskins* (Boston and New York, 1929), pp. 45–56; and M. Dominica Legge, 'L'influence littéraire de la cour d'Henri Beauclerc', in *Mélanges offerts à Rita Lejeune* (Gembloux, 1969), i. 680). He may, however, have been learned after the fashion of the knights of Maule (above, iii. 206), with a taste for speculative discussion rather than a sound grounding in Latin grammar.

So a bargain was struck between the brothers.[1] Henry provided the duke with three thousand pounds in silver, and received from him the whole of the Cotentin, which is a third part of Normandy. In this way Henry first acquired Avranches and Coutances and Mont Saint-Michel in peril of the sea, and the whole fee which Hugh, earl of Chester, held in Normandy.[2] He governed the Cotentin well,[3] and employed the years of his youth admirably. When Henry was a child he had been put to the study of letters by his parents, and he was well instructed in both natural philosophy and knowledge of doctrine.[4] When he attained manhood Lanfranc, archbishop of Canterbury, presented him for knighthood for the defence of the kingdom, invested him with the hauberk, placed the helmet on his head and girded him with the belt of knighthood[5] in the name of the Lord as a king's son born in the purple.[6] During the twelve years of William Rufus's reign over the English he led a difficult life, enduring the ups and downs of fortune, and gained wide experience through the alternations of prosperity and adversity. Finally after his brother's death he succeeded to the government of the kingdom, which he has now exercised for thirty-three years.[7] I will fully describe his character and deeds in their proper place, if God wills and my life lasts. But now I must return to my chronological narrative, and will instruct future generations in the deeds of our own times.

2

In the first year of the two brothers' government the magnates of both principalities met together for the purpose of discussing the division of the two realms which had formerly been held by one hand.[8] 'A great burden', they said, 'has suddenly been thrust

[5] Both the Anglo-Saxon Chronicle (1086) and William of Malmesbury say that he was knighted by his father at the Whitsuntide court at Westminster in 1086 (*GR* ii. 468). Lanfranc probably had some share in the ceremony.

[6] The insistence of chroniclers that Henry was born in England after his parents were crowned is so marked that the claim was probably made by Henry himself. Cf. Adrian Morey and C. N. L. Brooke, *Gilbert Foliot and his Letters* (Cambridge, 1965), pp. 111–12.

[7] If the figure is correct this passage was written *c.* 1133.

[8] This imaginary debate sums up Orderic's views on the evils of division; such opinions were certainly prevalent at the time he wrote, though the attitude of the nobility in 1088 is more open to question. See J. H. Le Patourel, 'The Norman Succession, 996–1135', in *EHR* lxxxvi (1971), 225–50, especially p. 247.

ingens subito creuit, et maxima diminutio potestatis nostræ opumque nobis incumbit. Hactenus enim in Normannia sub ducibus magnis honorifice potiti sumus paterna hereditate.ʼ quam parentes nostri qui de Dacia cum Rollone ante cc et xii annos[1] uenere nacti sunt cum magna strenuitate. Deinde nos cum Guillelmo duce pontum transfretauimus.ʼ et Saxones Anglos uiribus armisque nostris prostrauimus, et fundos eorum cum omnibus diuitiis non sine magno cruoris nostri discrimine optinuimus. Pro dolor en uiolenta nobis orta est mutatio, et nostræ sullimitatis[a] repentina deiectio. Quid faciemus? Ecce defuncto seniore nostro duo iuuenes succedunt, iamque dominatum Angliæ et Normanniæ subito segregarunt. Quomodo duobus dominis tam diuersis et tam longe ab inuicem remotis competenter seruire poterimus? Si Roberto duci Normannorum digne seruierimus, Guillelmum
iii. 269 fratrem eius offendemus.ʼ unde ab ipso spoliabimur[b] in Anglia magnis redditibus et precipuis honoribus. Rursus si regi Guillelmo congrue paruerimus.ʼ Robertus dux in Normannia penitus priuabit nos paternis hereditatibus. Summopere cauendum est ne tale diuorcium contingat nobis sub principibus his.ʼ quale sub Roboam et Ieroboam contigit Israhelitis. Vnus populus per duos principes in sese diuisus est.ʼ et lege templo cerimoniisque Dei pessundatis in apostasiam lapsus est.[2] Sic Hebrei per detestabile discidium in sua uiscera nequiter armati sunt.ʼ et seruientes Baalim multa suorum milia trucidarunt. Ad postremum uero pars eorum qui nunquam postea redierunt sub Assiriis in Mediam captiuata est.ʼ et alia pars sub Caldeis Babilonicam captiuitatem passa est. Et Thebeis quid contigit sub duobus fratribus Ethiocle et Polinice?[3] Nonne multa milia utriusque partis corruerunt, ad ultimum uero ipsi fratres mutuis uulneribus conciderunt, et extraneis successoribus hereditarium ius dimiserunt? Hæc et multa huiusmodi sollerter intueri debemus, et prudenter precauere ne per consilium iuuenile pereamus. Inuiolabile fedus firmiter ineamus, et Guillelmo rege deiecto uel interfecto qui iunior est et proteruus, et cui nichil debemus.ʼ Robertum ducem qui maior natu est[4] et tractabilior moribus, et cui iamdudum uiuente patre amborum

[a] sullimitas, *Caen MS.* [b] spoliabimus, *Caen MS.*

[1] This calculation is based on the erroneous statement, taken by Orderic from the *Annals of Saint-Évroul* (Le Prévost, v. 153), that Rollo first attacked Normandy in 876.
[2] Cf. 1 Kings xii–xiv.

upon us, and we are crippled by a sharp decline in our power and wealth. Our ancestors, who came from Denmark with Rollo two hundred and twelve years ago,[1] won by their valour lands in Normandy which we have honourably enjoyed by right of inheritance under the great dukes up to now. Later we crossed the Channel with Duke William, defeated the Anglo-Saxons by force of arms, and gained possession of their estates and considerable wealth at the cost of great bloodshed and heavy loss. Now, alas, we have suffered a sudden and violent change of fortune and an abrupt decline of our power. What are we to do? Now that our old leader is dead two young men have succeeded him, and now they have suddenly divided the government of England from that of Normandy. How can we provide adequate service to two lords who are so different and who live so far apart? If we serve Robert duke of Normandy as we ought we will offend his brother William, who will then strip us of great revenues and mighty honors in England. Again, if we obey King William dutifully, Duke Robert will confiscate our inherited estates in Normandy. We must take great care to avoid the kind of division under these princes which befell the Israelites under Rehoboam and Jeroboam. Then one people was divided against itself under two princes, abandoned the law and the temple and worship of God, and lapsed into apostasy.[2] Through this abominable division the Jews fell into the evils of civil war and the servants of Baal slew them in their thousands. Finally a part of them was carried away in captivity to Media by the Assyrians, never to return; and the other part endured the Babylonian captivity under the Chaldeans. And what happened to the Thebans under the two brothers Eteocles and Polynices?[3] Did not many thousands fall on both sides while the brothers slew each other in their fight to the death, leaving their inheritance to foreign successors? We should ponder deeply on these and similar examples, and be wise enough to avoid being destroyed by youthful counsels. Let us form an inviolable league; since King William is the younger of the two and very obstinate and we are under no obligation to him he must be deposed or slain. Then let us make Duke Robert ruler over England and Normandy to preserve the union of the two realms, for he is older by birth[4] and of a more

[3] Stories based on the *Thebais* of Statius were well known in lay circles at the time that Orderic was writing. Cf. above, iii. 100 n. 2.

[4] For Orderic's insistence on the right of the eldest son cf. above, ii, p. xxxvii.

fidelitatem iurauimus; principem Angliæ ac Neustriæ ad seruandam unitatem utriusque regni constituamus.'

iii. 270 Hoc itaque consilium Odo presul Baiocensis et Eustachius comes Boloniensis[1] atque Robertus Belesmensis aliique plures communiter decreuerunt; decretumque suum Roberto duci detexerunt. Ille uero utpote leuis et inconsideratus ualde gauisus est promissis inutilibus, seseque spopondit eis si inchoarent affuturum in omnibus; et collaturum mox efficax auxilium ad perpetrandum tam clarum facinus. Igitur post natale Domini[2] predicti proceres in Angliam transfretauerunt, et castella sua plurimo apparatu munierunt; multamque partem patriæ contra regem infra breue tempus commouerunt.

Odo nimirum ut supradictum est palatinus Cantiæ consul erat; et plures sub se comites uirosque potentes habebat.[3] Rogerius comes Scrobesburiensis et Hugo de Grentemaisnil qui presidatum Legrecestræ regebat; ac Robertus de Rodelento nepos eius aliique plures fortissimi milites seditiosis fauebant; et munitiones suas fossis et hominibus atque alimentis hominum et equorum abundanter instruebant. Iam auidi predones inuadebant predas pagensium ouanter prestolantes ducem Robertum; qui statuerat præcursores suos uere redeunte sequi cum multis legionibus
iii. 271 militum. Tunc Osbernus Ricardi cognomento Scrop filius, et Bernardus de Nouo Mercato[4] gener eius, aliique complices eorum qui fines Merciorum possidebant; in territorio Wigornensi rapinis et cedibus prohibente et anathematizante uiro Dei Vulfstano episcopo nequiter insistebant. Rex uero Guillelmus ut uidit suos in terra sua contra se pessima cogitare, et per singula crebrescentibus malis ad peiora procedere; non meditatus est ut timida uulpes ad tenebrosas cauernas fugere, sed ut leo fortis et audax rebellium conatus terribiliter comprimere. Lanfrancum itaque archiepiscopum cum suffraganeis presulibus et comites Anglosque naturales conuocauit; et conatus aduersariorum ac uelle suum expugnandi eos indicauit. At illi regem ut perturbatores pacis comprimeret

[1] Eustace II, count of Boulogne, had become reconciled with William the Conqueror after his attempt at invasion in 1067, and held extensive honors in England, some of which lay in Kent. See Frank Barlow, *Edward the Confessor*, pp. 307–8; above, ii. 204–6, 266; Douglas, *Domesday Monachorum*, p. 28 n. 7. Subsequently, in 1092, he appears in Robert Curthose's entourage in Normandy (Haskins, *Norman Institutions*, p. 68).

[2] Sources disagree on the exact moment of the uprising: the Anglo-Saxon Chronicle (1088) placed it at Easter. Details of the evidence are given in David, *Robert Curthose*, pp. 45–7 and Freeman, *William Rufus*, i. 22 ff.; ii, Appendixes B, C, D, E. Different writers specify particular rebels known to them. Orderic includes Robert of Rhuddlan, who was well known at Saint-Évroul; he makes

tractable character, and we have already sworn fealty to him during the lifetime of the father of both men.'

This was the agreement reached in common by Odo bishop of Bayeux, Eustace count of Boulogne,[1] and Robert of Bellême and many others; and they informed Duke Robert of their decision. Being thoughtless and improvident, he was delighted by their empty promises and undertook to give them his full support in their enterprise, and swift and effective aid in carrying out this shameless crime. So after Christmas[2] these magnates crossed to England, fortified and provisioned their castles, and had soon roused a considerable part of the kingdom against the king.

Odo, as I have described, was a most influential earl palatine of Kent, and had several earls and powerful men under him.[3] Roger earl of Shrewsbury, Hugh of Grandmesnil who was sheriff of Leicester, Hugh's nephew Robert of Rhuddlan and many other distinguished knights supported the rebels, and prepared their castles by digging fortifications, strengthening the garrisons and laying in provisions for men and horses. Rapacious brigands at once eagerly attacked the property of peasants, relying on Duke Robert who had said that when spring came he would follow them with many troops of men-at-arms. At that time Osbern, son of Richard called Scrop, and Bernard of Neufmarché[4] his son-in-law and their supporters who held lands in the marches of Wales iniquitously invaded the territory of Worcester, slaying and robbing the inhabitants and ignoring the prohibition and anathema of the man of God, Bishop Wulfstan. When King William realized that his subjects in his own land were planning treason and going from bad to worse in their lawless acts, he never for one moment thought of slinking away to some dark refuge like a timid fox, but resolved to crush the rebellion with the utmost ferocity, like a brave, strong lion. He therefore summoned Archbishop Lanfranc with the suffragan bishops and earls and the native English, and gave them an account of his enemies' uprising and his own determination to overthrow them. They urged the king to suppress

no mention of William of Saint-Calais, bishop of Durham, who was widely suspected of implication. The accounts of Orderic, William of Malmesbury (*GR* ii. 360–2), and the Anglo-Saxon Chronicle seem to have been written independently of each other; and Florence of Worcester, though using the Chronicle, also provided a good deal of west-country information of his own (FW ii. 21–6).

[3] See Douglas, *Domesday Monachorum*, pp. 28–30.

[4] For Bernard of Neufmarché's part in the rebellion cf. *Regesta*, i, no. 300.

adhortati sunt.' seseque promptissimos ad adiuuandum polliciti sunt. Anglorum uero triginta milia tunc ad seruitium regis sponte sua conuenerunt.'[1] regemque ut perfidos proditores absque respectu puniret admonuerunt dicentes, 'Viriliter age ut regis filius, et legitime ad regnum assumptus.' securus in hoc regno dominare omnibus. Nonne uides quod tecum sumus, tibique gratanter paremus? Passim per totam Albionem impera.' omnesque rebelles deice regali iusticia. Vsque ad mortem pro te certabimus.' nec
iii. 272 unquam tibi alium preponemus. Stultum nimis est et prophanum.' noto regi preferre hostem extraneum. Detestabilis gens est.' quæ principi suo infida est. Phalanx morti sit uicina.' quæ domini sui gaudet ruina. Sollerter Anglorum rimare historias.' inueniesque semper fidos principibus suis Angligenas.'

Rex ergo Rufus indigenarum hortatu promptior surrexit.' et congregato exercitu magno contra rebelles pugnaturus processit. Tunc Odo Baiocensis cum quingentis militibus intra Roffensem urbem se conclusit.'[2] ibique Robertum ducem cum suis auxiliaribus secundum statuta quæ pepigerant prestolari proposuit. Non enim seditiosi quamuis essent plurimi, multisque gazis et armis et ingenti apparatu stipati.' ausi erant contra regem in regno suo preliari. Oppidum[3] igitur Rouecestræ sollicita elegerunt prouisione, quoniam si rex eos non obsedisset in urbe.' in medio positi laxis habenis Lundoniam et Cantuariam deuastarent, et per mare quod proximum est insulasque uicinas pro auxiliis conducendis nuncios cito dirigerent. Animosus autem rex conatus eorum preuenit, oppidumque Maio mense cum grandi exercitu potenter obsedit, firmatisque duobus castellis omnem exeundi facultatem hostibus abstulit. Predictum ut prelibauimus oppidum Odo presul et Eustachius comes atque Robertus Belesmensis cum multis nobili-
iii. 273 bus uiris et mediocribus tenebant.' auxiliumque Roberti ducis qui desidia mollicieque detinebatur frustra expectabant. Rogerius uero Merciorum comes[4] multique Normannorum qui cum rege foris

[1] The support of many of the English for William Rufus is a well-attested fact (*GR* ii. 362; Anglo-Saxon Chronicle E 1088 (1087)); but Florence of Worcester (FW ii. 24–5) includes some Englishmen in the rebel forces fighting in the west country. Orderic's figure of 30,000 must be taken simply to mean a very large number.

[2] Orderic fails to give any account of Odo's earlier resistance with Robert of Mortain at Pevensey, or the apparent trick by which he entered Rochester on the pretext of negotiating its surrender. In a later summary of Odo's career (Le Prévost, iv. 17) he mentions the sieges of Pevensey and Tonbridge, but treats Odo as inspiring rather than taking part in the resistance.

[3] The great Norman castle at Rochester had not been built at that date: Rochester was a town with ancient fortifications, and it was behind these that the rebels gathered (cf. the reference of William II's charters of 1088 to the city of Rochester: *Regesta*, i, nos. 301, 302).

the disturbers of the peace and promised to give him immediate aid. On that occasion thirty thousand Englishmen assembled voluntarily for the king's service,[1] and urged the king to punish the traitors without respect of persons, saying, 'Act resolutely, as befits a king's son lawfully raised to the throne, so that you may govern all your subjects in this kingdom in safety. Do you not see that we are with you, and gladly obey you? Make your authority felt over the whole of England, and force all the rebels to submit to royal justice. We will fight for you to the death, and will never support another against you. It is both foolish and wicked to prefer a foreign enemy to a known king. A people who betrays its prince is utterly despicable. An army that welcomes the ruin of its lord is ripe for destruction. Study the pages of English history: you will find that the English are always loyal to their princes.'

King Rufus, greatly encouraged by the support of the English, raised a strong army and marched against the rebels. At that time Odo of Bayeux had shut himself up in the town of Rochester with five hundred knights,[2] and proposed to wait there until Duke Robert reinforced him with his troops according to the agreement they had made. For although the rebels were numerous and well supplied with treasure and arms and abundant equipment, they did not dare to engage the king in open battle in his own kingdom. Therefore with careful forethought they chose the fortified town[3] of Rochester as their base, so that if the king had not besieged them they could have broken out to plunder the two cities of London and Canterbury on either side of them, and have taken advantage of the sea, which was not far off, and the neighbouring islands to send messengers for help without loss of time. But the energetic king anticipated their intentions, and in May blockaded the walled town with a great army, and by fortifying two siege-towers cut off the enemy's egress. As we have said, Bishop Odo and Count Eustace and Robert of Bellême and many men of high and medium rank held the town of Rochester, waiting in vain for help from Duke Robert, who was delayed through his inertia and love of ease. It is true that Roger, earl of the Mercians,[4] and many Normans who were assisting the king in the siege attempted

[4] Roger of Montgomery, earl of Shrewsbury. He had supported the conspirators in the early stages of the rebellion, but, according to William of Malmesbury (*GR* ii. 361), William Rufus had persuaded him to change sides.

obsidebant clam adminiculari quantum poterant inclusis satagebant, non tamen palam contra regem arma leuare audebant. Omnes episcopi Angliæ cum Anglis sine dolo regem iuuabant.' et pro serena patriæ pace quæ bonis semper amabilis est laborabant. Hugo comes Cestrensis et Robertus de Molbraio[1] Nordanhimbrorum comes et Guillelmus de Guarenna ac Robertus Haimonis filius, aliique legitimi maturique barones regi fideliter adherebant.' eique armis et consilio contra publicos hostes commode fauebant.

In oppido Rofensi plaga similis Ægiptiorum plagæ apparuit.' qua Deus qui semper res humanas curat et iuste disponit, antiqua miracula nostris etiam temporibus recentia ostendit. Nam sicut sciniphes importunitate sua Ægiptios infestabant, et nec ad momentum ab infestatione sua circa ipsos cessabant.' ita muscæ obsessos incessanti molestia importune uexabant.[2] Obsessi nempe extra castellum exire nequibant.' et plures eorum ex diuersis infortuniis grassante morbo interibant. Innumerabiles ergo muscae hominum et equorum ceno nascebantur, et tam estatis quam
iii. 274 anhelitus cohabitantium calore confouebantur.' et oculis ac naribus et cibis ac potibus inclusorum horribiliter ingerebantur. Tanta itaque importunitate muscarum stimulabatur cohors superba rebellium.' ut nunquam die uel nocte possent capere cibum, nisi magna pars ipsorum ab inquietudine muscarum uicissim flabellis defenderet ora sociorum. Igitur Odo Baiocensis et complices sui diutius obsidionem pati non potuerunt, unde Guillelmum regem nunciis petierunt.' ut pacem cum eis faceret, ac oppidum ab eis reciperet.' tali tenore ut terras fundos et omnia quæ hactenus habuerant ab ipso reciperent, et ipsi eidem ut naturali domino fideliter amodo seruirent. His auditis rex iratus est et ualde rigidus intumuit.' et in nullo flexus legatorum postulationibus non adquieuit, sed perfidos traditores in oppido uirtute potenti capiendos iurauit.' et mox patibulis suspendendos et aliis mortium diuersis generibus de terra delendos asseruit. Videntes autem hi qui obsidebant cum rege ad necem parentum et amicorum qui obsessi erant tam ualide regis animum furere.' cum ingenti supplicatione ad eum accesserunt.' eique multa prece multoque fauore blandiri conati sunt. Dicunt itaque,

'Laudetur Deus qui semper adiuuat sperantes in se.' et dat

[1] William of Malmesbury, the Anglo-Saxon Chronicle, and Florence of Worcester number Robert of Mowbray among the rebels, and if he veered to the side of William Rufus towards the end of the rebellion his loyalty was not to last long (cf. below, pp. 278–82).

[2] Cf. Exodus viii. 16–32 for the plagues of lice and flies. Orderic appears to have had both in mind.

secretly to help the besieged as far as they could, but they dared not openly raise arms against the king. All the bishops of England together with the English gave whole-hearted support to the king, and worked to bring back to their country the peace and order that good men always cherish. Hugh earl of Chester, Robert of Mowbray,[1] earl of Northumbria, William of Warenne, Robert fitz Hamon, and other loyal barons of mature age remained faithful to the king, giving him practical help with arms and counsel against the rebels.

In the town of Rochester a plague like one of the plagues of Egypt broke out. In this way God, who always directs and justly disposes human affairs, repeated old miracles in modern times. Just as lice molested the Egyptians, biting them without a moment's respite from their persecution, so flies incessantly plagued the besieged.[2] For the men could not go outside the fortifications, and as disease spread many of them died from various infections. Consequently myriads of flies were generated in the rotting flesh of men and horses, and breeding rapidly in the heat of the summer and the breath of over-crowded men, they filled the eyes and nostrils of the besieged and contaminated their food and drink in a horrible way. The proud troop of rebels were so harassed by the torment of the flies that they could eat nothing either by day or night unless a great number of them took turns to protect their comrades' mouths by beating away the flies with whisks. In the end Odo of Bayeux and his accomplices could endure the siege no longer, and sent messengers to ask King William to make peace and receive the surrender of the town from them. The terms they asked were that they might receive from him the fiefs and lands and all the property they had previously held, and faithfully serve him as their rightful lord in future. The king heard these proposals with anger and gave full vent to his fury; he would not yield an inch to the requests of the intermediaries, but swore that the perjured traitors in the town must be captured by force and instantly hung on gibbets, or by some other form of execution utterly removed from the face of the earth. But when those taking part in the siege with the king saw how passionately the king in his rage desired the death of their kinsfolk and friends among the besieged, they approached him with a humble petition, and tried to appease him with earnest prayers and soft words. They spoke thus:

'Praise be to God who always helps those who put their trust

bonis patribus eximiam sobolem succedere. Ecce turgidi iuuenes et cupiditate cecati senes iam satis edocti sunt.ʼ quod regiæ uires in hac insula nondum defecerunt. Nam qui de Normannia tanquam milui ad predam super nos cum impetu aduolarunt, et in Anglia regiam stirpem defecisse arbitrati sunt.ʼ iam Guillelmum iuuenem Guillelmo sene non debiliorem cohibente Deo experti sunt. Iam pene uicti uiribus tuis succumbunt.ʼ et fatiscentes magnitudinem
iii. 275 tuam supplices exposcunt. Nos quoque qui tecum maximis in periculis sicut cum patre tuo perstitimus.ʼ nunc tibi humiliter astamus, et pro compatriotis nostris obnixe supplicamus. Decet nimirum ut sicut tumidos et uecordes uicisti fortitudine.ʼ sic humiliatis et penitentibus parcas mansuetudine. Seueritatem regiam temperet clementia.ʼ et gloriæ uirtutis tuae sufficiat celebris uictoria. Dauid rex magnus Semei maledicenti se pepercit.ʼ[1] et Ioab atque Abisai aliosque bellatores pro aduersante sibi Absalon ne perimerent eum obnixe rogauit.[2] In diuinis uoluminibus abundant exempla huiuscemodi.ʼ a quibus non discrepat sagax poeta in libello de mirabilibus mundi,[3]

> Parcere prostratis scit nobilis ira leonis.ʼ
> Tu quoque fac simile quisquis dominaris in orbe.'

Hæc ita dicentibus Guillelmus rex ait, 'Fateor me uiribus uestris hostes expugnasse.ʼ et per auxilium Dei cum labore uestro gratanter tropheo appropinquasse. Verum tanto cautius precauere debetis.ʼ ne me precibus uestris a rigore rectitudinis deuiare cogatis. Quisquis parcit periuris et latronibus, plagiariis et execratis proditoribus.ʼ aufert pacem et quietem innocentibus, innumerasque cedes et damna serit bonis et inermibus. Quid sceleratis peccaui? quid illis nocui? quid mortem meam totis nisibus procurauerunt, et omnes pro posse suo contra me populos cum detrimento multorum erexerunt? Omnia sua illis dimisi, nulloque
iii. 276 reatu contra me commoui.ʼ et illi summopere michi facti sunt inimici. Vnde reor omnino esse iustum, ut Dauid magni regis quem michi proposuistis imitandum.ʼ irrefragabiliter teneamus iudicium. Sicut Baana et Rechab filii Remon Berotitæ qui regem Isboseth in domo sua decollauerunt, iudicante Dauid in Hebron

[1] 2 Samuel xvi. 5–11. [2] 2 Samuel xviii. 5.

[3] The 'De mirabilibus mundi', a poem inspired by Solinus, was probably the work of Thierry, abbot of Saint-Trond from 1099 to 1107 (see J. G. Préaux, 'Thierry de Saint-Trond, auteur du poème pseudo-ovidien *De mirabilibus mundi*' in *Latomus*, vi (1947), 353). Most medieval writers wrongly attributed it to Ovid.

in him, and gives good fathers a worthy offspring to succeed them. Surely these presumptuous youths and blindly ambitious old men have now fully learnt the lesson that the royal might has not yet faltered in this island. Those who swooped down on us from Normandy like hawks on their prey, imagining that the royal stock was weakened in England, have now discovered with God's aid that young William is no less powerful than old William. Now on the point of defeat they yield to your forces; they are worn out and throw themselves as suppliants on your mercy. We who have stood beside you no less than your father in grave perils, now approach you humbly and plead the cause of our fellow countrymen. It is most proper that, just as you conquered them in their pride and folly by your strength, you should by your graciousness spare them now that they are humbled and penitent. Temper your royal rigour with mercy and let the fact of victory proclaim the triumph of your might. King David spared Shimei when he cursed him,[1] and besought Joab and Abishai and his other captains not to slay Absalom when he rebelled against him.[2] There are many similar examples in the holy Scriptures, and a wise poet speaks to the same purpose in the book of the *Wonders of the World*:[3]

> The noble lion's wrath can spare the vanquished;
> Do likewise, all who govern on this earth.'

King William replied to this, 'I grant that I have defeated the enemies with your forces, and by God's aid and your endeavours I have almost gained the prize of victory. You ought therefore to be all the more careful not to try by pleading to turn me from the path of justice. He who spares traitors and robbers, oppressors and accursed men, destroys the peace and security of the innocent and sows the seeds of endless massacres and troubles for good, defenceless people. What wrong did I do these villains? How did I harm them, that they should seek my death relentlessly, and devote all their efforts to stirring up all my people against me, causing harm to thousands? I restored all their estates and gave them no cause for rebellion by any injustice, yet they have become my bitterest enemies. So I judge it wholly right to imitate the judgement of David, the great king whom you hold up as an example for me. As Baanah and Rechab, the sons of Rimmon the Beerothite, who beheaded King Ishbosheth in his house, were hanged in Hebron

suspendio perempti sunt:[1] sic isti insidiatores regni puniantur terribili animaduersione ut presentes et futuri terreantur et castigentur huius ultionis relatione.'

Ad hæc optimates regi dixerunt, 'Omnia quæ dicis domine rex uera et iusta esse censemus: nec uni uerbo rationis tuæ contradicere ualemus. Beniuolentia tamen cogente potentiam tuam humiliter oramus: ut consideres qui sunt pro quibus tantopere rogamus. Baiocensis Odo patruus tuus est: et pontificali sanctificatione preditus est. Cum patre tuo Anglos subiugauit: eique in multis anxietatibus periculose subuenit. Quid tanto uiro agendum est? Absit ut in sacerdotem Domini manus inicias, uel sanguinem eius effundas. In tali causa reminiscere quid fecerit Saul in Nobe:[2] et quid pertulerit in monte Gelboe.[3] Quis presumet tibi nefarius suadere, ut antistitem Domini patruumque tuum uelis condemnare? Nemo. Omnes ergo precamur ut illi beniuolentiam tuam concedas, et illesum in Normanniam ad diocesim suam abire permittas. Comes etiam Boloniensis patri tuo satis fuit fidelis, et in rebus arduis strenuus adiutor et contubernalis.[a] Robertus
iii. 277 quoque Belesmensis qui patri tuo fuit ualde dilectus, et multis honoribus olim ab ipso promotus: nunc magnam Normanniæ partem[4] possidet, fortissimisque castellis corroboratus pene omnibus uicinis suis et Neustriæ proceribus preeminet. His itaque si animi tui rancorem indulseris, et tecum benigniter retinueris, aut saltem a te cum pace dimiseris: eorum adhuc amicicia seruitioque in multis euentibus utiliter perfrueris. Idem qui ledit: fors post ut amicus obedit. In horum comitatu pollent seseque tibi offerunt eximii tirones: quorum seruitutem inclite rex paruipendere non debes. Igitur quos iam superasti potestate diuitiis et ingenti probitate: subiuga tibi magnificentia et pietate.'

Magnanimus itaque rex fidelium suorum precibus uictus assensit, exitium et membrorum debilitationem obsessis indulsit: et de opido exeundi facultatem cum equis et armis concessit, sed omnem spem habendi hereditates et terras in regno eius quamdiu ipse regnaret funditus abscidit. Tunc Odo pontifex a rege Rufo impetrare temptauit: ne tubicines in eorum egressu tubis canerent, sicut moris est dum hostes uincuntur: et per uim oppidum capitur. Rex autem iratus quod petebatur omnino denegauit: nec se

[a] conturbernalis, *Caen MS.*

[1] 2 Samuel iv. 2–12. [2] 1 Samuel xxii. 19. [3] 1 Samuel xxxi. 1, 2.

[4] Robert of Bellême, the eldest son of Roger of Montgomery, appears to have held the Norman lands of the Bellême family from the time of his mother Mabel's death in 1077 (cf. above, iii. 136), in his father's lifetime.

by David's judgement,[1] so these traitors to the kingdom ought to be terribly punished, so that the knowledge of their fate may chasten and restrain present and future generations.'

The magnates of the kingdom made this reply, 'We acknowledge everything that you say, lord king, to be true and just, and cannot contradict any of your arguments. But pity compels us to beg you humbly to consider in your triumph who these men are for whom we are so solicitous. Odo of Bayeux is your uncle, and is a consecrated bishop. He helped your father to dominate the English and stood by him in many dangers and anxieties. What is to be done with such a man? God forbid that you should lay hands on a priest of the Lord, or shed his blood. In such an undertaking remember what Saul did in Nob[2] and what he suffered in Mount Gilboa.[3] Who could be so wicked as to persuade you to condemn a bishop of the Lord who is also your uncle? No one. We all beg you therefore to be merciful to him and allow him to return to Normandy to his see. The count of Boulogne also was loyal enough to your father, and was his helper and comrade in arms in many tight places. Robert of Bellême too, who was much favoured by your father and given great estates and dignities by him, now holds a great part of Normandy,[4] and from within his circle of strong castles now dominates almost all his neighbours and the magnates of Normandy. If you temper your rancour towards these men and restore them to positions of trust, or at least allow them to depart in peace, you will earn their gratitude and service on many future occasions. The man who does an injury today may perhaps serve as a friend in the future. Among these men are many distinguished knights, ready to offer their service to you, and you ought not, great king, to underrate its worth. Now that you have defeated them by your strength, resources, and great courage, win their hearts by your generosity and compassion.'

The generous king was convinced and, giving way to the petitions of his men, guaranteed life and limb to the besieged and allowed them a safe conduct to leave the town with their horses and arms; but he absolutely refused to give them any hope of recovering their inheritances or lands in his kingdom as long as he reigned. Bishop Odo next tried to win from the king the concession that the trumpeters should not sound their trumpets as the men came out, as is customary when an enemy is defeated and a stronghold taken by force. But the king in anger utterly rejected

concessurum etiam propter mille auri marcos palam asseruit. Oppidanis ergo cum merore et uerecundia egredientibus, et regalibus
tubis cum gratulatione clangentibus·/ multitudo Anglorum quæ
regi adherebat, cunctis audientibus uociferabatur et dicebat,
'Torques torques afferte, et traditorem episcopum cum suis complicibus patibulis suspendite. Magne rex Anglorum, cur sospitem
iii. 278 pateris abire incentorem malorum? Non debet uiuere periurus
homicida, qui dolis et crudelitatibus peremit hominum multa
milia.' Hæc et alia probra mestus antistes cum suis audiuit·/ sed
quamuis acerba minaretur indignationi suæ satisfacere non potuit.
Sic irreligiosus presul de Anglia expulsus est·/ et amplissimis
possessionibus spoliatus est. Tunc maximos questus quos cum
facinore optinuit, iusto Dei iudicio cum ingenti dedecore perdidit·/
et confusus Baiocas rediit, nec in Angliam postmodum repedauit.

iii. 279 Anno itaque primo Guillelmi Rufi regis, in inicio estatis[1]
Rofensis urbs ei reddita est·/ omniumque qui contra pacem enses
acceperant nequam commotio compressa est. Nam iniqui et omnes
malefactores ut audaciam regis et fortitudinem uiderunt, quia
predas et cedes aliaque facinora cum auiditate amplexati fuerant
contremuerunt·/ nec postea xii annis quibus regnauit mutire ausi
fuerunt. Ipse autem callide se habuit·/ et uindictæ tempus opportunum expectauit. Quorundam factiones seuissimis legibus puniit·/
aliquorum uero reatus ex industria dissimulauit. Antiquis baroni-
iii. 280 bus quos ab ipso aliquantum desciuerat nequitia, uersute pepercit
pro amore patris sui cui diu fideliter inheserant et pro senectutis
reuerentia·/ sciens profecto quod non eos diu uigere sinerent
morbus et mors propera.[2] Porro quidam quanto grauius se errasse
in regiam maiestatem nouerunt, tanto feruentius omni tempore
postmodum ei famulati sunt·/ et tam muneribus quam seruitiis ac
adulationibus multis modis placere studuerunt.

3

Cum supradicta tempestate uehementer Anglia undique concuteretur, et mutuis uulneribus incolæ regni cotidie mactarentur·/

[1] The exact date of the surrender is uncertain. The chronology of the Anglo-Saxon Chronicle, allowing for a siege of Tonbridge and a six-week siege of Rochester after Easter (April 16), suggests early July for the surrender of Rochester. A charter of Robert Curthose issued on Friday, 7 July 1088, in which he describes himself as about to cross to England (Haskins, *Norman Institutions*, pp. 288–9) corroborates this date, though in fact he failed to make the crossing.

[2] This applies to such men as Hugh of Grandmesnil, Eustace of Boulogne, and perhaps Roger of Montgomery (who had temporarily defected), all of whom gave no further trouble and were dead by the end of the reign.

the petition, loudly asserting that he would not grant it even for a thousand marks in gold. As the garrison came out in sorrow and shame, and the king's trumpets sounded triumphantly, the crowd of Englishmen who had supported the king shouted out loudly for all to hear, 'Halters, bring halters, and hang this traitor bishop and his accomplices from the gallows. Great king of England, why do you allow the fomentor of our troubles to go free? This traitor and murderer, who has caused the death of thousands by his schemes and cruelties has no right to live.' The unhappy bishop and his men heard these abuses and many more, but though he voiced dire threats he had to swallow his indignation. In this way the worldly bishop was banished from England, and stripped of his vast possessions. So by the just judgement of God he lost with every kind of humiliation the great gains he had accumulated by iniquity. He returned in confusion to Bayeux and never set foot in England again.

So in the first year of the reign of William Rufus, early in the summer,[1] the town of Rochester was recaptured by him, and the foul conspiracy of those who had taken up arms against him was put down. When evil-doers and criminals of all kinds saw the king's courage and daring they regretted the eagerness with which they had resorted to plunder and slaughter and other crimes, and for the remaining twelve years of his reign never dared to murmur against him. He bided his time and waited for the right moment to take vengeance. He punished some of the rebels with severe penalties, and deliberately turned a blind eye to the guilt of others. He shrewdly spared the older barons, although the conspiracy had temporarily weakened their allegiance to him, out of love for his father whom they had served long and faithfully, and through respect for their grey hairs. In any case he knew that disease and speedy death would soon put a term to their activities.[2] Consequently some of those who had gone furthest in their treachery obeyed him with all the more devotion in the years that followed, and endeavoured to appease him with gifts and services and flattery.

3

While the English everywhere were being shaken by these storms, and the inhabitants of the kingdom were fighting and

quia hi regem deicere temptabant, illi e contra pro rege uiriliter dimicabant.' Grithfridus rex Gualorum cum exercitu suo fines Angliæ inuasit, et circa Rodelentum magnam stragem hominum et incendia fecit. Ingentem quoque predam cepit.' hominesque in captiuitatem duxit. Robertus autem Rodelenti princeps[1] de obsidione Rofensi rediens, et tam atroces damnososque sibi rumores comperiens.' uehementer dolens ingemuit, ac terribilibus minis iram suam euidenter aperuit. Erat enim miles fortis et agilis, facundus et formidabilis.' largus et multis probitatibus laudabilis. Hic Eduardi regis armiger fuit.' et ab illo cingulum militiæ accepit.[2] Vnfridus pater eius fuit filius Ansfridi de progenie Dacorum.'
iii. 281 Adeliza uero mater eius soror Hugonis de Grentemaisnil de clara stirpe Geroianorum.[3] Hic precipuus agonitheta inter militiæ labores æcclesiæ cultor erat.' et clericos ac monachos ualde diligens honorabat, ac elemosinis pauperum pro modulo suo libenter instabat.

Porro Vticense cœnobium ubi fratres sui Ernaldus et Rogerius monachi erant, et pater suus ac mater aliique parentes eius tumulati quiescebant.' ualde dilexit, ac pro uiribus suis locupletauit. [4]Hinc illi æcclesiam de Telliolo et hoc quod habebat in æcclesia de Dambleinuilla et presbiterum dedit.' et hoc quod habebat in æcclesia de Torneor cum presbitero concessit, decimamque molendinorum et omnium exituum suorum et redecimationem promptuariorum suorum addidit. Idem uero Robertus in Anglia dedit sancto Ebrulfo et monachis eius ad Biuellam terram duarum carrucarum, et xx uillanos, et æcclesiam cum presbitero decimamque totam, et uillam quæ Chercabia dicitur cum æcclesia et presbitero, æcclesiamque de insula, et in ciuitate Cestra æcclesiam sancti Petri de mercato et tres hospites.[5] Quæ omnia ut sanctus
iii. 282 Ebrulfus solide et quiete sicut ea ipse dederat possideret.' in capitulum Vticense uenit, et de his omnibus quæ dicta sunt coram Mainerio abbate et conuentu monachorum concessionem suam confirmauit. Tunc ibidem cum eo fuerat Razso decanus et Hugo de Millaio, Guillelmus pincerna filius Grimoldi, et Rogerius filius

[1] For the events leading up to the death of Robert of Rhuddlan see above, Introduction, pp. xxxiv–xxxviii.

[2] Robert was one of a number of foreigners attracted to the court of Edward the Confessor after 1052 (F. Barlow, *Edward the Confessor*, p. 191).

[3] See genealogical table, above, ii, facing p. 370, and L. Musset, 'Les origines

slaying each other daily, as some tried to overthrow the king and others fought with determination in his support, the Welsh king Gruffydd invaded England with his army, burning and slaying mercilessly around Rhuddlan. He seized much booty and led away some captives. So when Robert, the commander of Rhuddlan,[1] returned home from the siege of Rochester and heard reports so terrible and damaging to him his heart was pierced with sorrow, and he openly showed his fury by his dreadful threats. He was a strong and agile knight, both eloquent and terrible, open-handed and admirable for his many good qualities. He had been a squire to King Edward, and had received the belt of knighthood from him.[2] His father, Humphrey, was the son of Ansfrid, of Danish stock; and his mother Adelina was a sister of Hugh of Grandmesnil, of the distinguished Giroie family.[3] This worthy champion remained a friend to the church in the midst of all his knightly duties; he truly loved and honoured clerks and monks, and gave alms freely to the poor according to his means.

Above all he loved the church of Saint-Évroul, where his brothers Arnold and Roger were monks, and his father and mother and kinsfolk lay buried, and he enriched it as far as his resources allowed. [4]He gave the church of Tilleul and what he had in the church of Damblainville with a priest, and what he had in the church of Le Tourneur with a priest, and the tithe of his mills and all his revenues, and added the second tithe of his store-rooms. Robert of Rhuddlan also gave St. Évroul and his monks in England the land for two ploughs at Byfield, and twenty villeins, and the church with a priest and all the tithe, and the manor called Kirby with the church and priest, and the church of Hilbre island, and in the city of Chester the church of St. Peter in the Market and three settlers.[5] In order that Saint-Évroul might hold all these things firmly and in peace, as he had given them, he came into the chapter-house and confirmed his grant of everything that had been listed, in the presence of Abbot Mainer and the community of monks. The other witnesses on that occasion were Razso the dean and Hugh of Mélay, William the butler, son of Grimold,

et le patrimoine de l'abbaye de Saint-Sever', in *La Normandie bénédictine au temps de Guillaume le Conquérant*, ed. J. Daoust (Lille, 1967), p. 358.

[4] Cf. Le Prévost, v. 186 for the text of Robert of Rhuddlan's charter, here cited verbally.

[5] Robert of Rhuddlan's English gifts were confirmed by William I in his charter of 1081 (above, iii. 238).

Geroii, Durandus et Burnellus, Osbernus de Orgeriis atque Gaulterius prepositus. Interfuerunt hi dum Robertus in basilicam
iii. 283 perrexit.' et donationem rerum supramemoratarum super altare posuit. Hæc breuiter tetigi de donis quæ prefatus heros Vticensi contulit æcclesiæ.' nec me uelit queso prudens lector inconsiderate subsannare, si titulum incepti operis dum tempus est prosequor in narratione.[1]

Robertus Vnfridi filius dum puer erat cum patre suo in Angliam transfretauit.' et Eduardo regi donec ab eodem miles fieret domi militiæque seruiuit. Deinde fulgentibus armis iam indutus, regiisque muneribus honorifice ditatus.' parentes suos reuisere concupiuit, et regis adepta permissione ad suos ouans repatriauit. Facto autem Senlacio bello, et rege Guillelmo multis hostium tumultibus occupato.' prefatus tiro cum Hugone consobrino suo Ricardi de Abrincis cognomento Goz filio iterum ad Anglos transiit, et semper in omnibus exercitiis quæ a militibus agenda erant inter precipuos uiguit. Deinde post multos agones predicto Hugoni comitatus Cestrensis datus est.' et Robertus princeps militiæ eius et tocius prouinciæ gubernator factus est.[2] Tunc uicini Britones qui Guali uel Gualenses uulgo uocitantur.' contra regem Guillelmum et omnes eius fautores nimis debachabantur. Decreto itaque regis oppidum contra Gualos apud Rodelentum constructum est.' et Roberto ut ipse pro defensione Anglici regni barbaris opponeretur datum est.[3] Bellicosus marchio contra inquietam gentem sepissime conflixit, crebrisque certaminibus multum sanguinis effudit. Incolis itaque Britonibus seuo marte repulsis fines suos dilatauit.' et in monte Dagannoth qui mari
iii. 284 contiguus est fortissimum castellum condidit. Per xv annos[4] intolerabiliter Britones protriuit, et fines eorum qui pristina libertate tumentes nichil omnino Normannis debuerunt inuasit, per siluas et paludes et per arduos montes persecutus hostes multis modis profligauit. Nam quosdam comminus ut pecudes irreuerenter occidit, alios uero diutius uinculis mancipauit, aut indebitæ seruituti atrociter subiugauit. Christicolæ non licet fratres suos sic opprimere.' qui in fide Christi sacro renati sunt baptismate.

Superbia et cupiditas quæ per totum orbem mortalium

[1] Orderic defends his inclusion of the history of the endowment of Saint-Évroul elsewhere in his work. Cf. above, iii. 6, 260.

[2] This description may possibly imply that Robert acted as Hugh's sheriff. Cf. J. Tait, *The Domesday Survey of Cheshire* (Chetham Society, N.S. lxxv (1916)), p. 46 n. 2.

[3] In 1086 the custody of the castle of Rhuddlan was divided between Hugh earl of Chester and Robert of Rhuddlan (*DB* i. 269a).

and Roger son of Giroie, Durand and Burnellus, Osbern of Orgères and Walter the provost. They were present when Robert entered the church and placed his gift of these things on the altar. I have touched very briefly on the gifts which Lord Robert granted to the church of Saint-Évroul, and I beg my judicious reader not to turn away with a sneer if I follow up the original purpose of the work I have undertaken in my narrative as occasion permits.[1]

Robert the son of Humphrey crossed to England with his father when still a boy, and served King Edward at home and at war until he was made a knight by him. When he had been girded with shining arms and honourably enriched with the king's gifts he wished to see his kinsfolk again, and with the king's permission returned home rejoicing. After the battle of Hastings, when King William was engaged in putting down rebellions of his enemies, the young knight Robert returned to England with his cousin, Hugh, the son of Richard Goz of Avranches, and at all times proved his distinction in the undertakings which fall to the lot of knights. Finally after many struggles the county of Chester was given to Hugh of Avranches, and Robert was made commander of his forces and governor of the whole province.[2] At that time the neighbouring Britons who are commonly called Gaels or Welsh were making savage attacks on King William and all his followers. So by the king's command a castle was built at Rhuddlan to contain the Welsh, and was given to Robert with the duty of defending the kingdom of England against these barbarians.[3] The warlike marcher lord often fought against this unruly people and slew many in battle after battle. After driving back the native Britons in fierce combat he enlarged his territories and built a strongly fortified castle on the hill of Deganwy which is near to the sea. For fifteen years[4] he harried the Welsh mercilessly, invaded the lands of men who when they still enjoyed their original liberty had owed nothing to the Normans, pursued them through woods and marshes and over steep mountains and found different ways of securing their submission. Some he slaughtered mercilessly on the spot like cattle; others he kept for years in fetters, or forced into a harsh and unlawful slavery. It is not right that Christians should so oppress their brothers, who have been reborn in the faith of Christ by holy baptism.

Pride and greed, which have a hold on the hearts of men

[4] See above, Introduction, p. xxxviii.

possident pectora, Robertum marchisum absque modo ad predas stimulabant et homicidia.' per quæ idem in horrendum precipitium mersus est postea. Nam tercio die Iulii[1] Grithfridus rex Gualorum cum tribus nauibus sub montem qui dicitur Hormaheua[2] littori appulsus est.' et mox piratarum exercitus quasi lupi rapaces ad depopulandam regionem diffusus est. Interim mare fluctus suos retraxit.' et in sicco littore classis piratarum stetit. Grithfridus autem cum suis per maritima discurrit, homines et armenta rapuit.' ac ad naues exicatas festine remeauit.

iii. 285 Interea clamor uulgi Robertum meridie dormitantem excitauit, eique hostilem discursum per terram suam nunciauit. Ille uero ut iacebat impiger surrexit.' et mox precones ad congregandum agmen armatorum per totam regionem direxit. Porro ipse cum paucis bellatoribus imparatus Gualos prosecutus est, et de uertice montis Hormaheuæ qui nimis arduus est.' captiuos a piratis ligari et in naues cum pecoribus precipitari speculatus est. Vnde marchisus audax ut leo nobilis uehementer infremuit.' hominesque paucos qui secum inermes erant ut antequam estus maris rediret super Gualos in sicco littore irruerent admonuit. Illi uero pretendunt suorum paucitatem.' et per ardui montis precipitium descendendi difficultatem. Denique Robertus dum uideret inimicum agmen cum preda sua prestolari reditum maris quo aufugeret nimis doluit.' impatiensque moræ per difficilem descensum sine lorica cum uno milite nomine Osberno de Orgeriis[3] ad hostes descendit. Quem cum uiderent solo clipeo protectum, et uno tantum milite stipatum.' omnes pariter in illum missilia destinant, et scutum eius iaculis intolerabiliter onerant.' et egregium militem letaliter uulnerant. Nullus tamen quamdiu stetit et parmam tenuit.' ad eum comminus accedere uel cum ense impetere ausus fuit. Tandem bellicosus heros spiculis confossus genua flexit et scutum missilibus nimis onustum uiribus effetus dimisit.' animamque suam Deo sanctæque Dei genitrici Mariæ commendauit. Tunc omnes in illum irruunt, et in conspectu suorum caput eius abscindunt.' ac super malum nauis pro signo uictoriæ suspendunt. Hoc plures de cacumine montis cum ingenti fletu et mesticia cernebant, sed hero
iii. 286 suo succurrere non ualebant. Deinde comprouinciales de tota

[1] The year has commonly been taken to be 1088; but Orderic gives no year and in fact 1093 is more consistent with the available evidence. Cf. above, pp. xxxiv–xxxviii.

[2] The identification with the Great Orme is accepted by J. E. Lloyd, *Trans. Hon. Soc. Cymmrodorion* (1899–1900), pp. 157–8.

[3] Osbern was a witness to Robert's charter to Saint-Évroul (above, p. 138).

everywhere, were the incentives that drove the marcher lord, Robert, to unrestrained plunder and slaughter; these deeds in time brought him to a terrible end. It happened that on 3 July[1] the Welsh king Gruffydd landed with three ships on the shore under the rocky height called the Great Orme,[2] and the army of pirates scattered at once to prey on the coastal region like ravening wolves. Meanwhile the tide went out, leaving the pirates' boats high and dry on the shore. Gruffydd and his men swooped on the lands near the sea, carried off men and beasts, and hurried back to the boats lying on the beach.

Meanwhile the cries of the crowd roused Robert from a midday sleep, and made him aware of the hostile raid on his land. He leapt up boldly just as he was, and immediately ordered the trumpeters to summon his troops from the whole district. He himself, all unprepared, pursued the Welsh with a few men-at-arms, and from the summit of the Great Orme, a precipitous rock, saw the captives being bound by the raiders and bundled into the boats with the animals. The fury of the lord marcher, a man bold as a lion, knew no bounds, and he ordered the few men with him, all unprepared as they were, to fall on the Welsh while they were stranded on the beach before the tide came in. They protested that they were too few and the way down from the summit of the rock too steep. Then Robert, seeing the enemy force waiting with the booty for the tide to carry them away, was sick at heart; unable to bear the delay, he flung himself down the difficult slope without his hauberk, accompanied by only one knight called Osbern of Orgères,[3] and rushed on the enemy. When they saw him with only a shield for protection, accompanied by only a single knight, with one accord they flung their javelins at this valiant lord, bore down his shield with the weight of their missiles, and fatally wounded him. But as long as he remained standing and held his shield none dared come to close quarters or strike him with a sword. At last the noble warrior, riddled with darts, fell to his knees, let fall his shield as his strength gave way under the weight of weapons, and commended his soul to God and St. Mary, the mother of God. Then all rushed upon him and, in full sight of his men, cut off his head and fixed it on the mast of a ship as a sign of victory. Many, weeping and lamenting bitterly, saw this from the summit of the hill, but they were powerless to help their lord. By the time their comrades from all over the province had

regione adunati sunt; sed frustra quia marchiso iam multato suffragari nequiuerunt. Classe tamen parata piratas per mare fugientes persequebantur; nimis tristes dum caput principis sui super malum pupis intuebantur. Cumque Grithfridus et complices sui respicerent et persecutores nimis iratos pro iniuria herili aduerterent; caput deposuerunt, et in mare proiecerunt. Hoc ut Roberti satellites conspexerunt; nequicquam prosequi homicidas desierunt. Corpus uero eius cum nimio luctu Anglorum et Normannorum sustulerunt, et Cestram detulerunt; ibique in cenobio sanctæ Warburgæ uirginis sepelierunt. Nuper illud cenobium Hugo Cestrensis consul construxerat;[1] eique Ricardus Beccensis monachus[2] abbas preerat, ibique Deo monachorum gregem inter beluinos cetus nutriebat.

Post aliquot annos Ernaldus monachus Vnfridi filius in Angliam transfretauit; et ossa Roberti fratris sui Roberto de Limesia Merciorum episcopo concedente sustulit, ac in Normanniam ad Vticense monasterium transtulit. Quæ Rogerius abbas cum conuentu fratrum honorifice suscepit; et in claustro monachorum secus æcclesiam in meridiana parte tumulauit. Prefatus Ernaldus cum quattuor nobilibus sociis Widone et Rogerio, Drogone et
iii. 287 Odone in adolescentia militiam deseruit,[3] et factus monachus plus cunctis sodalibus suis in monachatu desudauit; et fere quinquaginta annis in ordine monachili feruidus uixit. Hic nimirum æcclesiæ suæ utilitatibus satis inhiauit, pro quibus Britannicum pelagus multotiens transfretauit, atque Apuliam et Calabriam Siciliamque ut de spoliis parentum suorum æcclesiæ suæ subsidium suppeditaret penetrauit. Tunc Guillelmum abbatem sanctæ Eufemiæ fratrem suum et Guillelmum de Grentemaisnil consobrinum suum,[4] aliosque cognatos suos in Italia locupletatos adiit; ipsisque benigna ui quantum potuit ut monasterio suo conferret abstulit. Sic de rebus parentum suorum ornatus et alia commoda æcclesiæ suæ procurauit; ipsosque consanguineos utilitatibus monasterii subiugauit. Multas iniurias atque repulsas plurimis in locis pertulit, sed ab incepto conatu licet plurimis aduersitatibus interdum et frequenter impediretur depelli non potuit. Predictus uir his et huiusmodi nisibus sat procaciter studuit; eiusque studio conditus super tumulum fratris sui lapideus arcus usque hodie consistit. Rainaldus pictor cognomento

[1] Hugh's refoundation took place in 1092–3 (see above, Introduction, p. xxxvi).

[2] Either Richard, first prior of St. Neot's, or Anselm's chaplain, Richard (see M. Chibnall, 'The relations of Saint Anselm with the English dependencies of the abbey of Bec', in *Spicilegium Beccense* (Paris, 1959), i. 524).

[3] See above, iii. 227.

[4] See above, ii. 128 and genealogical table facing p. 370.

assembled it was too late to give any help to the lord marcher, for he was already slain. However they launched ships and pursued the pirates by sea, bitterly distressed when they saw the head of their leader on the ship's mast. When Gruffydd and his accomplices looked back and saw how maddened the pursuers were because of the insult to their lord they took down the head and threw it into the sea. Seeing this Robert's men abandoned the futile pursuit of the murderers. They took up the body, both English and Normans mourning greatly, and carried it to Chester, where they buried it in the monastery of St. Werburgh the virgin. Earl Hugh of Chester had recently built the abbey;[1] he established Richard, monk of Bec,[2] as its abbot, and cherished a community of monks for God's service in the midst of a brutal people.

Some years later the monk Arnold, Humphrey's son, crossed to England and obtained permission from Robert of Limesey, bishop of the Mercians, to remove the bones of his brother Robert, which he took back to Normandy to the monastery of Saint-Évroul. Abbot Roger and the whole community of brethren received them with reverence and buried them in the cloister of the monks against the south side of the church. Arnold himself, together with four noble companions, Guy and Roger, Drogo and Odo, had renounced his life as a knight in his youth;[3] becoming a monk he surpassed all his companions in his struggle for monastic perfection and followed the monastic way of life most fervently for almost fifty years. He was entirely devoted to the needs of his church, for whose sake he often crossed the English Channel; and he travelled as far as Apulia and Calabria and Sicily to ask for support for his church from the loot acquired by his kinsmen. He visited his brother William, abbot of St. Eufemia, and his cousin William of Grandmesnil[4] and other wealthy kinsfolk in Italy, and by gentle coercion secured from them all that he could in order to bestow it on his monastery. In this way he procured ornaments and other valuables for his church from the goods of his kinsmen, and made them recognize the needs of the monastery. He endured many insults and refusals in different places, but in spite of all the many difficulties that at times lay in his way nothing could deflect him from his purpose. He pursued all undertakings of this kind with considerable determination; thanks to his endeavours a stone arch was erected over the tomb of his brother, where it stands to this day. Reginald called Bartholomew, a painter,

Bartholomeus uariis coloribus arcum tumulumque depinxit.' et Vitalis[1] angligena satis ab Ernaldo rogatus epitaphium elegiacis uersibus hoc modo edidit.

Hoc in mausoleo Robertus de Rodelento
Conditur humano more soli gremio
Filius Vnfredi Dacorum spermate nati,
Fortis et illustris iste fuit iuuenis.
Dapsilis et pugnax, agilis formosus et audax
iii. 288 Miles in orbe fuit.' uiuere dum licuit
Marchio munificus sociisque fidelis amicus.'
Vt Christi sponsæ paruit æcclesiæ.
Presbiteros, monachos, pupillos et peregrinos.'
Semper honorabat, largaque dona dabat.
Construxit castrum tenuitque diu Rodolentum.'
Firmiter indigenis oppositum rabidis
Barbaricas contra gentes exercuit arma.'
Mille pericla probo sponte ferens animo
Montem Snaudunum fluuiumque citum Coluenum
Pluribus armatus transiliit uicibus.
Precipuam pulchro Blideno[2] rege fugato.'
Predam cum paucis cepit in insidiis.
Duxit captiuum lorisque ligauit Hoellum.'[3]
Qui tunc Walensi rex preerat manui.
Cepit Grithfridum regem,[4] uicitque Trehellum,[5]
Sic micuit crebris militiæ titulis,
At tamen incaute Walenses ausus adire.'
Occidit estiui principio Iulii.
iii. 289 Prodidit Owenius,[6] rex est gauisus Hoellus.'
Facta uindicta monte sub Hormaeua.
Ense caput secuit Grithfridus et in mare iecit,
Soma quidem reliquum possidet hunc loculum.
In claustro sancti requiescit patris Ebrulfi.'
Pro meritis cuius sit sibi plena salus,
Quondam robustus iacet hic nunc exanimatus.'
Hinc dolor in tota personat hac patria.
Hic modo fit puluis, iam nil agit utilitatis,
Ergo pie lector eius adesto memor,
Hunc ut in etherea locet arce.' roga prece digna,

[1] Orderic Vitalis.

[2] King Bleddyn was killed, probably in 1075, by Rhys ap Owain (J. E. Lloyd in *Trans. Hon. Soc. Cymmrodorion* (1899–1900), p. 151; though Lloyd's dating in this period depends partly on dates derived from a misreading of Orderic; cf. above, p. xxxviii).

[3] Hywel ap Ithel (J. E. Lloyd, *History of Wales*, 3rd edn., ii. 384 n. 87).

[4] Gruffydd ap Cynan ap Iago, who secured the kingdom in 1081.

painted the arch and tomb in different colours, and the Englishman Vitalis,[1] at Arnold's earnest request, composed this epitaph in elegiac verse:

Here in this tomb Robert of Rhuddlan lies,
Dust now to dust returned, like humans all;
The son of Humphrey, born of Danish stock,
Brave and illustrious always in his youth;
Courteous and warlike, handsome, swift and bold,
While life remained, a true knight in this world.
Most generous lord, faithful and loyal friend,
Obedient ever to Christ's bride, the Church;
All priests, all monks, orphans and homeless men,
Honourably held by him, received his gifts.
Rhuddlan his seat; he built the castle there
And held it long against wild, native foes.
Arming himself to fight barbarian hordes
He bore incessant perils undismayed;
Snowdon's high mountain, Conway's rapid river
Never deterred his oft-adventuring arms.
With a few men he ambushed great king Bleddyn[2]
And made him fly abandoning rich booty;
While Hywel,[3] who once as king led the Welsh forces,
Was bound with thongs and dragged away a captive.
He took King Gruffydd[4] prisoner, vanquished Trahaearn,[5]
And shone in many such deeds of knightly valour;
Finally, in a rash onslaught on the Welsh,
Death claimed him in the first heat of July.
Owain[6] proclaimed the news, King Hywel gloried,
When vengeance struck under the Great Orme's mount;
Gruffydd cut off his head: the deep sea claimed it;
His other bones are guarded in this tomb.
Now in the cloister of blessed father Évroul
He rests; may the saint's merits earn salvation
For him who, once so strong, now lies here lifeless;
Mourning for him re-echoes through our country.
Now he is turned to dust, powerless for action;
Reader, in Christian duty, think to help him,
Pray humbly that he may find room in heaven,

[5] Trahaearn ap Caradog, hereditary prince of the cantref of Arwystli, killed in 1081 at the battle of Glyn Cyfing (ibid. ii. 380–1).

[6] Owain ap Edwin, who gave his services to Hugh of Chester in 1098 and for a time exercised some authority in North Wales; he died in 1105 (ibid. ii. 408, 410, 416).

Cum lacrimis uerum qui regit omne Deum.
Christe Dei splendor, uitæ dator et reparator
Orbis:ʼ huic famulo propiciare tuo.
Eripe Tartareis Robertum Christe caminis:ʼ
Est nimis ipse reus, terge precor facinus.
Parce quod ipse piam rogitans clamore Mariam:ʼ
Consutus rigidis occubuit iaculis,
Indulge culpas, mansuras annue gazas:ʼ
Vt queat ymnidicis semper inesse choris. Amen.

4

Guillelmo Rufo per omnes Anglorum regiones dominante, et ubique rebelles principali censura fortiter comprimente:ʼ turgidus Odo de Anglia eiectus Baiocensem diocesim repetiit, et Roberto duce molliter agente toti Normanniæ dominari sategit. Prouincia tota erat dissoluta, et predones cateruatim discurrebant per uicos et per rura:ʼ nimiumque super inermes debachabatur latrunculo-
iii. 290 rum caterua.[1] Robertus dux nullam super malefactores exercebat disciplinam, et grassatores per viii annos sub molli principe super imbecillem populum suam agitabant furiam. Importune sanctam æcclesiam uexabant:ʼ et possessiones quas antecessores boni liberaliter dederant, uiolenter auferebant aut deuastabant. Desolata gemebant monasteria:ʼ et monachi ac sanctimoniales grandi premebantur penuria. In tantarum simultatuum pestilentia:ʼ nullus honos Deo sacratis exhibebatur seu reuerentia. Cotidie fiebant incendia:ʼ rapinæ et homicidia:ʼ et lugebat plebs nimiis calamitatibus anxia. Filii nequam emergebantur in Normannia:ʼ qui enormi cum auiditate ad cuncta prompti erant facinora, et crudeliter materna depascebantur uiscera. Inter hæc impune procedebat petulans illecebra molles flammisque cremandos turpiter fedabat uenus sodomestica:ʼ maritalem thorum publice polluebant adulteria, et erga diuinæ legis obseruantiam multiplex aderat negligentia. Episcopi ex autoritate Dei exleges anathematizabant, theologi prolatis sermonibus Dei reos admonebant:ʼ sed his omnibus tumor et cupiditas cum satellitibus suis immoderate resistebant. Adulterina passim municipia condebantur:ʼ et ibidem filii latronum ceu catuli luporum ad dilacerandas bidentes nutriebantur. Occasiones inimiciciarum ab iniquis querebantur, ut mutuis conflictibus

[1] For the disorders after the death of William I see the evidence of the Cartulary of Holy Trinity, Caen, printed in Haskins, *Norman Institutions*, pp. 63–4.

With tears importune God, who governs all things.
O Christ, glory of God, life-giver and Redeemer
Of the world, have mercy on your servant here.
O Christ, save Robert from Hell's fiery furnace,
His guilt is great, yet pardon his transgressions.
Spare him, I beg, who called on blessed Mary
Even as he fell transfixed with many weapons;
Forgive his guilt; grant him abiding treasures
That he may chant with the eternal chorus. Amen.

4

While William Rufus reigned securely over the whole of England and firmly repressed the rebels everywhere by his royal judgements, the proud Odo, banished from England, returned to his diocese of Bayeux and applied himself to gaining supreme power in Normandy, since Duke Robert was weak and ineffectual. The whole province was in disorder; troops of bandits were at large in the villages and all over the countryside, and robber bands pillaged the weak mercilessly.[1] Duke Robert made no attempt to bring the malefactors to justice, and for eight years under the weak duke scoundrels were free to treat the innocent with the utmost brutality. They sorely abused Holy Church, seizing by violence or devastating the properties which their worthy ancestors had freely given. The ruined monasteries lamented; monks and nuns suffered great privation. As these outrages spread like a plague no honour or reverence was shown to consecrated persons or things. Crimes of arson, rapine, and murder were committed daily, and the wretched populace bewailed its unspeakable misfortunes. Sons of iniquity rose to power in Normandy, ready and eager for all evil-doing, and cruelly devoured the bowels of their mother. In such times as these sodomy walked abroad unpunished, flaunting its tender allurements and foully corrupting the effeminate, dragging them down to Hell. Acts of adultery openly defiled the marriage bed and the divine law was neglected in every way. Bishops pronounced anathema on the outlaws by God's authority, theologians preached the word of God as a warning to sinners, but Pride and Avarice and their minions totally ignored all these. Unlicensed castles were built in many places, and there sons of iniquity—or rather wolf-cubs—were reared to tear the flocks to pieces. They found pretexts for quarrelling so that they might

iii. 291 finitimæ sedes[a] frequentarentur.' et rapacitates cum incendiis irreuerenti conatu agitarentur. Grauiter hæc sentit et michi attestatur depopulata regio.' et gemens uiduarum debiliumque pluribus oppressa malis concio. Sic per desidiam ignaui ducis in breui disperiit.' et in magnam egestatem ac perturbationem dedecusque cecidit, quicquid per uiuacitatem studiumque sollertis eri et fautorum eius actum est.' longoque tempore in Neustria propagatum est.

In estate postquam certus rumor de Rofensis deditione citra mare personuit.' Henricus clito Constantiniensis comes in Angliam transfretauit,[1] et a fratre suo terram matris suæ requisiuit. Rex autem Guillelmus benigniter eum ut decuit fratrem suscepit.' et quod petierat fraterne concessit.[2] Deinde peractis pro quibus ierat in autumno regi ualefecit.' et cum Roberto Belesmensi qui iam per amicos potentes cum rege pacificatus erat in Normanniam remeare disposuit. Interea quidam maliuoli discordiæ satores eos anticipauerunt, et falsa ueris miscentes Roberto duci denunciauerunt.' quod Henricus frater suus et Robertus Belesmensis cum rege Rufo essent pacificati, ac ad ducis dampnum sacramenti eciam obligatione confederati. Dux igitur illos potentes ac fortissimos milites sciens, eorumque conatus ualde pertimescens.' cum Baiocensi episcopo consilium iniit, et prefatos optimates preoccupauit. Nam antequam aliquid molirentur, cum securi ad littus maris de nauibus egrederentur.' ualida militum manu missa
iii. 292 illos comprehendit, uinculis coartauit.' et unum Baiocis[3] aliumque Noilleio sub manu Baiocensis tiranni custodiæ mancipauit. Rogerius comes Scrobesburiæ ut Robertum filium suum captum audiuit.' accepta a rege licentia festinus in Neustriam uenit, et omnia castella sua militari manu contra ducem muniuit. Porro Baiocensis Odo uelut igniuomus draco proiectus in terram, nimis iratus contra regis insolentiam.' uariis seditionibus commouebat Normanniam, ut sic aliquo modo nepoti suo a quo turpiter expulsus fuerat machinaretur iniuriam. Ipsum nempe dux multum metuebat.' et quibusdam consiliis eius adquiescebat, quedam uero floccipendebat.

[a] cedes, *Caen MS.*

---

[1] Henry witnessed his brother's charter at Fécamp on 7 July 1088 (see above, p. 134 n. 1) and probably crossed to England soon afterwards.

[2] There is no record that Henry ever received any of his mother's land.

[3] According to William of Malmesbury Henry was imprisoned at Rouen

overrun the surrounding settlements in their conflicts with each other, and be free to plunder and burn without respect for anyone. The devastated region, with mourning widows and cripples in all their afflictions, in itself bears witness to me of the extent of its suffering. So all that had been achieved by the activity and zeal of a far-sighted lord and his supporters and preserved in Normandy for a long time past was ruined by the inactivity of the slothful duke, and want, disorder and shame abounded.

In the summer, when positive news of the surrender of Rochester was heard in Normandy, Prince Henry, count of the Cotentin, crossed to England,[1] and asked his brother for his mother's lands. King William received him kindly as a brother should, and fraternally granted his petition.[2] In the autumn, after completing the business that had brought him, he said good-bye to the king and began preparations for returning to Normandy with Robert of Bellême, who had already been reconciled with the king through the intercession of powerful friends. In the interval some hostile mischief-makers arrived ahead of them and, mingling truth with falsehood, announced to Duke Robert that his brother Henry and Robert of Bellême had made their peace with King Rufus and had formed a sworn confederation against the duke. Since the duke knew that they were powerful and courageous knights and stood in great fear of an attack by them, he took counsel with the bishop of Bayeux and seized the two lords as a precaution. Before they could take any action, when they were peacefully disembarking from the ships on the sea-shore, he sent a strong force of knights to seize them, fettered them and threw them into prison under the guard of the tyrannical bishop of Bayeux, the one at Bayeux[3] and the other at Neuilly-l'Évêque. When Roger earl of Shrewsbury heard that his son Robert had been arrested, he secured the king's permission and hurried into Normandy, where he fortified all his castles with strong garrisons against the duke. Thereat Odo of Bayeux, like a fire-breathing dragon that has been vanquished, grew very angry at the king's contempt for him, and stirred up a number of troubles in Normandy, so that by some means or other he might contrive to injure his nephew who had banished him in disgrace. The duke certainly stood in great fear of Odo, and consented to some of his proposals though he disregarded others.

(*GR* ii. 468). The conflicting accounts of his movements are discussed by David, *Robert Curthose*, pp. 52–3.

5

Vndique furentibus in Normannia seditiosis, et multa mala cupientibus addere pessimis: presul Odo ad ducem Rotomagum uenit, et consideratis totius prouinciæ negotiis duci ait, 'Quisquis gubernaculum regni debet tenere, populoque Dei qui diuersis in moribus diffusus est preeminere: mitis et asper prout ratio expetit sit ubique. Sit mitis ut agnus bonis, et subiectis ac humilibus: asper autem ut leo prauis et rebellibus ac contumacibus. Hoc domine dux sagaciter perpende, ut bene nobili presis ducatui Normanniæ: quem diuinitus suscepisti ex paterna successione. Conforta te: et uiriliter age. Ecce proterui et exleges per totam terram debachantur: et pessimis assiduisque actionibus pene paganis assimilantur, et enormitate scelerum si dici fas est ad-
iii. 293 equantur. Clamant ad te monachi et uiduæ et dormis: inaudita facinora frequenter audis et paruipendis. Non sic egit sanctus Dauid nec magnus Alexander, non sic Iulius Cesar nec Seuerus Afer: non sic Anniba Cartaginiensis nec Scipio Affricanus, non Cirus Persa nec Marius Romanus. Quid moror in relatione barbarorum obscura, quorum eciam nomina tibi sunt incognita? Replicemus notiora, et sanguini nostro propinquiora. Reminiscere patrum tuorum et proauorum: quorum magnanimitatem et uirtutem pertimuit bellicosa gens Francorum. Rollonem dico et Guillelmum Longam Spatam atque tres Ricardos et Robertum auum tuum: postremo Guillelmum patrem tuum cunctis antecessoribus sullimiorem. Horum queso rigorem emulare et efficaciam sicut illi predecessorum suorum sectati sunt uigorem et industriam: qui regna mundi per immensos labores optinuerunt, tirannos compresserunt: et seuas gentes edomuerunt. Expergiscere et inuictum aggrega exercitum Normanniæ: et in urbem Cenomannicam proficiscere. Ibi sunt municipes tui in arce quam pater tuus condidit: et tota ciuitas cum uenerabili Hoello episcopo tibi gratanter obedit.[1] Iube ut illuc omnes Cenomannensium proceres ueniant ad te: et obsecundantibus letis affatibus et beniuola mente congratulare. Contempnentes uero cum uirtute militari aggredere, et munitiones eorum nisi cito dediderint se: protinus obside.

[1] William I built the keep and the two towers of Mont-Barbet and Petit-Mont-Barbet at Le Mans soon after the conquest of 1063 (Latouche, *Maine*, pp. 34, 38, 90). Bishop Hoel was certainly a loyal supporter of the Normans as long as circumstances allowed: the citizens, however, were turbulent and shifting in their allegiances. All these speeches are imaginary (cf. ibid., p. 44 n. 7).

5

While disturbers of the peace were troubling every part of Normandy, and the worst of them were ready to cause many other evils, Bishop Odo came to see the duke at Rouen. After considering all the business of the province he said to the duke, 'Whoever is ordained to direct the ship of state and to govern God's people, who differ greatly one from another in their conduct, needs to be both gentle and severe as occasion requires. He should be gentle as a lamb to good men and to the obedient and humble, but harsh as a lion to evil men and rebels and law-breakers. Give serious thought to this, my lord duke, so that you may provide good government for the fair duchy of Normandy, which you have received from God by hereditary succession. Take heart and act boldly. See how miscreants and outlaws pillage all over the country, showing themselves no better than pagans by their repeated atrocities and the enormity of their crimes, if I may say so. Monks and widows cry out to you, and you slumber; you hear of unspeakable outrages again and again and take no notice. This is not how the holy David acted, or Alexander the Great, or Julius Caesar, or Septimius Severus; Hannibal the Carthaginian, or Scipio Africanus, or Cyrus the Persian, or Marius the Roman. But why do I waste time with an obscure recital of foreigners, whose names even mean nothing to you? Let us reflect on better known men, nearer to us in blood. Remember your fathers and ancestors, whose spirit and courage brought terror to the warlike Franks. I refer to Rollo and William Longsword; the three Richards and Robert your grandfather; finally to your father William, greater than all his forebears. I ask you to imitate their justice and their achievements, just as they imitated the vigour and determination of those predecessors of theirs who conquered the kingdoms of the world by prodigious efforts, restrained tyrants, and civilized barbarous peoples. Rouse yourself, summon the unconquered Norman army, and march to the city of Le Mans. There you will find your castellans in the castle which your father built, and the whole city as well as the venerable Bishop Hoel is obedient to you.[1] Command all the magnates of Maine to assemble there with you, and reward those who obey with a ready welcome and your goodwill. But march on those who refuse with your forces, and lay siege to any castles that are not handed over to you at once. When

Cenomannensibus subiugatis Rogerium comitem aggredere.' et
ipsum cum progenie sua de finibus Normanniæ funditus exclude.
iii. 294 Ne timeas, sed in uirtute Dei confidas. Virile robur arripe.' et consiliis sapientum utere. Iam Robertum Rogerii primogenitum tenes
in carcere, iam si pertinaciter ut bonum ducem decet perstiteris
in agone.' Talauacios subuersores de ducatu tuo poteris penitus
expellere. Maledicta est prosapia eorum.' alit nefas et machinatur
quasi ius hereditarium. Hoc nimirum horrenda mors eorum
attestatur.' quorum nullus communi et usitato fine ut ceteri
homines defecisse inuenitur. Talauaciana propago nisi nunc eam
eradicaueris.' adhuc ut opinor noxia tibi erit et inexpugnabilis.
Habent quidem fortissima castella, Bellismum, Lubercionem,
Axeium, Alencionem, Damfrontem, Sanctum Senericum, rupem
de Ialgeio pro qua ab audaci Hugone digladiata est Mabilia,[1]
Mamercias et Vinacium[2] et alia plura, quæ Guillelmus Bellismen-
iii. 295 sis et Robertus, Iuo et Guarinus aliique successores eorum
superbe construxerunt.' aut ui seu fraude dominis suis uel finitimis
surripuerunt. Dolis et scelestis machinationibus semper inhiaue-
runt.' nec ulli amicorum uel affinium fidem seruauerunt. Simplici-
bus itaque uicinis nece seu captione supplantatis admodum
creuerunt.' et ingentes domos ac fortissimas munitiones cum
nimio sudore pagensium condiderunt. Nunc omnia optime dux
iure illis auferre poteris.' si magnanimi patris tui et operum eius
fortis emulator extiteris. Pater enim tuus omnia predicta munimenta in uita sua habuit.' et quibuscumque uoluit ad tutandum
commendauit.[3] Verum Robertus quem iam ligatum coherces mox
ut regem defunctum audiuit.' municipes tuos de munitionibus tuis
per superbiam suam expulit, suæque ditioni ut exhereditaret te
munimina subegit. Hæc omnia quæ dixi sapienter inspice.' ac ut
bonus princeps pro pace sanctæ matris æcclesiæ, et pro defensione
pauperum debiliumque laudabiliter exurge.' et resistentes uirtute
contere. Confractis cornibus primorum qui ceruicem erexerunt
contra te.' reliqui uisa deiectione contubernalium formidabunt te,
iii. 296 et iussis tuis famulabuntur sine contradictione. Tunc populus
Dei sub tutela protectionis tuæ securus in pace lætabitur.' et pro

[1] See above, iii. 136.
[2] For the castle of Vignats see L. Musset in *BSAN* lii (1952–4), 225 n. 10.

the Manceaux have been subdued, attack Earl Roger and banish him and his seed for ever from the soil of Normandy. Fear nothing, trust in God's strength. Be strong in your actions and rely on wise counsellors. Now you hold Robert, Roger's eldest son, in captivity; now if you continue resolutely with the struggle as a good duke should you can utterly extirpate the rebellious sons of Talvas from your duchy. Their stock is accursed: it nourishes evil and conspires almost by right of inheritance. This is proved by their horrible ends; you will find that none of them has met an ordinary or normal death like other men. I consider that unless you root out the family of Talvas now it will become more menacing to you and invincible later. They have strongly fortified castles: Bellême, Lurson, Essay, Alençon, Domfront, Saint-Céneri, La Roche Mabille, for the sake of which the daring Hugh cut off Mabel's head,[1] Mamers, Vignats,[2] and many others, which William of Bellême, Robert, Ivo, and Warin, and other successors of theirs either built in their pride or wrested by force or fraud from their lords or neighbours. They have always been addicted to deceits and evil plots; they have never kept faith with any of their friends or neighbours. They have grown excessively powerful by annexing the possessions of the innocent neighbours they have killed or taken prisoner, and have built great houses and almost impregnable castles by the sweated labour of peasants. Now, noble duke, you are in a position to take all this from them by right, if you courageously follow in your great father's footsteps and imitate his actions. For your father while he lived held all these castles in his own hand and entrusted the guard of them to men of his own choice.[3] But Robert, whom you now hold captive, on receiving the news of the king's death, in his arrogance drove your castellans out of your castles, subjected them to his sway and disinherited you. Reflect carefully on all that I have said; and stand up worthily as a good prince should for the peace of holy Mother Church and for the defence of the poor and helpless; put down all opponents with resolution. Once you have broken the horns of the leaders who raise their heads against you the rest, seeing the overthrow of their comrades, will fear you and obey your commands without opposition. Then the people of God will be able to flourish in peace under your protection, and will dutifully offer prayers to

[3] For William the Conqueror's control of private castles see J. Yver in *BSAN* liii (1955–6), 62–3.

salute tua omnipotentem Deum pie deprecabitur. Cultus diuinitatis in regione tua cunctis ab ordinibus iugiter celebrabitur.' et lex Dei cum securitate communi salubriter obseruabitur.'

Exhortatoriam antistitis allocutionem omnes qui aderant laudauerunt.' et sese ad ducis officium pro defensione totius patriæ hilariter optulerunt. Dux igitur Robertus aggregato exercitu Cenomannis profectus est.' et tam a clero quam a ciuibus tripudianter susceptus est.[1] Deinde legationibus eius auditis conuenerunt ad eum Goisfredus Madeniensis.' Robertus Burgundio et Helias filius Iohannis,[2] aliique plures parati ad seruitium ducis. Agminibus uero Normannorum preerant presul Baiocensis et Guillelmus comes Ebroicensis.' Radulfus de Conchis et nepos eius Guillelmus Bretoliensis, aliique militares uiri multis probitatibus precipui. Paganus de Monde Dublahelis[3] cum aliis contumacibus castrum
iii. 297 Balaonem tenebat.' et uenienti duci cum turmis suis acriter resistebat. Ibi Osmundus de Guaspreio pulcherrimus miles et honorabilis kal' Septembris occisus est.' cuius corpus ab Ernaldo monacho Vticum deductum est, et in porticum ante ualuas æcclesiæ sepultum est.

Post plurima damna utriusque partis Balaonenses pacem cum duce fecerunt, et postmodum Normanni simul ac Cenomannenses cum duce castrum Sancti Serenici obsederunt. Ibi familia Roberti Belesmensis erat, cui Robertus Quadrellus[4] acerrimus miles et multo uigore conspicuus preerat.' qui hortatu Rogerii comitis obsidentibus fortiter obstabat. Verum deficiente alimonia castrum captum est.' et prefatus municeps iussu irati ducis protinus oculis priuatus est. Aliis quoque pluribus qui contumaciter ibidem restiterant principi Normanniæ debilitatio membrorum inflicta est ex sentencia curiæ.[5]

Tunc Gaufredus Madeniensis cum Cenomannensium tribunis ad ducem accessit.' eique Robertum Geroium Roberti Geroiani filium presentauit. 'Iste' inquit 'tiro domine dux consobrinus tuus est.' sed in Apulia cum parentibus suis qui magna ibidem potentia pollent iamdudum conuersatus est. Nunc autem ad te dominum
iii. 298 suum et consanguineum fiducialiter accedit, seruitiumque suum tibi fideliter offerens hoc a te castrum iure requirit.' quod pater

[1] Robert's expedition probably took place in August 1088 (Latouche, *Maine*, p. 40).

[2] Robert was lord of Sablé and Craon (see above, p. 48 n. 2); Helias was the son of John of La Flèche.

[3] For Pain see Latouche, *Maine*, p. 40.

[4] His name suggests that he may have been a crossbowman.

almighty God for your salvation. The divine offices will be celebrated regularly by all orders in your duchy, and both the law of God and the general peace will be maintained for the good of all.'

All who were present applauded the bishop's persuasive speech, and gladly offered their service to the duke for the defence of their native land. So Duke Robert summoned an army and set out for Maine, where he was received by the clergy and citizens with rejoicing.[1] After hearing his messages Geoffrey of Mayenne, Robert the Burgundian, Helias son of John,[2] and many others answered the summons, ready for the duke's service. The Norman forces were commanded by the bishop of Bayeux and William count of Évreux, Ralph of Conches and his nephew William of Breteuil, and other warriors of conspicuous courage. Pain of Mondoubleau[3] and other rebels held the castle of Ballon and put up a fierce resistance to the duke when he arrived with his troops. There Osmund of Gaprée, a most noble and honourable knight, was killed on 1 September; his body was brought to Saint-Évroul by the monk Arnold, and was buried in the porch outside the doors of the church.

After both sides had suffered losses on many occasions the defenders of Ballon made peace with the duke; and afterwards the Normans and Manceaux together led by the duke laid siege to Saint-Céneri. Robert of Bellême's garrison was there, under the able command of a most courageous and resourceful knight, Robert Quarrel.[4] Encouraged by Earl Roger he put up a stout defence against the besiegers. However when food supplies failed the castle was taken, and at the command of the angry duke the castellan was blinded on the spot. Many others too who had contumaciously resisted the duke of Normandy at Saint-Céneri were mutilated by sentence of the duke's court.[5]

Then Geoffrey of Mayenne and the leaders of the Manceaux approached the duke, and presented Robert Giroie the son of Robert Giroie to him. 'This young knight', they said, 'is your kinsman, my lord duke; but he has spent many years in Apulia with his relatives, who are powerful lords there. Now he approaches you in loyalty as his lord and kinsman and, offering you his service and fealty, asks you for this castle which is rightly his, which his father justly possessed and held all his life by hereditary

[5] This is one of the very few references to any activities by Robert Curthose's *curia*; cf. Haskins, *Norman Institutions*, p. 77.

suus omni uita sua hereditario iure possedit, tenuit, et istic obiit.'[1] Tunc Robertus dux ista poscentibus facile annuit.' et Roberto Geroio castellum Sancti Serenici reddidit. Ille uero fere xxvi annis postmodum tenuit, muris et uallis zetisque muniuit, et moriens Guillelmo et Roberto filiis suis dereliquit.

Habitatoribus huius municipii quies et pax pene semper desunt.' finitimique Cenomannenses seu Normanni iurgiis et seditionibus insistunt. Scopulosum montem anfractus Sarte fluminis ex tribus partibus ambit.' in quo sanctus Serenicus uenerandus confessor tempore Milehardi Sagiorum pontificis habitauit.[2] Ibi monachile cœnobium fundauit, cum glorioso cetu diu domino militauit.' uitæque cursu beatæ peracto nonis Maii feliciter ad dominum migrauit. Denique Karolo simplice regnante dum Hastingus Danus cum gentilium phalange Neustriam depopulatus est.' sanctum corpus a fidelibus in castrum Teoderici translatum est, et dispersis monachis monasterium destructum est. Succedenti uero tempore incolarum facta est mutatio. Sanguinarii predones ibi speluncam latronum condiderunt, ubi sub regimine sancti Serenici contemptores mundi modeste conuersati sunt.' et in ordine monachico iugum domini fine tenus gesserunt. Centum quadraginta ut fertur sub prefato archimandrita cultores ibidem in
iii. 299 uinea Domini Sabaoth laborauerunt, quorum lapidea sepulchra[3] palam aduentantibus intra basilicam et in circuitu eius testimonio sunt.' cuius meriti et reuerentiæ homines inibi requiescunt. Scelesti ergo habitatores multa infortunia merito perpessi sunt.' et cedibus ac combustionibus multimodisque pressuris ac deiectionibus frequenter afflicti sunt.

Municipes Alencionis et Bellismi aliarumque munitionum ut audierunt quam male contigerit Rodberto Quadrello et complicibus qui cum eo fuerunt, ualde territi sunt.' ac ut debitas uenienti duci munitiones redderent consilium inierunt. Verum Robertus dux ab incepta uirtute cito defecit, et mollicie suadente ad lectum et quietem auide recurrit, exercitumque suum ut quisque ad sua repedaret dimisit. Rogerius igitur comes dissolutis agminibus Normannorum atque Cenomannensium gauisus est et per dicaces legatos a duce pacem filiique sui absolutionem postulans multa

[1] See above, ii. 28, 80–2; iii. 134 for the earlier history of Saint-Céneri.

[2] Cf. *AA.SS.*, May, ii. 161–6. Probably Milehard bishop of Séez either is to be identified with Amlecharius, who occurs from 650 to 663, or succeeded him (L. Duchesne, *Fastes épiscopaux de l'ancienne Gaule* (Paris, 1894–1915), ii. 229, 231–3). See also L. Musset in *Bull. soc. hist. et archéol. de l'Orne*, 1970, p. 12.

right, and where he died.'[1] Duke Robert readily granted their request and restored the castle of Saint-Céneri to Robert Giroie. He held it for about thirty-six years afterwards, fortified it with walls and ramparts and watch-towers, and left it to his sons William and Robert when he died.

The dwellers in this fortress have hardly ever enjoyed peace and quiet; and the Normans and Manceaux of this frontier region are constantly involved in conflicts and uprisings. A loop in the river Sarthe flows round three sides of the rugged hill where the venerable confessor St. Céneri lived in the time of Milehard, bishop of Séez.[2] He founded a monastic cell there and for many years served the Lord with a glorious company; when the course of his holy life had come to a close he departed gladly to the Lord on 7 May. Later, in the reign of Charles the Simple, when Hasting the Dane with a war band of pagans devastated Normandy, the holy body was translated by the faithful to Château-Thierry, the monks were dispersed, and the monastery was destroyed. In the period that followed the local inhabitants changed. Bloodthirsty bandits made a den of robbers in the place where men who had abandoned the world had once lived quietly and, as disciplined monks, had carried the yoke of the Lord to their life's end. Tradition tells us that a hundred and forty monks laboured in the vineyard of the Lord of Hosts there when Céneri was abbot; their stone sarcophagi,[3] remaining inside and around the church, bear witness to all comers of the man whose merits and venerable life brought together the monks who rest in that place. The brutal later settlers deserved the crop of misfortunes they suffered, and often had to endure bloodshed and fire and violence and disasters of every kind.

When the castellans of Alençon and Bellême and other castles heard of the terrible fate of Robert Quarrel and his companions their nerve gave way, and they began to discuss surrendering the fortresses entrusted to them when the duke arrived. However Duke Robert soon abandoned his show of energy and, giving way to voluptuousness, sank back with relief into idle dalliance, and disbanded his army, sending all his men home. Earl Roger, delighted by the dismissal of the Norman and Manceaux troops, sent smooth-tongued envoys to ask for peace and pardon for his

[3] Some of these early sarcophagi can still be seen built into the foundations of the romanesque church.

falso pollicitus est. Dux autem qui improuidus erat et instabilis, ad lapsum facilis, ad tenendum iusticiæ rigorem mollis, ex insperato friuolis pactionibus infidorum adquieuit:' et pace facta Rogerio comiti petita concessit, atque Robertum Belesmensem a uinculis absoluit. Ille uero iam liberatus intumuit, iussa ducis atque minas minus appreciauit:' preteritæque memor iniuriæ diutinam multiplicemque uindictam exercuit. Nam per quindecim annos[1] quibus postmodum in Neustria[a] simul manserunt admodum
iii. 300 furuit, totamque terram eius pluribus modis turbauit. Multos ab auxilio eius et famulatu callidis tergiuersationibus auertit:' et dominium ducis quod antecessores eius possederant et copiose auxerant imminuit. Erat enim ingenio subtilis, dolosus et uersipellis, corpore magnus et fortis, audax et potens in armis, eloquens nimiumque crudelis, auaricia et libidine inexplebilis. Perspicax seuorum commentor operum, et in exercitiis mundi grauissimorum patiens laborum. In extruendis ædificiis et machinis aliisque arduis operibus ingeniosus artifex:' et in torquendis hominibus inexorabilis carnifex. Sanctam æcclesiam non ut filius matrem honorauit, adiuuit atque uestiuit, sed uelut priuignus nouercam deturpauit, oppressit ac spoliauit. Hunc denique post innumeros reatus et dolosas factiones iusto Dei iudicio in uinculis artauit Henricus rex:' ut equissimus censor et ad hoc specialiter a Deo inspiratus miserorum strenuus uindex. Verum de his alias.

Prefatus uir procurante Guillelmo rege qui multum eundem dilexerat propter amorem parentum eius Rogerii et Mabiliæ, filiam Guidonis Pontiui comitis Agnetem nomine uxorem duxit, ex qua filium nomine Guillelmum progenuit:' qui hereditario iure amplas possessiones in Neustria et Pontiuo postmodum late possedit. Robertus enim ut diuitiis sic tirannide omnes fratres suos superauit, et omne antecessorum suorum in Normannia et Cenomannico rure patrimonium exhereditatis fratribus[2] inuasit, et
iii. 301 longo tempore solus optinuit. Contribules suos nobilitate pares sibi subiugare summo nisu laborauit, et quosdam prout insatiabilis cupiditas dictauit:' dolis uel intolerabilibus bellis aut insidiosis assultibus suæ ditioni curuauit. Hoc experti sunt Hugo de Nonanto, Paganellus et Robertus de Sancto Serenico, Bernardus de Firmitate et alii multi quos idem sepe contristauit multisque modis

[a] Neustriam, *Caen MS.*

[1] Fifteen years seems to be an approximate round figure rather than a calculation; moreover Robert Curthose made peace with Robert of Bellême in 1103 (David, *Robert Curthose*, p. 148).

[2] Here Orderic seems to imply that the Norman lands ought to have been divided.

son from the duke in return for many worthless promises. So the duke, who was imprudent and changeable, easily persuaded, and weak in enforcing justice, unexpectedly agreed to a precarious peace with the traitors and, remitting his rancour, granted Earl Roger's petitions and freed Robert of Bellême from his fetters. His presumption grew all the greater after his release; he showed even less respect for the commands and threats of the duke and, nursing a grievance for past wrongs, took vengeance daily in every way he could. During the fifteen years[1] that the two afterwards remained in Normandy he was thoroughly disorderly and found many ways of causing disturbances all over the duke's domains. By his cunning subterfuges he prevented many men from giving the duke help or service and was a continual threat to the domains which Robert had inherited, greatly enlarged, from his ancestors. He was a man of keen intelligence, treacherous and devious, strong and well-built, bold and victorious in battle, ready in speech and appallingly cruel, insatiable in his greed and lust. He was ingenious in devising difficult enterprises and ready to endure unremitting toil in worldly ventures. He showed great skill both in planning buildings and devising siege-weapons and other such things; but he was a merciless butcher in the way he tortured men. He never honoured, aided, or clothed holy Mother Church as a son should, but like a stepson shamed, oppressed, and plundered her. Finally when he had been guilty of countless crimes and treacherous plots King Henry threw him into fetters by the righteous decree of God, so proving himself a just judge and bold avenger of the poor, specially directed by God to this end. But more of this later.

King William, who had a great regard for this man because of his love for his parents Roger and Mabel, arranged a marriage for him with Agnes, daughter of Guy count of Ponthieu, and he had by her a son called William, who later came into his far-flung lands in Normandy and Ponthieu by hereditary right. Robert indeed, being richer and more tyrannical than all his brothers, forcibly disinherited them;[2] he seized all the patrimony of his ancestors in Normandy and Maine and enjoyed sole possession of it for many years. He did his utmost to dominate his fellow countrymen of equal rank, and reduced many of them to submission by cunning or cruel wars or treacherous attacks. This was the fate of Hugh of Nonant, Painel and Robert of Saint-Céneri, Bernard of La Ferté-Bernard and many others, whom Robert repeatedly attacked

terruit et afflixit. Multos nimirum demptis honoribus et combustis munitionibus humiliauit, seu depopulatis possessionibus in nimiam egestatem redegit.' uel quod est peius debilitatis membris mancos uel loripedes uel orbatis luminibus inutiles reddidit. Misera itaque regio in desolationem redibat, dum flagrans tirannis cruenti marchionis omnes finitimos conculcare ambiebat.' contra quem animositas ingenuitate pari tumentium pristinam libertatem usque ad mortem defensare satagebat. Sic inmensa cotidie detrimenta crescebant.' et pro uindicta uel adquisitione damna damnis adiecta res mortalium conterebant, terrigenasque ad inediam minabant.

Goisfredus Rotronis Mauritaniæ comitis filius[1] contra Robertum
iii. 302 arma sustulit.' et Excalfoium multasque alias in circuitu uillas combussit, multasque predas hominesque captos aduxit. Erat idem consul magnanimus, corpore pulcher et ualidus, timens Deum et æcclesiæ cultor deuotus, clericorum pauperumque Dei defensor strenuus, in pace quietus et amabilis bonisque pollebat moribus.' in bello grauis et fortunatus, finitimisque intolerabilis regibus et inimicus omnibus. Hic nobilitate parentum suorum et coniugis suæ Beatricis[2] inter illustres spectabilis erat.' strenuosque barones et in armis acres oppidanos suæ ditioni subditos habebat. Filias quoque suas consularibus uiris dedit in matrimonio, Margaritam Henrico comiti de Guarenico.' et Iulianam Gisleberto de Aquilæ oppido, ex quibus orta est elegans sobolis generosæ[a] propago. Goisfredus itaque comes tot stemmatibus exornabatur.' et armis animisque cum diuitiis et amicis fulciebatur.' et quod est super omnia timore Domini stipatus neminem timens ut leo pro- grediebatur. Damfrontem fortissimum castrum aliosque fundos iure calumniabatur.' et Roberto cognato suo auferre nitebatur.[3] Contristabatur quod inermes et immeritos premebat, sed in campo publicum hostem reperire nequibat.' contra quem debitam
iii. 303 ultionem exercebat. Nam ille qui pene omnes comprimebat.' omnes nichilominus metuebat, ideoque publicum certamen cum hoste cominus agere non audebat. In munitionibus igitur suis callide latitabat, et predones discurrere per fines suos plerunque merens sinebat.' nec eis obuiam procedere quamuis militiæ

[a] generosa, *Caen MS.*

---

[1] Geoffrey of Mortagne II, count of Perche. For his career see above, ii. 266 n. 4. His father Rotrou had married Adeline, daughter of Warin of Bellême (above, ii. 363–4).

[2] She was a daughter of Hilduin, count of Montdidier and Roucy (GEC xii (2), 360).

and terrorized, making their lives a misery. He humbled many by seizing their honors and burning their castles, or reduced them to penury by ravaging their lands, or, still worse, mutilated them, leaving them maimed or halt or blind and utterly helpless. The wretched province was reduced to a desert, while the terrible lord marcher in his open tyranny strove to crush all his neighbours and they for their part, proud of their equal birth, endeavoured to defend their former liberty against him to the death. So the terrible disturbances increased daily, vengeance or greed caused injury to be heaped on injury, destroying all men's property and bringing the wretched populace to the verge of starvation.

Geoffrey, the son of Rotrou count of Mortagne,[1] took up arms against Robert, burnt Échauffour and many other villages in the neighbourhood, and carried off captives and much booty. He was a distinguished count, handsome and brave, God-fearing and devoted to the church, a staunch defender of the clergy and God's poor; in time of peace he was gentle and lovable and conspicuous for his good manners; in time of war, harsh and successful, formidable to the rulers who were his neighbours, and an enemy to all. He stood out among the highest in the land because of the high birth of his parents and his wife Beatrice,[2] and kept valiant barons and warlike castellans in firm subjection to his government. He gave his daughters in marriage to men of high rank: Margaret to Henry earl of Warwick, and Juliana to Gilbert, lord of the castle of Laigle, from whom sprang a worthy line of noble descendants. So Count Geoffrey, being blessed with such descendants and supported by arms and men, wealth and friends, and, most important of all, filled with the fear of the Lord, feared no man and advanced bold as a lion. He claimed as his right the strong castle of Domfront and other properties, and struggled to win them from his kinsman Robert.[3] Though it distressed him to injure defenceless and innocent people, he could not force the public enemy to meet him in open battle and so punish him as he deserved. Robert of Bellême, who oppressed all men, feared all men and so dared not engage in open battle at close quarters with his enemy. So his plan was to lie in wait behind his fortifications, regretfully allowing plundering bands to range at large over his lands and never venturing to go out and fight them although he was most

[3] Geoffrey presumably thought that he was entitled to a share of the Bellême inheritance through his mother Adeline, a first cousin of Mabel of Bellême.

fortissimus esset presumebat. Callidus enim precauebat ne si progrederetur.' a domesticis suis in manibus hostium relinqueretur. Sic longa lis inter duos potentes marchisos perdurauit, et multa subditis detrimenta cedesque generauit. Par equidem malorum fomes inter alios proceres undique per Normanniam pullulauit.' et enormem tragedis farraginem preparauit.

6

Perturbata undique procerum turgidis seditionibus Neustria sub molli principe pacificisque inter incendia crebrasque depredationes gementibus filiis æcclesiæ.' clementissimus humani generis rector seruis suis condoluit, emeritosque quosdam de lacu miseriæ et conualle lacrimarum consortio mortalium exemit, et in amenitate desiderabilis paradisi ut remur notis in consimili studio religionis commilitonibus pie associauit. Durandus siquidem Troarnensis abbas grandeuus, ab infantia monachus, religione et sapientia precipuus, æcclesiastici cantus et diuini dogmatis doctor peritissimus, sibi durus carnifex, aliisque mitis opifex, post multos in Dei cultu labores in lectum decubuit, et bene ut prudens et fidelis seruus ire ad curiam domini sui paratus, iii° idus Februarii de seculo migrauit.[1] In eius transitu res non silenda contigit. In
iii. 304 corpore prefati patris dum obiret bipartitus color uisus est. Nam in sinistra parte uultus eius et totius corporis usque ad pedes niueus candor apparuit.' totamque dexteram partem plumbeus liuor obtexit, et omnino dexteram medietatem ut albedo sinistram a uertice capitis usque ad pedes optinuit. Insolitum itaque discrimen conspecti coloris terrorem intuentibus incussit.' et inusitatæ rei causam studiosis inquisitoribus ad exprimendam subtilitatem perspicacitatis suæ ingessit. Inde diuersi diuersa dixere, sed non est nostrum huic breuiloquio singula inserere.' quæ multipliciter eloquentes ex habundantia sensus sui protulere. Quidam quidem leuam et dexteram ad actualem et contemplatiuam uel presentem et futuram uitam interpretati sunt.' alii uero prodigium hoc presagium fore futurorum opinati sunt.[2]

[1] 11 February 1088.

[2] This condition is medically less remarkable than was imagined by Orderic's contemporaries; it can be produced by lying heavily on one side at the time of death. I owe this information to Dr. G. H. Wright.

powerfully equipped for battle. He shrewdly foresaw that if he ventured out he might be abandoned by his servants in the enemy's hands. So a protracted struggle dragged on between the two powerful border lords and caused severe losses and casualties to their subjects. Everywhere throughout Normandy similar seeds of discord were sown between other lords, and provided a fertile source of tragedies.

6

While Normandy under its weak duke was everywhere disturbed by the factious quarrels of its nobles, and the peaceable sons of the church lamented in the midst of conflagrations and continual plunder, the merciful ruler of the human race took pity on his servants, raised a few worthy veterans from the pit of wretchedness and vale of tears which is this mortal life, and—as we believe—brought them to the joys of Heaven in the fellowship of other famous men who likewise served and toiled under monastic discipline. One was Durand, the aged abbot of Troarn, who had been a monk from childhood. He was wonderfully pious and learned, and had a profound knowledge of church liturgy and theology. To himself he was harsh and relentless, to others gentle and persuasive. After many years of service in the worship of God he took to his bed, prepared himself well as a wise and faithful servant does to go to his Lord's court, and departed from this life on 11 February.[1] At his passing occurred a marvel which should not go unrecorded: the two halves of father Durand's body when he died were of different colours. A snowy whiteness appeared in the left half of his face and his whole body down to the feet; and the whole right side was the colour of lead, which extended from the top of his head to his feet as did the white on the left. This exceptional variation in colour alarmed those who saw it, and by its strangeness provided ingenious investigators with an opportunity of demonstrating the subtlety of their intelligence. Different men had different explanations: but it is not my intention to include in this brief notice everything that the eloquent have fully expounded in their wisdom. Some interpreted the left and right sides as the active and contemplative, or present and future, life; whereas others concluded that this wonder was a prognostic of future events.[2]

Venerabiles discipuli glebam religiosi doctoris in capitulo suo reuerenter sepelierunt.' et in candido lapide qui superpositus est epitaphium hoc addiderunt.

Hac tegitur tumba bonus ac uenerabilis abba
Durandus nostri norma monasterii.
Ad Domini laudem presentem condidit edem.'
Qua sibi propicium credimus esse Deum.
Luce sub undena Februi resolutus habena
Carnis ad angelicam dirigitur patriam.

Sepulto pastore Troarnensis grex Arnulfum Sagiensis monasterii priorem elegit, ac ut sibi preponeretur a rectoribus æcclesiasticis et principibus suis expetiit. Illis autem congratulantibus et libenter quod postulabatur annuentibus.' Arnulfus Troarnensium regimen suscepit, quod fere xxii annis sollerter tenuit,[1] et tam
iii. 305 uerbis quam scriptis et salutaribus exemplis subiectos erudiit. Prefata nimirum duo monasteria sicut ab uno principe primordium fundationis ceperunt.'[a] sic ex uno fonte usus diuinæ seruitutis et monastici ordinis institutionem sumpserunt.[b] Rogerius enim de Monte Gomerici utrumque cenobium monachis dicauit.' et Fiscannensis norma utrumque monachico ritui applicauit. Vnus ergo amor hos pariter cenobitas connexuit.' signipotensque Martinus Turonensis archipresul suo mancipatui commissos custodit. Sagienses a Troarnensibus primum sibi abbatem sumpserunt.'[2] et nunc eodem adhuc patre uiuente amicabilem sibi uicissitudinem de discipulis eius repetierunt. Quo adepto Deo gratias egerunt.' bonique pastoris sollertia bene profecerunt.

Tunc[3] Robertus Normanniæ dux optimatum suorum supplicationibus adquiescens Henricum fratrem suum concessit.' et a uinculis in quibus cum Roberto Belesmensi constrictus fuerat absoluit.

7

Circa hæc tempora Gregorius papa in urbe Beneuentana defunctus est.'[4] et Desiderius Cassiniensis abbas in Victorem Romanum papam electus et intronizatus est.[5] Defuncti uero

[a] cepit, *Caen MS.* [b] sumpsit, *Caen MS.*

[1] He was abbot from 1088 to 1112 (R. N. Sauvage, *L'abbaye de Saint-Martin de Troarn* (Mém. Soc. Ant. Norm. xxxiv (1911)), 291–2).

[2] Robert I, who died in January 1089 (below, p. 168).

Durand's devout followers reverently buried the body of their pious teacher in their chapter-house, and inscribed this epitaph on the marble slab which was placed over it:

Here in this tomb, worthy and virtuous,
Lies Abbot Durand, pattern of our house.
This abbey, built by him to show God's might,
Now, surely, justifies him in God's sight.
February's eleventh day dawned, when he came
From fleshly prison to share the angels' home.

After the abbot's funeral the community of Troarn elected Arnulf, prior of Séez, and sought permission to have him as their abbot from the ecclesiastical and secular rulers. As they were of like mind and willingly agreed to the request, Arnulf took up the government of Troarn and exercised it wisely for twenty-two years,[1] instructing his monks by his teaching and writing and exemplary life. These two monasteries both owed their foundation to the same lord and their monastic customs and ritual to the same source. Roger of Montgomery established monks in both; and the custom of Fécamp provided them with their monastic rites. So there was close affection between the communities, and Martin, the miracle-working archbishop of Tours, in whose name they were dedicated, protected them. The monks of Séez had taken their first abbot from those of Troarn;[2] and now in this man's lifetime they were able in their turn to provide an abbot through friendship from among his disciples. They received him, giving thanks to God, and prospered well through the care of their good shepherd.

About that time[3] Robert duke of Normandy yielded to the petitions of his magnates, pardoned his brother Henry, and freed him from the imprisonment which he had shared with Robert of Bellême.

7

About this time Pope Gregory died in the city of Benevento,[4] and Desiderius, abbot of Monte Cassino, was elected as Roman pope and enthroned with the name of Victor.[5] The body of the

[3] Henry was probably freed early in 1089 (David, *Robert Curthose*, p. 53 n. 57).

[4] Gregory VII died at Salerno on 25 May 1085.

[5] Victor was elected on 24 May 1086 and enthroned on 9 May 1087.

papæ corpus in confessione sancti Bartolomei apostoli tumulatum
iii. 306 est.'[1] ubi meritis eius fideque petentium copia miraculorum diuinitus ostensa est. Nam leprosi de aqua unde corpus eius ablutum fuerat petierunt, qua consecuta fideliter loti sunt.' et opitulante Deo protinus mundati sunt. Victor papa postquam apicem pontificatus ascendit, primam missam in die sancto Pentecostæ[2] solenniter cantare cepit.' sed occulto Dei nutu grauem morbum subito incurrit. Nam diarria cogente ter ad latrinam de missa ductus est.' et sic in papatu uix una tantum missa perfunctus est[a]. Hic magnæ nobilitatis et sapientiæ fuit ac religionis.' cenobiumque sancti patris Benedicti quod in Monte Cassino constructum est longo tempore rexit.[3] Inde ad presulatum assumptus repente ut diximus infirmatus est.' in egritudine tamen a Pentecoste usque ad Augustum languens defunctus est.[4] Quo defuncto Romanus clerus conuenit.' et Odonem ex monacho presulem Ostiensem in Vrbanum Romanum papam elegit.[5] Hunc Deus Israel maximum principem contra allophilos constituit.'[6] turremque Dauid cum propugnaculis contra faciem Damasci commisit.[7] Hic erat natione Gallus, nobilitate et mansuetudine clarus.' ciuis Re-
iii. 307 mensis, monachus Cluniacensis.' etate mediocris, corpore magnus.' modestia discretus, religione maximus.' sapientia et eloquentia precipuus. Adhuc Guitbertus inuasor apostolicæ sedis æcclesiam Dei conturbabat.' ac adulando uel persequendo cunctos quos poterat ab unitate pacis ad suum scisma pertrahebat. Odo nimirum comes Sutriæ nepos eius erat.'[8] et æcclesiasticæ pacis fautores pluribus pressuris cohercebat.

Vrbanus papa confisus in Domino cœlorum, qui non relinquet uirgam peccatorum super sortem iustorum.'[9] misit legatos et epistolas Romanæ auctoritatis Francis et Grecis,[10] aliisque gentibus per orbem constitutis.' ut in fide catholica irrefragabiliter persisterent, et omnem scissuram a lege Dei et corpore Christi quod

[a] *Omit* est, *Caen MS.*

---

[1] Gregory was buried in the cathedral of St. Matthew at Salerno, not in the church of St. Bartholomew at Benevento.

[2] 16 May 1087. His illness in Rome was dramatized by historians of the early twelfth century, who gave varying and highly-coloured accounts. For different versions see A. Fliche, *La réforme grégorienne* (Louvain, 1924–37), iii. 213 n. 1.

[3] Desiderius was abbot of Monte Cassino from 1058 to 1087. His abbacy was one of the great periods of building and scholarship there, though he himself was not a profound scholar. See F. Hirsch, 'Desiderius von Monte Cassino als Papst Victor III' (Forschungen zur deutsche Geschichte (Göttingen, 1867), vii. 3 ff.); F. J. E. Raby, *A History of Christian Latin Poetry* (Oxford, 1953), p. 238.

[4] He died on 16 September 1087.

[5] Odo, prior of Cluny, became bishop of Ostia in 1078 and was elected pope as Urban II on 12 March 1088.

dead pope was buried in the crypt of St. Bartholomew's church,[1] where many miracles have been divinely performed through his merits and the faith of those who prayed. Lepers begged for the water in which his body had been washed, and on obtaining it washed in it with faith, and by God's grace were instantly cleansed. When Pope Victor had mounted the papal throne he began to sing his first Mass with all solemnity on the day of Pentecost;[2] but by God's mysterious will he was suddenly afflicted with a serious illness. Diarrhoea forced him to be escorted three times to the latrine in the course of the Mass; and so he barely celebrated one Mass as pope. He was a man of very high birth and great wisdom and piety, and governed the abbey of our holy father Benedict which is at Monte Cassino for many years.[3] Raised from there to the papacy he suddenly became ill, as I have related, and after lingering in sickness from Pentecost until August he died.[4] After his death the Roman clergy met and elected Odo, bishop of Ostia and formerly a monk, as Roman pope with the name of Urban.[5] The God of Israel appointed him a mighty leader against the Moslems,[6] and set him up as the tower of David with its armouries to oppose Damascus.[7] He was French by race, of high birth and great courtesy, a citizen of Rheims and a monk of Cluny, middle-aged and tall in stature, unassuming in his modesty, of great piety, conspicuously learned and eloquent. At that time Wibert the anti-pope disturbed the Church of God, and by cajolery or persecution won over all he could from peaceful unity to his schism. Otto, count of Sutri,[8] was his nephew and in various ways persecuted the supporters of the Church's peace.

Pope Urban, trusting in the Lord of Heaven, who will not allow the rod of the wicked to rest upon the lot of the righteous,[9] sent legates to carry papal letters to the French and Greeks[10] and other peoples all over the world, urging them to hold resolutely to the catholic faith and advisedly to shun all schism from the law of

[6] A reference to his preaching of the crusade in 1095–6. For the term 'allophylus' see Ducange, i. 188.

[7] Cf. Song of Solomon iv. 4.

[8] See above, p. 10 n. 4.

[9] Psalm cxxiv (cxxv). 3.

[10] Urban II began his pontificate with conciliatory approaches to the princes of the west, and to Alexius Comnenus. His letter to Alexius asked for the restoration of his name in imperial documents (cf. Fliche et Martin, viii. 229–37; W. Holtzmann, 'Die Unionverhandlung zwischen Kaiser Alexios I und Papst Urban II im Jahre 1089', in *Byzantinische Zeitschrift*, xxviii (1928), 38–67).

est æcclesia callide precauerent. Solus Henricus Teutonum princeps et pedissequi eiusdem Guitberto coherebant.' Galli uero et Angli aliæque gentes pene omnes per orbem Vrbano pie obsecundabant.[1]

In Apulia omnes Normanni catholico papæ concorditer fauebant.' uerum inter se truculenter dissidebant, et fratres plus quam ciuilia bella uicissim conserebant. Rogerius enim cognomento Crumena id est Bursa ducatu Calabriæ solus cum matre potiebatur.' quod Buamundus frater eius apud Iordanum principem Capuæ exulans egre patiebatur.[2] Vnde auxilio eiusdem Iordani sororii sui aliorumque parentum amicorumque suorum arma contra
iii. 308 fratrem suum arripuit.' partemque paterni honoris quam ipse cum patre bello subegerat uiriliter repetere cepit. Cuius guerram frater et nouerca tolerare nequiuerunt.' commodiusque consilium ab amicis expetere coacti sunt. Persuasione igitur Rogerii Siciliæ comitis aliorumque affinium pacem fecerunt.' eique Barum atque Tarentum aliasque duas urbes cum multis oppidis tradiderunt.[3] Fratres itaque postquam talem concordiam fecerunt.' Mabiliam sororem suam Guillelmo de Grentemaisnil in matrimonium dederunt, et ditioni eius quia ualde probus erat plurima castra submiserunt.[4] Connexione huiuscemodi necessitudinis Normanni prouide mutuo religati sunt.' et magnam Italiæ partem quam Drogo et Vnfridus atque Ricardus et super omnes Robertus Wiscardus optinuerant usque hodie possederunt.

8

Anno ab incarnatione Domini M°LXXXIX° indictione xiiª Robertus primus abbas Sagiensis monasterii uir bonus et simplex mense Ianuario in lectum cecidit.' et perceptis dominicis sacramentis xviii° kal' Februarii de seculo migrauit, cui Radulfus Seifredi de
iii. 309 Scurris filius eiusdem cenobii monachus in regimine successit. Hic litteris admodum fuit imbutus, eloquens et iocundus.' ideoque amabilis omnibus. In iuuentute de illustri familia monachilem ad conuersationem uenit, et decem annis in monasterio per

[1] William Rufus hesitated for some years before recognizing Urban II in 1095 (Southern, *Saint Anselm*, pp. 154–5; F. Liebermann, 'Lanfranc and the anti-pope', in *EHR* xvi (1901), 328–32).

[2] The course of Bohemond's struggle to obtain a share of the inheritance of his half-brother, Roger Borsa, has been traced by R. Manselli, 'Normanni d'Italia alla prima Crociata', in *Japigia*, xi (1940), 55–9.

[3] The territory ceded to Bohemond included Oria, Taranto, Otranto, and the whole fee of Geoffrey of Conversano (*Japigia*, xi (1940), 56).

[4] William's fifteen 'castella' were situated in the valleys of the Crati and

God and the Church, which is the body of Christ. Only Henry, king of Germany, and his adherents upheld Wibert; the French and English and almost all the other peoples of the world dutifully obeyed Urban.[1]

In Apulia all the Normans were united in their support of the catholic pope; but they were deeply divided among themselves and brothers clashed with each other in worse than civil wars. Roger called Crumena (Borsa), which means a purse, was with his mother sole ruler in Calabria; and this his brother Bohemond, living in exile with Jordan prince of Capua, bitterly resented.[2] With support from Jordan, who was his first cousin, and other kinsmen and friends he took up arms against his brother, and made a determined attempt to recover the share in his father's honor which he had helped his father to conquer by force of arms. His brother and stepmother were unable to hold back his attack, and were forced to seek practical counsel from their friends. They were persuaded by Roger, count of Sicily, and other neighbours to make peace, and surrendered to Bohemond Bari and Taranto and two other towns, as well as many fortresses.[3] After the brothers had agreed to this settlement they gave their sister Mabel in marriage to William of Grandmesnil, and placed several castles under his command on account of his great valour.[4] By forming a relationship of this kind the Normans prudently became closely reunited, and they still remain in possession of a great part of Italy, which Drogo and Humphrey and Richard and, above all, Robert Guiscard had won.

8

In the year of our Lord 1089, the twelfth indiction, Robert, the first abbot of Séez, a simple and good man, took to his bed in January and, after receiving the Lord's sacraments, passed from the world on 15 January. Ralph son of Seifred of Escures, a monk of the same monastery, succeeded him as abbot. He was very well versed in letters, eloquent and agreeable, and therefore universally beloved. As a young man of a noble family he was converted to the monastic life, and for ten years he served humbly in various monastic

Coscile, and at Cotrone. Orderic omits to mention his rebellion in 1093–4 and his flight to Constantinople (ibid., pp. 57–8; E. M. Jamison, 'Some notes . . .', p. 199).

diuersorum gradus officiorum humiliter ministrauit. Vndecimo tandem anno abbatiæ curam iubente et consecrante Girardo Sagiensi presule suscepit.' et xvi annis inter seuos bellorum turbines strenue rexit, Deique fretus auxilio pro temporis opportunitate res æcclesiæ diligenter auxit. Deinde Roberti Belesmensis seuicia nimis imminente in Angliam confugit.' quem rex Henricus honorifice secum detinuit, et post Gundulfum presulem Rofensi episcopio prefecit. Inde post aliquot annos promotus uenerabili Anselmo archipresuli successit.' et ix annis Doroberniæ metropoli prefuit.[1]

Anno tercio Guillelmi Rufi regis Anglorum Lanfrancus Cantuariensis metropolis episcopus[a] defunctus est.'[2] et in basilica Sanctæ Trinitatis quam ipse mirifico opere construxerat ante crucifixum sepultus est. Beccensis autem Anselmus suprascriptam[3] compatriotæ sui memoriam heroico carmine uolumini lacrimabiliter indidit.' Deique nutu post triennium in cathedram Doroberniæ æcclesiastica electione promotus ascendit.[4] Deinde intra decem annos quibus postmodum regnauit Guillelmus Rufus.' Thomas Eborachensis metropolita coepiscopum suum morte
iii. 310 secutus est, cum aliis multis episcopis et abbatibus.[5] Nam Vulstanus presul Guigornensis, et Robertus Herfordensis, Osmundus Salesburiensis, et Gualchelinus Guentoniensis, Balduinus quoque archiater et abbas sancti Edmundi regis et martiris, Turstinus Glestoniensis, et Rainaldus Abundoniensis, aliique plures episcopi et abbates obiere, quos singillatim pro fastidio legentium nolo nominare.

His temporibus quidam clericus nomine Ranulfus familiaritatem Rufi regis adeptus est.'[6] et super omnes regios officiales ingeniosis accusationibus et multifariis adulationibus magistratum a rege consecutus est. Erat enim ingenio acer.' corpore pulcher, lingua disertus, comessationibus et ebrietatibus, libidinique nimis deditus, crudelis et ambitiosus, suisque prodigus, extraneis autem predo rapacissimus. Hic de obscura satis et paupere parentela

[a] Anno tercio . . . episcopus *over an erasure in Caen MS.*

[1] Ralph d'Escures was bishop of Rochester, 1108–1114, and archbishop of Canterbury, 1114–22.

[2] Lanfranc died on 28 May 1089.

[3] The epitaph is printed in Migne, *PL* clviii. 1049–50; cf. Southern, *Saint Anselm*, p. 26. Probably Orderic included a copy of it in his work, but the Caen copyist omitted it. The erasure at the beginning of the paragraph suggests that he began to copy something and changed his mind.

[4] He was nominated on 6 March 1093, and consecrated on 4 December 1093.

[5] Thomas of Bayeux, archbishop of York, died on 18 November 1100, three

offices. Finally in his eleventh year he undertook the duties of abbot, at the command of Gerard bishop of Séez, who blessed him; he governed capably for sixteen years amid the violent storms of war, and with God's aid assiduously increased the prosperity of his church as far as the evil times allowed. At last, when the brutality of Robert of Bellême became too dangerous he fled to England. King Henry received him with respect and made him bishop of Rochester after Gundulf. Some years later he was further promoted to succeed the venerable Anselm as archbishop, and he ruled the see of Canterbury for nine years.[1]

In the third year of the reign of William Rufus in England Lanfranc, archbishop of Canterbury,[2] died and was buried before the rood in the cathedral church of the Holy Trinity which he himself had built in a magnificent style. Anselm of Bec, deeply mourning, composed the above-written[3] memorial to his fellow countryman in heroic verse, and by God's will was elected three years later to succeed him in the church of Canterbury.[4] Subsequently during the ten years of William Rufus's reign Thomas archbishop of York likewise died, together with many bishops and abbots.[5] Wulfstan bishop of Worcester and Robert of Hereford, Osmund of Salisbury and Walchelin of Winchester; Baldwin too, physician and abbot of the abbey of St. Edmund, king and martyr, Thurstan of Glastonbury and Reginald of Abingdon and many other bishops and abbots died, whom I shall not name individually to avoid wearying my readers.

At this time a certain clerk named Ranulf gained a position in the household of King Rufus;[6] and by his cunning accusations and insidious flatteries obtained authority over all the royal officials from the king. He was a man of keen intelligence, handsome and ready in speech, but too addicted to feasts and carousals and lusts; cruel and ambitious, prodigal to his own adherents, but rapacious in seizing the goods of other men. He was born of poor and obscure

months after William Rufus. Wulfstan of Worcester died on 19/20 January, 1095; Robert Losinga of Hereford, on 26 June 1095; Osmund of Salisbury, on 3/4 December 1099; Walchelin of Winchester on 3 January 1098; Baldwin of Bury St. Edmunds probably on 29 Dec. 1097; Thurstan, abbot of Glastonbury, probably before 1100; and Reginald of Abingdon in 1097.

[6] All the leading contemporary historians comment on the career of Ranulf Flambard; all agree that he was the chief financial and legal agent of the king. See R. W. Southern, 'Ranulf Flambard', in *Medieval Humanism* (Oxford, 1970), pp. 183–205. Orderic's account is valuable, for he had an opportunity to observe Flambard at close quarters when he controlled the diocese of Lisieux.

prodiit, et multum ultra natales suos ad multorum detrimentum sullimatus intumuit. Turstini cuiusdam plebii presbiteri de pago Baiocensi filius fuit, et a puerilibus annis inter pedissequos curiales
iii. 311 cum uilibus parasitis educatus creuit.' callidisque tergiuersationibus et argutis uerborum machinationibus plusquam arti litteratoriæ studuit. Et quia semetipsum in curia magni regis Guillelmi[1] arroganter illustribus preferre ardebat.' nesciente[a] non iussus multa inchoabat.' infestus in aula regis plures procaciter accusabat.'[2] temereque maioribus quasi regia ui fultus imperabat. Vnde a Roberto dispensatore regio[3] Flambardus cognominatus est.' quod uocabulum ei secundum mores eius et actus quasi prophetice collatum est. Flamma quippe ardens multis factus intulit genti nouos ritus.' quibus crudeliter oppressit populorum cetus, et æcclesiæ cantus temporales mutauit in planctus. Hic iuuenem fraudulentis stimulationibus inquietauit regem, incitans ut totius Angliæ reuiseret descriptionem.' Anglicæque telluris comprobans iteraret particionem, subditisque recideret tam aduenis quam indigenis quicquid inueniretur ultra certam dimensionem. Annuente rege omnes carrucatas quas Anglice hidas uocant funiculo mensus est et descripsit, postpositisque mensuris quas liberales
iii. 312 Angli iussu Eduardi regis largiter distribuerant imminuit.' et regales fiscos accumulans colonis arua retruncauit.[4] Ruris itaque olim diutius nacti diminutione, et insoliti uectigalis graui exaggeratione.' supplices regiæ fidelitati plebes indecenter oppressit, ablatis rebus attenuauit.' et in nimiam egestatem de ingenti copia redegit.

Huius consilio iuuenis rex morientibus prelatis æcclesias cum possessionibus olim sibi datis inuasit, et tam in abbatiis cenobitas

[a] *The sense requires* rege

[1] He had become keeper of the royal seal under the chancellor, Maurice, by 1085, and held some scattered estates worth £30 in Domesday Book (Southern, *Medieval Humanism*, p. 187).

[2] He acted as the king's advocate in the local courts (ibid., p. 194).

[3] Robert, son of Thurstan, the Dispenser, witnesses a number of charters of William I and William II (*Regesta*, i, nos. 148, 205, 220, and *passim*).

[4] Orderic's account of administrative and financial organization, of which he had no practical experience, tends to be imprecise. Even if by 'descriptio' he meant Domesday Book we do not know what information he believed Domesday Book to contain; he may have imagined that the findings of more than one inquest were included in it. The language, here as elsewhere, suggests a belief that it incorporated material actually in the geld rolls (see V. H. Galbraith, *The Making of Domesday Book* (Oxford, 1961), pp. 86–101). There is certainly no evidence of a general reassessment of any kind early in the reign of William Rufus. But the king attempted to increase gelds, scots, and military services on some lands, including those of the Fenland abbeys; Flambard was active in the

parents and, rising far above his origins, prospered by the ruin of many men. He was the son of Thurstan, a parish priest from the region of Bayeux, and since he was educated from boyhood with base parasites among the hangers-on of the court he was better instructed in cunning deception and the specious manipulation of words than in literary studies. Burning with ambition to thrust himself above the eminent men in the court of King William the Great,[1] he undertook many things on his own initiative, without the king's knowledge. He boldly began hostile proceedings against a number of men in the king's hall,[2] and presumptuously issued orders to the greatest men as though he acted on the king's behalf. Consequently he was nicknamed 'torch-bearer' (Flambard) by Robert the king's Dispenser;[3] the name proved prophetic in the light of his character and actions and it stuck to him. Like a devouring flame he imposed innovations on the people, by which he cruelly oppressed the country and changed the daily chants of the Church into lamentations. This man unsettled the young king with his fraudulent suggestions, inciting him to revise the survey of all England, and convincing him that he should make a new division of the land of England and confiscate from his subjects, natives and invaders alike, whatever was found above a certain quantity. With the king's consent he measured all the ploughlands, which in English are called hides, with a rope, and made a record of them; setting aside the measures which the open-handed English freely apportioned by command of King Edward, he reduced their size and cut back the fields of the peasants to increase the royal taxes.[4] So by reducing the land which had long been held in peace and increasing the burden of the new taxation he brutally oppressed the king's helpless and faithful subjects, impoverished them by confiscations, and reduced them from comfortable prosperity to the verge of starvation.

On this man's advice the young king took possession of churches with their endowments after the death of prelates, and imposed

Fens, and Orderic later visited Thorney and Crowland and no doubt learnt of his activities there (Southern, *Medieval Humanism*, pp. 190–1). Instances of the division of lands in Normandy by measuring with ropes are reported by Dudo of Saint-Quentin (Lair, pp. 171, 182) and it may have been a Scandinavian practice (cf. J. Yver, 'Les premiers institutions du duché de Normandie', in *Settimane di studio del Centro Italiano di Studi sull'alto medioevo* (Spoleto, 1969), p. 321 n. 52. Cf. also a story in Robert of Torigny (Marx, p. 289) about the measurement of the *banlieu* around Tonbridge).

quam in episcopiis episcopales decanos et canonicos cuilibet satellitum suorum subegit. Parcam autem ad uictum suum distributionem rerum eis delegabat.' et reliquos redditus suæ dicioni mancipabat.[1] Sic auaricia regis in æcclesia Dei nimis exarsit.' et nefarius mos tunc inceptus usque in hodiernum diem perseuerans multis animabus exitio fit. Hac enim de causa cupidus rex pastores æcclesiis imponere differebat, et populus rectore, ceu grex pastore carens, lupinis dentibus patebat.' et multimodarum toxicatis missilibus culparum sauciatus interibat. Princeps itaque nimia cupiditate flagrans suo infert erario largas opes.' quas æcclesiæ Dei gratanter et deuote dederunt antiqui Anglorum reges, Edilbertus scilicet ac Eduinus, Offa quoque ac Athulfus, Elfredus et Edgarus aliique principes cum suis optimatibus. Illi nimirum ad fidem nouiter conuersi Deum fideliter coluerunt, et de suis abundantiis monachis et clericis affluenter largiti sunt.' ut speciales ministri sacræ legis copioso uictu pasci gauderent, Deique cultum absque ulla [ex]cusatione[a] nocte dieque alacriter peragerent.' et in locis constitutis celebres excubias Deo indesinenter exhiberent. Illuc
iii. 313 peregrini et uiatores securi ueniebant, et ibidem post laborem tutam repausationem sumebant, atque post inediam uberem alimoniam ex institutione principali reperiebant. Igitur ex insperato sic consolati Deo gratias agebant et pro benefactoribus qui longe ante tantum sibi suffragium preparauerant creatorem omnium pie exorabant.

Antequam Normanni Angliam optinuissent mos erat ut dum rectores æcclesiarum obirent.' episcopus cenobiorum quæ in sua diocesi erant res sollicite describeret, et sub dicione sua donec abbates legitime ordinarentur custodiret. Similiter archiepiscopus episcopii res antistite defuncto seruabat.' et pauperibus uel structuris basilicarum uel aliis bonis operibus cum consilio domesticorum eiusdem æcclesiæ distrahebat.[2] Hunc profecto morem Guillelmus Rufus ab inicio regni sui persuasione Flambardi aboleuit.' et metropolitanam Cantuariæ sedem sine pontifice tribus annis esse fecit, eiusque redditus suis thesauris intulit. Iniustum

[a] *Inserted in the margin: the first two letters are now cut off. The transcript of La Porte du Theil reads* excusatione (*Le Prévost, v. 214*)

---

[1] William of Malmesbury (*GR* ii. 369) and the Abingdon chronicler (*Chronicon Monasterii de Abingdon*, ed. J. Stevenson (RS 1858), ii. 42) also comment on William Rufus's innovation in seizing the lands of prelates during vacancies. See M. E. Howell, *Regalian Right in Medieval England* (London, 1962), pp. 10–19.

[2] There is very little evidence of pre-Conquest practice during vacancies;

the authority of his satellites on monks in monastic churches and deans and chapters of cathedrals in bishoprics. He assigned a frugal share of their property for their food, and applied the remaining revenues to his own purposes.[1] In this way the king's avarice drained the churches of God dry; the evil custom introduced at that time still persists and causes the loss of many souls. For the sake of profit the grasping king delayed appointing prelates to churches, and the leaderless people or shepherdless flock fell victim to the teeth of wolves, or died while wounded by the poisoned darts of their many sins. So the king, a slave to greed, filled his treasure-house with the great wealth that in former years had been freely given to the Church of God by the pious kings of England, namely Æthelbert and Edwin, Offa and Ethelwulf, Alfred and Edgar and others, and the English magnates. These men, when they were newly converted to Christianity, worshipped God faithfully, and generously gave from their abundant wealth to monks and clergy, so that the appointed ministers of the holy law might enjoy adequate sustenance and devote themselves wholeheartedly, day and night, to the service of God without any impediment, continually rendering their sleepless offices to God in the places appointed for that purpose. Pilgrims and travellers used to come there in safety; they received peaceful refreshment after their labours and, after a time of want, found abundant sustenance from the royal endowments. When these men found rest and recuperation beyond their dreams they gave thanks to God and dutifully offered prayers to their creator for the benefactors who, so long before, had laid up a store for them in their need.

Before the Normans conquered England the custom was that when the rulers of churches died the bishop made a careful inventory of the possessions of monasteries in his diocese, and had the custody of them until abbots were lawfully established. In a similar way the archbishop took charge of the revenues of a bishopric on the prelate's death, and after consulting the bishop's household assigned them to the poor, or the fabric of the church, or other good works.[2] But William Rufus, through Flambard's persuasion, abandoned this custom from the beginning of his reign. He kept the metropolitan see of Canterbury without an archbishop for three years, and added its revenues to his treasure. It is manifestly

Orderic's statement may be true of some cases, though it is likely that priors administered monastic property. See Knowles, *MO*, pp. 612–13.

quippe uidetur omnique rationi contrarium, ut quod Deo datum est fidelium liberalitate principum.' uel sollertia dispensatorum æcclesiasticæ rei laudabiliter est auctum, denuo sub laicali manu retrahatur.' et in nefarios seculi usus distrahatur. Indubitanter credendum est quod sicut illi qui Deo de suis opibus pie dederunt, iam retributionem meritorum donante Deo receperunt.' sic sacrilegi sacrorum inuasores ultore Deo punientur, opibusque quas iniuste possident cum iugi dedecore spoliabantur. Omnipotentis
iii. 314 enim lex æterna est et uera.' unde sicut iusticiæ cultoribus graciosa pollicetur stipendia, sic transgressoribus pro nequitiis dira comminatur supplicia. In omni pagina diuinæ auctoritatis misericordia et ueritas predicantur.' et luce clarius omni erudito manifestantur. Mirum ergo est quod humanum cor in nefas tam facile labascit, et plus presentia et caduca quam futura et perpetua concupiscit.' dum omnia diuino patere optutui et nichil e diuino examine indiscussum euadere nouerit.

Postquam Dorobernensium metropolis presule uiduata in timore et luctu exegerit triennium.' tandem iustus arbiter qui de cœlo prospicit super filios hominum et uidet omnes amplecti uanitates uanitatum.' acerba passione perculit regem Anglorum multimoda scelerum fæce coinquinatum. Egritudine igitur multatus sacerdotes Domini aduocauit, spiritualibus archiatris animæ suæ ulcera confessione denudauit, emendationem uitæ promisit, et æcclesiasticos rectores secundum uoluntatem Domini archiepiscopum eligere precepit. Tunc forte Anselmus Beccensium abbas pro utilitatibus æcclesiæ suæ in Angliam transfretauerat.[1] Audita iussione regis de metropolitani electione sancta æcclesia exultauit.' conuentum seniorum una congregauit, et de negotio pro quo conuenerant tractare cepit. Tandem considerata sanctitate et sapientia uenerabilis Anselmi, concorditer omnes ipsum elegerunt in nomine Domini.' multumque renitentem secundum morem æcclesiasticum preposuerunt Cantuariorum metropoli. Intronizatus itaque sollers pastor frequenter ingemuit.' prudenter perpendens quam graue et periculosum pondus ad portandum susceperit. Non intumescebat pro sui sullimatione, sed trepidabat pro
iii. 315 multorum perditione.' quos a lege Dei uidebat aberrare sua sub

[1] Anselm came to England in September 1092, and saw the king before going to Chester to assist Earl Hugh in the foundation of St. Werburgh's Abbey. William became ill at the beginning of March 1093, and Anselm was elected on 6 March. These events are fully described by Eadmer in his *Historia Novorum* (ed. M. Rule, RS, pp. 27–37) and his *Life of Anselm* (ed. R. W. Southern (Edinburgh, 1962), pp. 63–5). For the brief account of Anselm's life Orderic may have relied on Eadmer's *Life*, which he had read, and on information from monks at Bec (see above, ii. 294 n. 3).

unjust and contrary to all reason that the things given to God by the generosity of Christian princes, or honourably increased by the care of stewards of the Church's goods, should revert to lay hands and be applied to unholy secular uses. We must believe unquestioningly that just as those who dutifully gave of their wealth to God have received a reward according to their deserts by God's grace, so sacrilegious men who appropriate holy things will be punished by God's vengeance and stripped of the wealth they have unjustly acquired, to their perpetual disgrace. For the law of the Omnipotent is eternal and just; as it promises pleasing rewards to the righteous it threatens terrible punishments to the wicked for their crimes. Mercy and truth are declared in every page of divine revelation, and appear more clearly than daylight to every well-informed mind. All the more remarkable, therefore, that the human heart so readily slips into evil, desiring fleeting present joys more than future, eternal ones, though knowing that everything is open for God to read and nothing escapes undetected from God's sight.

After the metropolitan see of Canterbury had spent three years without a prelate, in fear and grief, the just Judge, who looks down from Heaven on the sons of men and sees that they all pursue vanities of vanities, struck down the king of England with a severe illness when he was defiled with the filth of many crimes. Chastised by sickness he sent for priests, revealed the ulcers in his soul to his spiritual physicians by confession, promised to live a better life, and ordered the governors of the Church to elect an archbishop in accordance with God's will. At that time as it happened Anselm, abbot of Bec, had crossed to England to attend to the affairs of his church.[1] The news of the king's command to proceed to the election of an archbishop caused great rejoicing in the Church; an assembly of leaders met and began to discuss the business that had brought them together. Finally, after considering the holiness and wisdom of the venerable Anselm, they all unanimously elected him in the name of the Lord. In spite of his earnest protests he was canonically raised to the archbishopric of Canterbury. After being enthroned the conscientious prelate often had cause to grieve, as he pondered on the burden and danger of the load he had agreed to bear. He did not become elated by his high office, but trembled for the ruin of many whom he saw turning away from the law of God under his rule. In his own diocese he found

gubernatione. In diocesi sua multa corrigenda perspexit. Peccantem regem toruosque proceres sepe corripuit.' unde plurima ab eis aduersa tulit, et pro zelo iusticiæ bis exulauit. Dictis et exemplis salutaribus peruersos mores subditorum emendare studuit.' sed obdurata quorundam iniquitate in multis non sicut uoluisset profecit. Peruersi quippe sicut Salomon ait difficile corriguntur.' et stultorum infinitus est numerus.[1]

In diebus illis lucerna ueræ sanctitatis obscurius micabat pene cunctis in ordinibus.' mundique principes cum subiectis agminibus inherebant tenebrosis operibus. Guillelmus Rufus Albionis rex iuuenis erat proteruus et lasciuus.' quem nimis inhianter prosequebantur agmina populorum impudicis moribus. Imperiosus et audax atque militaris erat.' et multitudine militum pompose tripudiabat. Militiæ titulis applaudebat.' illisque propter fastum secularem admodum fauebat. Pagenses contra milites defendere neglegebat.' quorum possessiones a suis tironibus et armigeris impune deuastari permittebat. Tenacis memoriæ et ardentis ad bonum seu malum uoluntatis erat, terribilis furibus et latrunculis imminebat.' pacemque serenam per subiectam regionem seruari ualenter cogebat. Omnes incolas regni sui aut illexit largitate, aut compressit uirtute et terrore.' ut nullus contra eum auderet aliquo modo mutire.

9

Confirmatus itaque in regno turmas optimatum asciuit, et Guentoniæ congregatis quæ intrinsecus ruminabat sic ore de-
iii. 316 prompsit.[2] 'Nostis' inquit 'egregii barones qualiter egerit erga me Roberti fratris mei fides.' et quantos michi procurauerit labores. Non opus est multis sermonibus referre, quod homines meos in regno meo excitauerit contra me.' et summopere machinatus fuerit me regno uitaque priuare. Satis omnibus liquet, quod intolerabile michi primo regni mei anno intulisset.' nisi diuina uirtus per pietatem suam illud a me repulisset. Ecce lacrimabilem querimoniam sancta æcclesia de transmarinis partibus ad me dirigit, quia ualde mesta cotidianis fletibus madescit.' quod iusto defensore et patrono carens inter malignantes quasi ouis inter lupos consistit. Terram meam fraudulentia et uiribus aufferre sategit.' qui

[1] Ecclesiastes i. 15.

[2] This cannot be taken literally: apart from inventing the speeches Orderic appears to have telescoped several events. If the decision to attack Robert's lands in Normandy was taken in a formal court there is no other evidence for it. For the fighting on the north-east frontier of Normandy in 1089 see above, Introduction, pp. xxxiii–xxxiv.

much to correct. He often reprimanded the erring king and his fierce vassals; by so doing he brought many troubles on his own head and was twice driven into exile for his pursuit of justice. He strove to reform the corrupt morals of his subjects by his preaching and good example, but some were so far gone in their iniquity that he could not make the impression he desired. For, as Solomon says, it is difficult to correct the unrighteous, and the number of fools is infinite.[1]

In those times the lamp of true holiness burned faintly among almost all ranks; the princes of the world and their subject masses were given over to works of darkness. William Rufus, the young king of England, was wanton and lascivious, and droves of his people all too readily imitated his corrupt morals. A masterful, bold and warlike man, he gloried in the display of many knights. He delighted in the honours of knighthood and granted them readily for the sake of worldly show. He failed to protect the peasants against his vassals, whose knights or squires and men-at-arms were allowed to ravage their possessions with impunity. Having a tenacious memory and a determined will, for both good and evil, he terrorized thieves and robbers, and successfully enforced internal peace throughout his realm. He bound some of his subjects to him by generosity, and held the rest in check by force and fear, so that no one dared to breathe a word against him.

9

Having secured his position in the kingdom he summoned the forces of his barons to Winchester, and when they were assembled told them what was in his mind.[2] 'You know,' he said, 'my worthy barons, what the loyalty of my brother Robert to me is worth, and what troubles he has brought on me. I do not need to describe in detail how he has incited my men in my kingdom to rebel against me, and has used every kind of intrigue to rob me of my kingdom and my life. All men know what grievous harm he would have done me in the first year of my reign, if the power of God that preserves right order had not averted the danger from me. And now the holy Church in Normandy has sent a cry of distress to me because, lacking a just defender and patron, its daily lot is mourning and weeping, for it is surrounded by enemies like a lamb among wolves. This man who tried by force and fraud to rob me

terram suam a malignis predonibus defendere neglegit. Nunc igitur commoneo uos omnes qui patris mei homines fuistis, et feudos uestros in Normannia et Anglia de illo tenuistis, ut sine dolo ad probitatis opus michi uiriliter unanimes faueatis. Non debemus pati latronum conuenticula, ut ab illis fideles opprimantur et sanctorum destruantur cenobia.ʼ quæ patres nostri summo nisu construxerunt in Neustria. Tota regio cedibus patet atque rapinis, sepius ex necessitate reminiscens Guillelmi magni principis.ʼ qui bellis eam eripuit externis et intestinis. Decet ergo ut sicut nomen eius et diadema gero.ʼ sic ad defensionem patriæ inhaeream eius studio. Colligite queso concilium, prudenter inite consilium.ʼ sententiam proferte, quid in hoc agendum sit discrimine. Mittam si laudatis exercitum in Normanniam.ʼ et iniuriis quas michi frater
meus sine causa machinatus est talionem rependam. Æcclesiæ
iii. 317 Dei subueniam.ʼ uiduas et orphanos inermes protegam.ʼ fures et
sicarios gladio iusticiæ puniam.'

His dictis omnes assensum dederunt, et magnanimitatem regis collaudauerunt. Tunc Guillelmus rex Guillelmum de Guarenna comitem Suthregiæ constituit.ʼ quem paulo post mors nulli parcens e medio rapuit.[1] Corpus uero eius Cluniacenses monachi quos
Laquis honorifice locauit[2] in capitulo suo sepelierunt.ʼ et quis uel
iii. 318 qualis uir ibidem requieuerit his uersibus super tumulum in albo
lapide scultis denotauerunt.

Hic Guillelme comes locus est laudis tibi fomes.
Huius fundator et largus sedis amator,
Iste tuum funus decorat.ʼ placuit quia munus,
Pauperibus Christi quod prompta mente dedisti.
Ille tuos cineres seruat Pancratius heres,
Sanctorum castris qui te sociabit in astris.
Optime Pancrati fer opem te glorificanti,
Daque poli sedem, talem tibi qui dedit ædem.

Prefati consulis filii Guillelmus et Rainaldus cum Gundreda matre sua successerunt.ʼ[3] et sub Guillelmo atque Henrico Angliæ

[1] Although Orderic had among his informants the monk Roger of Warenne, William's nephew, his statements about the family are not entirely reliable; he wrote nearly fifty years after the events described, when Roger had died after forty-six years as a monk (cf. above, iii. 228–30). Although the Hyde Chronicle is often an unreliable source, the very circumstantial account given by the chronicler of how William received a fatal wound at the siege of Pevensey in 1088 and was taken to Lewes to die commands confidence (*Liber monasterii de Hyda*, ed. E. Edwards (RS, 1886), p. 299). Apart from David (*Robert Curthose*, p. 54 n. 62), who takes Orderic's account literally, most historians have dated William's death on 24 June 1088 (*EYC* viii. 5; *Regesta*, i. 325; GEC xii (1). 494; Sanders, p. 128). The grant of the earldom of Surrey at this date may have been a reward for his loyalty during the critical period of Odo of Bayeux's rebellion.

of my land is unable to protect his own land from lawless bandits. Now therefore I urge all of you, who were my father's vassals and held your fees in Normandy and England from him, to unite behind me without any guile to undertake this righteous task. We ought not to allow bands of robbers to grow strong enough to oppress the faithful and destroy the monasteries of holy men which our fathers founded by their labours in Normandy. The whole region is exposed to slaughter and rapine, and is often forced to regret the great Duke William, who saved it from internal and external wars. It is proper therefore that I, who bear his name and crown, should imitate him in the determined defence of his country. I ask you to meet together in a council, discuss measures wisely among yourselves, and tell me what you decide should be done in this crisis. If you approve I will send an army to Normandy, and will pay back my brother in his own coin for the injuries that he has brought upon me without provocation. I will bring help to the Church of God, protect helpless widows and orphans, and punish thieves and murderers with the sword of justice.'

When he had finished speaking all gave their approval and praised the king's spirit. Then King William made William of Warenne earl of Surrey; death which spares no man claimed him shortly afterwards.[1] The Cluniac monks he had established at Lewes[2] buried his body honourably in their chapter-house, and recorded who and what manner of man he was by carving these verses on a marble slab over his tomb:

Earl William, in this place your fame is kindled,
You built this house and were its generous friend;
This was a gift freely and gladly given
To the poor of Christ; it honours now your urn.
The saint himself, Pancras, who guards your ashes,
Will raise you to the mansions of the blessed.
Saint Pancras, give, we pray, a seat in heaven
To him who for your glory gave this house.

Earl William's sons William and Reginald succeeded him with their mother Gundreda;[3] they were distinguished for their

[2] William of Warenne founded the priory of St. Pancras at Lewes as a Cluniac priory in 1072–7 (Knowles, *MO* 151–8; *VCH Sussex*, ii. 64–5).
[3] Gundreda had died in childbirth at Castle Acre in 1085 (*EYC* viii. 5–6).

regibus probitate et potentia diu claruerunt. Roberto quoque Haimonis filio rex Guillelmus magnos honores tribuit.' et inter maximos optimates Angliæ ipsum sullimauit. Hic Sibiliam Rogerii comitis filiam uxorem duxit, quæ filiam eius[a] nomine Mathildem peperit.' quam postmodum Robertus Henrici regis filius in matrimonium sibi coniunxit.[1]

iii. 319 Primus Normannorum Stephanus de Albamarla filius Odonis Campaniæ comitis[2] regi adhesit, et regiis sumptibus castellum suum[3] super Aucium flumen uehementer muniuit.' in quo ualidissimam regis familiam contra ducem suscepit. Quem mox Gornacensis Girardus[4] secutus est. Nam Gornacum et Firmitatem et Goisleni-fontem aliasque munitiones suas regi tradidit.' finitimosque suos regiæ parti subicere studuit. Deinde Robertus Aucensium comes et Gualterius Gifardus atque Radulfus de Mortuomari et pene omnes qui trans Sequanam usque ad mare habitabant Anglicis
iii. 320 coniuncti sunt.' et de regiis opibus ad muniendas domos suas armis et satellitibus copiosam pecuniam receperunt.[5]

Tunc Robertus dux contra tot hostes repagulum parauit, filiamque suam quam de pelice habuerat Helie filio Lamberti de Sancto Sidonio coniugem dedit, et Archas cum Buris et adiacente prouincia in mariagio tribuit.' ut aduersariis resisteret, Talogiique comitatum defenderet. Ille uero iussa uiriliter complere cepit, Roberto enim duci et Guillelmo filio[6] eius semper fidelis fuit, et sub duobus regibus Guillelmo et Henrico multa pertulit.' labores uidelicet et exheredationis damna, exilium et multa pericula.

10

Audientes Cenomanni discidium Normannorum, cogitauerunt fastuosum excutere a se iugum eorum.' quod olim facere multociens conati sunt sub Guillelmo magno rege Anglorum.[7] Hoc

[a] *Possibly an error for* ei

[1] Robert fitz Hamon (d. 1107), son of Hamo the steward and grandson of Hamo-aux-Dents (cf. J. H. Round in *EHR* xxix (1914), 349), received the honor of Gloucester; his daughter Matilda married Robert of Caen, probably the oldest of King Henry I's natural children, who became earl of Gloucester (Sanders, p. 6; GEC v. 683–9; xi, Appendix D, p. 106). He founded the abbey of Tewkesbury (see above, iii. 228).

[2] Eudo, count of Champagne, was the third husband of William the Conqueror's sister Adelaide (above, ii. 264 n. 3).

[3] At Aumâle. The castle of Eu was taken by the duke's forces in 1089, 'secundo anno principatus Roberti', i.e. before September (*Regesta*, i, no. 310).

[4] This passage is evidence that the twenty-four parishes of the 'conquêts Hue de Gournay' were acquired by Gerard's father, the elder Hugh of Gournay

integrity and might under both William and Henry, kings of England. King William also conferred great honors on Robert fitz Hamon, and made him equal to the greatest magnates in England. Robert married Sibyl, the daughter of Earl Roger, and she bore him a daughter Matilda, whom later King Henry's son Robert took to wife.[1]

Stephen of Aumâle, the son of Eudo count of Champagne,[2] was the first of the Normans to support the king, and he fortified his castle on the river Bresle[3] at the king's expense, and established a strong garrison of king's men to hold it against the duke. Gerard of Gournay[4] soon followed suit; handing over his castles of Gournay and La Ferté-en-Bray and Gaillefontaine to the king, he tried to win his neighbours to the king's side. Then Robert, count of Eu, and Walter Giffard and Ralph of Mortemer and almost all the lords between the Seine and the sea joined the English and received large sums of money from the king's resources to provide arms and men for the defence of their homes.[5]

Thereupon Duke Robert, to put up a barrier against his numerous enemies, gave his daughter by a concubine in marriage to Helias the son of Lambert of Saint-Saëns, and provided Arques and Bures and the adjoining province as her marriage portion, so that Helias would resist his enemies and defend the county of Le Talou. Helias undertook with courage the duty imposed on him, and always remained faithful to Duke Robert and his son William,[6] for whom he endured much under the two kings, William and Henry; for he suffered labours and the evil of disinheritance, exile and many dangers.

10

When the men of Maine learnt of the civil strife among the Normans they thought that the moment had come to shake off their burdensome rule, as they had often tried to do before under William the Great, King of England.[7] On hearing of this Duke

(Lemarignier, *L'hommage en marche*, pp. 20–1), since Gerard was firmly established in this disputed region at this date.

[5] For the events of these years cf. Fliche, *Philippe I*, pp. 292–5.

[6] William Clito, Robert's son by his wife Sibyl of Conversano.

[7] If Orderic is correct in stating (below, p. 186) that Fulk le Rechin of Anjou kept the peace for a year, these events took place in 1089. Fulk certainly married Bertrade some time before 24 April 1090 (Halphen, *Anjou*, p. 318 no. 256).

Robertus dux ut comperiit, legatos et exenia Fulconi Andegauorum satrapæ destinauit.' obnixe rogans ut Cenomannos a temerario ausu compesceret, ac in Normanniam ad se grauiter egrotantem ueniret. At ille obsecranti libenter adquieuit.' ducemque iam conualescentem reperiit. Post plurima pacis et amiciciæ colloquia Fulco comes dixit duci Roberto, 'Si michi quam ualde cupio rem feceris unam.' Cenomannos tibi subiciam, et omni tempore tibi ut amicus fideliter seruiam. Amo Bertradam sobolem Simonis de
iii. 321 Monteforti neptem scilicet Ebroicensis comitis Guillelmi.' quam Heluisa comitissa nutrit, et sua sub tutela custodit. Hanc michi coniugem trade obsecro.' et quæque tibi pepigi semper seruabo.' Protinus ex parte ducis super hac re comes Ebroicensis requisitus est. Qui mox cum suis necessariis amicis consilium iniit.' et exitum rei sollicite inuestigauit. Tandem negotio diligenter indagato ad curiam ducis accessit.' et inter cetera sic duci dixit, 'Rem domine dux postulas a me michi ualde contrariam, ut neptem meam quæ adhuc tenera uirgo est digamo tradam.' quam sororius meus michi commendauit nutriendam. Verum prouide commodum tuum queris.' meumque paruipendis. Cenomannensem comitatum uis tibi optinere per neptem meam.' et tu michi aufers hereditatem meam. Iustumne est quod moliris? Non faciam quod poscis, nisi reddideris michi Bathuentum et Nogionem, Vaceium et Craventionem, Scoceium aliosque fundos Radulfi patrui mei,[1] qui pro magnitudine capitis et congerie capillorum iocose cognominatus est Caput Asini, nepotique meo Guillelmo Bretoliensi[2]
iii. 322 Pontem Sancti Petri, et reliqua quæ rationabiliter et legaliter poterimus approbare, quod nostra debeant esse hereditario iure. Legitimi siquidem michi testes sunt et in omnibus idonei, quod Robertus de Guaceio filius prefati Radulfi patrui mei.' me totius iuris sui heredem constituit, sed Guillelmus rex consobrinus noster quia potentior nobis fuit.' omnes hereditatis nostræ partes sicut leo in particione cerui suas fecit.[3] His domine dux sapienter consideratis, tene rectitudinem nobis.' et nos tuis iuste optemperabimus iussis.'

Dux autem huiusmodi responsione audita, ex consultu sapientum

[1] Ralph Tête d'Âne and William's father Richard, count of Évreux, were both sons of Robert, archbishop of Rouen.

[2] Adeliza, the mother of William of Breteuil, was a half-sister of William, count of Évreux, by their mother Godeheut (GEC xii (1), 756–7). But if William of Breteuil had any rights in the inheritance of Robert of Gacé they would have come through his father, William fitz Osbern, who was a grandson of Count Ralph, the half-brother of Duke Richard I.

Robert sent envoys with presents to Fulk count of Anjou, importuning him to restrain the Manceaux from such a rash action, and come to see him in Normandy, where he was seriously ill. Fulk readily agreed to this request, and found the duke already convalescing. After several discussions on the question of peace and alliance, Count Fulk said to Duke Robert, 'If you will do for me one thing on which my heart is set, I will subdue the Manceaux for you and help you at all times as your faithful ally. I love Bertrade, the daughter of Simon of Montfort, who is the niece of William count of Évreux; the Countess Helwise has charge of her and is bringing her up. Give her to me as my wife, I ask you, and I will always keep faith in what I have promised you.' The duke immediately sent to inform the count of Évreux of this request. The latter consulted his closest friends, and carefully examined the probable consequences. Finally when the matter had been thoroughly sifted he went to the duke's court and said to him, among other things, 'My lord duke, you ask something that is repugnant to me, for you wish me to give my niece, who was entrusted to my guardianship by my brother-in-law and is a young virgin, in marriage to a man who has already been twice married. The truth is that you are solely concerned with your own interests and think nothing of mine. You wish to use my niece as a pawn to secure the county of Maine for yourself, and you propose to take away my inheritance from me. Is this a just proposal? I will not grant your request unless you restore to me Bavent and Noyon-sur-Andelle, Gacé and Gravençon, Écouché and the other estates of my uncle Ralph[1] (who was nicknamed *Tête d'âne* in jest because of his huge head and shaggy hair), and restore to my nephew William of Breteuil[2] Le Pont-Saint-Pierre and other properties which we can reasonably and lawfully prove to be ours by hereditary right. I can produce thoroughly law-worthy witnesses to say that Robert of Gacé, the son of my uncle Ralph, named me as heir to all his inheritance; but our cousin King William, being stronger than we are, took, as it were, the lion's share of the stag and appropriated for himself all our share in our inheritance.[3] Weigh these matters carefully, my lord duke; do justice to us, and we will obey your commands justly.'

When the duke had heard this reply he took counsel with

[3] Robert of Gacé died without direct heirs and Duke William added his lands to his own demesne (above, ii. 118).

decreuit dare minora.' ne perderet maiora. Tunc Edgarus adelinus et Robertus Belesmensis atque Guillelmus de Archis monachus Molismensis[1] precipui ducis consiliarii erant. Guillelmi ergo Ebroicensis et Guillelmi Bretoliensis nepotis eius petitionibus dux adquieuit, et prenominata cum territoriis suis oppida tribuit.' preter Scoceium quod Girardus de Gornaco possidebat, qui de eadem parentela prodierat.[2] Filius enim Basiliæ Girardi Fleitelli filiæ erat.' tantæque potentiæ cui nemo uim inferre poterat. Deinde Andegauensis consul concupitam puellam gaudens suscepit, et uiuentibus adhuc duabus uxoribus[3] terciam desponsauit, quæ filium ei nomine Fulconem peperit. Pacti quoque sui memor Fulco Cenomannos adiit, eosque plus precibus et pro-
iii. 323 missis quam ui compescere studuit.' et conspiratam rebellionem in annuum saltem spacium distulit. Hic in multis reprehensibilis et infamis erat.' multisque uitiorum pestibus obsecundabat. Ipse nimirum quia pedes habebat deformes, instituit sibi fieri longos et in summitate acutissimos subtolares.' ita ut operiret pedes, et eorum celaret tubera quæ uulgo uocantur uniones. Insolitus inde mos in occiduum orbem processit.' leuibusque et nouitatum amatoribus uehementer placuit. Vnde sutores in calciamentis quasi caudas scorpionum quas uulgo pigacias[4] appellant faciunt.' idque genus calciamenti pene cuncti diuites et egeni nimium expetunt. Nam antea omni tempore rotundi subtolares ad formam pedum agebantur.' eisque summi et mediocres clerici et laici competenter utebantur. At modo seculares peruersis moribus competens scema superbe arripiunt, et quod olim honorabiles uiri turpissimum iudicauerunt, et omnino quasi stercus refutauerunt, hoc moderni dulce quasi mel estimant, et ueluti speciale decus amplectentes gestant.

Robertus quidam nebulo in curia Rufi regis prolixas pigacias primus cepit implere stuppis.' et hinc inde contorquere instar

[1] William of Arques, monk of Molesme, not to be confused with William, count of Arques, witnessed charters of Robert Curthose in 1088 and 1089 (*Regesta*, i, nos. 299, 310; Haskins, *Norman Institutions*, pp. 76–7, 289; *GC* xi, col. 77). Edgar Atheling, grandson of Edmund Ironside, frequently changed his allegiance, but appears to have had too little ability or influence to be regarded as a political danger (see above, ii. 180, 182, 196, 222, 226; Anglo-Saxon Chronicle, 1086, 1091, 1097, 1106).

[2] Basilie, daughter of Gerard Fleitel, married first Ralph of Gacé and then Hugh of Gournay, the father of Gerard of Gournay (Robert of Torigny (Marx, p. 325)).

prudent men and decided to give the smaller so as not to lose the greater part. At that time Edgar Atheling and Robert of Bellême and William of Arques, a monk of Molesme,[1] were the duke's chief counsellors. The outcome was that he granted the requests of William of Évreux and his nephew William of Breteuil, and handed over all the strongholds named with their dependent territories, apart from Écouché which Gerard of Gournay, who came of the same stock, then held.[2] Gerard was the son of Gerard Fleitel's daughter Basilie, and so powerful that no one could force his hand. Afterwards the count of Anjou jubilantly received the girl he desired, and married her as his third wife though the two former wives were still living.[3] She bore him a son named Fulk. To fulfil his share of the bargain, Fulk approached the Manceaux, attempted to bring them under control more by pleas and promises than by force, and succeeded at least in postponing the planned rebellion for a year.

Count Fulk was a man with many reprehensible, even scandalous, habits, and gave way to many pestilential vices. Being a man with deformed feet he had shoes made with very long and pointed toes, to hide the shape of his feet and conceal the growths that are commonly called bunions. This encouraged a new fashion in the western regions, which delighted frivolous men in search of novelties. To meet it cobblers fashioned shoes like scorpions' tails, which are commonly called 'pulley-shoes',[4] and almost all, rich and poor alike, now demand shoes of this kind. Before then shoes always used to be made round, fitting the foot, and these were adequate to the needs of high and low, both clergy and laity. But now laymen in their pride seize upon a fashion typical of their corrupt morals. What honourable men once thought shameful and utterly rejected as filth, the men of this age consider sweet as honey and flaunt abroad as though it were a special grace.

Robert, a certain worthless fellow at King Rufus's court, first began to stuff the long 'pulley-toes' and in this way bend them

[3] Fulk le Rechin had been married at least three times: first to a daughter of Lancelin of Beaugency, and after her death to Ermengarde of Bourbon and Orengarde of Châtelaillon, both of whom he had repudiated. It is possible that he had also married a daughter of Walter I of Brienne and repudiated her (Fliche, *Philippe I*, p. 44 n. 2; Halphen, *Anjou*, pp. 169–70). At least two of his former wives were alive at the time of his marriage to Bertrade.

[4] These shoes, which persisted in France into the seventeenth century, were known as 'souliers à la poulaine'. A specimen may be seen in the Musée de Cluny in Paris.

cornu arietis. Ob hoc ipse cornardus cognominatus est.ʼ cuius friuolam adinuentionem magna pars nobilium ceu quoddam insigne probitatis et uirtutis opus mox secuta est. Tunc effeminati passim
iii. 324 in orbe dominabantur indisciplinate debachabantur sodomiticisque spurciciis fœdi catamitæ flammis urendi turpiter abutebantur. Ritus heroum abiciebant, hortamenta sacerdotum deridebant.ʼ barbaricumque morem in habitu et uita tenebant. Nam capillos a uertice in frontem discriminabant, longos crines ueluti mulieres nutriebant, et summopere comebant, prolixisque nimiumque strictis camisiis indui tunicisque gaudebant. Omne tempus quidam usurpabant, et extra legem Dei moremque patrum pro libitu suo ducebant. Nocte comesationibus et potationibus uanisque confabulationibus aleis et tesseris aliisque ludibriis uacabant, die uero dormiebant. Sic post obitum Gregorii papæ et Guillelmi Nothi aliorumque principum religiosorum.ʼ in occiduis partibus pene totus abolitus est honestus patrum mos antiquorum.[1] Illi enim modestis uestiebantur indumentis, optimeque coaptatis ad sui mensuram corporis.ʼ et erant habiles ad equitandum et currendum, et ad omne opus quod ratio suggereret agendum. Ast in diebus istis ueterum ritus pene totus nouis adinuentionibus commutatus est. Femineam mollitiem petulans iuuentus amplectitur.ʼ feminisque uiri curiales in omni lasciuia summopere adulantur. Pedum articulis ubi finis est corporis colubrinarum similitudinem caudarum imponunt.ʼ quas uelut scorpiones præ oculis suis prospiciunt. Humum quoque puluerulentam interularum et palliorum
iii. 325 superfluo sirmate uerrunt.ʼ longis latisque manicis ad omnia facienda manus operiunt, et his superfluitatibus onusti celeriter ambulare uel aliquid utiliter operari uix possunt. Sincipite scalciati sunt, ut fures.ʼ occipitio autem prolixas nutriunt comas ut meretrices. Olim penitentes et capti ac peregrini usualiter intonsi erant, longasque barbas gestabant.ʼ indicioque tali penitentiam seu captionem uel peregrinationem spectantibus pretendebant. Nunc uero pene uniuersi populares cerriti sunt et barbatuli.ʼ palam manifestantes specimine tali quod sordibus libidinis gaudeant ut fœtentes hirci. Crispant crines calamistro, caput uelant uitta siue pilleo. Vix aliquis militarium procedit in publicum capite discooperto.ʼ legitimeque secundum apostoli preceptum

[1] Cf. William of Malmesbury's denunciation of the fashions and morals of the court of William Rufus (*GR* ii. 369–70).

into the shape of a ram's horn. As a result he was nicknamed Cornard. The frivolous fashion he had set was soon imitated by a great part of the nobility as if it had been an achievement of great worth and importance. At that time effeminates set the fashion in many parts of the world: foul catamites, doomed to eternal fire, unrestrainedly pursued their revels and shamelessly gave themselves up to the filth of sodomy. They rejected the traditions of honest men, ridiculed the counsel of priests, and persisted in their barbarous way of life and style of dress. They parted their hair from the crown of the head to the forehead, grew long and luxurious locks like women, and loved to deck themselves in long, over-tight shirts and tunics. Some of them frivolled away their time, spending it as they chose without regard for the law of God or the customs of their ancestors. They devoted their nights to feasts and drinking-bouts, idle chatter, dice, games of chance, and other sports, and they slept all day. In this way, after the death of Pope Gregory and William the Bastard and other pious leaders, the healthy customs of our fathers almost wholly disappeared in the regions of the west.[1] Our ancestors used to wear decent clothes, well-adapted to the shape of their bodies; they were skilled horsemen and swift runners, ready for all seemly undertakings. But in these days the old customs have almost wholly given way to new fads. Our wanton youth is sunk in effeminacy, and courtiers, fawning, seek the favours of women with every kind of lewdness. They add excrescences like serpents' tails to the tips of their toes where the body ends, and gaze with admiration on these scorpion-like shapes. They sweep the dusty ground with the unnecessary trains of their robes and mantles; their long, wide sleeves cover their hands whatever they do; impeded by these frivolities they are almost incapable of walking quickly or doing any kind of useful work. They shave the front part of their head, like thieves, and let their hair grow very long at the back, like harlots. Up to now penitents and prisoners and pilgrims have normally been unshaven, with long beards, and in this way have publicly proclaimed their condition of penance or captivity or pilgrimage. But now almost all our fellow countrymen are crazy and wear little beards, openly proclaiming by such a token that they revel in filthy lusts like stinking goats. They curl their hair with hot irons and cover their heads with a fillet or a cap. Scarcely any knight appears in public with his head uncovered and decently shorn according to the

tonso.[1] Exterius itaque habitu gestuque monstrant.' quales interius conscientias habeant et qualiter per artum callem[2] ad Deum percurrant.

Altissimus igitur iudex e sullimi uidens solio, quod nimium flagitiis inheret humana intentio.' populum ineruditum plebemque indisciplinatum multiplici percutit flagello. Morbis enim macerari et bellis inquietari terrigenas permittit, hipocritisque presidibus subigit.' quos sibi contrarios suæque legis spontaneos preuaricatores perspicit. Electi autem qui zelo Phinees[3] inflammantur, inter reprobos crebro irascuntur.' ac ad Dominum cum propheta conqueruntur, 'Vidi preuaricantes et tabescebam.' quia eloquia tua non custodierunt.'[4] Vnde a bonis doctoribus arguuntur.' obsecran-
iii. 326 tur, increpantur in omni patientia et doctrina.'[5] sed his omnibus
pertinaciter obstat maliuoli cordis obduratio nefaria, quæ solet omnium fouere ac defendere scelerum contagia. Si Persius et Plautus aliique mordaces satirici nunc adessent, et curiose indagarent.' qualiter nostrates clam palamque libitus suos perpetrent, immensam reprehendendi materiam et subsannandi in propatulo reperirent.

Innumeris itaque lapsibus perspectis in mundo.' Geroius Grossiuus[6] in quadam epistola scripsit inter reliqua Gisleberto Maminoto Luxouiensium episcopo,

Virtutum lampas qua pristina splenduit ætas.'
Transtulit omne suum prorsus in astra iubar.
Temporibus nostris tenebris inuoluitur orbis.'
Nec ualet extinctus iam releuare caput.
Nec probus est hodie nec curans de probitate.'
Nec precium nec honor, nec probitatis amor.

Enormitati maliciæ quam passim grassari perspexit.' ardens scolasticus yperbolice detraxit. Blittero quoque Flandrita in poemate quod super Henrico Cesare nuper edidit.'[7] ruinam mundi et miseros mortalium euentus elegiacis modis luculenter denotauit. Alii quoque plures litterati sophistæ magnos questus pro-
iii. 327 tulerunt de flagitiis et erumnis huius seculi, quos secutus in
presenti opusculo breuiter memini.' quo tempore cisalpes cepit

[1] Cf. 1 Corinthians xi. 7, 14.
[2] Cf. Matthew vii. 14.
[3] Cf. Numbers xxv. 11.
[4] Psalm cxviii (cxix). 158.
[5] Cf. 2 Timothy iv. 2.
[6] I have been unable to find any other information about this writer; it is possible that the name was copied wrongly. The style is not unlike that of Geoffrey Grossus, author of the *Life of St. Bernard of Tiron.* The question remains open.

apostle's precept.[1] So in their outward dress and bearing they reveal their character and show in what fashion they follow the narrow path[2] of God.

So the most high Judge, seeing from his heavenly throne that the human heart is greatly given to deeds of shame, chastises the ignorant people and undisciplined herd with many scourges. He suffers mortals to be tormented by disease, harassed by wars and subjected to false rulers if he finds that they disobey him and wilfully transgress his law. Meanwhile the elect, living among the reprobate and burning with the zeal of Phineas,[3] often grow angry and complain to God in the words of the prophet, 'I beheld the transgressors and was grieved, because they kept not thy word.'[4] Learned and good men reprove, rebuke, and exhort the transgressors with all long-suffering and doctrine;[5] but the hardened wickedness of an evil heart obstinately resists all these, for it fosters and preserves the contagion of every kind of sin. If Persius and Plautus and other bitter satirists were now living, and made a careful study of how the men of our time openly and secretly practise their vices, they would find abundant matter to criticize and expose to public mockery.

When Giroie Grossivus[6] saw how many men of his day fell away from virtue, he wrote in one of the letters that he addressed to Gilbert Maminot, bishop of Lisieux,

The lamp of virtue, which in former days
Shone brightly, lends the distant stars its rays.
Darkness broods thickly over all the earth;
The light, extinguished, has no power or worth.
No virtue now remains, nor quest for grace,
No value, honour, love of righteousness.

The zealous scholar hyperbolically denounced the tremendous evil that he saw increasing all around. And Blitherus the Fleming has vividly described the ruin of the world and the wretched fate of mortal men in elegiac verses in a poem he wrote recently about the Emperor Henry.[7] Also many other learned writers have composed long laments about the sins and sorrows of this age. Following their example, I have given a brief account in this modest work of the time when men in northern parts adopted the foolish

[7] The poem of Blitherus the Fleming, who was possibly a canon of Utrecht, is now lost (Manitius, *Geschichte der lateinischen Literatur des Mittelalters* (Munich, 1911–31), iii. 659, 764, 768).

ineptia pigatiarum, et superflua prolixitas capillorum atque uestium terræ sordes frustra scopantium.

De sanctitate et miraculis sanctorum mallem scribere multo libentius quam de nugis infrunitorum friuolisque nepotationibus.' si principes nostri et antistites sanctis perfecte insisterent carismatibus, et prodigiis pollerent sanctitatem preconantibus. Ast ego uim illis ut sanctificentur inferre nequeo.' unde his omissis super rebus quæ fiunt ueracem dictatum facio. Nunc autem ad narrationis ordinem redeo.

II

Anno ab incarnatione Domini M°XC° indictione xiiiª Cenomanni contra Normannos rebellauerunt, eiectisque custodibus eorum de munitionibus nouum principem sibi constituerunt. Nam qui uiuente Guillelmo rege contra eum rebellare multociens conati sunt.' ipso mortuo statim de rebellione machinari ceperunt. Legationem igitur filiis Azonis marchisi Liguriæ[1] direxerunt.' eisque uelle suum intimantes per legatum dixerunt, 'Cur tam segnes et ignaui estis, ut hereditatem uestram non repetatis, quam nos ultro seruamus uobis? Mortui sunt omnes Cenomannensis
iii. 328 principatus legitimi heredes, iamque nullus uobis uicinior est heres. Guillelmus eciam uiolentus multorum inuasor iam decidit, qui per Margaritam Herberti filiam quam Roberto filio suo sociare uoluit.' suæ diutius ditioni nos mancipauit.[2] Ecce filii eius quorum unus regno preest Angliæ, alter ducatui Normanniæ.' mutuis cedibus conturbantur, sibi inuicem aduersantur, rapinis et incendiis malignantur, et pene usque ad internecionem seuientes labuntur. Nos autem Cenomannicam urbem et oppida eius in pace possidemus, uobisque fideliter mandamus.' ut huc confestim ueniatis, et hereditario iure nobis presideatis.' Hæc itaque Cenomanni Liguribus mandauerunt non pro amore eorum.' sed ut aliqua rationabili occasione iugum excuterent a se Normannorum.' quod fere xxx annis fortiter detriuerat turgidas ceruices illorum.

Ligures germani audita legatione gauisi sunt.' initoque consilio

[1] Azzo of Este, marquess of Liguria, married Gersendis, sister of count

fashions of pulley-toes and long and flowing hair and garments that sweep up all the filth on the ground for no useful purpose.

I would far rather write of holiness and the miracles performed by the saints than of the trifles of fools and frivolous extravagances, if only our princes and bishops devoted themselves wholly to lives of spiritual grace and performed miracles that proclaimed their sanctity. But I have no power to force them to live holy lives; and so leaving these matters aside I write a factual account of what they really do. Now, however, I return to the course of my narrative.

II

In the year of our Lord 1090, the thirteenth indiction, the men of Maine rebelled against the Normans, expelled their castellans from the castles, and set up a new prince. The men who had often attempted to rebel against King William during his lifetime lost not a moment in plotting rebellion when he was dead. With this intent they sent an embassy to the sons of Azzo, marquess of Liguria,[1] and made their wishes known to him through their envoy, saying, 'Why are you so idle and complacent that you make no attempt to recover your heritage, which we are freely guarding for you? All the legitimate heirs of the county of Maine are dead, and no man is now a closer heir than you. William, who violently seized so many men's lands and by the right of Herbert's daughter Margaret whom he wished to marry to his son Robert has for many years held us in his grip,[2] is dead. And now his sons, one of whom rules the kingdom of England, the other the duchy of Normandy, are locked in deadly combat, plundering and burning each other's territories, and ferociously tearing each other to pieces. We however are in peaceful possession of the city of Le Mans and all its strongholds, and send to you as your liege men, urging you to come at once and rule over us by hereditary right.' This is what the men of Maine proposed to the Ligurians; not from any love of them, but to find any reasonable excuse for shaking off the Norman yoke which had rubbed sorely on their proud necks for almost thirty years.

The Ligurian brothers were delighted by the envoys' message, and took counsel with their most intimate friends to determine

Hugh IV of Maine. Hugh's other sister, Paula, married John of La Flèche. See above, ii. 304 n. 2; Latouche, *Maine*, Appendix III, pp. 113–15.

[2] See above, ii. 116–18.

cum necessariis amicis quid agendum esset perscrutati sunt. Tandem diffinierunt ut Fulco qui maior natu erat patris honorem in Italia possideret./ Hugo autem frater eius Cenomannensem principatum ex matris hereditate sibi reposceret.[1] Denique Gaufredus Madeniensis et Helias[2] aliique ciues et oppidani uenientem Hugonem susceperunt./ eique ad optinendum ius ex materna hereditate competens aliquandiu suffragati sunt.

Venerabilis autem Hoellus antistes qui dono Guillelmi regis
iii. 329 presulatum habuit./[3] ipsi filiisque eius semper fidelis extitit, et in quantum potuit./ truculentam recalcitrationem dissuasit. Pertinaces uero interdixit, pontificali iure anathematizauit, et a liminibus sanctæ matris æcclesiæ sequestrauit. Qua propter rebellionis incentores contra eum nimis irati sunt./ et iniuriis eum terribiliter afficere comminati sunt. Interea dum per diocesim suam cum clericis suis equitaret, et episcopali more officium suum sollerter exerceret./ Helias de Flechia eum comprehendit, et in carcere donec Hugo in urbe Cenomannica susceptus fuisset uinctum presulem tenuit.[4] Porro æcclesia Dei pontificis sui afflictioni ualde condoluit, Dominique sanctas imagines in crucibus et sanctarum scrinia reliquiarum ad terram deposuit./ et portas basilicarum spinis obturauit,[a] et a clangore signorum celebrique cantu solitisque solenniis ut uidua merens cessauit, lacrimisque uacauit.

Cenomanni postquam nouum comitem suum diuitiis et sensu ac uirtute inopem esse cognouerunt./ imprudentes facti sui pœnitentes eum sicut Sichimitæ Abimelech despicabilem et exosum habuerunt.[5] Imprudens enim et ignauus ac deses erat./ tantæque dignitatis habenas moderari nesciebat. Hic filiam Roberti Wiscardi coniugem habuit./[6] sed generosæ coniugis magnanimitatem uir ignauus ferre non ualens ipsam repudiauit, pro qua re papa Vrbanus eum palam excommunicauit. Omnes igitur Allobroges ipsum execrati sunt./ et inuenta occasione ferocibus cisalpinis extorrem destinauerunt. Inscius inter gnaros et timidus inter
iii. 330 animosos milites consul constitutus uilis habebatur./ multiplicique terrore frequenter exanguis angebatur, et fugam quod precipuum

[a] opturauit, *Caen MS.*

[1] Hugh probably arrived in Le Mans in April 1091 (Latouche, *Maine*, p. 41 n. 10).

[2] Helias, son of John of La Flèche and son-in-law of Gervase of Château-du-Loir.

[3] The rights of patronage were contested by the count of Anjou. See above, ii. 300–2; Latouche, *Maine*, pp. 79–80.

[4] Hoel's imprisonment did not last long; he had already been released by the time Count Hugh reached Le Mans (Latouche, *Maine*, pp. 42, 86).

[5] Judges, ch. ix.

what they should do. In the end they decided that Fulk, who was the elder, should hold his father's honor in Italy, and his brother Hugh should claim the county of Maine by inheritance from his mother.[1] When Hugh reached Maine he was welcomed by Geoffrey of Mayenne, Helias,[2] and other citizens and castellans, who for some time provided him with adequate help towards recovering his maternal inheritance.

The venerable Bishop Hoel, however, who held the see by King William's gift,[3] had always remained loyal to him and his sons, and had done his best to discourage the savage revolt. Laying an interdict on the obstinate rebels, he excommunicated them by episcopal authority, and utterly excluded them from the precincts of their holy Mother Church. Consequently the leaders of the rebellion turned their wrath against him, and threatened him with terrible acts of vengeance. Whilst he was riding one day through his diocese with his clergy, discharging his episcopal duties with his customary care, Helias of La Flèche seized him and kept him securely in prison until such time as Hugh might be received in the city of Le Mans.[4] Meanwhile the church of God shared in the affliction of its bishop. The holy images of the Lord on the crucifixes and shrines containing the relics of saints were taken down, the doors of the churches blocked up with thorns, the ringing of bells, the chanting of offices and all the accustomed rites ceased as the widowed church mourned and gave itself up to weeping.

When the men of Maine discovered that their new count had neither riches nor judgement and courage to commend him, the hotheads began to regret their action, and they treated him with scorn and loathing as the Shechemites did Abimelech.[5] He was foolish, cowardly, and idle, and had no idea how to hold the reins of high office. He had taken a daughter of Robert Guiscard as his wife,[6] but being a contemptible creature who could not endure the spirit of his high-born wife he repudiated her without cause, thereby incurring public excommunication by Pope Urban. All the Italians therefore regarded him as accursed, and welcomed the opportunity of banishing him among the fierce northern races. An ignoramus among learned men, a coward among brave knights, he became a count only to be held in contempt; continually trembling with fear of everything he suffered torments and

[6] See Latouche, *Maine*, p. 115 n. 8; Chalandon, *Domination normande* i. 251, 285.

sibi remedium putabat meditabatur. Hoc aduertentes Cenomanni ualde lætati sunt; et maiorem ei metum sempectas[a] incusserunt.[1]

Tandem Helias consobrinus eius ad eum accessit; et cum eo de imminentibus causis tractans dixit, 'Audio musitantem populum domine, quod in patriam tuam uis redire; durosque mores et comitatum indomitæ gentis relinquere. Hoc profecto nullus amicorum tuorum tibi debet dissuadere. Nam sicut mores tui placidi sunt amantque tranquillitatem pacis; sic huius incolæ regionis continuis uacant bellis, et impatientes sunt quietis. Preterea impacabiles Normanni Cenomanniam calumniantur; et cum ingenti feritate Cenomannicis dira comminantur. Nam filii regis Guillelmi qui olim inter se dissidebant nunc reconciliati sunt; et in Normanniam cum grandi exercitu conueniunt, ut in terram nostram repente irruant; et nos qui contra illos rebellauimus atrocibus armis impugnent et puniant. Hanc sine dubio
iii. 331 crede precipuam causam pro qua Guillelmus rex cum ingenti pompa uenit in Neustriam,[2] cuius ut reor aduentus nobis pariet grauem metum et occupationem maximam.' Hæc ita dicenti Hugo manifeste propalauit Heliæ, quod suum uellet consulatum uendere; patriosque penates reuisere. Helias dixit, 'Cognatus tuus sum domine, suffragioque meo sullimatus es in consulatus honore; quem nulli potes nisi michi dare uel uendere. Nam filia Herberti comitis Lancelino de Balgenceio nupsit;[3] eique Lancelinum Radulfi[4] patrem et Iohannem meum genitorem peperit. Hoc itaque disserui manifeste; ut me sicut te scias ortum de comitis Herberti progenie. Nunc igitur de meo quod inter nos conuenerit accipe; et consulatus stemma michi dimitte, quod meum debet esse consanguinitatis iure. Graue quidem et laboriosum est quod appeto; quia uix aut nunquam dum tres filii regis Guillelmi aduixerint in pace possidebo. Valde indignum uidetur tantis principibus qui nos circumuallare possunt militum centum milibus; ut a collimitaneis contribulibus impune patiantur aliquod dedecus, uel aliquo modo amittant sine terribili calumnia quodlibet

[a] *Sic in Caen MS.; possibly* per sempectas *is meant*

[1] In the Rule of St. Benedict (cap. 27) the term used for a veteran monk is 'sempecta'. Unless the copyist has completely misread some such word as 'semper' or 'temperius' the meaning seems to be that the older counsellors played on Hugh's fears.

[2] In January 1091.

[3] Orderic's various references to the family of the counts of Maine are confused and vague. Latouche (*Maine*, pp. 113–15) has reconstructed a more probable genealogy; according to his hypothesis Paula, daughter of Herbert

contemplated flight as the sovereign remedy for his troubles. When the men of Maine perceived this their spirits rose, and they worked on his fears through the intervention of their senior statesmen.[1]

Finally his kinsman Helias came to him, and as they discussed urgent matters said, 'There is a rumour among the people, my lord, that you would like to return to your own country and leave behind you the harsh customs and company of this untamed people. Surely no one who is your friend should try to dissuade you from this. You are a peaceloving man of tranquil character, whereas the inhabitants of this county spend their time in wars and grow restive in peace. Besides this, the Normans are relentless in their claim to Maine, and fiercely utter terrible threats against the Manceaux. And the sons of King William who were formerly at each other's throats have now become reconciled and are meeting in Normandy with a great army, with the intention of suddenly invading our country, overcoming us by force of arms, and punishing us for our rebellion against them. You may be quite sure that this is the real reason why King William has crossed to Normandy with a great retinue,[2] and I fear that his coming will expose us to grave dangers and require superhuman efforts.' In reply to this Hugh made it plain to Helias that he would be glad to sell his title and return to the home of his fathers. Helias said, 'I am your kinsman, my lord, and it was by my voice that you were raised to the honourable office of count; this office can be given or sold to none but me. For the daughter of Count Herbert married Lancelin of Beaugency,[3] and bore him Lancelin the father of Ralph[4] and John, my father. I have explained this to you so that you may recognize that I, no less than you, am sprung from the stock of Count Herbert. So take whatever we may agree upon from my possessions and restore the count's rights to me by right of kinship. What I seek is burdensome and laborious, for I shall rarely or never hold it in peace as long as the three sons of King William live. It seems shameful to princes such as these, who can hem us in with a hundred thousand knights, that they should endure any slight from their neighbours and associates, or should surrender, without making the most formidable claim, one jot of the right

'Wake-Dog' and sister of Count Hugh IV, married John of La Flèche, son of Lancelin of Beaugency, but Lancelin did not marry into the family of the counts of Maine. If so, Helias was a first cousin of Count Hugh V.

[4] Ralph of Beaugency.

ius.' quod pater eorum qualicumque pacto fuerit nactus. Me quoque libertatis amor nichilominus stimulat.' et hereditatis auitæ rectitudo dimicandi pro illa fiduciam in Deo michi suppeditat.'

His dictis ignauus Allobrox annuit.' et pro comitatu Cenomannensi decem milia solidorum Cenomannensis monetæ recepit.[1]
iii. 332 Helias uero recedente Ligure comes Cenomannorum factus est.' et xx annis adepto consulatu strenue potitus est.[2] Heres quoque soceri sui Geruasii de Castro Ligeri factus est, cuius filiam habuit, ex qua filiam nomine Eremburgem genuit.' quam domini sui filio Fulconi Andegauorum comiti in matrimonium copulauit.[3] Hic in accepta potestate uitam suam multum emendauit.' et multiplici uirtute floruit. Clerum et æcclesiam Dei laudabiliter honorauit.' et missis seruitioque Dei cotidie feruenter interfuit, subiectis æquitatem seruauit.' pacemque pauperibus pro posse suo tenuit.

12

His temporibus in Normannia nequitiæ rabies nimium creuit.' et in cunctis climatibus eius ultra modum redundauit, miserosque regionis indigenas miserabiliter conturbauit. Armorum crebra collisio in conflictibus frenduit, et multorum sanguine tellus maduit.

Anno secundo postquam Guillelmus rex obiit.' Ascelinus cognomento Goellus Guillelmo Bretoliensi domino suo arcem Ibreii furto surripuit, et Roberto duci prodidit.[4] Guillelmus autem pro
iii. 333 redemptione arcis qua carere noluit.' mille quingentas libras duci erogauit. Recepta uero turri presidatum Ibreii pro uindicta Goello abstulit.' et omnibus rebus quas sua sub dicione habebat eum spoliauit. Inde diutinum inter eos bellum fuit.' et rapinis incendiisque cum cædibus hominum uicina regio luxit. Amalricus de Monteforti qui fortis cognominabatur pro uirtute

[1] For these events cf. *Cartulaire de l'abbaye de Saint-Vincent du Mans*, ed. R. Charles and S. Menjot d'Elbenne, i (Mamers and Le Mans, 1886), no. 117. In 1095 Hugh was equally ready to sell off his claim to some of his father's property in Italy to his brother Fulk (Latouche, *Maine*, p. 115 n. 8).

[2] He became count of Maine between 29 June and 27 July 1092 (Latouche, *Maine*, p. 44) and died on 11 July, according to Orderic in 1110 (ibid., p. 53), eighteen years later.

[3] Helias married as his first wife Matilda, daughter of Gervase of Château-du-Loir (Latouche, *Maine*, p. 115). The marriage of Eremburge to Fulk's son, Fulk V, marked a definite alliance with Anjou, which finally led to the union of Maine and Anjou after Eremburge's death in 1126 (ibid., pp. 47, 52–3).

that their father acquired by any kind of treaty. Notwithstanding this, love of liberty animates me and the justice of my struggle for my ancestral inheritance enables me to put my trust in God.'

The craven Italian agreed to these proposals and received ten thousand shillings in the money of Maine for the county of Maine.[1] Helias became count of Maine after the Ligurian had withdrawn, and for twenty years governed the county he had acquired with energy.[2] He was made the heir of Gervase of Château-du-Loir, whose daughter he had married. He had by her a daughter called Eremburge whom he gave in marriage to Fulk count of Anjou, his lord's son.[3] Once established in power Helias showed a great improvement in his way of life, and was outstanding for his many virtues. He deserves praise for the honour that he showed the clergy and the Church of God, and for his daily, devout attendance at Mass and other divine offices; he showed justice to his subjects and gave peace to the poor as far as he was able.

12

At this time uncontrolled wickedness was on the increase in Normandy, causing turmoil in every part of the country and crushing the wretched inhabitants into still greater wretchedness. Armed clashes continually broke out, and the earth was watered with the blood of many men.

The second year after King William died Ascelin Goel feloniously took the castle of Ivry away from his lord, William of Breteuil, and surrendered it to Duke Robert.[4] William, who was unwilling to lose the castle, offered fifty thousand livres to the duke for it. After recovering the castle he avenged himself by depriving Goel of the castellanship and confiscating all the property which he held of him. As a result there was prolonged war between them, and the entire neighbourhood was troubled by plundering, burning and slaughter. Amaury of Montfort, who was

[4] The castle of Ivry, originally built by Aubrée, wife of Ralph of Ivry, count of Bayeux, was taken from her son, Hugh bishop of Bayeux, by Robert the Magnificent, and remained in the ducal demesne until the death of William the Conqueror. Ascelin Goel's grandmother, Aubrée, may have been a daughter of Hugh bishop of Bayeux; if so his claim to the castle was based on hereditary right (GEC viii. 208; above, iii. 208; Robert of Torigny in William of Jumièges (Marx, pp. 288–91)). William of Breteuil's claim was based on his descent from Emma, daughter of Count Ralph of Bayeux (Douglas, *WC*, pp. 89–90; J. Yver, in *BSAN* liii (1955–56), 67).

qua uigebat.' et cunctis affinibus qui secus eum commorabantur audacia et feritate formidabilis erat, dum in terram Guillelmi Bretoliensis ut seuiens leo irrueret.' et solus contra duos milites certamen iniret, ab uno eorum lancea in latere percussus est.' ipsoque die mortuus est. Quo defuncto Ricardus frater eius paternum honorem adeptus est.' et perniciem germani super Guillelmum ulcisci summopere molitus est.[1]

Robertus dux Gisleberto Ingenulfi de Aquila filio militaria quoniam ualde probus erat seruitia crebro iniunxit.' eique pro remuneratione patriæque tuicione castrum de Oximis donauit. Vnde Robertus Belesmensis felle liuoris et iræ commotus exercitum aggregauit.' et in prima Ianuarii septimana[2] castrum per
iii. 334 quattuor dies obsedit, et inter hibernos imbres et pruinas acerrimis assultibus impugnauit. Gislebertus autem cum paucis sed animosis pugnatoribus fortiter intus obstitit, iactisque missilibus et lapidibus hostes relisit.' in uallum precipitauit, quosdam uulnerauit.' nonnullos etiam exanimauit. Interea Gislebertus tiro Aquilensis erus[3] ei suppetias uenit.' cum lxxx militibus noctu castrum introiuit,· alimentis et armis ac propugnatoribus illud muniuit, adminiculoque tali patruum suum corroborauit. Porro Belesmensis tirannus uidens loci munitionem ualidamque defensorum obstinationem.' commorari non ausus in obsidione diutina, furibundus recessit cum ingenti mesticia.' nichil lucratus preter suorum uulnera. Sequenti anno dum prefatus eques Gislebertus[4] de Sancta Scolastica ueniret, et Molinis colloqui cum Duda eiusdem castri domina[5] diuertisset.' post colloquium Antonio cognomento Haren ibidem arma sua forte dimisit, et inermis ipse cum armigeris suis circa uesperam festinanter abscessit. Protinus eum Gerardus Capreolus et Rogerius de Ferrariis aliique Corbonienses milites fere xiii persecuti sunt.' uiuumque comprehendere conati sunt. Qui dum ueloci equo ueheretur.' et manus inimicorum effugere niteretur, ab uno eorum lancea in latere
iii. 335 punctus est.' ipsisque merentibus qui hoc perpetrarant nobilis heros ipso die mortuus est. In crastinum autem bissextili die corpus eius ad Sanctum Sulpicium delatum est.' ibique cum parentibus suis a

[1] The pedigree of the Montfort family is traced in GEC vii, Appendix D.

[2] Probably in January 1090.

[3] Gilbert's nephew, the son of Richer and Judith. 'Tiro' may mean here either a squire or a knight.

[4] The elder Gilbert, son of Engenulf; 'eques' here implies a seasoned, warrior knight.

called 'the strong' on account of his courage and energy and was respected by all his neighbours because of his daring and ferocity, attacked the land of William of Breteuil like a raging lion; while he was engaging two knights in combat single-handed he was struck in the side by one of their lances and died the same day. After his death his brother Richard acquired their paternal inheritance; he was relentless in his attempts to take vengeance on William for Amaury's fate.[1]

Duke Robert often commanded Gilbert, son of Engenulf of Laigle, to perform military service because he was conspicuously courageous; in recompense he gave him the castle of Exmes so that he could defend his country. Upon this Robert of Bellême, roused to bitter envy and anger, brought together an army, besieged the castle for four days in the first week of January,[2] and launched a series of fierce attacks amid the storms and snows of winter. Inside the castle Gilbert held out stoutly with defenders few in number but brave in spirit, struck back at the enemy by hurling weapons and stones, and threw them back into the ditch, wounding some and killing others. Meanwhile the young knight Gilbert, lord of Laigle,[3] came to his aid, entered the castle by night with eighty men-at-arms, supplied it with food and arms and defenders, and with these reinforcements strengthened his uncle's position. Then the tyrant of Bellême, seeing that the fortifications were strong and the defenders determined, dared not continue the siege any longer, and retired in grief and fury having gained nothing but the wounds of his men. Next year when the veteran knight Gilbert[4] was travelling from Sainte-Scholasse he turned aside at Moulins-la-Marche to visit Duda, the lady of the castle;[5] after the visit he chanced to leave his armour there with Anthony Haren and galloped off unarmed with his attendants towards evening. Immediately Gerard Capreolus and Roger of La Ferrière and about thirteen other knights of the Corbonnais pursued him, wishing to take him alive. He rode a swift horse and did his utmost to escape from the hands of his enemies, but a lance thrown by one of them pierced him in the side. The noble lord died the same day, to the great grief even of those who had done the deed. On the morrow, which was an intercalary day, his body was taken to Saint-Sulpice-sur-Risle, and he was buried there beside his

[5] Duda, daughter of Waleran I of Meulan and second wife of William of Moulins-la-Marche (see above, iii. 132).

Gisleberto Ebroicensium episcopo et Serlone Vticensi abbate cum multorum luctu tumulatum est.[1] Porro Goifredus Mauritaniæ comes[2] perpendens quod homines sui graue facinus peregerint, et ex occisione strenuissimi baronis ingentium detrimentorum terræ suæ seminarium procreauerint: cum Gisleberto Aquilensi nepote eius pacem fecit, eique Iulianam filiam suam in matrimonium coniunxit: quæ Richerium et Goisfredum ac Gislebertum ipsi peperit. Sapiens itaque consul subiectis et heredibus suis commode consuluit, dum dulcedine coniugalis amplexus exortum scelus occauit, ne de radice prauæ actionis multiplicius nefas pullularet, et rediuiuum inter posteros semper in peius excresceret. Fœdus itaque inter consobrinos heredes nunc usque indissolubile persistit: et serena pax eos blande salubriterque connectit.

Eadem septimana qua Gislebertus ut dictum est inter Molinos et Aquilam interiit: Goellus contra Guillelmum Bretoliensem dominum suum campestri certamine dimicauit, et secum habens Ricardum de Monteforti magnamque multitudinem Francorum
iii. 336 hostilem exercitum contriuit.[3] Guillelmum autem cum multis aliis captum uinculis iniecit: et in squalore carceris sequenti quadragesima crudeliter afflixit, et rigorem quadragesimalis penitentiæ inuitum pro peccatis suis subire coegit. Denique per hanc occasionem Ricardus de Monteforti et Hugo de Monte Gomerici, Geruasius de Nouo Castello aliique plures Francorum et Normannorum una conuenerunt: et pacem inter Guillelmum et Goellum apud Breheruallum composuerunt. Tunc Guillelmus ut pactum exigebat Goello Isabel filiam suam in coniugium sociauit: et pro redemptione sua mille drocensium libras et equos et arma et alia multa donauit, quin etiam arcem Ibreii tristis et inuitus adiecit. Nefarius itaque predo his opibus admodum ditatus intumuit, et castellum suum quod reuera spelunca latronum erat fossis et densis sepibus ad multorum damna conclusit: ubi totam uitam suam rapinis et cedibus finitimorum exercuit. Ex coniuge sua septem filios genuit, quorum nequitia nimis excreuit, et multos fletus ex oculis uiduarum et pauperum seuis operibus exciuit.

[1] Serlo was abbot of Saint-Évroul from 1089 to July 1091, when he became bishop of Séez; the nearest leap year was 1092. These statements are, therefore, incompatible. Since Orderic places the capture of William of Breteuil by Goel in the same week, and this was certainly not as late as 1092 (below, p. 203 n. 3), 28 February 1091, is the most probable date for Gilbert's death, though 1090 is not impossible.

[2] Geoffrey was a relentless enemy of Robert of Bellême; see above, p. 160.

parents by Gilbert, bishop of Évreux and Serlo, abbot of Saint-Évroul, mourned by many people.[1] Afterwards Geoffrey count of Mortagne,[2] considering that his men had committed a serious crime and had sown the seeds of terrible troubles for his land by murdering such a warlike baron, made peace with his nephew Gilbert of Laigle, and gave him his daughter Juliana in marriage. She bore him Richer and Geoffrey and Gilbert. So the wise count took prudent precautions for the welfare of his subjects and heirs when with the sweetness of a marriage alliance he stifled the evil that had been sown, so that multiple crime did not proliferate from the root of evil and put out new and worse shoots continually in future generations. The alliance between the two lines of cousins has remained unbroken up to now, and unruffled peace binds them in amity for the general good.

In the same week in which Gilbert lost his life, as I have described, between Moulins and Laigle, Goel engaged his lord William of Breteuil in battle in the open field and, having Richard of Montfort and a great company of Frenchmen on his side, defeated the enemy army.[3] Taking William captive with many others he flung him into prison and cruelly ill-treated him in his foul dungeon through the following Lent, forcing him to endure involuntarily the hardship of a lenten penance for his sins. Finally this led to a meeting between Richard of Montfort, Hugh of Montgomery, Gervase of Châteauneuf-en-Thimerais, and many other Frenchmen and Normans, who succeeded in bringing about a truce between William and Goel at Bréval. Then William, as the treaty required, gave his daughter Isabel in marriage to Goel and for his own ransom paid a thousand livres in the money of Dreux, with horses and arms and many other things to which, sadly and against his will, he even added the castle of Ivry. The infamous brigand triumphed in his new excess of wealth and encircled his castle—or rather his den of thieves—with ditches and thick hedges, to the sorrow of many; for he passed the remainder of his life there robbing and slaughtering his neighbours. He had by his wife seven sons, who continually grew in wickedness and caused widows and poor people to weep bitterly by their brutal acts.

[3] Probably in February 1091, provided that the siege of Conches at which Richard of Montfort lost his life took place in November 1091, not in 1090 (below, p. 214). In 1091 Lent began in the last week of February.

13

Eodem tempore[1] alia turbatio in Neustria surrexit. Robertus
iii. 337 comes Mellenti muneribus et promissis Guillelmi regis turgidus de Anglia uenit, Rotomagum ad ducem accessit.' et ab eo arcem Ibreii procaciter repetiit. Cui dux respondit, 'Equipollens mutuum patri tuo dedi.' Brionnam nobile castrum pro arce Ibreii.' Comes Mellenti dixit, 'Istud mutuum non concedo.' sed quod pater tuus patri meo dedit habere uolo. Alioquin per sanctum Nigasium faciam tibi quod displicebit.' Iratus igitur dux ilico eum comprehendi et in carcere uinciri precepit.' et Brionnam Roberto Balduini filio custodiendam commisit.[2] Callidus senex Rogerius de Bellomonte ut captam prolem audiuit per aliquot dies aliis actionibus quasi infortunium pignoris non curasset specie tenus intendit.' suique merorem tristis animi leto uultu dissimulauit. Deinde ut mitigatum ducem estimauit.' premissis muneribus eum adiuit, et honorifice salutauit. Cumque ab illo resalutatus fuisset.' dixit, 'Gratias ago domine dux uestræ sullimitati.' quia filii mei superbiam principali seueritate castigasti. Hoc ego iamdudum debuissem facere.' si necessaria michi uirtus inesset in hac senili etate.
iii. 338 Crebro nempe nimia eius proteruia me contristauit.' monitusque meos multociens contempsit. Corripiendus ergo erat et docendus.' qualiter loqui debeat dominis suis et maioribus.'

Hæc et alia huiuscemodi Rogerius ad fauorem ducis leniter locutus est.' et ille futura non precauens adulanti congratulatus est. Ad omnia ducis consilia familiariter iam admissus est.' et sic postmodum de sobolis ereptione prudenter agere nisus est. Erat enim ex antiquis et precipuis Roberti ducis et Guillelmi regis optimatibus.' gener Gualeranni comitis Mellentici et Hugonis sororius[3] fidei et legalitatis probabili laude dignus.' amicis fultus et parentibus, diuitiis et amplis honoribus munitis oppidis atque probis hominibus, ualidisque filiis et sullimibus, quorum unus

[1] Almost certainly in 1090; charter evidence shows that in 1089 Robert was occupied in hostilities in eastern Normandy (above, Introduction, p. xxxiii). This date is accepted by J. Yver in his account of the castle of Brionne (*BSAN* liii (1955–6), 67–8).

[2] Robert, son of Baldwin of Meules, grandson of Count Gilbert. He appears to have been placed in Brionne as the duke's castellan. In these imaginary speeches Orderic shows that in his time at least the Norman barons claimed rights of

13

At about this time[1] another disturbance broke out in Normandy. Robert, count of Meulan, over-confident because of the gifts and promises of King William, came from England, approached the duke at Rouen, and haughtily demanded the tower of Ivry from him. The duke replied, 'I gave a fair exchange to your father: the noble castle of Brionne for the tower of Ivry.' The count said, 'I do not accept the exchange; instead I wish to have what your father gave to my father. Otherwise, by St. Nicaise, I will give you cause to regret it.' At this the duke flew into a rage and ordered him to be seized and thrown into prison, giving Brionne to Robert son of Baldwin to guard.[2] When the wily old Roger of Beaumont heard of his son's imprisonment he put up a show for some days of being occupied with other affairs, as though he were indifferent to the misfortune of his offspring, and concealed his mental distress under a cheerful face. Then when he judged that the duke was mollified he sent gifts in advance, came into his presence and greeted him reverently. The duke returned his greeting and he said, 'My lord duke, I thank your highness for punishing my son's pride with a severity becoming in a prince. This I myself would have done before now if I had had the necessary strength in my feeble old age. His stubbornness has caused me great sorrow on many occasions; he has often spurned my advice. He needed correction and a lesson in how to speak to his lords and seniors.'

By such smooth speeches as these Roger ingratiated himself with the duke who, giving no thought to the future, fawned on his flatterer. Once he was admitted to all the duke's most intimate counsels, Roger attempted to work cautiously for his son's release. He was one of the most distinguished older magnates from the days of Duke Robert and King William, a son-in-law of Waleran count of Meulan and brother-in-law of Hugh;[3] because of this distinction he was entitled to trust and authority, blessed with friends and kinsmen, wealth and great honors, fortified castles and stout vassals, and brave and noble sons, one of whom was count of

inheritance in the castles where William the Conqueror had given them only custodianship.

[3] Roger of Beaumont married Adeline, daughter of Waleran, count of Meulan and sister of Hugh, count of Meulan; see GEC vii. 520–3 for the early history of the Beaumont family.

Mellenti comes erat in Gallia,[1] et alter Gaureguici consul in Anglia.[2] Hic itaque sensu et opibus et amicis stipatus.' accedens ad ducem dixit, 'Debes domine dux mecum clementer agere.' et frequenter recolere, quod omni tempore fidelis extiterim dominis Normanniæ. Nunquam domino meo fraudem feci.' sed pro illo magnos et periculosos labores sustinui. Hoc nimirum potest in bello luce clarius intueri.' quod in puericia patris tui contra rebelles gessi, in quo corruerunt Rogerius de Hispania et filii eius Elbertus et Elinantius atque plures alii.[3] In fide semper persistere ab infantia elegi, et hoc hereditarium ius a Turolfo auo meo et
iii. 339 Vnfrido patre meo[4] accepi.' omnique uita mea in aduersis et prosperis feruenter seruaui. Absit ut amodo cum sim silicernius incipiam deseruire fraudibus.' quas odiui hactenus et ab ineunte semper ætate totis deuitaui nisibus. Et quia pater tuus nunquam inuenit me deuiantem a suo latere, sed fortiter in sua perdurantem fidelitate.' nimiasque pro illo aduersitates tolerantem uirili robore præ ceteris optimatibus suis ad omnia secreta sua semper habuit me.' Rogerio talia dicenti dux dixit, 'Magnam legalitatem tuam domine Rogeri, qua tempore patrum meorum magnifice uiguisti.' multis attestantibus optime noui. Vnde sicut illi te dilexerunt.' consiliisque tuis probabilibus utiliter adquieuerunt.' ego nichilominus prudentiæ tuæ congratulor, monitusque tuos amplector. Quod uero filium tuum uinculis inieci, hoc sine dubio pro contemptu tuo non feci.' sed pro eius stomachatione stulta nimiumque procaci qua minaciter et importune insistebat michi.' Rogerius dixit, 'Quia temerarium iuuenem castigasti letus gratias egi.' magnasque iterum gratias ago uestræ sullimitati. Amodo si placet uestræ serenitati.' parcendum est illi. Relaxa castigatum.' et fidelem tibi exhibebit famulatum.' Delibutus itaque dux huiuscemodi uerbis Mellenticum comitem a uinculis absoluit.' et cum patre liberum abire permisit.

Non multo post Rogerius cum filio suo ducem ut Brionnam sibi redderet requisiuit.' et ob hoc ingens pecuniæ pondus promisit. Dux autem pecuniæ cupidus poscenti facile annuit.' et prefato municipi oppidum Rogerio reddi precepit. Ille uero duci remandauit dicens, 'Brionnam si tibi uis retinere, sicut eam pater tuus
iii. 340 in sua tenuit proprietate.' tibi non differo reddere. Alioquin hereditatem meam seruabo.' nec alicui tradam dum aduixero. Omnibus

[1] Robert of Beaumont, count of Meulan and later earl of Leicester.

[2] Henry, earl of Warwick.

[3] See above, ii. 40.

[4] Turold, lord of Pont-Audemer, and Humphrey of Vieilles.

Meulan in France[1] and the other earl of Warwick in England.[2] So, relying on his good sense and wealth and friends, he went to the duke and said, 'My lord duke, you ought to use me kindly and constantly keep in mind that I have remained at all times faithful to the dukes of Normandy. I have never deceived my lord; on the contrary I have borne much toil and peril for his sake. This indeed is as clear as daylight; witness the war that I fought against the rebels in your father's minority, when Roger of Spain and his sons Elbert and Elinand and many others perished.[3] From my childhood I have always chosen the path of loyalty; this is the inheritance that I received from my grandfather Turold and my father Humphrey[4] and have treasured all my life long in adversity and prosperity. God forbid that now, when I am grey with age, I should try my hand at deceits, which up to now I have loathed and have utterly shunned from my earliest years. And because your father found that I never turned from his side, but always stoutly persevered in loyalty and endured great misfortunes for his sake with manly courage, he always admitted me to his most intimate counsels before all his other magnates.' Duke Robert replied, 'Indeed I know, lord Roger, the great loyalty that you showed so splendidly in the days of my ancestors, for it is well attested. So just as they loved you and followed your sound counsel to their profit, I likewise rejoice in your wirdom and accept your advice. When I threw your son into prison I did it, believe me, not out of contempt for you, but because of his foolish pride and the rash presumption with which he made threatening and importunate demands of me.' Roger said, 'I gladly thanked you for punishing the rash young man, and I thank your highness once again most heartily. But now, if it please your lordship, let him be spared. Free him now that he has been punished, and he will give you loyal service.' The duke thereupon, placated by speeches of this kind, released the count of Meulan from prison and allowed him to leave with his father in freedom.

Not long afterwards Roger went with his son to the duke's court, and asked for Brionne to be restored to him, promising a considerable sum of money in return. The duke, coveting the money, readily agreed and commanded the castellan to restore the castle to Roger. He hesitated, saying to the duke, 'If you wish to keep Brionne for yourself, as your father held it, I will restore it at once. Otherwise I will protect my inheritance, and will surrender it

enim huius prouinciæ indigenis euidenter innotuit, quod Ricardus senior dux Normannorum Godefredo filio suo Brionnam cum toto comitatu donauit, quam ipse nichilominus Gisleberto filio suo moriens dimisit. Deinde Gisleberto comite nequiter interfecto a malignis hominibus, et pedagogis filiorum eius cum eisdem pueris ad Balduinum Flandrensem timore inimicorum fugientibus.' pater tuus aui mei comitatum partim dominio suo mancipauit, partim extraneis ad libitum suum distraxit.[1] Post longum tempus dum ipse filiam Balduini Flandritæ coniugem accepit, precibus eiusdem Balduini Balduino patri meo Molas et Sappum reddidit.' et filiam amitæ suæ uxorem dedit, Ricardo autem fratri eius Benefactam et Orbeccum restituit. Denique gratia uestra domine cui per omnia parere desidero, Brionnam Gisleberti comitis aui mei principale oppidum nunc possideo.' Deoque rectitudini meæ adminiculante fine tenus tenebo.'

His auditis Rogerius ducem acriter stimulauit ne deficeret, sed ut repente armatorum manu aggregata rebelles comprimeret, et munitissimum castrum quod in meditullio terræ situm est obsidione
iii. 341 sibi subigeret. Igitur Robertus dux in ebdomada Pentecostes[2] Brionnam obsedit, quod Robertus Balduini filius cum sex tantum militibus[3] contra phalanges armatas defendere sategit. Cæterum Belmonticus heros et Mellenticus comes ingentes bellatorum turmas adunauerant, et prefatum munionem ne sociorum adminiculis et alimentis prestrueretur subito cinxerant, et uiriliter instantes oppidum post nonam acerrime impugnabant. Tunc calor ingens incipientis estatis et maxima siccitas erant.' quæ forinsecus expugnantes admodum iuuabant. Callidi enim obsessores in fabrili fornace quæ in promptu structa fuerat ferrum missilium calefaciebant.' subitoque super tectum principalis aulæ in munimento iaciebant, et sic ferrum candens sagittarum atque pilorum in arida ueterum lanugine imbricum totis nisibus figebant.[4] Inde magnus ignis celeriter confotus est.' et defensoribus oppidi ualide pugnantibus dolumque nescientibus nimis confortatus est, donec flamma super capita eorum extimplo progressa
iii. 342 est. Quam mox ut super se cunctam corripere uiderunt collapsis

[1] The castle of Brionne was granted for a time to Guy of Burgundy, but after his rebellion Duke William took it back into his demesne (J. Yver in *BSAN* liii (1955–6), 49).

to no man as long as I live. It is common knowledge in this land that Richard the elder, duke of Normandy, gave Brionne with the whole county to his son Godfrey, and that he at his death handed it on in like fashion to his son Gilbert. Then after Count Gilbert had been brutally assassinated by evil men, and the guardians of his sons had fled with the boys to Baldwin of Flanders for fear of their enemies, your father kept a part of my grandfather's county in his own hand and alienated part to outsiders at his will.[1] Long afterwards your father, having married the daughter of Baldwin of Flanders, at his request restored Meules and Le Sap to my father Baldwin, and gave him his aunt's daughter in marriage. He also restored Bienfaite and Orbec to Baldwin's brother Richard. Finally by your favour, my lord, whom I wish to serve in all things, I now hold Brionne, my grandfather Gilbert's chief castle, and will continue to do so while God upholds my right.'

After hearing this Roger sharply pressed the duke not to be inactive, but to muster an armed force at once, suppress the rebels and, by laying siege to this most powerful castle in the heart of his land, to force it into submission. So in the week of Pentecost[2] Duke Robert besieged Brionne, which Robert son of Baldwin had difficulty in defending against the armed hosts with only six knights.[3] Meanwhile the lord of Beaumont and the count of Meulan assembled large forces of fighting men, suddenly surrounded the castellan to cut him off from relieving forces or supplies, and made a most determined and violent attack on the castle after the ninth hour. The heat of early summer was then intense and the drought severe; and this gave a great advantage to the attackers. For the ingenious besiegers heated the metal tips of their missiles in a smith's furnace built for the purpose, and suddenly hurled them on to the roof of the great hall of the castle, so that the red-hot iron of the arrows and darts showered down and was riveted into the dry and crumbling wood of the old shingles.[4] From this a great fire soon broke out, which increased in fury, for the defenders of the castle, occupied in their determined struggle, knew nothing of the trick until the fire suddenly spread above their heads. As soon as they saw it sweeping above them their power to resist

[2] The week beginning 9 June, if the year was 1090.

[3] The figure is not impossible, if it implied trained, hauberked knights; the greater part of the garrison may have consisted of auxiliary soldiers.

[4] This vivid detail indicates that the eleventh-century castle of Brionne was roofed with wooden shingles, and not with tiles.

uiribus defecerunt.' et furentibus per omnia intrinsecus flammarum globis clementiæ ducis sese dediderunt. Sic Robertus dux ab hora nona Brionnam ante solis occasum optinuit.' quam Guillelmus pater eius cum auxilio Henrici Francorum regis sibi uix in tribus annis subigere potuit, dum Guido filius Rainaldi Burgundionis post prelium Vallisdunensis illic presidium sibi statuit.[1]

In expugnatione predicti castri Gislebertus de Pino princeps militiæ erat,[2] et obsidentium turmas de Ponte Aldemari et Bellomonte prouide ordinabat, ac ut intolerabilem assultum darent audacter incitabat. Interea pilo desuper ruente letaliter in capite percussus est, et protinus a sociis lugentibus pene exanimis de pressura preliantium eiectus est. Deinde post breue spacium saucius de lipotosmia rediit.' et terribiliter ad circumstantes uociferari cepit, 'O miseri, miseri quid facitis, cur tempora uestra perditis? Cur mundi uanitates diligitis, et ea quæ uere salubria
iii. 343 sunt et permansura obliuioni traditis? Si miserias et tormenta quæ male uiuendo meremini sciretis, et horrenda quæ modo uidi una saltem hora sentiretis.' omnia profecto labentis seculi delectamenta pro nichilo estimaretis.' Hæc dicens et his addere plura uolens obmutuit.' et famosus optio sic inter uerba deficiens hominem exuit.

His ita gestis dux Brionnam Rogerio reddidit.'[3] et Roberto municipi compatiens patruum feudum permisit.[4] Amicis enim et parentibus admodum stipatus erat.' et erga ducem plurimos
iii. 344 adiutores habebat. Nam sicut supradictum est Guillelmus rex filios Gisleberti comitis Ricardum et Balduinum caros habuit, et tam pro uicinitate sanguinis quam pro strenuitate amborum eos sullimauit, et pluribus fundis atque honoribus et potestatibus in Anglia et in Normannia ditauit.[5] Prefati quoque fratres bonis

[1] See Douglas, *WC*, pp. 54–5; William of Poitiers (Foreville, pp. 18–20). The late eleventh-century keep now standing on a hill at Brionne is not on the site of the first castle, destroyed by William the Conqueror (*Congrès archéologique de France*, 56e session, 1889 (Paris, 1890), p. 103).

[2] Probably Gilbert, son of Maurice of Le Pin, who witnessed a charter of Roger of Beaumont *c.* 1087 (*CDF*, no. 368). Le-Pin-au-Haras was in the honor of Meulan (see W. E. Wightman, *The Lacy Family in England and Normandy* (Oxford, 1966), pp. 221–2). Pont-Audemer and Beaumont-le-Roger were the two chief lordships of the Beaumont family, each supplying a contingent of knights. Gilbert's function may have been that of constable.

[3] It is very likely that Roger now secured the castle as a fief, not simply as a custody.

[4] Robert inherited his father's English honor in 1096, after the death of his elder brother William; he died without heirs in 1101 (Sanders, p. 69). Robert

collapsed and they gave up the struggle, throwing themselves on the duke's mercy while masses of flames roared through the castle. So between the ninth hour and sunset Duke Robert captured Brionne, which his father William, even with the help of Henry, king of France, had scarcely been able to subdue in three years, when Guy son of Reginald the Burgundian made it his centre of resistance after the battle of Val-ès-Dunes.[1]

Gilbert of Le Pin was commander of the forces[2] during the attack on the castle of Brionne; he disposed the contingents of besiegers from Pont-Audemer and Beaumont strategically and urged them on to attack boldly in an irresistible assault. During the course of the battle he was fatally wounded in the head by a spear thrown from above and, at the point of death, was hastily dragged out of the press of combatants by his stricken comrades. A few moments later the wounded man recovered from his swoon, and began to cry out in a terrible voice, 'O wretches, wretches, what are you about? Why are you wasting your time? Why do you love worldly vanities and forget the things that redeem and are eternal? If you knew the woes and torments which you earn by evil living, and were to experience for only one hour the horrors that I have just seen, from that moment you would regard all the delights of the fleeting world as nothing.' As he spoke these words and attempted to say more, speech failed him, and so, dying as he spoke, the famous captain gave up the ghost.

After these events the duke restored Brionne to Roger[3] and in compensation granted to Robert, who had been the castellan, his ancestral fee.[4] He was in fact a man strongly supported by friends and kinsmen, and had a number of adherents among the duke's companions. For, as I have explained above, King William had a great affection for Richard and Baldwin, the sons of Count Gilbert, showed great honour to them both because of their kinship to him and because of their valour, and enriched them with many estates and honors and offices of authority in England and Normandy.[5] Besides this the brothers were blessed with good wives

of Torigny, who calls Robert the son of Richard, says he was compensated with land in the Cotentin (Marx, p. 289).

[5] Richard fitz Gilbert received the lordship of Clare and extensive estates in England during the Conqueror's reign; Baldwin fitz Gilbert was sheriff of Devon in Domesday Book (see Michael Altschul, *A Baronial Family in Medieval England: the Clares* (Baltimore, 1965), pp. 18–19; GEC iii. 242; iv. 308–9; J. H. Round, 'The family of Clare', in *Archaeological Journal*, lvi (1899), 221–31).

uxoribus et honorabili sobole donati sunt. Ricardus enim Roaldem Gaulterii Gifardi[1] filiam accepit.' quæ filios ei et filias peperit, Rogerium et Gislebertum, Gaulterium et Robertum, atque Ricardum Beccensem monachum, cui Henricus rex comisit Eliense cœnobium.[2] Balduinus uero genuit Robertum et Guillelmum, Ricardum nothumque Guigerium.[3] Isti nimirum tempore Guillelmi regis et filiorum eius laboriosa seculi probitate uiguerunt, uariisque flatibus instabilis fortunæ agitati in pelago huius mundi periculose; fluctuauerunt. Wigerius autem nouissimus horum mundialis militiæ discrimen sponte deseruit, in Beccensi cœnobio comam deposuit, et in monachatu fere xl annis sub uenerabilibus archimandritis Guillelmo et Bosone uixit.[4]

14

Perstrepentibus undique præliis in Neustria.' securitate pacis perfrui non potuit Ebroicensis prouincia. Illic nempe plus quam
iii. 345 ciuile bellum inter opulentos fratres exortum est.' et maligna superbarum emulatione mulierum malicia nimis augmentata est. Heluisa nanque comitissa[5] contra Isabelem de Conchis[6] pro quibusdam contumeliosis uerbis irata est.' comitemque Guillelmum cum baronibus suis in arma per iram commouere totis uiribus conata est. Sic per suspiciones et litigia feminarum, in furore succensa sunt fortium corda uirorum.' quorum manibus paulo post multus mutuo cruor effusus est mortalium, et per uillas ac uicos multarum incensa sunt tecta domorum. Ambæ mulieres quæ talia bella sciebant.' loquaces et animosæ ac forma elegantes erant, suisque maritis imperabant, subditos homines premebant.' uariisque modis terrebant. Magna tamen in eisdem morum diuersitas erat. Heluisa quidem sollers erat et facunda, sed atrox et auara.' Isabel uero dapsilis et audax atque iocosa, ideoque coessentibus amabilis et grata. In expeditione inter milites ut miles equitabat armata, et loricatis equitibus ac spiculatis satellitibus non minori prestabat audacia.' quam decus Italiæ

[1] For the family of Giffard, originally from Longueville-sur-Scie, see Loyd, p. 45, and Round, *Feudal England*, pp. 468–74.

[2] Richard was the last of the abbots before Ely became a bishopric and the monastery a priory in 1109 (*Liber Eliensis*, ed. E. O. Blake (Camden Third Series, xcii (1962)), p. 225). Richard of Clare had at least two daughters, Rohais and Adeliza. The sentence as it stands seems incomplete, and Orderic may have named the daughters in his original text.

[3] Later records (Dugdale, *Mon. Ang.* v. 269, 377) name Robert, William, Richard, and three daughters and call Baldwin's wife Aubrée.

[4] Wiger occurs in the list of monks of Bec almost at the end of the list of those

and worthy offspring. Richard married Walter Giffard's daughter[1] Rohais, who bore him sons and daughters; Roger and Gilbert, Walter and Robert and Richard, monk of Bec, whom King Henry made abbot of Ely.[2] Baldwin's sons were Robert and William, Richard and a bastard called Wiger.[3] The first three won worldly distinction in the time of King William and his sons by their determination and integrity, and were perilously tossed to and fro on the ocean of this life by the varying winds of fickle fortune. But Wiger, the youngest, voluntarily renounced the battle of knighthood in the world, received the tonsure in the monastery of Bec, and lived as a monk for about forty years under the venerable abbots, William and Boso.[4]

14

While battles were raging all over Normandy the province of Évreux could not hope to enjoy peace and security. There indeed a more than civil war broke out between powerful brothers and the evil was fomented by the malignant rivalry of two proud women. The Countess Helwise[5] was incensed against Isabel of Conches[6] for some slighting remarks, and in her anger used all her powers to urge Count William and his barons to take up arms. So the hearts of brave men were moved to anger through the suspicions and quarrels of women, which led to great bloodshed on both sides and the burning of many homes in towns and villages. Both the ladies who stirred up such bitter wars were persuasive, high-spirited, and beautiful; they dominated their husbands and oppressed their vassals, whom they terrorized in various ways. But they were very different in character. Helwise on the one hand was clever and persuasive, but cruel and grasping; whereas Isabel was generous, daring, and gay, and therefore lovable and estimable to those around her. In war she rode armed as a knight among the knights; and she showed no less courage among the knights in hauberks and sergeants-at-arms than did the maid

admitted in the time of Anselm (Porée, ii. 631); probably, therefore, he entered the monastery just before William of Beaumont became abbot in 1093 and died about 1133. Boso was abbot from 1124 to 1136.

[5] Helwise, wife of William, count of Évreux, was a daughter of the count of Nevers (Le Prévost, iv. 279).

[6] Isabel (Elizabeth), wife of Ralph of Tosny, was a daughter of Simon of Montfort. See above, iii. 128.

Turni commanipularibus uirgo Camilla.[1] Emulabatur Lampedionem et Marseppiam, Ippolitem et Pentesileam.' aliasque reginas Amazonum bellatrices[2] quarum certamina Pompeius Trogus[3] et Maro Virgilius referunt aliique historiarum scriptores.' quibus
iii. 346 attinuerunt Asiæ reges, et per xv annos armis edomuerunt Asiaticas gentes. Ebroicenses multos adiutores habebant.' et incendia multa predasque Concanis plerumque faciebant, sed interdum illi non dispares inimicis taliones reddebant. Radulfus Robertum ducem adiuit.' querelas damnorum quæ a contribulibus suis pertulerat intimauit, et erile adiutorium ab eo poposcit.' sed frustra quia nichil optinuit. Hinc alias conuersus est.' et utile sibi patrocinium querere compulsus est. Regem Angliæ per legatos suos interpellauit eique sua infortunia mandauit.' et si sibi suffragaretur se et omnia sua promisit.[4] His auditis rex gauisus est.' et efficax adminiculum indigenti pollicitus est. Deinde Stephano comiti[5] et Girardo de Gornaco aliisque tribunis et centurionibus qui preerant in Normannia familiis eius.' mandauit ut Radulfum totis adiuuarent nisibus, et oppida eius munirent necessariis omnibus. Illi autem regiis iussionibus alacriter obsecundauerunt.' et Radulfo per omnia regi placere nitentes suffragati sunt.

Mense Nouembri Guillelmus comes ingentem exercitum aggregauit.' et Concas expugnare cepit.[6] Duo nepotes eius uiri potentes Guillelmus de Britolio et Ricardus de Monteforti[7] cum eo erant.'
iii. 347 et cum turmis suis Concheios impugnabant. Ibi Ricardus de Monteforti dum cenobialem curiam beati Petri Castellionis inuaderet nec pro reuerentia monachorum qui cum fletibus uociferantes Deum interpellabant ab inceptis desisteret, hostili telo

[1] Turnus, king of the Rutuli, appears in Book xi of Virgil's *Aeneid* with the maiden warrior Camilla as his ally.

[2] Hippolyta, queen of the Amazons, was said to have been captured by Theseus, and Penthesilea to have been killed by Achilles in the Trojan War. Lampeto and Marpesia were among the other great Amazon queens of legend, mentioned by Pompeius Trogus (ed. O. Seel (Leipzig, 1935), II. iv. 12, 24, 31).

[3] Some fragments of the *Histories* of Pompeius Trogus remain, but he was known chiefly in the Middle Ages through the epitome of Justin. See *M. Iuniani Iustini epitoma historiarum Philippicarum Pompeii Trogi*, ed. O. Seel (Leipzig, 1935).

[4] The course of fighting in the war between William count of Évreux and Ralph of Tosny is difficult to establish. William of Malmesbury (*GR* ii. 363), Florence of Worcester (FW ii. 27), and Robert of Torigny (Marx, p. 270) agree, though with some imprecision of date, that after William Rufus came to Normandy in January 1091, Robert Curthose reached an agreement ceding to him certain fortresses and territories of which he had gained control. These certainly included Eu, Fécamp, and the lands of Gerard of Gournay and Count Stephen of Aumâle; Orderic is alone in mentioning the lands of Ralph of Tosny. Ralph's transfer of allegiance may have taken place about this time, though he

Camilla, the pride of Italy, among the troops of Turnus.[1] She deserved comparison with Lampeto and Marpesia, Hippolyta and Penthesilea and the other warlike Amazon queens,[2] whose battles, in which they held in check the kings of Asia and subdued the Asian peoples by force of arms for fifteen years are described by Pompeius Trogus[3] and Virgil and other writers of histories. The faction of Évreux had many supporters, and often plundered and burnt in the territory of the men of Conches, who in their turn repaid their enemies in the same coin. Ralph went to Duke Robert to complain to him of the injuries inflicted by his fellow countrymen and ask him as his liege lord for help; but he wasted his time, for nothing was done. Therefore he looked elsewhere, since he had to seek effective patronage. He sent envoys to describe his misfortunes to the king of England and promised to submit himself and all he owned to William if help were forthcoming.[4] This message was most welcome to the king, and he promised effective support to Ralph in his need. Then he commanded Count Stephen[5] and Gerard of Gournay and the other military leaders who were in charge of his retainers in Normandy to lend Ralph full support, and garrison and provision his fortresses. They obeyed the king's commands at once, and to please him gave support to Ralph everywhere.

In the month of November Count William collected a great army and began to besiege Conches.[6] Two powerful men who were his nephews, William of Breteuil and Richard of Montfort,[7] accompanied him and attacked Conches at the head of their troops. There Richard of Montfort was struck down by an enemy shaft while he was seizing possession of the monastic buildings of St. Peter of Conches, without respect for the monks who vainly implored him with tears and appeals to God to desist from the

witnessed two of Robert's charters dated not earlier than June, 1091 (Haskins, *Norman Institutions*, pp. 68, 292).

[5] Stephen of Aumâle.

[6] Le Prévost (iii. 346) dates the siege of Conches in November 1090, and is followed by David (*Robert Curthose*, p. 58). There is, however, no clear evidence in favour of 1090, and the date is difficult to reconcile with other events. William, count of Évreux, was active during the rising at Rouen on 3 November, probably in 1090 (below, pp. 220–2); and Richard of Montfort, who was killed during the siege of Conches, is said by Orderic to have taken part in the capture of William of Breteuil, probably in February 1091 (above, p. 202). November, 1091 or 1092, would be a more acceptable date; 1092 is suggested in GEC vii. 712.

[7] Richard was the son of William's sister Agnes; William of his half-sister, Adeliza (see genealogical tables in GEC vii. 709, and Douglas, *WC*, Table VIII).

repente percussus est.' ipsoque die cum maximo luctu utriusque partis mortuus est. Germanus[1] enim fratris erat Isabelis, et ex sorore nepos Guillelmi comitis.' unde formidabilem marchisum utraque pars luxit, qui pro nimio tumore et procacitate pertinaciter malum faciens interiit. Cadauer autem predicti militis ad natale solum a suis translatum est.' et Asparlone in cimiterio sancti Thomæ apostoli sepultum est. Ibi nempe Maioris Monasterii regulares monachi Deo seruiunt, ibique senior Simon Amalrici filius et filii eius tumulati sunt.[2]

Non multo post Ebroicenses denuo conglobati sunt.' et dolorem suum ulcisci cupientes Conchense territorium depredari aggressi sunt. Tunc Radulfus preualidum agmen de suis et de familia regis[3] habuit.' cupidisque tironibus foras erumpere dixit, 'Armamini, et estote parati.' sed de munitione non exeatis, donec ego iubeam uobis. Sinite hostes preda onerari, et discedentes mecum uiriliter insectamini.' Illi autem principi suo qui probissimus et militiæ gnarus erat obsecundarunt, et abeuntes cum preda pedeten-
iii. 348 tim persecuti sunt.' eisque seuientibus Ebroicenses relicta preda fugerunt. Tunc Guillelmus Bretoliensis cum aliis pluribus captus est.' et uictoriam huiusmodi pax secuta est. Ebroicenses enim erubescentes quod guerram superbe ceperant, et inde maximi pondus detrimenti cum dedecore pertulerant.' conditioni pacis post triennalem guerram[4] adquieuerunt, et in unum conuenientes huiusmodi pactum confirmauerunt. Guillelmus auunculo suo Radulfo tria milia librarum pro redemptione sua dedit, et Rogerium consobrinum suum Radulfi filium[5] totius iuris sui heredem fecit. Ebroicensis quoque comes eundem Rogerium utpote nepotem suum consulatus sui heredem constituit.' sed diuina dispositio quæ nutibus humanis non subicitur aliud prouidit. Idem iuuenis moribus egregiis pollebat.' et cunctis sodalibus ac subiectis clientibus et uicinis admodum amabilis erat. Clericos et monachos diligebat, et competenter honorabat. Preciosis uestibus quibus superbi nimis insolescunt uti dedignabatur.' et in omni esse suo sese modeste regere nitebatur.

Quondam milites ociosi simul in aula Conchis ludebant et

[1] Because Le Prévost printed 'frater' G. H. White took 'germanus' to mean a legitimate brother of the half-blood (*TRHS* xxii (1940), 85 n. 4). But if the correct reading is 'fratris', 'germanus' here could have its normal meaning of a full brother, and 'fratris' could mean 'half-brother'.

[2] The priory of Épernon was founded in 1053 by Amaury of Montfort, as a dependency of Marmoutier (Cottineau, i. 1056).

[3] i.e. King William Rufus.

[4] The dates are uncertain; fighting began about 1090 and ended in 1091 or 1092.

attack. He died the same day, greatly mourned by men on both sides. He was a brother of Isabel's half-brother[1] and a nephew of Count William on his sister's side, so both parties had cause to mourn for this warlike marcher lord, who had met his end through the great presumption and recklessness with which he carried out an evil deed. The knight's body was carried back to his native place and buried at Épernon in the cemetery of St. Thomas the apostle. There Benedictine monks from Marmoutier serve God; and the elder Simon, son of Amaury, and his sons are buried there.[2]

Not long afterwards the men of Évreux assembled a second time anxious to avenge their loss, and invaded and plundered the lands of the men of Conches. On that occasion Ralph commanded a very powerful contingent of his own men and the king's[3] retainers, and he said to the knights, who were eager to make a sortie, 'Arm yourselves and be ready for action, but do not leave the castle until I give the command. Let our foes load themselves with booty, and when they turn back come with me boldly in pursuit.' They obeyed their leader, who was a very brave man with considerable experience of warfare, and followed with such fury on the heels of the forces, who were creeping away with their booty, that the men of Évreux dropped their loot and fled. On that occasion William of Breteuil and many others were captured, and peace followed this victory. The men of Évreux in fact, who were ashamed at having entered the war with pride and then shamefully endured great loss, sought grounds for peace after the three years' war,[4] and after meeting together confirmed this pact. William gave his uncle Ralph three thousand livres for his ransom, and made his cousin Roger, Ralph's son,[5] the heir of all his right. The count of Évreux also appointed Roger, who was his nephew, to be heir to his office of count; but God's providence, which is not subject to human wills, intended otherwise. Young Roger was a man of excellent character, well-liked by all his kinsmen and vassals and neighbours. He loved clerks and monks, and showed proper reverence to them. He scorned to wear the extravagant clothes in which vain men flaunt themselves, and in all his bearing he showed moderation and self-discipline.

On one occasion some knights were taking their ease, amusing

[5] Roger (II) of Tosny, elder son of Ralph and Isabel, who died before his father (GEC xii (i). 760).

colloquebantur.' et coram dominam Elisabeth de diuersis tematibus ut moris est huiuscemodi confabulabantur. Tunc quidam eorum dixit, 'Nuper uidi somnium.' quo ualde territus sum. Videbam Dominum in cruce fixum et toto corpore liuentem, seseque quasi præ angustia nimis torquentem, meque terribili uisu aspicientem.' Talia narranti qui aderant dixerunt, 'Hoc somnium graue est ac
iii. 349 terribile.' et uidetur horrendum Dei iudicium tibi portendere.' Balduinus autem Eustachii Boloniæ comitis filius[1] dixit, 'Et ego nuper in somniis uidebam Dominum Ihesum in cruce pendentem.' sed clarum et pulchrum ac michi alacriter ridentem, dexteraque sua me benedicentem.' signumque crucis super caput meum benigniter facientem.' Astantes uero responderunt, 'Tali ostensione dulcedo magnæ gratiæ uidetur tibi fulgere.'

His auditis Rogerius adolescens matri suæ dixit, 'Noui hominem nec longe est.' qui similia per uisum contemplatus est.' Cumque mater insisteret, et diligenter inquireret, quis aut quæ uidisset.' adolescens erubuit, et manifeste rem publicare noluit. Tandem a genitrice et presentibus amicis multum rogatus respondit, 'Quidam in uisione sua nuper uidit Dominum Ihesum capiti suo manum imponentem.' et clementer benedicentem, hisque uerbis eum uocantem, "Veni cito dilecte meus ad me.' et dabo tibi gaudia uitae." Audacter igitur eum in hac uita non diu uicturum assero.' quem sic a Domino uocatum cognosco.'

Non multo post tres prefati tirones ut diuersa retulerunt.' uarios euentus experti sunt. Primus enim in expeditione quadam male sauciatus est.' et sine confessione ac uiatico mortuus est. Balduinus autem gener Radulfi de Conchis in dextero humero Domini crucem sumpsit.' et Vrbani papæ iussu sanctam contra
iii. 350 ethnicos peregrinationem arripuit. In illo itinere super omnes compares suos exaltatus est.' et uirtute cruciferi opificis prout in somnio speculatus fuerat gloriose suffultus est. Prius enim Rages id est Edissæ nobilissimæ urbis dux factus est.' et post aliquot annos defuncto Godefredo fratre suo diu regno Ierusalem potitus est. Hic contra paganos multociens preliatus est.' multisque triumphis adminiculante Deo gloriatus est. Rogerius uero eodem anno quo hæc uisa fuerant in lectum decubuit.' et deuote completis in eo quæque fideli uiro competunt, idus Maii de mundo migrauit, et cum luctu multorum Castellionis cum parentibus suis sepultus quiescit.

[1] Baldwin of Bouillon, who married Ralph and Isabel's daughter, Godechilde, in 1096 (above, iii. 128).

themselves and chatting together in the hall of Conches, and were discussing various topics in the presence of the lady Isabel, as men do. One of them said, 'Recently I had a dream which greatly alarmed me. I saw our Lord nailed to the cross, his whole body livid, writhing in agony and fixing a terrible look on me.' The others said to the narrator, 'This is a solemn and terrible dream, and seems to portend some dreadful judgement of God towards you.' Then Baldwin, son of Eustace count of Boulogne,[1] said, 'I also recently saw our Lord Jesus in a dream, hanging on the cross; but he was fair and beautiful and smiled on me, blessing me with his right hand and making the sign of the cross graciously over my head.' His hearers said, 'Such a manifestation seems to promise you great spiritual joy.'

After hearing this young Roger said to his mother, 'I know a man, not far away, who saw similar sights in a vision.' As his mother pressed him, and earnestly inquired who the man was and what he had seen the young man grew confused and plainly had no wish to reveal the matter. But at last, after repeated requests from his mother and friends there, he replied, 'A certain man recently saw in a vision the Lord Jesus laying his hand on his head in gentle benediction, and calling him with these words, "Come quickly, my beloved, to me, and I will give you the joys of life." I confidently assert that the man whom I know to have been called by the Lord in this way has not long to live on earth.'

Not long afterwards the three knights suffered different fates corresponding to what they had told. The first was badly wounded on some foray or other, and died without confession or viaticum. Baldwin, however, the son-in-law of Ralph of Conches, took the Lord's cross on his right shoulder and, at Pope Urban's command, set off on a crusade against the infidel. In that journey he was exalted above all his peers, and by the power of Christ working as he had seen in his dream he was gloriously sustained. First he became duke of Rages, that is Edessa, a famous city; and when his brother Godfrey died a few years later he ruled the kingdom of Jerusalem for a long time. He frequently fought the pagans in battle, and was rewarded with many victories by God's help. But Roger fell sick in the same year in which the visions were seen, and after piously performing all that a good Christian should he died on 15 May, and was laid to rest with his ancestors, greatly mourned by the people of Conches.

15

Eodem tempore Constantinienses Henricus clito strenue regebat.' rigidusque contra fratres suos persistebat. Nam contra ducem inimicicias agitabat.' pro iniusta captione quam nudius tercius[1] ut predictum est ab illo perpessus fuerat. Regi nichilominus Angliæ hostis erat, pro terra matris suæ qua rex eundem in Anglia dissaisiuerat, et Roberto Haimonis filio dederat. His itaque pro causis oppida sua constanter firmabat.'[2] et fauctores sibi de proceribus patris sui plurimos callide conciliabat. Abrincas et
Cesaris burgum, et Constantiam atque Guabreium, aliasque muni-
iii. 351 tiones possidebat, et Hugonem comitem[3] et Ricardum de Radueriis[4]
aliosque Constantinienses preter Robertum de Molbraio secum habebat.' et collectis undique uiribus prece precioque cotidie crescebat. Tot pestibus inquietabatur Neustria.' et cedibus ac flammis homines ac uicos et casas tradebat gehennalis furia.

Vis Anglici regis pene per totam Normanniam discurrebat, et Normannicis optimatibus ei fauentibus propter eius pecuniam, rectore desolatam sibi mancipabat prouinciam. Ciues etiam Rotomagi regiis muneribus et promissis illecti de mutando principe tractauerunt.' ac ut Normanniæ metropolim cum somnolento duce regi proderent consiliati sunt. Huius nimirum fauctionis[a] incentor Conanus Gisleberti Pilati filius[5] erat.' qui inter ciues utpote ditissimus eorum precellebat. Is cum rege de tradenda ciuitate pactum
iii. 352 fecerat, et immensis opibus ditatus in urbe uigebat.' ingentemque
militum et satellitum familiam contra ducem turgidus iugiter pascebat. Maxima pars urbanorum eidem adquiescebant.' nonnulli tamen pro fide duci seruanda resistebant, et opportunis tergiuersationibus detestabile facinus impediebant. Ceterum Conanus de suorum consensu contribulium securus terminum constituit, dieque statuto exercitum regis de Gorniaco aliisque regalibus castris accersiit.' et Rotomagum confestim uenire precepit. Dux autem ubi tantam contra se machinationem comperiit, amicos in

[a] *Possibly an error for* factionis; *but possibly coined by Orderic to mean 'conspiracy'*

---

[1] In classical usage this meant 'three days earlier'; Orderic seems to have intended the meaning to be 'about three years earlier'.

[2] The nuns of Holy Trinity, Caen, complained that Henry forced their men to work on his castles (Haskins, *Norman Institutions*, p. 63).

[3] Earl Hugh of Chester.

[4] Richard of Reviers held an honor with its *caput* at Néhou in the Cotentin; he was one of Henry's most loyal followers and was rewarded with the honor of Plympton in Devon (Sanders, p. 137; Loyd, p. 85).

15

At the same time Prince Henry was effectively governing the Cotentin, and remained relentless towards his brothers. He nursed enmity towards the duke because of the unjust imprisonment which he had endured some three years before[1] at his hands, as I have described. He was no less a foe of the king of England, who had disseised him of his mother's land in England and given it to Robert fitz Hamon. So for these reasons he resolutely fortified his castles[2] and shrewdly won over many of his father's nobles to the support of his cause. He held Avranches and Cherbourg, Coutances and Gavray and other castles, and had on his side Earl Hugh[3] and Richard of Reviers[4] and the other barons of the Cotentin except Robert of Mowbray. As forces were collected from all sides by persuasion or payment he daily grew in strength. Hellish passions troubled Normandy with many plagues, and men were put to the sword and houses and villages to the flames.

The power of the English king was effective almost everywhere in Normandy, and since the Norman magnates supported him because of his wealth he laid hands on the province, neglected by its duke. Even the citizens of Rouen, won over by the king's gifts and promises, considered the possibility of changing their ruler, and decided to betray both the chief city of Normandy and the slumbering duke to the king. The prime mover in this faction was Conan, the son of Gilbert Pilatus,[5] who was the richest of the citizens and so held a leading position among them. He made a pact with the king to hand over the city; and since he was extremely wealthy he grew powerful in the city, and arrogantly maintained against the duke a huge permanent household of men-at-arms and dependants. Most of the townsmen leant to his party; some however preserved their fealty to the duke by resisting him, and hindered his vile treachery by well-timed subterfuges. None the less Conan fixed a date for action with the agreement of his fellow citizens, and on the appointed day sent to the king's forces at Gournay and other royal castles, telling them to advance immediately on Rouen. When the duke heard of this formidable plot against him, he called to his presence friends whom he trusted.

[5] A later judgement of the court of Henry I referred to the troubles of 1090 as 'gravis dissensio inter partes Pilatensium . . . et Calloensium' (Haskins, *Norman Institutions*, pp. 91–2; cf. also J. J. Vernier, *Chartes de l'abbaye de Jumièges* (Rouen and Paris, 1916), i. 157–61).

quibus confidebat ad se conuocauit. Tunc etiam cum Henrico fratre suo et cum aliis quibusdam qui ab eo desciuerant fœdus amiciciæ pepigit.' et Guillelmo comiti Ebroarum et Roberto Belesmensi atque Guillelmo Bretoliensi et Gisleberto de Aquila aliisque fidelibus suis desolationem sui cita legatione intimauit. Henricus igitur primus ei suppetias uenit.' et primo subsidium fratri contulit, deinde uindictam uiriliter in proditores exercuit.

Tertio die Nouembris[1] Gislebertus de Aquila militum turmam ducis ad seruitium duxit, et per pontem Sequanæ ad australem portam urbis accessit.' et tunc ex alia parte Rainaldus de Guarenna[2]
iii. 353 cum ccc^tis^ militibus ad Calcegiensem portam[3] properauit. Tunc Conanus dixit suis, 'Surgite confestim et armamini.' quia tempus non est ulterius prestolandi. En a meridie ueniunt hostes nos impugnare.' et ab occidente feruentes socii nos adiuuare. Festinanter ergo fauctoribus.' et inimicis ut decet occurrite, aditum sodalibus aperite.' et hostibus armis acriter obserate.' Pars igitur ciuium cucurrit ut Gislebertum cum suis repelleret.' et alia pars conata est occidentalem portam reserare, ut Rainaldum cum suis intromitteret. Preterea iam pridem quidam de regiis satellitibus in urbem introierant.' et parati rebellionem tacite prestolantes seditionis moram egre ferebant.

Denique dum militaris et ciuilis tumultus exoritur.' nimius hinc et inde clamor attollitur, et tota ciuitas pessime confunditur, et in sua uiscera crudeliter debachatur. Plures enim ciuium contra cognatos uicinosque suos ad utramque portam dimicabant.' dum quædam pars duci et altera regi fauebant. Dux autem ubi furentes ut dictum est in ciuitate aduertit.' cum Henrico fratre suo et commanipularibus suis de arce prodiit, suisque uelociter suffragari[a] appetiit. Sed dum perturbationis ingens tumultus cuncta confunderet.' et nesciretur quam quisque ciuium sibi partem eligeret,
iii. 354 dux persuadentibus amicis ne perniciem inhonestam stolide incurreret.' cunctisque Normannis perenne opprobrium fieret, fugiens cum paucis per orientalem portam egressus est.' et mox a suburbanis uici qui Malapalus[4] dicitur fideliter ut specialis erus susceptus est. Deinde cimba parata Sequanam intrauit.' et relicto post terga conflictu trepidus ad Ermentrudisuillam[5] nauigauit.

[a] suffrari, *Caen MS.*

---

[1] The date is so precise that presumably Orderic took it from a written source, perhaps from an obit, though the only obit celebrated at Saint-Évroul on 3 Nov. was that of Queen Matilda (above, p. 45 n. 3).

[2] The second son of William of Warenne.

[3] The west gate of the city.

Then he made a treaty of friendship with his brother Henry and other men who had broken with him, and sent messengers in haste to inform William count of Évreux, Robert of Bellême, William of Breteuil, and Gilbert of Laigle and his other loyal vassals of his predicament. Henry was the first to come to his aid; he first sent help to his brother and later actively took vengeance on the traitors.

On 3 November[1] Gilbert of Laigle brought a contingent of knights for the duke's service, coming to the south gate of the city over the Seine bridge; meanwhile Reginald of Warenne[2] hurried to the Cauchoise gate[3] with three hundred knights in support of Conan. Then Conan said to his men, 'Take action; to arms! We must lose no more time. See, enemies are coming to attack us from the south, and our allies hasten from the west to help us. Hurry to receive friends and foes as they deserve: open the gates to our comrades and bar the enemy's path with armed resistance.' So one body of the citizens ran to drive back Gilbert and his men, while another attempted to unbar the west gate and let in Reginald with his men. In addition to this, a number of royal retainers who had already infiltrated into the city stood ready in silent support of the revolt, champing at the delay.

In time, as the military and civil tumult swelled, an appalling din rose everywhere; the whole city was thrown into dire confusion and fierce civil fighting broke out. Many of the citizens were fighting against their kinsmen and neighbours at both gates, for one part favoured the duke and the other the king. When the duke came to know of the combat raging in the city he burst out of the castle with his brother Henry and his bodyguard, and prepared to give aid to his men. But since the tumult of the chaotic action caused confusion everywhere, and none of the citizens knew which party to choose, the duke was persuaded by his friends not to invite an ignoble death in the mêlée and thereby make himself an object of scorn to all Normans afterwards. Escaping with a few men, he left by the east gate and was at once welcomed by the loyal inhabitants of the suburban village called Malpalu[4] as their liege lord. A boat was launched and from there he embarked on the Seine and, much alarmed, sailed to Émendreville,[5] leaving the conflict behind him. There he was

[4] Around the church of Saint-Maclou.

[5] Now the suburb of Saint-Sever.

Tunc ibidem a Guillelmo de Archis Molismensi monacho[1] susceptus est.' ibique in basilica Sanctæ Mariæ de Prato[2] finem commotæ seditionis prestolatus est.

Postquam Gislebertus Aquilensis[3] tam uirtute sua suorumque quam iuuamine ciuium qui proditionis participes non erant australem portam optinuit, et Henrico aliisque ducis auxiliaribus associatus contra rebelles in urbe certamen iniit, tumidis et reis presumptoribus in nefario conatu deficientibus pars ducis creuit, atque aduersarios ferro fortiter feriens superior preualuit. Tunc uehemens burgensium cedes facta est.' et Conanus proditorum signifer cum aliis multis captus est. Timor et luctus erat ingens in ciuitate.' uirisque certantibus aut cadentibus aut fugientibus flentes uociferabantur feminæ. Innocentes et rei passim cedebantur.'
iii. 355 aut fugiebant aut capiebantur. Ciuibus ut prelibatum est uicissim dissidentibus et tristis infortunii procellis periclitantibus.' regia cohors territa fugit, latebrasque siluarum quæ in uicinio erant auide poscens delituit.' et subsidio noctis discrimen mortis seu captionis difficulter euasit. Conanus autem a uictoribus in arcem[4] ductus est.' quem Henricus per solaria turris ducens insultando sic allocutus est, 'Considera Conane.' quam pulchram tibi patriam conatus es subicere. En ad meridiem delectabile parcum patet oculis tuis.' et saltuosa regio siluestribus abundans feris. Ecce Sequana piscosum flumen Rotomagensem murum allambit.' nauesque pluribus mercimoniis refertas huc cotidie deuehit. En ex alia parte ciuitas populosa menibus sacrisque templis et urbanis edibus speciosa.' cui iure a priscis temporibus subiacet Normannia tota.' Conanus yronica insultatione Henrici pauidus ingemuit.' et supplex clementiam exorans ait, 'Proprio reatu domine damnandus sum.' sed nunc misericordiam posco propter Deum creatorem omnium. Pro redemptione mei domino meo aurum dabo et argentum.' quantum reperire potero in thesauris meis meorumque parentum, et pro culpa infidelitatis fidele usque ad mortem rependam seruitium.' Cui Henricus dixit, 'Per animam

[1] See above, p. 186.

[2] The church of Notre-Dame-du-Pré was a priory of Bec-Hellouin. Possibly in gratitude for his shelter there, Robert shortly afterwards granted a charter to the abbey confirming the grants his parents had made for the church of Émendreville, and adding the tithe of his park at Rouen (Haskins, *Norman Institutions*, p. 68; *Regesta*, i, no. 327).

[3] It is not clear whether Gilbert, son of Engenulf, or his nephew, Gilbert, son of Richer, is intended. The index to Le Prévost's edition assigns the action to

received by William of Arques, a monk of Molesme,[1] and there he awaited the end of the rebellion in the church of Notre-Dame-du-Pré.[2]

Subsequently Gilbert of Laigle,[3] thanks to both his own and his men's courage and to the help of the citizens who were not supporters of the revolt, captured the south gate. Joining forces with Henry and the other adherents of the duke, he attacked the rebels in the city itself. The duke's party grew in size and confidence as the guilty perpetrators of the treacherous revolt collapsed, and proved its superiority over its adversaries in determined hand-to-hand fighting. A ferocious slaughter of the townsmen took place, and the arch-traitor Conan was captured with many others. Grief and fear walked abroad in the city, as men struggled and fell or fled, and women wept and wailed. Innocent and guilty alike perished, or took to flight, or were captured. While the citizens were tearing each other to pieces in this way and the storms of the terrible disaster were raging, the royal troops panicked and fled, anxiously seeking out hiding-places in the nearby woods, where they lay low and barely escaped death or capture under cover of darkness. Conan himself was taken by the victors to the castle;[4] and Henry led him through the rooms of the tower, mocking him in these words, 'Admire, Conan, the beauty of the country you tried to conquer. Away to the south there is a delightful hunting region, wooded and well-stocked with beasts of the chase. See how the river Seine, full of fishes, laps the wall of Rouen and daily brings in ships laden with merchandise of many kinds. On the other side, see the fair and populous city, with its ramparts and churches and town buildings, which has rightly been the capital of all Normandy from the earliest days.' Conan grew pale with dread as he heard Henry's ironical mockery and, humbly begged for mercy, saying, 'My lord, I deserve condemnation for my own guilt, but now I ask mercy for the sake of God who created all things. For my ransom I will give my lord all the gold and silver that I can find in my own and my kinsmen's treasure-stores, and in compensation for my treachery I will give him faithful service until I die.' To this Henry answered, 'By my mother's soul, there

the younger Gilbert; but as Orderic (above, p. 200) speaks of the conspicuous military service given to Duke Robert by Gilbert, son of Engenulf, it is possible that he was the leader of the troops on this occasion.

[4] The tower stood near the river, on the site of the modern Place de la Haute-Vieille-Tour.

iii. 356 matris meæ traditori nulla erit redemptio.' sed debitæ mortis acceleratio.' Tunc Conanus gemens clamauit alta uoce.' 'Pro amore' inquit 'Dei confessionem michi permittite.' Verum Henricus acer fraternæ ultor iniuriæ præ ira infremuit, et contemptis elegi supplicationibus ipsum ambabus manibus impulit, et per fenestram turris deorsum precipitauit. Qui miserabili casu in momento confractus est.' et antequam solum attingeret mortuus est. Deinde cadauer illius iumenti caudæ innexum est.' et per omnes Rothomagi uicos ad terrendos desertores turpiter pertractum est. Locus ipse ubi uindicta huiusmodi perpetrata est 'saltus Conani' usque in hodiernam diem uocitatus est.[1]

Robertus autem dux ut de Prato ad arcem rediit, et quæ gesta fuerant comperit.' pietate motus infortunio ciuium condoluit, sed fortiori magnatorum censura preualente reis parcere nequiuit. Tunc ibi Robertus Belesmensis et Guillelmus Bretoliensis affuerunt.' et Rodomanos incolas uelut exteros predones captivos abduxerunt, et squaloribus carceris grauiter afflixerunt. Guillelmus Ansgerii filius[2] Rodomensium ditissimus a Guillelmo Bretoliensi ducitur captiuus, et post longos carceris squalores redimit se librarum tribus milibus. Sic Belesmici et Aquilini ceterique ducis
iii. 357 auxiliarii contra se truculenter seuiunt, ciuesque metropolis Neustriæ uinculatos attrahunt.' cunctisque rebus spoliatos ut barbaros hostes male affligunt.

Ecce quibus erumnis superba profligatur Normannia, quæ nimis olim uicta gloriabatur Anglia.' et naturalibus regni filiis trucidatis siue fugatis usurpabat eorum possessiones et imperia. Ecce massam diuitiarum quas aliis rapuit, eisque pollens ad suam perniciem insolenter tumuit.' nunc non ad delectamentum sui sed potius ad tormentum miserabiliter distrahit. Nunc sicut Babilon de eodem bibit tribulationum calice.' unde nequiter alios solita est inebriare.[3] Visis tot malis pauper gemit clerus, monachorum plorant cetus.' et desolatus ubique meret inermis populus. Soli gaudent sed non diu nec feliciter, qui furari seu predari possunt

[1] William of Malmesbury (*GR* ii. 469) tells a very similar story of the execution of summary justice, adding that Henry's companions helped him to throw Conan from the window. The murderers of Charles the Good of Flanders suffered a similar fate in 1127, and summary execution by precipitation may have had a place in Norman custom as a penalty for heinous crimes, though J. le Foyer sees this example as an act of war rather than as an execution of justice. See J. le Foyer, *Exposé du droit pénal normand au xiiie siècle* (Paris, 1931), pp. 114, 231–2; R. C. van Caenegem, *Geschiedenis van het strafrecht in Vlaanderen* (Brussels, 1954), p. 168 n. 3; Galbert of Bruges, *The Murder of Charles the Good*, trans. James Bruce Ross (New York, 1967), pp. 47, 250–2.

shall be no ransom for a traitor, only more rapid infliction of the death he deserves.' Then Conan, groaning aloud, cried in a loud voice, 'For the love of God, allow me to confess my sins.' But Henry, stern avenger of his brother's wrong, trembled with rage and, scorning the wretch's prayers, thrust him violently with both hands, hurling him down from the window of the tower. Shattered by this frightful fall, he was dead before he reached the ground. His body was then tied to a horse's tail and dragged shamefully through all the streets of Rouen as a warning to traitors. The place where this punishment was inflicted is called 'Conan's leap' to this day.[1]

When Duke Robert returned from Notre-Dame-du-Pré to the castle and learnt what had been done he was moved by compassion for the citizens' misfortune; but the sterner judgement of his magnates prevailed and he did not spare the guilty men. Robert of Bellême and William of Breteuil were both there; they carried off the citizens of Rouen captive like foreign raiders and imprisoned them harshly in dreadful dungeons. William son of Ansger, the richest of the citizens,[2] was among William of Breteuil's prisoners, and after long suffering in a foul dungeon he ransomed himself with three thousand livres. In like manner the men of Bellême and Laigle and the other supporters of the duke stubbornly showed their cruelty against his wishes, carried off in chains the citizens of the capital of Normandy and, stripping them of all their possessions, ill-treated them as if they had been foreign enemies.

What disasters now overwhelmed proud Normandy, which once had boasted of the conquest of England, and now that the native English were slain or put to flight usurped their goods and authority! See how Normandy now uses the great wealth which she plundered from others and proudly flaunted as she triumphed over them to her own destruction, not for her own delight but only to cause grief and torment. Now like Babylon she drinks from the same cup of sorrows that she used unrighteously to force on others.[3] At the sight of such evils the poor clergy groan, the communities of monks lament, and the helpless and innocent populace everywhere is sunk in grief. Only those who can plunder continually have cause to rejoice, and even they, neither long nor

[2] Probably the William, son of Ansger, who acted as a justice for Henry I (Haskins, *Norman Institutions*, p. 98; *CDF*, no. 167). [3] Cf. Jeremiah li. 7.

pertinaciter. Proh dolor sacerdotalis pene adnichilatur reuerentia, cui pene omnis denegatur obedientia: uehementer insurgente et furente malorum uiolentia. Vt quid in Neustria tantum effrenata furit Erinis, indigenasque Normannos proculcat subigitque ruinis? Quia in diebus illis non erat rex neque dux in Israel, aureisque uitulis Ieroboam rebellis plebs immolabat in Dan et Bethel:[1] unde transgressores legis ab eruca et brucho et locusta et rubigine comesos plangit et hortatur Iohel.[2] Quattuor his cladibus a propheta prolatis denotantur quattuor animi passiones, metus et cupiditas, dolor et gaudium. Metus et cupiditas humana precordia stimulant
iii. 358 et corrodunt: eademque lætali gaudio seu dolori subdentes deiciunt. Læta obsecundant libidini: tristia[a] uero inherent crudelitati. Horum meminit Virgilius in poemate sua dicens,

> Hinc metuunt cupiuntque, dolent, gaudentque neque auras
> Respiciunt clausi tenebris et carcere ceco.[3]

Qui enim perturbationum tenebris inuoluuntur clarum sapientiæ lumen iam non ualent intueri: nec uitiorum glutino exui.

16

Multa intueor in diuina pagina, quæ subtiliter coaptata nostri temporis euentui uidentur similia. Ceterum allegoricas allegationes et idoneas humanis moribus interpretationes studiosis rimandas relinquam: simplicemque Normannicarum historiam rerum adhuc aliquantulum protelare satagam.[4] Iam descriptis laboribus Ebroicensium, et factionibus periculisque Rotomagensium: expediam conflictus et damna Oximensium. Robertus Belesmensis in eminenti loco qui Furcas uulgo dicitur castellum condidit, et illuc habitatores Vinacii transtulit,[5] omnesque finitimos tirannide sua sibi subigere sategit. Aliud quoque oppidum quod castellum Gunterii nuncupant super Olnam fluuium ad Curbam construxit: per quod Holmetiam regionem sibi licet iniuste penitus subiugare putauit. Sic ultra natales suos et auorum ius nimium

[a] tristicia, *Caen MS.*

[1] 1 Kings xii. 28–30.

[2] Joel i. 4.

[3] Cf. Virgil, *Aeneid*, vi. 734–5; the second line, however, begins 'Despiciunt clausae tenebris'. 'Respiciunt' originates in a commentary of Servius, *c.* 400 (Hans Wolter, *Ordericus Vitalis*, p. 225 n. 520).

[4] Here as elsewhere Orderic shows the indebtedness of his training in historical method to the methods of biblical study. In a different way his contemporary, Hugh of St. Victor, was trained in the same school; cf. R. W. Southern, 'Hugh of St. Victor and the idea of historical development', in *TRHS* 5th ser. xxi (1971), 164.

prosperously. Sad to tell, respect for the priesthood has almost wholly disappeared together with obedience to it; evil and violence erupt and ravage everywhere. Why did such a Fury rage in Normandy, destroying the Normans and reducing the land to ruin? Because in those days there was neither king nor duke in Israel and the rebellious people sacrificed to the golden calves of Jeroboam in Dan and Bethel,[1] so that Joel had cause to lament and give warning that the transgressors of the law had been eaten by the canker-worm and the locust and the grub and the hopper.[2] These four plagues revealed by the prophet signify four passions of the mind, fear and greed, sorrow and joy. Fear and greed both stir up and eat away human hearts and, by enslaving them to fatal joy or grief, cause their destruction. For joys encourage lust, and sorrows lead to cruelty. Virgil testifies to this in the poem where he says,

And so they fear, yearn, grieve, rejoice; and never
Breathe the pure air, imprisoned deep in darkness.[3]

For those who are enveloped in the darkness of strong emotions cannot look on the bright light of wisdom, nor escape from the slime of vice.

16

I find many things in the pages of Scripture which, if they are subtly interpreted, seem to resemble the happenings of our own time. But I leave the allegorical implications and explanations appropriate to human customs to be interpreted by scholars, and propose now to relate a little further the simple history of Norman affairs.[4] Now that I have described the struggles of the men of Évreux and the factions and perils of those of Rouen, I will unfold the conflicts and sufferings of those of Exmes. Robert of Bellême built a fortified town on a crag known as Fourches, moved the inhabitants of Vignats there,[5] and set about subduing all the local people by his tyranny. He built another fortress called Château Gontier above the river Orne at La Combe, planning to use it as a base in bringing the region of Houlme under his heel, though he had no legal right there. So, swollen with pride, he grew in power

[5] See above, p. 152 n. 2. Robert of Bellême later created a new stronghold in a similar way in Shropshire, by transporting the inhabitants of Quatford to the better-placed site of Bridgnorth (cf. J. Mason, in *TSAS* lvii (1961–4), p. 41).

elatus insurrexit.' et pene per totam iusti patrocinio aduocati
iii. 359 carentem Normanniam paribus suis obstitit, et collimitaneos omnes comprimere cepit.[1] Quibus uisis Normannici proceres turbati sunt.' nimioque merore afflicti de resistendo diu multumque tractauerunt. Precipue quia uiciniores erant tiranni terminis et conatui nefario.' insurrexerunt primi Hugo de Grentemasnilio et Ricardus de Curceio, et municipia sua munierunt armis et alimentis et militum auxilio. Præfati quippe uiri etate canebant.' audacia et nobilitate pollebant, uicinitate ac necessitudine connexi uigebant. Robertus enim Ricardi filius uxorem duxerat filiam Hugonis.' quæ marito suo quinque filios peperit.

Magnanimus Hugo in iuuentute sua magna probitate floruerat coniugemque pulcherrimam Adelidem filiam Iuonis comitis de Bello Monte duxerat.' quæ peperit ei Robertum, Guillelmum, Hugonem, Iuonem et Albericum, Adelinam et Haduisam, Rohesiam et Mathildem et Agnetem.[2] Tantam progeniem et tam speciosam multifida sors inuoluit.' et nullum ex his preter Robertum ad canos usque uiuere permisit. Ipse nimirum primogenitus extitit.' cunctisque fratribus suis et sororibus defunctis trigamus consenuit. Primo duxit Agnetem Ranulfi Baiocensis[3] filiam, deinde
iii. 360 Emmam Roberti de Stoteuilla[4] filiam, denique Luciam Sauarici filii Canæ filiam.[5] Guillelmus autem et Iuo coniuges habuerunt, quorum unus in Apulia duxit uxorem Mabiliam Roberti Wisgardi
iii. 361 filiam,[6] et alter in Anglia Gisleberti de Ganda filiam.[7] Adelina uero nupsit Rogerio de Ibreio,[8] et Rohes Roberto de Curceio.'[9] Mathildis Hugoni de Monte Pincionis,[10] et Agnes Guillelmo de Saia.[11] Haduisa autem iam nubilis innupta obiit.

Precipuus itaque Hugo filiis generisque et pluribus amicis fretus, acriter bellum contra Robertum cepit, tirannidique illius insignium uirtute auxiliatorum fortiter restitit. At ille fratrum suorum

[1] Robert seems to have aimed at establishing an independent territory, directly under the king of France. See Lemarignier, *L'hommage en marche*, pp. 63–4.

[2] Cf. above, ii, genealogical table facing p. 370, and below, pp. 338–40.

[3] Ralph (Ranulf), vicomte of Bayeux, nephew and heir of Hugh earl of Chester.

[4] For the family of Robert of Stuteville see *EYC* ix. 1 ff.

[5] Cana was the second wife of Ralph IV, vicomte of Maine: Savaric was Ralph's fifth child (Latouche, *Maine*, pp. 130–1).

[6] Mabel, daughter of Robert Guiscard and Sichelgaita.

[7] For the family of Gilbert of Gand see *EYC* ii, p. ix; the name of this daughter is not known.

[8] Roger of Ivry, William the Conqueror's butler. See Douglas, *Domesday Monachorum*, pp. 56–7.

far beyond the right of his ancestors or of his own birth, challenging his peers almost everywhere in Normandy, which was unprotected by any just champion, and trying to overpower all his neighbours.[1] The Norman magnates grew alarmed when they realized what was happening, and in great anxiety held many long discussions on how best to resist. In particular Hugh of Grandmesnil and Richard of Courcy, because they were nearest to the tyrant's boundaries and most threatened by his evil ambitions, took to arms, provisioning their castles with arms and food and reinforcing their garrisons. Although these men were both grey-haired, they were distinguished by courage and magnanimity and throve in a necessary alliance against imminent danger. Richard's son Robert took Hugh's daughter to wife, and she bore him five sons.

The noble Hugh was distinguished by remarkable valour in his youth, and married a beautiful wife, Adeliza, the daughter of Ivo count of Beaumont, who bore him Robert, William, Hugh, Ivo, and Aubrey; Adelina, Hawise, Rohais, Matilda, and Agnes.[2] Various fates befell this numerous and promising family, so that none of them except Robert survived to old age. Robert was the first-born, and after the deaths of all his brothers and sisters he grew old, a thrice-married man. First he married Agnes, daughter of Ralph of Bayeux;[3] next Emma, daughter of Robert of Stuteville;[4] and finally Lucy, daughter of Savaric son of Cana.[5] Both William and Ivo had wives; one of them married Mabel, daughter of Robert Guiscard,[6] in Apulia, and the other a daughter of Gilbert of Gand[7] in England. Adelina married Roger of Ivry[8] and Rohais, Robert of Courcy;[9] Matilda, Hugh of Montpinçon;[10] and Agnes, William of Sai.[11] Hawise died when she had reached marriageable age but was still unmarried.

The good Hugh, therefore, relying on the support of his sons, sons-in-law, and many friends, plunged vigorously into a war against Robert, and thanks to the courage of his distinguished allies put up an impressive resistance to Robert's tyranny. But the latter, strengthened by the forces of his brothers Roger and

[9] Son of Richard of Courcy; see above, p. 230.

[10] Son of William the Conqueror's steward, Ralph of Montpinçon; see above, iii. 164–6.

[11] The family came from Sai, near Argentan (Loyd, p. 96); one branch was settled in Shropshire under Roger of Montgomery (R. W. Eyton, *Antiquities of Shropshire* (London, 1854–60), vi. 225 ff.). William of Sai witnessed a charter of Henry I in 1113 (Le Prévost, v. 199).

Rogerii et Arnulfi[1] multorumque sibi subiectorum uiribus tumens finitimos despexit.' multisque conatibus illos pessundare et posses-
iii. 362 siones eorum deuastare cœpit. Ad conflictus istorum conuenerunt Matheus comes de Bellomonte[2] et Guillelmus de Guarenna aliique plures.' ut in tali ginnasio suas ostentarent probitates. Ibi Tedbaldus Gualeranni de Britolio filius[3] et Guido Rubicundus occisi sunt.' quorum prior quia cornipes et omnia indumenta eius candida erant candidus eques appellabatur.' sequens quoque rubeus quia rubeis opertus erat cognominabatur. Robertus autem uidens quod insignes uicinos per se uincere non posset.' quia nobilitas in eis et audacia et robur ad perferendum uel agendum ardua preualeret.' ducem Normannorum supplex promissis deliniuit, et contra emulos uenire suos obnixis precibus exorauit.

Anno igitur ab incarnatione Domini MºXCºIº indictione xiiiª Robertus dux Normannorum mense Ianuario Curceium obsedit, sed ingenuis optimatibus suis parcens coartare obsessos neglexit. Robertus uero per tres septimanas dolis et uiribus in hostes omnimodis surrexit.' et diuersis machinationibus municipium infestauit, sed copia militum fortiter intus obstante multociens repulsus erubuit. Ingentem machinam quam berfredum[4] uocitant
iii. 363 contra munitionem erexit, et copiose bellicis apparatibus instruxit.' sed nec sic oppidanos ad libitum suum coartauit. Quotiens enim assultum contra Curceium inchoabat, totiens militaris uirtus de Grentonis mansione suppetias festinabat, et assultores ab incepto uiolenter retrahebat. Interea castellani Guillelmum de Ferrariis[5] et Guillelmum de Ruperia et alios plures comprehenderunt.' quorum redemptionibus opime adiuti sunt. Sed bellica sors uariatur.' et uictor a uicto plerunque superatur. Iuo filius Hugonis et Ricardus Gulberti[6] filius a forinsecis hostibus capti sunt.' aliique plures qui Roberti dirum carcerem experti sunt. Tunc Hugo arma pro senio non ferebat.' sed sapientia consilioque acutus omnibus eminebat. Hic obsidione diutina grauari uehementer doluit.' ideoque obsidienti duci mandauit, 'Patri tuo et auo

[1] See above, iii. 150 n. 1.

[2] Matthew count of Beaumont-sur-Oise, one of the lords of the Île-de-France. Prince Louis was to lead an expedition against him in 1101–2 (Lemarignier, *Le gouvernement royal*, pp. 165–6; Le Prévost, iv. 286–7). He was a kinsman of Hugh's wife Adeliza, but his presence also suggests that French contingents may have been involved in these 'more than civil wars'.

[3] Waleran of Breteuil in Beauvaisis; cf. above, ii. 106.

[4] For the siege-tower cf. below, p. 289 n. 7.

Arnulf[1] and many of his dependants, held his neighbours in contempt and made many forays to ruin them and plunder their lands. Matthew count of Beaumont[2] and William of Warenne and many others joined in these skirmishes, anxious to show their prowess in such a school of knighthood. Theobald, son of Waleran of Breteuil,[3] and Guy 'the red' were killed there; the first was called 'the white knight' because his horse and all his trappings were white; the second 'the red' because he was covered with rubies. Robert however realized that he could never conquer his eminent neighbours, because their excellence and the daring and strength with which they carried through difficult tasks were bound to prevail in the end. He therefore placated the duke of Normandy with promises, and humbly entreated and begged him to come to his aid against his rivals.

So in the year of our Lord 1091, the thirteenth indiction, Robert duke of Normandy laid siege to Courcy in the month of January; but he spared his native barons and did not press the besieged closely. Robert of Bellême molested the enemy for three weeks with every kind of trick or violence, and attacked the castle with various kinds of siege-machines, but he was often driven back in shame by the great force of men-at-arms stoutly resisting within. He built a huge contraption called a siege-tower[4] against the fortress, and equipped it with an abundance of weapons; but the garrison was not to be bent to his will in this way. As often as he began an assault on Courcy, the military force of Grandmesnil hastened to the rescue, and violently forced back the defenders. During the siege the garrison captured William of Ferrières,[5] William of Rupierre, and many others, and gained much wealth from their ransoms. But the fortunes of war are variable, and often the vanquished turn the tables on the victors. Ivo the son of Hugh and Richard the son of Goubert[6] were captured by the enemy without, as well as many others who experienced Robert's grim dungeons. Hugh no longer bore arms on account of his age, but his wisdom and good counsel enabled him to take the lead. He was much distressed by the burden of the long siege, and sent to the duke who was besieging him saying, 'I have seen years of service

[5] William of Ferrières-Saint-Hilaire, son of Henry of Ferrières (Ferrers), castellan of Tutbury (see above, ii. 264; Le Prévost, *Eure*, ii. 80 ff.; GEC iv. 190–203; Loyd, p. 42).

[6] His identity is uncertain; Le Prévost's suggestion that he was Richard of Bienfaite (Le Prévost, iii. 363 n. 5) was corrected in the index.

diu seruiui.' et in eorum seruitio multa grauia pertuli. Tibi quoque semper fidelis extiti. Quid egi, quid in te peccaui? Vnde promerui tam hostiliter a te impugnari? Dominum meum te publice fateor, et iccirco contra te non preliabor. Sed nunc a me ducentas libras accipe et uno tantum die quo uis recede.' ut te absente liceat
michi cum Roberto Belesmensi dimicare. Patet itaque Rober-
iii. 364 tum sub protectione ducis admodum confidere.' et obsessos plus
coherceri erilis reuerentia fidelitatis quam hostilium armorum terrore.'

Clibanus extra munitionem inter machinam oppidique portam stabat ibique panificus ad subsidium inclusorum panes coquebat.' quia pro acceleratione obsidionis in nouo munimento construere furnum oppidanis fas non fuerat. Contigit ergo ut circa clibanum creberrimæ cedes fierent, et plurimo sanguine fuso plures animæ de carcere carnis atrociter exirent. Curceienses enim panes in furno armis tuebantur, eisque Belesmenses auferre nitebantur.' et hac de causa multæ strages crudeliter agebantur. Quadam die dum panis in furno coqueretur.' et inter inimicas partes ex procacitate uehemens ira oriretur, armatæ acies utrinque conuenerunt, initoque conflictu fere xx homines occisi sunt.' multique uulnerati qui de panibus emptis cruore suo non gustauerunt. In conspectu obsidentium comilitones obsessorum in castellum cotidie intrabant.' et armis ac alimentis non curante duce socios ne deficerent confortabant.

Quondam de conflictu Roberto cum suis fugiente.' insecutores armigerum quendam fecerunt in berfredum ascendere, et a boreali plaga ignem immittere. Iusto itaque Dei iudicio machina combusta est.' quæ tirannico iussu in diebus sanctæ Natiuitatis
Domini proterue fabricata est. Ad obsidionem sollers Girardus
iii. 365 Sagiensis episcopus[1] ut dissidentes parrochianos suos pacificaret
uenit.' hospitiumque suum apud Diuense cenobium constituit. Pacem dissidentibus proposuit.' sed discordia preualente repulsus ingemuit. Robertus insuper iniuriam ei maximam fecit, eumque nimis contristauit. Nam puerum quendam qui presuli ministrabat, dum per exercitum puerili more ludens equitabat.' eiectum de equo comprehendit, et in carcere trusit, sibique cornipedem retentauit. Idem puer Ricardus de Guaspreia filius Seuoldi uocitabatur.' cuius

[1] Gerard, bishop of Séez, *c.* 1082–91.

under your father and grandfather and suffered many misfortunes then; to you I have always been faithful. What is my fault? What wrong have I done you that I should be so bitterly attacked by you? I publicly acknowledge you my lord, and therefore I will not fight against you. But accept two hundred livres from me now, and withdraw just for one day, whenever you wish, so that in your absence I may join combat with Robert of Bellême. It seems that Robert trusts too much in your protection and keeps the besieged in check more through their respect for their fealty to their lord than from fear of enemy arms.'

An oven stood outside the fortress, between the siege-tower and the castle gate, where the baker made bread for the use of the besieged, because the siege had begun so suddenly that there had been no chance of building an oven for the garrison inside the new defences. Consequently the greatest slaughter took place round the oven: much blood was shed and many souls were released from the prison of the flesh in a terrible way. The men of Courcy fought to guard the bread in the oven, those of Bellême to carry it off, consequently there was much cruel slaughter. One day while the bread was being baked in the oven a fierce clash began because of the boldness of the warring factions; armed contingents met together and, when battle was joined, about twenty men were killed and many wounded, who never tasted the bread bought with their blood. Companions of the besieged daily entered the castle under the eyes of the besiegers and brought succour by replenishing the supplies of arms and food, while the duke turned a blind eye.

Once as Robert and his men fled from an engagement the pursuers made one of their men-at-arms climb up into the siege-tower and set fire to it on the north side. So by God's just decree the machine, which by the tyrant's command had been unrighteously built at Christmas time, was burnt. Gerard bishop of Séez[1] came to the siege, anxious to make peace between the warring parties in his diocese, and lodged in the abbey of Saint-Pierre-sur-Dives. He made proposals for peace to the factions, but their enmity was too great and he withdrew in sorrow. In addition Robert did him a great injury, which caused him particular distress. One of the boys attending on the bishop was riding through the army in sport, after a boy's fashion, when he was thrown from his horse; Robert seized him and threw him into prison, keeping the horse for himself. The boy's name was Richard of Gaprée, son of

parentela contra Robertum sese iamdudum defendere totis uiribus nitebatur. Episcopus autem ut clericum suum sine reatu a Roberto captum audiuit, sibi eundem protinus reddi precepit.' et nisi redderetur totum exercitum interdixit. Post aliquot igitur dies inberbis clericus liber dimissus est.' et antistes languens Sagium ad propriam sedem reportatus est. Ibi dominicis sacramentis munitus est.' et inter manus discipulorum xº kal' Februarii defunctus est, cuius corpus in æcclesia sancti Geruasii martiris[1] tumulatum est.

In eadem septimana[2] Guillelmus Rufus Anglorum rex cum magna classe in Normanniam transfretauit.' cuius aduentu audito
iii. 366 territus dux cum Roberto aliisque obsidentibus actutum recessit, et unusquisque propria repetiit. Mox omnes pene Normannorum optimates certatim regem adierunt.' eique munera recepturi maiora cum summo fauore contulerunt. Galli quoque et Britones ac Flandritæ ut regem apud Aucum in Neustria commorari audierunt.' aliique plures de collimitaneis prouinciis ad eum conuenerunt. Tunc magnificentiam eius alacriter experti sunt.' domumque petentes cunctis eum principibus suis diuitiis et liberalitate preposuerunt. Denique duo fratres Rotomagum pacifice conuenerunt.' et in unum congregati abolitis prioribus querimoniis pacificati sunt.[3] Tunc ingentia Robertus dux a rege dona recepit, eique Aucensem comitatum et Albamarlam totamque terram Gerardi de Gornaco et Radulfi de Conchis cum omnibus municipiis eorum eisque subiectorum concessit.' ubi prefatus rex a Ianuario usque ad kalendas Augusti regali more cum suis habitauit.

17

iii 367 Quid in episcopatu Lexouiensi in capite Ianuarii contigerit cuidam presbitero.' pretereundum non estimo, nec comprimendum silentio.[4] In uilla quæ Bonauallis dicitur Gualchelinus sacerdos erat.' qui æcclesiæ sancti Albini Andegauensis ex monacho episcopi et confessoris deseruiebat. Hic anno dominicæ incarnationis MºXCIº in capite Ianuarii accersitus ut ratio exegit.' quendam egrotum in ultimis parochiæ suæ terminis noctu uisitauit. Vnde

[1] The cathedral church of Séez.

[2] Orderic may mean within a week of the burial: William was certainly at Dover on 27 January (*Regesta*, i, no. 315). The Anglo-Saxon Chronicle dates his crossing at Candlemas (1091); cf. David, *Robert Curthose*, p. 58 n. 75.

[3] Orderic omits all mention of hostilities before the peace. But this is the most

Sewold, and his family had for some time put up a tremendous struggle to defend itself against Robert. When the bishop heard that his innocent clerk had been made prisoner by Robert he immediately demanded his restoration, laying an interdict on the whole army if he were not released. A few days later therefore the beardless boy was set free, and the bishop, then gravely ill, was carried back to his own seat at Séez. There he received the holy sacraments and died in the arms of his followers on 23 January. His body was buried in the church of St. Gervase the martyr.[1]

Within a week[2] William Rufus, king of England, crossed to Normandy with a great fleet. At the news of his coming the duke in alarm immediately withdrew with Robert and the other besieging forces and each one returned home. Soon almost all the Norman magnates eagerly flocked to the king, ingratiatingly offering him gifts in the hope of receiving greater ones. Frenchmen too, Bretons, Flemings and many others from the neighbouring provinces, on hearing that the king was staying at Eu in Normandy, flocked to him. They soon experienced his munificence, and on returning home declared him to be far above all their princes in wealth and generosity. Finally the two brothers met amicably at Rouen, and renouncing all their former differences were united in a bond of peace.[3] Duke Robert then received great gifts from the king, and granted him the county of Eu with Aumâle and the whole territory of Gerard of Gournay and Ralph of Conches, with all the castles held by them or their vassals; and there the king lived with his followers in royal style from January until 1 August.

17

I am sure that I should not pass over in silence or consign to oblivion something that happened to a priest in the diocese of Lisieux on 1 January.[4] There was a priest called Walchelin, who served the church of St. Aubin the confessor, bishop of Angers and previously monk, in the village of Bonneval. On 1 January 1091, this man was sent for by night, as his office required, to visit a sick man on the fringes of his parish. As he was returning alone,

likely date for the siege of Eu, when according to William of Malmesbury and the Anglo-Saxon Chronicle Philip I came to the help of his vassal Robert. There was no serious fighting and William Rufus may have been bought off (Fliche, *Philippe I*, pp. 294–6; David, *Robert Curthose*, pp. 59–60).

[4] See above, Introduction, pp. xxxviii–xl.

dum solus rediret, et longe ab hominum habitatione remotus iret, ingentem strepitum uelut maximi exercitus cepit audire.' et familiam Roberti Belesmensis putauit esse, quæ festinaret Curceium obsidere. Luna quippe octaua in signo arietis tunc clare micabat, et gradientibus iter demonstrabat. Prefatus presbiter erat iuuenis, audax et fortis, corpore magnus et agilis. Audito itaque tumultu inordinate properantium timuit, et plurima secum tractare cepit.' an fugeret ne a uilibus parasitis inuaderetur, et inhoneste spoliaretur.' aut ualidam manum pro defensione sui erigeret si ab aliquo impeteretur. Tandem quattuor mespuleas[a] arbores in agro procul a calle prospexit.' ad quas latitandi causa donec equitatus
iii. 368 pertransiret cito diuertere uoluit. Verum quidam enormis staturæ ferens ingentem maxucam presbiterum properantem preuenit.' et super caput eius leuato uecte dixit, 'Sta nec progrediaris ultra.' Mox presbiter diriguit.' et baculo quem baiulabat appodiatus immobilis stetit. Arduus uero uectifer iuxta eum stabat.' et nichil ei nocens pretereuntem exercitum expectabat. Ecce ingens turba peditum pertransibat.' et pecudes ac uestes multimodamque suppellectilem et diuersa utensilia quæ predones asportare solent super colla scapulasque suas ferebat. Omnes nimirum lamentabantur.' seseque ut festinarent cohortabantur. Multos etiam uicinorum suorum qui nuper obierant presbiter ibidem recognouit.' et merentes pro magnis suppliciis quibus ob facinora sua torquebantur audiuit. Deinde turma uespillionum secuta est, cui prefatus gigas repente associatus est. Feretra fere quingenta ferebantur et unumquodque a duobus baiulis ferebatur. Porro super feretra homines parui uelut nani sedebant.' sed magna capita ceu dolia habebant. Ingens etiam truncus a duobus Ethiopibus portabatur, et super truncum quidam misellus dire ligatus cruciabatur.' et inter angores diros ululatus emittens uociferabatur. Teterrimus
iii. 369 enim demon qui super eundem truncum sedebat.' igneis calcaribus in lumbis et tergo sanguinolentum importune stimulabat. Hunc profecto Gualchelinus interfectorem Stephani presbiteri[1] recognouit, et intolerabiliter cruciari pro innocentis sanguine uidit.' quem ante biennium idem effudit, et tanti non peracta pœnitentia piaculi obierat.

Deinde cohors mulierum secuta est, cuius multitudo innumerabilis presbitero uisa est.' femineo more equitabant.' et in

[a] *Possibly an error for* mespileas

[1] His identity is uncertain; he was probably a local priest known to

in a spot far from human habitation, he heard a sound like the movement of a great army, and took it to be the household troops of Robert of Bellême, hurrying to the siege of Courcy. The eighth moon was shining brightly in the sign of the Ram, and showed the road clearly to travellers. This priest was a young man, strong and brave, well-built and active. But on hearing the sound of men in disorderly haste he trembled and hesitated between several courses of action, undecided whether to take to his heels to avoid being attacked by low minions and shamefully robbed, or whether to stand his ground and defend himself if anyone accosted him. As he noticed four medlar trees in a field far from the path he made up his mind to hurry there and hide until the troop of horse had passed by. But a man of huge stature, carrying a great mace, barred the priest's way as he ran and, brandishing the weapon over his head, cried out, 'Stand; go no further.' The priest obeyed at once and stood motionless, leaning on the staff he was carrying. The stern mace-bearer stood beside him without harming him, waiting for the army to pass by. A great crowd on foot appeared, carrying across their necks and shoulders animals and clothes and every kind of furnishing and household goods that raiders usually seize as plunder. But all lamented bitterly and urged each other to hurry. The priest recognized among them many of his neighbours who had recently died, and heard them bewailing the torments they suffered because of their sins. Next came a crowd of bearers, and the giant suddenly fell in with them. They were carrying about five hundred biers, two men to each bier. On the biers sat men as small as dwarfs, but with huge heads like barrels. One enormous tree-trunk was borne by two Ethiopians, and on the trunk some wretch, tightly trussed, was suffering tortures, screaming aloud in his dreadful agony. A fearful demon sitting on the same trunk was mercilessly goading his back and loins with red-hot spurs while he streamed with blood. Walchelin at once recognized him as the slayer of the priest Stephen,[1] and realized that he was suffering unbearable torments for his guilt in shedding innocent blood not two years earlier, for he had died without completing his penance for the terrible crime.

Next came a troop of women, who seemed to the priest to be without number, riding in women's fashion on side-saddles which

Walchelin. Since the slayer was undergoing penance, but there is no mention of civil punishment, he may have been accidentally killed in the civil wars.

muliebribus sellis sedebant, in quibus claui ardentes fixi erant. Frequenter eas uentus spacio quasi cubiti unius sulleuabat, et mox super sudes relabi sinebat. Illæ autem candentibus clauis in natibus uulnerabantur, et punctionibus ac adustione horribiliter tortæ 'Væ uæ' uociferabantur.' et flagitia pro quibus sic penas luebant palam fatebantur. Sic nimirum pro illecebris et delectationibus obscenis quibus inter mortales immoderate fruebantur.' nunc ignes et fetores et alia plura quam referri possunt supplicia dire patiuntur, et eiulantes miserabili uoce penas suas fatentur. In hoc agmine prefatus sacerdos quasdam nobiles feminas recognouit.' et multarum quæ uitales adhuc auras carpebant mannos et mulas cum sambucis muliebribus prospexit.

Stans presbiter talibus uisis contremuit.' et multa secum reuoluere cœpit. Non multo post numerosum agmen clericorum et monachorum uidit.' atque rectores eorum episcopos et abbates cum pastoralibus cambutis aduertit. Clerici et episcopi nigris cappis induti erant.' monachi quoque et abbates nigris nichilominus
iii. 370 cucullis amicti erant. Gemebant et plangebant.' et nonnulli Gualchelinum uocitabant.' ac pro pristina familiaritate ut pro se oraret postulabant. Multos nimirum magnæ estimationis ibi presbiter se uidisse retulit.' quos humana opinio sanctis in cœlo iam coniunctos astruit. Hugonem nempe uidit Luxouiensium presulem, et abbates precipuos Mainerium Vticensem[1] atque Gerbertum Fontinellensem.' aliosque multos quos nominatim nequeo recolere, neque scripto nitor indere. Humanus plerunque fallitur intuitus.' sed Dei medullitus perspicit oculus. Homo enim uidet in facie.' Deus autem in corde. In regno æternæ beatitudinis perpetua claritas omnia irradiat.' ibique perfecta sanctitas omne delectamentum adepta in filiis regni exultat. Ibi nichil inordinate agitur.' nichil inquinatum illuc intromittitur, nichil sordidum honestatique contrarium illic reperitur. Vnde quicquid inconueniens fæx carnalis commisit purgatorio igne decoquitur, uariisque purgationibus prout æternus censor disponit emundatur. Et sicut uas excocta rubigine mundum et diligenter undique politum in thesaurum reconditur.' sic anima omnium uitiorum a contagione mundata paradisum introducitur, ibique omni felicitate pollens sine metu et cura lætatur.

Terribilibus uisis presbiter admodum trepidabat.' baculoque innisus terribiliora expectabat. Ecce ingens exercitus militum

[1] Orderic had a high regard for Hugh of Lisieux and Mainer of Saint-Évroul (above, iii. 14–18, 118–24).

were studded with burning nails. Caught by gusts of wind they would rise as much as a cubit from the saddle, and then fall back on the sharp points. So their buttocks were wounded by the red-hot nails, and as they suffered torments from the stabs and burning they cried out, 'Woe, woe', loudly bewailing the sins for which they endured such punishment. Indeed it was for the seductions and obscene delights in which they had wallowed without restraint on earth that they now endured the fire and stench and other agonies too many to enumerate, and gave voice to their sufferings with loud wailing. The priest recognized a number of noble women in this troop, and also saw the horses and mules with empty women's litters belonging to many who were still alive.

The priest stood shaking from head to foot at these terrible apparitions and began to reflect on their meaning. Not far behind he saw a great troop of clergy and monks, and noticed their rulers, both bishops and abbots, with pastoral staffs. The clergy and bishops wore black caps; the monks and abbots too were attired in black cowls. They groaned and lamented, and some greeted Walchelin and asked him for the sake of past acquaintance to pray for them. The priest related that he had seen there many of high repute, who in human estimation are believed to have joined the saints in heaven. Indeed he saw Hugh bishop of Lisieux, and the notable abbots, Mainer of Saint-Évroul[1] and Gerbert of Saint-Wandrille, and many others whose names I cannot recall and will not attempt to commit to writing. Human judgement is often in error, but nothing is hidden from God's sight. For men judge from outward appearances; God looks into the heart. In the kingdom of eternal blessedness light eternal illumines all things; there true sanctity is won and every delight brings joy to the heirs of the kingdom. Nothing there is disorderly, no trace of guilt enters in, nothing evil or wrong can be found there. So all unseemliness of which base humanity is guilty is burned away in purgatorial fire and the soul is purified by every kind of purgation that the eternal judge deems right. And just as a vessel, cleansed from rust and well-polished, is placed in the treasury, so the soul, purified from the stain of every sin is led into paradise, where it enters into perfect blessedness and the joy that knows no fear or shadow.

The priest, trembling at the fearful sights he had seen, stood leaning on his staff and waiting for still worse. Behold, next

iii. 371 sequebatur.' et nullus color nisi nigredo et scintillans ignis in eis uidebatur. Maximis omnes equis insidebant, et omnibus armis armati uelut ad bellum festinabant, et nigerrima uexilla gestabant. Ibi Ricardus et Balduinus filii Gisleberti comitis qui nuper obierant[1] uisi fuere.' et alii multi quos non possum enumerare. Inter reliquos Landricus de Orbecco qui eodem anno peremptus fuerat presbiterum alloqui cepit, eique legationes suas horribiliter uociferando intimauit, ac ut mandata sua uxori suæ referret summopere rogauit. Subsequentes autem turmæ et quæ precedebant.' uerba eius interrumpendo impediebant, presbiteroque dicebant, 'Noli credere Landrico.' quia mendax est.' Hic Orbecci uicecomes et causidicus fuerat[2] et ultra natales suos ingenio et probitate admodum excreuerat. In negociis et placitis ad libitum iudicabat, et pro acceptione munerum iudicia peruertebat, magisque cupiditati et falsitati quam rectitudini seruiebat. Vnde merito in suppliciis turpiter denotatus est.' et a complicibus suis mendax manifeste appellatus est. In hoc examine nullus ei adulabatur.' nec pro ingeniosa loquacitate sua eum aliquis precabatur. Verum quia dum poterat aures suas ad clamores pauperis opturare solitus est.' nunc in tormentis ut execrabilis auditu indignus omnino iudicatus est. Gualchelinus autem postquam multorum milium ingens cohors pertransiit.' intra semetipsum sic cogitare cepit, 'Hæc sine dubio familia Herlechini est.[3] A multis
iii. 372 eam olim uisam audiui, sed incredulus relatores derisi.' quia certa indicia nunquam de talibus uidi. Nunc uero manes mortuorum ueraciter uideo.' sed nemo michi credet cum uisa retulero, nisi certum specimen terrigenis exhibuero. De uacuis ergo equis qui sequuntur agmen unum apprehendam, confestim ascendam.' domum ducam, et ad fidem optinendam.' uicinis ostendam.' Mox nigerrimi cornipedis habenas apprehendit, sed ille fortiter se de manu rapientis excussit aligeroque cursu post agmen Æthiopum abiit. Presbiter autem uoti compotem se non esse doluit. Erat enim etate iuuenis animo audax et leuis.' corpore uero uelox et fortis. In media igitur strata paratus constitit.' et uenienti paratissimo

[1] Richard of Bienfaite, or of Tonbridge, and Baldwin of Meules. 'Nuper' is a vague term, which can refer to events several years before; cf. Douglas, *Domesday Monachorum*, p. 39.

[2] This story of Landry illustrates the vicomte's duty of administering justice in the duke's name (Haskins, *Norman Institutions*, p. 46 n. 201).

[3] Various explanations have been offered for the origins of the name Herlequin or Hellequin; they range from the suggestion of L. Sainéau (*Revue des*

followed a great army of knights, in which no colour was visible save blackness and flickering fire. All rode upon huge horses, fully armed as if they were galloping to battle and carrying jet-black standards. Among them appeared the sons of Count Gilbert, Richard and Baldwin, who had recently died,[1] as well as many others whom I cannot enumerate. Among them Landry of Orbec, who had died within the year, began to speak to the priest, shouting out his messages in a terrible voice, and peremptorily bidding him take his commands to his wife. But the troops in front and behind interrupted, shouting him down and saying to the priest, 'Don't believe Landry; he is a liar.' He had been vicomte and advocate of Orbec[2] and had risen far above his low origin through his intelligence and merit. But in suits and pleas he determined the case as he chose, and perverted justice by taking bribes, showing greater devotion to greed and dishonesty than to right. Consequently he deserved to be shamed in his torments, and openly called a liar by his fellow sufferers. In that judgement there was no one to flatter him or beg for the help of his ingenious pleading; indeed, because he had stopped his ears to the cries of the poor as long as he was able, now in his torments he was judged beneath contempt, not even worthy of a hearing. Walchelin, after the great army of many thousands had passed by began to say to himself, 'This is most certainly Herlechin's rabble.[3] I have heard many who claimed to have seen them, but have ridiculed the tale-tellers and not believed them because I never saw any solid proof of such things. Now I do indeed see the shades of the dead with my own eyes, but no one will believe me when I describe my vision unless I can show some sure token to living men. I will catch one of the riderless horses following the host, quickly mount it and take it home, to compel the belief of my neighbours when I show it to them.' At once he seized the reins of a coal-black steed, but it proudly shook off his detaining hand and galloped after the dark host as if it were winged. The priest regretted his failure to carry out his resolution; but he was young in years, bold and nimble, and physically swift and strong. He placed himself therefore in the middle of the road, holding out his hand to a horse that approached

traditions populaires, xx (1905), pp. 184–5) that it is derived from 'hèle-chien' (setting a hunting dog on its prey) 'de sorte que *mesnie hellequin* paraît signifier "équipage de chiens bruyants"', to the hypothesis of Grimm, favoured by F. Lot (*Romania*, xxxii (1903), 437–9) that it is derived from the Dutch *hellequin*, a diminutive of *helle* (hell).

cornipedi obuius manum extendit. Ille autem substitit ad suscipiendum presbiterum.' et exalans de naribus suis proiecit nebulam ingentem ueluti longissimam quercum.[1] Tunc sacerdos sinistrum pedem in teripedem misit, manumque arreptis loris clitellæ imposuit.' subitoque nimium calorem uelut ignem ardentem sub pede sensit, et inedicibile frigus per manum qua lora tenebat eius precordia penetrauit.

Dum talia fiunt quattuor horrendi equites adueniunt.' et terribiliter uociferantes dicunt, 'Cur equos nostros inuadis? Nobiscum
iii. 373 uenies. Nemo nostrum lesit te.' cum tu nostra cœpisti rapere.' At
ille nimium territus caballum dimisit tribusque militibus eum prendere uolentibus quartus dixit, 'Sinite illum, et permittite loqui mecum.' quia coniugi meæ filiisque meis mea mittam mandata per illum.' Deinde nimium pauenti presbitero dixit, 'Audi me queso.' et uxori meæ refer quæ mando.' Presbiter respondit, 'Quis sis nescio.' et uxorem tuam non cognosco.' Miles dixit, 'Ego sum Guillelmus de Glotis filius Barnonis[2] qui famosus fuit quondam dapifer Guillelmi Bretoliensis.' et patris eius Guillelmi Herfordensis comitis. Præiudiciis et rapinis inter mortales anhelaui.' multisque facinoribus plus quam referri potest peccaui. Ceterum super omnia me cruciat usura. Nam indigenti cuidam pecuniam meam erogaui, et quoddam molendinum eius pro pignore recepi, ipsoque censum reddere non ualente tota uita mea pignus retinui, et legitimo herede exheredato heredibus meis reliqui. Ecce candens ferrum molendini gesto in ore.' quod sine dubio michi uidetur ad ferendum grauius Rotomagensi arce. Dic ergo Beatrici uxori meæ et Rogerio filio meo ut michi subueniant.' et uadimonium unde multo plus receperunt quam dedi uelociter heredi restituant.' Presbiter respondit, 'Guillelmus de Glotis iamdudum mortuus est.' et huiusmodi legatio nulli fidelium acceptabilis est. Nescio quis es.' nec qui tui sunt heredes. Si Rogerio de Glotis uel fratribus eius aut matri eorum presumpsero talia
iii. 374 enarrare.' ut amentem deridebunt me.' Porro Guillelmus obnixe
insistens rogabat.' et plurima notissimaque signa diligenter inculcabat. Presbiter autem intelligens ea quæ audiebat.' omnia tamen se scire dissimulabat. Tandem multa prece uictus adquieuit.' et iturum ut rogatus fuerat se promisit. Tunc Guillelmus cuncta recapitulauit.' et longa confabulatione multa eidem replicauit. Interea sacerdos cepit secum tractare.' quod non auderet execrabilis

[1] There is no doubt that this is the word in the text as it stands, though the image is an unusual one.

[2] See above, iii. 130 and n. 2.

and seemed ready to be taken. The horse stopped for the priest to mount, breathing from its nostrils a great cloud of steam in the shape of a tall oak-tree.[1] The priest put his left foot in the stirrup and, seizing the reins, placed his hand on the saddle; immediately he felt an intense burning like raging fire under his foot, and an indescribable cold struck into his heart from the hand that held the reins.

While this was happening four fearsome knights came up and said, in voices of thunder, 'Why are you molesting our horses? Come with us. None of our people has harmed you, yet you try to take what is ours.' Terrified he let go of the horse, and as three of the knights were on the point of seizing him the fourth said, 'Let him be, and allow him to talk to me, so that I may send messages to my wife and sons through him.' Then he said to the priest, who stood aghast, 'Hear me, I beg, and take my message to my wife.' The priest answered, 'I neither recognize you nor know your wife.' The knight said, 'I am William of Glos, the son of Barnon,[2] who was the renowned steward of William of Breteuil and his father William, earl of Hereford, before him. I have been guilty of unjust judgements and annexations in the world, and have committed more sins than I can tell. But most of all usury torments me. For I lent my money to a poor man, receiving a mill of his as a pledge, and because he was unable to repay the loan I retained the pledge all my life and disinherited the legitimate heir by leaving it to my heirs. See, I carry a burning mill-shaft in my mouth which, believe me, seems heavier than the castle of Rouen. Therefore tell my wife Beatrice and my son Roger that they must help me by quickly restoring to the heir the pledge, from which they have received far more than I ever gave.' The priest answered, 'William of Glos died long ago and no true believer can carry a message of this kind. I do not know who you are, or who are your heirs. If I presume to tell such things to Roger of Glos and his brothers or their mother they will deride me as a madman.' William persisted in his demands, resolutely pressing many visible proofs on him; but the priest, though understanding what he heard, pretended that he knew nothing of all this. Finally, worn down by repeated prayers, he consented and promised to attend to what was asked. Then William repeated everything, and in a long discourse unfolded many things to him. Meanwhile the priest began to turn over in his mind that he would never dare

biotanati mandata cuilibet annunciare. 'Non decet' inquit 'talia promulgare. Nullatenus quæ iniungis cuilibet referam.' Mox ille furibundus manum extendit.' et presbiterum per fauces apprehendit, secumque per terram trahens minare cepit. Captiuus autem manum qua tenebatur ardentem uelut ignem persensit.' et in tali angustia repente exclamauit, 'Sancta Maria gloriosa mater Christi adiuua me.' Protinus ad inuocationem piissimæ genitricis filii Dei auxilium presto affuit.' quale Omnipotentis ordinatio disposuit. Nam quidam miles solum ensem dextra ferens superuenit.' gladiumque nudum quasi ferire uellet uibrans dixit, 'Cur fratrem meum interficitis maledicti? Sinite illum et abite.' Mox illi auolarunt.' Æthiopicamque phalangem prosecuti sunt.

Abeuntibus cunctis miles in uia cum Gualchelino demoratur.' et ab eo sciscitatur, 'Cognoscisne me?' Presbiter respondit, 'Non.' Miles dixit, 'Ego sum Robertus filius Rodulfi cognomento Blondi.'[1]
iii. 375 et sum frater tuus.' Cumque presbiter pro tam insperata re uehementer admiraretur, nimiumque pro his quæ uiderat ut dictum est uel senserat angeretur.' miles ei de puericia utriusque multa cepit recensere, et notissima signa recitare. Sacerdos autem audita optime recolebat.' sed ore confiteri non ausus omnia denegabat. Tandem prefatus eques ait, 'Miror duriciam et hebetudinem tuam. Ego te post mortem utriusque parentis nutriui, et super omnes mortales dilexi. Ego te ad scolas in Galliam direxi, et uestes nummosque tibi copiose porrexi, aliisque multis modis tibi prodesse satis elaboraui. Nunc horum immemor efficeris.' meque tantummodo recognoscere dedignaris.' Tunc presbiter ueridicis faminibus ubertim prolatis conuictus est allegationibus certis.' palamque cum lacrimis fassus est affamina fratris. Tunc miles dixit ei, 'Merito debuisses mori nostrarum particeps pœnarum nunc nobiscum uehi.' quia res nostras nefaria temeritate inuasisti. Hoc nullus alius inchoare ausus fuit.' sed missa quam hodie cantasti ne perires te saluauit. Michi quoque nunc permissum est
iii. 376 tibi apparere.' meumque miserum esse tibi manifestare. Postquam in Normannia tecum locutus fui, a te salutatus in Angliam porrexi.' ibique finem uitæ iussu creatoris accepi, et pro peccatis quibus nimis oneratus eram immania supplicia pertuli. Arma quæ

[1] His identity is uncertain. In 1086 the lords of Ashfield in Suffolk (cf. Sanders, p. 3) and Lavington in Wiltshire (cf. *VCH Wilts.* ii. 158, 192) were both called Robert 'blundus'; but this was a common nickname and it is not even certain, from Orderic's account, that Robert son of Ralph was still alive in 1086.

to transmit the messages of the accursed reprobate to anyone. 'It is not right', he said, 'to declare such things. In no circumstances will I carry your orders to anyone.' The knight in a terrible rage then put out his hand and seized the priest by the throat, dragging him along the ground and threatening him. His victim felt the hand that held him burning like fire, and in his great anguish cried out suddenly, 'Blessed Mary, glorious Mother of Christ, help me.' No sooner had he invoked the compassionate Mother of the Son of God than help was at hand, of a kind that the Omnipotent's law ordained. A knight appeared, carrying only a sword in his right hand; brandishing the naked blade as though about to strike, he said, 'Wretches, why are you murdering my brother? Leave him and be gone.' At once the knights sped on, following the dark host.

When the rest had gone the knight remained alone in the path with Walchelin and inquired of him, 'Do you not recognize me?' The priest answered, 'No.' Then the knight said, 'I am Robert, son of Ralph the Fair,[1] and your brother.' And as the priest stood thunderstruck at such an unexpected thing, greatly tormented by all that he had seen and felt, as I have described, the knight began to recall many things that had happened when they were boys, and to reveal many proofs to him. The priest had a clear recollection of all he heard, but dared not confess it and denied everything. At last the knight said, 'I am amazed by your hardness and obstinacy. I brought you up after both our parents died, and loved you more than any living person. I sent you to the schools of France, kept you well-provided with clothes and money, and in many other ways furthered your progress. Now you have forgotten all this and disdain even to recognize me.' When so many true words had been spoken the positive proofs at last convinced the priest, and with tears he admitted his brother's assertions. The knight said to him, 'You deserved by right to die and be carried along with us to share in our punishment, for you rashly tried to seize things that are ours. No other man has ever dared to attempt this; but the Mass which you sang today has saved you from death. Also I have now been permitted to show myself to you, and to reveal my wretched condition to you. After I last spoke to you in Normandy I left for England with your blessing; there I reached my life's end when my Creator willed, and I have endured severe punishment for the great sins with which I am heavily burdened.

ferimus ignea sunt.' et nos fœtore teterrimo inficiunt, ingentique ponderositate nimis opprimunt, et ardore inextinguibili comburunt. Hactenus itaque huiuscemodi pœnis inenarrabiliter cruciatus sum. Sed quando in Anglia ordinatus fuisti, et primam missam pro fidelibus defunctis cantasti, Radulfus pater tuus suppliciis ereptus est.' et scutum meum quo uehementer angebar elapsum est. Ensem hunc ut uides adhuc fero.' sed in hoc anno relaxationem ab hoc onere fiducialiter expecto.'

Dum miles hæc et alia huiuscemodi diceret, et diligenter ad eum presbiter intenderet.' quasi strumam sanguinis instar humani capitis ad eius talos circa calcaria uidit, stupensque sic interrogauit, 'Vnde tanta coagulatio cruoris imminet calcaneis tuis?' At ille respondit, 'Non est sanguis sed ignis.' et maioris michi uidetur esse ponderis quam si ferrem super me Montem Sancti Michahelis. Et quia preciosis et acutis utebar calcaribus ut festinarem ad effundendum sanguinem.' iure sarcinam in talis baiulo enormem, qua intolerabiliter grauatus nulli hominum depromere ualeo penæ quantitatem. Hæc indesinenter meditari mortales deberent.' et timere immo cauere ne pro reatibus suis tam dira luerent. Plura
iii. 377 michi non licet tecum frater fari.' quia miserabile agmen festinanter cogor prosequi. Obsecro memento mei.' precibusque piis et elemosinis succurre michi. Nam a Pascha florum usque ad unum annum spero saluari, et clementia creatoris ab omnibus tormentis liberari. Tu uero sollicitus esto de te.' uitamque tuam prudenter corrige, quæ pluribus uitiis sordescit, scitoque quod diuturna non erit. Ad presens sile. Res quas nunc ex insperato uidisti et audisti silentio comprime.' et usque ad tres dies nemini presumas enarrare.'

His dictis miles festinus abcessit, presbiter autem tota septimana grauiter egrotauit. Deinde postquam conualescere cepit.' Luxouium adiit, Gisleberto episcopo cuncta ex ordine recitauit, et ab eo medicamenta sibimet necessaria impetrauit.[1] Postmodum fere xv annis uegetus uixit, et hæc quæ scripto tradidi.' aliaque plurima quæ obliuione abolita sunt ab ore ipsius audiui, et faciem eius horrendi militis tactu lesam perspexi. Hæc ad ædificationem

[1] Gilbert Maminot was both doctor and bishop, and was capable of providing physical as well as spiritual remedies.

The arms which we bear are red-hot, and offend us with an appalling stench, weighing us down with intolerable weight, and burning with everlasting fire. Up to now I have suffered unspeakable torture from these punishments. But when you were ordained in England and sang your first Mass for the faithful departed your father Ralph escaped from his punishments and my shield, which caused me great pain, fell from me. As you see I still carry this sword, but I look in faith for release from this burden within the year.'

When the knight had said this and more to the same purpose the priest, who was gazing intently at him, noticed what seemed to be a mass of blood like a human head at his heels around his spurs. Horrified he asked, 'How do you come to have that great clot of blood around your heels?' His brother replied, 'It is not blood, but fire, and it weighs more heavily on me than if I were carrying the Mont Saint-Michel. Because I used bright, sharp spurs in my eager haste to shed blood I am justly condemned to carry this enormous load on my heels, which is such an intolerable burden that I cannot convey to anyone the extent of my sufferings. Living men should constantly have these things in mind and should tremble and take heed not to incur such dire penalties for their sins. I cannot speak longer with you, my brother, for I am compelled to hasten after this wretched host. Remember me, I beg: help me with your prayers and compassionate alms. In one year from Palm Sunday I hope to be saved and released from all torments by the mercy of my Creator. Take thought for your own welfare: correct your life wisely, for it is stained by many vices, and you must know that it will not be long enduring. For the present, do not speak. Keep silent about all that you have inadvertently seen and heard, and do not venture to reveal it to anyone for three days.'

When he had finished speaking the knight galloped away. The priest was seriously ill for a whole week. Then, when he began to recover, he went to Lisieux, related everything to bishop Gilbert just as it had happened, and received from him the remedies he needed.[1] He lived in good health for about fifteen years afterwards; I heard from his own mouth all that I have written and much more which I have now forgotten, and saw the scar on his face caused by the touch of the terrible knight. I have recorded these things for the edification of my readers, so that just men may be

legentium scripsi: ut in bonis consolidentur iusti, et a malis resipiscant peruersi. Amodo inceptam repeto materiam.

18

Anno ab incarnatione Domini MºXCIº indictione xiiii[a] mense Ianuario Guillelmus Rufus rex Anglorum cum magna classe in Normanniam transfretauit, et Robertus dux audito regis aduentu statim obsidionem Curceii reliquit: et Robertus de Belismo cum suis complicibus aufugit. Rex autem in Neustria usque ad Augustum[1] permansit: et dissidentes qui eidem adquiescere uoluerunt regali
iii. 378 auctoritate pacauit. Henricus uero quia ingentes querelas contra utrumque fratrem promebat, partemque de ampla possessione magnifici patris sui requirebat, sed eorum tenacitate nimium perdurante nil impetrabat, aggregatis Britonibus et Normannis Constantiam et Abrincas aliaque oppida muniuit, et ad resistendum totis nisibus insurrexit. Verum Hugo Cestrensis comes aliique fauctores eius paupertatem perpendentes, et amplas opes terribilemque potentiam Guillelmi regis metuentes: egregium clitonem in bellico angore deseruerunt, et municipia sua regi tradiderunt. In medio igitur quadragesimæ Guillelmus rex et Robertus dux Montem Sancti Michahelis obsederunt,[2] ibique Henricum fratrem suum incluserunt, et fere xv diebus eum cum suis aquæ penuria maxime cohercuerunt. Porro callidus iuuenis dum sic a fratribus suis coartaretur, et a cognatis atque amicis et confederatis affinibus undique destitueretur, et multimoda pene omnium quibus homines indigent inedia angeretur: prudenter secum tractans uarios mortalium casus precogitauit, et infrunito impetu pessumdato sese ad meliora tempora reseruare decreuit. Liberum tandem sibi sociisque suis exitum de Monte ab obsidentibus poposcit. Illi admodum gauisi sunt: ipsumque cum omni apparatu suo egredi honorifice permiserunt. Henricus itaque
iii. 379 redditis munitionibus suis per Britanniam transiit, Britonibus qui sibi solummodo adminiculum contulerant gratias reddidit,[3] et confines postmodum Francos expetiit. In pago Vilcassino nobilis

[1] Florence of Worcester also dates his return in August (FW ii. 28); he was certainly still in Normandy at Caen on 18 July 1091 (*Regesta*, i, no. 316). The 'condominium' of the brothers in Normandy brought only a brief and precarious peace. See John Le Patourel, *Normandy and England, 1066–1144* (Stenton Lecture, Reading, 1971), p. 5.

[2] In 1091 Lent lasted from 26 February to 12 April. For accounts of the siege see David, *Robert Curthose*, pp. 63–4; Fliche, *Philippe I*, p. 296.

encouraged in good, and vicious men may repent of evil. Now I will return to my subject.

18

In the year of our Lord 1091, the fourteenth indiction, in the month of January, William Rufus, king of England, crossed to Normandy with a great fleet. Duke Robert, hearing of his arrival, at once raised the siege of Courcy, and Robert of Bellême retreated with his followers. The king then remained in Normandy until August,[1] and used his royal authority to pacify those of the insurgents who were ready to listen to him. Henry, however, who had brought important pleas against both brothers, demanding a share in the far-flung possessions of his noble father, and had got nothing in the face of their persistent tenacity, raised a following of Bretons and Normans, fortified Coutances and Avranches and other strongholds, and prepared with all his might to uphold a rebellion. In fact Hugh, earl of Chester, and other supporters of his, after weighing his poverty against the great resources and terrible power of King William, whom they feared, deserted the noble prince in his military need and handed over their castles to the king. So in the middle of Lent King William and Duke Robert besieged the Mont Saint-Michel,[2] closely invested their brother Henry there, and blockaded him and his men for about fifteen days under great pressure because of the shortage of water. Finally the shrewd young man, being harshly constrained by his brothers, weighed up his predicament: he had been deserted everywhere by his kinsmen and friends and allies and was suffering from extreme want of most of the necessities of life, and as he mused on the various fates that can befall human beings he decided to abandon his ill-advised rebellion and save himself for better days. He therefore asked the besiegers for a safe-conduct to leave the Mount with his companions. They welcomed the approach and allowed him to leave honourably with all his baggage. Henry then surrendered his castles and passed through Brittany, where he thanked the Bretons for the support which they and they alone had given him,[3] before crossing the frontier into France. A noble

[3] Henry I certainly received Breton help and as king rewarded his Breton supporters, who included Alan fitz Flaald and Richard of Reviers, with extensive estates.

exul non plenis duobus annis[1] commoratus diuersa hospicia quesiuit, unoque tantum milite unoque clerico cum tribus armigeris contentus pauperem uitam exegit. Sic regia proles in exilio didicit pauperiem perpeti, ut futurus rex optime sciret miseris et indigentibus compati.' eorumque deiectioni uel indigentiæ regali potentia seu dapsilitate suffragari, et ritus infimorum expertus eis pie misereri.

Nunc Robertus dux magnam partem Normanniæ Guillelmo regi concessit.' fereque duobus annis[2] a bellis Normannia quieuit. Post solennitatem Pentecostes[3] Guillelmus archiepiscopus sinodum episcoporum et abbatum apud Rotomagum aggregauit.' et cum duce Roberto suffraganeisque presulibus de Sagiensi presulatu tractare cepit. Tandem finito consultu Serlonem Vticensium rectorem elegit, eique Salariensem episcopatum ualde renitenti commisit. Denique decimo kal' Iulii prefatum cenobitam Rotomagum conuocauit.' et in æcclesia sanctæ Dei genitricis Mariæ canonice consecrauit. Porro uenerandus Serlo suscepti pontificatus
iii. 380 sarcinam xxvii[a] annis et iiii mensibus strenue gessit,[4] æcclesiæque Dei sollerti studio inter prospera et aduersa prodesse sategit. Sed duros nimis ac proteruos habuit parrochianos, Robertum scilicet Bellesmensem et Rotronem Mauritaniensem eorumque complices.' qui crudeliter inter se dissidebant.' et pacem æcclesiæ Dei frequenter uiolabant.' ouesque dominici gregis quas Christus sanguine suo redemit bellicis tumultibus dispergebant, et multimodis factionibus opprimentes dilaniabant. Contra eos gladium uerbi Dei audacter exeruit, obduratos in nequitia multociens excommunicauit.' sed in pace firma rebelles discipulos erudire uel seruare uix aut nunquam potuit. Vnde nimirum quamdiu pontificatum tenuit.' semper in tumultu et perturbatione laborauit, et plerumque furia Roberti nimium seuiente in Anglia uel Italia exulauit, multoque metu anxius gemuit.

Vticensis autem abbatia postquam prefatus rector suus episcopatum suscepit, de pastore sollicita predictum pastorem suum

[a] xxxii, *Caen MS.*

[1] If Henry ever went to the Vexin he cannot have been there for long. The Durham charter of 1091–2 that might seem to be evidence of his presence in England at that time (*Regesta*, i, no. 318) has recently been rejected as spurious (*Durham Episcopal Charters*, ed. H. S. Offler (Surtees Society, vol. clxxix, 1968), pp. 48–53); but his appearance at Domfront may have been as early as 1092 (below, p. 256).

[2] This is true only if taken to mean that William II did not again threaten Robert Curthose for two years.

exile, he lived in poverty for rather less than two years[1] in the Vexin, seeking lodging where he could find it, and contenting himself with only one knight, one clerk, and three attendants. In this way the king's son learnt to endure poverty in exile, so that the future king might have a better knowledge of misfortune and be compassionate to the poor, alleviating their deprivations and needs by his royal power and generosity. Having experienced the way of life of humble men, he could show mercy to them according to his duty.

On this occasion Duke Robert ceded a great part of Normandy to King William, and for almost two years[2] Normandy was free from wars. After the feast of Pentecost,[3] Archbishop William held a synod of bishops and abbots at Rouen, and raised the question of the bishopric of Séez with Duke Robert and his suffragan bishops. When they had fully discussed it he elected Serlo, abbot of Saint-Évroul, and in spite of his protests committed the bishopric of Séez to him. Afterwards on 22 June he summoned the monk Serlo to Rouen, and consecrated him canonically in the church of St. Mary, the Mother of God. After the venerable Serlo had taken up the burden of episcopal office he ruled the see actively for twenty-seven years and four months,[4] giving all his care to the welfare of the Church of God in prosperity and adversity. But he had grim and disobedient subjects in his diocese, namely Robert of Bellême and Rotrou of Mortagne and their confederates, who were in bitter conflict with each other and frequently violated the peace of the Church of God, scattering in their fierce affrays the sheep of the Lord's flock, whom Christ redeemed with his blood, and tearing them to pieces as their warring factions plundered each other. Serlo boldly drew the sword of God's word against them, and when they grew hardened in their wickedness repeatedly excommunicated them, but he could rarely or never bring his rebel subjects to make a firm peace, or keep them to it. Consequently he led a hard life of disturbance and anxiety as long as he remained bishop, and on several occasions when Robert's outbursts became too terrible he went into exile in England or Italy, where he lived in anxiety and sorrow.

After the abbot had been made a bishop, the community of Saint-Évroul, anxious to find a successor, invited their former

[3] Whit Sunday was on 1 June in 1091.

[4] Until 27 October 1118.

xii kal' Augusti accersiit, factoque triduano ieiunio de eligendo abbate tractare cepit. Affuerunt eciam tres abbates, Fulco Diuensis, Arnulfus Troarnensis, et Radulfus Sagiensis. Lecta autem lectione de ordinando abbate secundum regulam sancti Benedicti.'[1] elegerunt
iii. 381 domnum Rogerium de Sappo monachum eiusdem cenobii, qui simplicitate pollebat, et peritia litterarum.' multaque honestate, et bonorum dulcedine morum. Tunc Hermannus prior et Ernaldus de Telliolo[2] aliique plures eum ad curiam ducis duxerunt.' sed ducem in Normannia non inuenerunt. Clandestinis enim factionibus quibus transmarini contra pacem et securitatem regni moliebantur subito auditis.' ambo fratres de Neustria in Angliam ex insperato transfretauerunt[3] mirantibus cunctis. Tunc Hermannus ad domum regendam Vticum regressus est.' et Ernaldus cum electo abbate principes regni per mare secutus est. Peruenientes autem in uillam regiam quam Windresorias[4] dicunt electionem monachilis conuentus cum auctoritate Sagiensis episcopi triumque abbatum duci ostenderunt. At ille gratanter assensum dedit.' et prefato Rogerio per baculum pastoralem ut eo tempore moris erat[5] cenobii curam in exterioribus rebus commisit, apicibusque suis Luxouiensi episcopo ut eum in omnibus canonice proueheret mandauit.[6] Guillelmus quoque rex eundem monachum tunc ibidem benigniter asciuit, et omnia quæ pater suus proceresque eius Vticensi æcclesiæ olim dederant concessit.' et regali auctoritate in carta firmauit.[7] Peractis itaque pro quibus ierat Rogerius Vticum xv° kal' Ianuarii rediit.' et a fratribus honorifice susceptus xxxiiii
iii. 382 annis abbatiæ prefuit. Hic centum et quindecim discipulos ad monachatum suscepit, quorum uitam mobilis fortuna uariabiliter agitauit. Nam quidam eorum uirtutibus florentes ad supernæ uocationis brauium Deo iuuante peruenerunt.' nonnulli uero insidiante Sathana in cenulentam uiciorum uoraginem relapsi sunt.' a iusto recepturi iudice quod meruerunt.

Sex nimirum ex his quos uenerabili Rogerio subiectos diximus abbates uidimus, id est Guarinum Sartensem, Goisfredum

[1] *RSB*, cap. 64.

[2] A son of Humphrey of Tilleul; see above, iii. 226.

[3] William and Robert returned to England together about the beginning of August at the news of a threatened invasion by King Malcolm of Scotland.

[4] The monks found Duke Robert with the king at Windsor after his return from Scotland.

[5] This is the last lay investiture of an abbot of Saint-Évroul (J. Yver in *BSAN* lvii (1963–4), p. 225 n. 3). The change in custom is reflected in Orderic's change of language: writing *c.* 1114 of the investiture of Abbot Thierry with the

abbot to come on 21 July; and after a three-day fast they took steps to elect an abbot. Three abbots were then present: Fulk of Dives, Arnulf of Troarn, and Ralph of Séez. After reading the chapter on the establishment of an abbot according to the Rule of St. Benedict,[1] they elected Dom Roger of Le Sap, a monk of their abbey, a man of simple life, considerable learning, great uprightness, and gentle manners. Then Herman, the prior, Arnold of Le Tilleul,[2] and several others took him to the duke's court, but they could not find the duke in Normandy. Both brothers had been roused by the sudden news of secret plots which threatened the English kingdom, and had caused general surprise by suddenly crossing from Normandy into England.[3] So Herman returned to Saint-Évroul to take charge of the house, and Arnold with the abbot-elect followed the princes of the realm across the sea. Reaching the royal residence at Windsor[4] they showed the duke the record of the election by the convent with the authority of the bishop of Séez and three abbots. He readily gave his assent and committed the temporal charge of the monastery to Roger by handing him the pastoral staff, as was customary at that time,[5] and sent letters to the bishop of Lisieux instructing him to admit him fully according to the canons.[6] At the same time King William received the monk Roger kindly, granted all that his father and his magnates had formerly given to the church of Saint-Évroul, and confirmed it in a charter with his royal authority.[7] So, having accomplished all that he set out to do, Roger returned to Saint-Évroul on 18 December. He was received with honour by the brethren, and governed the abbey for thirty-four years. He admitted a hundred and fifteen new monks, whose lives were subject to varying fortunes. Some of them grew in virtue, and with God's help attained the prize of their holy calling; but others, at Satan's tempting slid back into the foul abyss of vice, for which they will receive their deserts from the just Judge.

We have seen six of those who were, as we said, monks under abbot Roger, become abbots: Warin of Les Essarts, Geoffrey of

pastoral staff by Duke William (above, ii. 18), he wrote 'sicut moris est'. Cf. O. Guillot, *Le comte d'Anjou et son entourage au xie siècle* (Paris, 1972), i. 184 n. 227.

[6] In fact the bishop of Lisieux did not bless him as abbot until 1099 (Le Prévost, iv. 63; J. Yver in *BSAN* lvii (1963–4), pp. 276–7). The Caen scribe failed to copy fully all the details of the history of Saint-Évroul; see above, Introduction, p. xiv.

[7] This charter has not survived.

Aurelianensem, Gislebertum Glotensem atque Robertum Pru-
neriensem, Guillelmum Bassum et Ludouicum. Guarinus enim
magistro successit.' et Vticensis æcclesiæ regimen pluribus annis
tenuit. Robertus autem Pruneriensis Tornense cenobium in Anglia
strenue gubernauit.'[1] Goisfredus uero Aurelianensis Crulandensi
æcclesiæ fere xv annis prefuit,[2] et Guillelmus Bassus Holmiense
iii. 383 monasterium sancti Benedicti diu rexit.[3] Porro Ludouicus iudicio
maiorum expulsis canonicis de Balcheriuilla.' primus monasticum
ordinem cum decem monachis cepit in sancti Georgii martiris
basilica.[4] Gislebertus uero de Glotis uir nobilis et facundus
Lirense cenobium fere x annis[5] rexit.' et in multis emendauit.
Vticenses itaque monachi de penetralibus monasterii regulariter
iii. 384 extracti sunt.' et ad plurimorum emolumentum in culmine pre-
lationis sullimati sunt.' ut dum quasi lucernæ super candelabrum
lucerent,[6] cupientibus ingredi domum Domini per semitam iusticiæ aditum salutis ostenderent. Sed exteriorum perturbationes
rerum quæ per desidiam seu nequitiam secularium principum
fiunt.' ordini æcclesiastico et rigori monastico multociens im-
pedimento sunt. Quod omnes qui in Normannia uel confinio
eius religioni seruire concupierunt.' tempore Roberti ducis et
Philippi regis Francorum nimis experti sunt.

19

Anno ab incarnatione Domini $\text{M}^{o}\text{XC}^{o}\text{II}^{o}$ indictione xv^{a} Henricus Guillelmi regis filius Danfrontem oppidum auxilio Dei suffragioque amicorum optinuit,[7] et inde fortiter hereditarium ius calumniari sategit. Nam idem dum esset iunior non ut frater a fratribus habitus est.' sed magis ut externus exterorum id est Francorum et Britonum auxilia querere coactus est.' et quinque annis diuersorum euentuum motibus admodum fatigatus est. Tandem Danfrontani nutu Dei erumnis tam preclari exulis

[1] From *c.* 1113 to 1151; here the sense is certainly 'has governed', rather than 'governed'.

[2] From 1109 to *c.* 1124; see above, ii. 346–8.

[3] 1127–34.

[4] For the substitution of monks for canons in the church of Saint-Georges-de-Boscherville see J. Yver in *BSAN* lvii (1963–4), 220. The charter of Henry I confirming and enlarging the possessions of the church and, at the request of his chamberlain William of Tancarville, consenting to its erection into an abbey was issued between September 1112 and June 1113 (*Regesta*, ii, pp. 324–6). Louis became abbot in 1114.

[5] Four earlier abbots of Lire had been monks of Saint-Évroul (*GC* xi. 645–6).

Orleans, Gilbert of Glos, Robert of Prunelai, William Basset, and Louis. Warin succeeded his master and ruled the church of Saint-Évroul for many years. Robert of Prunelai has governed the abbey of Thorney in England with firmness;[1] Geoffrey of Orleans was abbot of the church of Crowland for about fifteen years,[2] and William Basset governed the abbey of St. Benet of Hulme for many years.[3] Then Louis, after the canons had been expelled from Boscherville by judgement of their superiors, was the first to establish the monastic order in the church of St. George the martyr, with ten monks.[4] And Gilbert of Glos, a man of high birth and great ability, governed the abbey of Lire for about ten years[5] and introduced many reforms. In this way monks of Saint-Évroul were brought from the seclusion of the cloister according to the Rule, and were raised to the peak of abbatial dignity to improve the lives of many, so that they might shine like candles on a candlestick[6] and show the way of salvation to those seeking to enter the house of the Lord by the path of righteousness. But ecclesiastical order and monastic discipline were often disturbed by outward disorders resulting from the neglect or malice of secular rulers. All who desired to follow a monastic way of life in Normandy or on its frontiers in the time of Duke Robert and King Philip of France learnt this to their cost.

19

In the year of our Lord 1092, the fifteenth indiction, King William's son Henry gained possession of the fortified town of Domfront with the help of God and the support of his friends,[7] and from there made a bold claim for his inheritance. Because he was the youngest he was not treated as a brother by his brothers, but rather as a stranger, so that he was forced to seek the support of strangers, namely the French and Bretons, and for five years had been wearied by constant changes of fortune. At last by God's will the men of Domfront took pity on the misfortunes of the noble

[6] Cf. Matthew v. 15.

[7] Orderic alone gives a date for Henry's acquisition of Domfront, but 1092 is consistent with other evidence (below, p. 292). The Anglo-Saxon Chronicle (1094) describes how King William sent to Domfront for Henry. He held the town without interruption to the end of his life (cf. Robert of Torigny, in Marx, p. 271).

compassi sunt.' et ipsum ad se de Gallia accersitum per Harche-
iii. 385 rium[1] honorifice susceperunt, et excusso Roberti de Belismo a quo diu grauiter oppressi fuerant dominio, Henricum sibi principem constituerunt. Ille uero contra Robertum Normanniæ comitem uiriliter arma sumpsit.' incendiis et rapinis expulsionis suæ iniuriam uindicauit, multosque cepit et carceri mancipauit. [2]Inter hæc dum quendam hominem nomine Rualedum de terra sancti Ebrulfi cepisset, apud Danfrontem castellum[3] deposuit. Qui cum sederet ad focum iemps enim erat.' cum lacrimis sanctum Ebrulfum cepit inuocare ac dicere, 'Deprecor te sancte Ebrulfe amice Dei.' ut me de ista captiuitate eripias. Scis enim quia semper tibi fideliter deseruiui.' Cumque hæc dixisset.' subito obdormiuit. Et ecce quidam manum eius apprehendens.' cepit eum trahere. Tunc expergefactus.' sensit omnem dolorem de corpore suo recessisse. Erat enim ualde debilitatus in tantum ut nec de loco absque adiutorio alterius mouere se posset. Ceciderat uero in itinere de iumento super quod ligatus fuerat. Itaque cepit intra semetipsum cogitare quid ageret.' quomodo de domo egredi posset. Viderat enim quod miles qui eum ibidem deposuerat, hostium per quod exitus in ortum patebat ualide cum cuneo obfirmasset. Tamen assumptis uiribus fidei.' accessit ad hostium, et manu repagulum tenuit. Tunc mirum dictu cuneus qui fortiter infixus fuerat ad terram decidit. Ille uero aperiens hostium.' peruenit ad exitum ortuli. Et aspiciens multitudinem militum ante se in platea uidit
iii. 386 consistere, et extendens manum dixisse fertur, 'Sancte Ebrulfe ducito me.' Sicque ut erat nudis pedibus linea tantum atque pallio amictus per medias acies transiuit, ac si oculos non habuissent. Nullus enim eum interrogauit quis esset, uel quo tenderet. Puto quod uirtute sanctissimi uiri eum uidere nequiuerunt. Circa sextam uero horam respiciens post se.' uidit militem qui eum ceperat concito cursu uenientem. Qui magno timore perculsus inter quædam fructeta quæ se oculis eius obtulerunt semet occuluit. Cumque predictus miles prope eundem locum aduenisset.' interrogauit bubulcos qui ibidem arabant si hominem quendam fugientem uidissent, promittens tres solidos illi absque mora se daturum qui ei insinuasset. At illi Dei timore admoniti quamuis illum scissent.'

[1] Probably Robert Achard, Henry's former tutor, who was later rewarded with lands in Berkshire (*Regesta*, ii, pp. xvii, xx, no. 1134).

[2] The miracle which follows is also to be found in a collection of *Vitae Sanctorum* in Bibl. nat. MS. lat. 1864, f. 191, at the end of a *Life* of St. Évroul. Delisle printed it in Le Prévost, v. 181; apart from the first sentence it corresponds exactly with Orderic's version, and was probably copied from it.

[3] The castle of Domfront stands on a rocky eminence separated from the fortified town: it is not, however, certain that Orderic deliberately meant to

exile, and sending for him from France by the hand of Achard[1] received him with honour. Throwing off the rule of Robert of Bellême, by whom they had been sorely oppressed for many years, they made Henry their lord. He took up arms energetically against Robert, duke of Normandy, avenging the injustice of his banishment with fire and plunder, and capturing and imprisoning many men. [2]Among these he took prisoner a certain man named Ruald from the territory of Saint-Évroul, and placed him in the castle[3] of Domfront. As he was sitting by the fire, for it was winter, he began to call on the name of St. Évroul with tears, and said, 'I pray you, St. Évroul, friend of God, to rescue me from this captivity; for you know that I have always served you faithfully.' As he spoke these words he suddenly fell asleep. And behold, someone took hold of his hand and began to lead him. Waking, he realized that all pain had left his body, although he had been so weakened that he could not move from the place without someone to help him, for in the course of the journey he had fallen from the horse to which he was bound. He began to wonder what he should do, and how he could escape from the house; for he saw that the knight who had left him there had fastened the door leading into the garden tightly with a wedge. However, emboldened by his faith, he went up to the door and took hold of the bolt. Wonderful to relate, the wedge, which had been tightly fixed to hold it, fell to the ground. So, opening the door, he went out to the gate of the little garden. Looking out he saw a great many knights standing in the courtyard, and stretching out his hand he is reputed to have said, 'St. Évroul, lead me.' Just as he was, barefooted and clad only in a linen shirt and cloak, he passed right through the ranks as though the men were blind. No one asked him who he was or where he was going. I think that they were prevented from seeing him by the saint's power. Towards the sixth hour, looking behind him, he saw the knight who had captured him hurrying in pursuit. As great fear seized him his eye fell on some bushes, and he hid himself among them. When the knight had come very near to his hiding-place, he asked the ploughmen who were ploughing there if they had seen the fugitive, and offered to give three shillings on the spot to the man who could give him any information. But they, restrained by the fear of God, said they had no knowledge of him,

contrast 'oppidum' and 'castellum'; the prisoner may have been taken to a house in the town rather than to the castle.

negauerunt se scire. Cumque ille recessisset.' de loco in quo se oculuerat captiuus surrexit, et fretus Dei adiutorio et beati Ebrulfi.' incolumis ad sua remeauit, perdurans in corpore usque ad nostra tempora. Hoc uero quod retulimus.' ex ipsius ore didicimus, eique quia legitimus et laudabilis uitæ est, sine scrupulo credimus.

20

Circa hæc tempora in regno Galliæ feda turbatio exorta est. Bertrada enim Andegauorum comitissa metuens ne uir suus quod iam duabus aliis fecerat sibi faceret,[1] et relicta cunctis contemptui ceu uile scortum fieret.' conscia nobilitatis et pulchritudinis suæ fidissimum legatum Philippo regi Francorum destinauit, eique quod in corde tractabat euidenter notificauit. Malebat enim ultro uirum relinquere, aliumque appetere.' quam a uiro relinqui omniumque patere despectui. Denique mollis princeps comperta lasciuæ mulieris uoluntate flagitio consensit.' ipsamque relicto
iii. 387 marito Gallias expetentem cum gaudio suscepit. Porro generosam et religiosam coniugem suam nobilis Florentii ducis Fresionum filiam[2] quæ Ludouicum et Constantiam enixa fuerat ei dimisit.' et Bertradam quæ fere quattuor annis cum Fulcone Andegauensi demorata fuerat sibi copulauit. Odo Baiocensis episcopus hanc execrandam desponsationem fecit.'[3] ideoque dono mechi regis pro recompensatione infausti famulatus æcclesias Madanti oppidi aliquandiu habuit. Nullus enim Francorum presulum execrabilem consecrationem dignatus est facere, sed in rigore stantes æcclesiasticæ rectitudinis Deo magis quam homini studuerunt placere, et omnes turpem copulam unanimiter detestati sunt pari anathe-
iii. 388 mate. Sic peculans pelex adulterum comitem reliquit, adulteroque regi usque ad mortem eius adhesit. Abominabile crimen mechiæ in solio regni Galliæ proh dolor perpetratum est.' unde inter opulentos riuales minarum ingens tumultus et preliorum conatus exortus est.[4] Verum uersipellis mulier inter riuales simultatem

[1] See above, pp. 184–6. The abduction of Bertrade took place at Pentecost (15 May) 1092 (Fliche, *Philippe I*, pp. 42–3). Although William of Malmesbury (*GR* ii. 293) also implies that the initiative came from Bertrade, Angevin chroniclers attribute the initiative to Philip with the connivance of Bertrade (P. Marchegay and A. Salmon, *Chroniques des comtes d'Anjou* (Paris, 1856–71), pp. 142, 192).

[2] Philip's first wife was Bertha, daughter of Florence I, count of Holland; he repudiated her, but was unable to obtain papal consent for the repudiation, and even after her death in 1094 his marriage with Bertrade could not be legalized (Fliche, *Philippe I*, pp. 36–40).

[3] The marriage was not solemnized by Odo of Bayeux, or, as William of

although in fact they had. When the knight had gone back, the captive rose from his hiding-place and, trusting to the help of God and St. Évroul, reached his home in safety. He is still alive at the present day; indeed I learnt all that I have related from his own mouth, and because he is a trustworthy man of upright life I have no hesitation in believing him.

20

About this time a disgraceful scandal began in the kingdom of France. Bertrade, countess of Anjou, feared that her husband might treat her as he had already treated two other wives,[1] and that if she were deserted she would be despised by all like a low harlot. Being fully conscious of her high birth and beauty, she sent a loyal messenger to King Philip of France, to tell him what she had in mind; for she thought it better to desert her husband voluntarily and seek another than to be deserted by him and exposed to public scorn. The outcome was that the weak prince, learning of the wanton woman's desire, agreed to the crime, and received her rapturously after she had left her husband and fled to France. Then he separated from his highly born and pious wife, the daughter of the noble Florence duke of Frisia,[2] who had borne him Louis and Constance, and took as his wife Bertrade, who had already lived for four years with Fulk of Anjou. Odo bishop of Bayeux performed the disgraceful marriage,[3] and received from the adulterous king as a reward for this infamous service the churches of the town of Mantes, which he held for some time. None of the French bishops would agree to perform this shocking ceremony; but respecting the rules of canon law they chose rather to please God than man, and all with one voice rejected and anathematized the shameful union. So the absconding concubine left the adulterous count and lived with the adulterous king until his death parted them. The detestable sin of adultery, sad to tell, was committed within the bounds of the kingdom of France, and led to terrible threats and preparations for war between the rival lords.[4] Then the cunning woman soothed the animosity of the

Malmesbury (*GR* ii. 480) alleged, by William Bonne-Âme. The letters of Pope Urban II and subscriptions to Philip's diplomas prove conclusively that the ceremony was performed by Ursion, bishop of Senlis (Fliche, *Philippe I*, p. 50; M. Prou, *Recueil des actes de Philippe I* (Paris, 1908), no. cxxxii).

[4] Fulk at first tried to accuse the king of incest (Halphen, *Anjou*, p. 171).

compescuit, ingenioque suo in tantam pacem eos compaginauit.' ut splendidum eis conuiuium prepararet, ambosque simul ad mensam discumbere faceret, et nocte sequenti ambobus in uno conclaui strata pararet.' et apte prout placuit illis ministraret.[1] Vrbanus papa legatos apostolicæ sedis in Galliam destinauit, per epistolas et sacerdotum predicationem erroneum regem arguit, obsecrauit et increpauit.'[2] qui legitimam coniugem repudiauit,
iii. 389 adulteramque sibi contra Dei legem sociauerit. Ceterum in flagitio grauiter obduratus ad instar surdæ aspidis[3] quæ opturat aures suas ad uocem incantantis.' corripientium hortamenta patrum spreuit, et in adulterii fetore diu putridus iacuit.' donec filios duos Philippum et Florum ex adultera genuit.[4] Tempore igitur Vrbani et Paschalis Romanorum pontificum fere xv annis interdictus fuit.[5] Quo tempore nunquam diadema portauit, nec purpuram induit neque solennitatem aliquam regio more celebrauit. In quodcumque oppidum uel urbem Galliarum rex aduenisset, mox ut a clero auditum fuisset.' cessabat omnis clangor campanarum, et generalis cantus clericorum. Luctus itaque publicus agebatur.' et dominicus cultus priuatim exercebatur.' quamdiu transgressor princeps in eadem diocesi commorabatur. Permissu tamen presulum quorum dominus erat, pro regali dignitate capellanum suum habebat.' a quo cum priuata familia priuatim missam audiebat.

His temporibus Gallia religiosis et eruditis presulibus florebat. Nam Leuterius senex Bituricensi preerat metropoli, et Daimbertus Senonensi.'[6] inclitus uero Rainaldus Remensi, eique defuncto
iii. 390 Radulfus cognomento Viridis successit in eadem diocesi.[7] Eruditissimus quoque Iuo Carnotensi[a] preerat æcclesiæ.' cui perhibet euidens testimonium laus bonæ uitæ et rectæ doctrinæ.[8] Walo etiam preerat Parisiensibus.'[9] aliique plures episcopi fulgebant in suis regionibus, quorum religione admodum Gallia gaudebat et sacris dogmatibus. Rex tamen Philippus eorum admonitionibus de corrigenda uita procaciter obstitit, adulterioque putidus in

[a] Carnotensis, *Caen MS.*

[1] Although details in Orderic's account seem to belong rather to romance than to history, Suger also says that she subdued her former husband by her wiles so that he sat on a stool at her feet like a slave (*Vita Ludovici*, ed. A. Molinier (Paris, 1887), p. 57). Certainly Fulk welcomed Philip and Bertrade at Angers in 1106 (Fliche, *Philippe I*, p. 45).

[2] Cf. 2 Timothy iv. 2 (cited in *RSB*, cap. 2).

[3] Psalm lvii (lviii). 5.

[4] Bertrade and Philip also had a daughter, Cecilia (Fliche, *Philippe I*, p. 90).

[5] In fact Urban II did not pronounce excommunication on Philip until October 1094; Philip was reconciled in 1096, excommunicated again in 1100, and absolved, on condition that he would renounce Bertrade, in 1104; he did not renounce her, but Paschal II turned a blind eye (see Fliche, *Philippe I*, pp. 56, 61–4, 67–75). William of Malmesbury (*GR* ii. 480) has similar stories of

rivals, and by her wiles brought them together in such close alliance that she was able to prepare a splendid banquet for them, persuade them both to recline at the same table, and on the following night prepare couches for them both in the same chamber, while she herself attended to all their wants in a fitting way.[1] Pope Urban sent papal legates into France and reproved the erring king both in his letters and through the remonstrances of priests, persuading and rebuking him[2] for repudiating his lawful wife and marrying an adulteress in defiance of God's law. But he grew hardened in his wickedness like the deaf adder[3] which blocks its ears to the voice of the charmer, spurned the arguments of the fathers who corrected him, and continued to wallow in his shameful adultery until he had got two sons, Philip and Florus, by the adulteress.[4] So for about fifteen years while Urban and Paschal were popes he was under an interdict.[5] During that time he never wore his crown, nor put on the purple, nor took part in any solemn celebration in royal state. As soon as the clergy heard of the king of France approaching any town or city, all the bells stopped ringing and all sung offices were silenced. So it was a time of public mourning, and the divine offices were performed only in private as long as the erring prince remained in that diocese. But on account of his royal dignity he was allowed by the bishops, whose lord he was, to have his own chaplain to recite private Masses for him and his immediate household.

At this time France was full of pious and learned bishops. The aged Leger was archbishop of Bourges, Daimbert of Sens,[6] and the renowned Reginald of Rheims; after Reginald's death Ralph called 'le Vert' succeeded him in the same diocese.[7] Ivo, a man of most profound learning, the fame of whose good life and sound doctrine is attested everywhere, governed the church of Chartres.[8] Walo was bishop of Paris,[9] and many other bishops added lustre to their dioceses, enriching France with their piety and holy teaching. But King Philip obstinately remained deaf to their exhortations to amend his life and continued to rot in his wickedness.

the suspension of divine service when the king and queen entered a town; these were probably exaggerated, for not all the bishops respected the papal interdict (Fliche, *Philippe I*, p. 66).

[6] Daimbert was elected in 1096.

[7] Reginald died in 1096 and was in fact succeeded by Manasses (II); Ralph le Vert became archbishop only in 1106.

[8] Ivo of Chartres, the distinguished canonist, was elected bishop in 1090.

[9] Walo became bishop of Paris only in 1104.

malicia perdurauit.' ideoque dolori dentium et scabiei multisque aliis infirmitatibus et ignominiis merito subiacuit. Ludouico igitur filio suo consensu Francorum Pontisariam et Madantum totumque comitatum Vilcassinum donauit.' totiusque regni curam dum primo flore iuuentutis pubesceret commisit.[1] Constantiam
iii. 391 uero filiam suam Hugoni Trecasino comiti prius dedit.' quam postmodum famosissimo duci Antiochiæ Buamundo apud Carnotum tradidit.[2] Hic nempe dux anno ab incarnatione Domini M°C°VI° Gallias uenit.' et ab occidentalibus populis utpote precipuus christiani exercitus signifer susceptus ubique claruit. Prefatam quoque regis filiam in Eoas partes secum duxit.' multa quoque occidentalium milia secum contra ethnicos produxit, sed in illa tunc profectione peregrinantibus ad uotum per omnia non contigit.[3]

21

[4]Anno ab incarnatione Domini M°C°VIII° indictione prima.' Guillelmus archiepiscopus concilium presulum et abbatum Rotomagi congregauit, et de necessariis æcclesiæ rebus cum suffraganeis suis per aliquot dies tractauit. Tunc Radulfus Constantiæ urbis episcopus ad hospicium Serlonis Sagiensis episcopi qui sapientior erat uenit, et cum eo de plurimis locutus copiosam rationem de propositis audiuit. Tandem inter cetera prefatus pontifex retulit dicens, 'In urbe nostra est basilica in honore beati Petri apostoli ab antiquis temporibus constructa, ubi diuinitus multa olim perpetrata sunt miracula. Multæ sanitates egrotis ibi contigerunt,
iii. 392 et multociens desursum ardentes candelæ demitti uisæ sunt. Quædam uero sanctimonialis magnæ ut creditur religionis hanc æcclesiam cotidie frequentat, et plurima huiuscemodi se uidisse sepius enarrat. Et ut certum specimen suæ narrationis exhiberet quondam dum in oratorio sola excubaret, et candelam ardentem de sullimi sine humana ope deponi uidisset.' reuerenter ad aram accessit, candelam extinxit, linteolo mundo inuoluit, et in scrinio

[1] Louis, in accordance with a well-established Capetian tradition, was associated with his father in the kingship not later than 1103. There is evidence that he granted charters in the Vexin as early as 1093–4 (Luchaire, *Louis VI*, pp. 4–5) and he was formally knighted in 1098 at Abbeville by Guy, count of Ponthieu. The evidence is considered in full by Fliche (*Philippe I*, pp. 78–86), but he distorts it through taking this passage in Orderic to refer to events in 1092, whereas Orderic implies that the events took place some years after Philip's marriage. No other chronicler repeats the gossip about Philip's infirmities.

[2] See above, iii. 182; H. Hagenmeyer in *Revue de l'Orient latin*, xii (1911), 324–6.

As a result he fell a prey to decaying teeth and scabies and many other infirmities and ignominies according to his deserts. Therefore, with the consent of the French, he gave his son Louis Pontoise, Mantes, and the whole county of the Vexin, and entrusted the administration of the whole kingdom to him when he was still an adolescent in the first flower of youth.[1] He gave his daughter Constance in marriage to Hugh count of Troyes, and afterwards at Chartres to Bohemond, the illustrious duke of Antioch.[2] Duke Bohemond came to France in the year of our Lord 1106, and his fame resounded everywhere as the peoples of the west acclaimed the noble standard-bearer of the armies of Christendom. He took the king's daughter Constance with him when he left for the eastern lands, leading many thousand westerners to fight the pagans; but in that expedition things did not fall out altogether as the crusaders desired.[3]

21

[4]In the year of our Lord 1108, the first indiction, Archbishop William summoned a council of bishops and abbots to Rouen, and treated of important ecclesiastical affairs with his suffragans for some days. During this time Ralph bishop of Coutances came to the lodging of Serlo bishop of Séez, who was more deeply learned than he, to discuss various matters with him, and heard his full explanations of them. At last among other things the bishop related this, 'In our city a church in honour of St. Peter the apostle has stood from early times, and many miracles have been performed there through God's power. Many sick persons have been healed there, and often burning candles have been seen descending from above. A certain nun who has a great reputation for piety worships daily in that church, and often tells how she has seen things of this kind. Here is one example of her stories: once when she was passing the night watching alone in the church she saw a burning candle coming down from on high without human agency. Reverently approaching the altar she put out the candle, wrapped it in a clean linen cloth, and put it away in her

[3] Bohemond began his crusade with an attack on the empire of Alexius Comnenus; in October 1107 he besieged Durazzo, but the expedition was a total failure and he was forced to make peace in September 1108. See R. Manselli, 'Normanni d'Italia alla prima Crociata', in *Japigia*, xi (1940), 179–81.

[4] This episode, out of place though it appears, is copied as an integral part of the text, and presumably was inserted at this point by Orderic.

suo reclusit. Cumque opportuno tempore quod uiderat retulisset, et scrinium aperuisset ut depositum ostenderet.' fauillam solummodo pro indicio concremationis inuenit, sed totam penitus candelam sine lesura mappulæ aliarumque rerum quæ ibidem erant combustam perspexit.

'Nuper in eadem basilica dum plebs Dei festiuitatem beati Petri apostoli celebraret, et clerus ad uespertinalem sinaxim in choro celebrandam astaret.' tres cereos clare ardentes desursum usque ad altare demitti omnes uiderunt, et pro re insolita admirantes obstupuerunt. Cerei autem usque ad finem matutinorum arserunt.' et tunc ad auroram consumpti sunt. In aere quidem super aram ordinate stabant.' sed tamen altaris mappulam non tangebant. Medius eorum maximus erat et quadratus.' alii uero duo mediocres erant et rotundi. Fama huius rei personuit in tota urbe, et pene omnes clerici et laici post uesperas ad spectaculum occurrere. Porro nullus cereos ausus fuit tangere.' sed in quadrato cereo clerici scripturam huiuscemodi legere. In primo latere.' "Manda Petre iram de cœlo". In secundo.' "populum tarisum[1]
iii. 393 peccato". In tercio.' "misererem ei". In quarto.' "lacrimas". Litteræ quidem optime formatæ erant ad legendum.' et litterati lectores studiose inquisierunt huius scripturæ sensum, et necessariis subauditionibus additis exposuerunt, secundum suum intellectum. Sic nimirum uisum est illis, ut diuinitus diceretur Petro qui caput est orbis, iudex seculi et clauiger regni cœlestis, "Manda Petre iram de cœlo ut effundatur super populum tarisum" id est totum aridum peccato. "Misererem" pro "misererer ei.' si lacrimas dignæ pœnitentiæ michi offerret." Diuina quippe locutio gramaticorum regulis subiecta non est, et humanæ loquacitatis idioma sequi ex necessitate cogi non potest. His itaque in Constantino uisis territi sumus, et inter pestilentias ac tempestates bellorum quas toleramus.' imminentia nobis pericula sentimus, et in futuro adhuc peiora formidamus.'

Hæc Radulfo Constantiensi episcopo referente audientes mirati sunt.' et in Normannia paulo post multæ calamitates bellorum ac tempestatum atque famis subsecutæ sunt. Nam idem presul non multo post defunctus est.'[2] et lætifera clades per totam diocesim eius debachata est.

[1] This strange 'word' is otherwise unknown (Ducange, viii. 34); it is doubtful if it is a word, as indeed Orderic suggests in the interpretation he records.

cupboard. When at a suitable time she described what she had seen and opened the cupboard to show what she had put there, she found only ashes as evidence of complete burning, the whole candle having been consumed without scorching the cloth or the other things with it.

'Recently while the populace was celebrating the feast of St. Peter the apostle in the same church, and the clergy were celebrating vespers in the choir, everyone saw three brightly burning candles descending above the altar, and gazed in astonishment at the marvel. The candles continued to burn until the end of matins, and at dawn were burnt out. They stood in a row floating above the altar, without touching the altar cloth. The middle one was thick and square; the other two were thinner and round. News of the marvel spread through the city and after vespers almost all the clergy and laity rushed to see the sight. Although no one dared to touch the candles, the clergy were able to read on the square candle the following words. On the first side, "Peter, summon wrath from heaven". On the second, "the *tarisum*[1] people from sin". On the third, "*misererem* the people". On the fourth, "tears". The letters were well formed and clearly legible, and learned readers pondered deeply on the meaning of the writing and, by supplying the lost words as the sense required, interpreted it as best they could. It seemed to them that a divine command came to Peter, who is head of the world and judge of the earth and holds the keys of heaven, saying, "Peter, summon wrath from heaven to descend on the people who are *tarisum*" (that is, parched with sin); "*misererem*" for "I will pity them, if they offer me the tears of true penitence." Indeed divine speech is not subject to the rules of grammar, and is not obliged to preserve the idioms of human speech. After these marvels were seen in Coutances we were greatly alarmed, and we believe that new dangers threaten us even among the plagues and storms of war that we endure, so that we must fear even worse things to come.'

Many who heard what Ralph, bishop of Coutances, told were amazed; and indeed many disasters befell Normandy not long afterwards through wars and tempests and famine. For Bishop Ralph died soon afterwards,[2] and murderous frays broke out everywhere in his diocese.

[2] Ralph bishop of Coutances died not long afterwards, possibly in 1110 (*GC* xi. 873).

22

Anno ab incarnatione Domini MºLXXXºIXº indictione xª uenerabilis Lanfrancus Dorobernensis archiepiscopus defunctus est.' et æcclesiastica possessio quæ metropolitæ competebat dominio regis per triennium subdita est. Deinde sacer Anselmus Beccensis
iii. 394 abbas dispensante Deo successit.' et multorum patiens laborum ac aduersitatum per xvii annos sancte rexit.

Eo tempore multa malicia in terris orta est.' et uehementer augmentata est. Militares uiri mores paternos in uestitu et capillorum tonsura derelinquerunt.' quos paulo post burgenses et rustici et pene totum uulgus imitati sunt. Et quia diuinæ legis preuaricatio nimis exuberauit.' cœlestis iræ animaduersio multis uariisque calamitatibus reos merito protriuit.

In illo tempore[1] Melcoma rex Scotorum contra regem Anglorum rebellauit.' debitumque seruitium ei denegauit. Porro Guillelmus rex postquam in Normannia ut supra retulimus cum Roberto fratre suo pacem fecerat, ipsumque contra infidos proditores qui contra regem conspirauerant secum duxerat.' exercitum totius Angliæ conglobauit, et usque ad magnum flumen quod Scotte Watra[2] dicitur perduxit, sed quia inaccessibilis transitus erat super ripam consedit. Rex autem Scottorum e regione cum legionibus suis ad bellandum paratus constitit.' regique Anglorum per internuncios ista mandauit, 'Tibi rex Guillelme nichil debeo.'
iii. 395 nisi conflictum si a te iniuriis lacessitus fuero. Verum si Robertum primogenitum Guillelmi regis filium uidero.' illi exhibere paratus sum quicquid debeo.' His auditis ex consultu sapientum Robertus dux cum paucis militibus transfretauit.' rex autem Scotorum benigniter illum suscepit, secumque tribus diebus amicabiliter detinuit. Tunc super quendam montem excelsum ducem deduxit.' et inde in quadam planicie ingentem exercitum armatorum ei ostendit. Deinde inter duos montes eundem ex alia parte minauit.' et in alio campo maiorem exercitum ei demonstrauit. 'Talibus' inquit 'stipatus cuneis Scottiæ, paratus sum fratrem tuum suscipere.' si huc ad me presumpserit transfretare. Vtinam uelit nos

[1] The rebellion occured in the summer of 1091, while William was in Normandy (Anglo-Saxon Chronicle, 1091). For the events which follow see Ritchie, *Normans in Scotland*, pp. 52–66; W. C. Dickinson, *Scotland from the Earliest Times to 1603* (2nd edn., Edinburgh, 1965), pp. 70–4. Malcolm had become the man of William the Conqueror in 1072.

[2] The name given to the Firth of Forth. The Anglo-Saxon Chronicle (1091), however, says that Malcolm came out of Scotland into Lothian, the region

22

In the year of our Lord 1089, the tenth indiction, Lanfranc, the venerable archbishop of Canterbury, died, and the church estates assigned to the archbishop remained in the king's hand for three years. Then the holy Anselm, abbot of Bec, succeeded him by God's grace and governed righteously for seventeen years, enduring many trials and adversities.

At that time great evils appeared and increased rapidly all over the world. Men of knightly rank abandoned the customs of their fathers in style of dress and cut of hair; in a little while townsmen and peasants and all the lower ranks followed their example. Because the divine law was broken everywhere the wrath of Heaven rightly brought down punishment on the heads of the guilty through disasters of many kinds.

In those days[1] Malcolm, king of Scotland, rebelled against the king of England and refused to perform the service that he owed. So King William, after he had made his peace with his brother Robert in Normandy as I have described, and had brought Robert with him to put down faithless traitors who were conspiring against the king, mustered the army of all England and marched to the great river called 'Scot's water'[2] where, because the crossing-place was inaccessible, he encamped on the bank. The king of Scotland meanwhile was waiting with his troops ready for battle on the other side, and he sent envoys with the following message to the king of England: 'I owe you nothing, King William, unless it be battle if you inflict any injuries on me. But if I could see King William's eldest son, Robert, I would be ready to offer him whatever I owe.' When the message had been discussed with the leading counsellors, Duke Robert crossed the river with a few knights. The king of Scotland welcomed him warmly and entertained him as a friend for three days. Then he led the duke up on to a high mountain and showed him a great army in the plain below. He then led him between two mountains and on the other side pointed out a still larger army in another plain. 'With the support of these Scottish battle-squadrons,' he said, 'I am ready to receive your brother if he presumes to cross to my side. If only

between Forth and Tweed which had formed part of the earlier English kingdom of Bernicia. The English army may have halted at the Tweed. The Anglo-Saxon Chronicle agrees that Duke Richard acted (with Edgar Atheling) as intermediary.

aggredi.' et missilium nostrorum acumen experiri. Fateor quod rex Eduardus dum michi Margaritam proneptem suam in coniugium tradidit[1] Lodonensem comitatum michi donauit. Deinde Guillelmus rex quod antecessor eius michi dederat concessit.' et me tibi
iii. 396 primogenito suo commendauit. Vnde quod tibi promisi conseruabo.'
sed fratri tuo nichil promisi et nichil debeo. Nemo ut Christus ait potest duobus dominis seruire.'[2] Robertus respondit, 'Vt asseris ita est. Sed mutationes rerum factæ sunt, et statuta patris mei a pristina soliditate in multis uacillauerunt. Nunc igitur inclite rex adquiesce michi, et mecum ad fratrem meum ueni.' inueniesque apud eum dulcedinem bonique affluentiam, quia uicinior est et potentior et maiorem habet diuitiarum copiam.' His itaque promissis rex credulus effectus est.' et peractis colloquiis cum rege pacificatus est. Deinde reges agmina sua remiserunt.' et ipsi simul in Angliam profecti sunt.[3] Post aliquot tempus dum Melcoma rex ad sua uellet remeare, muneribusque multis honoratus a rege rediret pacifice.' prope fines suos Robertus de Mol-
iii. 397 braio cum Morello nepote suo et militibus armatis occurrit, et ex
inesperato inermem interfecit. Quod audiens rex Anglorum regnique optimates ualde contristati sunt.' et pro tam feda re tamque crudeli a Normannis commissa nimis erubuerunt. Priscum facinus a modernis iteratum est. Nam sicut Abner filius Ner a Ioab et Abisai de domo Dauid pacifice rediens dolose peremptus est.'[4] sic Melcoma rex de curia Guillelmi regis cum pace remeans a Molbraianis trucidatus est.

Margarita Scottorum regina tam tristi nuncio de morte uiri sui perculsa contremuit, omnesque regni sui proceres conuocauit.' eisque filios suos Edgarum et Alexandrum et Dauid commendauit, ac ut eos sicut filios regis honorarent obsecrauit. Susceptis autem precibus eius cum ingenti fauore a curia, iussit aggregari pauperum

[1] Margaret was the granddaughter of Edmund Ironside, half-brother of King Edward the Confessor. She fled to Scotland after the Conquest, and did not marry King Malcolm until *c.* 1068.

[2] Matthew vi. 24; Luke xvi. 13.

[3] The two brothers met Malcolm just before Michaelmas and were back at Windsor by early December 1091. Orderic has telescoped the events of two years into a few weeks, omitting William Rufus's second expedition against Malcolm in 1092. Malcolm did not come to William's court until 1093, when the king was sick at Gloucester. More reliable accounts in the Anglo-Saxon Chronicle (1093) and Florence of Worcester (FW ii. 28) show that King Malcolm returned safely to Scotland and was murdered by Robert of Mowbray in the course of

he would attack us he would learn how sharp our weapons are! I acknowledge that when King Edward gave me his great-niece Margaret in marriage[1] he gave me the county of Lothian. King William later confirmed what his predecessor had given me, and required my fealty to you as his first-born son. What, therefore, I have sworn to you I will honour, but I have promised nothing to your brother and owe him nothing. No man, as Christ says, can serve two masters.'[2] Robert replied, 'What you allege is true. But conditions have changed and my father's decrees have been undermined in many ways and are less rigid than they were. So now, great king, do as I ask you and come with me to my brother; you will find him kind and bountiful, for he is more powerful and has a greater store of riches, and his kingdom is nearer to yours.' The credulous king was won over by promises of this kind, and after holding conference with King William made peace with him. Then the kings dismissed their armies and set out for England together.[3] Some time later Malcolm, desiring to return home, took leave of the king honourably and received many gifts. Robert of Mowbray, with his nephew Morel and a troop of knights, fell in with him near the borders of his kingdom and killed him without warning when he was unarmed. At the news of this the king of England and his magnates were grieved beyond measure and felt deep shame that such a disgraceful and cruel deed should have been perpetrated by Normans. The crime of a former age was repeated in our own time: for just as Abner son of Ner was treacherously slain by Joab and Abishai while returning peacefully from the house of David,[4] so King Malcolm was murdered by Mowbray's men as he made his way home in peace from King William's court.

Margaret, queen of Scotland, was wounded to the heart and shattered by the terrible news of her husband's death. She summoned all the nobles of her kingdom, commended her sons Edgar, Alexander, and David to them, and begged them to treat them with respect as the king's sons. When her court had given full approval to all her requests, she asked for a great crowd of

a border raid on 13 November 1093. Florence's account of the cause of the rupture between Malcolm and William suggests that Malcolm, having made peace and performed homage in the marches of his kingdom, was unwilling to undergo justice anywhere but in the marches (cf. Lemarignier, *L'hommage en marche*, pp. 81–5).

[4] Cf. 2 Samuel iii. 22–7.

agmina.' eisque pro amore Dei omnem thesaurum suum distribui,
iii. 398 omnesque rogauit ut pro se maritoque suo proleque sua[a] Dominum studerent deprecari. Hæc nimirum filia fuit Eduardi regis Hunorum,[1] qui fuit filius Edmundi cognomento Irneside fratris Eduardi regis Anglorum.' et exul coniugem accepit cum regno filiam Salomonis regis Hunorum. Generosa quippe mulier de sanguine regum a proauis orta pollebat, sed morum bonitate uitæque sanctitate magis precluebat. Denique competenter ordinatis rebus et gazis distributis pauperum cœtibus.' æcclesiam intrauit, missam a capellanis celebrari rogauit. Sacris deinceps deuote solenniis interfuit, et post sacræ perceptionem Eucharistiæ inter uerba orationis exspirauit.[2]

Inter cætera bona quæ nobilis hera fecerat, Huense cenobium quod seruus Christi Columba tempore Brudei regis Pictorum filii
iii. 399 Meilocon construxerat.'[3] sed tempestate preliorum cum longa uetustate dirutum fuerat, fidelis regina reedificauit.' datisque sumptibus idoneis ad opus Domini monachis reparauit.

Duas filias Edit[4] et Mariam Christianæ sorori suæ quæ Rumesiensis abbatiæ sanctimonialis erat.' educandas sacrisque litteris imbuendas miserat. Illic diutius inter monachas enutritæ sunt.' et tam litteratoriam artem quam bonorum obseruantiam morum edidicerunt, nubilemque ætatem pertingentes solatium Dei deuotæ uirgines prestolatæ sunt. Nam utroque ut dictum est parente orbatæ, et fratrum aliorumque amicorum seu parentum auxilio destitutæ.' cuncta bene disponentis Dei clementiam sibi promptam
iii. 400 auxiliatricem persensere. Alannus enim Rufus Britannorum comes Mathildem quæ prius dicta est Edith.' in coniugem sibi a rege Rufo requisiuit, sed morte preuentus non optinuit.[5] Deinde Guillelmus de Guarenna Suthregiæ comes Mathildem expetiit.' sed diuinitus reseruata celebrius alteri nupsit. Henricus enim adepto Anglorum regno.' prefatam uirginem desponsauit.' ex qua Guillelmum Adelinum et Mathildem imperatricem genuit. Mariam

[a] maritumque suum prolemque suam, *Caen MS.*

[1] Edward Atheling was brought up at the Hungarian court, but was never king; see above, ii. 180 n. 2.

[2] Margaret died only three days after her husband, on 16 November 1093.

[3] Cf. Bede, *HE* iii. 4 (p. 222).

[4] Later called Matilda. It is interesting to note that Orderic does not suggest that either sister may have taken monastic vows: in 1100 many alleged that Edith (Matilda) was not free to marry Henry I, and Anselm was called in to judge the case. His decision, reached with some difficulty, was that she had taken no vows; and possibly Orderic knew this. For discussions of the case see Southern, *St. Anselm*, pp. 188–90; A. Morey and C. N. L. Brooke, *Gilbert Foliot and his Letters*, pp. 121–2.

poor people to be brought together and all her treasure given to them for God's sake, and asked all to pray to the Lord for her and her husband and children. This lady was a daughter of Edward, king of the Magyars,[1] who was the son of King Edward the Confessor's brother Edmund Ironside, and when in exile had married the daughter of Solomon king of the Magyars, receiving the kingdom with her. This noble lady, descended from a long line of kings, was eminent for her high birth, but even more renowned for her virtue and holy life. When she had made provision for the kingdom and distributed her wealth to the throngs of beggars, she entered a church and asked the chaplains to celebrate Mass. She took part most devoutly in the celebration, and after receiving the holy Eucharist died with a prayer on her lips.[2]

Among the other good deeds which this noble lady performed was her restoration of the cell of Iona, which the servant of Christ, Columba, had founded in the time of Bruide son of Malcolm, king of the Picts.[3] It had fallen into ruins as a result of its great age and the ravages of war, but the pious queen restored it for the use of monks and made sufficient provision for the service of the Lord.

She sent her two daughters, Edith[4] and Mary, to her sister Christina, who was a nun in Romsey abbey, to be brought up and taught sound doctrine. There they were cared for by the nuns for a long time, and educated both in letters and in good morals; and when they reached marriageable age the pious maidens looked to God for succour. For, having lost both parents as I have described, and being deprived of the help of brothers and other friends and kinsmen, they learnt to depend on the mercy of God, who orders all things well, for the help they needed. Alan the Red, a Breton count, asked for the hand of Matilda (who had previously been called Edith) from King Rufus, but was prevented by death from obtaining it.[5] Next William of Warenne, earl of Surrey, sued for Matilda, but she was destined by Heaven for a more illustrious marriage. When Henry became king of England he wedded this maiden, and had by her Prince William and the Empress Matilda.

[5] The story of this betrothal probably stems from a remark attributed by Eadmer (*Historia novorum* (RS), p. 122) to King Malcolm that he had decided that his daughter should rather marry 'Count Alan' than enter a nunnery. Dom Wilmart in *Annales de Bretagne*, xxxviii (1929), 601, supposed that the words were used of Alan the Black and were ironical; but Southern, *St. Anselm*, pp. 183–5 argued that Malcolm intended the marriage with Alan the Red.

uero Eustachius Boloniensis comes coniugem accepit.' quæ filiam ei unicam peperit, quam Stephanus Moritoliensis comes cum paterna hereditate sibi sociauit.

Interfecto a Normannis Melcoma rege Scottorum.' seditio de successore grauis orta est in regno eorum. Edgarus enim primogenitus regis paternos fasces iure assumpsit, sed Dwanaldus frater Melcomæ regis arrepta tirannide per aliquot tempus crudeliter ei restitit.[1] Tandem strenuus iuuenis a patruo suo peremptus est.' sed Alexander eius frater occiso Dwanaldo regnum sortitus est. Vltor itaque et successor fratris aliquot annis Alexander regnauit, et filiam Henrici regis Anglorum ex concubina uxorem duxit,[2]
iii. 401 moriensque sine liberis Dauid fratri suo regnum dimisit. Sic omnes isti fratres uicissim in Scotia regnauerunt, bonisque moribus et amore Dei pollentes uiguerunt, atque pro modulo suo utpote adolescentes uirique seculares laudabiliter uixerunt.

Dauid autem minimus fratrum.' sagaci consultu deuitans atroces incursus Scottorum, expetiit curiam Henrici regis Anglorum. Qui dum intestina clades Scottos uexaret, et bellica rabie in sua uiscera impacabiliter armaret.' curiæ sororii sui inseparabilis inhesit, et inter domesticos educatus pueros creuit, regisque sapientis
iii. 402 et potentis familiarem amiciciam promeruit. Vnde ab illo preclara militiæ arma recepit, et multiplicibus exeniis muneratus inter precipuos optimates penes illum consedit. Filiam quoque Gualleui comitis et Iudith consobrinæ regis uxorem duxit,[3] binosque comitatus Northamtonæ et Huntendonæ quos Simon Siluanectensis comes cum prefata muliere possederat habuit. Illa uero peperit ei filium nomine Henricum.' duasque filias Clariciam et Hodiernam. Porro primogenitam eius sobolem masculini sexus.' ferreis digitis crudeliter peremit quidam miserabilis clericus, qui ob inauditum quod apud Northwigenas perpetrauerat scelus.' oculorum priuatione et pedum manuumque precisione fuerat multatus. Illic enim

[1] Donald Bane (Donald III) was elected king according to the Scottish custom of tanistry, normal at that date, whereby brothers had a stronger claim than sons; Orderic wrongly assumes that descent should have been by primogeniture. Edgar was Malcolm's third son by Margaret; the eldest, Edward, was murdered with his father, and the second, Edmund, supported Donald Bane and after his defeat entered a monastery. The wars that followed immediately after Malcolm's death were between Donald III and Duncan, Malcolm's son by his first wife, Ingiborg; it was Duncan, not Edgar, who was killed by his uncle. Edgar gained the throne with Norman help in 1097 (Ritchie, *Normans in Scotland*, pp. 60–6). He died a natural death in 1107.

Eustace, count of Boulogne, took Mary to wife, and she bore him an only daughter, who was given in marriage to Stephen, count of Mortain, along with her paternal inheritance.

After Malcolm, king of Scotland, was murdered by the Normans a rebellion broke out in the kingdom over the succession. The king's eldest son Edgar rightly took up his father's sceptre, but King Malcolm's brother Donald Bane made a tyrannical bid for power and resisted him cruelly for some time.[1] The outcome was that the brave young man was slain by his uncle, but his brother Alexander was chosen king after killing Donald Bane. Alexander reigned for some years, the successor and avenger of his brother; he married a natural daughter of King Henry of England[2] and, dying without children, left the kingdom to his brother David. In this way all these brothers in turn reigned in Scotland, giving abundant evidence of their good character and love of God; and they led praiseworthy lives in the way appropriate for young laymen.

David, the youngest of the brothers, by taking good counsel escaped from the fierce attacks of the Scots and took refuge at the court of Henry, king of England. While the Scots were troubled with civil strife, and the fury of war raged relentlessly in the heart of their country, he was in constant attendance at the court of his brother-in-law, grew up among the boys of the royal household, and earned the close friendship of a wise and powerful king. He received the arms of knighthood from the king's hand, and after being loaded with gifts sat at his side among the greatest magnates. He married the daughter of Earl Waltheof and the king's kinswoman Judith,[3] and held the two counties of Northampton and Huntingdon which Earl Simon of Senlis had received when he married Judith. David's wife bore him a son called Henry, and two daughters, Clarice and Hodierna. They had had another boy, their first-born child, who was cruelly murdered by the iron fingers of a certain wretched clerk. This man was punished for an appalling crime which he had committed in Norway, by having his eyes put out and his hands and feet cut off. He had attacked

[2] Sibyl, whose mother may have been Sibyl Corbet, daughter of Robert Corbet of Alcester (GEC xi, App. D, p. 118); Ritchie, *Normans in Scotland*, pp. 134–5). William of Malmesbury speaks slightingly of her charms (*GR* ii. 476).

[3] See above, ii. 262. Judith married Simon of Senlis after the execution of her first husband, Waltheof.

quendam sacerdotem dum missam celebraret.' post perceptionem sacramentorum dum populus recessisset.' ingenti cultello fortiter in aluo percussit, et intestinis horribiliter effusis super aram
iii. 403 mactauit. Hic postmodum a Dauid comite in Anglia pro amore Dei susceptus, et uictu uestituque cum filia paruula sufficienter sustentatus.' digitis ferreis quibus utebatur utpote mancus, biennem filium benefactoris sui quasi mulcere uolens immaniter pupugit.' et sic instigante diabolo inter manus nutricis uiscera lactentis ex insperato effudit. Prima itaque proles Dauid sic enecata est. Homicida igitur ad caudas quatuor indomitorum equorum innexus est.' quibus in diuersa ualide trahentibus ad terrorem sceleratorum discerptus est.[1]

Anno ab incarnatione Domini MºCºXXVº[2] Alexander rex Scotorum uita exiuit, et Dauid frater eius regni gubernacula suscepit. Melcofus autem nothus Alexandri filius[3] regnum patruo preripere affectauit, eique duo bella satis acerrima instaurauit.' sed Dauid qui sensu et potentia diuitiisque sullimior erat illum cum suis superauit.

Anno ab incarnatione Domini MºCºXXXº dum Dauid rex in curia
iii. 404 Henrici regis caute iudicium indagaret, et de reatu perfidiæ quam Goisfredus de Clintonia ut dicunt contra regem agitauerat diligenter discuteret.'[4] Aragois comes Morafiæ cum Melcolfo et quinque milibus armatorum Scotiam intrauit, totamque regionem sibi subigere studuit. Porro Eduardus Siwardi filius[5] qui sub Eduardo rege tribunus Merciorum fuit, princeps militiæ et consobrinus Dauid regis exercitum aggregauit.' et hostili repente exercitui obuiauit. Tandem facta congressione Aragois consulem occidit.' eiusque turmas prostrauit, cepit atque fugauit.[6] Deinde cum cohortibus suis iam triumpho elatis fugientes auide insecutus est.' et Morafiam defensore dominoque uacantem ingressus est, totumque regionis spaciosæ ducatum Deo auxiliante nactus est.
iii. 405 Sic Dauid aucta potestate super antecessores suos exaltatus

[1] This terrible story occurs in no writer but Orderic, and has generally been regarded as untrue (Ritchie, *Normans in Scotland*, p. 252 n. 3).

[2] An error: Alexander died on 23 April 1124.

[3] His parentage is uncertain; he may have been a son of Angus, earl of Moray (Ritchie, *Normans in Scotland*, pp. 401–2).

[4] For the career of Geoffrey of Clinton, one of Henry I's 'new men', see R. W.

a certain priest who was celebrating Mass, and when the people had withdrawn after receiving the sacraments he had struck him in the stomach with a huge knife and murdered him, horribly scattering his bowels over the altar. Afterwards Earl David took him into his care in England for the love of God, and provided him and his small daughter with food and clothing. Using the iron fingers with which he was fitted, being maimed, he cruelly stabbed his benefactor's two-year-old son while pretending to caress him, and so at the prompting of the devil he suddenly tore out the bowels of the suckling in his nurse's arms. In this way David's first-born child was killed. The murderer was bound to the tails of four wild horses and torn to pieces by them, as a terrible warning to evil-doers.[1]

In the year of our Lord 1125[2] Alexander, king of Scotland, died, and his brother David took up the government of the kingdom. Malcolm Macbeth, a bastard son of Alexander,[3] made a bid for his father's kingdom, and instigated two bitter wars against him; but David, being wiser, more powerful and wealthier, defeated him and his supporters.

In the year of our Lord 1130, while King David was carefully investigating a case in the court of King Henry, and meticulously examining a charge of treason which Geoffrey of Clinton was said to have committed against the king,[4] Angus earl of Moray and Malcolm Macbeth entered Scotland with five thousand armed men, attempting to gain control of the kingdom. Then Edward, son of Siward[5] who had been a thane of Mercia in King Edward's time, himself a constable and a kinsman of King David, mustered the army and fell without warning on the enemy forces. In the course of the conflict he killed the earl of Moray and shattered his troops, killing some and putting the rest to flight.[6] He and his forces, triumphant at their victory, hotly pursued the fugitives into the territory of Moray which no longer had a lord and defender, and with God's aid conquered the whole of that extensive duchy. In this way David grew more powerful than his predecessors, and the

Southern, *Medieval Humanism*, pp. 214–17. Geoffrey later succeeded in making his peace with the king.

[5] Edward, possibly the son of Siward Barn, occurs as King Alexander's constable (Ritchie, *Normans in Scotland*, p. 161); here 'princeps militiae' appears to carry the meaning of 'constable'.

[6] The victory was at Stracathro in the Mearns; see Anglo-Saxon Chronicle (D, 1130); Ritchic, *Normans in Scotland*, p. 230.

est.' studioque eius religionis et eruditis personis regio Scottorum decorata est.[1] En causa Scottorum qui ab antiquis temporibus adheserunt catholicæ fidei, et christianæ gratanter seruierunt simplicitati.' inceptam epanalempsim[2] aliquantulum protelaui, sed nunc ad propositum nitor opus de nostris regredi.

23

Plerique Normannorum qui diuitiis labore aliorum quesitis in Anglia ditati nimis intumuerunt.' ardentioris cupiditatis et superbiæ molesta inquietudine admodum stimulati sunt. Inuidebant quippe et dolebant, quod Guillelmus Rufus audacia et probitate precipue uigeret, nullumque timens subiectis omnibus rigide imperaret. Arrogantes ergo conglobati sunt.' et in regem nefariam
iii. 406 conspirationem fecerunt, fideique immemores quam domino suo promiserunt.' in facinus proditionis turpiter prolapsi sunt.

Robertus Rogerii de Molbraio filius potentia diuitiisque admodum pollebat.' audacia et militari feritate superbus pares despiciebat, et superioribus optemperare uana uentositate turgidus indignum autumabat. Erat enim corpore magnus, fortis, niger et hispidus, audax et dolosus, uultu tristis ac seuerus, plus meditari quam loqui studebat, et uix in confabulatione ridebat. Hic nimirum cc.lxxx uillas in Anglia possidebat.'[3] quas Guillelmus rex magnus Goisfredo Constantiniensi episcopo dederat. Prefatus enim presul nobilitate cluebat, magisque peritia militari quam clericali uigebat, ideoque loricatos milites ad bellandum quam reuestitos clericos ad psallendum magis erudire nouerat. Conflictibus ergo contra Dacos et Anglos sepe interfuit.' et ingentes[a] subactis hostibus possessiones optinuit, quas moriens Roberto nepoti suo comiti Nordanhimbrorum dimisit.

Robertus autem ut fines suos undique dilataret, et ditissimis contubernalibus affinitate potentum sibi copulatis robustior ardua temptaret.' Mathildem generosam uirginem filiam Richerii de

[a] ingenges, *Caen MS.*

[1] The practices of the Celtic Church in Scotland were slowly eroded in the early twelfth century. During David's reign the organization of bishoprics and parishes made considerable progress and there was a notable increase in religious houses. See W. C. Dickinson, *A New History of Scotland*, pp. 121 ff.

kingdom of Scotland became famous for its religious zeal and learning.[1] This is why I have somewhat prolonged this digression[2] on the Scots, who have adhered to the catholic faith from ancient times, and have had great regard for the Christian religion. Now however I propose to return to my intended work on our own people.

23

Many of the Normans who had acquired riches in England by the labour of others grew in their pretensions, goaded on by the restless prick of their insatiable greed and pride. They felt aggrieved and disappointed because William Rufus was a bold and active man, who feared no man and ruled all his subjects strictly. The ambitious therefore drew together, formed a treacherous conspiracy against the king, and regardless of the fealty they had sworn to their lord shamefully lapsed into the crime of treason.

Robert, the son of Roger of Mowbray, was a man of great power and wealth, proud of his daring and military prowess, who looked with contempt on his equals and was so puffed up with empty vanity that he thought it shameful to show obedience to his superiors. He was a man of great bodily stature, strong, dark and shaggy, bold and crafty, with an austere and melancholy countenance; more given to thought than to speech he scarcely ever smiled when he spoke. He held two hundred and eighty manors in England,[3] which King William the Great had given to Geoffrey, bishop of Coutances. Bishop Geoffrey was a man of noble birth, devoted more to knightly than to clerical activities, and so better able to instruct knights in hauberks to fight than clerks in vestments to sing psalms. He often took part in battles against the Danes and English, and after the enemies had been defeated secured huge possessions, which he handed on at his death to his nephew Robert, earl of Northumbria.

Robert was anxious to extend his territories on all sides, and by forming connections with the wealthiest of his fellow countrymen through an influential marriage alliance he became powerful enough for the most arduous undertakings. He married a highly

[2] Probably Orderic derived this strange word from the Greek ἐπανάληψις; there were some short Greek glossaries at Saint-Évroul (cf. above, iii. 8 n. 3).

[3] See above, ii. 266.

Aquila uxorem duxit,[1] quæ neptis erat Hugonis Cestrensis comitis ex sorore nomine Iudith. Hic itaque primus cum complicibus suis futile consilium iniit, et manifestam rebellionem sic inchoauit.

Quattuor naues magnæ quas canardes uocant[2] de Nothuegia in
iii. 407 Angliam appulsæ sunt.' quibus Robertus et Morellus nepos eius ac satellites eorum occurrerunt, et pacificis mercatoribus quicquid habebant uiolenter abstulerunt. Illi autem amissis rebus suis ad regem accesserunt.' damnique sui querimoniam lacrimabiliter deprompserunt. Qui mox imperiose mandauit Roberto, ut mercatoribus ablata restitueret continuo.' sed omnino contempta est huiusmodi iussio. Magnanimus autem rex quantitatem rerum quas amiserant inquisiuit.' et omnia de suo eis erario restituit. Deinde ad curiam suam Robertum accersiit.' sed ille uenire noluit.[3]

Tunc rex nequitiam uiri ferocis intelligens exercitum aggregauit.' et super eum ualidam militiæ uirtutem conduxit. Denique ut rex finibus Roberti appropinquauit.' Gislebertus de Tonnebrugia miles potens et diues regem seorsum uocauit, et pronus ad pedes eius corruit.' eique nimis obstupescenti ait, 'Obsecro domine mi rex ignosce quod deliqui.' et ingens tuæ saluationis emolumentum insinuabo tibi.' Cumque rex miraretur et hesitaret, et intra se
iii. 408 aliquantulum deliberaret.' tandem supplicanti leniter ignouit, et promissum auidus expectauit. Gislebertus ait, 'Siste pedem queso rex nobilis.' et hanc siluam quæ ante nos est ne ingrediaris. Hostes enim illic in armis parati prestolantur.' qui te nunc iugulare conantur. Contra te conspirationem fecimus.' et mortem tuam iureiurando machinati sumus.' His auditis rex substitit.' et prefato barone indicante quot et qui fuerant proditores agnouit.[4]

Delusis itaque sicariis qui regem occidere moliti sunt.' armatæ phalanges prospere loca insidiarum pertransierunt, et munitissimum castrum quod Babbenburg dicitur obsederunt. Et quoniam

[1] See above, p. 50.

[2] An unusual name for the large Scandinavian trading ships. See A. Jal, *Glossaire nautique* (Paris, 1848), *canardus*.

[3] Orderic alone tells this story; the Anglo-Saxon Chronicle (1095) also says, without stating the cause, that Robert was summoned to the king's court at Whitsuntide 1095, but failed to appear.

[4] This story occurs only in Orderic; other sources do not mention Gilbert of Tonbridge by name. Florence of Worcester says that there was a sworn conspiracy of Robert of Mowbray, William of Eu, and many others to place Stephen of Aumâle on the throne; and William of Malmesbury (*GR* ii. 372)

born maiden, Matilda, the daughter of Richer of Laigle,[1] who was a niece of Hugh, earl of Chester, through his sister Judith. He was the initiator of an ill-fated plot with his fellow conspirators, and sparked off open rebellion.

When four great ships called *canardes*[2] were on their way from Norway to England, Robert and his nephew Morel with their minions waylaid them and violently robbed the peaceful merchants of their goods. The merchants, spoiled of their property, went to the king in great distress and laid a complaint about their loss. Immediately the king sent a peremptory order to Robert to restore the stolen property to the merchants without delay, but Robert paid no attention to his command. The generous king asked the merchants the value of the goods they had lost, and paid them the full sum out of his own treasure-store. He then summoned Robert to his court, but he declined to come.[3]

At this the king, who knew how perverse and headstrong a man he was, mustered an army and led a strong force of knights against him. As they were approaching the bounds of Robert's domains Gilbert of Tonbridge, a rich and powerful knight, drew the king aside and, to his utter amazement, threw himself at his feet, saying, 'My lord king, pardon, I beg, the wrong I have done you, and I will recommend something that will contribute greatly to your safety.' The king at first hesitated in his astonishment, and debated with himself what he should do; but finally he graciously pardoned the suppliant and eagerly awaited the fulfilment of his promise. Gilbert said, 'Stay your foot, I beg, great king, and do not enter the wood which lies ahead of us. For enemies, fully armed, are lying in ambush there, hoping to cut your throat. We have conspired against you, and have taken a sworn oath to achieve your death.' On learning this the king halted the march, and learnt the names and number of the traitors from information that Gilbert of Tonbridge gave.[4]

After outwitting the assassins who had designed to kill the king, the armed forces passed safely by the place of the ambush and laid siege to the strongly fortified castle of Bamburgh. Since the

also speaks of a conspiracy. A letter of Anselm, written in July 1095, to Walter, cardinal-bishop of Albano, shows that an invasion of Kent was feared (Southern, *St. Anselm*, p. 131; *S. Anselmi Opera Omnia*, ed. F. S. Schmitt, iv. 77, ep. 191). Orderic omits the first stages of the campaign, which began with the siege of Robert of Mowbray's household knights in Tynemouth castle (Anglo-Saxon Chronicle, 1095; FW ii. 38), and the siege of Newcastle (*Regesta*, i, nos. 366–7).

illa munitio inexpugnabilis erat quia inaccessibilis uidebatur.' propter paludes et aquas et alia quædam itinerantibus contraria quibus ambiebatur, rex nouam munitionem[1] ad defensionem prouinciæ et coartationem hostium construxit, et militibus armis ac uictualibus impleuit. Conscii autem perfidiæ et fauctores eorum detegi uerentes conticuerunt, et metu exangues quia conatus suos nichil ualere perpenderunt, regiis cohortibus immixti eius seruitium cuius exitium optauerant prompte aggressi sunt.

Interea dum rex in armis cum agminibus suis ad bellum promptus constaret, et chiliarchos ac centuriones aliosque proceres Albionis cum subditis sibi plebibus operi nouæ munitionis indesinenter insistere compelleret.' Robertus de propugnaculis suis contrarium sibi opus mestus conspiciebat, et complices suos alta uoce nominatim compellebat, ac ut iusiurandum de proditionis societate conseruarent palam[a] commonebat. Rex autem cum
iii. 409 fidelibus suis hæc audiens ridebat et conscia reatus publicati mens conscios et participes timore et uerecundia torquebat.

Rege autem ad sua prospere remeante, et de moderamine regni cum suis amicis sollerter tractante.'[2] Robertus longæ obsidionis tedio nauseatus noctu exiluit, et de castro in castrum migrare uolens in manus inimicorum incidit. Captus itaque a satellitibus regis Robertus finem belli fecit, et fere xxx annis in uinculis uixit, ibique scelerum suorum penas luens consenuit.

Mathildis uero uxor eius quæ cum eo uix unquam leta fuerat, quia in articulo perturbationis desponsata fuerat, et inter bellicas
iii. 410 clades tribus tantum mensibus cum tremore uiri thoro incubuerat, maritali consolatione cito caruit, multisque meroribus afflicta diu gemuit. Vir eius ut dictum est in carcere uiuebat, nec ipsa eo uiuente secundum legem Dei alteri nubere legitime ualebat. Tandem permissu Paschalis papæ cui res a curiosis enucleata patuit, post multos dies Nigellus de Albineio[3] ipsam uxorem accepit, et pro fauore nobilium parentum eius aliquandiu honorifice tenuit. Verum defuncto Gisleberto de Aquila fratre eius uafer occasionem diuortii exquisiuit, eamque quia consanguinei

[a] pallam, *Caen MS.*

[1] This castle was called Malveisin, according to the Anglo-Saxon Chronicle (1095) and Florence of Worcester (FW ii. 38).

[2] After Michaelmas the king undertook a campaign against the Welsh and the rebels in the marches (FW ii. 38–9; W. E. Wightman, *The Lacy Family in England and Normandy*, p. 170).

[3] For Matilda of Laigle's marriage to Nigel of Aubigny, and his subsequent

fortress was impregnable, being virtually inaccessible on account of the marshes and pools and other obstacles to advancing forces by which it was surrounded, the king built a new castle[1] to defend the region and blockade the enemy, garrisoned it, and filled it with arms and supplies. Those who were conscious of their treachery and their adherents kept silent for fear of discovery; pale with fear because they realized that their attempt had failed, they mingled with the royal forces and readily entered the service of the man whose ruin they had planned.

The king kept the field with his army mobilized and ready for battle at any moment, and compelled his generals and captains and other nobles of England with the populace subject to them to work unremittingly on the new castle. Robert, meanwhile, mournfully watched from the battlements the progress of the castle that threatened him, loudly shouting to his fellow conspirators by name and openly inciting them to respect the sworn conspiracy that they had made. Hearing this the king and his faithful vassals smiled to themselves, while the conspirators, knowing that their guilt was made public, were tormented by fear and shame.

Finally when the king had returned home safely and was actively occupied in the business of governing the kingdom with his friends,[2] Robert, wearied by the tedium of the long siege, slipped out by night and fell into enemy hands as he attempted to travel from one castle to another. Robert's capture by the king's men put an end to the war; he lived for about thirty years in captivity and paid the penalty for his crimes as he grew old.

His wife Matilda, who had scarcely ever known any joy with him, for she had been married at the beginning of the rebellion and had shared his bed, fearfully, for three months only amid the clash of arms, was soon deprived of marital solace, and for many years led an unhappy life in great distress. Her husband being alive in prison, as I have described, she could not lawfully marry another without transgressing the law of God. Finally, long afterwards, with the permission of Pope Paschal to whom the affair was made known by men of the court, Nigel of Aubigny[3] took her as his wife, and out of respect for her noble kinsmen treated her honourably for a while. But after the death of her brother, Gilbert of Laigle, her cunning husband sought an excuse for divorce and,

fortunes see D. E. Greenway, *Charters of the Honour of Mowbray, 1107–1191* (Oxford, 1972), pp. xvii–xx.

sui coniunx fuerat repudiauit, et Gundream sororem Hugonis de
iii. 411 Gornaco uxorem duxit.[1] Morellus autem domino suo uinculis indissolubiliter iniecto de Anglia mestus aufugit,[2] multasque regiones peruagatus pauper et exosus in exilio consenuit.

Exhilaratus nacto de rebellibus trophæo rex amicos remunerauit, factiosos conuenit, diuersisque modis conuictos puniuit. Rogerium de Laceio penitus exheredatum de Anglia fugauit, et hereditatem eius Hugoni fratri eius qui fideliter iusticiæ seruierat tribuit.[3] Hugonem Scrobesburiensium comitem[4] priuatim affatus corripuit, et acceptis ab eo tribus milibus libris in amiciciam callide recepit. Sic et alios plures ingentem pecuniæ massam accipiendo castigauit: et pro nobilium reuerentia parentum qui talionem in Normannia recompensare possent uelle suum prouide dissimulauit.

Tunc Guillelmus de Auco[5] palam de nequitia conuictus fuit: quem rex luminibus priuauit, et amputatis testiculis euirauit. Hoc nimirum Hugone Cestrensium comite pertulit instigante cuius sororem habebat: sed congruam fidem ei non seruauerat, quia secus eam trinam sobolem de pelice genuerat.

iii. 412 Consules et consulares uiri nefandæ coniurationis gnari incentores erant, sed praua conspiratione detecta secum plura pertractantes erubuerant: et potentissimo eorum confracto ne similiter quaterentur contabuerant. Porro hæc subtiliter rex comperiit, et consultu sapientum huiusmodi uiris pepercit, nec eos ad iudicium palam prouocauit, ne furor in peius augmentaretur, iterumque in generale facinus contra rem publicam lacesserentur, et multa multis inde damna pernicies et luctus publice gignerentur.

[1] Nigel of Aubigny married Gundreda, daughter of Gerard of Gournay by Edith, daughter of William of Warenne, in 1118 (*EYC* ix. 200).

[2] According to the Anglo-Saxon Chronicle, Morel informed the king of the names of the chief conspirators.

[3] See W. E. Wightman, *The Lacy Family in England and Normandy*, pp. 170–1.

[4] Hugh of Montgomery is not named in any other source. Florence of Worcester says that Philip of Montgomery was imprisoned (FW ii. 39).

[5] William of Eu held extensive estates in England in 1086, and frequently subscribed royal charters. Although D. C. Douglas has claimed (Douglas, *Domesday Monachorum*, pp. 64–5), following E. Chester Waters, *Genealogical Memoirs of the Counts of Eu* (1886), that he was not the same man as William, count of Eu, he has not produced any convincing evidence for this assertion or suggested who he could have been, if not the son of Robert, count of Eu. Robert died between 1089 and 1093; his successor William was certainly dead by 1101 (*Cartulaire de l'abbaye de Saint-Michel du Tréport*, ed. P. Laffleur de Kermaingant (Paris, 1880), pp. 20–2), and probably by the summer of 1096 when, according to Guibert of Nogent, the widowed countess of Eu, Hélisende, and her son saved a Jewish boy in a pogrom in Rouen (Guibert of Nogent, *Self and Society in Medieval France*, ed. J. F. Benton (1970), pp. 135–6). That

repudiating her because she had been the wife of one of his blood-relatives, he married Gundreda,[1] the sister of Hugh of Gournay. As for Morel, after his master had been condemned to perpetual imprisonment, he fled wretchedly from England[2] and, wandering through many lands, grew old in exile, poverty-stricken and despised.

The king, jubilant at his victory over the rebels, rewarded his friends and, summoning the disturbers of the peace, punished those who were found guilty in various ways. He confiscated all the land of Roger of Lacy and banished him from England, giving his inheritance to his brother Hugh, who had remained loyal to the cause of justice.[3] He reproached Hugh, earl of Shrewsbury,[4] privately, and shrewdly took him back into his favour for three thousand pounds. He punished many others similarly, receiving huge pecuniary fines from them, and out of respect for their exalted kinsfolk who might have sought vengeance in Normandy he carefully concealed his real wishes.

At that time William of Eu[5] was publicly found guilty of treason, and the king had him blinded and castrated. This sentence was carried out at the instigation of Hugh earl of Chester, whose sister he had married; he had not remained faithful to her, but, neglecting her, had had three children by a concubine.

Earls and men of similar rank had knowingly been parties to the treacherous confederacy, but after the foul conspiracy had been unmasked they were ashamed to think of their part in it, and when the most powerful of them had been ruined they lay low for fear of a similar punishment. The king was perceptive enough to recognize this, and on the advice of his counsellors spared men of this kind. He refrained from publicly bringing them to trial for fear of fomenting their discontent still more, and goading them to another unlawful insurrection against the state, which could only cause general distress and great harm and loss to many persons.

William of Eu was William, count of Eu, is accepted by J. F. Benton (ibid., p. 135 n. 3), GEC v. 153–4; Sanders, p. 119 and n. 7; Jean le Foyer, *Exposé du droit pénal normand au xiiie siècle* (Paris, 1931), pp. 232–3, *V.C.H. Sussex*, ii. 101; ix. 1–2, 14. William of Eu was defeated by Geoffrey Baynard in a judicial duel in January 1096 (Anglo-Saxon Chronicle, 1096). All sources agree on his punishment; the story about Hugh of Chester's sister is peculiar to Orderic. The savage penalty was in line with a judicial pronouncement attributed to William the Conqueror, 'Interdico etiam ne quis occidatur aut suspendatur pro aliqua culpa, sed eruantur oculi et testiculi abscidantur' (F. Liebermann, *Gesetze der Angelsachsen* (Halle, 1903), i. 488).

24

Anno ab incarnatione Domini M°XC°IIII°[1] rebellium conatus in
Anglia compressus est.' et Guillelmus potens nullo resistente in
sui regno patris confirmatus est. Verum Normannia incolis ubique
territis et commotis misere turbata est.' et Robertus dux seditionibus[a] admodum seuientibus pro mollicie sua despicabilis effectus
est. Tunc nimia guerra inter Guillelmum Bretoliensem et Asceli-
num Goellum orta est.' cuius occasio talis est. Guillelmus frater
Goelli iuuenis miles cuidam apud Paceium iniuriam mulieri fecit,
unde conquerenti Guillelmus Bretoliensis ut iustum principem
decuit.' de contumaci adolescente legitimam rectitudinem tenuit.
Ascelinus igitur iratus est contra dominum suum.' quod publice
placitare coegerit fratrem suum. Non multo post arcem de Ibreio
ingeniosa fraude illi surripuit, et Roberto duci Normannorum
tradidit.' a quo ille ingenti pondere argenti dato redemit.[2] Post-
iii. 413 modum inter illos pro huiusmodi furto immanis simultas furuit.'
et uterque alteri nocere concupiuit.

Mense Februario[3] Ascelinus Ricardum de Monteforti et familiam Philippi regis sibi asciuit, et Guillelmum dominum suum contra se ad pugnam uenientem audacter excepit, uicit et comprehendit, et exercitum eius captis quibusdam militibus fugauit. Hac itaque uictoria elatus nimis intumuit.' dominumque suum et Rogerium de Glotis aliosque quos ceperat crudeliter cruciauit. Nam per tres menses in castro Breheruallo eos in carcere strinxit, et multociens dum nimia hiemps seuiret.' in solis camisiis aqua largiter humectatis in fenestra sullimis aulæ boreæ uel circio exposuit, donec tota uestis circa corpus uinctorum nimio gelu diriguit. Tandem intercurrentibus amicis pax inter eos facta est.' ac tali tenore Guillelmus egredi de carcere permissus est. Isabel filiam suam Goello coniugem dedit, et tria milia librarum cum equis et armis aliisque multis sumptibus erogauit, et arcem de Ibreio permisit. His ita compositis Guillelmus liber extitit.' sed pax quam pepigerant parum durauit.

Sequenti anno[4] Guillelmus inquietudine stimulante guerram

[a] seditionis, *Caen MS.*

[1] A mistake for 1095.

[2] See above, p. 198.

[3] Probably February 1091; 1090 is just possible (cf. above, p. 202, where the death of Gilbert of Laigle is put in the same week). All Le Prévost's dates for these events are too late.

[4] The latest possible date for this, since it was before the siege of Bréval (1092), is summer 1091; if William of Breteuil was captured in Lent 1091, 'sequenti anno' is not strictly true.

24

In the year of our Lord 1094[1] the rebellion in England was put down, and William's authority was strengthened in his father's kingdom as there was no further resistance. But Normandy was in a state of great unrest; its inhabitants lived wretchedly in fear and disorder, and with brutal rebellions everywhere Duke Robert became an object of contempt because of his weakness. At that time a terrible war broke out between William of Breteuil and Ascelin Goel: the cause of it was as follows. Goel's brother William, a young knight, had done an injury to a certain woman at Pacy, and when she lodged a complaint with William of Breteuil he, as a just lord should, sat in judgement on the contumacious youth. Consequently Ascelin was offended with his lord because he had dragged his brother into a public suit. Not long afterwards he took the castle of Ivry from him by a cunning trick and handed it over to Robert duke of Normandy, from whom William of Breteuil reclaimed it in return for a large sum of money.[2] Afterwards great rivalry smouldered between them on account of this act of robbery, and each waited his chance to harm the other.

In the month of February[3] Ascelin secured the support of Richard of Montfort and the household troops of King Philip, and in a bold attack intercepted his lord William, who was marching to make war on him, defeated and captured him, and after taking prisoner a number of knights scattered his army in flight. He grew bold in his presumption as a result of this victory, and cruelly tormented his lord and Roger of Glos and the other prisoners. He kept them for three months in his dungeon in the castle of Bréval, and often, in the most severe cold of winter, he would expose them to the north or north-west wind in the window of his upper hall, clad only in shirts soaked with water, until the whole garment was frozen stiff round the prisoners' bodies. At length with friends acting as mediators peace was made between them, and William was released from prison on the following terms. He gave his daughter Isabel in marriage to Goel, paid him three thousand livres as well as giving him horses and arms and many other things, and ceded the castle of Ivry to him. When the agreement had been made William was released, but the peace then established was of short duration.

In the following year[4] William, who had remained restive,

iii. 414 iterauit, et munitionem in cenobio monachorum quod Rogerius de Ibreio in honore sanctæ Mariæ construxerat militibus suis constituit.[1] Porro Goellus qui arcem tenebat copiam militum conduxit, ad cenobium quod tunc spelunca latronum proh dolor effectum fuerat[2] appropinquauit, et estiuis ardoribus circa Pentecosten torrentibus acriter impugnauit, ignem iniecit, et edacibus flammis basilicam et edes monachorum cum suppellectili sua consumpsit. Tunc Guillelmus Alis[3] et Ernaldus Popelinæ filius[4] aliique octo milites capti sunt.' qui diu Goelli crudelitatem in eius carcere nimis experti sunt. Guillelmus autem Bretoliensis fugiendo uix euasit.' ultionemque de tantis iniuriis summo nisu concupiuit. Diues erus intrinsecus nimio dolore punctus irascebatur, quod homo suus contra se tanta ui grassabatur.' et uires eius per iii annos[5] redemptionibus captorum spoliisque pagensium nimis
iii. 415 augebantur. Tandem Philippo regi Francorum dcc libras pepigit, et Roberto duci Normannorum aliisque pluribus ingentem pecuniam promisit.' si fideliter sibi adminicularentur, et hostiles copiæ subigerentur.

Igitur quadragesimali tempore rex Franciæ et dux Normanniæ Breheruallum obsederunt,[6] ibique fere duobus mensibus laborauerunt. Illuc presbiteri cum parochianis suis uexilla tulerunt.' et abbates cum hominibus suis coacti conuenerunt. Illuc Robertus Belesmensis ingeniosissimum artificem adduxit,[7] cuius ingeniosa sagacitas ad capiendam Ierusalem Christianis profecit. Hic machinas construxit, contra munimentum hostile super rotulas egit, ingentia saxa in oppidum et oppidanos proiecit, bellatores assultus dare docuit.' quibus uallum et sepes circumcingentes diruit, et culmina domorum super inhabitantes deiecit, tantisque calamitatibus aduersarios ad deditionem coegit. Vetus odium inter Robertum et Goellum diu pro antiquis reatibus inoleuerat, ideoque Robertus ut tempus ultionis opportunum uiderat.' Guillelmum

[1] William seems to have used the abbey buildings as a siege-work for the purpose of investing the castle of Ivry. There was no attempt to establish an *avouerie* here (cf. J. Yver, in *BSAN* liii (1955–6), p. 75).

[2] Cf. Jeremiah vii. 11; Matthew xxi. 13.

[3] A vassal of William of Breteuil; see above, iii. 130.

[4] Also a vassal of William of Breteuil; see Le Prévost, iii. 414 n. 3.

[5] Orderic's time sequence is very confused; three years appears to be a round number, which he uses frequently.

[6] There is no doubt that the siege of Bréval took place in 1092, earlier than May, and therefore probably, as Orderic says, in Lent. An authentic surviving charter of Philip I was dated at the siege of Bréval in 1092; and, since it was attested by Ivo bishop of Chartres and Fulbert bishop of Beauvais, it was

reopened hostilities, and turned the abbey which Roger of Ivry had built in honour of St. Mary into a fortress garrisoned with his knights.[1] So Goel, who held the castle of Ivry, hired a force of knights, led them against the abbey, which at that time, sad to tell, had been made a den of thieves,[2] attacked it fiercely about the time of Pentecost when the summer heat was scorching and, setting fire to the place, burnt down the church and monastic buildings with all that they contained. At that time William Alis[3] and Arnold son of Popeline[4] and eight other knights were taken prisoner, and for a long time they had bitter experience of Goel's cruelty in his dungeon. William of Breteuil, however, just managed to escape by taking flight, and nursed a passionate longing to revenge all his wrongs. This wealthy lord was sick at heart and full of anger, because his vassal had risen up so mightily against him and had built up his power formidably in the course of three years,[5] with the help of the ransoms of captives and plunder taken from the country people. Finally he gave seven hundred livres to King Philip of France and promised great subsidies to Robert, duke of Normandy and many others if they would give him loyal support to destroy the enemy forces.

So during Lent the king of France and duke of Normandy besieged Bréval[6] and pressed it hard for about two months. The priests, carrying banners, came with their parishioners, and the abbots were compelled to bring their men. Robert of Bellême, whose engineering skill was to help the Christians capture Jerusalem, brought a most ingenious invention to the siege.[7] He built contrivances which were wheeled against the enemy's fortress, hurling great stones at the castle and its garrison, and taught the attackers how to make assaults by which the boundary wall and palisades surrounding the castle could be smashed to pieces, the roofs of the buildings brought down on the heads of the inhabitants, and the enemy forced to surrender by such calamities. There was an old feud between Robert and Goel, which had originated long before in ancient grievances, and so when Robert saw

presumably earlier than his marriage with Bertrade in May (Prou, *Recueil des actes de Philippe I*, no. cxxviii; Fliche, *Philippe I*, p. 298).

[7] Robert of Bellême may have been a skilful siege engineer, but he was certainly not the inventor of siege-towers or catapults. Robert Guiscard made use of a siege-tower, with a catapult placed on top, at the siege of Durazzo in 1081. See William of Apulia, iv. 249–51 (Mathieu, p. 218); Anna Comnena, *Alexiad*, IV. i. 2.

Bretoliensem consilio et auxilio plus quam omnes alii pares sui adiuuerat. Goellus autem probus et callidus et predo malignus æcclesiarumque uiolator erat, nobiles et animosos parentes habebat, quorum adminiculis Breheruallum in deserta et siluestri regione castrum firmauerat, et magnanimitate subsidiisque tanta preliorum pondera strenue pertulerat. Denique ut tam magnos principes et animosos sibi summopere aduersari prospexit.' pacem
iii. 416 a domino soceroque suo petiit et gaudente Guillelmo impetrauit, eique tunc regibus et ducibus diu uexatis arcem de Ibreio honorifice reddidit.[1]

Hæc nimirum est turris famosa, ingens et munitissima.' quam Albereda uxor Radulfi Baiocensis comitis construxit, et Hugo Baiocensis episcopus frater Iohannis Rotomagensis archiepiscopi contra duces Normannorum multo tempore tenuit.[2] Ferunt quod prefata matrona postquam multo labore et sumptu sepefatam arcem perfecerat.' Lanfredum architectum cuius ingenii laus super omnes artifices qui tunc in Gallia erant transcenderat, qui post constructionem turris de Pedueriis[3] magister huius operis extiterat, ne simile opus alicubi fabricaret decollari fecerat. Denique ipsa pro eadem arce a uiro suo perempta est, quia ipsum quoque ab eadem munitione arcere conata est.

En uolubilis fortuna cotidie rotatur.' et mundi status uariabiliter agitatur. Insipiens nimis excecatur.' qui talia uidet assidue nec castigatur, sed confidit in eo qui cito precipitatur. Mortalis mortalem in mortem impellit, parique cursu sequitur illum quem in exitium premisit, meritoque sibi uel aliis suffragari posse proh dolor amittit.

iii. 417 Pace facta inter pugnaces aduersarios multis gaudentibus solus Robertus Belesmensis admodum fuit iratus, quia ipse ad consilium pacis ne impediret non fuerat inuitatus, qui precipuus presederat ad bellicos apparatus, ut atrox et proteruus hostis confunderetur superatus. Roberti enim argutiæ et uires formidandæ super omnes alios preualuerunt, et insignem sensu militiaque predonem mirandis

[1] According to Robert of Torigny (Marx, p. 290) William then held it until his death 'sicut proprium'.

[2] See above, p. 114; J. Yver in *BSAN* liii (1955–6), 67. Hugh, bishop of Bayeux, was the son of Aubrée and Count Ralph.

[3] For the castle of Pithiviers, built in the late tenth century by Heloïse of Champagne, see J.-F. Lemarignier, 'Aspects politiques des fondations de collégiales dans le royaume de France au XIe siècle', in *La vita comune del clero*

a chance of vengeance he assisted William of Breteuil with his counsel and support far above all his other peers. Goel was brave and cunning as well as being a merciless robber and despoiler of churches, and he had brave and noble kinsmen, with whose aid he had fortified the castle of Bréval in a remote, wooded region; thanks to their courage and support he had vigorously borne the brunt of many conflicts. But at last, seeing that such powerful and courageous lords were set on his defeat, he sought peace from his lord and father-in-law, secured it on terms favourable to William, and restored the castle of Ivry honourably to him after it had long been a source of trouble to kings and dukes.[1]

This is the famous castle, mighty and almost impregnable, which Aubrée, wife of Ralph count of Bayeux built, and Hugh, bishop of Bayeux and brother of John archbishop of Rouen, held for a long time against the dukes of Normandy.[2] The story goes that Aubrée had as architect Lanfred, who was then famous above all other architects in France for his skill, and after his construction of the tower of Pithiviers[3] had been appointed as master of the works; and that after she had completed the castle of Ivry with great toil and expense she had had him executed so that he could never design a castle like it anywhere else. Afterwards she herself was slain by her own husband on account of that very same castle, because she had attempted to expel him from it.

So the wheel of fortune turns each day and the condition of the world is subject to many changes. The fool is blind indeed if, constantly seeing such things he is not chastened, but puts his trust in that which crumbles in a moment. Man sends his fellow man to death, and, having driven him to his ruin, follows by the same path, deservedly, alas, losing the power to help himself or others.

There was general rejoicing when peace was made between the warring parties; Robert of Bellême alone remained disgruntled. He had not been invited to the peace negotiations for fear that he might impede them, although he had taken the principal part in directing the siege-machines which had led to the defeat of the grim and determined enemy. Robert's inventions and formidable strength had turned the scale, and by means of his marvellous contraptions he had struck terror into a bandit renowned for his

nei secoli XI e XII (Milan, 1959), pp. 22–3; J. Devaux, *Essai sur les premiers seigneurs de Pithiviers* (Orleans, 1887), pp. 15–18.

machinationibus terruerunt, quem antea reges et duces in asilo suo ludentem et inimicos multis uersutiis subsannantem a cachinnis cohibere nequiuerunt. Denique prefatus miles ut concordiam inter discordes factam cognouit.' cuneos suos protinus conuocauit, nullique fraudem sui cordis detegens festinanter remeauit, ac ad sanctum Serenicum super Robertum Geroianum ex improuiso conuolauit.[1] Municipes autem Robertum in expeditione generali cum duce putantes exierant.' et sparsim per agros securi pro libitu suo discurrebant. Cumque uafer insidiator cum copiis suis repente irrueret, et oppidum ingredi castellanosque sibi subire satageret.' Geroianus nutu Dei hostilem impetum preuenit, et munitionem cum suis celeriter intrauit, et Belesmensis quod uelle suum de capiendo castrum frustratum est doluit. Deinde ad predandum sese conuertit, unum militem occidit.' et plurima damna fecit. Sic nequitia eius et fraus detecta est.' et exinde manifesta guerra inchoata est. Geroianus autem Goisfredum de Madenia et Guillelmum de Silleio aliosque plurimos auxiliatores habuit, totamque
iii. 418 circa Alencionem per tres menses prouinciam deuastauit. Henricus Guillelmi magni regis Anglorum filius Danfrontem possidebat,[2] et super Robertum cui prefatum castellum abstulerat.' immo super fratres suos regem et ducem guerram faciebat, a quibus extorris de cespite paterno expulsus fuerat.

In initio mensis Iulii[3] Robertus Geroianus cum familia Henrici aliisque commanipularibus suis expeditionem fecit, et ingenti preda direpta Belesmenses hostes cum copiis suis insectari cepit. Cumque Geroianus auxiliarios suos ad sua properantes conduceret.' et alacriter confabulando cum notis et amicis longius iret.' subito rumor ortus est, quod occisus esset. Mox dolor ingens omnes perculit, et terribilis clamor in castro personuit. Castrenses expalluerunt.' et omne consilium ac uirile robur amiserunt. Paganus itaque de Mondublel, et Rotro de Monteforti aliique muniones castri defecerunt.' ac ut Belesmensi fauerent sicut quidam ferunt.' nemine cogente castrum sine defensore deseruerunt. Radegundis
iii. 419 autem uxor tam diris perculsa rumoribus expalluit, et in castro certitudinem rei cum suis prestolari decreuit, sed sola mulier

[1] For Robert Giroie's recovery of the castle of Saint-Céneri from Robert of Bellême in 1088 see above, p. 156.

[2] See above, p. 256. This implies that *c.* 1092 Henry was in Domfront.

[3] July 1092.

cunning and fighting qualities, who up to that time had resisted all efforts of kings and dukes to silence his guffaws as he sported in his den, mocking his enemies with great ingenuity. So when Robert of Bellême learnt that peace had been made between the rivals he quickly gathered his troops together and started for home without telling anyone of the deceit he had in mind; then, turning aside, he attacked Robert Giroie at Saint-Céneri without warning.[1] The garrison, thinking that Robert was sharing in the general military service with the duke, had left the castle and were scattered about the countryside where they pleased, believing themselves secure. When the crafty assailant suddenly appeared with his troops, and attempted to force his way into the stronghold and overpower the occupants, Robert Giroie, by God's grace, arrived ahead of the attacking force and quickly got inside the castle with his men, leaving Robert of Bellême to bewail the frustration of his plan to seize the castle. The latter then turned his attention to plundering, killed one knight, and did much damage. In this way he revealed his malevolence and treachery, with the result that open war broke out. Robert Giroie had Geoffrey of Mayenne and William of Sillé-le-Guillaume and many others as allies, and for three months he laid waste the country all round Alençon. Henry, the son of William the Great, king of England, was holding Domfront,[2] and he made war on Robert, from whom he had taken that fortress, and more particularly on his brothers the king and duke, by whom he had been exiled and driven from his paternal inheritance.

At the beginning of the month of July[3] Robert Giroie took part in an attack with Henry's household troops and his other forces, and after capturing much booty set off in pursuit of the hostile forces of Bellême. As Giroie was accompanying his auxiliary forces to their home, and was riding along cheerfully talking with his companions and friends, a rumour suddenly sprang up that he had been killed. At once there was general alarm, and a fearful uproar broke out in the castle. The garrison were beside themselves and lost all their nerve and judgement. Pain of Mondoubleau, Rotrou of Montfort-le-Rotrou, and other defenders of the castle defected and, as some say, in order to win favour with Robert of Bellême left the castle undefended. Robert Giroie's wife, Radegunde, grew pale at the terrible news, and resolved to wait with her followers in the castle for confirmation of it, but one woman

contra procaces uiros quod sibi bonum uidebatur defendere non potuit. Porro illis de castro egredientibus, et impudenter uociferantibus.' Robertus Belesmensis comperta huiusmodi re statim affuit, munitionem propugnatore uacuam reperit, facile intrauit, penitusque spoliauit, flammisque reliqua concremauit. Ingressi castrum lebetes super ignes feruentes inuenerunt carnibus plenas.' et mensas mappulis coopertas, et escas cum pane super appositas. Sagienses quoque monachi brachium sancti Senerici de æcclesia tulerunt.' et in sancti Martini cenobium reuerenter transtulerunt. Nam reliqua pars corporis eius in Castello Teoderici super Maternam fluuium seruatur.' et a Gallis celebri deuotione ueneranter excolitur.

Cumque Geroianus ab amicis letus reuerteretur, et de damno inimicis iterum inferendo frustra meditaretur, quia nulla potentia mortalium longa est.' aduersis rumoribus perceptis ex insperato confractus est. Sic nobilis miles protinus exheredatus est.' et extraneorum hospitia exul reposcere coactus est. Eodem anno Radegundis uxor eius proba femina et honesta defuncta est.' quam paulo post Guillelmus infans filius eius moriendo secutus est, quem Robertus Belesmensis obsidem habuerat, et per manus Roberti de Poileio ut dicunt ueneno extinxerat.

Geroianus itaque tot infortuniis lesus ad amicos confugit,
iii. 420 auxilium petiuit, solatioque parentum et amicorum corroboratus spem ad meliora erexit. Deinde castellum sequenti anno super Montem acutum firmauit.' acerrimamque ultionem contra Belesmensem exercuit. At ille nimis furens ad ducem concurrit, multis questibus ac promissis exciuit, atque ad obsidendum Montem acutum cum exercitu Normanniæ adduxit. Tunc Gaufredus Madeniensis aliique optimates Cenomannorum ducem conuenerunt, eique pro Geroiano cognato scilicet suo blande supplicauerunt, a quo protinus quia flexibilis erat ad misericordiam impetrauerunt, ut castrum quod nuper constructum fuerat dirueretur,[1] eique tota hereditas eius cum pace restitueretur. Quod et ita factum est.

Sicut post nimiam tempestatem serenitas redit, hominesque lætificat.' sic diuina iusticia reos plerumque uerberat, et clemens bonitas afflictos mitigat et penitentes iustificat, purgatosque pie remunerat. Geroianus itaque multis calamitatibus eruditus Deo

[1] An earlier castle built at Montaigu (probably Saint-Pierre-des-Nids) by Robert's uncle, William Giroie, had been pulled down at the insistence of the lord of Bellême (see above, ii. 26–8).

could not uphold what she believed to be right against determined men. Then, as they were leaving the castle with disorderly shouts, Robert of Bellême got wind of the matter and was on the spot at once. He found the fortress undefended, entered without resistance and sacked the place, burning everything that remained. Entering the castle the troops found cauldrons full of meat cooking over the fires, tables covered with cloths, and dishes of food with bread set out on them. The monks of Séez took the arm of St. Céneri from the church, and reverently translated it to the abbey of St. Martin. The remainder of the body was already treasured in Château-Thierry on the river Marne, and was venerated by the French with great devotion.

When Giroie returned from his friends in good spirits, planning how to inflict further harm on his enemies—vainly in the end, for no human power is long-enduring—he was shattered by the disastrous news that he heard so suddenly. So at one blow the noble knight was utterly disinherited and forced to live as an exile in the homes of strangers. In the same year that upright and courageous woman, his wife Radegunde, died, and a little later his young son followed her in death. Robert of Bellême was holding him as a hostage, and is said to have poisoned him by the hand of Robert of Poillé.

Heart-broken by so many disasters, Giroie took refuge with friends, sought help from them and then, strengthened by the support of his kinsmen and friends, planned hopefully for the future. In the following year he built a castle above Montaigu and wreaked fierce vengeance on Robert of Bellême. The latter however in great anger turned to the duke for help, stirred him to action with repeated complaints and promises, and induced him to come with the army of Normandy to invest Montaigu. Then Geoffrey of Mayenne and the other magnates of Maine met the duke, quietly pleaded with him for Giroie who was his kinsman, and soon secured from him—for he was very pliable—pardon on these terms: the castle, which had just been built was to be pulled down,[1] and Giroie's whole inheritance was to be restored in peace; and this is what was done.

Just as calm returns after great storms and gladdens the hearts of men, so divine justice often chastises sinners, and merciful goodness tempers their punishments, pardons the penitent, and gently rewards them when they have been purified. So Giroie,

gratias egit.' cuius ope post multos agones pristinum honorem recuperauit, et fere xxx annis postmodum inter læta uel tristia uitæ cursum peregit. Feliciam uero Guarnerii de Coneraia[1] filiam coniugem accepit.' quæ tres filios totidemque filias peperit, Guillelmum scilicet et Robertum ac Mathæum, Agatham, Damatam et Auelinam.

iii. 421 Belesmensis munio nouum castellum totis nisibus destruere studuit, et pagenses de omni potestate sua et uicinitate ad angariam ceptæ deiectionis compulit. Et quia homines sancti Ebrulfi ad dissipationem castri non affuerunt, quia ditioni eius subdi minime debuerunt, uehementer contra monachos intumuit, et per unum annum ingentia damna eis intulit. Homines sancti patris Ebrulfi ad suorum opera castrorum uiolenter cogebat, diffugientium uero predas diripiebat.' et ipsum cenobium se destructurum crudeliter minabatur, nisi omnino sibi ut domino in omnibus manciparentur. Denique in tantum creuit eius uesania.' ut pene omnes æcclesiasticæ possessiones in uicinio eius depopularentur insolentia. Vnde monachi claustrales graui artati sunt penuria, et Rogerius abbas compulsus est Guillelmi regis subsidium deposcere in Anglia, ad usus egenorum quibus tiranni depopulatio alimenta sustulerat necessaria. Aliis quoque Dei famulis qui sub eo uel in eius uicinio crudeliter imminebat, eosque pluribus damnis et afflictionibus absque misericordia sepe contristabat. Hoc Sagienses et Troarnenses, hoc etiam attestantur Cenomannenses.'[2] qui per eius seuitiam et iniustas exactiones frequenter ira tristiciaque expalluere lugentes.[3]

Sagiense quoque episcopium Robertus contra ius et fas comprimebat, et Guillelmo Belesmensi auo eius a Ricardo duce datum
iii. 422 asserebat.' et multis oppressionibus ac detrimentis æcclesiasticas possessiones ualde aggrauabat.[4] Vnde uenerandus Serlo episcopus

[1] Felicia was the daughter of Avejot, lord of Connerré (Latouche, *Maine*, p. 41 n. 1); she occurs in a charter of 1100 as Robert's wife (*Cartulaire de Saint-Vincent-du-Mans*, ed. S. Menjot d'Elbenne (Mamers/Le Mans, 1913), no. 139, p. 89).

[2] There is some evidence of Robert providing for his men out of the property of Troarn; conditions appear to have been so bad in 1106 that the abbot, Arnulf, in sickness and despair, asked for Anselm's advice on resigning his charge. But he made some liberal gifts to other churches, including Saint-Vincent-du-Mans (R. N. Sauvage, *L'abbaye de Saint-Martin de Troarn* (Mém. Soc. Ant. Norm. 1911), pp. 22–3; *S. Anselmi Opera Omnia*, ed. F. S. Schmitt (Edinburgh, 1946–61), v. 370–2 (ep. 425)).

[3] Robert's claims to rights in church lands probably resulted from an attempt to usurp the general protection that Duke William had exercised over the monasteries of the duchy and a confusion of temporal and spiritual rights; there

schooled by much suffering, gave thanks to God, by whose aid he had recovered his former honor after many struggles, and for some thirty years lived a life that had its share of joys and sorrows. He took to wife Felicia the daughter of Garner of Connerré,[1] who bore him three sons and as many daughters: William, Robert, and Matthew; Agatha, Damata, and Aveline.

The lord of Bellême set about the destruction of the new castle with all his resources, and compelled all the peasants on his own and his neighbours' lands to forced labour to pull it down. Because the men of Saint-Évroul did not come to help in pulling down the castle, since they were in no way subject to his rule, he nursed bitter hatred for the monks, and for a whole year inflicted injuries on them. He compelled the men of the holy father St. Évroul by force to help in the work on his own castles, seizing the possessions of any who defaulted, and even cruelly threatened to destroy the abbey itself unless they would be subject to him in all things as their lord. Finally his madness reached such a pitch that almost all the church lands in his neighbourhood were laid waste through his excesses. As a result the monks suffered acutely from want, and Abbot Roger was obliged to seek for supplies from King William in England for the use of the needy who had lost all their means of sustenance through the tyrant's ravages. He ill-used other communities of God's servants also, who were under his rule or in his neighbourhood, and often distressed them through his merciless injuries and persecutions. To this the monks of Séez and Troarn and even Le Mans[2] bear witness, for through his cruelties and unjust exactions they often had cause to fear and lament in sorrow and anger.[3]

Robert also oppressed the bishopric of Séez in a way contrary to right and justice; alleging that it had been given to his ancestor William of Bellême by Duke Richard he burdened all the lands of the church with repeated oppressions and injuries.[4] For this the venerable bishop, Serlo, excommunicated him, and by his episcopal

is no proof that he was trying to introduce the non-Norman practice of 'avouerie' (*advocatus*) into Norman lands. See J. Yver, 'Autour de l'absence de l'avouerie en Normandie', in *BSAN* lvii (1965), 217.

[4] Robert of Bellême asserted his claims so successfully that in 1101 Duke Robert surrendered his rights in the bishopric of Séez to him (Le Prévost, iv. 104); this was presumably one of the acts that provoked the letter of Paschal II to the duke in 1102, complaining of his injuries to the Church in the words, 'tutela enim et patrocinia ecclesiarum secularibus potestatibus commissa sunt' (*PUF* no. 4, pp. 56–8).

eum excommunicauit, et pontificali rigore totam terram eius interdixit.' ne diuinum ibidem officium celebraretur, nec mortuorum corpora humarentur. Robertus autem qui pro duricia iure Talauacius uocabatur,[1] induratus ut Pharao,[2] pontificalibus plagis siue unguentis non emolliebatur, sed ad omne nefas cotidie detestabiliter augmentabatur. Ipse sicut Ismahel contra omnes uicinos manus armatas atrociter erigebat.' monachos et clericos et inerme uulgus seua tirannide terrebat, et damnis contumeliisque frequenter illatis miserabiliter affligebat. Temporibus illis principalis censura super illum preualere nequibat, quem secularis potentia nimium extollebat, et malorum immanitas morum intolerabilem familiaribus amicis et clientibus faciebat. Homines priuatione oculorum et amputatione pedum manuumue deformare paruipendebat, sed inauditorum commentatione suppliciorum in torquendis miseris more Siculi Falaris tripudiabat. Quos in carcere pro reatu aliquo stringebat, Nerone seu Decio uel Datiano seuior inedicibiliter cruciabat, et inde iocos cum parasitis suis et cachinnos iactabundus exercebat.[3] Tormentorum quæ uinctis inferebat delectatione gloriabatur, hominumque detractione pro penarum nimietate crudelis lætabatur.' magisque affectabat supplicia miseris inferre, quam per redemptionem captiuorum pecunias augere. Plerumque de uinculis eius auxi-
iii. 423 liante Deo multi euaserunt, suasque postmodum iniurias fortiter ulti sunt.' pro quibus si humana ratione et clementia tactus uoluisset, ingentem censum et honorifica percipere seruicia potuisset. Terribilis multis multos metuebat, et quia plures conscientia mordaci stimulante suspectos habebat, nocte dieque meticulosus in erumnis ubique laborabat, sibique uix aliquem fidum credebat. Miles quidem magnus erat in armis et acerrimus, ingenio et eloquentia cum fortitudine pollebat, sed nimio tumore et crudelitate omnia polluebat, scelerumque nefaria congerie dona sibi diuinitus prestita obscurabat. Ob insolentiam et cupiditatem plurima contra collimitaneos prelia cepit, sed sepe uictus cum damno et dedecore aufugit. Hoc bene nouerunt Corbonienses et

[1] A 'talvas' was a kind of shield; the nickname was first applied to Mabel of Bellême's father William, who was never called 'of Bellême', probably because his brother Ivo, bishop of Séez, held Bellême. Later 'Talvas' became an honorific suffix among his descendants (see G. H. White, 'The first house of Bellême', in *TRHS* 4th ser. xxii (1940), 82–3).

[2] Exodus vii. 12 and *passim*.

[3] William of Malmesbury also denounced the cruelty of Robert of Bellême (*GR* ii. 475–6). Phalaris, tyrant of Agrigentum, was notorious for the cruelty of

authority placed all his lands under an interdict so that the divine office could not be celebrated, nor the bodies of the dead buried, in them. Robert, however, who for his hardness was justly called Talvas,[1] hardened his heart like Pharaoh[2] and was not softened by either the bishop's blows or his balm, but daily increased in his abominable proclivity to evil. Like Ishmael he mercilessly sent out his armed bands against all his neighbours and terrorized monks, clerks, and the defenceless populace by his fierce tyranny, reducing them to the verge of ruin by his continual injuries and injustices. In those days no ducal censure could touch him, for he was exceedingly powerful and the perversion of his evil character made him intolerable even to his closest friends and dependants. He thought nothing of mutilating men by putting out their eyes and cutting off their hands or feet, and took delight in devising unheard-of punishments for torturing unhappy wretches, after the fashion of Phalaris the Sicilian. He tormented those who were thrown into his dungeons for any offence in unspeakable ways, more cruelly even than Nero or Decius or Domitian, boasting of what he had done as he laughed and joked with his sycophants.[3] He took pride in his enjoyment of the torments of his prisoners, and laughed at men's condemnation of the excessive cruelty of his punishments; he greatly preferred inflicting torture on his wretched captives to increasing his wealth with their ransoms. By God's help many men escaped from his fetters at different times and later avenged their wrongs to the full; whereas if he had allowed humanity and mercy to touch his heart he might instead have received from them great revenues and honourable services. Terrible to many, he feared many; and because he knew in his heart that he had cause to regard most men as potential enemies he went in fear by night and day, never out of danger, and was convinced that scarcely anyone was loyal to him. He was a renowned knight, of great enterprise in the field, and was endowed with quick wits and a ready tongue as well as courage; but everything was marred by his excessive pride and cruelty, and he hid the talents with which Heaven had endowed him under a sombre mass of evil deeds. He engaged in many wars against his neighbours as a result of his arrogance and ambition, but was often defeated and put to flight with loss and dishonour. This is well known to the

his punishments (cf. Pliny, *Naturalis Historia*, xxiv. 89); Nero, Decius, and Domitian persecuted Christians.

Cenomannenses, Normanni affines proximique Oximenses, qui tiranno fugiente facti sunt uictores. Hoc feliciter experti sunt Goisfredus Moritoniæ comes et Rotro filius eius,[1] Helias quoque Cenomannensis aliique affines.' quibus ipse semper infestus detrimenta moliebatur, sed iudicante Deo duriora iure patiebatur. Triginta quatuor castella munitissima possidebat, multisque milibus hominum dominatu preeminebat.' Hugo tamen de Nonanto pauper oppidanus et uicinus multis annis ei restitit, et ingentia damna iniuriasque frequenter intulit.

Agnetem filiam Guidonis Pontiui comitis uxorem habuit, quæ
Guillelmum Talauantium totius honoris eius heredem peperit.
Seuus maritus generosam coniugem non ut decuit propter dile-
iii. 424 ctam sobolem honorauit, immo multis eam afflictionibus ut odibi-
lem ancillam[2] contristauit, quin etiam multo tempore in arce
Belesmensi uelut latronem custodiæ mancipauit. Tandem auxilio
industriaque fidelis cubicularii erepta de carcere clanculo exiuit.'
et ad Hadalam Carnotensem comitissam confugit, et inde nunquam
ad tirannum reditura in Pontiuum secessit.

Diris conatibus et tergiuersationibus prefati lanionis Neustria
sepe turbata est.' et Cenomannica regio uicinitasque circumiacens
predis ac cedibus incendiisque feraliter profligata est. Episcopatus
et cenobia super illo ad Dominum Sabaoth clamauerunt, in
quorum terris castella uiolenter consita sunt.' et possessiones
sanctorum temeraria inuasione eius diminutæ uel spoliatæ sunt.
Vticenses uero monachi post multa damna et labores metusque
guerram eius ferre non potuerunt, unde coacti dicam per totam
terram suam quæ hactenus a malis consuetudinibus libera fuerat
fecerunt, et lx libras cenomannensium de censu pagensium
iii. 425 Roberto dederunt, ne monasterium et colonos eius ulterius
uexaret, sed in pace Dei cultores legali theusebia[a] tripudiare
sineret. Alii quoque monachi et inermes clerici simili precio se
redemerunt, datisque magnis sumptibus frendentem tirannum
sibi placauerunt, quia tunc ingentem sæuitiam eius reges seu duces
principali censura corrigere ad quietem æcclesiarum nequiuerunt.

[a] teusebia, *Caen MS.*

---

[1] There is an account of Rotrou's harsh imprisonment in the *Vita beati Bernardi Tironensis* of Geoffrey Grossus (Migne, *PL* clxxii. 1413–16).

[2] A similar comparison was made by Paschal II, when he accused Robert Curthose of treating the Church not as a spouse but as a slave (*PUF* no. 4, p. 57).

men of the Corbonnais and Maine, to his Norman neighbours and to the men of Exmes who were nearest of all, for they triumphed over the tyrant and put him to flight. Geoffrey of Mortagne and Rotrou his son[1] experienced this to their profit, as did Helias and his other neighbours in Maine; for though he was their constant enemy and repeatedly wronged them, by God's will he himself suffered an even harsher judgement. He held thirty-four very strong castles and ruled over many thousands of men; yet his neighbour Hugh of Nonant, a poor castellan, held out against him for many years and often caused him to suffer great harm and loss.

He had as his wife Agnes, the daughter of Guy count of Ponthieu, who bore him William Talvas, the heir of all his honors. The harsh husband did not honour his highly-born wife as he should have done because of this beloved child, but instead made her suffer many afflictions as if she had been a hateful slave-girl,[2] and even kept her imprisoned like a thief in the castle of Bellême for a long time. But in the end she was saved by the help and ingenuity of a faithful chamberlain, escaped in secret from imprisonment, and fled to Adela countess of Chartres. From there she betook herself to Ponthieu, never again to return to the tyrant.

Normandy was often disturbed by the foul plots and changes of allegiance of this butcher, while the county of Maine and all the neighbourhood around was mercilessly ravaged by his looting, slaying, and burning. Pleas against him were raised to the Lord of Hosts by the episcopal clergy and monasteries, in whose lands he had forcibly established his castles, diminishing or plundering the possessions of the saints by his reckless usurpations. The monks of Saint-Évroul, after enduring many injuries and difficulties, could no longer bear the terror of his raids; so under duress they raised a tallage on all their estates, which had previously been exempt from evil customs, and gave Robert sixty livres of the money of Maine from the peasants' dues. In return he was not to disturb the monastery or its peasants in future, but would allow the servants of God to perform their pious offices in peace. Other monks and defenceless clerks ransomed themselves with a similar payment and placated the bloodthirsty tyrant by giving large sums of money; for at that time kings and dukes were unable to restrain his ferocity and secure the peace of the Church by any authority of theirs.

25

In diebus illis antiqui optimates qui sub Roberto duce uel filio eius Guillelmo rege militauerunt.' humanæ conditionis more hominem exuerunt. Rogerius de Montegomerici apud Scrobesburiam monachile scema deuotus suscepit, et in basilica sancti Petri apostoli quam[a] extra urbem inter duo flumina Meolam et Sabrinam condidit, tribus diebus in colloquiis diuinis et oratione inter seruos Dei permansit. Tandem vi° kal' Augusti mortuus est,[1] et in basilica sancti Petri sepultus est. Post quem Hugo de Monte Gomerici filius eius comes in Anglia factus est.' et Robertus de Belismo totum honorem eius in Normannia nactus est. Porro Rogerius Pictauinus et Arnulfus, Philippus et Ebrardus de paterna hereditate nichil habuerunt.' quia duo priores ut dictum est, Robertus et Hugo citra mare et ultra totum patris ius optinuerunt. Rogerius tamen et Arnulfus qui militiæ probitatumque titulis inter contubernales ualuerunt, consilio patris suaque procura-
iii. 426 tione generosas coniuges acceperunt.' et ambo comites potentia diuitiisque pollentes aliquandiu floruerunt, sed ante mortem pro perfidia sua honores adeptos perdiderunt. Philippus autem et E[brardus] litterarum studio trad[iti in] puericia.' labe[ntis] uitæ cursum sa[te]gerunt uaria.[b] Philippus enim cum Roberto duce peregre profectus est.' et Antiochiæ mortuus est. Ebrardus uero qui de Adelaide comitissa natus est.' in capella Henrici regis clericali officio inter mediocres functus est.

Rogerius quoque de Bellomonte sapiens et modestus heros qui dominis suis ducibus Normanniæ fidelis semper extitit.' in cenobio Pratellensi post emeritæ militiæ tempus colla monachatui submisit. Illud enim Vnfredus de Vetulis pater eius in proprio fundo fundauerat.' et ipse post patris obitum multis possessionibus et ornamentis ditauerat. Ibi Robertus de Bellomonte filius Vnfredi
iii. 427 quem Rogerius de Clara occiderat tumulatus quiescit.' et ipse Rogerius iam senex frater eius post aliquot annos conuersionis suæ bono fine quieuit.[2] Filios uero suos Robertum et Henricum honoris sui sensatos heredes dereliquit, quos in hoc seculo gratia Dei multum sullimauit. Amicicia siquidem et familiaritate regum comitumque potentum illustrati sunt.' generosis et fecundis coniugibus et insigni prole utriusque sexus multisque diuitiis cum

[a] quod, *Caen MS.* [b] Philippus . . . uaria *inserted in the margin; the edge is cut off and some letters are missing*

[1] In 1094; see above, iii. 138. For his sons see J. F. A. Mason in *TRHS* 5th ser. xiii (1963), 1–28.

[2] He died on 3 December; the year is uncertain (GEC vii. 522–3).

25

In those times the old magnates who had fought under Duke Robert and his son William died, as all humans must. Roger of Montgomery piously put on the monastic habit at Shrewsbury, and lived for three days devoted to spiritual discourse and prayer among the servants of God in the church of St. Peter the apostle, which he had founded outside the town between the two rivers Meole and Severn. Finally on 27 July he died[1] and was buried in the church of St. Peter. After his death his son Hugh of Montgomery became an earl in England and Robert of Bellême acquired his whole honor in Normandy. Roger of Poitou, Arnulf, Philip, and Evrard had no share in the paternal inheritance because the two eldest received the whole of it, as I said, Robert on one side of the Channel and Hugh on the other. However Roger and Arnulf, who were much regarded among their companions for their knightly skill and reputation for valour, married highly-born wives through their father's advice and their own efforts. Both throve for a while with comital rank, enjoying power and wealth, but before their deaths they lost by their treachery the honors they had won. Philip and Evrard on the other hand were educated in letters from boyhood, and experienced different fates in the course of this transient life. Philip set out with Duke Robert on crusade and died at Antioch; Evrard, who was the son of the Countess Adelais, served as a clerk among the humbler officers in King Henry's chapel.

Then Roger of Beaumont, a wise and moderate lord who had always been faithful to his lords the dukes of Normandy, bowed his neck to monastic discipline in the monastery of Préaux when he was a veteran knight. His father Humphrey of Vieilles had founded this abbey on his own land, and he himself had enriched it with many lands and ornaments after his father's death. There Robert of Beaumont, son of Humphrey, who was killed by Roger of Clères, lies buried; and his brother Roger in his old age made a good end there a few years after his conversion to monastic life.[2] He left his sons Robert and Henry as his designated heirs, and God by his grace has raised them to great dignity in this world. They have been marked out by the friendship and trust of kings and powerful counts, and have been blessed with noble and fruitful wives and worthy children of both sexes, and with great wealth

honoribus ditati sunt. Robertus enim comitatum de Mellento in pago Vilcassino hereditario iure post Hugonem Adelinæ matris suæ fratrem possedit, et in Anglia comitatum Legrecestræ cum aliis pluribus et gazis Henrici regis dono feliciter optinuit.[1] Henricus autem frater eius strenuitate sua et legalitate comitatum de
iii. 428 Guarewico promeruit,[2] et elegantem Margaritam Goisfredi Moritoniæ[3] comitis filiam coniugem accepit.' cuius religionis et honestatis fama celebris habetur, et longe lateque in uicinis regionibus inter precipuas mulieres diuulgatur. Hæc marito suo Rogerium et Robertum de Nouoburgo[4] peperit.' quorum sullimitas in Anglia et Neustria tempore Henrici regis perspicue fulsit. Prefati consules Pratellense monasterium iure dilexerunt, et multis opibus locupletatum honorauerunt, quod antecessores eorum in optimo loco prope portum maris et Pontem Aldemari ubi rapide pontum Risela petit construxerunt. Ibi monachi ad laudem et cultum omnipotentis Dei diuinitus conuocati sunt.' et a religiosis ac sapientibus pedagogis regulari disciplina pie instituti sunt.

iii. 429 Primus abbas Pratellensis æcclesiæ[5] quis quantusue fuerit, epitaphium quod in claustro super tumulum eius nitescit.' ad hostium basilicæ in australi climate sic intuentibus ostendit.

Ecce sub hac tumba tegitur sine felle columba,
Abbas Anfridus uir probus atque pius.
Peruigil implebat quod lex diuina iubebat.'
Eius consilium quæ fuit et studium.
Debilibus, dubiis, cecis, claudis, peregrinis.'
Tectum, pes, oculus, consilium, baculus.
Triginta Phebus dum decidit iste diebus
Torruerat pisces, cui Deus esto quies.

Ricardus autem de Crumellis[a] moderno tempore idem monasterium rexit.' quem Robertus Tumbaleniensis ad monachatum Baiocis in æcclesia sancti Vigoris suscepit. Verum Odone presule qui noui cenobii fundator erat in carcere Guillelmi regis gemente, et Roberto sophista non Montem sancti Michahelis de periculo
iii. 430 maris unde cenobita erat repetente, sed potius in Latias partes ut supra retuli migrante, noua constructio et imperfecta celeriter

[a] *An error for* Furnellis

[1] Leicester was first mortgaged to him by Ivo of Grandmesnil *c.* 1102. For his career see GEC vii. 524–6; Depoin, *Cartulaire de Pontoise*, pp. 311–13; G. H. White in *Genealogist*, N.S. xxxvi. 173–8.

[2] For his career and family see GEC xii (2). 357–60 and Appendix A.

[3] Margaret was a daughter of Geoffrey count of Perche and Mortagne and a sister of Rotrou of Mortagne.

and honors. Robert received the county of Meulan in the Vexin by hereditary right after Hugh, the brother of his mother Adeline; and as he prospered he was given the county of Leicester and many other estates and riches in England by King Henry.[1] His brother Henry, thanks to his courage and his lawful rights, acquired the county of Warwick[2] and received as his wife the beautiful Margaret, daughter of Geoffrey count of Mortagne,[3] who is renowned for her piety and virtue and is praised far and wide in these parts as one of the most distinguished of women. She bore her husband Roger and Robert of Neubourg,[4] whose high reputation was outstanding in England and Normandy in the time of King Henry. These earls and counts loved the abbey of Préaux as was right, and enriched it bountifully with great wealth. Their ancestors had founded it on an excellent site near to the seaport and Pont-Audemer, where the river Risle flows swiftly to join the sea. There by divine will monks were brought together for the praise and worship of almighty God, and were duly established under a monastic rule by pious and learned teachers.

The name and character of the first abbot of Préaux[5] are proclaimed to all who read it by the epitaph engraved over his tomb in the cloister, by the south door of the church:

Beneath this tomb, dove without spot, lies Ansfrid,
An upright, virtuous abbot; day and night
Fulfilling all God's holy law commands
He made that law his study and pursuit.
Staff to the weak he was; to the doubtful, counsel;
Eyes to the blind, foot to the lame, and pilgrim's roof.
For thirty days the sun had burnt in Pisces
When Ansfrid died; God grant him perfect peace.

In recent times Préaux has been governed by Richard of Fourneaux, whom Robert of Tombelaine received as a monk in the church of St. Vigor at Bayeux. But while Bishop Odo, the founder of the new cell, languished in King William's prison and the learned Robert, instead of returning to Mont Saint-Michel in peril of the sea where he had been a monk, travelled to Italy as I have described above, the new and still unfinished building was quickly pulled down and the community of the faithful who had

[4] Roger became earl of Warwick; Robert succeeded to his father's lands in Normandy; there were three other sons and two daughters.

[5] Ansfrid, abbot of Préaux, died in 1078.

dissipata est: et concio fidelium quæ illuc confluxerat de diuersis locis rectore carens cito dispersa est.[1] Ricardus itaque unus ex illis diuinis in litteris eruditissimus fuit, et in tanta deuastatione teneri gregis religiosos sophistas quesiuit: in quorum contubernio dogmatibus almis inherens reuerenter habitauit.

Ea nempe tempestate in Normannia florebant Anselmus Beccensis, Gerbertus Fontanellensis, Guntardus Gemmeticensis, aliique plures in templo Dei lucentes lucernæ, a quibus insigniter illustratus salubris hauriebat ubertatem doctrinæ. Defuncto autem Goisfredo abbate[2] Ricardus ad regimen Pratellensis abbatiæ electus est: quod Roberti ducis et Henrici regis tempore fere xxiiii annis tenuit ibique defunctus est. Hic in diuinis codicibus apprime studuit, in uia Dei per antiquorum uestigia patrum psallens ab adolescentia cucurrit, famelicisque pueris enigmaticum panem in domo Dei benigniter fregit, manumque tendentibus alacriter et ubertim distribuit, torpentibus quoque et recusantibus ut manderent uim intulit. Commentarium super Genesim Mauricio sancti Launomari Blesensium eruditissimo abbati edidit, et aliud domno Adelelmo eruditissimo presbitero conscripsit: Flauiacensi[3] quidem
iii. 431 monacho qui cum Fiscannensibus sanctæ Trinitati reuerenter militans consenuit. Egregio Cluniacensium abbati Poncio eximiam explanationem super Parabolas Salomonis contexuit: aliisque uenerabilibus personis Æcclesiasten et Cantica Canticorum ac Deuteronomium luculenter exposuit, multosque tractatus super obscura prophetarum problemata allegorice seu tropologice disseruit.[4]

Nicholaus leuita et abbas sancti presulis Audoeni tercii Ricardi ducis Normannorum filius fuit, multaque benignitate et caritate aliisque uirtutibus floruit, et in æcclesia Dei usque ad quartum annum post mortem Guillelmi regis consobrini sui specialiter effulsit. Hic compellente Roberto duce patruo suo puer monachus in cenobio Fiscannensi sub Iohanne abbate factus est: sed post aliquot annos a Guillelmo duce ad prefatæ regimen abbatiæ in adolescentia assumptus est. In regimine uero positus subiectis intus exteriusque magis prodesse quam preesse studuit, et postquam adorato in Ierusalem sepulchro Domini remeauit, quinquagesimo

[1] See above, pp. 116–18.

[2] Abbot of Préaux, 1096–1101 (*GC* xi. 838).

[3] Saint-Germer-de-Fly (or Flaix).

[4] For a description of Richard's works, which are unpublished, see *Histoire littéraire de la France* (Paris, 1733–1949), xi. 169–76; B. Smalley, 'Some

flocked there from different places, having no superior, was soon scattered.[1] Richard, who was one of their number, was deeply learned in sacred studies, and when the young community was broken up he sought out men of piety and learning and settled in their company, reverently studying holy doctrine.

At that time Anselm of Bec, Gerbert of Saint-Wandrille, and Gontard of Jumièges flourished in Normandy, as well as many others who shone like lanterns in the temple of God, and thanks to their distinguished teaching he gained a rich store of sacred learning. When Abbot Geoffrey[2] died Richard was elected abbot of Préaux; he ruled the abbey for about twenty-four years in the time of Duke Robert and King Henry and died there. He made a particular study of Holy Scripture, and from the time of his adolescence had travelled swiftly along the way of God in the footsteps of the fathers of old, singing psalms. He broke the enigmatical bread for the hungry children in the house of the Lord with a blessing, distributing it gladly and bountifully to all who held out their hands, compelling those who were either indifferent or reluctant to eat. He dedicated a Commentary on Genesis to Maurice, the learned abbot of Saint-Laumer of Blois, and another to a learned priest, Athelelm, who was a monk of Fly[3] but in his old age followed the monastic way of life with the monks of Holy Trinity, Fécamp. He composed a remarkable Commentary on the Proverbs of Solomon for Pontius, the renowned abbot of Cluny, wrote clear expositions of Ecclesiastes, the Song of Songs, and Deuteronomy for other reverend persons, and in many treatises discussed the difficult passages of the prophets allegorically or figuratively.[4]

Nicholas, priest and abbot of Saint-Ouen, was a son of Richard III, duke of Normandy; he was distinguished by great kindness and charity and other virtues and was a shining light in the Church of God until the fourth year after the death of King William, his cousin. He was compelled by his uncle, Duke Robert, to become an oblate monk in the abbey of Fécamp under Abbot John; but some years later, while still an adolescent, he was made abbot of Saint-Ouen by Duke William. Placed in a position of authority, his constant care was to secure the good of his subjects both internally and externally rather than to dominate them; and after he returned from a pilgrimage to worship at the Holy Sepulchre in

thirteenth-century commentaries on the Sapiential Books', in *Dominican Studies*, ii (1949), 318–20.

sexto regiminis sui anno[1] iiii° kalendas Martii obiit, et in æcclesia sancti Petri apostoli quam ipse a fundamentis ceperat, ante altare sanctæ Dei genitricis Mariæ sepultus esse melius in resurrectione
iii. 432 expectat. Super ipsum structura de lignis pulchre depictis condita nitescit, cuius in culmine Mauricius cenobita huiusmodi epitaphium litteris aureis eleganter inseruit.

Hic amor et pietas, monachorum flos et honestas,
Deponens artus Domino uiuit Nicholaus.
Rexit amore gregem, quam cernis condidit edem,
Hæc lux occubuit, dum pisces Phebus adurit.

Helgotus Cadomensis prior eruditione et uirtutum exercitio pollens uenerabili Nicholao subrogatus est.' et gubernaculo abbatiæ sancti Audoeni fere xx annis potitus est.' cuius tempore conuentus eiusdem æcclesiæ numero et religione laudabiliter auctus est. Tunc Gislebertus quidam laicus de Ierusalem Rotomagum uenit, et a prefato patre ad monachatum susceptus æcclesiæ suæ digniter profecit. Opus enim basilicæ quod iamdudum pro admiranda magnitudine intermissum fuerat assumpsit, ibique pecuniam
iii. 433 Alberadæ Grossæ dominæ suæ quæ in uia Dei moriens thesaurum ei suum commendauerat largiter distraxit, et inde aliorum quoque fidelium subsidiis adiutus insigne opus perficere sategit. Helgoto autem abbate xii° kalendas Decembris defuncto,[2] et ante altare sancti Stephani prothomartiris sepulto, quod in uestibulo in aquilonali plaga est.' Guillelmus Balotensis[a] eiusdem æcclesiæ a puericia monachus in ordine regiminis per annos fere xiiii subsecutus est. Ipsius quidem tempore basilica ingens olim a Nicholao cepta uix in annis lx[3] consummata est.' et a Goisfredo archiepiscopo cum aliis pluribus prelatis et subditis xvi° kalendas Nouembris dedicata est.[4]

Eodem anno Guillelmus abbas obiit, et Ragemfredus eiusdem monachus æcclesiæ regimen suscepit, cuius tempore claustrum cum aliis monachorum officinis consummatum specialiter emicuit.

[a] Calotensis, *Caen MS.*

---

[1] The date was 27 February (not 26) because 1092 was a leap-year. In his interpolations in William of Jumièges (Marx, p. 153), Orderic stated that Nicholas was abbot for about fifty years during the rule of William the Conqueror, and subsequently died in February 1092, in the time of Duke Robert II. This could just be reconciled with the statement that he died in the fifty-sixth year of his rule, if we allow that the years after the Conqueror's death were not included in his earlier rough figure, and that Nicholas became abbot of Saint-Ouen about 1036 or 1037 and died in 1092.

[2] The date 1112 given for his death in *GC* xi. 144 rests on no clear evidence. Apart from this episode, the last datable reference to him is in a letter of St.

Jerusalem he died on 27 February in the fifty-sixth year of his rule.[1] Buried before the altar of Mary, the blessed Mother of God, in the church of St. Peter the apostle, which he had completely rebuilt, he waits for a better life in the resurrection. A canopy of wood, beautifully painted in glowing colours, has been raised over his tomb, and on the top of it the monk Maurice inscribed this epitaph exquisitely in letters of gold:

Here, loved and mourned, of monks the flower and glory,
Nicholas laid his bones, to live with God.
By love he ruled his flock, he built this temple;
Light left him when the sun through Pisces burnt.

Helgot, prior of Caen, outstanding for his learning and virtuous life, was elected in place of the venerable Nicholas, and ruled the abbey of Saint-Ouen for about twenty years. The number of monks in the abbey and its reputation for piety greatly increased in his time. Then a layman named Gilbert came from Jerusalem to Rouen, and after being received as a monk by Helgot gave worthy service to the church. He revived work on the fabric of the church, which had been interrupted for some time on account of its exceptional size, applied to that purpose the greater part of the money of Aubrée Grossa, his lady, who had died on pilgrimage and bequeathed her wealth to him; and endeavoured to bring the noble work to completion with the aid of additional gifts from other believers. After Helgot had died on 20 November[2] and been buried before the altar of St. Stephen the first martyr, which is in the vestry on the south side, William Belot, an oblate monk of the same church, succeeded as abbot and ruled for about fourteen years. In his time the huge church which had been begun by Nicholas was finished after a full sixty years,[3] and was dedicated on 17 October[4] by Archbishop Geoffrey, in the presence of many prelates and lower clergy.

In the same year Abbot William died and Rainfred, a monk of the same church, became abbot. In his time the cloister and other monastic buildings were completed to be a special glory of the

Anselm of 1106–7 (*Sancti Anselmi opera omnia*, ed. F. S. Schmitt (Edinburgh, 1946–61), v, ep. 407, pp. 352–3). His successor occurs in 1119 (*GC* xi. 144).

[3] This could be a scribal error for seventy, since Orderic later gives the figure of eighty years before 1136 for the building period (Le Prévost, v. 66); work may have begun *c.* 1056.

[4] In 1126. Presumably this passage was written before 1136, since Orderic does not mention the disastrous fire of that year (Le Prévost, v. 66).

Tunc Fulbertus archidiaconus[1] et decanus Rothomagensis egrotauit, et monachile scema deuotus suscepit. Defunctus autem in claustro sancti Audoeni ante capitulum tumulatus est, et albo lapide decenter coopertus est. Titulus uero qualis fuerit, illic ita insculptus ostendit.

Gloria metropolis, cleri decus et diadema,
Morte tua Fulberte ruit, ruit illa profunda
Fontis inexhausti sapientia lingua diserta.
Metropolitanus fuit archidiaconus iste,
Canonicus primum postremo cœnobialis,
Quarta dies erat ante diem qua claruit orbi
iii. 434 Virgine de sacra Christus cum tanta columna
Decidit æcclesiæ nulli pietate secundus.

26

[2]Felici patrum decessione in Christo migrantium, pius in terris meret amor filiorum, qui quamuis eos regnum indubitanter speret ascendere supernum, affectuose tamen absentiam plangit eorum metuens nimiam desolationem hic exulantium. Verum diuina pietas æcclesiam suam crebro uisitat, et inuisibili tactu dulcedinis suæ consolatur ne in uia deficiat, cotidieque missis ad eam fortibus agonithetis ad luctam corroborat. Hinc ait per prophetam, 'Pro patribus tuis nati sunt tibi filii.'[3] Apostolis enim astra transuolantibus apostolici doctores successerunt, qui uerbis et operibus in atriis Ierusalem stantes[4] fulserunt, Deoque suorum fructus laborum huc usque acceptabiles offerunt.[5] En abundante iniquitate in mundo, uberius crescit fidelium in religione deuotio, et multiplicata seges in agro surgit dominico. In saltibus et campestribus passim construuntur cenobia, nouisque ritibus uariisque scematibus trabeata, peragrant orbem cucullatorum examina. Albedine in habitu suo precipue utuntur, qua singulares ab aliis notabilesque uideantur. Nigredo in plerisque locis sanctæ Scripturæ humilitatem

[1] Fulbert had been archdeacon of Rouen at the time of the 1096 council of Rouen, which he attended (Mansi, xx. 926). He was the author of a life of St. Romanus, bishop of Rouen (E. Martène and U. Durand, *Thesaurus novus anecdotorum*, i (Paris, 1717), 181–3).

[2] Orderic's treatise on the new orders may have circulated apart from the bulky *Ecclesiastical History*; Robert of Torigny copied verbatim from it. See above, Introduction, p. xiv, and M. Chibnall, 'Orderic Vital et Robert de Torigni', in *Millénaire monastique du Mont Saint-Michel* (Paris, 1966–71), ii. 137.

[3] Psalm xliv (xlv). 17 (16).

[4] Psalm cxxi (cxxii). 2.

church. In those days Fulbert, archdeacon and dean of Rouen,[1] fell sick and devoutly took monastic vows. When he died he was buried in front of the chapter-house in the cloister of Saint-Ouen, and was reverently covered with a marble slab. His epitaph, carved on it, tells in these words what manner of man he was:

The clergy's crown and honour by your death,
Fulbert, is sunk in ruin, with the fame
Of this cathedral; ruined too the calm
Deep fount of wisdom in your eloquence.
Canon, then monk; archdeacon of this town,
Second to none in virtue; with his death
Four days before the feast-day of Christ's birth
A mighty column of the Church crashed down.

26

[2]The blessed end of the fathers who depart in Christ brings mourning to their dutiful and loving sons on earth who, although they confidently hope that these men have risen to the heavenly kingdom, nevertheless lament their absence out of affection, dreading the terrible desolation that remains after they are gone. But God in his divine mercy often visits his Church, consoling it with the unseen touch of his kindness lest it should faint by the way, and strengthens it to bear sorrow by sending it brave champions day after day. So he speaks through the prophet, 'Instead of thy fathers shall be thy children.'[3] When the apostles were taken up into Heaven the apostolic doctors came in their place; they became glorious through their words and deeds as they stood within the gates of Jerusalem,[4] and offered God the fruits of their labours which are still acceptable.[5] See, though evil abounds in the world, the devotion of the faithful in cloisters grows more abundant and bears fruit a hundredfold in the Lord's field. Monasteries are founded everywhere in mountain valleys and plains, observing new rites and wearing different habits; the swarm of cowled monks spreads all over the world. They specially favour white in their habit, and thereby seem remarkable and conspicuous to others. Black represents humility in many places in Holy

[5] Cf. 1 Peter ii. 5.

designat,[1] quem iccirco colorem religiosorum feruor hactenus
gratanter gestat. Nunc autem nigredinem qua prisci patres tam
regulares clerici in cappis quam monachi in cucullis ob humilita-
tis specimen usi sunt.' moderni tanquam ob maioris iusticiæ
iii. 435 ostentationem abiciunt, inusitata quoque pannorum sectione
suorum ab aliis discrepare appetunt. Voluntaria paupertas mundique contemptus ut opinor in plerisque feruet ac uera religio,
sed plures eis hipocritæ seductoriique simulatores permiscentur
ut lolium tritico. [a]Paganus Carnotensis canonicus cognomento
Belotinus pulchrum carmen adonico metro nuper edidit, in quo
palliatas horum hipocrisi superstitiones subtiliter et copiose propalauit.[2] Ego autem in presenti chronographia nunc nitor palam
enucleare, qualiter et a quibus antiqui scematis mutatio nuper
ceperit pullulare, quia posteris lectoribus hoc autumo gratum fore.

In Burgundia locus est qui dicitur Molismus, unde Rainardus ait Linguonensis episcopus,[3]

Est quasi baptismus quibus est in amore Molismus.

Ibi tempore Philippi regis Francorum uenerabilis Robertus abbas
cenobium condidit,[4] et inspirante gratia Spiritus Sancti discipulos
magnæ religionis aggregauit, studioque uirtutum in sancta paupertate iuxta usum aliorum cenobiorum comiter instruxit. Post
aliquot annos sancti Benedicti regulam diligenter perscrutatus
est.' aliorumque sanctorum documentis patrum perspectis conuocans fratres sic affatus est, 'Nos fratres karissimi secundum
iii. 436 normam sancti patris Benedicti professionem fecimus.' sed ut
michi uidetur non eam ex integro tenemus. Multa quæ ibi non
precipiuntur obseruamus, et de mandatis eiusdem plura negle-
gentes intermittimus. Manibus nostris non laboramus, ut sanctos
patres fecisse legimus. Si michi non creditis o amici.' legite gesta
sanctorum Antonii, Macharii, Pachomii, et ante omnes alios
doctoris gentium Pauli apostoli. Abundantem uictum et uestitum ex
decimis et oblationibus æcclesiarum habemus, et ea quæ competunt

[a] *lat. 4861 omits* Paganus . . . gratum fore

---

[1] Orderic had previously expressed the same praise of black as the colour of humility in the death-bed speech attributed to Ansold of Maule (above, ii. 196). Cf. also *The Letters of Peter the Venerable*, ed. Giles Constable (Cambridge, Mass., 1967), i. 57, 288–90. White had been regarded in the early Church as a festive colour.

[2] Pain Bolotin, or Pain de Mongerville, was a canon of Chartres in the period 1121–36, and possibly considerably longer. His poem, 'De falsis heremitis qui uagando discurrunt' has been published, and the circumstances which produced it discussed, in an illuminating article by J. Leclercq, 'Le poème de Payen

Scripture;[1] therefore up to now monks in their devotion have chosen to wear that colour. Now however, as if to make a show of righteousness, the men of our time reject black, which the earlier fathers always adopted as a mark of humility both for the cloaks of the clergy and for the cowls of monks, and also by cutting their garments in a novel way seek to differentiate themselves from others. In my opinion voluntary poverty, contempt for the world, and true religion inspire many of them, but many hypocrites and plausible counterfeiters are mixed with them, as tares with wheat. Pain, called Bolotinus, a canon of Chartres, recently wrote a beautiful song in adonic metre, in which he exposed the covert superstitions of their hypocrisy subtly and at length.[2] But I will now attempt to make plain in this present chronicle how and by whose efforts the change from the ancient custom recently began to spread, for I believe this will be welcome to later readers.

In Burgundy is a place called Molesme, of which Reginald, bishop of Langres,[3] says,

> Molesme, to those who love the place, is like a baptism.

There in the time of King Philip of France the venerable Abbot Robert founded a monastery,[4] and by the grace of the Holy Spirit gathered followers of true piety and instructed them carefully in the pursuit of virtue in holy poverty, according to the custom of other monasteries. After some years he examined the Rule of St. Benedict very carefully; and after studying the writings of other holy fathers he called the brethren to him and spoke as follows: 'We have made our profession, my dear brethren, according to the rule of our holy father Benedict, but it seems to me that we have not observed it in every point. We have many customs which are not laid down there, and we carelessly overlook a number of its precepts. We do not work with our hands as we read that the holy fathers did. If you do not believe me, my friends, read the acts of St. Anthony, St. Macharius, and St. Pachomius, and in particular of St. Paul, the learned apostle of the Gentiles. We receive abundant food and clothing from the tithes and oblations of churches, and by casuistry or force take for ourselves the things that belong

Bolotin contre les faux ermites', in *Revue bénédictine*, lxviii (1958), 52–86. The poem shows strong sympathy with the older monasticism. Cf. above, Introduction, pp. xli–xlii.

[3] Reginald bishop of Langres (1065–85).

[4] Robert, previously abbot of St. Michael of Tonnerre, became the first abbot of Molesme *c.* 1075.

presbiteris ingenio seu uiolentia subtrahimus. Sic nimirum sanguine hominum uescimur, et peccatis participamur.[1] Laudo igitur ut omnino regulam sancti Benedicti teneamus.' cauentes ne ad dexteram uel ad sinistram ab ea deuiemus. Victum et uestitum labore manuum nostrarum uendicemus,[a] a femoralibus et staminiis pelliciisque[2] secundum regulam abstineamus. Decimas et oblationes clericis qui diocesi famulantur relinquamus, et sic per uestigia patrum post Christum currere feruenter insudemus.'

His dictis monachorum conuentus non adquieuit, immo predecessorum quorum uita euidentibus miraculis insignita manifeste refulsit exempla et instituta uenerabilium uestigiis trita uirorum immoderatis nouitatibus obiecit. 'Viam' inquiunt 'uitæ qua sancti patres olim in Gallia religiose uixerunt, quorum sanctitatem Deo placitam in uita et post humationem prodigia contestata sunt.' iuxta ritum et traditiones eorum iamdiu obseruauimus, et usque ad mortem toto conatu conseruare peroptamus. De hoc quod redarguimur a te pater uenerande quia exorbitamur a rigore
iii. 437 monachilis regulæ, nec aspero gradimur Ægiptiorum patrum tramite qui in Thebaida et Sciti Nitriaque commorabantur,[3] inter barbaros antiquo tempore, necessariam rationem subtili considera examinatione.

'Nullus doctor iure cogit fideles omnia pati pacis tempore quæ sancti martires compulsi sunt in persecutionibus paganorum tolerare, quoniam nec ipsi eadem ante pressuram impiorum ultro perpessi sunt.' quæ necessitate postmodum cogente pro fide certantes sustinuerunt. Hoc nimirum Dominus Petro manifeste declarauit dicens, "Cum esses iunior cingebas te.' et ambulabas ubi uolebas. Cum autem senueris.' extendes manus tuas et alius te cinget et ducet quo tu non uis."[4] Secundum precepta diuinæ legis prudenter intuere, quam discrete in uia Dei deceat te illos dirigere, qui sponte sua conuersi a mundana prauitate, sub tuo magistratu

[a] uendicamus *Caen MS.*; uendicemus *lat. 4861*

---

[1] For the rejection of tithes by the Cistercians see Giles Constable, *Monastic Tithes from their origins to the twelfth century* (Cambridge, 1964), pp. 136–9.

[2] Possibly 'furs'; but Walter Map, in reporting the Cistercian criticisms of the Black Monks, says that the latter occasionally wore 'pellicias agninas', which are certainly lambskins (cf. Walter Map, *De nugis curialium*, ed. M. R. James, Oxford, 1914, p. 41; and the translation of the passage by M. R. James (Cymmrodorion Record Society, ix (1923), 46)).

[3] This region was the centre of early eremitic and monastic life. St. Anthony was one of the first hermits to live in the Thebaid, a province of considerable size in Upper Egypt. Paul the Hermit's retreat was in Nitria and the desert of Scete, a shallow desert valley about fifty miles south of Alexandria. St. Anthony was regarded from an early date as the initiator of monastic life and St. Paul

to the priests. In this way we are gorged with the blood of men and are participators in sin.[1] I propose therefore that we should observe the Rule of St. Benedict in everything, taking care not to turn aside either to the left or to the right. Let us earn our food and clothing by the labour of our hands, and abstain from wearing breeches and shirts and lambskins[2] according to the Rule. Let us surrender tithes and oblations to the clergy who serve parishes, and in this way let us fervently strive to follow after Christ in the footsteps of the fathers.'

The community of monks did not agree to these proposals; indeed they preferred the examples of predecessors whose worthy lives were made glorious by proved miracles, and the well-tried paths long trodden by venerable men, to exaggerated innovations. 'The way of religious life', they said, 'which was once followed in France by the holy fathers whose sanctity was pleasing to God in life and after death, as miracles clearly prove, is the one which up to now we have observed according to their customs and traditions, and we wish to preserve it until we die. As to your rebuke, reverend father, about our departure from the letter of the monastic Rule and our failure to follow the rough path of the fathers of Egypt, who dwelt in the Thebaid and Scete and Nitria[3] among the barbarous peoples of ancient times, reflect with care and precision on the true explanation.

'No learned doctor attempts by law to compel the faithful to suffer in time of peace all that the holy martyrs had to endure during the persecutions of the pagans, for the martyrs themselves did not voluntarily suffer before the attacks of the impious those hardships that they endured afterwards of necessity in fighting for the Faith. Indeed the Lord openly proclaimed this, when he said to Peter, "When thou wast young, thou girdedst thyself and walkedst whither thou wouldest: but when thou shalt be old, thou shalt stretch forth thy hands and another shall gird thee and carry thee whither thou wouldest not."[4] Meditate in your heart according to the precepts of the divine law how carefully you should direct in the way of God those who, having of their own free will turned from worldly corruption, desire to lead a better life

was closely associated with him. Both Cluniacs and Cistercians looked to St. Anthony and ancient Egypt as the source of monasticism. See J. Leclercq, 'Saint Antoine dans la tradition monastique medíévale', in *Studia Anselmiana*, xxxviii (1956), 229–47.

[4] John xxi. 18.

emendatiorem uitam uolunt arripere. Qua ratione potes approbare ut illos qui ultro uolunt suum nequam esse in bonum mutare,[a] ad latebras Pauli uel Antonii uiolenter debeas effugare? Illi quippe parentum etiam suorum timore, de paternis laribus ne occiderentur fugere.[1] Prouidus archiater egrotum fouet temperato medicamine, ne si nimis importunæ medicationis uexat infirmum cruciamine, quem curandum susceperat uideatur extinguere. Nullus prudens inualido infert onus importabile, ne lassus portitor uel oppressus sarcina pereat in itinere.'

Sic palam monachis repugnantibus dixit abbas Robertus, 'Imitabilem[b] Ægiptiorum patrum uitam ad informationem boni com-
iii. 438 memoro, sed inde nulla uobis uiolenta imponitur exactio, immo salubris proponitur persuasio. Verum ad tenendam per omnia sancti Benedicti regulam uos inuito.' quam in pluribus preuaricari secundum id quod professi estis uos ueraciter agnosco. Vnde superni iudicis animaduersionem pertimesco, ne in nos deseuiat pro reatu transgressionis in tremendo iudicio.'

Ad hæc monachi responderunt, 'Beatus pater Benedictus ut nobis omnibus euidenter patescit, beatum Maurum monasterii sui priorem quem a puericia nutrierat in Galliam misit.' et librum regulæ quem ipse uir Dei propria manu conscripsit, et libram panis eminamque uini per eum Francis destinauit.[2] Hic a Teodeberto rege[3] susceptus usque ad obitum suum in Gallia permansit, atque Floro regis consiliario adiuuante cenobium construxit ibique centum quadraginta monachos in loco qui Glannifolium dicitur regulariter instruxit. Discretus autem pater Maurus non mores Ægiptiorum qui nimio solis ardore iugiter estuant imitatus est, sed ritus Gallorum qui sepe brumali gelu in occidente contremiscunt pie intuitus est, sicut a spirituali magistro salubriter edoctus est. Dicit enim sanctus Benedictus, "Vestimenta fratribus secundum locorum qualitatem ubi habitant uel aerum temperiem dentur, quia in frigidis regionibus amplius, in calidis uero minus

[a] commutare *lat. 4861* [b] Imitabilem *in both Caen MS. and lat. 4861; Duchesne and Le Prévost print* inimitabilem

[1] Paul fled to the desert to escape betrayal by his brother-in-law during the persecutions of Decius and Valerian (Jerome, *Vita S. Pauli eremitae,* in Migne, *PL* xxiii. 20). Anthony, however, went voluntarily.

[2] The story that Benedict's pupil, Maur, brought the Rule to Gaul and founded the monastery of Glanfeuil depends on one source only, the *Vita Sancti Mauri* attributed to Faustus, which is a ninth-century forgery by Abbot Odo of Glanfeuil (L. Halphen, 'La *Vie de Saint Maur*; exposé d'une théorie de M. Auguste Molinier', in *Revue historique,* lxxxviii (1905), 287–95). Its authen-

under your guidance. By what argument can you maintain that those who voluntarily seek to change their sinful life for a better one should be violently driven to the retreats of Paul or Anthony? They indeed fled from their fathers' homes to avoid death, fearing even their kinsmen.[1] A wise physician treats a sick man with a mild medicine, for fear that if he goads the sick man with the pain of too drastic a remedy he may kill instead of curing him. No wise man imposes an intolerable burden on a weakling for fear that the porter, growing weary or weighed down by the burden, will perish on the journey.'

Abbot Robert replied to the monks who openly protested in this way, 'I remind you of the life of the Egyptian fathers, which can be imitated, as an example of virtue, but without attempting to force any part of it on you, only a desire to persuade you for your good. Instead I invite you to observe the Rule of St. Benedict in every detail, for in truth I see that you have departed in many ways from that Rule to which you professed obedience. Therefore I fear the condemnation of the supreme Judge, and dread that he will censure us for the guilt of this transgression in the Last Judgement.'

To this the monks answered, 'Our blessed father Benedict, as is well known to all of us, sent to Gaul St. Maur, the prior of his monastery, whom he had brought up from boyhood; and sent a book of the Rule, which the man of God had written with his own hand, a pound of bread, and a measure of wine through him to the Franks.[2] St. Maur was welcomed by King Theodebert[3] and remained in Gaul until his death; with the help of Florus, the king's counsellor, he founded a monastery in the place called Glanfeuil, and instructed a hundred and forty monks there in the observance of the Rule. Our prudent father, Maur, did not imitate the customs of the Egyptians, which are appropriate to the great heat of the sun there; he had more respect for the customs of the Gauls, who often shiver in the wintry frosts of the west. This accords with what our spiritual master himself taught for our good. St. Benedict says, "Let clothing be given to the brethren according to the nature of the place where they live and the climate; for more is necessary in cold, and less in warm, regions. It is the

ticity was accepted without question in the twelfth century, and Orderic copies it here (*Vita S. Mauri abbatis*, in *AA.SS.*, January, i. 1042).

[3] Theodebert, king of Austrasia (d. 547) had no authority in Anjou.

indigetur. Hæc ergo consideratio penes abbatem est."[1] Sic etiam
iii. 439 de cibo et potu et omni conuersatione humana prouide temperat
ac disponit, ut omnia mensurate fiant propter pusillanimes,[2] ut
absque murmurationibus sint.[3] Abbatem quoque summopere
admonet, ut omnium imbecillitatem consideret.[4] Fratribus infirmis
aut delicatis talem operam uel artem iubet iniungi ut nec ociosi
sint.' nec uiolentia laboris opprimantur ut[a] effugentur.[5] Paulus et
Antonius aliique plures qui primitus heremum expetierunt, et in
abditis deserti locis monasteria sibi construxerunt.' timore paganorum ut supradictum est illuc compulsi artam nimis uitam elegerunt,
et cooperante gratia Dei necessitatem in uoluntatem trans-
mutauerunt.[6] Deinde laudabili eorume xemplo admodum creuit
renunciantium seculo numerus, et pro diuersitatibus locorum ac
moribus hominum uariis incessit institutionibus. Sed in una fide
ut dicit Gregorius papa.' nil officit sanctæ æcclesiæ consuetudo
diuersa.[7] Magna pars hominum in calidis regionibus caret
femoralibus, tunicisque fruitur ut mulieres laxis et talaribus,
quorum consuetudinem non abhorret sed amplectitur inde
propagatus, ibique consistens monachorum cuneus. Ast omnes
populi bracis utuntur in occiduo climate, nec eis tam pro frigore
quam pro dedecore norunt carere, quibus pro causis idem mos est
in nostro ordine, nec illum quia utilis et honestus est uolumus
relinquere. Sic de omnibus aliis rationabiles causas nobis tradiderunt, eruditi doctores qui nos in sacro scemate precesserunt. In
Italia et Palestina et aliis regionibus quibusdam satis abundant
oliuæ, cuius fructu ditati ad diuersos esus condiendos non indigent
iii. 440 sagimine, quod nobis hic clementer concessum est carentibus olei
pinguedine. Quod uero manibus nostris cotidie non laboramus
plurimorum dire stimulamur redargutionibus, sed sincerum in
diuino cultu laborem audacter obicimus, quem ab autenticis
magistris diutina diuinæ legis obseruantia probatis olim didicimus.
Dagobertus rex et Teodericus atque Carolus Magnus imperator
aliique reges et augusti cenobia deuote condiderunt, et de suis
redditibus ad uictum et uestitum seruorum Dei ubertim erogaue-
runt, multitudinemque clientum ad exteriora ministeria pleniter
explenda subegerunt, monachosque lectionibus et sacris orationibus

[a] aut *RSB* (*in the sense of* et)

---

[1] *RSB*, cap. 55. [2] *RSB*, cap. 48. [3] *RSB*, cap. 40.
[4] *RSB*, cap. 37. [5] *RSB*, cap. 48.
[6] Cf. Jerome, *Vita S. Pauli*, cap. 5 (Migne, *PL* xxiii. 20–1), 'necessitatem in voluntatem vertit.' As before, Orderic has generalized from the life of Paul.
[7] Cf. the reply of Pope Gregory I to one of St. Augustine's questions; Bede, *HE* i. 27 (pp. 80–2).

abbot's business to take thought for this matter."[1] In a similar way he makes due adjustment for food and drink and all the human needs of monastic life, so that everything may be done in moderation on account of the faint-hearted[2] and they may abstain from murmuring.[3] He particularly enjoins the abbot to bear in mind the weakness of all;[4] commanding him to assign such work or craft for sick or delicate brothers that they shall neither be idle nor exhausted by heavy work and driven away from the monastery.[5] Paul and Anthony and many others, who were the first to fly to the desert and build monasteries for themselves in the remote parts of the desert, were driven there, as we have said, by fear of the pagans; they adopted a rigorous way of life and, by God's grace, turned necessity into choice.[6] Afterwards because of their laudable example the number of those who renounced the world greatly increased; this gave rise to different foundations according to the differences in regions and human customs. But, as Pope Gregory says, the varying custom of Holy Church does not impede the unity of the Faith.[7] Most men in warm climates dispense with breeches and like women, prefer loose, ankle-length tunics: the groups of monks that spread thence and are established there do not regard such dress as unseemly, but adopt it themselves. But all peoples in the western region wear breeches, and could not do without them both for warmth and for decency's sake. Therefore the same custom exists in our order, and we are unwilling to give it up, for it is both useful and modest. Similarly the learned doctors who have lived before us according to the holy Rule teach us sound reasons for all other divergences. In Italy and Palestine and other regions where olive trees grow freely those who use their fruit to cook various dishes do not need lard, which has been reasonably permitted for those who have no olive oil. It is true that we are severely criticized by many because we do not engage in daily manual labour; but we openly offer in its place our earnest toil in the worship of God, as we have been taught to do by true masters of former ages, who have proved their worth by their long-continued observance of the divine law. King Dagobert and Theodoric and the Emperor Charlemagne and other kings and emperors piously founded monasteries and made ample provision for the food and clothing of the servants of God. They introduced numerous dependants to carry out all the external duties and established monks to devote their time to sacred reading, devout

pro cunctis benefactoribus suis et cœlestibus misteriis intentos esse constituerunt. Exinde principum institutione et diuturna consuetudine usitatum est in Gallia, ut rustici ruralia sicut decet peragant opera, et serui seruilia passim exerceant ministeria. Monachi autem qui sponte relictis huius mundi uanitatibus regi regum militant: claustralibus septis ut filiæ regis quiete insideant, archana sacræ legis legendo perquirant, et inde semper meditantes taciturnitati delectabiliter[a] insistant, a prauis et ociosis sermonibus os suum coherceant, dauiticos ymnos aliasque misticas modulationes nocte dieque creatori concinant, aliisque mundis et idoneis actibus cotidie agendis prout ratio exegerit secundum precepta maiorum intendant. Hæc in occidente monachi hactenus operari solent, ac studia eorum huiuscemodi esse debere omnes procul dubio norunt et perhibent. Absit ut rustici torpescant ocio, saturique lasciuientes cachinnis et inani uacent ludicro, quorum genuina sors labori dedita est assiduo: egregii uero milites et
iii. 441 arguti philosophi ac dicaces scolastici si renunciant seculo, cogantur seruilibus et incongruis more uilium mancipiorum studiis seu laboribus occupari pro uictu proprio. Decimæ fidelium uel oblationes generali auctoritate conceduntur clericis et Dei ministris: sicut Paulus apostolus ait Chorinthiis, "Qui in sacrario operantur: quæ de sacrario sunt edunt. Qui altari deseruiunt, cum altari participantur."[1] Ita et Dominus ordinauit his qui ewangelium annunciant, de ewangelio uiuere. Nos autem et ordine et officio clerici sumus, et clericale seruitium summo pontifici qui penetrauit celos[2] offerimus, ut sortem supernæ hereditatis ipso adiuuante[b] optineamus. Æcclesiastica igitur beneficia iure possidemus, et communi sanctione semper tenere decernimus. Hoc o reuerende pater sanctitati uestræ indubitanter notum sit. Quæ a prioribus cenobitis qui religiose uixerunt seruanda didicimus, ac ut heredes ordinis et possessionis habemus, quamdiu Cluniacenses siue Turonenses[3] aliique regulares uiri ea nacti fuerint non dimittemus, nec ut temerarii nouitatum adinuentores a fratribus nostris longe lateque condemnari uolumus.'

[a] laudabiliter *lat. 4861* [b] adminiculante *lat. 4861*

[1] 1 Cor. ix. 13. [2] Cf. Hebr. iv. 14.
[3] St. Martin's abbey of Marmoutier, at Tours, had many dependent priories (Odile Gantier, 'Recherches sur les possessions et les prieurés de l'abbaye de

prayers for all their benefactors, and the divine office. So, through the foundations of princes and long-established custom, it is the practice in France for peasants to perform work in the fields, as is seemly, and servants to perform the duties suitable for servants. Monks, however, who have voluntarily renounced the vanities of this world for the service of the King of kings, live peacefully in their enclosed cloisters like the daughters of kings, seek out by study the hidden meanings of Scripture, and, as they meditate continually on them, gladly preserve silence, keep their lips from foolish and idle words, sing the psalms of David and other mystical chants night and day to their Creator, and devote themselves each day to other pure and suitable activities, as is fitting according to the precepts of the fathers. These are the works which monks in the west have performed up to now, and everyone knows and testifies without a shadow of doubt that such should be their activities. God forbid that peasants, whose true lot is continual toil, should grow useless through idleness and should lounge lasciviously, wasting their time in coarse laughter and idle sport; or that noble knights and gifted philosophers and learned scholars who have renounced the world should be compelled to spend their time in servile and unbecoming labours and occupations like low-born servants in order to earn their bread. The tithes and oblations of the faithful are by general approval granted to the clergy and ministers of God; as Paul the apostle says to the Corinthians, "They which minister about holy things live of the things of the temple. They which wait at the altar are partakers with the altar."[1] So, as the Lord ordained, they that preach the Gospel live by the Gospel. We indeed are clergy both by order and by office and offer a priestly service to the high priest who has gone into the Heavens,[2] so that by his aid we may obtain a share of the heavenly kingdom. So we hold ecclesiastical benefices by right and believe that we should hold them always by common approval. This, reverend father, is certainly well known to you. The things that we have learnt to value from earlier monks who lived by the Rule, the things that we hold as heirs of the order and its possessions, we will not renounce as long as the Cluniacs and the monks of Tours[3] and other monks preserve them; and we do not choose to be condemned far and wide by our brethren as rash innovators.'

Marmoutier du xe au xiiie siècle', in *Revue Mabillon*, liii (1963), 93–110, 161–7; lv (1965), 65–79), and had sent out colonies of monks to Battle and other abbeys.

Hæc et plura his similia monachis constanter dicentibus abbas
iii. 442 in sua satis pertinax sententia recessit ab eis cum xii[1] sibi assentientibus, diuque locum quesiuit idoneum sibi suisque sodalibus, qui sancti decreuerant regulam Benedicti sicut Iudei legem Moisi ad litteram seruare penitus. Tandem Odo filius Henrici Burgundiæ dux illis compassus est.ʼ et predium in loco qui Cistercius dicitur in episcopatu Cabilonensi largitus est. Ibi Robertus abbas cum electis fratribus aliquandiu habitauit in heremo nimiæ districtionis et religionis cenobium construere cepit, Deoque donante in breui plerosque sanctitatis emulatores habuit. Cumque Molismenses cenobitæ per aliquot tempus pastore carerent, uiroque Dei uirtutibus famoso discedente despicabiliores erga uicinos et notos fierent.ʼ Vrbanum papam supplices adierunt, eique prorsus enodata serie rerum quas supra retuli consilium et auxilium ab eo postulauerunt. Ille uero paterno affectu utrisque consuluit. Abbati enim apostolica iussit auctoritate ut prius monasterium repeteret, et ne laberetur regulariter regeret.ʼ ac in alio quod postmodum ceperat quemlibet de suis idoneum substitueret.[a] Deinde firma statuit sanctione ut in primis quisque quam uellet institutionem uitæ arriperet, ipsamque omni uita sua irrefragabiliter teneret.[2]

Sic nimirum sollers papa utile super hoc decretum promulgauit dicens,[3] 'Summopere cauendum est, ne horridum scisma in domo Dei nutriatur, multorumque ad detrimentum scaturiat atque grassetur, et rursus ne bonum culpabiliter prefocetur, quod
iii. 443 diuinitus ad salutem animarum inspiratur. Salubriter ergo paterno more prouidemus, et apostolica auctoritate iubemus.ʼ ut Molismenses qui generales monachorum ritus eligunt inuiolabiliter illos custodiant, ne amodo relicta sede sua transire ad alios ritus audeant. Cistercienses[4] uero qui sese sancti Benedicti regulam per omnia seruaturos iactitant, denuo relapsi ad ea quæ spontaneo despectu

[a] sustitueret *Caen MS.*

---

[1] Since MS. lat. 4861 reads 'cum duodecim' this is unlikely to be a copyist's error. But Robert of Torigny, who based his account on Orderic, says 'cum xx et uno' (*Chronique de R. de Torigni*, ed. L. Delisle, ii. 185).

[2] William of Malmesbury (*GR* ii. 383–4) suggests that the initiative to return to Molesme came from Robert himself. The official Cistercian account in the *Exordium parvum* states, like Orderic, that a papal command brought Robert back to Molesme; it differs from Orderic, however, in the statement that Alberic was canonically elected (cf. J. A. Lefèvre, 'Le vrai récit primitif de Cîteaux . . .', in *Le Moyen Âge*, lxi (1955), 329–61; 'Saint Robert de Molesme dans l'opinion monastique . . .', in *Anal. boll.* lxxiv (1956), 72–3). Whence Orderic derived the suggestion that Robert appointed his own successor is uncertain; but he records a number of cases of abbots virtually designating their successors, and there is no reason to suppose that he questioned the legality of the proceedings.

As the monks resolutely argued along these lines the abbot, who held firmly to his opinion, retired with twelve[1] men of like mind and for a long time looked for a place suitable for himself and his companions, who were resolved to observe the Rule of St. Benedict according to the letter as the Jews observed the law of Moses. At length Odo, the son of Henry duke of Burgundy, took pity on them and gave them an estate in the place called Cîteaux in the diocese of Châlons. Abbot Robert and his chosen brethren lived there for some time in the wilderness and began to found a monastery of great austerity and piety; in a short time God sent many others to imitate their holiness. When the monks of Molesme had been for some time without an abbot, since the departure of the man of God, renowned for his virtues, made them seem contemptible to men everywhere, they went as petitioners to Pope Urban and, after describing the course of events which I have related, asked for his advice and help. Out of paternal affection he gave consideration to both sides. By his apostolic authority he commanded the abbot to return to his former monastery and govern it as the Rule requires to save it from decline, and to appoint as abbot in the new house he was founding a suitable man from among the monks there. Then he firmly decreed that every man should make an initial choice of the way of life he desired and should be indissolubly bound to abide by it all his life.[2]

So this most judicious pope promulgated a wise decretal to this end, declaring,[3] 'We must at all costs avoid allowing a shocking schism to appear in God's house and to spread and increase, bringing ruin to many; but equally we must avoid wrongly smothering something good, which has been inspired by God to save souls. So, in fatherly fashion, we make sound provision and, by apostolic authority, we command that the monks of Molesme who choose the established customs of monks shall observe them and shall not hereafter venture to leave their house and follow other customs. The Cistercians[4] on the other hand, who publicly profess to follow the Rule of St. Benedict in all things, shall never

[3] J. A. Lefèvre believes this 'pseudo-bull' to be based on knowledge of the existence of a bull of 1100, which Orderic had not seen (*Anal. boll.* lxxiv (1956), 73). It appears to be as freely composed as the speeches Orderic attributes to the monks.

[4] The term 'Cistercienses' was never used in genuine documents as early as 1100. J. A. Lefèvre argues that it came into use at the chapter of 1119, replacing 'monachi novi monasterii' (in *Le Moyen Âge*, lxi (1955), 110–13).

nunc deserunt nunquam redeant. Stabilitas quippe in congregatione et in omni bono perseuerantia semper attollenda et firmiter tenenda est: quia conditori qui caudam hostiæ in sacrificio exigit,[1] acceptabilis est, et hominibus qui uiso sanctitatis exemplo ad uirtutum apicem prouocantur commode grata est.'

Coactus itaque Robertus abbas Molismum repedauit, ibique laudabiliter usque ad finem uitæ suæ Deo militauit. Albericum uero magnæ religionis uirum ad opus Cistercii uicarium sibi elegit, et Iohanni ac Hilbodo Atrebatensibus aliisque xxii fratribus abbatem Cistercii constituit.[2] Qui in magna egestate per decem annos ibi deguit, et cum suis contubernalibus Deo laboriose militauit, a quo securus inestimabile premium expectauit. Quo
iii. 444 defuncto Stephanus natione Anglicus uir magnæ religionis et sapientiæ successit:[3] et plus quam xxiiii annis doctrina et operatione sancta gloriose pollens tenuit, cuius tempore monasterium in heremo multipliciter creuit. Ipso adhuc uiuente et iubente Guido abbas Trium Fontium[4] electus est: et non multo post uenerabilis predecessor eius defunctus est. Guido autem assumptum patris officium aliquandiu uituperabiliter tenuit: et post duos annos insipienter reliquit. Deinde Rainardus iuuenis filius Milonis comitis de Bar super Sequanam electus est:[5] et abbas a Gualterio Cabilonensi presule[a] consecratus est.

Iam fere xxxvii anni sunt[6] ex quo Robertus abbas ut dictum est Cistercium incoluit,[b] et in tantillo tempore tanta uirorum illuc copia confluxit, ut inde lxv abbatiæ consurgerent,[7] quæ omnes cum abbatibus suis Cisterciensi archimandritæ subiacent. Omnes femoralibus pelliciisque carent,[8] ab adipe et carnium esu abstinent,
iii. 445 multisque bonis in mundo ut lucernæ lucentes in caliginoso loco[9] renitent. Omni tempore silentio student, fucatis uestibus non utuntur. Manibus propriis laborant, uictumque sibi et uestitum uendicant. Omnibus diebus preter dominicum[c] ab idibus

[a] episcopo *lat. 4861* [b] incolere cepit *lat. 4861* [c] dominicam *lat. 4861*

---

[1] Leviticus iii. 9.

[2] Alberic became abbot in 1099; there is no early evidence that Robert appointed him (cf. J. A. Lefèvre in *Anal. boll.* lxxiv (1956), 72–3). Robert of Torigny, who copied Orderic, here departs from his text and says simply, 'primus Albericus factus est abbas Cisterciensis post ipsum' (R. Tor. ii. 186).

[3] Stephen Harding, elected in 1109 (*DHGE* xii. 866).

[4] In 1133. Guy's rule lasted only a few months; the Cistercians regarded his offence as so serious that his name was struck from all their records (E. Vacandard, *Vie de Saint Bernard*, 4th edn. i. 160).

[5] He was abbot from 1133/4 to 1150 (*DHGE* xii. 866).

from this time return to the custom which they now abandon of their own free will. For stability in a community and perseverance in whatever is good should be extolled and resolutely maintained because it is acceptable to the Creator, who requires even the fat-tail of the offering in the sacrifice;[1] also it is useful and salutary to men, who may be inspired to greater virtue by seeing an example of sanctity.'

So under compulsion Abbot Robert returned to Molesme and there worthily served God until the end of his life. He chose Alberic, a man of great piety, to take his place in the Cistercian enterprise, and made him abbot of Cîteaux over John and Hildebod of Arras and twenty-two other brothers.[2] He remained there for ten years in great poverty, and with his companions faithfully served God, in the assurance of receiving a priceless reward from him. After his death Stephen, an Englishman remarkable for his piety and wisdom, succeeded him[3] and held office for more than twenty-four years, giving a shining example by his holy works and teaching. In his time the monastery in the wilderness grew in every way greater. At Stephen's command, while he was still living, Guy, abbot of Trois-Fontaines,[4] was elected; shortly afterwards the venerable Stephen died. After Guy took up the office of abbot he held it in a disgraceful way for some time, and after two years relinquished it through his folly. Then Reginald, the young son of Milo count of Bar-sur-Seine, was elected;[5] he was blessed as abbot by Walter bishop of Châlons.

It is now about thirty-seven years[6] since Abbot Robert founded Cîteaux in the way I have described, and in that time such a great multitude of men has flocked there that sixty-five abbeys have been founded from it,[7] all of which with their abbots are subject to the chief abbot of Cîteaux. All dispense with breeches and lambskins,[8] abstain from eating fat and flesh-meat, and by the great good they do shine out in the world like lanterns burning in a dark place.[9] They maintain silence at all times and wear no dyed garments. They toil with their own hands and produce their own food and clothing. From 13 September until Easter they fast every

[6] This implies that Orderic was writing *c.* 1135.

[7] The number of Cistercian abbeys reached sixty-five in 1134/5 (J. A. Lefèvre in *Anal. boll.* lxxiv (1956), 72–3).

[8] For Cistercian dress see E. Vacandard, *Vie de Saint Bernard* (4th edn.), i. 41–2.

[9] 2 Peter i. 19.

Septembris usque ad Pascha ieiunant. Aditus suos satis obserant, et secreta sua summopere celant. Nullum alterius æcclesiæ monachum in suis penetralibus admittunt, nec in oratorium ad missam uel alia seruitia secum ingredi permittunt. Multi nobiles athletæ et profundi sophistæ ad illos pro nouitate singularitatis concurrerunt, et inusitatam districtionem ultro complexantes in uia recta læti Christo ymnos læticiæ modulati sunt. [a]In desertis atque siluestribus locis monasteria proprio labore condiderunt, et sacra illis nomina sollerti prouisione imposuerunt, ut est Domus Dei, Clarauallis, Bonus Mons et Elemosina, et alia plura huiusmodi, quibus auditores solo nominis nectare inuitantur festinanter experiri, quanta sit ibi beatitudo, quæ tam speciali denotetur uocabulo.

iii. 446 Multi ex eorum fonte sitientes hauserunt, et inde plures riuuli per diuersas Galliarum regiones deriuati sunt. Nouæ institutionis emulatores dispersi sunt in Aquitania, in Britannia, Guasconia, et Hibernia[b]. Mixti bonis hipochritæ procedunt, candidis seu uariis indumentis amicti homines illudunt, et populis ingens spectaculum efficiunt.[1] Veris Dei cultoribus scemate non uirtute assimilari plerique gestiunt, suique multitudine intuentibus fastidium ingerunt, et probatos cenobitas quantum ad fallaces hominum obtutus attinet despicabiliores faciunt.

27

Eodem tempore uenerabilis Andreas de Valle Bruciorum monachus effloruit.' et in Bituricensi pago monasterium quod Casale Benedicti nuncupatur construxit, et discipulos in magna paupertate et continentia Deo famulari docuit.[2] Hic erat genere Italus, litterarum eruditione pleniter instructus, et lucrandis Deo animabus per eius gratiam idoneus.

Tunc Hildebertus[c] Dolensis abbas ad archiepiscopatum Bituricensem promotus est.'[3] multisque pollens uirtutibus sanctitatis

[a] In desertis . . . despicabiliores faciunt *om. lat. 4861* [b] *Probably an error for Hiberia.* [c] *An error for Aldebertus*

[1] There is an example of the hostility aroused by false hermits in the *Vie de Saint Étienne d'Obazine*, ed. M. Aubrun (Clermont-Ferrand, 1970), p. 52; see also J. Leclercq, 'Le poème de Payen Bolotin contre les faux ermites', in *Revue bénédictine*, lxviii (1958), 52–86.

[2] The Florentine, Andrew, undertook the foundation of a small monastery at Cornilly about 1087, and transferred it a few years later to Chézal-Benoît, with the usages of Vallombrosa. It had a few small dependencies, but was without great influence (Jean Becquet, 'L'érémitisme clérical et laïc dans l'ouest de

day except Sunday. They bar their gates and keep their private quarters completely enclosed. They will not admit a monk from another religious house to their cells, nor allow one to come with them into the church for Mass or any other offices. Many noble warriors and profound philosophers have flocked to them on account of the novelty of their practices, and have willingly embraced the unaccustomed rigour of their life, gladly singing hymns of joy to Christ as they journey along the right road. They have built monasteries with their own hands in lonely, wooded places and have thoughtfully provided them with holy names, such as Maison-Dieu, Clairvaux, Bonmont, and L'Aumône and others of like kind, so that the sweet sound of the name alone invites all who hear to hasten and discover for themselves how great the blessedness must be which is described by so rare a name.

Many who were parched with thirst have drunk from their spring; many streams have flowed out of it through all parts of France. Imitators of the new foundations have spread through Aquitaine, Brittany, Gascony, and Spain. Among the good men are some hypocrites who, clothed in white or other distinctive habits, have deceived men and made a great show to the masses.[1] Many seek to be numbered with the true servants of God by their outward observance, not their virtue; their numbers disgust those who see them and make true monks seem less worthy in the faulty judgement of men.

27

The venerable Andrew, monk of Vallombrosa, flourished at the same time; he founded a monastery called Chézal-Benoît in the diocese of Bourges and taught his followers to serve God in great poverty and austerity.[2] He was an Italian by birth, very learned in the literary arts, and by God's grace skilful in saving souls.

Audebert, abbot of Déols, was promoted to the archbishopric of Bourges at this time;[3] distinguished by many virtues he set an

la France', in *L'eremitismo in Occidente nei secoli XI e XII* (Milan, 1962), p. 187; L. Raison et R. Niederst, 'Le mouvement érémitique . . .', in *Annales de Bretagne*, lv (1948), 30 n. 178).

[3] Audebert became abbot of Déols in 1087 and archbishop of Bourges in 1092 (P. R. Gaussin, *L'abbaye de la Chaise-Dieu* (Paris, 1962), p. 123 n. 24).

documentum sequentibus Christum uerbo et actione largitus est. Guarnerius de Monte Maurilionis prefati presulis frater miles
iii. 447 illustris fuit, et postmodum Casæ Dei monachus fere xl annis Deo militauit.[1] Hic dum adhuc in armis mundo seruiret quondam dum de sancti Iacobi peregrinatione rediret.ʼ[a] in introitu cuiusdam siluæ solus cum armigero suo languenti mendico repente occurrit, et poscenti stipem nummos quos daret ad manum non habuit, sed preciosas cirothecas ab amica sibi directas deuote porrexit. Deinde post longum tempus cuidam religioso Dei seruo post matutinos in oratorio supplicanti angelica uisio apparuit.ʼ et ei quædam agenda specialiter iniunxit. Cumque monachus diligenter inquireret, cuius auctoritate talia sibi preciperet.ʼ 'Ille' inquit 'me misit ad te, et hæc tibi mandauit, quem Martinus parte clamidis suæ uestiuit, et cui Guarnerius cirothecas suas donauit.' Frater hæc abbati retulit et senioribus. Historia de Martini diuisa clamide satis claruit, cuius parte Ambianis adhuc catecuminus Christum in paupere texerit,[2] sed res de Guarnerii cirothecis omnino diu latuit. Tandem ipse quibusdam percunctantibus simpliciter detexit, qualiter inopi pro amore Christi subuenerit, et ab illis nichilominus reuelationem audiuit, Deoque qui bona facientibus semper presto est gratias egit.

Circa hæc tempora Bernardus Quinciaci abbas Pictauense solum reliquit,[3] quia prefatum monasterium quod hactenus liberum extiterat Cluniaco subiugare noluit. Et quia sicut scriptum est 'iustus ut leo confidit',[4] in Romana sinodo contra Paschalem
iii. 448 papam pro libertate æcclesiæ[b] litigauit, ipsumque quia plenarium sibi rectum non fecerat ad diuinum examen prouocauit. Cuius formidandam animositatem papa reueritus est.ʼ ipsumque ut secum ad Romanæ tutelam æcclesiæ commoraretur precatus est. Ille uero mundanas omnino curas deseruit, et plura cum quibusdam religiosis fratribus ipsum auide sequentibus loca perlustrauit. Denique post plures circuitus ad uenerabilem episcopum Iuonem diuertit, et ab eo benigniter susceptus in predio Carnotensis

[a] quondam . . . rediret *om. lat. 4861* [b] pro libertate æcclesiæ *om. lat. 4861*

[1] Garnier of Montmorillon and Audebert were kinsmen of Judith, daughter of Robert II, count of Auvergne. They connived at her disappearance on the night of her betrothal to St. Simon of Crépy in 1077, when she and Simon both entered religious houses (P. R. Gaussin, *L'abbaye de la Chaise-Dieu*, p. 123). The date of Garnier's entry to Chaise-Dieu is not known.

[2] Cf. Sulpicius Severus, *Vita beati Martini*, c. 3 (Migne, *PL* xx. 162).

[3] Bernard of Tiron was abbot of St. Cyprian, Poitiers, at the time of its long

example to the followers of Christ in words and deeds. Garnier of Montmorillon, his brother, was a famous knight, who later served God for about forty years as a monk of Chaise-Dieu.[1] Once, during the time he still lived in the world as a knight, he was returning from a pilgrimage to Santiago di Compostella. Entering a wood alone with his squire, he came suddenly upon a sick beggar, who asked for money. He had no money that he could give, but piously offered him a pair of very precious gloves that he had received from his lady. Long after this had happened an angel appeared in a vision to a certain pious monk who was praying in his church after matins, and charged him to perform certain tasks. When the monk sought to know by whose authority these duties were laid on him the angel said, 'He who sent me to you and bade you do these things is the same whom Martin clothed in half his cloak, and to whom Garnier gave his gloves.' The brother related this to the abbot and senior monks. They were familiar with the history of Martin's divided cloak, and how, when he was still only a catechumen at Amiens, by clothing a beggar in half of it he clothed Christ;[2] but the reference to Garnier's gloves was unintelligible to them. At length Garnier happened to give a simple account of how he had helped the beggar for the love of Christ to some who asked him and, learning from them about the vision, he gave thanks to God, who is always near to those who do good.

About this time Bernard, abbot of Saint-Cyprian, left Poitiers[3] because he did not wish to subject his monastery, which up to that time had been independent, to Cluny. Since, as it is written, 'the righteous man is bold as a lion',[4] he fought an action in the Roman synod before Pope Paschal for the liberty of his church and challenged him to face the judgement of God because he had not done full justice in the matter. The pope respected his impressive courage and begged him to remain with him to further the interests of the Roman church. But he utterly spurned all worldly cares and travelled through many parts with a few pious monks who gladly followed him. Finally, after long wandering, he visited the venerable Bishop Ivo and was so well received by him that he

and unsuccessful suit for independence from Cluny. Orderic's brief account is consistent with the *Vita sancti Bernardi Tironensis* of Geoffrey Grossus (Migne, *PL* clxxii. 1367–1446), written probably a little later, and it has independent value as a source. See L. Raison and R. Niederst in *Annales de Bretagne*, lv (1948), 8–9.

[4] Cf. Proverbs xxviii. 1.

æcclesiæ cum fratribus quibusdam constitit, et in loco siluestri qui Tiron dicitur cœnobium in honore sancti Saluatoris construxit.[1] Illuc multitudo fidelium utriusque ordinis[2] abunde confluxit, et predictus pater omnes ad conuersionem properantes caritatiuo amplexu suscepit: et singulis artes quas nouerant legitimas in monasterio exercere precepit.[3] Vnde libenter conuenerunt ad eum fabri tam lignarii quam ferrarii, sculptores et aurifabri, pictores et cementarii, uinitores et agricolæ, multorumque officiorum artifices peritissimi. Sollicite quod eis iussio senioris iniungebat operabantur: et communem conferebant ad utilitatem quæ lucrabantur. Sic ergo ubi paulo ante in horribili saltu latrunculi solebant latitare,
iii. 449 et incautos uiatores repentino incursu trucidare:[a] adiuuante Deo in breui consurrexit monasterium nobile. Teobaldus comes palatinus et Adala mater eius, et Rotro comes Moritoniæ[4] ac Beatrix mater eius, illustres quoque ac mediocres Carnotenses, Drocenses, Corbonienses, aliique fideles uicini ut innocentium simplicitatem monachorum ueraciter experti sunt benigniter illos[b] in timore Domini coluerunt, sumptibus et consiliis ad corroborandum quod ceperant Dei castrum summopere adminiculati sunt.

Venerandus Vitalis qui quondam fuerat Roberti comitis Moritolii capellanus,[5] et apud Moritolium sancti Ebrulfi canonicus, secularium curarum ac diuitiarum depositis oneribus leue iugum[6] Christi per apostolorum uestigia ferre decreuit, et in desertis locis aliquandiu cum religiosis quibusdam habitauit. Ibi mollioris uitæ pristinas consuetudines edomuit, et rigidioris obseruantiæ cultus edidicit. Denique Sauineium uicum ubi antiquorum ingentes edificiorum ruinæ apparent considerauit, sedemque sibi suisque ad habitandum elegit, et in contiguo saltu monasterium in honore

[a] trepidare *lat. 4861* [b] eos *lat. 4861*

[1] Tiron was founded in 1107×1109 (Raison and Niederst, *Annales de Bretagne*, lv (1948), 9; Ivo of Chartres, *Epistolae*, no. 283 (Migne, *PL* clxii. 283).

[2] Probably clerks and laymen; but possibly secular clergy and monks.

[3] Cf. *Vita sancti Bernardi* (Migne, *PL* clxxii. 1419), 'Erant etenim inter eos plures artifices, qui singulas artes cum silentio exercebant . . . quibus semper custodes ordinis praeerant, qui jubente Patre districtionem regularis observationis diligenter observarent.' L. Genicot ('L'érémitisme du xie siècle dans son contexte économique et social', in *L'eremitismo in Occidente nei secoli XI e XII* (Milan, 1962), p. 56 n. 51) considers that Orderic drew on the same source as the author of the *Vita*, and that the details of trades given by him may be drawn from his imagination. Nevertheless he was well informed about his neighbour, Rotrou of Mortagne, and possibly also had personal knowledge of Tiron; there is nothing improbable in his list of crafts practised.

[4] Cf. *Vita sancti Bernardi Tironensis* (Migne, *PL* clxxii. 1413–14) for Bernard's relations with Adela of Blois and Rotrou of Mortagne.

settled with some brethren in the territory of the church of Chartres. Here in a wooded spot called Tiron he built a monastery in honour of our holy Saviour.[1] A multitude of the faithful of both orders[2] flocked to him there, and Father Bernard received in charity all who were eager for conversion to monastic life, instructing individuals to practise in the monastery the various crafts in which they were skilled.[3] So among the men who hastened to share his life were joiners and blacksmiths, sculptors and goldsmiths, painters and masons, vine-dressers and husbandmen and skilled artificers of many kinds. They industriously carried out the tasks imposed on them by their superior and handed over for the common good whatever they earned. So in the place where, shortly before, robbers had normally lain hidden in the grim wood, waiting to fall on unwary travellers and murder them, a noble monastery rose by God's aid in a short space of time. The count palatine, Theobald, and Adela his mother, Rotrou count of Mortagne[4] and Beatrice his mother, as well as faithful persons of high and low rank from Chartres, Dreux, and the Corbonnais and other neighbouring parts, came to value at its true worth the simplicity of the innocent monks. Next they cherished them in the fear of the Lord, and by providing goods and counsel gave them every assistance to complete the citadel of God, which they had begun to build.

The venerable Vitalis, who had formerly been a chaplain of Robert, count of Mortain,[5] and a canon of the church of Saint-Évroul at Mortain, determined, on putting aside the burdens of worldly cares and riches, to bear the easy yoke[6] of Christ in the footsteps of the apostles and lived for some time in the wilderness with a few monks. There he conquered the habits belonging to the easier life he had known before and learnt the discipline of a strict observance. Finally he discovered the village of Savigny, where the huge ruins of old buildings remain, chose it as a dwelling-place for himself and his followers, and began to establish a monastery

[5] Orderic's account of Vitalis, the founder of Savigny, is earlier than the *Vita* by Stephen of Fougères (d. 1178) (ed. E. P. Sauvage in *Anal. boll.* i (1882), 355–90). He may have taken some facts from the mortuary roll of Vitalis (L. Delisle, *Rouleaux des morts du ixe au xve siècle*, Paris, 1866, pp. 282–4). Though his account is rhetorical, the vivid details of the preaching of Vitalis may have been drawn from the life (cf. Raison and Niederst, in *Annales de Bretagne*, lv (1948), 15–16, 24).

[6] Cf. Matthew ii. 30.

sanctæ et indiuiduæ Trinitatis condere cepit.[1] Ritus Cluniacensium uel aliorum qui monachilibus obseruantiis iamdudum mancipati fuerant imitatus non est: sed modernas institutiones neophitorum
iii. 450 prout sibi placuit amplexatus est. Hic eruditione litterarum erat apprime imbutus, fortitudine ac facundia preditus, ac ad proferendum quicquid uolebat animosus, non parcens in populari sermone infimis nec potentibus. Quasi tuba exaltabat uocem suam iuxta Isaiæ uaticinium, annuncians populo Christiano scelera eorum, et domui Iacob peccata eorum.[2] Reges igitur ducesque reuerebantur illum. Plures turbæ manicabant ut audirent uerba eius, quæ postmodum auditis ab illo latenter olim actis facinoribus, lugubres et confusæ redibant a facie ipsius. Omnis ordo intrinsecus pungebatur eius ueridicis allegationibus, omnis plebs contremiscebat coram illo ad correptiones eius, et uterque sexus rubore infectus uerecundabatur ad improperia illius. Nuda quippe uitia manifeste promebat: et occultorum conscios probrosis redargutionibus stimulabat. Sic nimirum superbos athletas et indomitos uulgi cœtus plerumque comprimebat, atque locupletes eras sericis uestibus et canusinis pellibus[3] delicate indutas trepidare cogebat, dum uerbi Dei gladio in scelera seuiret, et spurciciis pollutas conscientias ualide feriret, grandisonoque diuinæ animaduersionis tonitruo terreret. Sollers itaque seminiuerbius multis profuit multos secum aggregauit, in cenobio quod construxerat per annos vii Deo militauit, et usque ad bonum finem bonæ uitæ permansit. In oratorio post aliquantam egritudinem in qua fideliter
iii. 451 confessus fuerat, et sacræ communionis uiaticum deuote perceperat, ad matutinos de sancta uirgine Maria lectori poscenti benedictionem dedit, et a cunctis qui aderant dicto 'Amen' mox spiritum exalauit.[4] Quo defuncto Baiocensis Goisfredus ac[a] Cerasiacensis monachus successit, qui et ipse immoderatis adinuentionibus studuit, durumque iugum super ceruices discipulorum aggrauauit.[b]

Notitiæ posterorum hæc annotaui de modernis preceptoribus, qui nouas traditiones priscorum preferunt patrum ritibus: aliosque monachos seculares uocitant, ac ueluti regulæ preuaricatores temere condempnant. Studium et rigorem eorum considerans illos

[a] *Om.* ac *lat. 4861* [b] *lat. 4861 ends here*

[1] Savigny was founded *c.* 1112.

[2] Isaiah lviii. 1.

[3] Canosa was famous for its fine fleeces in Roman times.

[4] On 16 September 1122 (*Rouleau mortuaire du B. Vital, abbé de Savigni*, ed. L. Delisle (facsimile edn. Paris, 1909), p. 15 n. 4). Compare the details of his death in the *Vita* by Stephen of Fougères (*Anal. boll.* i (1882), 383).

in honour of the holy and undivided Trinity in a wood nearby.[1] He did not imitate the customs of the Cluniacs or others who had submitted themselves to monastic observances for some time, but adopted the recent institutions of the new monks as he chose. He was a man who had studied deeply, was endowed with great courage and eloquence, sought what he believed right with passion, and spared neither rich nor poor in his public sermons. He raised his voice like the trumpet of Isaiah's prophecies, showing the Christian people their transgressions and the house of Jacob their sins.[2] Because of this kings and dukes held him in great reverence. Many multitudes journeyed to hear his words and, after hearing from his lips the shameful deeds that they had done in secret, withdrew in sorrow and confusion from his presence. Every rank was mortified by his true allegations, every crowd trembled before him at his reproaches; men and women alike blushed with confusion at his taunts. He laid bare vices and exposed them to the light, stabbing those who were aware of hidden faults with his pungent reproofs. So he often restrained haughty warriors and undisciplined rabbles, and caused wealthy ladies delicately clad in silk garments and fine lambskins[3] to tremble when he attacked their sins with the sword of God's word, striking deeply into consciences defiled with filth and bringing terror with the rolling thunder of divine rebuke. So by assiduously scattering words abroad he saved many and brought many to his side; he served God for seven years in the monastery he had founded and remained steadfast in his good life until its holy close. After he had been ill for some time and had made his confession and reverently received the viaticum of holy communion, he was taken to the church. He heard the matins of the Holy Virgin Mary and gave a blessing to the reader when he asked for it; after all present had said 'Amen' he breathed his last.[4] After his death Geoffrey of Bayeux, a monk of Cérisy, succeeded him; he introduced new practices of excessive strictness and increased the burden of the hard yoke on the necks of his followers.

I have noted down for the information of posterity this account of present-day teachers, who prefer new traditions to the customs of the fathers of old, calling other monks seculars and presumptuously condemning them as violators of the Rule. I shall not abuse them, out of respect for their zeal and asceticism; nevertheless

magnopere non uitupero, at tamen maioribus et probatis patribus non antepono. Arbitror ignorant quod beatus pater Columbanus de Hibernia ortus sancto Benedicto contemporaneus fuerit,[1] paternam domum patriamque relinquens cum precipuis monachis in Gallias nauigauerit, et a Childeberto rege Francorum filio Sigisberti susceptus in Burgundia Luxouii cenobium construxerit, ac postmodum ab impiissima Brunichilde regina expulsus in Italiam secesserit, et ab Agilulfo Langobardorum rege receptus Bobiense monasterium condiderit. Hic admirandæ sanctitatis pater
iii. 452 inter precipuos laborauit, signis et prodigiis gloriose inter terrigenas effulsit, et Spiritu Sancto edoctus monachilem regulam edidit, primusque Gallis tradidit. Florentissimi de scola eius monachi prodierunt, et in mundo uelut astra in firmamento uirtutibus micuerunt. Eustasius enim Luxouiensis, Agilus Resbacensis, Faro Meldensis, Audomarus Bononiensis, Philibertus Gemmeticensis, aliique plures episcopi et abbates excellentissimæ processere religionis, quorum sanctitas euidentibus miraculis cœlitus ostensa est, ipsorumque studio in filiis æcclesiæ insigniter propagata est. Ipsi reor beatum Maurum[2] eiusque socios et discipulos nouerunt utpote uicini, et ab ipsis sicut ab aliis scripta doctorum ædificationis causa sancti normam suscepere Benedicti, ita tamen ut non abhorrerent sui statuta magistri, almi uidelicet Columbani.[3] Ab ipso siquidem modum diuinæ seruitutis et ordinem didicerunt, et formam orationum pro cunctis ordinibus qui in æcclesia Dei sunt.ʼ nigredinem uestium aliasque obseruationes sumpserunt, quas pro religione et honestate ipsi tenuerunt, et sequaces eorum usque in hodiernum diem reuerenter obseruare appetunt.

iii. 453 Qualis predictus doctor ante Deum et homines quantusque fuerit.ʼ liber uitæ eius signis plenus et uirtutibus ostendit.[4] In gestis etiam sepe memoratur Audoeni Rotomagensis archiepiscopi, et Nouiomensis Eligii,[5] aliorumque uirorum qui ab illo educati sunt.ʼ ac ad apicem uirtutum per eius documenta prouecti sunt.

Materiam scribendi nuper ab Vticensi æcclesia cepi, sed ampla

[1] This mis-statement is surprising, for the Annals of Saint-Évroul (Le Prévost, v. 146–7) show that they were not contemporaries. St. Benedict died *c.* 547 (the Annals wrongly say 509), and St. Columbanus in 615. Orderic himself used the Annals for early dates (above, iii, p. xxvi).

[2] See above, p. 316 n. 2.

[3] Many Merovingian monasteries did in fact preserve Columbanian customs after the introduction of the Benedictine Rule. See J. Laporte, 'Les origines du monachisme dans le province de Rouen', in *Revue Mabillon*, xxxi (1941), 1–41; James O'Carroll, 'Monastic rules in Merovingian Gaul', in *Studies*, xlii (1953), 407–19; M. Chibnall, 'The Merovingian monastery of Saint-Évroul in the light of conflicting traditions', in *Studies in Church History*, viii (Cambridge, 1971), pp. 35–6, 38.

I do not think them better than the early fathers, whose worth is proved. I think that they do not know about the blessed father Columbanus, who was born in Ireland, a contemporary of St. Benedict.[1] Leaving his own country and his father's house, he sailed with some chosen monks to Gaul and, being received by Childebert son of Sigebert, king of the Franks, he established the monastery of Luxeuil in Burgundy. After his banishment by the impious Queen Brunechildis he moved to Italy, where he was received by Agilulf, king of the Lombards, and founded the monastery of Bobbio. This abbot of marvellous holiness toiled among the great, was glorified among men by signs and miracles, and, inspired by the Holy Spirit, composed a monastic rule, which he was the first to give to the Franks. Under him were trained distinguished monks, whose virtues shone in the world like stars in the heavens. Among them were Eustace of Luxeuil, Agilus of Resbais, Faro of Meaux, Omer of Boulogne, Philibert of Jumièges, and many other bishops and abbots of exemplary piety, whose holiness was proclaimed by heaven-sent miracles and whose zeal was widely spread among the sons of the Church. I believe that they knew the blessed Maur[2] and his companions and followers, who were their neighbours, and, as they received from others the writings of the masters designed for edification, received from them the Rule of St. Benedict, but in such a way that they did not reject the precepts of their master, the beloved Columbanus.[3] From him they learnt the ritual and sequence of the divine offices, and the form of prayers for all orders in the Church of God; they also adopted their black habit and other customs cherished for their appropriateness for monastic life: these their successors up to the present day have endeavoured to observe with respect.

What kind of man the master Columbanus was, and how he was esteemed before God and men is told in the book of his life, which is full of miracles and proofs of his virtue;[4] also in the acts of the renowned Ouen, archbishop of Rouen, and Eloy of Noyon[5] and other men who were trained by him and rose to the highest virtues through his example.

A little while ago I began the subject-matter of my book with the

[4] See *Vita Columbani abbatis*, ed. B. Krusch (*MGH SS Rer. Meroving.* iv. 65–152).

[5] See *Vita Audoini episcopi Rotomagensis* (*MGH SS Rer. Meroving.* v. 536–67); *Vita Eligii episcopi Noviomagensis* (ibid. iv. 634–741).

terrarum regna uelut in extasin raptus prospexi, longe lateque oratione uolitaui, et per plura perlustrans longissimam epanalempsim[1] protelaui. Nunc autem stratum meum quod est Vtici fessus repetam, et quiddam de rebus ad nos pertinentibus in libri calce liquido retexam.

28

Anno ab incarnatione Domini M°XCVIII° indictione I[a]. Hugo de Grentemaisnil inclitus heros in Anglia in lectum decidit, senioque et infirmitate fractus ultimis appropinquauit.[2] Tunc a Goisfredo Aurelianensi Vticensium priore quem Rogerius abbas pro tutela eiusdem in Anglia iam pridem dimiserat monachatum suscepit, sextaque postmodum die viii° scilicet kalendas Martii obiit. Inde Bernardus et Dauid Vticenses cenobitæ[3] cadauer illius sallitum et in corio bouum optime consutum in Normanniam conduxerunt,
iii. 454 quod supramemoratus abbas et conuentus monachorum in capitulo secus Mainerium abbatem in australi plaga honorifice tumulauit. Porro Ernaldus de Rodelento[4] nepos eius lapidea sarcofagum lamina cooperuit, et Vitalis[5] hoc heroicis uersibus epitaphium edidit.

Ecce sub hoc titulo requiescit strenuus Hugo.
Qui uiguit multos multa probitate per annos.
Mansio Grentonis munitio dicitur eius.
Vnde fuit cognomen ei multis bene notum.
Guillelmi fortis Anglorum tempore regis.
Inter precipuos magnates is cluit heros.
Militia fortis fuit et uirtute fidelis,
Hostibus horribilis et amicis tutor erilis.
Sumptibus officiis augens et pinguibus aruis.
Cenobium sancti multum prouexit Ebrulfi.
Dum cathedram sancti celebrabat plebs pia Petri.
Occidit emeritus, habitu monachi trabeatus.

[1] Cf. above, p. 279 n. 2.

[2] The indiction does not correspond with the year; Le Prévost considered that in such cases Orderic's indiction numbers were more reliable than his dates, and for this reason and no other gave the date of Hugh's death as 1093. But this could easily be a copyist's error. The year 1098 is given both in the Annals of Saint-Évroul (Le Prévost, v. 159) and in the necrology of the abbey (Bibl. nat. MS. lat. 1006, f. 36[v]: 'Anno ab incarnatione Domini millesimo nonagesimo octavo ix kal. Martii obiit Hugo de Grentemesnil, comes Lekcestrie (*sic*), fundator huius cenobii, monachus nostre congregacionis, cuius anniversarium

church of Saint-Évroul; but I have surveyed the wide kingdoms of the earth like one caught up in a trance; I have flown hither and thither in my speech and, traversing many of them, I have prolonged an extensive digression.[1] But now, weary, I return to my bed, which is Saint-Évroul, and will give a simple account of some things concerning us at the end of this book.

28

In the year of our Lord 1098, the first indiction, the famous lord, Hugh of Grandmesnil, fell ill in England and, worn out with old age and sickness, drew near to death.[2] Then he was received as a monk by Geoffrey of Orleans, prior of Saint-Évroul, whom Abbot Roger had sent to England for his spiritual welfare a little while before, and on the sixth day afterwards, which was 22 February, he died. Then Bernard and David, who were monks of Saint-Évroul,[3] had his body preserved with salt and sewn securely into an ox-hide, and brought it to Normandy. It was buried with honour by the abbot and convent of Saint-Évroul in the chapter-house, on the south side, beside Abbot Mainer. Arnold of Rhuddlan,[4] his nephew, covered the tomb with a stone facing and Vitalis[5] composed this epitaph in heroic verse:

This verse declares the place where great Hugh rests;
Through many years his many virtues shone.
Grandmesnil was the name his castle bore,
From which his name earned honour with all men.
When William in his might was England's king
This lord was great among the greatest lords;
In battle brave, and faithful in his strength,
Terrible to the foe, shield to his friends.
His wealth enriched the ritual; on the cell
Of Saint-Évroul he lavished fertile fields.
While Christians kept the feast of Peter's Chair,
In habit of a monk this veteran died;

instituit dominus abbas Rogerius fieri per omnes prioratus nostros festive ubi sunt duo et eo amplius monachi'); there is no early evidence for 1093, and no good reason for rejecting 1098. The Caen copyist may easily have written *i* for *vi* in the indiction year.

[3] The presence of two monks in attendance on Hugh suggests that by this date the priory of Ware was coming into existence at Hugh's principal residence in England. See above, iii. 236 n. 1.

[4] Arnold, son of Humphrey of Tilleul.

[5] Orderic Vitalis.

Æcclesiæ cultor largus dator et releuator.'
Blandus egenorum, letetur in arce polorum. Amen.

Ante vii annos Adeliza prefati optimatis uxor Rotomagi v° idus Iulii obierat,[1] et in capitulo Vticensi ad dexteram Mainerii abbatis tumulata fuerat. Hæc Iuonis de Bellomonte comitis de Iudea
iii. 455 genitrice filia fuit,[2] uiroque suo quinque filios et totidem filias peperit, quibus uaria sors in mundanæ instabilitatis uaga fluctuatione incubuit.

Robertus qui maior natu erat trigamus consenuit.'[3] sub cuius manu patrimonium quod satis amplum a patre receperat decidit. Ipse tandem post xxxviii annos a morte patris kalendis Iunii mortuus est.'[4] et in Vticensi capitulo cum duabus uxoribus suis Agnete et Emma sepultus est. Guillelmus frater eius in curia Guillelmi regis magnæ estimationis fuit, ipsumque rex adeo dilexit, ut ei neptem suam Roberti scilicet Moritolii comitis filiam offerret, quatinus sic iuuenem in magno honore consanguinitati suæ coniunctum retineret. Denique superbus tiro consilium regis respuit, et leuitate ductus cum Roberto Gifardo[5] aliisque pluribus Apuliam expetiit, ibique Mabiliam Roberti Guiscardi filiam quæ Curta Lupa cognominabatur cum quindecim castellis coniugem accepit, ibique post reditum de Antiochia obiit, filiosque suos Guillelmum et Robertum honoris sui heredes dimisit.[6] Hugo strenuus et honestus miles in iuuentute defunctus est.' et in capitulo
iii. 456 sancti patris Ebrulfi honorifice sepultus est. Iuo paternum honorem in Anglia primo aliquandiu tenuit, sed postmodum tempore Henrici regis Roberto consuli de Mellento inuadiauit. Iter in Ierusalem bis iniit, et in prima profectione apud Antiochiam dura cum sociis tolerauit.' in secunda uero uita decessit.[7] Albericus qui etate iunior erat in puericia litteris studuit, sed in adolescentia relicto clericatu ad militiam se contulit, in qua strenue plura patrare sategit. Tancredum Odonis Boni Marchisi[8] filium multarum

[1] Presumably in 1091.

[2] Ivo count of Beaumont-sur-Oise and Judith, his second wife.

[3] See above, p. 230 for details of his marriages.

[4] Probably *c.* 1136.

[5] See above, p. 16.

[6] William's career has been traced in E. M. Jamison, 'Some notes . . .', pp. 199–200; see above, pp. 16, 32 for his part in Robert Guiscard's campaign against Durazzo in 1081. William's lands were situated in the valleys of the Crati and the Coscile and at Cotrone; he died before 1114 and his son William

Friend, donor, and refounder of the church,
Balm of the poor, may he in Heaven find joy. Amen.

Seven years previously Adeliza, Hugh's wife, had died in Rouen on 11 July,[1] and had been buried in the chapter-house of Saint-Évroul on the right side of Abbot Mainer. She was the daughter of Ivo count of Beaumont and Judith,[2] and she bore her husband five sons and as many daughters, to whom different lots fell in the uncertain chances of the changing world.

Robert, who was the eldest, lived to old age and was thrice married;[3] in his hands the patrimony, which had been very extensive when he inherited it from his father, declined. He finally died thirty-eight years after his father's death,[4] on 1 June, and was buried in the chapter-house of Saint-Évroul with two of his wives, Agnes and Emma. His brother William had a high reputation in the court of King William; the king had so great an affection for him that he offered him the hand of his niece, the daughter of Robert count of Mortain, hoping in this way to bind the youth to him by the signal honour of kinship. But the proud young knight thought nothing of the king's proposal and for frivolous reasons went to Apulia with Robert Giffard[5] and many others. There he married Robert Guiscard's daughter, Mabel, called Courte Louve, and received fifteen castles with her; and there after returning from Antioch he died, leaving his sons William and Robert as heirs to his honor.[6] Hugh, a brave and upright knight, died in his youth and was honourably buried in the chapter-house of Saint-Évroul. Ivo held his father's honor in England for a little while; but later, in the time of King Henry, he pledged it to Robert count of Meulan. He went twice to Jerusalem: in the first crusade he endured great hardships with his companions at Antioch, and on his second journey he died.[7] Aubrey, who was the youngest, learnt his letters as a boy; but when he reached adolescence he abandoned a clerical life for the life of a knight, in which he strove vigorously to do many deeds of valour. He wounded Tancred, the son of Odobonus the Marquis,[8] who was renowned for his valiant achievements, so

did not long survive him. Robert is said to have abandoned his fiefs after a dispute about military service and returned to his kinsfolk north of the Alps in 1129.

[7] Orderic deals with his career later (Le Prévost, iv. 168–9).

[8] See above, p. 32. This story is uncorroborated. There is, however, no doubt of William of Grandmesnil's hostility to Tancred, and his brother Aubrey accompanied him on crusade (E. M. Jamison, 'Some notes . . .', p. 199).

titulis probitatum insignem uulnerauit, unde prefatus optio postmodum omni uita sua claudicauit. Omnes isti Hugonis filii corpore formosi et proceri strenuique fuerunt, sed infortunio infestante nec longeuitate preter Robertum nec placida felicitate diutius potiti sunt.[1]

[1] The extract from Orderic's *Ecclesiastical History* in MS. Vat. Reg. 703[B] ends at this point. If Orderic wrote an epilogue, it is lost.

severely that the young lord was lame for the rest of his life. All these sons of Hugh were tall and handsome and brave; but misfortune dogged them so that not one of them except Robert lived to old age or enjoyed peaceful prosperity for very long.[1]

APPENDIX I

THE fragment printed here has, since the sixteenth century, been regarded as the first part of Book VII of the *Historia Æcclesiastica*. There are strong reasons for rejecting it,[1] though the traditional attribution earns it a place in the Appendix.

The first part is printed from Bibl. nat. MS. lat. 10913, ff. 1–4. Where this breaks off I have used Bern MS. Bongars 555, ff. 276–283v. I have compared this with Bibl. nat. MS. lat. 5122, but there are no significant variations. Rouen MS. 1176 (Y 170) is a slightly abbreviated copy taken apparently from MS. lat. 5122 or the same original.

I

[2]Anno ab incarnatione Domini DCmoLXXXoVIIIo Pippinus Auster maior domus regiæ principatum Francorum suscepit.

Anno Domini DCCoXIo obiit Childebertus rex Francorum.

Anno Domini DCCoXIIo obiit Pippinus senior et filius eius qui dicebatur Karolus Martellus principatum usurpauit.

Anno Domini DCCoXVo obiit Dagobertus rex iunior xiiiio kal. Februarii, qui regnauit in Francia annis v. Secundo anno post mortem eius pugnauit primum Karolus Martellus princeps contra Radbodum ad Coloniam, regnante Theoderico filio suprascripti Dagoberti iunioris. Eo tempore gens impia Wandalorum Galliam deuastare coepit. Quo tempore destructæ æcclesiæ, subuersa monasteria, captæ urbes, desolatæ domus, diruta castra, strages hominum innumeræ factæ, et multus ubique humani generis sanguis effusus est. Ea tempestate grauissime per totam Galliam detonabat Wandalis omnia flammis et ferro proterentibus. Peruenientes Senones ciuitatem cœperunt eam omni arte iaculis et machinis infestare. Quæ cernens presul eiusdem urbis Eboba nomine exiens de ciuitate cum suis fretus diuina uirtute exterminauit illos ab urbis obsidione. Fugientibus illis persecutus est eos usque dum egrederentur de finibus suis.

Anno Domini DCCoXLIo obiit Karolus Martellus princeps, sepultusque est in basilica sancti Dionisii Parisius. Hic res æcclesiarum propter assiduitatem bellorum laicis tradidit. Quo mortuo Karlomannus et Pippinus filii eius principatum suscipiunt.

[1] See above, Introduction, pp. xv–xviii.

[2] The following extract (pp. 343–50) is a version of the *Historia Francorum Senonensis*, printed in *MGH SS* xi. 364–9. It is not one of the MSS. used in the preparation of that edition and there are some small variant readings; only one is sufficiently important for comment.

Anno Domini DCC^{o}L^{o} Pippinus electus est in regem, et Childericus qui de stirpe Clodouei regis remanserat tonseratus est. Hic deficit progenies Clodouei regis.

Anno Domini DCC^{o}LXVIII° Pippinus rex moritur et filii eius Karolus qui dictus est imperator magnus et Karlomannus eliguntur in regno.

Anno Domini DCC^{o}LXXI° uir Karlomannus obiit.

Anno Domini DCCC^{o}IX° obiit Alcuinus phylosophus abbas sancti Martini Turonorum.

Anno Domini DCCC^{o}XIV° obiit Karolus imperator magnus et Ludouicus filius eius qui Pius dicitur regnum Francorum et imperium Romanorum suscepit. Huius in tempore pagani diffusi sunt in prouincia quæ Pontiuus pagus appellatur. Vicesimo igitur anno regni domni Hludouici piissimi imperatoris, rebellauit contra eum Hlotarius filius eius, auferens illi regnum Francorum. Ipso anno collecto exercitu copioso ualde, Hludouicus pater restituit sibi regnum quod illi abstulerat filius.

Anno Domini DCCC^{o}XL° obiit Hludouicus pius imperator xii^{o} kal. Iulii. Eodem anno facta est eclipsis solis feria quarta ante Ascensionem Domini hora diei nona ii^{o} nonas Maii. Vertente igitur anno in die Ascensionis Domini fit bellum Fontanetum in Burgundia a quattuor filiis supradicti Hludouici, Karolo scilicet.' Lothario, Hludouico et Pippino, ubi multus effusus est sanguis humanus. Ex quibus Karolus qui appellatus est Caluus regnum Francorum et imperium Romanorum optinuit. Lotharius uero partem Franciæ sibi uendicauit, quæ usque in hodiernum diem ex suo nomine Lotharii regnum appelatur. Hludouicus autem Burgundiam sibi uendicauit unctus est in regem.

Anno Domini DCCC^{o}LXVII° Karolus imperator qui Caluus uocabatur filius Hludouici piissimi imperatoris.' cum secunda profectione Romam peteret iii^{o} kal. Octobris in ipso itinere obiit Vercellis ciuitate, ibique sepultus in basilica beati Eusebii martiris requieuit annis vii. Post hæc autem per uisionem delatum est corpus eius in Francia, et honorifice sepultum in basilica beati Dyonisii martiris Parisius. Suscepit autem regnum Hludouicus filius eius. Sequenti uero anno, Iohannes papa Romanus ad Gallias ueniens cum Formoso episcopo Portuensi ferens secum pretiosissimas reliquias, primo Arelatum nauigio est aduectus, per Lugdunum aliasque ciuitates ad Tricasinam urbem accessit. Ibique cum Hludouico rege filio Karoli Calui locutus, ad Italiam repedauit. Post hæc defunctus est Hludouicus rex Francorum filius Karoli Calui.' relinquens filium suum paruulum Karolum nomine qui Simplex apellatur cum regno in custodia Odonis principis.

Eo tempore gens incredula Normannorum per Gallias sese diffudit.' cedibus, incendiis, atque omni crudelitatis genere debachata. Deinde Franci Burgundiones, et Aquitanienses proceres congregati in unum, Odonem principem elegerunt sibi in regem. Obeunte uero Odone, kal. Ianuarii, recepit regnum Karolus simplex filius Hludouici. Sub

ipso tempore, uenerunt Normanni in Burgundia ad sanctum Florentinum. Occurrit autem illis Ricardus dux Burgundiae cum suo exercitu in territorio Tornoderense irruensque in eos percussit multitudinem ex eis more gladii; et reliqui fugerunt v nonas Iunii. Tempore illo factus est terræ motus circa cenobium sanctæ Columbæ uirginis v idus Ianuarii. Eo tempore pagani obsederunt Carnotinam ciuitatem. Collecto igitur exercitu, Ricardus dux Burgundiæ et Rodbertus princeps, irruerunt in eos peremptis ex paganis sex millibus octingentis, et paucis qui remanserant obsides capientes xiii° kal. Augusti in sabato; auxiliante illis superna clementia per intercessionem sanctæ Dei genitricis Mariæ.

Post hæc igitur mediante mense Marcio aparuit stella a parte Circii emittens radium magnum fere diebus xiiii. Sequenti anno fuit fames magna per totam Galliam. Deinde post quinque fere annos kal. Februarii igneæ acies uisæ sunt in celo diuersorum colorum quod mirum fuit, alternis se insequentes. Ipso anno fuit magna dissensio inter regem et principes eius. Ob hanc causam; plurimæ strages perpetratæ sunt Christiani populi, sed fauente Deo omnis illa contradictio cessauit.

Tercio autem anno post hanc persecutionem defunctus Ricardus dux Burgundiæ kal. Septembris, sepultusque est in basilica sanctæ Columbæ uirginis; in oratorio sancti Symphoriani martyris. Secundo anno post eius mortem, Rodbertus princeps rebellauit contra Karolum Simplicem, unctusque est in basilica in regem iii° kal. Iulii. Et nondum anno expleto xvii kal. Iulii factum est bellum Suessionis ciuitate inter Karolum Simplicem et ipsum Rotbertum; qui inuaserat Francorum regnum, ubi interfectus est ipse Rotbertus. Karolo uero a cæde belli uictore reuertente, occurrit illi Herbertus infidelium nequissimus, et sub fictæ pacis simulatione in castro quod Parrona dicitur ut ospitandi gratia diuerteret compulit, et sic cum dolo captum retinuit. Habebat enim idem Rotbertus sororem istius Herberti in coniugio, de quo ortus est Hugo Magnus. Hic itaque positus Karolus Rodulfum nobilem filium Ricardi Burgundionum ducem quem de sacro fonte susceperat, una cum consilio Hugonis magni filii supradicti Rotberti et procerum Francorum in regnum sublimauit. Isdem autem Karolus Simplex post longam carceris macerationem defunctus est in ipsa custodia, et sepultus in basilica sancti Fursei confessoris quæ est in ipsa Parrona castro. Vnctus est in regem ipse Rodulfus iiii° idus Iulii Suessionis ciuitate.

His temporibus pagani Burgundiam uastauerunt, factumque est bellum inter Christianos et paganos in monte Chalo peremptis a paganis ex Christianis multis millibus viii° idus Decembris. Igitur defuncto Rodulfo rege xviii° kal. Februarii sepelierunt eum in basilica sanctæ Columbæ uirginis. Post mortem igitur Rodulfi regis, Hugo magnus una cum Francis accersiens Guillelmum ducem qui Longa Spata dicitur[1] misit illum ad Ouiam uxorem iam dicti Karoli Simplicis

[1] *ducem qui Longa Spata dicitur* is substituted for *archiepiscopum*, the normal

ut inde reduceret Hludouicum filium eius. Fugerat enim ad patrem suum regem Anglorum ob timorem Herberti et Hugonis. Veniensque illuc Guillelmus datis obsidibus sub sacramenti titulo matri eius reduxit Hludouicum in Franciam. Igitur xiii° kal. Iulii unctus est in regem Hludouicus filius Karoli Simplicis apud Laudunum. Secundo post hæc anno xvi kal. Martii circa gallorum cantum usque illucescente die, sanguineæ acies per totam celi faciem apparuerunt. Sequenti autem mense viiii kal. Aprilis Hungri adhuc pagani, Franciam, Burgundiam, atque Aquitaniam ferro et igne depopulari cœperunt. Post hæc rebellauerunt Francorum proceres contra Hludouicum regem, super omnes autem Hugo magnus.

In ipso anno facta est fames ualida per totum regnum Francorum, ita ut modus frumenti uenundaretur xxiiii. Deinde non post multos dies captus est Hludouicus rex filius Karoli simplicis dolo Baiocas ciuitate a Normannis, multis ex Francorum populo interemptis, consentiente Hugone magno. [1]Post haec mense Maio feria iii[a] pluit sanguis super operarios. Et ipso anno mense Septembrio, Hludouicus rex totum tempus uitae suae plenum ducens angustiarum et tribulationum diem claudit extremum, sepultusque est Remis in basilica sancti Remigii. Sequenti quoque mense ii° idus Nouembris, Lotarius iam iuuenis filius eius unctus est in regem Remis et Hugo magnus factus est dux Francorum. Secundo autem anno post hæc mense Augusti obsedit supradictus Hugo magnus Pictauis ciuitatem sed nichil ei profuit, dum enim obsideret eandem urbem quadam die intonuit Dominus terrore magno disrupitque turbo papilionem eius a summitate usque deorsum, stuporque magnus inuasit illum cum exercitu suo, ita ut uiuere nequirent. Statimque in fugam uersi, recesserunt ab urbis obsidione. Fecit autem hoc Deus per intercessionem beati Hylarii⌟ qui semper tutor et defensor illius est urbis.

[2]In ipso anno defunctus est Gislebertus dux Burgundiæ relinquens ducatum Ottoni filio Hugonis Magni. Habebat namque Otto filiam illius Gisleberti in coniugio. Secundo anno, obiit Hugo magnus dux Francorum apud Drodingam uillam xvi° kal. Iulii sepultusque est in basilica beati Dionisii martyris Parisius. Cui successerunt filii eius Hugo uidelicet, Otto, et Hainricus, nati ex filia Ottonis regis Saxoniæ. Hugo dux Francorum effectus est, et Otto dux Burgundionum. Defuncto Ottone duce Burgundionum successit Hainricus frater eius. Sub ipso tempore, oritur contentio inter Ansegisum episcopum Trecarum, et Robertum comitem. Eiectus uero ex ciuitate Ansegisus episcopus a Rodberto comite, porrexit in Saxoniam ad Ottonem imperatorem,

reading in other MSS. of the *Historia Francorum Senonensis*. Dudo of Saint-Quentin also made William Longsword the king's envoy (cf. above, iii. 80 n. 1).

[1] Cf. Le Prévost, i. 166.

[2] Cf. Le Prévost, i. 167.

adductosque Saxones mense Octobrio, obsedit ciuitatem Trecas longo tempore. Venientes autem in predam Senonis, occurrerunt illis Archenbaldus archiepiscopus et Rainardus comes uetulus cum magno exercitu in loco qui uocatur Villare, interfectosque Saxones cum duce suo Helpone nomine Senonenses extiterunt uictores. Dixerat enim Helpo incensurum se æcclesias et uillas quæ sunt super Venena fluuium usque ad ciuitatem, infigereque lanceam suam in portam sancti Leonis. Interfectus autem cum populo suo a Senonensibus, reportatus est in patriam suam Ardennam, a seruis suis, sic enim iusserat mater ipsius Helponis nomine Warna. Planxerunt autem eum planctu magno Rainardus comes et Archembaldus archiepiscopus, consanguineus enim illorum erat. Videns itaque Bruno dux socius eiusdem Helponis qui obsederat Trecas ciuitatem quod mortuus esset socius suus Helpo cum suis reuersus est in patriam suam. [1]Deinde post non multos dies Hlotharius rex congregans exercitum copiosum ualde, renouauit in dicione sua Hlotharium regnum. Veniensque ad palatium quod uocatur Aquisgrani ubi manebat Otto imperator cum uxore hora prandendi, ingressusque in palatium nemine contradicente, comederunt et biberunt quicquid illi ad suos usus parauerant. Otto imperator cum uxore sua et populo fugiens, reliquit palatium. Depredato itaque Lotharius rex palatio et tota prouincia, reuersus est in Franciam cum pace, nemine prosequente. Post hæc Otto imperator congregans exercitum suum, uenit Parisius, ubi interfectus nepos ipsius Ottonis cum aliis pluribus ad portam ciuitatis, incenso suburbio illius. Iactauerat namque se extollendo dicens, quod lanceam suam infigeret in ciuitatis portam. Conuocans igitur Hlotharius rex Hugonem ducem Francorum et Hainricum ducem Burgundionum irruensque in eos, fugientibus illis persequtus usque Suessionis ciuitate. Illi autem ingressi fluminis alueum quod dicitur Axonam, nescientes uadum plurimi ibi perierunt. Et multo plures consumpsit aqua, quam gladius uorasset. Et tanti ibi perierunt, ut etiam aqua redundaret cadaueribus mortuorum. Aqua enim inpleuerat ripas suas, Hlotharius uero rex constanter persequens illos tribus diebus et tribus noctibus usque ad fluuium quod fluit iuxta Ardennam siue Argonam, interfectis ex hostibus maxima multitudine. Desinens autem prosequi illos Hlotharius rex reuersus est in Franciam cum magna uictoria. Otto uero imperator cum his qui euaserant cum magna confusione reuersus est ad propria. Post hæc non aposuit ultra Otto imperator uenire aut ipse uel exercitus eius in Franciam. In ipso anno pacificatus est Hlotharius rex cum Ottone rege Remis ciuitate contrà uoluntatem Hugonis et Hainrici fratris eius, contra uoluntatem exercitus sui, dedit Hlotarius rex Ottoni regi in beneficio Lotharium regnum, quæ causa magis contristauit corda principum Francorum.

[1] Cf. Le Prévost, i. 168–9.

[1]Anno DCCCC°LXX°VI° obiit Hlotharius rex senex plenus dierum, sepultusque est in basilica beati Remigii Remis. Cui successit Hlodouicus filius eius iuuenis. Anno DCCCC°LXXX°II° obiit Hludouicus rex iuuenis qui regnauit in Francia annis vi. Sepultus est uero in basilica beati Cornelii Compendio. Cui successit Karolus frater eius, filius Hlotharii regis. Eodem anno rebellauit contra Karolum Hugo dux Francorum eo quod accepisset Karolus filiam Herberti comitis Trecarum. Collecto igitur Hugo exercitu copioso ualde, obsedit Laudunum ubi commanebat Karolus cum uxore sua. Exiens uero Karolus de ciuitate, fugauit Hugonem cum exercitu suo, incensa hospicia ubi manebant hostes. Cernens itaque Hugo dux quod minime posset Karolum uincere, consilium habuit cum Ascelino traditore uetulo qui erat episcopus falsus Lauduni et consiliarius Karoli. Itaque tradens Ascelinus episcopus Laudunum noctu quiescentibus cunctis Hugoni duci Francorum uinctus est Karolus cum uxore sua et ductus in custodia Aurelianis ciuitate. Nondum autem ipse Karolus erat unctus in regem, resistente Hugone duce. Manens uero idem Karolus in custodia Aurelianis in turrim, genuit illi uxor sua filios duos Ludouicum et Karolum. Eodem anno unctus est in regem Remis ciuitate Hugo dux, et in ipso anno Rodbertus filius eius rex ordinatus est. Hic deficit regnum Karoli Magni.

[2]In illis diebus erat Remensium ciuitate archiepiscopus uir bonus et modestus frater Lotharii regis ex concubina nomine Arnulfus. Hugo autem rex inuidebat ei, uolens exterminare progeniem Lotharii regis. Congregansque in urbe Remensi sinodum isdem Hugo rex, inuitauit archiepiscopum Senonicæ urbis nomine Sewinum cum suffraganeis suis. In quo concilio fecit degradare domnum Arnulfum archyepiscopum Remorum dolo nepotis sui quem tenebat in carcere, dicens non debere esse episcopum natum ex concubina. In loquo uero eius consecrari fecit domnum Gerbertum monachum phylosofum. Qui Gerbertus magister fuit Rodberti regis filii istius Hugonis, et domni Leotherici archyepiscopi successoris uenerabilis Sewini. Arnulfum autem fecit mancipari custodiæ Aurelianis ciuitate. Venerabilis itaque Sewinus archyepiscopus non consensit in degradatione Arnulfi neque in ordinatione Gerberti. Iussio autem regis urgebat. Alii uero episcopi licet inuiti, tamen propter timorem regis degradauerunt Arnulfum et ordinauerunt Gerbertum. Sewinus autem plus timens Deum quam terrenum regem noluit consentire regis nequiciae, sed magis in quantum potuit redarguit ipsum regem, propter quam causam ira regis contra eum efferbuit. Cum magno itaque dedecore expelli iussit rex Arnulfum de æcclesia beatæ Dei genitricis Mariæ Remensis, et sic alligatum retrudi in carcerem. Alligatus autem in carcere Aurelianis ciuitate ubi detinebatur nepos eius Karolus mansit ibi annis tribus.

Nuntiantur hæc omnia presuli Romano. Qui ualde indignatus super

[1] Cf. Le Prévost, i. 169–70. [2] Cf. Le Prévost, i. 172–3.

hoc.' interdixit omnes episcopos qui Arnulfum deiecerant.' et Gerbertum ordinauerant. Misit quoque Leonem abbatem a sede apostolica ad domnum Sewinum archyepiscopum urbis Senonicæ, qui uice sua in urbe Remensi sinodum congregaret, mandans illi ut sine dilatione reuocaret de carcere Arnulfum, et degradaret Gerbertum. Collecto igitur concilio iterum in urbe Remensi ex iussione apostolica, reuocatus est Arnulfus de custodia, et cum honore magno receptus in propria sede. Gerbertus autem intelligens quod iniuste pontificalem dignitatem suscepisset.' pœnitentia ductus est. Altercationem uero Gerberti pontificis et Leonis abbatis ualde utilem, plenius inuenies in gestis pontificum Remorum. Post hæc domnus Gerbertus electus est pontifex in urbe Rauenna ab Ottone imperatore, et a populo eiusdem urbis. Residensque in eadem urbe pontifex quam plurimos annos, defunctus est papa urbis Romæ. Statimque omnis populus Romanus, sibi dari adclamat domnum Gerbertum. Assumptus autem de urbe Rauenna, ordinatus est pontifex summus in urbe Roma.

Anno ab incarnatione Domini dccccºxcviiiº, obiit Hugo rex.' sepultus est in basilica beati Dionisii martiris Parisius. Cui successit Rodbertus filius eius, regum piissimus et modestus.

Anno Domini dccccºxcviiii uenerabilis Sewinus archyepiscopus ab imo cœpit restaurare cœnobium sancti Petri Milidunensis, et monachos ibi mittens, abbatem Gauterium eis prefecit. In ipso anno tradidit Gaulterius miles et uxor eius castrum Milidunum Odoni comiti. Congregans uero Rodbertus rex exercitum copiosum ualde et Burchardus comes, conuocansque Normannos cum duce suo Ricardo obsedit castrum Milidunum. Castro igitur capto suspensus est Gaulterius et uxor illius in patibulo. Burchardus autem comes recepit castrum Milidunum sicuti ante possederat. Igitur Rainaldus comes uetulus Senonum post multa mala perpetrata defunctus est, et sepultus in basilica Sanctæ Columbæ uirginis. Cui successit Fromundus filius eius, habens in coniugio filiam Rainaldi comitis Remorum.

Anno Domini mº indictione xiiiª xvi kal. Nouembris transiit ad Christum uenerabilis Seguinus metropolitanus episcopus. Post transitum uero illius, stetit æcclesia Senonica sine benedictione sacerdotali anno i. Adclamabat autem omnis populus sibi ordinari domnum Leothericum nobilissimis ortum natalibus tunc archydiaconum, omni bonitate conspicuum, sed resistebant quamplurimi clerici, cupientes episcopalem conscendere gradum. Precipue uero Frotmundus comes filius Rainardi uetuli natus ex mala radice hoc non permittebat fieri, eo quod haberet filium clericum nomine Brunonem, uolens de eo facere episcopum. Dei autem nutu congregati suffraganei episcopi Senonicæ æcclesiæ.' cum uoluntate et auctoritate apostolica, sublato omni timore humano solleniter ordinauerunt domnum Leothericum in sede pontificali ut preesset æcclesiæ Senonensi.

Anno Domini M°I° obiit Hainricus dux Burgundiæ sine filiis. Rebellaueruntque Burgundiones contra regem Rodbertum nolentes eum recipere. Ingressus itaque Landricus comes Autissiodorum, tenuit ciuitatem.

Anno Domini M°III° Rodbertus rex assumptis Normannis cum duce suo Ricardo et exercitu copioso ualde, uastauit Burgundiam, obsidens Autissiodorum diebus multis. Burgundiones autem nullo modo ei se subdere uolentes, unanimiter resistebant ei. Obsedit uero Auallonem castrum tribus fere mensibus et famis necessitate eum cepit, tunc reuersus est in Franciam. Mortuo itaque Frotmundo comite Senonum, successit ei Rainardus filius eius, infidelium nequissimus. Hic persecutionem intulit æcclesiis Christi et fidelibus eius, quanta non est audita a tempore paganorum usque in odiernum diem. Archyepiscopus autem Leothericus nimis angustiatus pro hac re, quo se uerteret omnino nesciebat. Totum uero se domino committens in orationibus et uigiliis exorabat Christum ut eius superna pietas dignaretur auxilium ministrare.

Igitur anno a passione domini M°XVI° indictione xiii^a x kal. Maii, capta est ciuitas Senonum ab archyepiscopo Leotherico per consilium[1] Rainoldi episcopi Parisiacensis et regi Rodberto reddita. Rainardus autem fugiens nudus euasit. Frodmundus uero frater eius et caeteri milites de ciuitate ingressi turrim quae est in ciuitate obtinuerunt. Rex autem oppugnans eam diebus multis cepit eam et Frodmundum fratrem Rainardi comitis quem duxit in carcerem Aurelianis ciuitate ubi et defunctus est.[2]

Rodbertus siquidem rex Francorum xxxvii annis regnauit et coniugem probitate ac sapientia famosam Constantiam habuit, quae generosam ei sobolem peperit, Henricum, Rodbertum et Adalam. [3]Anno autem dominicae incarnationis M°XXX°I° indictione x^a iv^a Rodbertus rex obiit, et Henricus filius eius fere xxx annis regnauit. Rodbertus autem ducatum Burgundiæ habuit et tres filios genuit Henricum, Rodbertum et Simonem. Henricus uero qui primogenitus erat Hugonem et Odonem genuit, sed ante patrem suum obiit. Hugo siquidem auo in ducatu successit, ingentique probitate pollens tribus annis tenuit, ac deinde Odonem fratrem suum ducem ultro constituit, et ipse Dei compunctus amore monachus Cluniacensis fere xv annis religiose Deo militauit. Adala uero filia Rodberti regis Balduino satrapæ Flandrensi in coniugio data fuit, quae multiplicem ei prolem peperit, Rodbertum Fresionem, Arnulfum et Balduinum consules, Vdonem Treuerensium archiepiscopum, et Henricum clericum, Matildem quoque reginam Anglorum et Iuditham Tostici ducis uxorem.

[1] Bibl. nat. MS. lat. 10913 breaks off here.

[2] The extract from the *Historia Francorum Senonensis* ends here.

[3] Cf. Le Prévost, i. 179.

His temporibus dum Robertus et Henricus Gallis praefuerunt decem papae in apostolica sede sibi successerunt, id est Gerbertus philosophus, qui Siluester dictus est, et Iohannes Benedictus et Iohannes frater eius, Benedictus quoque nepos eorum, Clemens et Damasus nobilitate et ardore boni feruidus, Leo et Victor, Stephanus et Nicolaus. Henricus autem Francorum rex Bertradam Iulii Claudii regis Russiæ filiam uxorem duxit quae Philippum et Hugonem Magnum Crispeii comitem peperit. Philippus uero post patris occasum xlvii annis comes regnauit, et Bertradam Florentii Frisiorum ducis filiam in coniugium duxit quæ Ludouicum Tedbaldum et Constantiam peperit.

2

[1]Anno ab incarnatione Domini M°XL°VII° indictione XV[a] Guillelmus Nothus dux Normannorum Henricum regem in Neustriam adduxit, eoque adiutore contra cognatos hominesque suos apud Vallesdunas pugnauit, et Guidonem Burgundionem aliosque rebelles superauit sibique subiugauit, aliosque fugauit. Post haec in potestate confirmatus Mathildem Balduini Flandriæ marchionis filiam uxorem duxit, quæ quatuor filios et quinque filias ei peperit, id est Rodbertum, Ricardum, Guillelmum et Henricum; Agatham ac Adelizam, Constantiam, Adalam et Ceciliam. Tam claram progeniem uaria fortuna per diuersos discursus egit, dieque suo quemque in occasum praecipitauit, sicuti stilus noster alias sufficienter notificauit. Seditiosis deinde insurgentibus, et inter præfatos principes dissensionem serentibus ingens guerra inter Francos et Normannos orta est, unde multorum nimia strages facta est.

[2]Tandem anno dominicæ incarnationis M°L°IV° Henricus rex in Ebroicensem pagum intrauit, et ingentia deprædando siue concremando detrimenta facere cœpit et Odonem fratrem suum cum multis millibus per Beluacensem pagum trans Sequanam direxit. Guillelmus autem dux cum turmis suis regem a latere comitabatur et resistere pro opportunitate præstolabatur. Porro Rogerium de Mortuomari et omnes Caletenses asciuit et in regalem exercitum abire uelociter praecepit. At illi iussis cito obsecundantur et occurrentes Gallis apud Mortuum Mare pugnauerunt et uictoriam nacti Guidonem Pontiui comitem ceperunt, Odonem uero et Radulfum comitem de Monte Desiderii pluribus peremptis fugauerunt. Eo tempore Leo papa sexto anno papatus sui obiit, cuius secundo anno Vticensis abbatia restaurata est et Teodoricus sancti Ebrulfi primus abbas nonis Octobris consecratus est. Qui post viii annos peregre profectus est et in Cypro insula kal. Augusti defunctus est. Ad cuius sepulcrum miraculorum copia celebrata est.

[1] Cf. Le Prévost, i. 182. [2] Cf. Le Prévost, i. 184.

3

Eduardus rex Anglorum postquam xxiii annis regnauit anno sexto Philippi regis Francorum hominem exiuit. Cuius genealogia de stirpe Sem filii Noe ita descendit. Sem genuit Arfaxat et Beadumg, et Beadumg genuit Wala. Wala genuit Hatra. Hatra uero genuit Itermod. Itermod autem genuit Heremod. Heremod autem genuit Sceldunea. Sceldunea genuit Beaw. Beaw genuit Cetuna. Cetuna uero genuit Geatam, quem Geatam pagani iamdudum pro deo uenerabantur. Hic genuit Findgoldwlf patrem Fidhulput. De quo Frealaf pater Frithowald. De quo Woden ortus est a quo Angli feriam quartam Wodenis diem nuncupant. Hic magnae sublimitatis inter suos et potentiae fuit.[1]

[1] All MSS. break off here.

APPENDIX II

The Translation of St. Nicholas of Myra to Bari

(above, pp. 54–68)

THE translation of the relics of St. Nicholas from Myra to Bari in 1087 was an event of world-wide importance, and accounts occur in Latin, Greek, and Russian sources.[1] The cult of the saint, widespread in the Greek empire, was firmly established in Bari, the residence of the catapan and the centre of Greek government in such parts of southern Italy as the Greeks could still control, from at least 1036.[2] Several churches were dedicated in his name before the middle of the eleventh century. After the Cerularian schism of 1054, the capture of Bari by the Normans in 1071, and the battle of Manzikert in the same year, which opened the way for the Turks to overrun Asia Minor and occupy Myra, the desire to secure the bones of the saint for Bari began to take shape in a plan of action. It is very likely that the seizure of the relics was premeditated, though the Latin chronicles deny this; and also that the plan was favoured by Elias, abbot of St. Benedict's abbey in Bari. Originally a monk of Cava, where he had become a friend of the future pope, Urban II, Elias was a staunch Gregorian. As Ursus, archbishop of Bari, a man of political ambitions, was in close contact with the now schismatical Greek elements in Trani and even in Bari itself, and had since the death of Robert Guiscard in 1085 given his support to the antipope, Clement III, Elias represented the Gregorian church which was to be so triumphantly reinforced by the acquisition of the relics of St. Nicholas. There is no doubt about his popularity, both with the merchant classes and with the people of Bari; all sources testify to it, and on the death of Ursus in 1089 he was unanimously elected to succeed him as archbishop of Bari, so gaining full authority to complete the building of the new church of St. Nicholas, the first stages of which had been delegated to him in 1087.

The Latin sources[3] for the translation consist of two main accounts:

1. The *De translatione* of John, archdeacon of Bari, written, he

[1] The historical background to the translation is fully discussed in Bernard Leib, *Rome, Kiev et Byzance à la fin du xie siècle* (Paris, 1924), F. Nitti di Vito, *La ripresa*; and id., 'La traslazione delle reliquie di san Nicola' in *Japigia*, N.S. viii (Bari, 1937), 295–411.

[2] Cf. *Anal. Boll.* xxii (1903), 354.

[3] Cf. also *BHL*, nos. 6179–90.

claims, at the command of Archbishop Ursus, and therefore before 1089.[1]

2. The account of Nicephorus, monk first of Cava and then of St. Benedict of Bari, composed from the depositions of the mariners.[2]

The two records agree in broad outline, though with variant details, and John softens the violence of the Normans that appears in Nicephorus. Both allege that the act was unpremeditated and undertaken only to forestall Venetians trading to Antioch, who were planning a similar seizure.

Among other sources the most important is the Kievan chronicle, possibly by Archbishop Ephraim of Kiev, written within a few years of the translation.[3] Leib believed that it was based on the work of John of Bari, with a few independent pieces of information, Nitti di Vito that it was independent. It shows some Greek influence. It corroborates the Latin narrative of events as far as the facts go, but differs in interpretation; the author believed that the translation had been planned before the ships left Bari, which in fact is likely to be true. The Russian church inaugurated the feast of the translation of St. Nicholas on 9 May, within a few years of the Latin church, and the Kievan account regards the translation as a voluntary cession of the relics by the Greeks, no longer able to protect them from the infidel.

Orderic's account is an abbreviation of the narrative of John of Bari, which circulated in Normandy at an early date.[4] For the most part he uses John's own words, merely adapting the sentences to his own rhythmic prose. At times—as always when he abbreviates—his account is so cryptic that it can be clearly understood only by reference to the fuller text of the original. Very occasionally he gives a different moral slant, as in his statement that the men of Bari decided to seize the relics out of love of their native land and of the saint, whereas John says unambiguously that they did not wish to allow the Venetians to anticipate them in the deed. Orderic adds independent material only when he describes the acquisition of relics by the abbey of Venosa and the priory of Noron.

[1] Printed, L. Surius, *De probatis sanctorum historiis*, iii (Cologne, 1579), 172–81; *Japigia*, viii (1937), 357–66.

[2] Printed in *Japigia*, viii (1937), 336–56; *Anal. boll.* iv (1885), 169–92.

[3] Printed, with translation, in *Japigia*, viii (1937), 387–98.

[4] An early copy from the abbey of Jumièges is now Rouen MS. 1382 (U 109). For early MSS. of the miracles of St. Nicholas cf. Porée, i. 35 n. 3.

ADDENDA AND CORRIGENDA

VOLUME II

p. 30 *n.* 1 and genealogical table. Agnes, wife of Robert of Moulins-la-Marche, was the daughter of Robert (III), son of Hugh of Grandmesnil, *not* of Robert (I) of Grandmesnil.

pp. 58 *n.* 3, 84 *n.* 3, and *index* (*p.* 400), *for* Roger Guiscard, *read* Roger count of Sicily.

p. 107 *line* 2, *for* Beauvoisis *read* Beauvaisis.

p. 134 *line* 13, *for* iv^{o} *read* iv^{a}.

p. 274 *n.* 2, *change to* Darius the Mede was a legendary character; see H. H. Rowley, *Darius the Mede and the Four World Empires* (Cardiff, 1935), pp. 5–9.

p. 317 *n.* 3, *add Fagaduna* has recently been identified by Professor Bruce Dickins, to whom I owe this information, as Fawdon in Whaddon (Cambs.).

p. 319 *lines* 24–5, *for* as long as he lives *read* as long as I live.

Genealogical table, *facing p.* 370. To the children of Hugh of Grandmesnil and Adeliza of Beaumont, *add* Matilda, wife of Hugh of Montpinçon.

VOLUME III

p. 93 *line* 5, *for* Arnold *read* Arnulf.

p. 127 *n.* 4, *for* Roger *read* Ralph.

p. 165 *lines* 26–7 and *index for* Émendeville *read* Émendreville.

p. 367 *line* 2, *for* Richard II *read* Richard III.

ADDENDA AND CORRIGENDA

INDEX OF QUOTATIONS AND ALLUSIONS

A. THE BIBLE

References to the Authorized Version are stated in parentheses where they differ from those in the Vulgate.

B. CLASSICAL, PATRISTIC, AND MEDIEVAL SOURCES

GENERAL INDEX

Persons and places named in the text are indexed under the form given in the translation. English places are identified by the county; French places by the department and, where necessary, the canton and commune.